FOREIGN INVESTMENTS IN CHINA

FOREIGN INVESTMENTS
IN CHINA

BY

C. F. REMER

NEW YORK

Howard Fertig

1968

First published in 1933
by The Macmillan Company

HOWARD FERTIG, INC. EDITION 1968
published by arrangement with the author

Copyright © 1968 by Charles F. Remer

Library of Congress Catalog Card Number: 67-24594

PRINTED IN THE UNITED STATES OF AMERICA
BY NOBLE OFFSET PRINTERS, INC.

TO THE MEMORY

OF

O. A. BRANDT

A teacher who delighted to free the
mind and who did not doubt that free
minds would play a noble part in the
building of a better world.

PREFACE

What is the true picture of the international economic relations of China as they are revealed in the statistics of foreign investment and of the international financial position of the country? This question was formulated at a meeting of a committee called together by the Social Science Research Council in New York in June, 1928. At this meeting, over which Professor James T. Shotwell of Columbia University presided, proposals were made for an investigation which was begun in October of that year. Mr. Robert S. Lynd and Mr. Robert T. Crane of the staff of the Council have taken an unfailing interest in the work. The Brookings Institution of Washington, D. C., was asked to appoint an advisory committee. Mr. Harold G. Moulton, Miss Cleona Lewis, and Mr. Robert R. Kuczynski served on this committee and I wish to thank them for the many hours they gave to the consideration of plans and problems. In addition, I am indebted to Mr. Moulton and Miss Lewis for criticism of the manuscript and for numerous suggestions as to its improvement.

Plans were made for an investigation to be carried on in each of the following countries: China, Great Britain, Japan, and the United States. The investigation in China brought together the information available in that country on the subject of foreign investments. It has provided the only estimates in some fields and it has made possible the checking and verification of estimates from other sources. Mr. D. K. Lieu, at the time the head of the statistical bureau of one of the departments of the Chinese government, was in charge of the Chinese investigation.

In each of the other countries a new estimate was made of the Chinese investments of its nationals. The Institute of Pacific Relations, whose secretary for research at the time, Mr. J. B. Condliffe, took a keen interest in the whole study from the beginning, was planning to deal with foreign investments in China at its meeting in Kyoto, Japan, in 1929. The Royal Institute of International Affairs in London undertook a study of British investments in China for this Kyoto meeting. The results of this investigation, together with later returns, were made available to me in London in 1931 under conditions which preserved the confidential nature of the original returns. This study and the general co-operation of the Royal Institute of International Affairs have been of the greatest value.

The Japanese investigation was begun in the hope that it would provide material for the Kyoto Conference of the Institute of Pacific Relations. A committee was appointed by the Japanese Council of the Institute and a preliminary report was presented at Kyoto. It was felt that further work was necessary and the continued labors of this Japanese committee form the basis of the chapter on Japanese investments to be found in Part II of this volume.

The American investigation was my direct responsibility. The attempt to measure American investments in China has involved the assistance of so many persons and of so many American firms and corporations that I cannot hope to make adequate acknowledgment or to thank individuals. The officials of the United States government went to much trouble to assist the investigation. American bankers in New York and in various Chinese cities gave help which was particularly valuable. I wish to acknowledge the interest and assistance of those in charge of mission and philanthropic organizations. The preliminary results of the American investigation were made available to the Kyoto Conference of the Institute of Pacific Relations.[1]

---

[1] And in addition a preliminary study of French and German investments in China which was undertaken by Howard S. Ellis with the co-operation of others engaged in the general study.

The outcome of these studies in the various countries was a considerable body of information. The material was not in a satisfactorily comparable form and there were inconsistencies which required further study. Preliminary work had revealed the need of an examination of Russian investments in China. There were the investments of other countries to be studied and estimated and there was the necessity of securing more adequate information concerning China's balance of international payments.

The years 1930–1931 were spent in a visit to the chief countries for the purpose of checking, verifying, and adding to the estimates which form the basis of the work. The visit enabled the subject of investments in China and China's international financial position to be discussed with a considerable number of informed persons. Most of the time was, of course, spent in China, but a discussion of the results of the preliminary study was undertaken in Japan and England. It proved possible, also, to arrange for a study of Russian investments by Mr. J. J. Serebrennikov, a Russian economist now living in Tientsin, China. The results of the German and French studies were considered with officials and business men and information was obtained which enabled reports to be worked out for other countries.

The whole of the collected material was brought together in Ann Arbor in the autumn of 1931. It was put into comparable form, in so far as this proved possible. A report on investments in China for each of the individual countries was written. The general analysis of the material was undertaken and the new estimates of China's balances of international payments were worked out. It was not until the end of the summer of 1932 that the chapters of the first part of the volume could be given their final form.

There lay behind the whole undertaking a conviction and a hope which has, I believe, been justified by the outcome. The hope was that the assembling of facts under the categories of economics would prove possible in a field which was charged with emotion and required the widest international co-operation. The fact that the work could be done at all seems to me, in looking back over the four years, something of a triumph.

The conviction was that the assembling of the facts called for by economic analysis would bring significant results. It is not maintained that any one person or any group of persons can be entirely objective when it comes to examining the acts of others and drawing conclusions from them. There is, I believe, no such remote imperturbability about the social sciences. It is maintained that the concepts generally accepted by economists in a variety of countries enable us to look for the facts, to bring them together, to analyze them, and to draw conclusions from them with the assurance that our conclusions do not merely reflect our prejudices and with the confidence that they will command the assent of persons who may differ widely as to the policy which they indicate. In a world in which complete objectivity is impossible, the social scientist must be as objective as he can.

It is probably more necessary to emphasize objectivity when a study of China is presented than in the case of any other country. This is not entirely because emotion and prejudice are strong and interests are involved, but, also, because there is among the practical students of China's economic problems a school of perverse mystics who maintain that principles do not hold for China. The student of China must, of course, freely acknowledge that caution is necessary when it comes to generalizing about the country, but he is tempted to answer those who hold that no rules apply by asking whether a bank account ought not to balance in Shanghai or Tientsin as well as in Tokyo or London.

The measurement of foreign investment in China is the task that occupied most of the time devoted to the

investigation. An inventory of foreign holdings enabled
an estimate to be made of important items in China's
balance of international payments. Further work on the
balance of payments involved a wholly new investigation
of remittances from Chinese abroad and estimates of
other items of importance. In connection with this investigation of remittances I wish to thank the bankers of
Hongkong, who deal in foreign exchange, for their assistance. Inpayments and outpayments in connection with
foreign investment, taken together with the remittances
to China from Chinese overseas and considered with other
items in the balance of payments, have made possible a
picture of China's international economic relations which
may with some justice be called a new picture.

The task is, of course, incomplete. Concentration upon
the important factors has led to the neglect of others,
and the important elements in China's balance of payments cannot be said to be known with certainty. We
need a more complete account of Chinese holdings abroad
and a current study of China's balance of international
payments carried on over a series of years. I venture to
predict that China will find in the holdings of her people
overseas a support for national economic policy whose
strength is not fully appreciated either by her own people
or by others. But one need not look to the future for
reasons to encourage further investigation. Properly
qualified, the assertion may be made that, for China, the
silver question is a problem in the balance of international payments.

I have made an attempt to indicate, in the chapters on
the different countries in Part II, how far I report the
findings of others. I have, however, given them new form
and I must therefore accept responsibility for these chapters. For the interpretation of Part I and for the analysis,
I am alone responsible.

The investigation has involved work in Japan, China,
Russia, Germany, France, and England, and in the

United States as well. It has meant conferences with business men, bankers, and political leaders in a large number of cities and with officials of the League of Nations at Geneva. There are so many persons to thank that I cannot hope to name them. I am indebted, for direct assistance, to several hundred persons in China. Among them are many of my former students at St. John's University in Shanghai, and many persons in the service of the Chinese government. I must be content to express my gratitude to every one who has helped the work forward.

I wish to acknowledge the great assistance of my wife throughout the study. A debt of gratitude for hospitality is due to Elbrook, Inc., an American firm which provided me with an office in Shanghai and Tientsin, to the North China Union Language School, and to Dr. and Mrs. H. H. Morris of Shanghai. I wish to thank the following who served as my secretaries: Miss Louise Boynton, now of St. Hilda's School, Wuchang, Mr. Koh Chinghung of Shanghai, Mrs. Betty Fraser of London, and Miss Florence Weaver of Ann Arbor.

The funds for the whole series of investigations have come from the Social Science Research Council of New York with a supplementary grant from the Faculty Research Fund of the University of Michigan.

C. F. REMER

Ann Arbor, Michigan
December, 1932

CONTENTS

CONTENTS

PART II

INDIVIDUAL STUDIES

CONTENTS

CHARTS

MAPS

INTRODUCTION TO THE 1968 EDITION

FORTY YEARS LATER

Nearly forty years ago work was begun on a study of foreign investments in China. The original text of the report of this study, published in 1933, is reprinted in the following pages. To it, as an appendix, is added a relevant paper written a few years later.

This study was an honest piece of work and might continue to look the world in the eye without any word from me. But years have passed since it was written and there are comments to be made on the study itself and on its significance in the light of the changes that have come about in these years within China, in eastern Asia, and in the world in which China plays a part.

The changes began at once. On September 18, 1931, I reached Ann Arbor, Michigan, after more than a year of field work which had been carried on not only in China but all the way from Tokyo to London with many stopovers. That was the very day on which Japanese troops marched into Manchuria. My information had been gathered, my statistics had been brought together, my interviews had been carried out, consultations had taken place with my collaborators, all this had been completed when the Japanese troops moved.

Consider the momentous changes which have followed that Japanese advance. It may be said to have been the first step toward the war in the Pacific and toward the Second World War. And communism was soon involved in China.

So my estimates of foreign investment in China may be said to have come at the end of a period and at the beginning of a period in the recent history of China. This has given my study a sort of footnote immortality. Even the Chinese Communist writers have made use of my figures. Since reference to the work will no doubt continue to be made, it is the more reasonable that a reprint edition should be made available.

I want to thank once more the many who assisted me in carrying out the study. Gratitude is felt for the help of some who are no longer living and of many with whom I have been unable to keep in touch. This is more than a perfunctory "thank you," for cooperation was essential to the success of the work. I will not repeat the detailed statement of thanks that appeared in the Preface to the original edition but I must repeat one statement. In view of the international situation at the time and of later developments in that situation, I am still somewhat astonished that the work could have been carried out at all.

While study of foreign investments was going forward, Japan was of overshadowing importance in the foreign relations of China. This had been true for years, certainly since the "Twenty-one Demands" of 1915 when Japan made a bid for a measure of control over China. Japanese intentions were continuously in the minds of Chinese and of foreigners living in the coastal cities of China. They were demonstrated with forceful clarity in 1931 when Japanese troops took over in Manchuria and separated the area from China. Japanese policy is indicated both by what is said and by what is left unsaid in the report of the study. It should however be mentioned concerning the attitude of my Japanese collaborators at a difficult time that they made no effort to influence in Japan's favor the nature or the general conclusions of the report. Japanese policy was, however, continuously in the minds of Chinese and of all those who had to do with China. When I left China in June, 1931 I was of the opinion that the greatest threat to the success of the new nationalist government lay in Japanese policy, and I believe it to have been a prime factor in the defeat of that government.

Within China the nationalist, or Kuomingtang, government was being established, extended, and consolidated. This had followed the northern march of the Kuomingtang armies during which there had been an uneasy cooperation between the Communists and the Kuomingtang, a cooperation that came to an end in 1927. The break with the Communists was accompanied by the withdrawal from China of Soviet advisers and experts. It was followed after a period by the setting up of a local Communist government in the province of Kiangsi and this local government was in existence when I was at work on my study in Shanghai and elsewhere on the coast of China.

The Kuomingtang government undertook to deal with regional warlords and independent leaders and was led by confidence in its efforts in Manchuria into an open quarrel with Soviet Russia over the control of the Chinese Eastern Railway. This railway I set down as the chief Soviet investment, or holding, in China, though the Soviet experts with whom I consulted in Moscow did not like the term "investments," preferring, as they said, to call the railway a Chinese-Soviet condominium.

The Western governments dealt with the new government of China in a conciliatory spirit. The United States led the way toward tariff autonomy for China which promised financial support at a time when the Kuomingtang government did not desire to borrow abroad. This government did however take preliminary steps in the direction of economic development by setting up a National Resources Commission and by inviting advisers and experts from the League of Nations to assist this commission.

I have said enough if I have given some impression of the Chinese scene during the years just before 1931. The dominant feature was, as I have stressed, the policy of Japan. To the confusion arising from domestic difficulties was added the serious threat arising from the increasing hostility of Japan.

The point of view from which the study was undertaken calls in the first place for a word on the relation between analysis and policy, or on the interplay of analysis and policy. My position was stated, somewhat awkwardly I now believe, in the very first paragraph of the Introduction to the original edition. Who, it was there asked, may see the world as a whole and China in its true place in such a general picture?

It would have been better, as I see it now, to say simply that economic analysis is a contribution to policy and that the search for appropriate policy is as broad as the wide world. The economist proceeds in the hope that effective analysis will play its part in wise policy but he must appreciate that policy is determined by many factors beyond the economic. It is policy which is the more general and the more inclusive. This is said without raising any question as to the importance of method, of theory, or of the tools of economic analysis. The test of method, however, is ultimately the wisdom of policy.

One application of this approach lies in the fact that I moved in my exposition from the history and assessment of foreign investments in China to an examination of the Chinese balance of international payments. A corollary is that I did not move from foreign investment to revolution in China as a struggle against the foreigner and against foreign imperialism. I did not see the Chinese revolution as chiefly a movement against the foreigner.

I had come to believe during my residence in China and my study of the Chinese economy that there were more important factors than foreign economic relations in the Chinese revolution. I had found foreign investments to be relatively small. They had been undertaken by the nationals of countries with highly divergent attitudes and policies toward China. Political interest as in Manchuria had in some cases preceded investment. I resented the tyranny and the oversimplification of the term "imperialism."

It was more important, however, that I had found in China a social, political, and economic organization which was accompanied by, if it had not brought into existence, a great population of poor peasants living under such conditions and such institutions as to explain and promote revolution. This situation called for policy and analysis in many fields beyond international economics and foreign policy. I had been in famine relief service in northern China and had studied the peasant villager. I believed that an effective Chinese revolution might be a gradual change or it might be violent, but that in any case it would give an important place to the peasants and to the countryside. Moreover I believed that the skilled industrial workers of Shanghai and Tientsin were a potential source of strength to the "new" China, as indeed the Communist government has discovered.

As a result of these opinions I may not have given sufficient weight to foreign investment and foreign-owned industrial plants as a factor in the Chinese revolution. I have more to say on that within a few pages. In any case my progress was from investments to the balance of international payments and it seems to me to have been reasonable. It was a defensible application of the principle of the priority of policy based on good sense and broad judgment. I have in recent years come to believe that this principle has a wide application, especially in the case of underdeveloped countries.

There was a second feature of the point of view from which I approached the study of foreign investments, the possibility of objectivity. This matter had led to much speculation on my part during the decade or more that I had spent in China before I wrote the Introduction to the original edition. I have no doubt that such speculation plays a part in the thought of every social scientist who has lived and worked in a culture different from his own. The danger is that he will find something normal about the social arrangements in his own culture and something not quite normal about arrangements which differ from those in his own culture. There is the further danger that he will do this without knowing that he is doing it.

The simple answer is a stern resolution to be objective. But further reflection on this matter leads to the conclusion that man cannot be entirely objective when he is engaged in the study of his fellow man. At the same time it seemed clear that mere prejudice ought to be avoidable though this is not as easy, even among scholars, as is frequently supposed. The solution that I reached was to accept the paradox: If you can't be objective, be as objective as you can. This might be given more elegant expression without being any clearer or any more adequate as a statement of my point of view.

When the study of foreign investment was planned it was greatly desired that quantitative estimates of the appropriate factors be made. There were many reasons for this insistence upon quantitative estimates. But there was one reason of a personal sort which helps to present the scene in which part of the work was done.

I had lived in Shanghai for a decade or more and my desire for quantitative measurement was, in part, a protest against the assertions about China and her international relations which expressed the attitude of many foreigners living in China and of many articulate Chinese. I came to the study weary of unsupported qualitative and subjective statements.

What's wrong with China was frequently the theme of the discussion of China among foreigners. And the discussion often revealed both smugness and condescension. Of course there were many honorable exceptions to this lofty attitude but it was general enough to lead one to give great weight to the objectivity promised by quantitative estimates.

The subjectivity of the Chinese, chiefly of course of the Chinese intellectuals, was in part a reaction to the attitude of the foreigners living in their country. The magnificence of China's past was emphasized in their statements and the "unequal treaties" denounced, often as the chief cause of China's troubles. This was sometimes carried to the point of presenting China as the innocent victim of the hostile schemes of others. It is not easy to see how this could have been the attitude of informed Chinese toward the international financial operations of Li Hung-chang or Yuan Shih-kai. In any case I was moved by the popular Chinese viewpoint to give great weight to objective measurement.

From the vantage point of forty or fifty years later it may be said that neither the Chinese nor the foreigner of my period of residence in China knew how uncertain was the ground on which he stood. What the Chinese did not see was that the foundation was fast being eroded from beneath the noble, beautiful, and, as he was likely to believe, eternal structure of China's traditions and social arrangements. What the Westerner and the Japanese did not see was that the stability and even the structure of empires were threatened. Confusian doctrine and modern empire building were soon to lose much of their power over the minds of men. But my purpose is not so much to reflect on the passing of what seemed, to the Easterner or the Westerner, a safe reliance; it is rather to offer the modest observation that there is something to be said for objective study and little to be said for smugness and airs of superiority.

The items for which quantitative estimates were made may be listed. This list shows the rounded account which I made an effort to present, and it provides a basis of reference for the comments on selected items which it seems desirable to offer.

The first item is the obligations of the Chinese government to foreigners. The second consists of the business or direct investments of the foreigner. The two items show what may be called the holdings in China of the foreigner at selected dates since 1900. This inventory of holdings may be looked upon as a series of instantaneous pictures.

The third item is inpayments into China on government account, that is, unilateral or capital inpayments. The fourth item is outpayments from China on government account.

The fifth and sixth items are the inpayments and outpayments associated with the business or direct investments. The four items of payments show in each case the flow over a period of time and stand in related contrast with the holdings.

These unilateral payments on capital account could be

given their general meaning only by drawing up balances of international payments for China, which is the seventh item on my list.

The eighth and final item, remittances from overseas Chinese, presents unilateral inpayments of great and peculiar importance in the Chinese case. The position of China could not be made clear or, for that matter, understandable without an estimate or a series of estimates of remittances. So a completely new estimate was worked out for each of the three years 1928 to 1930, and a re-examination was made of estimates over the years since 1902.

This set of interrelated estimates must stand as it was presented in the original edition. Modification or attempted correction is now impossible and any attempt to make changes would destroy the value of this reprint.

Reflecting now on these estimates my first comment concerns the place of the Chinese government as a borrower. It is true that the government during the early years of the century borrowed for railway construction and made some progress in this field. But, as I pointed out in my study, the Chinese government was, overall, an indemnity-paying institution and not a capital-importing institution. Railway building, a highly important step toward economic development, was marred by bickering among the foreign powers and checked by the anti-Manchu revolutionists who saw in it a means of unifying the country under the Manchus.

The usual situation in the international financial operations of the Chinese government was a large annual excess of outpayments, which was to be expected of an indemnity-paying institution. There were, however, two years when there were great net inpayments, 1913 and 1918. The net inpayments of 1918 were associated with the Nishihara Loans. I suppose that no one, looking back on these operations, will defend them.

The great net inpayment of 1913 was associated with the so-called Reorganization Loan. This loan must have been finally signed, as I said to Chinese friends at the time, in the dark of the moon and in the back room of the issuing bank. It provided funds for the government under Yuan Shih-kai and assisted in the reorganization of the Salt Revenue Administration. But in a whole variety of ways it was a failure on the Chinese and on the foreign side. This was not fully brought out at the time nor has it been brought out since with the devastating clarity it deserves. An excellent factual account of this loan, including the negotiations and the immediate consequences, might have had some good effect at an earlier time, and an adequate study even at this late date would be most revealing of the conditions that made for dissension and civil strife in China and aroused strong feelings against the foreigner. It would be more enlightening than general assertions about corruption and unequal treaties.

The Reorganization Loan was the last effort of international banking institutions of the period before the First World War to set the Chinese government on its feet and start it along the path of economic development. The whole episode shows the awkwardness of traditional China in meeting the new conditions after the fall of the monarchy and the remoteness of the Western governments and of Japan from any acceptance of true and general responsibility. This loan, I may add, was my introduction to international finance in China and I have always regarded it as an outstanding example of how not to do it.

I turn from the obligations of the Chinese government to deal with direct, or business, or entrepreneur investments. More might have been said in the original edition on the subject of the ownership by foreign governments of direct investment in railways in China. Such ownership was the strongest evidence of empire building, of steps toward political control in China on the part of foreign governments. But my present purpose is not to say more than has been said on railroad construction in Manchuria and Shantung. It is rather to call attention to the fact that direct investment meant the introduction into China of capital, technical effectiveness, and management in one balanced bundle, in one appropriately proportioned package. By 1931 such investment had been the chief means of developing in China whatever there was in the way of modern industry in the country. Direct investment met the needs of the Chinese economy. The circumstances surrounding the growth of direct investment included the treaty port extraterritoriality system which was characteristic of the situation in China. But it did bring in capital and technical competence in transportation, mining, manufacturing, and public utilities.

The intensification of Chinese nationalism which accompanied the successful establishment of the Kuomingtang government at Nanking was, in my opinion, certain to bring attacks on foreign direct investment. It followed that my speculation on the prospects for economic development in China included the examination of the possibilities of importing into China the capital and the technical competence required for such development in ways which were consistent with the continued rise of nationalism.

This explains my careful examination of the prospects for the effectiveness of the Chinese corporation. It seemed to me that it might be the means by which the Chinese could get many of the advantages associated with direct investment. I held the opinion that the course of events in Japan had included early direct investment by the foreigner, followed by the shrewd use of foreign capital and foreign technicians in building up Japanese corporations. And in any case it was a possible path toward the solution of the problem for China which would be consistent with private enterprise and the increasing maturity of the Chinese businessman. I found that the Japanese had had experience with investment in Chinese corporations. This experience I examined carefully even though the investments of this sort were small. After interviews with both Chinese and Japanese I came to the conclusion that early progress along this line was not to be expected. I need not go into the reasons here; they are set forth in the book.

A second possibility which was briefly reported in the book was the possibility of introducing foreign capital into China through a Chinese banking syndicate organized to borrow abroad and lend in China. I did not sufficiently emphasize the importance of technique and management as I now see it, though these factors came up in discussion with the Chinese bankers. This plan may be regarded as a variation on the idea of investment through the Chinese corporation and it gave importance to the groups who were both nationalist and keenly aware of the difficulties. There was grave doubt among the bankers of the workability of any such plan.

A third possibility was suggested in Shanghai. I have not at any time reported this elsewhere but it may be desirable to say a word about it here since it reveals the thinking of businessmen who knew China and were seriously concerned over the importance of investment in the business and industry of the country. During the winter of 1930-1931 I met a number of times with a small group of such businessmen in Shanghai, who explored in their discussions the possibility that Shanghai, or a part of Shanghai, might be made into a great and accepted international center.* This was to be done with the consent and cooperation of the Chinese government. They

---

* The meetings of foreign businessmen in Shanghai were the counterpart of an initiative taken by the British members of the Institute of Pacific Relations Conference at Honolulu in 1927, and taken to London by Mr. Lionel Curtis, who was then Secretary of the Royal Institute of International Affairs. As a result, the Hon. Mr. Justice Feetham, C.M.G. (a South African Judge) was commissioned to study the status of the International Settlement at Shanghai. Judge Feetham's study was published as "Report of the Hon. Mr. Justice Feetham, C.M.G. to the Shanghai Municipal Council, 1931." It was extensively discussed at the Fourth Conference of the Institute of Pacific Relations held at Hangchow and Shanghai, October-November, 1931. These discussions are reported in Bruno Lasker (ed.) *Problems of the Pacific, 1931*, University of Chicago Press, 1932, Ch. X.

called it the free city of Shanghai or the international city of Shanghai. It was to include a free port but that was only part of the plan. It was to be a financial and banking center and to offer facilities for technical assistance and advice. There was talk of legal service and research. It was to be established by international agreement. I do not now remember further details but it was to constitute a great international center to assist in the development of China. When the strong nationalism of the time is remembered and it is borne in mind that this was very shortly before the separation of Manchuria from the rest of China by the Japanese, any plan of this sort seems to have been a totally unrealistic dream. Even under the conditions of 1930 it did not seem to call for serious investigation. In part it reflected fear for the future of Shanghai as well as interest in the future of China. I have mentioned this to show how far Japan and the West and China herself were in 1930 from anything like the suggestions considered by the group with whom I met in Shanghai. Cooperation to bring about the economic development of China semed to me both necessary and impossible.

When the Chinese Communist government, after it took over, undertook to get forward in the industrial field, it met the same shortage of capital and technical competence which had brought direct investments into China at an earlier time. The underlying economic problem had not been solved by changing names. The solution, or the attempted solution, in the Chinese Communist case, is indicated by the phrase "complete sets of equipment."

When the Soviet government undertook to provide, during the Chinese first Five Year Plan, a considerable number of industrial plants, it agreed to do so, we are told by an official of the Chinese Communist government, from start to finish. The Soviet government provided a loan from which payments were made. It sent its experts to conduct surveys, to select construction sites, to design the particular plant, to order the equipment needed which came as one shipment or one series of related shipments and thus gave rise to the term "complete sets." The Soviet experts and technicians then set up the plant in China or supervised its construction. They brought it into operation and carried the responsibility for this operation over a period of time.

As early as 1931, I was taken to see an electric light and power plant in Swatow which in its beginning had been a foreign direct investment and had later been taken over by Chinese interests. One section of the Peking-Mukden Railway was a direct investment by a foreign mining corporation when it was taken over by the Chinese government interested in the creation of the Peking-Mukden line. The newspapers in 1967 have reported sales to China of industrial plants by corporations in non-Communist countries under short-term credits and with provision for technical aid in getting these "complete sets" constructed and into operation. I mention these arrangements to show the similarity and to suggest that there might at an earlier time have been more imagination and flexibility in the use of foreign direct investments in China.

The studies of remittances to China by the overseas Chinese which I carried on in Hongkong, Amoy, and Swatow during 1930 and 1931 finally convinced me that large estimates of such remittances were not unreasonable. I had made estimates of such remittances at an earlier time in connection with my studies of the foreign trade of China and I had always had some misgivings. I had feared that my estimates might be too large. This fear was removed by the studies reported in this volume of inpayments from overseas Chinese during the years 1928, 1929, and 1930. I was convinced that during these years the remittances came to about U. S. $100 million a year.

The immediate application of this was to the balance of international payments. I found inpayments of overseas remittances to be as great as outpayments from China on foreign business earnings and the service of the foreign obligations of the Chinese government. When I tried to translate overseas remittances into Chinese holdings in foreign countries, I found my efforts futile. It was not possible to discover how far these remittances were the wages of Chinese workers and how far they were returns on business assets. A better way of putting it is to say that my difficulties were due to the differences between the Chinese family and the Western business corporation.

I wish to record once more my astonishment at the failure of China to make more effective use of the overseas Chinese as a means of importing capital, technical skill, and business experience from the outside. The loyalty of the overseas Chinese to family and community in China was great. Their business success was obvious and their banks were in touch with banking institutions abroad. It was to be expected that the leadership would be found either in China or among the Chinese overseas themselves who would employ their qualifications in the industrial and more general economic development of their country. But neither the Manchu government nor the Kuomingtang government nor the Chinese Communist government has made effective use of the overseas Chinese.

It is true that the overseas Chinese supported the revolutionary activities of Sun Yat-sen, which did not make for cooperation with the Manchu government. It is true that there was an interest in education, as in the case of Amoy University, and that there were some small investments in business and industry. While the Japanese were creating a mining and industrial complex in Manchuria and the foreign businessman was building a modest but impressive assortment of industrial enterprises in Shanghai and Tientsin, the overseas Chinese were adding to family land holdings and providing competencies for grandmothers in the villages of Southeast China, and the exchange made available paid for an excess of imports of consumer goods into the area. In 1932 I set this down as a legacy from traditional China and a reflection of the position of the foreigner in the treaty ports and in Manchuria. I am puzzled that the Chinese Communist government has not made a serious effort to deal more favorably with the overseas Chinese who have had their troubles in Southeast Asia. I believe that there has been increased investment in recent years by the overseas Chinese in Taiwan and a more favorable attitude on their part toward the Chinese government on Taiwan. When this volume was published in 1933 I believed that cooperation between the overseas Chinese and the businessmen and authorities of China might become an important feature of the economic development of China.

There is a final comment on investment in China which touches matters that proved to be fundamental to this study and which are, I believe, of significance at the present time for much of Southeast Asia.

When I set out to measure foreign investments in China I tried to take and hold a territorial point of view. I looked upon Hongkong as a part of China. I counted the sale of the obligations of "foreign" municipalities, such as Shanghai, in countries other than China as foreign investment in China. Payment of overseas remittances into Hongkong I looked upon as payment into China. I was required by experience to modify this territorial outlook.

The neatest example of the difficulty I encountered was in Harbin. There were in Harbin flour mills, to give the case that actually came to my attention, owned by "white" Russians who felt themselves excluded from their own country by the Communist revolution. The flour mills had been built very largely by the reinvestment of profits over a considerable period of time. There had been little inpayment into China. The firms that owned the mills had remitted a little to Russia at an earlier time and by 1930 they had for years made no remittances. The owners expected, or hoped, to live out their lives in China and to have their children take over when they had passed on. From the territorial point of view these flour mills were Chinese just as the flour mills of Minneapolis were American even though the first of these mills were the result of a British business investment. The Harbin Mills were part of the flour-milling industry of China and their increase in numbers a part of the industrial growth of China. But my

Chinese friends would not have it so. The Chinese looked upon these mills as Russian. This seemed to them obvious, since the owners were not Chinese. The viewpoint of the Chinese may not be correctly described as racial but I cannot think of a better word. It seemed to me that its origin was to be found in the Chinese family or family-village attitude.

Now it was not difficult to solve the problems presented by this and by similar situations elsewhere in China for purposes of the compilation of statistics or for classification and comparison. I could use the distinction between holdings and payments. Holdings could be, and were, classified and measured on the basis of the nationality of the ownership. Payments were the subject of separate investigation. And I did not feel it desirable to put aside the problems of holdings as non-economic while payments were accepted as economic, for the holdings presented a whole assortment of economic problems in addition to those of a political and legal kind.

It is clear that a racial point of view toward holdings carries with it problems of policy which are different, in important respects, from those associated with the balance of international payments. There are certain feelings that go with the concepts of nation and race. Patriotism has been defined as a dislike for foreigners and the Chinese, along with others, have their full measure of this sort of patriotism.

At the same time it seems equally clear that economic development requires foreign capital and foreign technical sophistication. This calls for some peaceful and friendly, or at least neutral, relations with foreigners. Few peoples have met this test well and I believe it fair to say that the Chinese have not. The Chinese attitude was shown in the early days at Canton in the foreign trade of China and it is shown today in the mainland of China under the Communists. It was usual at an earlier time to put the blame for this on extraterritoriality and the unequal treaties but it seems to lie much deeper, perhaps in the very family system that has given the Chinese great power in many international economic and political relations.

The progress of economic development in many countries of Southeast Asia has been slow. One of the reasons for this may well be a point of view similar to that of the Chinese toward foreign investment and the presence of foreigners associated with the introduction of foreign technique. The overseas Chinese themselves may be suffering from a viewpoint not so different from that applied to foreigners in their own country. This problem is of special importance in countries where peoples of different cultures and races occupy the same territory. The Chinese have experienced and are experiencing the results of their racial viewpoint in the Philippines, Indonesia, Malaysia, and, with some modifications, in Thailand. But my point is not that the Chinese are suffering from discrimination and prejudice; it is to emphasize that a racial viewpoint toward foreign economic relations may be retarding, as it did in China, the economic progress of the Southeast Asian countries. Perhaps the real revolutionists in this area will prove to be leaders who are able to persuade peoples of different "streams," as the term is used in Singapore, to work together effectively and in their foreign economic relations to take a geographical view of the economy of the country. Greater progress would have been made in China in the past and might be made today over much of Asia if an economy could be regarded as an economy and a flour mill, or a fertilizer plant, were not looked upon as if it were a member of the family.

In conclusion I propose to ask how the course of events since 1931, and especially since 1949, may be related to the observations and the analysis presented in this volume for which the work was done nearly forty years ago. This was before the war with Japan, before the Pacific war and the Second World War, and long before the Communists came to power on the mainland of China.

The argument of the book may be briefly restated. The fundamental proposition is that China is poor. The poverty of the Chinese people is emphasized again and again. This means that there are sharp limitations on surplus and savings.

Economic development is taken to mean improvement in the living conditions of the Chinese people. It is a matter of increasing per capita consumption; of food, clothing, and shelter for the people of China's villages.

Economic development requires increased capital equipment, a greatly increased supply of capital equipment, together with improved methods and new techniques. These requirements cannot be adequately met within China nor can they be financed from within China in sufficient supply.

The capital equipment must come in large measure from abroad. In some part it may be procured by trade. This gives importance to the possibility of increased exports and to the terms on which the exports are exchanged for imports. The import of capital equipment must, however, be financed in large measure by foreign credits, that is by foreign investment. The means must be found to solve technical problems. These means I had found largely in direct investments, and I thought they might be found for the future in modified direct investments.

So I reached the conclusion that foreign investment, using the term in its broadest sense, was not only an essential factor in the economic development of China but a factor of critical importance.

I ought to add that it was understood, in connection with this argument, that a great increase in the population of China might make population the critical factor. If I had known in 1932 that the population of China in 1967 would be estimated at some 700 million, I would no doubt have given greater emphasis than I did to the problem of population.

What has been said in the preceding paragraphs was clearly stated in the study of foreign investments which was published in 1933. What I did not expressly state was the opinion which I held that a serious effort to bring about economic development in China without foreign investment or foreign credits on a large scale would call for a large measure of regimentation. This was the term I used in my thinking. Regimentation,

as I put it, would be called for since development would require great savings from a poor people.

There was only a remote possibility in my mind, when I
wrote in 1932, that this regimentation would take the form
of Communist totalitarianism. The increasing efforts of Japan
to dominate China filled my horizon. Even after Japan entered
Manchuria in 1931, I still believed that Japan's efforts would
be limited. I thought that the very large amounts of foreign
capital required for the development of China would probably
bring it about that the Japanese business community would
urge restraint on the Japanese government in its pursuit of a
unilateral policy in China. I felt that the Japanese businessman might see that Japan needed cooperation in the development of China and that American cooperation was to be
preferred to American opposition.

The whole scene, including the Japanese, the Communists,
and the Kuomingtang government, suggested to me the importance of the introduction of foreign capital into China by
means which were adapted to the nationalism of China and
the group individualism and private enterprise of its people. I
hoped that, in the international field, these means would not
include an assertion of exclusiveness on the part of any one
foreign power.

So I examined, as I have said, the prospects for the development of the Chinese corporation. I considered the possibilities
of investment through Chinese modern banking and looked
for restraint upon the intervention of Chinese officials in the
field of business. I speculated upon such modification of direct
investment as would promote the introduction of technical
effectiveness and innovation as well as capital. I looked for
efforts to maximize the flow of funds into China from overseas
Chinese and through overseas Chinese bankers. I gave attention to the promotion of technical education in China and
hoped for more general application of science to Chinese
agriculture.

But it is pointless to dwell further on possibilities of this
sort. What came to China was Japanese invasion, devastating

war, and a Communist régime. The Communists after 1949 were soon faced with the problem of the economic development of the country. Mao Tse-tung has said that revolution is not a dinner party. This was said in a different context but when a Chinese leader invites his people to revolution, it may be well for him to include in this program more food, more consumers' goods, and better living conditions for these people. And the Communist program brought into China a new and related organization which had economic development as one of its chief features.

Under communism the economy of China became a planned economy. This has meant regimentation far beyond that which I had in mind as a possibility at an earlier time. I was thinking of regimentation compatible with the growth of reliance on the strength of private enterprise in China. But the Communist program called for complete control.

Among its features were planned pricing, the related "profits" of government enterprises, compulsory deliveries in kind of agricultural products, the sale of these products at controlled prices, taxes and the sale of bonds, the allocation of equipment and raw materials, the control of exports and imports, and a planned banking and financial system.

Under such an organization the pressure on the people to bring about "capital accumulation" was the result of the policies of the planning authorities. And the priorities which these policies embodied were set by the authorities. Even with higher wages it was not possible to buy consumers' goods beyond the quantity that had been planned.

Among the policies which have put pressure on the Chinese people have been the arming of the country and the development of nuclear weapons. China is certainly the poorest country to have turned out nuclear weapons, and one wonders how and after what discussion that decision was made. The quarrel with the Soviet Union has, no doubt, delayed for some time the economic development of the country. The policy of economic self-sufficiency may be regarded as a check on development. The great planned exports have put consumers' goods beyond the reach of the people. Circumstances, including domestic measures under communism, have made it necessary in recent years to use available foreign exchange for the purchase of food grain abroad. I am not condemning all of these policies indiscriminately. They have, however, increased the pressure on a poor people.

During the period of the first Five Year Plan there were loans from Soviet Russia and there was valuable technical assistance from the same source. During the years since Soviet aid came to an end, there has not been even that relief. After the Great Leap Forward and the difficulties which followed and after further troubles with the Soviet Union, it was to be expected that policy would be adjusted and that Communist China would turn to Japan and western Europe. There has been some increased attention to these areas and to other export markets. There is talk of small credits from western Europe and from Japan. The newspapers have carried reports of the equivalent of "complete sets" from western European countries on short-term credits.

But there has not been, so far as I have learned, any large effort to get capital and technology from the West or from Japan. No high priority seems to be attached to any such effort even when it appears to the observer that the need is greater than at any time in the past.

Reflecting upon the course of events, I am of the opinion that the argument of my book still holds. The economic development of a poor country requires foreign capital and technical assistance, if the pressure upon the people is not to be great, perhaps unbearably great.

The economic policy of Communist China seems to be held within limits which are in large measure beyond the control of the Communists. There is a limit to the pressure on the Chinese people. If there is to be domestic peace, this pressure cannot become intolerable. There is also a limit which lies in the foreign policy of the Chinese Communist government. The policies of that government cannot be so harsh or so doctrinaire as to prove intolerable to the foreigner from whom the capital, the capital equipment, and the technical assistance is to come.

If there should prove to be sufficient adjustment over the coming years on the part of Communist China and on the part of other countries as well to bring about significant economic development in China, I can imagine an economist dealing with my subject in, say, the year 2000 and giving his study this title: Foreign Aid and Technique From Abroad in Chinese Economic Development.

C. F. REMER

Oakland, California
June 1, 1968

PART I

GENERAL: FOREIGN INVESTMENTS AND CHINA'S
INTERNATIONAL ECONOMIC AND FINANCIAL
POSITION

CHAPTER I

INTRODUCTION

Foreign investment in China is but one aspect of the international economic relations of the country and of China's international relations in general. To see these relations in their proper perspective is to see the world in which China plays a part; to understand these relations is to understand the modern world. Who can count or measure all the factors that enter into China's relations with other countries? Who may claim to see the world as a whole, understand the trends of its economic development, and see China in her true place in the general picture?

In every field of the social sciences examples are at hand of efforts to establish a perspective which later events have proved false, or to sketch a background which the passage of time has made meaningless. It is usually unnecessary to go back more than a few years to find examples of the sort which may be cited to the discomfiture of the economist. Those who wrote of world problems, during the period of prosperity before 1929, frequently permitted an easy optimism to lead them into generalizations which were contradicted by the depression of later years. Those who wrote at an earlier time of the economic troubles of the world after the war often provided a background so gloomy that it may be said to reflect an easy pessimism.

The writings on the Far East at the turn of the century offer additional examples which are closer to the subject at hand. The historian was inclined to set the stage for his account by picturing the eastward pressure of Russian expansion and the clash of interests between

Russia and Great Britain along a front that stretched across Asia from Persia to the Amur River. More than one economist saw in the industrialization of Europe and in the declining interest rates of the western world a reason to believe that imperialism would dominate the immediate future and that Asia would be the scene of the ensuing struggle. After the event it is easy to see that the historian failed in many cases to give due weight to the rise of Japan. After 1914 it was easy to refer to the opening years of the century as the pre-war years, but it is to be noted that the war was fought in Europe and that Great Britain and Russia were allies. The economist could hardly have foreseen in 1900 that, within a few decades, the motor car would bring about the investment in roads and factories within the western world of many times the amount of capital which was to find use in the railways of China.

The task of setting the stage or sketching the background seems often to be dealt with as if it were a matter of taste. In Soviet Russia the preference is for a version of current events in China trimmed with red. The imperialist or the apologist for imperialism prefers to decorate his account of China with the colors of his country's flag. The young and emotional Chinese nationalist finds in the black flag of piracy a more appropriate symbol of the attitude of the foreign powers toward his country. It is not a matter, however, of a well-chosen figure of speech but a difficult venture in the field of analysis.

One may not enter lightly upon the task of making a world picture in which the place of China shall be truly shown. A view which gives undue emphasis to recent events is not easily avoided. One cannot escape the powerful influences of country, class, and race. The result of these and other influences is that many undertake an exposition of Chinese affairs and provide a background which carries with it a ready-made solution of the most difficult and important problems to be attacked. Nevertheless, in spite of the risks, the task may not be avoided if anything is to be offered as to the meaning of the current situation and if the information which has been brought together is to be interpreted.

As an approach to a classification of the world's countries which shows the place of China, I venture to accept the traditional distinction which sets off the East from the West. This distinction has found a place in the literature and in the ordinary conversation of both the East and the West. The general acceptance of this distinction means, I believe, that it is based upon real differences of importance.

It is often supposed that the differences between the East and the West are of the same sort as those between the medieval and the modern West. It is, of course, true that China and the medieval West show many similarities in technique as well as in economic and social organization. But even here "the hackneyed reference to the Middle Ages is sadly overworked and leaves a good deal unsaid."[1] The fact of outstanding importance from the viewpoint of international economic relations is that China lives in a world which includes a West that is not medieval. The modern West plays an important, often a dominant, part in every aspect of China's foreign relations. It is the existence of the West which gives form and content to many of China's present problems. We may be assisted in our efforts to understand the social and economic life of the Chinese if we know the West of an earlier time, but we miss the point if we allow ourselves to reflect upon China as if the results of the Industrial Revolution were not present in the world and as if powerful modern national states did not exist.

When we come to ask what the differences are which make the distinction between East and West so common a matter of comment, we find a variety of answers.

[1] Tawney, R. H., *A Memorandum on Agriculture and Industry in China*, Honolulu, 1929, p. 13.

Eastern civilization, we are told by Hu Shih, is "wheel-barrow civilization," and Western is "motor-car civilization." The boundary line between the two he claims to have found in the city of Harbin where rickshas are used in one section and automobiles in another.[2] In the contrast between human labor and machinery as the source of power we have the difference most frequently mentioned.

We are told by others that the extensive use of minerals in the West marks it off from the East, that the East has a "vegetable" civilization. A Chinese economist finds the important difference, taking his cue from Veblen, in the matter-of-factness of Western civilization. He contrasts with this the power over the Eastern mind of such abstractions as propriety and benevolence. Examples might be multiplied, for every one who knows the East has probably felt himself impelled, at some time, to generalize.

For the purposes of economic analysis I propose to carry this distinction between East and West into a division of the world by the test of industrial advance and economic organization. If the word "development" may be used in a neutral sense, we may say that the world presents developed and relatively undeveloped countries. To be significant the division must be carried further and, I believe, we may distinguish the following: (1) the highly developed West, that is, western Europe and the United States, (2) the relatively undeveloped West which presents few obstacles to development, including such countries as Canada, Argentina, and Jugo Slavia, (3) the Tropics, including such tropical regions as offer permanent obstacles to development, for example, Central

[2] Hu Shih, "Civilizations of the East and West" in Beard, Charles A. (Ed.), *Whither Mankind*, New York, 1928. "Here I made my great discovery in modern geography. I discovered the border line between the Eastern and Western civilizations. The city of Harbin separates the East from the West by separating the jinricksha (man-power-carriage) civilization from the motor-car civilization."

Africa, (4) Russia, which is relatively undeveloped and offers to development along Western lines resistance based upon an alternative program, and finally, (5) the East, including such countries as China, India, and Japan.

The East is relatively undeveloped but differs in important ways from the other groups which have been set off from the developed West. The undeveloped West presents sparse populations and much unused land; the East, dense populations and little unused land. The East offers to development on Western lines the obstacle, not of a vigorous alternative program, as does Russia, but of an economic and social organization based upon a civilization and culture different from that of the West.

Broadly speaking, the East shows in its political life the persistence of government based upon some special sort of religious sanction. In its social and economic life the family stands out as of supreme importance. Just as an Easterner who would understand the West must bear in mind the overwhelming importance of the national state, so the Westerner, who would understand the East, must not lose sight of the importance of the family. The peasant family is the foundation and support of the agricultural village and it is the agricultural village which is the characteristic social and economic phenomenon of Asia. We see in China a peasant village civilization which must find a way to live in the modern world. This is the key to the great revolution which is going on in China.

An outstanding difference between the East and the modern West lies in the abundance and effectiveness of the capital equipment at the disposal of the West. It is, in general, the absence of such capital equipment that is characteristic of undeveloped countries. We ought, therefore, to find that capital moves from the highly developed countries of the world to those relatively undeveloped. This is, in fact, what we do find in the world as it was before 1914. The flow of capital has been greatly altered by the war but the classification of the world's countries, which I have presented, leads to the conclusion that we may look forward in the future to a continuance of the pre-war flow of capital. If this is true, we may take certain important things for granted in the economic and political relations of the next century.

Among the undeveloped countries a distinction has been set up between the West and the East. The undeveloped West offers few obstacles to the inflow of capital. Consider the facility of its movement to Canada or Argentina. The East, on the other hand, presents checks and barriers of a variety of sorts. These hindrances are of such importance in the Chinese case as to lead to the generalization that the flow of capital to undeveloped Eastern countries is in accordance with the capacity of these countries to receive the capital and make effective use of it.

The place of Russia in the classification which I have offered enables still another application to be made. The economic development of the West is capitalistic, that of Russia is being attempted under communism. What shall we say of the East? The economic development of China, and of India and Japan as well, has in the past been under a social organization which makes the family the owner of the land and the capital equipment. Efforts have been made to find an appropriate name for this Eastern organization. It may, if there is such a term, be called familistic. The course of events in Russia on the one hand and in Japan on the other makes it reasonable to suppose that Chinese development must be either communistic or capitalistic. This is not to be accepted too easily. Neither capitalism nor communism can spread in China without undergoing changes. It is to be borne in mind, also, that the East may work out a modification of the familistic system which will be something new.

It is sometimes maintained that the world is moving toward a Pacific era and that this tendency offers the best introduction to an exposition of China's international economic relations.[3] This view seems to me unsupported by the facts and misleading in that it often serves as the basis of a narrow regional view of Eastern and of Chinese economic problems. The drainage area of the Pacific Ocean is much smaller than that of the Atlantic. The Atlantic is more easily reached from the whole of Europe and from most of North and South America. The geographical situation has been greatly altered by the opening of the Panama Canal. These are facts which need to be considered.

It is true that we have seen, especially since 1914, a vigorous growth of trade and production in the Pacific area. It is to be expected that in the future the Pacific will take a place of co-ordinate importance with the Atlantic, but it seems impossible to suppose that the Atlantic will be overshadowed or supplanted. China, along with other Eastern countries, may be expected to play a more important part in world economic relations, but no easy generalization based upon an over-simplification of history and geography will serve as a true perspective.

Analysis, based upon the classification of the world's countries, which I have offered, may be pushed somewhat further. We may consider differences within the group of Eastern countries, such as those between China and Japan. It is a matter of common observation that Japan has adapted herself to modern ways more rapidly than has China. Her history, her political system, and her economic organization have made the problem of securing capital at home or abroad less difficult than in the case of China. Japan has carried her development to the point at which she faces the difficulty of finding markets for the products which her adoption of modern

[3] It is usual in American works to support this with a quotation from Wm. H. Seward, "The Pacific Ocean, its shores, its islands, and the vast region beyond will become the chief theatre of events in the world's great hereafter," or from Theodore Roosevelt, "The Mediterranean era died with the discovery of America. The Atlantic era is now at the height of its development and must soon exhaust the resources at its command. The Pacific era, destined to be the greatest of all, is just at the dawn."

methods enables her to turn out. The key to Japan's international economic relations seems to be found in her foreign trade.

China, on the other hand, is in the midst of a great revolution which touches every aspect of her life. She faces economic changes, and many of the changes in this field require a surplus. The poverty of her people makes it unlikely that she will be able to find any large surplus at home. Her social organization makes it difficult to secure it abroad. The key to China's economic relations may well be found in foreign investment.

CHAPTER II

CHINA'S POPULATION AND RESOURCES

GEOGRAPHY

The facts about China may be stated confidently enough so long as we are satisfied with the very general. We may say with some confidence that China, with about a fifth of the world's population, occupies about a thirteenth of the world's land area. If we exclude Tibet, Sinkiang, and Mongolia, we may say that in China a fifth of the world's population occupies less than a twenty-fifth of the world's land.

The size and position of the territory may be most easily grasped if, following the example of others, we superimpose a map of China upon that of North America without departing from correctness as to latitude. The whole of the territory of China will be found to cover a slightly greater distance from east to west and a considerably greater distance from north to south than does the United States. Shanghai will fall east of the coast of southern Georgia; Vladivostok, in Siberia just beyond the Chinese border, will fall near Boston; and Canton not far from Havana. Peking and Tientsin find a place in central Ohio and Hankow near Mobile, Alabama. The northern extension of Heilungkiang province in Manchuria will touch the southern end of Hudson Bay and the western extension of Sinkiang will fall west of San Francisco. The eighteen provinces of China and the Manchurian provinces taken together cover a territory about equal to the territory of North America between Hudson Bay and Havana and east of central Kansas.

But China differs from the United States. She has but one sea coast and her only outlet on the west is by a long

overland journey.[1]   Another important difference between China and the corresponding North American region may be brought out if we imagine ourselves seizing
Florida as a handle and turning North America, east of
the Rocky Mountains, until we make of the Mississippi
a river flowing east. If we then combine New Orleans and
New York to make a great city at the mouth of this river,
we shall have a territory somewhat like China and a city
similar in importance to Shanghai.

China presents greater variations in temperature than
does the corresponding North American region.   The
summers are likely to be hotter and the winters colder.
The rainfall is not unlike that of the United States east
of the Rocky Mountains. America has an arid west and
China an arid northwest.[2] The extreme northwest of the
provinces of China lies beyond the line of 20 inches of
rainfall and thus approaches in dryness the desert regions
of central Asia.

A final point of difference between China and the
United States is that China is much more mountainous.
There is nothing in China to correspond to the great,
fertile, and level valley of the Mississippi. The plain of
North China presents a great expanse of fertile land but
it is little larger than Iowa and Illinois in the United
States. If we add the plain of Manchuria and that of the
Yangtze we have a territory to be compared in size with
the western part of the Mississippi valley rather than
with the whole.[3] The mountains of China reduce the proportion of usable land, make communication difficult,

---

[1] Bain, H. F., *Ores and Industry in the Far East*, New York, 1927, p. 35,
points this out.   Bain uses the device of the superimposed map.

[2] The average annual rainfall in Hongkong is 84 inches, in Shanghai
44 inches, and in Peking 24 inches. See Stamp, L. Dudley, *Asia*, New York,
1929, p. 456.   See also Buck, J. L., *Chinese Farm Economy*, Shanghai,
1930, pp. 8, 13.

[3] I take the area of these plains from Cressy, George B., "The Geographic Regions of China," in the *Annals of the American Academy*, Nov.,
1930, p. 3. See also Stamp, L. Dudley, *China*, p. 446, "A far larger portion of the surface is mountainous and incapable of utilization than is
the case with India."

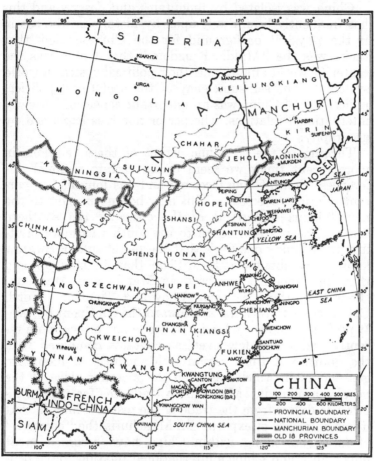

CHINA: PRESENT POLITICAL DIVISIONS, THE CHIEF CITIES, AND
THE BOUNDARY OF THE OLD EIGHTEEN PROVINCES

reinforce regionalism, and have served to cut China off from Burma and India.

China was isolated by mountains and deserts and this has frequently been dwelt upon by historians who see in it the physical background for the Chinese view that theirs was the "Middle Kingdom," that China was the center of world affairs, and their political system a world system.[4] The self-sufficiency of the social and political philosophy of China was an important aspect of her early international relations, whether or not it is explained by geography.

Turning to the economic aspect of these relations in more recent times we seem to see certain regional differences. South China faces out and has long had important relations overseas. This may be due in part to the mountainous hinterland of the cities of the southern coast. The peaceful ocean to the south was more inviting. Even today one finds that the merchants of Swatow know more about events in Siam than in Hankow and that the economic ties between Manila and Amoy are closer than those between Amoy and Tientsin. North China seems to turn its face toward the continent of Asia. It prefers to move by land. Its trade has grown more recently and it has few overseas contacts compared with the South. A third region is Manchuria, a mountain guarded plain which has been the meeting place of the peoples around it. Manchurian trade has features of its own. It differs from the trade of the rest of China in that it has an excess of exports. In Manchuria the "colonies" of foreigners living within China have assumed great importance and China's international relations have usually been concerned with events within China's boundaries.

---

[4] A recent writer has found in the effect of geography upon communications the basis for the antagonism between North and South which runs through Chinese history. Bishop, C. W., "The Geographical Factor in the Development of Chinese Civilization," *The Geographical Review*, New York, Jan., 1922, vol. 12, no. 1, pp. 19–41.

RESOURCES

The provinces of China, we have said, have a fifth of
the world's population upon a twenty-fifth of the world's
land. If we inquire more closely we soon find ourselves
on uncertain ground. It is not known, for example, what
proportion of the land of China (I include the old eighteen provinces and Manchuria) is capable of cultivation.
There is no doubt that it is considerably less than in the
United States, where it is about 50 per cent, and considerably greater than in Japan, where it is about 15 per cent.

The land under cultivation in China is usually estimated at somewhat less than 25 per cent of the total
area.[5] If we accept some such figure as this and accept
400 million as an estimate of the population, we find
that China has approximately two persons to every acre
of cultivated land, that is, about 1,280 persons to every
square mile. Comparing China with the West we may
say that she has a larger population per unit of cultivated
land than any Western country, except Great Britain,
Holland, and Belgium, larger, that is, than in the case of
any Western country mainly dependent upon agriculture. Comparing China with Eastern countries, we may
say that China has about half the population of Japan per
unit of cultivated land. Other comparisons require attention to particular regions. The island of Cebu in the
Philippines and the island of Java in the Dutch East

[5] Jamieson put the total land under cultivation at 400 million acres in
1905. This is an unbelievably high figure. (*China Year Book*, 1914, p. 436.)
Efforts to make use of the report (in Chinese) of the Ministry of Commerce
and Agriculture for the year 1918 resulted in an estimate of 172.5 million
acres by La Fleur, Foscue, and Baker. (La Fleur, Albert, and Foscue,
Edwin J., "Agricultural Production in China," *Economic Geography*,
vol. 3, no. 3, pp. 297–308. Baker, O. E., "Land Utilization in China,"
Problems of the Pacific, 1927, pp. 324–38, table on p. 326. Earlier issues of
the same Chinese report put the total as high as 250 million acres (see
Lieu, D. K., *China's Industries and Finance*, Peking, 1927, pp. 84–6, for
the totals for 1914–1921 and a discussion of the reliability of the reports).
A more recent estimate puts the total cultivated land about the same
area dealt with above at 323,000 square miles or 207 million acres (Cressy,
George B., "The Geographic Regions of China," *Annals of the American
Academy*, Nov., 1930, p. 3).

Indies are examples of regions largely dependent upon agriculture which show about as large a population per unit of cultivated land as China.

The students of China's land resources agree that there is unused land in China capable of cultivation. It is difficult to believe there is much land of this sort, outside of Manchuria, which does not require capital expenditure and the solution of technical problems to make it usable. Here we touch the possibilities of scientific agriculture, irrigation, the control of rivers, and reforesting. Attention to these problems will, no doubt, increase the available land. It needs to be emphasized that the problem of China's resources in land is not entirely, perhaps not predominantly, a matter of acres but one in which many factors play a part. There is enough land within the wide boundaries of China to make possible, under proper utilization, a higher standard of living for as many people as now live within those boundaries.

The mineral resources of China are not as great as was formerly supposed. The German geologist, Richthofen, said of Shansi, about 1870, that it presented "an extraordinary wealth of the finest iron ore" and that production was capable of an "enormous increase." Of the coal fields of the same province he said that "there were no others in the known world to be compared with them."[6] Such opinions have been drastically revised as the result of later work and the tendency today is probably toward an under-estimate.

It may be said, with some degree of confidence, that China has a fairly adequate supply of coal. The coal reserves of China were estimated in a compilation for the year 1913 at about a billion tons. China was given second

[6] The quotations are from Wittvogel, K. A., *Wirtschaft und Gesellschaft Chinas*, Leipzig, 1931, pp. 96, 115. Richthofen traveled in China in 1870–1872. His reports took the form of letters to the Shanghai Chamber of Commerce and a later work on the geology of China. The value of his work is not to be judged from these references. Richthofen estimated the coal reserves of Shansi alone at 1,260,000 tons.

place among the world's countries following the United States and ahead of Canada.[7] The coal reserves of the Far East, as they were then estimated, show that China holds an overwhelming proportion. Later estimates center about the work of the Geological Survey of China

TABLE 1
COAL RESERVES OF THE FAR EAST IN MILLIONS OF METRIC TONS *

	Proved	Probable	Total
China (without Manchuria)	18,666	976,921	995,587
Manchuria	409	799	1,208
Japan (including Korea)	981	7,070	8,051
Indo-China		20,002	20,002

* Bain, *Ores and Industry in the Far East*, p. 33, from figures compiled for the International Geological Congress in 1913.

and more recent corrections of that work. An estimate of 217.6 million metric tons was made public in 1928,[8] and a revision of this estimate by W. H. Wong placed the total at 302 million metric tons.[9] Mines northeast of Tientsin (Kaiping) provide coking coal in quantities sufficient to support a considerable iron and steel industry. Taking our available information into account we may say that China's coal resources are ample for the needs of the country. Coal is not the limiting factor in the possible development of a metallurgical industry in China.[10]

[7] The figures were compiled for the International Geological Congress at Toronto and published in *Coal Resources of the World*, Toronto, 1913, and are reprinted in Bain, H. F., *Ores and Industry in the Far East*, New York, 1927, p. 33.

[8] *Far Eastern Review*, May, 1928, p. 237.

[9] *China Year Book, 1929–1930*, p. 53. The great discrepancy between these figures and that for 1913 is due largely to differences in definition and, in part, to a tendency on the part of the Geological Survey to be extremely conservative. Professor George B. Cressy in a lecture at Ann Arbor on June 12, 1930, reached the conclusion that an estimate of 864 million metric tons was reasonable.

[10] In support of this conclusion see Bain, H. F., *Ores and Industry in the Far East*, pp. 33, 56, and Smith, Wilfred, *A Geographical Study of Coal and Iron in China*, Liverpool, 1926, pp. 76–7, "although not inexhaustible, China's coal resources are amply sufficient to meet her own needs and those of the Far East and, in spite of the fears of the Geological Survey, her iron resources seem sufficient to supply the requirements of her own, but not, however, of her neighbors', iron industries."

Iron and coal have been the chief supports of modern industry and it seems unlikely that substitutes will be found for them. When we turn from coal resources to those of iron ore we must give serious attention to the opinion that China's resources are quite inadequate as a basis for modern industry.[11] Competent observers are now of the opinion that Richthofen and those who followed him were completely mistaken as to the available iron ore in China. The iron ore deposits of China must be regarded as small. Tegengren, who is widely accepted as an authority, has estimated the iron ore reserves at 950 million metric tons. China's iron ore resources, says Tegengren, "must be termed very modest, or even scant, when her potentialities of industrial development are taken into consideration and the strictest economy would be indispensable to guard against future unpleasant contingencies. By way of illustration it may be pointed out that the total quantity of iron ore (both actual and potential) . . . would be consumed by the iron industry of the United States within less than nine years."[12]

In the second place China's iron ore deposits are widely scattered. It is this fact, perhaps, which explains earlier over-estimates of their total. The more important deposits are to be found in about twelve of the twenty-one provinces into which Manchuria and the rest of China were formerly divided. For this and for other reasons the iron ores of China present difficulties when it comes

[11] Professor Edwin F. Gay in a preface to Bain, H. F., *Ores and Industry in the Far East*, pp. v–viii, states the economic implications of this conclusion as to the inadequacy of Chinese and Far Eastern mineral resources. Bain and C. K. Leith (*Foreign Affairs*, April, 1926) have stated the estimates of the mining engineers upon which this conclusion is based. V. K. Ting and W. H. Wong were among the first to publish such estimates. See their *General Statement of the Mining Industry*, Special Report of the Geological Survey of China, no. 1, June, 1921. T. T. Read and F. R. Tegengren are generally regarded as competent authorities in this field. Tegengren's chief work was done for and published by the Geological Survey of China.

[12] Quoted by Bain, H. F., *Ores and Industry in the Far East*, p. 84, from Tegengren, F. R., *Iron Ores and Iron Industry of China*, Memoirs of the Geological Survey of China, Peking, 1921–1924.

to large scale operations. The Manchurian deposits are of such low grade that study and experiment have failed to turn out cheap pig iron in great quantities and the Japanese are turning to other parts of the Far East for their supplies.[13] Ore of comparatively high grade is to be found at many places in the Yangtze valley. This ore, although scattered, [14] is fairly close to a satisfactory means of transportation and it has been in the past the chief source of China's iron production.

The inadequacy of China's iron ore supply is considered by Professor Gay from the point of view of the industrial development of the Far East. It may well be that the Far East gives no promise of a development like that of the Ruhr-Lorraine region or like that which has resulted in the United States from the bringing together of the resources of Pennsylvania and Minnesota. It does not follow from this that the iron ore of China presents immediate limitations to industrial development. China has the ore for an industrial development which may seem modest to the Western student and may, at the same time, be of great significance to China.

Turning to minerals of minor importance it may be said that China has in recent years produced no less than 70 per cent of the world's antimony and about 50 per cent of the world's tungsten. Tin and ores containing manganese are of some importance as well.

The petroleum resources of China are held to be small by every investigator. It is the opinion of W. B. Heroy that the oil resources of China are "probably less than 1 per cent of those of the United States."[15] The oil shale deposits of Manchuria may be extensive but the petroleum content is low and the capacity of the one plant small. An American corporation in 1914 held options upon the exploitation of the oil resources of the provinces of Chihli

[13] Japanese Investments, pp. 465–66, 491.
[14] Tegengren lists 17 deposits along the Yangtze, the largest being that at Tayeh in Hupeh. Bain, H. F., *Ores and Industry in the Far East*, p. 81.
[15] Bain, H. F., *Ores and Industry in the Far East*, p. 116.

and Shensi. These options were permitted to lapse after
an investigation by mining engineers. It is most unlikely
that petroleum will count for much among China's power
resources, though we may add, as do most of the writers,
a reference to the deficiencies in our knowledge.

The water power resources of China can hardly be said
to be known at all. The only estimate which has come to
my knowledge puts the potential resources below those
of the United States and India and slightly higher than
those of Canada, and the developed resources at so small
a total as not to be worth considering.[16] It seems certain that the resources of China are scattered, that they
will be developed, but slowly, and that they count for
relatively little in the present situation.

The inadequacy of the natural resources of China are
to be seen as a distant or ultimate limitation upon the
economic and industrial development of the country rather
than as a limitation which is immediate or close at hand.
In so far as there is this limitation, it is a limitation also
upon the possibilities of foreign investment in the country,
or upon what may be called China's capacity to receive
capital. The economic development of China may be
carried far without meeting any ultimate barrier in the
natural resources. To appreciate this one need but reflect upon the changes that would be brought about by
an adequate system of transportation. The reason for
China's lack of railways is not to be found in her modest
resources of coal and iron. And there is always the possibility that modern industry will be so altered by the
progress of invention as to require natural resources somewhat different from those which it has required in the past
or to use resources which have not been used in the past.[17]

[16] Shing, T., and Wong, W. H., "An Outline of the Power Resources
of China," *Transactions of the First World Power Conference*, London,
1924, vol. 1, pp. 739–47.

[17] This point has been made by J. B. Condliffe, "Industrial Development
in the Far East," *Chinese Social and Political Science Review*, July, 1928,
vol. 12, no. 3.

The limitations upon economic development and capital movement which lie in the institutions and traditions of the Chinese people seem to me of more immediate significance, but it is not to be forgotten that changes in traditions and customs, such as land tenure, may have the effect of making the natural resources more abundant. We may attack the problem of the next half century in China with some degree of assurance that the land and resources are adequate for considerable development and that they do not constitute the limiting factors.

POPULATION

The widest variety of figures for China's population may be brought together. Consider those for recent years only. A survey carried out by a group of co-operating mission organizations under the "China Continuation Committee" arrived at a total for the eighteen provinces and Manchuria of 440.9 million in 1919. The estimate of the Chinese Post Office for 1920 was 427.7 million. The Post Office estimate for 1926 was 485.5 million. The estimate of the Chinese Maritime Customs for 1928 was 451.8 million and for 1930 it was 438.9 million. Recent work by the Bureau of Statistics of the Chinese government indicates that a final total of about 480 million will be reached.[18]

Estimates of competent students of China's population vary even more widely than do the figures which have been quoted. The problem was given attention at the 1930 session of the International Institute of Statistics in Tokyo. Dr. W. F. Willcox, well known for his earlier studies in this field, presented an estimate of 323 million for the old eighteen provinces. Dr. Willcox does not in-

[18] Post Office estimates are printed in the *China Year Book*. For the China Continuation Committee's estimate see *The Christian Occupation of China*, Shanghai, 1922, p. 298, and other places. Customs estimates are in the *Annual Report on the Foreign Trade of China*. Figures from the Bureau of Statistics have appeared from time to time in recent years in the *China Critic* (Shanghai).

clude Manchuria. Taking a figure for the Manchurian provinces which is certainly not too high, we may round out his total to 350 million for the eighteen provinces and Manchuria. Papers were prepared for the same conference by two Chinese students. Warren H. Chen estimated "the probable population of all China" at 445 million for 1929 and Chen Chang-heng reached the conclusion that "the present total population of China is in the neighborhood of 461.7 million."[19]

The discrepancies in such estimates are due to a difference of opinion upon a number of points. The reliability of earlier censuses, the decline in numbers as the result of the wars and famines of the last century, the recovery which may have taken place in more recent years have been matters of dispute. The outstanding differences touch the reliability of the census of 1910 and the number of persons per household which ought to be accepted for the purpose of turning figures of households, compiled after the Chinese manner, into figures showing the number of persons. It is significant that Professor Willcox has seen fit to increase his estimate of the average number of persons per household from 4.3, in his earlier studies, to 5. Others insist that the average is somewhat higher. Chen Chang-heng, for example, adopts 5.2 as a reasonable figure.[20] To point out that there are such differences is to be quite convincing upon one point, the lack of accurate information. We can do no better than to accept the popular figure of 400 million and to acknowledge that, as Willcox says, "no one knows what the population of China is within many millions."

[19] Chen, Warren H., "An Estimate of the Population of China in 1929" and Chen Chang-heng, "China's Population Problem." These papers were first printed in Shanghai in 1930. They appear in the *Bulletin of the International Institute of Statistics*.

[20] The farm families studied by Buck, J. Lossing, *Chinese Farm Economy*, Shanghai, 1930, averaged about 5.6 persons per family. The figures for 102 villages in Chihli province, collected at a famine relief station with which the writer was connected during the famine of 1920–1921, showed an average of 4.8 persons per family. Professor Willcox mentions studies which show 5.2, 5.3, and 5.7.

If we accept a figure of 400 million as the population of China and 200 million acres as a reasonable estimate of the land under cultivation in China, we may bring out the significance of the situation by further comparisons between China and the United States. The United States is reported in the census of 1930 to have a population of 122.8 million and land under cultivation to the number of 522.4 million acres.[21] These figures show the United States to have nearly nine times the cultivated land per capita that China has. If the United States had a population of about 1,000 million, the number of persons in the country per acre of cultivated land would be approximately equal to that in China. The population of the world is usually reported to be about 2,000 million; it may then be said that half the total population of the world could live within the boundaries of the United States and have at their disposal about as much cultivated land per person as the Chinese now have. These facts must be borne in mind constantly when China is being considered. It is difficult to give them sufficient emphasis. Practically every economic and political problem which China faces is made more difficult—it sometimes seems hopelessly difficult—by the very numbers of the Chinese people.

The process of sampling shows us some additional things about the population of China. There is good reason for believing that the population is not growing rapidly, if it is increasing at all, that China has a high birth rate, a high death rate, and an extremely high rate of infant mortality, so high, indeed, as to lead to the conclusion that infanticide is by no means rare.[22]

[21] I have taken for comparison with land under cultivation in China the total for the United States of "crop land," 413.2 million acres, and "plowable pasture land in farms," 109.2 million acres. *Fifteenth Census of the United States: Agriculture*, vol. 1, pp. 1, 8.

[22] It is reported that the bodies of at least 18,000 children are picked up for burial in the streets of Shanghai and its suburbs every year (see p. 158 of Professor Willcox' paper) and that 1,300 are picked up in the streets of Hongkong. (See *North China Daily News*, Shanghai, March 27, 1931.)

The percentage of rural population is usually put at about 80. Figures purporting to show the percentage of farm households to all households by provinces were recently made public. They show variations from 63.7 per cent in Kwangtung province in the south to 88.9 per cent in the northern province of Shantung. The average was 74.5 per cent.[23] According to the estimate of Leonard Hsu "66 per cent of our population live in villages below 2,500, 22 per cent in small cities between 10,000 and 50,000, and 6 per cent in large cities above 50,000."[24] Recent estimates show a slightly larger percentage of urban population than earlier ones, but it is hardly safe to draw the conclusion from this that there is a measurable drift toward the cities.

The outstanding fact concerning the regional distribution of population is that the densest population is to be found in the richest and most fertile agricultural regions. There simply are no industrial regions such as we find in western Europe and the United States. The outstanding fact concerning the occupational distribution of the population is the overwhelming percentage engaged in agriculture. It is probable that the percentage in transportation is unusually high but we can do no more than guess at this.

There is no word more commonly used in the discussion of these matters than over-population, but over-population does not explain everything any more than does the lack of iron ore. Over-population is relative to the "state of the arts." There is no doubt that the final solution of many of China's problems is impossible without control of population. There is little doubt that much may be done toward a higher standard of living which does not depend upon such control.

[23] *China Critic*, June 2, 1932, vol. 5, no. 22, p. 548. The statistics are from a special agricultural number of the *Chinese Statistical Monthly* (in Chinese).

[24] Hsu, Leonard, "Population Problems in China," *Sociology and Social Research*, vol. xiii, no. 5, p. 431.

The strongest objective evidence of over-population seems to me to lie in the fact, shown by a number of Chinese studies, that small families go with small incomes in town and with small farms in the country, and that the smallest families go with the smallest incomes and the smallest farms. Dittmer's study of a village near Peking, Tao's study of the standard of living in Peking, Buck's study of a number of farms in Shantung province, the work of the China Famine Relief Commission, all lead to the same conclusion that the average size of families was smallest among those who had the smallest farms and incomes.[25] A relation of this sort between size of income and size of family would be regarded in the West—and is so regarded in Sweden—as proof of the desirable results of birth control. Where no evidence is found of conscious birth control, what is it that maintains the close relationship between the size of the family and the size of the farm or income? Among the fairly well-to-do it may be, as Sarvis points out, that income determines the number of the members of the "large" family who live together [26] but among the very poor there is no choice of the sort. Among the poor the obvious explanation of the facts is the pressure of population upon the means of livelihood or rather the constricting influence of inadequate incomes upon the population. Here we find high rates of infant mortality, premature deaths from privation, lack of vigorous physical and mental development, the absence of any surplus of funds or energy upon which to bring about a change, the practice of infanticide, in short, life under such hard conditions as to make survival a difficult matter. The adjustment of

[25] Dittmer, C. G., "An Estimate of the Standard of Living in China," *Quarterly Journal of Economics*, November, 1918, vol. 33, no. 1. Tao, L. K., *Livelihood in Peking*, Peking, 1928. Buck, J. Lossing, *An Economic and Social Survey of 150 Farms in Yenshan County*, Nanking, June, 1926, pp. 63–4. Gamble, S. D., *Peking: A Social Survey*, New York, 1921, p. 351, where conclusions are presented from two surveys conducted by churches.

[26] Sarvis, G. W., "The Standard of Living in China and Its Meaning," *Journal of Applied Sociology*, vol. 9, 1924–1925, p. 187.

family to income is made and we are forced to the conclusion that it is the result of what may truly be called grinding poverty.

The population of China seems to the observer to have crept into and filled every crack and cranny of opportunity. No surplus emerges and any change seems to carry with it the probability that it will make worse the immediate condition of certain groups of Chinese. From the point of view of capital movements and economic development, this means that every development which can be brought about without the import of foreign capital is highly important but that, at the same time, the possibilities of development without foreign capital are fairly narrow.

We have in China a great mass of poor people, dependent upon agriculture, in a country without great mineral resources for a rapid industrial development, and so adapted to present opportunities as to make change difficult, perhaps costly in human terms, and dependent upon the acceptance and application of new ideas and new methods. The new ideas and methods require education, the continued study of China's economic problems by men of a practical turn of mind, leadership which will seize upon every opportunity for improvement, and foreign capital which must be used with the wisest economy.[27]

[27] Migration to countries outside of China is hardly to be taken seriously as a means of solving China's population question. Migration from the southeastern coast plays an important part in the importation of ideas and in the balancing of China's financial accounts with the rest of the world.

CHAPTER III

TRADITIONAL CHINA

GENERAL

The social, economic, and political organization which China brought to her contacts with modern nations in recent times may be called that of traditional China.[1] The changes which began with modern foreign trade and which have brought about foreign investment and the development of modern industry and modern means of communication are exerting a profound and, I believe, a disintegrating effect upon traditional China. The fundamental nature of the changes which are taking place and which seem to be in prospect has influenced Chinese thinking in many fields. It is true to say, as Sir Frederick Whyte does,[2] that there are many revolutions going on in China today; it is also true to say that there is but one revolution in prospect, that is the adaptation of traditional China to the modern world. "How," says Hu Shih, "can we Chinese feel at ease in this new world which at first sight appears to be so much at variance with what we have long regarded as our own civilization."[3]

It is difficult for the foreigner to see traditional China objectively. The Westerner, critical of his own civilization, has often created a China to suit his needs. The earliest of modern economists, the Physiocrats, learned that China was a state resting upon agriculture, private property in land, and upon an idea of nature. From their point of view these were the foundations of an ideal social

[1] Here I follow the example of T'ang Leang-li. See the title of Chapter VI of his *The Foundations of Modern China*, London, 1928.

[2] *The Times* (London), January 5, 1928.

[3] Hu Shih, *The Development of Logical Method in Ancient China*, Shanghai, 1922, p. 6.

27

life and they proceeded to make of China an "image idyllique."[4] On the other hand, the student, critical of Chinese civilization, has often created a China which must come to the good or bad end for which his thought has predestined it. A French banker explained to me recently that China must inevitably develop a vigorous capitalism. An expert on China at the Communist Academy in Moscow was equally certain that the next step in China will be the success of communism. Both of these men know China well and in each case the conclusion rested upon a sweeping analysis of the social and economic life of the country. Examples might be multiplied but these are, no doubt, sufficient to give renewed emphasis to the difficulties.

The government of traditional China was, in theory, an absolute monarchy ruled over by a supreme lord who, as the Son of Heaven, was invested with a certain sacredness and moral authority. In practice the government was a sort of constitutional monarchy without representation.[5] The unwritten constitution lay in the customs of the Chinese family, in the traditions of peasant villages, and in the ancient rules of guild and club and association. The monarchy was represented by the officials, and the government may, therefore, be described as a bureaucracy placed over families and guilds who were in most respects self-governing. The Emperor and his officials were, according to the Confucian tradition, above all else exemplars of virtue. Good government was held to be the exhibition of virtue so moving as to command the reverence and win the loyalty of the subject. The West is familiar with the doctrine that the end of government is the good life; in the Chinese classics it is presented as the means of government as well. One might quote from the classics at some length in support of this.

[4] See the account in Daszyńska-Golińska, Sophie, *La Chine et le système physiocratique en France*, Varsaviae, 1922.
[5] Erkes quotes a statement to this effect by Ku Hung-ming in his *China*, Gotha, 1919, p. 103.

I offer a single example. "May not Shun be instanced as having governed efficiently without exertion? What did he do? He did nothing but gravely and reverently occupy his imperial seat."[6] The officials of such an Emperor were his ministers who were supposed to represent or reflect the exemplary virtue of the Son of Heaven in all parts of the empire, and this meant in all parts of the civilized world. This doctrine of the exemplary virtue of the Son of Heaven carried with it a theoretical basis for the government of the world.

Traditional China thus had its solution of the problem of nationalism, and the Chinese political system with its philosophy had a universal quality. The officials of China were at the same time a tax collecting bureaucracy who started on its way to the imperial court the contributions of the people. The theory of taxation was that of the payment of tribute. There was no thought of payment for services rendered. The officials saw to it that they themselves brought together competences upon which to retire and live as landed gentlemen. What may be called the constitutional limitations upon the theoretically absolute monarchy operated through the passive resistance of family and village and guild. The conventional fiction of the Mandate of Heaven justified rebellion, for the Mandate of Heaven was held to be withdrawn from any emperor or a dynasty whose rule had offended against custom and tradition, especially if the offense carried with it evidence that the welfare of the people was being destroyed. The Chinese had a political system based upon custom which, at the same time, made room for rebellion. It did not, however, make room for such revolutionary changes as must be brought about if China is to be a modern state. A shrewd observer has said of the Chinese that of all nations they are "the least revolutionary and the most rebellious."[7]

[6] *The Analects of Confucius*, Book XV, chapter 4.
[7] Meadows, T. T., *The Chinese and Their Rebellions*, p. 25.

The inadequacy of the political organization of traditional China and the fact that the government was in the hands of a dynasty which the Chinese regarded as alien brought about early disintegration in the political field. It is not to be forgotten, however, that the political conditions of modern economic relations go back very largely to the political philosophy of an earlier time. The doctrines of China's great teachers and the political experience of the Chinese people express themselves today in ways that are important for our purposes.

In the first place philosophical anarchism plays a part in the ideal state as it is conceived by many Chinese.[8] The Chinese have a profound scepticism as to the desirability of governmental interference in social and economic life.

The rule of the righteous man appeals strongly to most Chinese. This carries with it the right of the official or, in modern terms, the government to interfere when the purpose is in accord with righteousness. Another way of saying it is that the righteous official is in some way above the law. It follows that the Western concept of constitutional limitation upon the acts of government is not easily grasped. At the same time the right to rebel is not a forgotten doctrine. There is a check upon official acts even under military dictatorship. The limitation lies where it did in the past, in the resistance of the people, rather than in any constitutional provision to which merchant or landowner may make an orderly appeal.

A third principle which follows from the practice of centuries is that orthodoxy is an important qualification for official position. This goes back to an idea that a pattern of rightness is to be found in nature and that it may be established by the exemplification of virtue. The unorthodox seem to have been rejected in China because they were leading the people astray. This tradition is still powerful in China today. The test of orthodoxy for

[8] The classical expression is in the *Tao Teh Ching* of Lao Tse.

official position, the importance attached to the acceptance of Dr. Sun's three principles, the idea that the
officials are to show forth the revolution in their lives—
matters of frequent comment in China today—go back
to traditions of long-standing in the political life of the
country.

In the field of social organization the family can hardly
be over-emphasized.[9] Filial piety, that is, the proper
conduct of younger persons in family relations, was ex-
tolled as the chief virtue in traditional China and incul-
cated in a thousand ways. It is the family solidarity of
China which made appropriate the doctrine of delegated
responsibility by which the head of the family was morally,
and so legally, responsible for the acts of its members.
The Chinese family is at once a group, small enough and
sufficiently disciplined, to have some of the advantages of
individualism. The success of the Chinese overseas and
in the settlement of Manchuria is in a large measure due
to this group individualism. On its economic side the
family solidarity of the Chinese makes the Western concept of private property inapplicable as well as the socialist
doctrine that land, for example, should be the property
of the state. The family lies behind the importance of the
partnership as a form of business organization. It makes
for nepotism in government and business. It provides for
old age and is a defense against employer and official.
The family system carries with it the need for children.[10]
In short, it may be said that whatever can be done through
the family the Chinese do well, and they do less well
whatever calls for greater individualism or wider solidarity.

The family in the agricultural village makes the chief
social unit the outstanding economic unit. The power of
the family explains and is the result of the subsistence
agriculture of China. Land is held as a means of securing

[9] That is the "great" family, not the individual or small family.
[10] "There are three unfilial acts," said Mencius, "and the greatest of
these is to have no offspring."

food for the family, not as a business investment. Surplus food was sold, but even this, under the granary system of traditional China, was dealt with on family principles.

There is no more frequent statement in China today than this, that the family is disintegrating. This statement is seldom followed by convincing proof but I must record it as the conviction of most Chinese and foreign residents of China that this is the case. One of the outstanding consequences of modern industry is said to be the weakening of family solidarity. There is much talk of divorce, of free choice in marriage, of young married persons setting up houses of their own, which a foreigner finds difficult to judge critically. The fate of the family under modern conditions in China must be one of the chief considerations not only of the student but of the political leader and business man.

The social classes of traditional China show the nature of the economic organization behind Chinese civilization. We may put the official class first. They represent at once the highest social position and the greatest opportunity for wealth. The next group consisted of the landed gentry. The officials were usually recruited from the children of the gentleman landlords and the officials took their place among them on retirement. It is commonly guessed in China that they owned a large fraction of the land of the country, though there were probably redistributions from time to time as the result of rebellions, and there is today a considerable variation from province to province in the proportion of land so held. The relation between landlord and tenant is today, as it has been for centuries, an economic problem of central importance. That which is called communism in China at the present time is frequently found to have its economic basis in the relation between tenant and landlord.

The merchant and banker, those whose prosperity rested upon trade and finance, probably came next in power and importance. They were frequently not of the city in which they carried on their business and lost some of the social prestige that went with landownership in the locality. They were not highly regarded by the literati of the official class and were in some degree more defenseless than the landed gentry against the demands of the officials. Their reliance in these matters was upon the guild and the provincial club.[11]

The master craftsman and his workers came next. Family and guild dominated their lives and they carried on an industry whose products and methods were fixed by custom. They were shielded from competition by the guild-supported system of apprenticeship.

The peasant farmers were, and are, of such importance by reason of their numbers that they ought to be put ahead of the craftsmen of the towns. Those who owned land were certainly in a better position but the great mass of the peasants were probably less well off. Among those who did not own land were some with security of tenure. China presents the greatest variety of arrangements when it comes to land tenure. But there were considerable numbers at all times of landless peasants and laborers who had nothing but their physical strength to offer in a society so numerous that it was pressing upon its means of subsistence, so dominated by the family as to check free movement, and so ruled by custom and tradition as to make any economic progress difficult. It is the landless peasants who are the day laborers of the country and the coolies of the city. They are the wheelbarrowmen, muleteers, and porters on the highways.

It is the peasant, the small landowner and tenant, who gives to China its outstanding characteristics. China was and is a peasant civilization. The Chinese peasant has had, and still has, a degree of sturdy independence, which is astonishing when his income and opportunities

[11] The "provincial club" is the English equivalent of a Chinese term which means an association in a particular city of those from another province or another city. The Shaohsing Club in Shanghai is an example.

are considered. This independence is to be explained, I believe, by the peasant's feeling that he does not stand alone, but is a member of a family and has his place in his home village.

In the various economic fields the Chinese people had, through long years of trial and error, carried their traditional methods to a considerable degree of excellence. It is true that the Chinese farmer did not, in all his years of experience, learn to control insects and pests, nor did he learn much about seed selection and animal breeding. He failed to make use of chemical fertilizers. He was, and is, slow to adapt his crops to changing demand and to new markets. Chinese agriculture did not find a way to overcome the wastefulness of the non-contiguous diminutive fields and the small size of the total individual holding. The Chinese farmer did, however, learn the lesson of maintaining soil fertility by the use of wastes of all kinds and by the use of legumes, and he learned these things before they were known in the West. He has learned much about the rotation of crops and the adaptation of crops to soil and climate.

Consider the skill of the Chinese weavers and artisans and smiths. Consider the early use of paper money, the wide circulation of bank paper, the system of canals and roads, and the great internal trade of traditional China.

BANKING AND FINANCE IN TRADITIONAL CHINA

Traditional China used brass and copper coins and silver in an uncoined form as money. No effort was made to bring copper and silver into a unified system, either on the principles of bi-metallism or on those of subsidiary coinage. There was no exclusion of gold and it was, in fact, used at times. China may be said to have had a "parallel" standard. Differences in practice and custom in the field of money were like local differences in custom. The imperial government paid some attention to these matters but, in general, they were the concern of merchants and bankers. The Chinese did not, as some writers seem to suppose, evince a perverse desire for senseless complications; it is merely that things happened so in their wide country.

Chinese banking of the traditional sort consisted, in the first place, of money changing. The characteristic institution was the "exchange shop." An important additional function was the facilitation of payments in other places by means of bank paper. The carrying on of this domestic exchange business was the chief activity of the Shansi bankers, who were, for a century or two before the revolution of 1911, the greatest bankers of China. The acceptance of deposits was a third function of the banks of traditional China. The usual risks of deposit holding were multiplied by the attitude of the officials, who had a keen interest, at all times, in every possible source of funds. The accepted standards of government offered little effective security to banker or merchant, and the actual practice frequently put such men at the mercy of official greed and rapacity. The deposits were ordinarily fixed for at least six months and the banks paid very low rates of interest or none at all.

We have little information as to the use of these funds. Banks provided credit for merchants at rates which after rather extended inquiry I would put at about 2 per cent a month. It is well known that they advanced money to pawnshops at 18 per cent, or more, a year. Local rice shops and silver dealers were probably among the borrowers who reloaned funds so secured. I have found no evidence of borrowing from the banks by local money lenders but, no doubt, such transactions took place.

The mass of the people secured the funds which they required in a variety of ways. The family was of first importance. Next in importance came the pawnshop. Its charges were from 2 to 5 or 6 per cent a month and it is not far from the truth to say that, in many a Chinese

community, everything pawnable was in a pawnshop.[12]
Local dealers in grain, merchants, and landowners were
frequently money lenders. Small societies were formed
to assist members, in rotation, on the occasion of an
unusual expenditure. Most of these advances were to
individuals and families for consumer's goods.

The provision of funds for capital equipment was
conspicuously lacking. I have found no evidence that
the craftsman of China secured funds for his purposes
either from his guild or from the banks. The system
under which the employer was also a merchant [13] enabled some bank funds to be used for industrial purposes. There were, no doubt, other ways of accomplish-
ing the same result, but it must be emphasized that the
relatively high development of banking and finance in
China carried with it practically no way by which the
financial institutions of traditional China regularly provided capital for the manufacturing industries of the
country. The master craftsman of China depended upon
the family for the meager capital which he required.

The public finance of traditional China consisted very
largely of the gathering of the land tax for remittance to
the imperial court. The government made some use of
the banking system but, in spite of the early use of paper
money, there was little development of public credit.
Government securities did not offer a convenient form
of investment nor did they work, as in the West, to create the concepts and point of view favorable to the collection and "productive" investment of funds. On the
contrary, the whole business of finance tended to be
driven underground by the unwelcome interest of officials in every possible source of funds. And when the
officials did succeed in getting together their fortunes, the
funds went into land and impressive or luxurious consumer's goods, rather than to trade and industry.

[12] To some extent the pawnshop served as a place for safe deposit.
[13] The "putting out" system, production under a merchant-manufacturer.

The Economics of Traditional China

The economy of traditional China was family economy and it illustrates the original and literal meaning of the term. It is significant that in the West we have felt obliged to call it political economy. An important aspect of the modern economic history of the West lies in the relation between politics and economics. Organized in national states, desiring to be powerful, and recognizing power to be, in important respects, economic, the West has created a national life which emphasizes the relation of the state to the economic activity of the people. In an atmosphere of nationalism, economics must be political economy. The right relation between economics and politics has been put by the West into such systems of thought and policy as mercantilism, *laissez faire*, and the neo-mercantilism or economic nationalism of the present day.

Traditional China presents these matters quite differently. Traditional China was a civilization, not a state. The Emperor was not in competition with rulers of equal states for power.[14] He did not concern himself, in any direct way, with economic policy or with the material welfare of his people. He was forced, by tradition and convention, to accept a general responsibility for want and suffering and to issue expiatory mandates at times when drought or flood made the miseries of his people acute. But, for all practical purposes, the Emperor was indifferent to matters of material welfare. The economic activities of traders, bankers, craftsmen, and farmers were uncontrolled by the State. The interest of the officials was expressed in ways that did not come to the open notice of the ruler and did not ordinarily have as

[14] When China consisted of warring and competing kingdoms her thinkers gave attention to matters of political economy. Compare the attitude toward population in the Chinese classics, in the writings of Mencius for example, and in the writings of the mercantilists of the West.

its purpose the control of economic activity for the general welfare. The control exercised in traditional China was that of family and guild. The Chinese system is frequently referred to as individualism or *laissez faire*. It may with equal truth be called family communism or guild socialism. The Chinese system must be understood for what it was, and in large part still is; it is not to be comprehended by giving it a Western label. The outstanding fact, in a world of economic nationalism, is the separation of economics and politics.

We are now prepared to view the Chinese system in rather complete outline. The Chinese brought to modern relations with the West and with the rising nationalism of Japan a political system which carried with it a solution of the problem of nationalism. Among the people nationalism was lost in the family system and its local loyalties. It was swallowed up in the political claims of the Son of Heaven to universal dominion. It was rejected by the philosophers, whose eyes were upon a universalism which was politically expedient and in accord with nature. The Chinese economic organization carried with it a solution of the insistent Western problem of the relation between economics and politics. The Son of Heaven was remote and the economic problem was left to the family system and the customs and traditions of the people, to what I have called the group individualism of China.

China could not meet the political system of the West without a revolution. Her political organization and philosophy were inadequate. Her Son of Heaven was either the potential ruler of the world or he was less than a Son of Heaven. The Manchu court, attempting to live up to its pretensions of universal dominion in a modern world, presents a pathetic spectacle. The fall of the Manchus and the disintegration of the Mandarinate are incidents in the political revolution now in progress. The economic aspect of this revolution lies in a necessary change in the relation of the State to the material welfare of the Chinese people.

When this question of the relation of the State to the "people's livelihood" is considered, there seem to be three possible answers. They may be stated in terms of the leadership under which the economic development will take place.

In the first place, China may proceed under the tradition that all power rests in the government and its officials. This will bring economic development under something like state socialism. The political traditions of China favor this, but the training and traditions of the official class are against its success.

The second possibility is the development of private enterprise under the group individualism of China. The economic traditions of China favor this. It means, however, that new concepts must be formed and private enterprise must be given freedom and assurance of its rights under a constitution binding upon the officials as well as upon the people.

A third possibility is some form of communism. The village traditions of China favor this and communism, if it is to have any measure of success, must be adapted to family and village. Communism as a movement among the peasants to secure land reform may have some power today, but it is difficult to imagine that a communist movement can provide the leadership for the economic development of the country.

One may proceed next to consider the problem of securing the necessary capital under the three possibilities. State socialism means government borrowing abroad on a large scale. Private enterprise, or capitalism adapted to China, means the creation of such legal and political conditions as to make possible successful borrowing abroad, on a large scale, by individuals, groups, and corporations. Communism, if it is to develop China, must undertake to borrow abroad, either from Russia, a country with no capital to lend, or by some method worked out on the present Russian model.

Other problems of China's industrial development might be considered under the three possibilities outlined. The problem must be considered once more, however, for it involves more than is to be discovered by a study of traditional China. It involves the international political situation and the consideration of the actual source of the capital. What can be done in China does not depend on China alone.

CHAPTER IV

MODERN ECONOMIC RELATIONS

THE EARLY TRADE

Traditional China came to know the West through commercial relations, but the immediate economic consequences of the early trade were slight. They must have been imperceptible before 1842, when the trade was confined to Canton, and it was not until the increase in trade during the last quarter of the nineteenth century that its effects upon the economic life of the Chinese people need be considered. The early trade was important for other reasons.

Behind this early demand for the right to trade, represented by a handful of Western merchants at Canton, lay the whole overseas expansion of Europe at the beginning of modern times. The slow opening of China to trade was a late accompaniment of the commercial revolution in the West, but Chinese trade did not count for much until the Industrial Revolution had worked its changes in the economic life of Europe. The merchant adventurer of the West insisted upon entrance into Canton, but it was the Western industrialist who was interested in the removal of the obstacles to trade during the latter half of the nineteenth century. The Chinese political and economic organization opposed a passive resistance to the insistence of the Westerner, which, in its turn, was the result of the political and economic organization of the West.[1] China could no more avoid meeting and being influenced by the West at an earlier time than

[1] It is not maintained that there was opposition to trade as such by the Chinese, especially the local officials and merchants.

41

the West can now avoid the consequences which flow from the rising tide of nationalism in Eastern countries.

The conditions of the early trade with the West brought it about that trade was carried on by foreign merchants who came to China for the purpose. The presence in China of groups different from the Chinese in race and political allegiance, occupying areas set apart for their residence, dependent for their success upon China's trade and economic development, is a characteristic feature of China's relations. Such foreign "colonies" in China, however much their significance may have changed in the course of years, are to be explained by the conditions that brought the Canton "factories" into existence. Modern Shanghai has its origin in early Canton.[2]

Foreign trade was a path, however narrow, to more general relations between China and the West. It brought on the long struggle on the part of the foreign powers for equality with China. Equality was contrary to the assumptions upon which the imperial government of traditional China was founded. To ask for equality seemed to the European no more than to ask for the establishment of an obviously necessary condition of international relations; to admit equality was, from the Chinese viewpoint and especially from that of the non-Chinese Manchu imperial house, to weaken the foundations upon which rested the political system of the Chinese world. This situation gave a psychological setting to Chinese-foreign relations which must be understood. Every arrangement in which the foreigner was involved was likely to be regarded by the Chinese as a concession forced from China or a special privilege which the foreigner enjoyed at some risk to China and for no other reason, in the last analysis, than his power to enforce his claim. The foreigner, as he saw it, encountered a continuous resistance to the establishment of the ordinary condi-

[2] It is to be noted that the trade between China and southeastern Asia is carried on by Chinese "colonies" living within those countries.

tions of peaceful trade. He was both puzzled and exasperated. The psychological background on both the foreign and the Chinese side has often been more important in shaping the course of events than the legal and economic complications which are more frequently the subject of comment. The emotion in such terms as "imperialism" and "unequal" treaties goes back, in part, to this psychological background.

CERTAIN IMPORTANT INSTITUTIONS

The general differences between China and the West have been dealt with at some length. They are, I believe, the best background for the understanding of the problems of China's international economic relations. The whole set of arrangements under which the foreigner lives and carries on his business in China and under which other nations trade with China, a system which stood without important modification until a few years ago, ought to be seen as a living and working adjustment.

Extraterritoriality was, and is, the most important institution in this system. Extraterritorial jurisdiction may be regarded as the extension of the jurisdiction of the governments of foreign states over their citizens in China, or as the removal of those citizens from the jurisdiction of the Chinese government.[3] The existing system of extraterritoriality is expressed in a series of treaties between China and foreign states, the first of which was entered into in 1843 and the last in 1919.[4] Extraterritoriality was so general that at the beginning of the World War there were practically no foreigners living in China under Chinese jurisdiction. At the present time the Germans, Austrians, Hungarians, and Russians have lost the extraterritorial status which they once had. The citizens

[3] Lobengier, Charles S., on Extraterritoriality, *Corpus Juris*, American Law Book Company, New York, 1921, vol. 25, p. 300.
[4] The pertinent treaty clauses are listed in Appendix I of the *Report of the Commission on Extraterritoriality in China*, Washington, 1926, pp. 113–4.

of the new states of eastern Europe and many of the Latin-American republics are subject to the jurisdiction of the Chinese courts. But so many foreign governments continue to exercise extraterritorial jurisdiction that it remains the foundation of the system under which the foreigner lives in China.

Extraterritorial jurisdiction applies to corporations and to civil suits and it is chiefly in this field that its economic significance lies. Foreign governments have courts to carry out the treaty provisions and they have, in some cases, enacted legislation concerning the creation of corporations to carry on business in China.[5] Such corporations may be formed in China with Chinese as well as foreign members. This greatly complicates the problem of measuring foreign investments in China. It creates diversity in the conditions of business competition and complicated problems of taxation. Such problems were difficult when the foreign corporation was confined to the import and export business at a seaport; consider the additional difficulties created by foreign ownership of an important railway in China by a corporation removed from the jurisdiction of the Chinese government. When such railways are owned by foreign governments the economic significance of investment may be overshadowed by the political.

A second institution is that of the treaty port or open port at which the foreign business man is permitted to reside, to acquire land, and to carry on his business. The establishment of such ports is in most cases the result of provisions in the treaties, but a number of them have been opened by the decree of the Chinese government.[6] I propose to use the term treaty port as a convenient name for the cities of China, whether on the coast or not, which are open to the foreign business man and to direct trade with foreign countries.[7] The treaty port brought it

[5] See for example the account of the China Trade Act in the chapter on American Investments in China, pp. 316–28.

[6] Willoughby, W. W., *Foreign Rights and Interests in China*, vol. 2, p. 736.

[7] Missionaries have had the right to acquire land in the "interior" of

about that the foreign "colonies" in China consisted of groups of foreigners living at a relatively few centers, where by the operation of extraterritoriality they were under foreign jurisdiction. The number of treaty ports, open ports, trade marts, that is of all places open to the trade and residence of foreign business men, was about eighty at the end of the year 1930. At fifty-two of these places there were Customs houses. The number of treaty ports had increased from the five in existence in 1842, to thirty-two in 1899 and forty-eight in 1913. Among them Shanghai was of outstanding importance after 1850, from the point of view of trade and investment, and is the chief financial center of the country.

At certain of the treaty ports areas were set aside for the residence of foreigners. Where, as in some cases, the whole administration of the local government is in the hands of the Chinese authorities, the operation of extraterritoriality gives to the area in which the foreigners live a degree of separateness. In certain cities the area set aside for foreign residence is under a government which rests upon an arrangement by which local government is in some degree in foreign hands. The foreign settlement at Shanghai may be regarded as having a sort of charter resting upon the land regulations proclaimed by the Chinese government.[8] Under this charter and under extraterritoriality a self-governing settlement has grown up with an elected council, subject in some degree to the local consuls of the foreign powers and the ministers of these powers at the capital.[9] At certain cities "concessions" have come into existence. The "settlement" has certain international features which the concession does not have. A concession is based upon an agreement be-

China, that is, at places which are not treaty ports, since 1860. Willoughby, W. W., *Foreign Rights and Interests in China*, vol. II, pp. 706–10.

[8] *Feetham Report*, vol. 1, p. 26, reprints the original proclamation of 1845.

[9] *Feetham Report*, chapter IV, pp. 84–9, presents the municipal "constitution" as embodied in the land regulations.

tween a foreign power and the Chinese government which gives to the foreign power concerned control of the land and municipal administration. There were at the beginning of the World War at least twenty-four concessions in China. At Tientsin, for example, there were no less than eight.[10] It is important to note that settlements and concessions are alike in this important respect, that the police power and the municipal administration are not in the hands of the Chinese authorities.

A fourth institution is that which may be called the "leased" area. Examples may be found in the Japanese leased area on the Liaotung Peninsula in southern Manchuria, the French leased area at Kuangchouwan, the British leased area at Kowloon, opposite Hongkong, the former British leased area at Weihaiwei, and the former German leased area at Kiaochow.[11] The leased area is completely under the control of the foreign power during the term of the lease. Provisions for military defense have been undertaken in such areas without consultation with the Chinese government, and the extraterritorial jurisdiction of other foreign powers is held not to apply.

The conventional or treaty tariff is to be listed among these institutions, although it is no longer in effect. In 1928 and 1929 China succeeded in securing tariff autonomy. A national tariff went into effect on February 1, 1929, and a second national tariff law on January 1, 1931. During the period of the conventional tariff, i.e. from 1842–1929, Chinese tariff rates were fixed by treaty on a basis of approximately 5 per cent *ad valorem*. The duties were, as a matter of fact, largely specific duties and the inflexibility of the system may be judged by the fact that there were but three revisions during the period; in 1858,

[10] The eight were: British, French, Japanese, Italian, German, Russian, Belgian, and Austrian. Of these, four have been recovered by China: the German and Austrian in 1917, the Russian in 1920, and the Belgian in 1930. Shanghai offers a striking contrast with its one concession (French) and its international settlement.

[11] Weihaiwei was restored to China on October 1, 1930, in accordance with a convention of April 18, 1930, *China, No. 2* (1930), Cmd. 3590.

1902, and 1919. The chief Chinese objections to the treaty tariff were that it greatly limited the income of the Chinese government and that it prevented higher duties upon luxuries or for protective purposes.

Silver has been the accepted means of payment in international transactions throughout the period of China's modern trade. Within the country copper has declined in importance, especially during the present century, and this decline is, in part, due to the growth of the foreign trade. The business man who deals with China thinks of silver in terms of its day-to-day fluctuations or of the rise and fall of silver over a few years, the rise during the World War or the fall since 1929. These fluctuations bring an element of uncertainty into trade and make speculation unavoidable. They serve to check the flow of funds between Shanghai, the chief financial center of China and foreign financial centers. There is less short-term investment in China than there would be if China were on a gold or gold-exchange standard. Fluctuations in the gold price of silver have added to the risk of long-term investment in China by the business man and of long-term borrowing by the Chinese government. The effect of the remarkable and fairly continuous fall in the gold price of silver since about 1870 is not so easily discovered either in the field of trade or of investment. In general I believe that less importance is to be attached to silver than is commonly supposed. For China the silver problem is the currency problem. A currency different from that of the great trading nations is not so significant as in the days before the World War when the West may be said to have been on an automatic gold standard. The monetary standard of a particular country is more a matter of national policy. Under such circumstances the important considerations may be the effect of silver on domestic prices and business conditions within China rather than its effects in the field of international economic relations.

FOREIGN TRADE DURING LAST QUARTER OF THE CENTURY

The trade of China really began to grow during the last quarter of the nineteenth century. In silver value the increase was threefold. This increase followed, or was accompanied by, the opening of the Suez Canal in 1869, a rapid increase in the use of the steam-driven steel ship, and the opening of telegraphic communication between London and Shanghai.[12]

The changes of the period touched every aspect of the trade. From the days of the Canton trade tea and silk had been the chief exports from China, and in the minds of the ordinary person in the West today China is still the land of tea and silk rather than the land of the soya bean. In the early 'seventies tea and silk together still accounted for more than 90 per cent of China's exports but by 1900 they formed no more than half. At the same time the export of tea from India and of silk from Japan was growing. During the early years of the present century China lost her position as the world's chief exporter of tea and silk.

During the closing quarter of the nineteenth century cotton goods took first place among the imports into China.[13] Kerosene oil was accepted by the Chinese and became an ordinary article of consumption and there was a great increase in the use within China of a wide variety of consumer's goods, such as window glass, soap, clocks, watches, and wheat flour.

The trade of the period was very largely with the British Empire and through two great distributing centers within the British Empire, Hongkong and London. In this, too, there were evidences of a significant change. No less

[12] In my *Foreign Trade of China*, pp. 38–44, I give a detailed account of the reasons for beginning the detailed study of China with the year 1871.

[13] Cotton goods displaced opium in 1885. The import of opium declined rapidly and disappeared altogether from the official reports in 1917, except that it is still imported into Dairen "for consumption in the Leased Territory." Opium is also imported into Hongkong for the use of the local opium monopoly.

than 85 per cent of China's foreign trade in 1871 had been with Great Britain, India, and Hongkong. By the end of the century the percentage had dropped to 60. There was more trade with other countries and a notable increase in the direct trade with other countries.

There was no importation of machinery or of railway equipment from abroad until about the end of the century. The beginning of such importation is but one more bit of evidence that the economic relations of China with the West were changing and that the trade of the present day really began at about the year 1900.

THE RECENT TRADE OF CHINA

The silver value of China's foreign trade was about five times as great in 1929–1931 as it had been at the turn of the century. About half of this increase took place before the World War and the other half in more recent years. This increase represents a real change in the economic position of China. The Chinese economy is being slowly drawn into the current of world trade. The swing in that direction has been strong during the past thirty years.

It is to be noted, however, that figures which enable comparisons to be made with other countries reveal the slowness of the change. China finds a place at the bottom of every list showing the per capita trade of the countries of the world. The per capita trade of China doubled between 1900–1913, it doubled once more between 1914 and 1930. Nevertheless the per capita trade of China has been no more than about half that of Russia and India in recent years, one-tenth that of Japan, and hardly more than 3 or 4 per cent of the per capita trade of the highly developed countries of the West.[14]

If we turn to figures showing the share which China

[14] Figures for recent years are to be found in the various numbers of the League of Nations *Memorandum* on International Trade and Balances of Payments.

takes in the trade of the world we find a similar situation. China's trade was about 1.5 per cent of world trade at the beginning of the century, about 1.7 per cent immediately before the World War, and about 2.2 per cent in recent years.[15] The increase is significant. The share of India in world trade has hardly increased at all during the century. Japan, however, has three times the share she had in 1900. And when the actual figure of 2.2 per cent is considered in relation to China's area, population, and resources, the conclusion is forced upon us that the changes which are important to China are still relatively small from the world point of view.

TABLE 2

The Foreign Trade of China (Customs Statistics)

In Millions of Haikwan Taels with Relatives

Year	Total Trade		Exports		Imports	
	Mills. Hk. Tls.	Rela- tives	Mills. Hk. Tls.	Rela- tives	Mills. Hk. Tls.	Rela- tives
1898	368.6	37.9	159.0	39.4	209.5	36.7
1899	460.5	47.3	195.7	48.5	264.7	46.4
1900	370.0	38.0	159.0	39.4	211.0	37.0
1912	843.6	86.7	370.5	91.9	473.0	83.0
1913	973.4	100.0	403.3	100.0	570.1	100.0
1914	925.4	95.0	356.2	88.3	569.2	99.8
1929	2,281.4	234.4	1,015.6	251.8	1,265.7	220.0
1930	2,204.4	226.5	894.8	221.9	1,309.6	229.7
1931	2,330.9	239.5	887.5	220.1	1,443.4	253.2

Among the exports from China there was a marked increase in raw materials, especially those which are the products of agriculture. The growth in the export of beans, bean cake, and bean oil, which is closely connected with the settlement and development of Manchuria, is a matter of general knowledge. It is not so commonly known that the export of a variety of oil-bearing seeds and nuts

[15] Figures for the earlier years are from the *Statistisches Jahrbuch für das deutsche Reich* and for later years from the League *Memorandum*.

has increased. During the past twenty-five or thirty years the developed countries of the West have purchased increasing quantities of vegetable oils from the tropics and the East, and China has played her part in this. There has been an increase in the export of eggs and cereals. Certain metals, such as antimony, are exported in greater quantities. Finally, the Customs authorities have, since 1921, presented a separate table of "factory products" exported from China. The chief of these is cotton yarn and in 1929 and 1930 the total value of such products came to about Hk. Tls. 75 million.

Among the imports, cotton manufactures of all sorts have continued to hold first place. In recent years there has been some decline. In the case of cotton yarn the import has become so small that China is now a net exporter of this commodity which was among the first manufactured products to find a wide market in China. Such new items among the imports as machinery, motor cars, and electrical equipment, show the progress of changes which were hardly discernible in 1900. In addition, food products have assumed some importance among China's imports.

The importance of the chief groups of imports and exports in recent years is shown in the table on page 52. It is to be borne in mind that the year 1926 was in many ways the last year which may be called normal. A boycott of British goods was then declining and the more recent boycotts of Japanese goods had not yet begun.

The outstanding changes in the direction of the foreign trade of China between 1900–1931 were a remarkable increase in the trade with Japan and a great increase in the trade with the United States. The trade with Great Britain increased somewhat in silver value, but as a percentage of China's total trade it declined. There was, also, a persistent decline throughout the period in the proportion of the trade which was with Hongkong. Finally, it is to be noted that the region to which the

TABLE 3

CHINA'S TRADE BY CLASSES OF COMMODITIES *

Percentage Distribution by Value

Year	Imports			Exports		
	Articles of Food and Drink	Materials Raw or Partly Man-ufactured	Manu-factured Articles	Articles of Food and Drink	Materials Raw or Partly Man-ufactured	Manu-factured Articles
1925	21.6	25.5	45.6	31.0	49.7	17.0
1926	23.0	25.1	45.3	30.6	48.7	16.7
1927	24.8	24.6	43.1	33.1	46.8	17.4
1928	20.7	24.1	46.3	35.0	47.6	16.4
1929	21.8	24.3	45.2	37.0	46.1	14.7
1930	22.0	28.3	42.4	36.8	41.6	15.3

* Sources: League of Nations *Memorandum* and Chinese Maritime Customs statistics.

Chinese give the name, the South Seas (*Nan Yang*), that is, the whole of southeastern Asia and the East Indies, has increased in its importance in China's trade.[16]

Attempts to show the distribution of Chinese trade are made difficult by the position of Hongkong. In the past they have been impossible. Hongkong trade figures are now available for the last nine months of 1930.[17] Calculations based upon these figures enable us to arrive at a clearer figure of the distribution than has been possible in the past. If Hongkong is taken as a part of China, we arrive at a percentage distribution which shows significant differences from that which is arrived at from the Chinese statistics alone. In the following table the first column shows the trade with the particular country as a percentage of the trade of China, while the second column shows the trade of the particular country with China and Hongkong taken together as a percentage of the appropriate total.

[16] The changes in the trade with the important countries are shown in the final tables of each chapter in Part II.

[17] Hongkong Trade and Shipping Returns: Noronha & Co., Dec., 1930.

TABLE 4

TRADE OF CERTAIN COUNTRIES WITH CHINA AND WITH CHINA AND
HONGKONG, 1930

	As a Percentage of the Total Trade of China	As a Percentage of the Total Trade of China and Hongkong
Japan	24.7	26.4
United States	16.5	17.6
United Kingdom	7.8	9.3
Germany	4.2	4.9
France	2.7	2.7
India	6.8	6.9
Dutch East Indies	2.7	5.0
French Indo-China	1.5	4.4
Straits Settlements	1.3	2.7
Philippines	0.6	0.9
Siam	0.4	2.2
Hongkong	17.1	—
	86.3	83.0

The three countries of greatest importance, Japan, the
United States, and the United Kingdom, accounted for
49 per cent of the trade of China and for 53.3 per cent of
the trade of China and Hongkong. There is more to be
said. There is trade between China and the United States
which goes through Japan and is reported in the statistics as Japanese when it is really American. There is
trade with Great Britain which goes through Singapore
and India and is not reported as British. If all the information could be assembled the three chief trading countries would be found to be well ahead of all others and
to account for nearly three-fifths of the trade of China.
There is no doubt that the three countries would be
more nearly equal in their importance in the foreign trade
of China than the figures which include Hongkong show
them to be. It is to be noted that trade with the South
Seas really comes to about 15 per cent if we include Hongkong rather than the 6.5 per cent shown by the Chinese
Customs figures. There are really four important countries in China's trade; Japan, the United States, the

South Seas, and Great Britain, in the order named. Such a statement enables us to see, more clearly than we can from the Chinese Customs statistics, the true picture of China's commercial relations.

A Note on Cotton Yarn

The story of the rise and fall of China's trade in cotton yarn throws a light upon changes in China and upon important aspects of the economic history of the Far East in recent years. Before the 'seventies of the last century cotton yarn was imported into China from Great Britain in small quantities. The trade did not develop until cotton spinning had made some headway in India. In the late 'seventies the number of cotton spindles reached a total of a million and there was a rapid increase in the export of Indian cotton yarn to China. The trade in cotton yarn continued to grow and by 1900 the value of the yarn imported into China was as great as that of the whole trade in piece goods. No less than 65 per cent of Hk. Tls. 55 million came from India in 1899.

In 1915 about as much cotton yarn was imported into China as in 1899. It counted for less in China's total imports, but the quantity was about the same and the value a little higher. The difference lay in the country of origin. More than half of the yarn came from Japan in 1915. Since 1915 there has been a fairly continuous decline in China's purchases of cotton yarn from foreign countries. In this declining trade Japan took an increasing share. In 1922 and 1923 over two-thirds of the yarn came from Japan.

After 1925 the drop in yarn imports was rapid, from Hk. Tls. 40 million in that year to Hk. Tls. 10 million in 1930. The Japanese share of the import in 1930 was no more than 40 per cent. The explanation of the drop in the Japanese share is probably the boycotting of Japanese goods.

A trade which amounted to 20 per cent of the total

imports into China at the turn of the century had dropped
to less than half of one per cent by 1930. Cotton yarn
was the first import, after opium, to grow remarkably.
The industrial development of India took place first; her
exports to China reached a high point in 1905 and then
declined. Japan came to play the chief rôle as she developed. Her exports reached a high point in 1915 and
then declined. Today mills in China supply practically
the whole of the demand for yarn and China has become
a net exporter since 1929. No other commodity provides
so neat and clear an illustration of the course which events
have tended to take in the general trade in cotton goods.
In the rise and fall of the trade in cotton yarn we see
reflected the early industrial development of India, Japan,
and China.

RECAPITULATION

China has been presented as an Eastern country, relatively undeveloped in the modern capitalistic sense. She
offers to economic development the resistance of a traditional organization which was powerful in its time, in
theory world-wide and in practice embracing the whole
of the world then known to her. China is a civilization
of peasant villagers governed by the family, dependent
upon agriculture, and with so great a population that
grinding poverty is the normal state of many. The capital
equipment is meager. The banking and financial institutions were organized at an early time and they have
assisted trade rather than industry. This Chinese civilization met the West in the field of trade. Its imperial
government could not stand the test of this meeting because it could not make good its claims to world dominion and because the Chinese regarded it as alien. The
political problem which the Chinese face is that of building a national state. The West has found the relation
between political organization and economic welfare, a
fundamental problem of national organization. The Chi-

nese national state must face this problem or, better, a Chinese national state will be built up around the answer to this problem. The Chinese must work out a political, social, and economic organization which will solve the problem, in Dr. Sun's language, of the people's livelihood. How far the disintegration of traditional China will go, no one is wise enough to say.

Applying this analysis to our problem, the question becomes that of the immediate means of economic development. Every possibility of advancement by importing ideas must be cultivated but, finally, foreign capital will be required. How will it come? The immediate possibilities of political organization seem to be state socialism under the official class or its successor, communism under the leadership of new men from the peasant class, or capitalism adapted to China under the leadership of the business men. Which of these possibilities is most likely to bring in adequate amounts of foreign capital, use the foreign capital wisely, avoid the political dangers of its use, and carry China forward past the early and most difficult stages of economic development? My object is not, at the moment, to ask questions which may be answered with any degree of certainty, but to put the questions of fundamental importance.

The task to which I turn next is an attempt to present a picture of foreign investment in China as it is. After an exposition of the facts about foreign investment, an attempt is made to fit these facts, and other available information in the field, into a balance of international payments for the country. I turn from judgment as to possibilities and probabilities to the analysis of the studies which are present in Part II below. The purpose is to make a picture of China's international financial position which is reasonable and logically consistent. If my judgment as to the world position in which the Chinese find themselves is quite wrong and my estimate of possibilities for the future mistaken, it may, nevertheless, be admitted that the facts concerning foreign investment in China are authentic and the balance of payments reasonable. The reader may know China well enough to be sceptical of any analysis which undertakes to estimate the future. He may have his own analysis which he does not propose to alter. In any case, he will find in the chapters which follow, new material on foreign investments in China and a new attack upon the difficult problem of China's balance of international payments.

CHAPTER V

A GENERAL PICTURE OF FOREIGN INVESTMENTS IN CHINA

The General Figures

Foreign investments in China, bringing into a single figure the estimates below, come to a total for 1931 of U. S. $3,242.5 million. Allowing for omissions the sum may be put at, roughly, U. S. $3,300 million. Taking into account the errors in any such estimate, it may still be said with some certainty that the total falls between U. S. $3,000 million and U. S. $3,500 million.

Totals may be offered for two earlier years. The first is for a year near the turn of the century. The actual year differs for different countries but 1902 may be taken as representative. The total foreign investment in China for 1902 is U. S. $787.9 million. The second is for 1914, selected to show the situation before the World War and before the general effects of the Chinese revolution had made themselves apparent. The total for 1914 is U. S. $1,610.3.

If it were possible to carry the estimate back to 1900, the total would, no doubt, be somewhat smaller than for 1902, say, U. S. $750 million. If estimates for every country were in existence for 1914, the figure would be somewhat larger, say, U. S. $1,650 million. Foreign investment in China doubled between the year of the Boxer uprising and the World War, and doubled once more between the beginning of the war and the beginning of the Japanese occupation of Manchuria in September, 1931.

FIGURES FOR OTHER COUNTRIES

The magnitude of the sums involved may be gauged by comparison with estimates for other countries, though it must be borne in mind that the figures for China are probably more inclusive. The size and population of China suggest a comparison with India. There are no generally accepted figures for India and totals may be found that run from U. S. $2,000 million to U. S. $3,500 million.

Sir George Paish in 1911 estimated the total British investment in India and Ceylon at £365 million.[1] H. F. Howard made an estimate for about the same year which reached a total of £450 million for India alone.[2] A widely quoted estimate is that of G. F. Shirras for 1918 which puts the total at approximately £570 million.[3] Sir Lionel Abrahams put the figures for about the same year at £400 million.[4] *The Economist* (London), in the course of an inquiry into the foreign investments of Great Britain, estimated British holdings in India in 1930 to be about £354 million, a total to which government and municipal bonds contributed £219 million and "commercial capital" £134 million.[5] An estimate of British holdings of Indian government securities only for 1929 by G. F. Shirras comes to no less than £353 million.[6] The divergences in these estimates suggest the difficulty of arriving at any satisfactory total. A committee appointed for the purpose of considering the flow of external capital to

[1] *Journal of the Royal Statistical Society*, Jan., 1911, vol. 74, Pt. II, p. 186.
[2] In his "India and the Gold Standard," 1911, quoted in Pillai, P. P., *Economic Conditions in India*, London, 1925, p. 282.
[3] *Indian Finance and Banking*, 1919.
[4] In his evidence before a Committee in 1919, "East India: Committee on Indian Exchange and Currency," vol. 2, *Minutes of Evidence*, p. 292. Cmd. 528, 1920.
[5] *The Economist* (London), Oct. 25, 1930, p. 751. *The Economist* accepted the total of Sir Robert Kindersley for "Government and Corporation" bonds. *The Economist* estimate was probably too low for investments of both sorts.
[6] Shirras, G. F., "Gold and British Capital in India," *Economic Journal*, Dec., 1929, p. 634.

India pointed out in 1925 that any calculation must be largely guess work.[7] Professor J. Coatman of the London School of Economics, who has been consulted, suggests the limits of £400 million and £700 million. It is his opinion that the truth is nearer to the smaller figure. We may conclude from this that no close estimate exists, that foreign investment in China is probably greater today than foreign investment in India, and we may guess that foreign investment has increased more rapidly in China than in India during the present century.

A recent estimate of foreign investment in Japan by H. G. Moulton puts the total for 1929 at U. S. $1,275 million. This is not a net sum but the total without the deduction of the offsetting item of Japanese investments abroad. The estimate for 1913 is U. S. $1,035 million. Concerning 1898 we are told that foreign investment in Japan was extremely small.[8] Accepting these estimates we may conclude that foreign investment in China is two and one-half times that in Japan. There is no doubt that the increase was much more rapid between 1900 and 1914 in the case of Japan and much less rapid between 1914 and the present day.

Comparison may be made with Russia before the World War. The total foreign investment in Russia is estimated by Pasvolsky and Moulton at about U. S. $3,882 million. This includes "State" debt, municipal loans, and guaranteed loans to the amount of U. S. $2,760 million and "private" investments to the amount of U. S. $1,122 million.[9]

Foreign investment in China, according to the inclu-

[7] The conclusion of the committee "we do not think that any practical purpose would be served by an attempt to estimate the amount of external capital operating in India" seems strange in view of its purpose. Indian Government: Legislative Council: *Report of the External Capital Committee*, 1925.

[8] Moulton, H. G., *Japan*, pp. 500, 510, 524.

[9] Pasvolsky, Leo, and Moulton, H. G., *Russian Debts and Reconstruction*, Washington, 1924, pp. 177, 179, 182. Apostal, P. N., *Russian Public Finance during the War*, New Haven, 1928, pp. 239, 243, gives figures for "debt" which are in substantial agreement.

sive estimate offered here, was considerably smaller than foreign investment in pre-war Russia, was somewhat larger than foreign investment in India, and has always been much larger than foreign investment in Japan. It may be added that the British holding of American railway securities in 1914 was about equal in value to the 1931 figure of total foreign investment in China.

The Chinese Study

The totals presented above and the picture of foreign investments in the chapters that follow rest upon a series of studies which are presented in Part II of this volume. Each of these studies carries a brief statement of the methods by which the results were reached in the particular case and, taken together, these statements indicate a considerable amount of international co-operation. In addition to the studies of the individual countries it is to be noted that a general study of foreign investments was undertaken in China by D. K. Lieu, a well-known Chinese economist.[10] The whole set of studies are the result of some years of effort in the field of international economic research in China, Great Britain, Japan, and the United States. While it was to have been expected, it is worth recording that no one actually engaged in the group of studies has at any time suggested a change in methods or questioned the results for reasons outside the field of our common interest in arriving at a truthful picture.[11]

[10] The results of this study and a further revision have been issued by the Chinese Council of the Institute of Pacific Relations under the title *Foreign Investments in China*. In my references to them I shall add the date, 1929 or 1931. The earlier publication has been the only available general work against which to check the results of the individual studies. Lieu's work is frequently based upon material available only in the Chinese language. No effort is made to indicate such sources, though a list of the chief titles, in translation, is to be found in the bibliography.

[11] It may be taken for granted at all times, when specific reference is not made to another source, that the information presented is from the individual studies in Part II. Lieu's work is usually given specific reference.

What Is Included in the Chinese Totals

The statement that foreign investment in China comes to U. S. $3,300 requires explanation. We must know what the figures mean and do not mean if we are to avoid unwarranted conclusions and if we are to make the necessary distinction between the study of investments and of the balance of payments.

The total includes a reasonable valuation of all sources within China from which an income is received or is normally to be expected by persons who are not Chinese. It is important to note that the test for the total is not that it leaves China, not that it is an outpayment from the Chinese economy, but that it is paid to someone who is not Chinese. Foreign investment is a source of income owned by a "foreigner" who may live in China or outside of China.

It follows from this that the total foreign investment is not a sum which has been remitted to China for the purchase or acquisition of the property or other source of income. For the study of balances of payment it is important to know how much in the way of inpayments into China have been involved in the creation of a foreign investment of U. S. $3,300 million, and an attempt is made to estimate this in the chapters devoted to that subject. It follows, also, from the meaning which is here given to foreign investment that the sum which is here reported as foreign investment is greater than the capital sum, the income from which is remitted abroad and constitutes an outpayment from the Chinese economy. Again, it is important, for the purpose of studying China's international accounts, to know how much in the way of outpayments is caused by foreign investments of U. S. $3,300 million and an estimate is made later when this subject is considered. My present task is the measurement of foreign investment as the term is here understood. The significance of this investment from the point of view of the annual flow of funds into and out of China is a matter which requires additional investigation and is separately dealt with below.

A foreigner may be defined as one who is not Chinese. Political allegiance to a government other than that of China is usually involved but this may not be the case. There are in northern Manchuria and elsewhere in China Russians, numbered by the thousand, who are the recognized citizens of no other state. These Russians are here regarded as "foreigners" and their property is included in the total of foreign investments in China.

I wish to make as emphatic as possible the statement that my present task is to show the total of the income producing holdings in China which are in the hands of foreigners, whether the foreign owners live in China or outside of China.[12] The definition of foreign investments used here is not usual but it is the only one which is appropriate to the Chinese situation. There is, in the first place, the practical reason that it was impossible to make distinctions in the original investigation. The total business property of an American firm, for example, could be measured with reasonable accuracy, but it was often impossible to get a report upon the inpayments and outpayments involved. The second reason is the importance of what I have called the foreign "colony" in China. The economic significance of the foreign colony is an aspect of China's international economic relations which could not be neglected even if it produced no inpayments or outpayments at all. Consider the problems of taxation presented by the existence of a foreign corporation under extraterritorial jurisdiction within China. Consider the complexity of labor problems in such a center

[12] Fortunately it has not been necessary to deal with Chinese who live abroad, i.e. beyond Hongkong, and own sources of income within China. There are cases of this sort. At Amoy, for example, eleven American firms are owned by Philippine Chinese and at both Amoy and Foochow there are investments owned by Formosan Chinese who are Japanese citizens. The sums involved are small and no attempt has been made to estimate them.

as Shanghai where there is a foreign settlement, a French Concession, and a surrounding city under jurisdiction which is completely Chinese. Such problems carry with them sufficient justification for the attempt to bring into one total the investments in China by foreigners whether they live and receive their income abroad or whether they live within China, receiving, spending, and investing their incomes without any effect upon the international financial position of the country.

The Fundamental Classification

The work of estimating the total foreign investment in China was done by studying the investments of the individual countries, and the figures presented go back to these studies. For each country the fundamental classification has been into business investments and government obligations. The first reason for this is, again, a practical one. The estimating of government obligations involves the study of loan contracts, loan issues, and the movement of securities among the lending countries. These obligations have been the subject of fairly frequent comment and report, and there is considerable published material.[13] Business investments in China, on the other hand, had never in the past been estimated carefully. The task was a new one and required carrying the study to the individual business unit for the chief countries. It was the necessity for such a study which made thorough co-operation necessary since it was fairly certain that firms of one nationality would hardly report the details of this business to investigators of a different nationality. Information had to be secured in such a way as to insure comparability, avoid prejudice and suspicion, scrupulously live up to pledges that the confidence of the individual firm would be respected, and at the same time to get results. In short, a new study in a difficult field had

[13] Certain unpublished estimates of Chinese government obligations have been made available also.

to be undertaken. Much of the information which is not to be found elsewhere is due to the degree of success with which this task of measuring business investments was carried out.

In addition to the practical there were other reasons of first importance for making the distinction between business investments and government obligations fundamental. There are three ways by which capital may come to China and has come. It may be brought by the foreign business man or the foreign corporation and may remain in the legal possession of the foreigner. It may come as the result of foreign borrowings by the Chinese government. Finally it may come as the result of foreign borrowings by the Chinese corporation. The third of these methods, which may well prove to be of great importance in the future, has been of little importance in the past. Investments of this sort were separately estimated only in the Japanese case. The subject of investment in China through the Chinese corporation is dealt with in the following chapter and may be dismissed from our analysis here.

The methods by which foreign capital has actually come are, then, business investments and government borrowings. The first of these I call direct, since the property remains under foreign control and management. The directness lies in the fact that no one stands between the foreign investor and the business risk involved in his investment. The second is indirect investment, since a legal obligation on the part of the Chinese government comes into existence and lies between the foreign investor and whatever risk may be involved in the actual use of the funds. This use of the terms direct and indirect is quite clearly appropriate in the Chinese case. To avoid any possible misunderstanding it should be added that in the few cases in which foreigners have invested in the obligations of a Chinese corporation we have a business investment which is indirect since capital equipment is not in the legal possession of the foreigner who has in his hands the obligation of a Chinese company.[14]

EARLY INVESTMENT IN CHINA

China offers a striking illustration of the truth of Hobson's statement that "the first foreign investors were merchants."[15] The first investments were the direct business investments of the foreign merchant on the coast of China. He required certain property and equipment to carry on his business and a considerable stock of silver as well. American investments at Canton about 1830 are estimated to have been about U. S. $3 million, of which silver stocks were five-sixths of the total.

As opportunity presented itself, the foreign merchant, at a later date, undertook to carry on simple industrial processes immediately associated with trade. There was some foreign interest in modern silk filatures, but the Chinese government was generally successful in maintaining that foreigners had, by treaty, no right to establish industrial plants in China until the right was granted in the treaty of 1895, which brought the war with Japan to an end.

In the field of shipping the foreigner took a leading part as soon as the five ports were opened to trade in 1842. Shipping in the foreign trade was, of course, in foreign hands but this is not regarded as an investment in China. In the steam shipping between the open ports, the "coastal" shipping of the Customs reports, the foreigner took a leading place at once. After the decline of American shipping from a place of importance in the 'seventies,

---

[14] The terms "direct" and "indirect" are used here in a way which is consistent with their use by others in this new field of business investments. Paul D. Dickens of the Bureau of Foreign and Domestic Commerce uses direct investments, without specifically saying so, to mean investments in which the business risk and, usually, the legal ownership remain with the investor. See the introduction to his "American Direct Investments in Foreign Countries," Washington, 1930, *Trade Information Bulletin*, No. 731.

[15] Hobson, C. K., *The Export of Capital*, London, p. 79.

practically the whole of the modern coast and river shipping of China was in British hands until about 1900. It is estimated that American investments in China in the 'seventies, before the sale of a large American fleet of river steamers to a newly organized Chinese company, the China Merchants Steam Navigation Company, reached a total of U. S. $7 million. In addition to shipping land holdings at Shanghai accounted for most of this total. At the same time "all the foreign banks but one, and three-fourths of the large business houses at Shanghai were British."[16] The Americans probably took second place in the 'seventies but British investments were many times the American total and probably considerably greater than those of all the other countries put together.

The public finances of traditional China involved the use of paper money but not that of loan bonds or other government securities. Chinese officials may at times have secured from local sources funds to make remittances in advance of actual tax collections, but there was no holding by the banks or the public of the obligations of the government. This absence of public credit helps to explain the failure of traditional China to develop facilities for investment and it was, I believe, a handicap, although it may well have worked to some advantage for China by checking early borrowing abroad.[17] There were other reasons, as well, for the slowness of the Chinese government to avail itself of foreign funds. Of modern Egypt it has been said that it was an unfortunate day when its autocratic government made the acquaintance of the credit facilities of western Europe.[18] The government of China, autocratic in theory, was restrained by its own traditions and by public opinion from making an early and reckless use of foreign funds. Harm was pre-

[16] Sargent, A. J., *Anglo-Chinese Commerce and Diplomacy*, Oxford, 1907, p. 141.
[17] Otte, Friedrich, *China: Wirtschaftspolitische Landeskunde*, Gotha, 1927, p. 2, expresses the opinion that absence of public credit was advantageous.
[18] The Earl of Cromer, *Modern Egypt*, New York, 1909, vol. 1, p. 58.

vented but the government was far from any idea of leadership in the development of the country.

There is some doubt as to when the foreign borrowing of the Chinese government began. Lieu reports a British loan of about £1,400,000 for the payment of an indemnity to Russia in 1865.[19] According to others [20] the first loans were in the early 'seventies, from British bankers, and for the purpose of providing funds for the suppression of the Mohammedan rebellion in northwest China. We see in these early loans certain outstanding features of later financing. They were from foreign banks in China, were secured on the Customs, were for wars and indemnities, and there seems to have been a considerable independence on the part of the officials who carried on the negotiations. Borrowing on a considerable scale began in 1894 with a group of loans connected with the Japanese war and the payment of the Japanese indemnity. These loans represent a very large fraction of the amount outstanding at the end of 1901.

BUSINESS INVESTMENTS AND GOVERNMENT OBLIGATIONS IN RECENT YEARS

The first analysis of the general figures for 1900, 1914, and 1931 turns upon the division into business investments and government obligations. Direct business investments are and always have been of overwhelming importance in China. China is probably the world's outstanding example of the preponderance of such investments. The situation is shown in the following figures.

Business investments form nearly 80 per cent of the total foreign investment in China and this percentage has increased. A fuller examination of these facts and their significance is to be found in the two chapters which follow.

[19] Lieu, D. K., *Foreign Investments in China*, 1929, p. 13.

[20] Morse and MacNair, *Far Eastern International Relations*, Shanghai, 1928, p. 500. I have been unable to find a reference to these loans in the edition issued in the United States. U. S. Department of State: *Report on the Commercial Relations of the U. S. with Foreign Countries for the Year 1878*, Washington, 1879, p. 225.

	Business Investments—in Millions of U. S. Dollars	Per Cent of Total	Government Obligations—in Millions of U. S. Dollars	Per Cent of Total
1902	503.2	63.9	284.7	36.1
1914	1,084.5	67.3	525.8	32.7
1931	2,531.9	78.1	710.6	21.9

It is to be noted that the obligation involved in the Boxer indemnity has been omitted from the figures for 1914. This has been done because the indemnity plays no part in the figures for the end of 1901 and a very small part at the end of 1930, and for the further reason that the Boxer indemnity has always been regarded in a different light from the other obligations of the Chinese government. If we were to include the Boxer indemnity under government obligations our figures would show business investments to be 56.5 per cent of the total and government obligations 43.5 per cent.

The first generalization to be noted and to be borne in mind at all times is that business investments,—and this means direct business investments in the legal possession of foreign business men and corporations, are the chief form of foreign investment in China. No study which leaves business investments out of account can give a true picture of the Chinese situation.[21]

How the Investments Have Been Used

Transportation has been the most important field of foreign investment throughout the present century. Here business investments and the investment of the funds borrowed abroad by the Chinese government combine to swell the total. The investments of British shipping firms, of the Japanese railway in Manchuria, of the Chinese government railways, and of the American companies

[21] Some effort has been made to compare the Chinese situation with that in other countries. My rough calculations show that foreign business investments, including both direct and indirect, form about a third of the foreign investments of India and pre-war Russia and about 10 per cent of the foreign investments in Japan.

interested in the motor industry all fall within this field. It was important in 1902 when it accounted for U. S. $284.8 million, 36.1 per cent of the total foreign investment in China. By 1914 it had reached U. S. $531.1 million, 33 per cent, of the total foreign investment for that year. Although there were new developments in other fields the total reached U. S. $845.1 million in 1931 and was 26.1 per cent of the whole.

Borrowings by the Chinese government for other purposes than railways and communications, have been brought together into one total under the heading, The General Purposes of the Chinese Government. This includes the early war and indemnity loans, the Reorganization Loan of 1913 and many of the "unsecured" loans of a more recent date. The general purposes of the Chinese government accounted for 31.5 per cent of the foreign investment in 1902, 20.5 per cent in 1914, and 13.2 per cent in 1931.

TABLE 5

FOREIGN INVESTMENTS IN CHINA, 1914 AND 1931

Distributed by Purpose or Nature of the Business

	1914		1931	
	Millions of U. S. Dollars	Per Cent Total	Millions of U. S. Dollars	Per Cent Total
General purposes of the Chinese government	330.3	20.5	427.7	13.2
Transportation	531.1	33.0	846.3	26.1
Communications and public utilities	26.6	1.7	128.7	4.0
Mining	59.1	3.7	128.9	4.0
Manufacturing	110.6	6.9	376.3	11.6
Banking and finance	6.3	0.4	214.7	6.6
Real estate	105.5	6.5	339.2	10.5
Imports and exports	142.6	8.8	483.7	14.9
Miscellaneous (undistributed)	298.2	18.5	282.8	8.7
Obligations of foreign municipalities			14.2	0.4
Total	1,610.3	100.0	3,242.5	100.0

It has been found impossible to make any further distribution of the total for 1902. The figures for 1914 and 1931 are found in the accompanying table. The vigorous increase in the fields of business investment is to be noted. The distribution is less complete for 1914 than for 1931.

GEOGRAPHICAL DISTRIBUTION

Foreign investments are here divided into those in Manchuria, in Shanghai, and in the rest of China, that is in China outside of Manchuria and Shanghai. The foreigner, it must be remembered, has not been free to invest where he pleased in China. His investments have been confined to the treaty ports, except as he has entered into special agreements with the Chinese government or has loaned money to the Chinese government for developments in the "interior." The legal conditions seem to dictate a classification into investments in the treaty ports and investments outside the treaty ports. The actual situation, however, seems to me to make the classification here offered more significant.

Shanghai is of such importance among the treaty ports as to justify giving it a special place. The amount of the investment in Manchuria and the conditions which have existed there make a separate consideration desirable. The existence of railway "zones," the varied activity of the two great foreign railway corporations, and the opening up of a large number of cities to trade make the distinction between the treaty port and the interior of much less significance here than elsewhere. All investments outside of Shanghai and outside of Manchuria are brought together under one heading. Most of these investments are in Chinese government railways but they include, also, those which have involved "concessions" granted by the Chinese government. The French railway in Yunnan and a number of mining ventures are among those that find a place here.

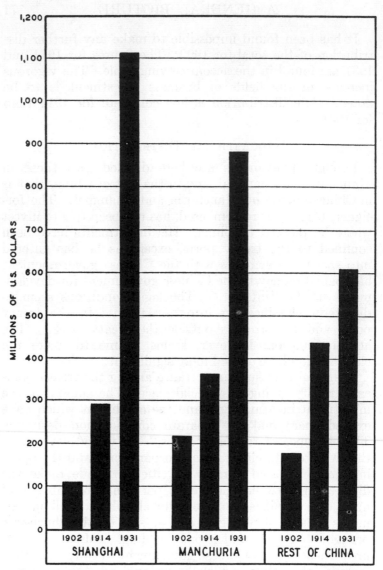

CHART 1.—GEOGRAPHICAL DISTRIBUTION OF FOREIGN INVESTMENTS
IN CHINA

Data in Table 6, p. 73

The geographical distribution of the investments is shown in the following table. It must be pointed out that distribution of the whole of the investment has been impossible. It is obvious that loans for the general purposes of the Chinese government could not be geographically distributed. The sums reported as undistributed in the table are very largely such loans. The percentages have been worked out on the basis of the whole foreign investment, including the undistributed amounts.

TABLE 6

GEOGRAPHICAL DISTRIBUTION OF FOREIGN INVESTMENTS IN CHINA, 1902–1931

	1902		1914		1931	
	Millions of U. S. Dollars	Per Cent of Total	Millions of U. S. Dollars	Per Cent of Total	Millions of U. S. Dollars	Per Cent of Total
Shanghai	110.0	14.0	291.0	18.1	1,112.2	34.3
Manchuria	216.0	27.4	361.6	22.4	880.0	27.1
Rest of China	177.2	22.5	433.1	26.9	607.8	18.8
Undistributed	284.7	36.1	524.6	32.6	642.5	19.8
Total	787.9	100.0	1,610.3	100.0	3,242.5	100.0

If our information enabled us to go back to the years before the Japanese war and the entrance of the Russians into Manchuria, we would find practically the whole of the foreign investment to be in the treaty ports with nearly one-half in Shanghai. By 1902 the building of the Russian railway and borrowings by the Chinese government had worked a change. Over a quarter of the total investments were in Manchuria in 1902 and Shanghai accounted for no more than 14 per cent.

Since 1902 the outstanding change has been an increase in the relative importance of Shanghai. Manchuria on the other hand declined in relative importance between 1902 and 1914 and held a slightly smaller share of the total in 1931 than it had in 1902. The increase in the case of

Shanghai is to some small extent due to more complete information in 1931 but there can be no doubt of the rapid increase in the relative importance of Shanghai throughout the thirty years, and especially since 1914. One-third of the total foreign investment in China was in Shanghai alone in 1931. Taking Shanghai and Manchuria together we find that they accounted for about 40 per cent of the total investment before the World War and the Chinese revolution, and that they account for 60 per cent at the present time. These facts go far to explain the increasing importance in recent years of Manchuria and Shanghai in China's international relations.

THE CREDITOR COUNTRIES

British merchants and British bankers lead the way both in business investments and in loans to the Chinese government. The political situation after the war between China and Japan brought in Russia and Germany. We find, as we should expect, that these countries were the chief investors in China in 1902. Great Britain held 33 per cent of the total, Russia 31.3 per cent, and Germany 20.9 per cent.

In 1914 no other country seriously threatened the leading position of Great Britain. There were now four countries of about equal importance, Germany, Russia, Japan, and France, but they were all far behind Great Britain. The most remarkable change was in the position of Japan, whose investments in China had amounted to nothing in 1902 and who held 13.6 per cent of the total in 1914.

The figures for 1931 show a number of changes. Japan now occupies the place that Russia had occupied in 1902. She stands next to Great Britain, still the leading creditor country, and the two are far ahead of all others. Russia, the United States, and France are now about equal and the other countries are of minor importance. Japanese and American investments have grown vigorously, Jap-

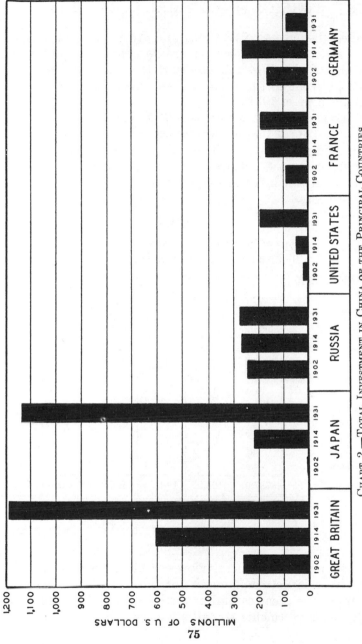

CHART 2.—TOTAL INVESTMENT IN CHINA OF THE PRINCIPAL COUNTRIES
Data in Table 7, p. 76

anese being over five times and American four times as
great as in 1914. German investments have fallen to a
third of the 1914 amount and the Germans, who held
20 per cent of the total in 1902, have dropped to about
3 per cent in 1931.

Looking at the whole period of thirty years, as shown
in the figures in the two tables below, we find the outstanding facts to be: the continuance of Great Britain in
first place, the remarkable rise of Japan—the increase
in American investments, and the decline of German investments.

TABLE 7

FOREIGN INVESTMENTS IN CHINA, 1902, 1914, 1931

By Creditor Countries—Percentage Distribution

	1902		1914		1931	
	Millions of U. S. Dollars	Per Cent of Total	Millions of U. S. Dollars	Per Cent of Total	Millions of U. S. Dollars	Per Cent of Total
Great Britain	260.3	33.0	607.5	37.7	1,189.2	36.7
Japan	1.0	0.1	219.6	13.6	1,136.9	35.1
Russia	246.5	31.3	269.3	16.7	273.2	8.4
United States	19.7	2.5	49.3	3.1	196.8	6.1
France	91.1	11.6	171.4	10.7	192.4	5.9
Germany	164.3	20.9	263.6	16.4	87.0	2.7
Belgium	4.4	0.6	22.9	1.4	89.0	2.7
Netherlands					28.7	0.9
Italy					46.4	1.4
Scandinavian countries					2.9	0.1
Others	0.6	0.0	6.7	0.4		
	787.9	100.0	1,610.3	100.0	3,242.5	100.0

THE IMPORTANCE OF CHINA IN THE INVESTMENTS OF
OTHER COUNTRIES

To make our general view complete we must see that
Chinese investments count for little in the foreign hold-
ings of the great capital exporting countries of the world.
British investments abroad are usually estimated at about

TABLE 8

FOREIGN INVESTMENTS IN CHINA, 1902, 1914, 1931

Relatives for the Chief Countries

Investments for 1914 = 100

	1902	1914	1931
Great Britain	42.8	100	195.8
Japan	0.5	100	517.7
Russia	91.5	100	101.4
United States	40.0	100	399.0
France	53.2	100	112.3
Germany	62.3	100	33.0
Total (all countries)	48.9	100	201.4

U. S. $20,000 million.[22] If we accept this estimate we find British investments in China to be 5.9 per cent of the British total.

The foreign investments of the United States are variously estimated. We may accept a total of U. S. $15,000 millions as reasonable. This is a recent estimate by the Department of Commerce of the United States government.[23] On the basis of this estimate we find that 1.3 per cent of American investments are in China. French and German investments may be taken at, roughly, U. S. $4,000 and U. S. $2,000 million respectively. French investments in China are 4.8 per cent and German 4.3 per cent of the totals given. The Chinese investments of Great Britain are of greater importance to her than is the case with any other of the developed countries of the West.

When we come to Japan the situation is quite different.

[22] A recent estimate is that of the London *Economist*, Oct. 25, 1930, which gives this total. The estimate of Sir Robert Kindersley, *Economic Journal*, June, 1930, is somewhat smaller. If direct investments in all countries were included the total would probably be larger than U. S. $20,000 million.

[23] Dickens, Paul D., "A New Estimate of American Investments Abroad," *Trade Information Bulletin*, No. 767, Washington, 1931. A somewhat larger estimate by Max Winkler is in the Information Service of the Foreign Policy Association of New York for Feb. 3, 1932.

The Japanese have investments in China and a few other investments.   Inouye reports the other investments to be yen 134 million in the South Seas, and certain war loans to Russia which need not be counted.[24]   Making an estimate of U. S. $250 million as sufficient to cover all Japanese investments abroad, outside of China, we arrive at a figure of 81.9 per cent as the share of the total which is in China.   The Soviet Union had no foreign investments.   Leaving out of account the Russian business investments in China which may be said to be those of the Russian colony in China, we have to consider the Chinese Eastern Railway which is the property of the Russian government and certain small holdings.   If the total of the income-producing property of the Soviet government held abroad were known, the share in China would probably be found to be a very large fraction of it.

The Russian case is peculiar.   The members of the Communist Academy at Moscow with whom I discussed this matter in June, 1931, maintained that the Soviet Union had no foreign investments abroad.   They intended to convey to me that the Soviet economy does not look to a return upon capital invested abroad as a normal source of income.   They were at the same time willing to admit that the Chinese Eastern Railway is owned by the Russian government, that it has been a source of some small income, and that the rights of the Russian government in this railway are a matter of some economic importance to Russia.   Russian political interest in China, it may be added, takes other forms than those, to use their language, of capitalistic imperialism.   Without raising the question of Russian business investments in China and without pressing the matter of the name, let us say that the Russian government has income-yielding property in China and that a very large fraction of the

[24] Inouye, Junnosuke, *Present Condition of Our International Financial Relations* (in Japanese), Tokyo, 1926, p. 232, and App. 10.

income-yielding property which it owns outside of Russia is located in China. The situation is, on the surface, similar to that in the case of Japan.

In short, China accounts for but a small fraction of the foreign investments of the capital exporting countries of the Western world. Investments in China are of great relative importance to the Japanese, four-fifths of whose foreign holdings are in China. So great a preponderance of investments in China on the part of a country which has been an importer of capital, except for a few years, needs to be explained. In part the explanation is the same for Japan and Russia and lies in the history of their relations with Manchuria.

Conclusion

The outline of the picture has been sketched. Taking foreign investments in China to mean the value of all sources of business income within the country owned by foreigners and foreign holdings of government obligations, we find these investments to have doubled between 1900 and 1914 and doubled again between 1914 and 1931, and to be worth today about U. S. $3,300 million. Business investments we find to be of predominant importance and to have been so since the foreign business man first made a place for himself on the coast of China. Nearly 80 per cent of the foreign investment in China, as I have here defined the term, is direct business investment. This is probably a greater percentage than in any other country in the world. The investments have gone, first of all, into the provision of transportation facilities. Shanghai and Manchuria account for about three-fifths of the investments and the relative importance of Shanghai has increased, especially since 1914. Great Britain has always been the chief creditor country, with Russia not far behind in 1902 and Japan not far behind in 1931.

It must be remembered in connection with this picture that my task has been to show what the foreigner owns in China and what claims to receive money he holds. I do not now make any distinction between the Russian who is permanently domiciled in China and owns a small shop in Harbin and the British country gentleman who has never seen China and owns a Chinese government bond. They are equally foreign investors in China. But for other purposes we must know what these foreign investments mean in China's international accounts. This is a matter which is reserved for later consideration. I turn now to a more complete account of foreign investments under each of the two major divisions.

CHAPTER VI

SURVEY OF BUSINESS INVESTMENTS

China is a country with undeveloped resources, a fairly high degree of economic organization, an industrious people, meager capital equipment, and high rates of interest. And yet foreign capital has failed to reach China except as it has been brought in by the foreigner. The characteristic form of foreign investment has been, and is, direct business investment.

Under the conditions which exist in China direct business investment is investment through the foreign "colony" or through the foreign "colonies" in the country. The capital has been brought to China by the foreigner, who is himself in China or who represents persons outside of China. It remains the legal property of the foreigner and it is under his management. In so far as extraterritoriality exists, the property and person of the foreigner are removed from the jurisdiction of the Chinese courts. In "settlement" or "concession" or "leased area" the territory is under the political control, in part or entirely, of one or more foreign governments.

The term "colonies" is to be understood as a neutral or colorless name for the groups of foreigners living in the country. It is inclusive, covering foreigners who are and those who are not under Chinese jurisdiction. It is intended to avoid legal complications and is used without political significance.

There is, of course, no desire to minimize the political implications of direct business investments under the conditions which exist in China. Such investments have at times been the tool of policy which has for its aim the acquisition of Chinese territory or the furtherance of other political ambitions. But, on the other hand, they have often been purely business ventures by men who were quite innocent of political designs of any sort.

JAPANESE INVESTMENTS IN CHINESE CORPORATIONS

The general figures of business investments which have been presented in the preceding chapter include certain small items which must be eliminated if we are to confine ourselves strictly to direct investments. These items are: a Japanese investment of U. S. $17.5 million in Chinese corporations in 1914 and a similar investment of U. S. $38.7 million in 1931. The items are small and it is not certain that they are correctly classified. The two important corporations involved are the Hanyehping Company and the Kiangsi Railway Company. In both cases the interest of the two governments lies just beneath the surface and the nature of the obligations may be modified at any time as the result of diplomatic negotiation. In addition, Japanese loans have been made to Chinese public utility corporations to the amount of U. S. $9.3 million and to Chinese cotton milling companies to the amount of about U. S. $4 million.

The above investments have been separated from direct business investments because they are reported to be financial transactions by which Japanese funds have been made available to Chinese corporations over a long term of years. It is significant that this form, which we may call *indirect* business investment, has been tried. The significance is diminished by the fact that the venture can hardly be called a success from the point of view of either the Japanese or the Chinese.[1] With these small sums eliminated we may proceed to consider direct business investments in China.

THE GENERAL FACTS

Direct business investments are estimated to have been U. S. $2,500 million in 1931, which is three-fourths of the

[1] The chapter on Japanese investments in China gives a detailed statement of such investments.

foreign investment in China. The figures for this and for the earlier years are as follows:

	Direct Business Investments		
	In Millions of U. S. Dollars	As a Percentage of the Total	Index Numbers
1902	503.2	63.9	47.2
1914	1,067.0	67.3	100.0
1931	2,493.2	78.1	233.7

If, instead of having figures for the above years only, we had figures for short intervals over the past century, it may be guessed that they would reveal a steady rise in business investments throughout the period. The rate would, no doubt, have been quickened by certain events. In 1895, for example, the foreigner secured the right to build and own industrial plants at the treaty ports. In 1897 the Russians began the building of the Chinese Eastern Railway which was pushed rapidly to completion. In 1907 Dairen was opened to trade and Japanese investments began a rapid increase. In contrast with the steady rise of business investments the borrowings of the Chinese government present quite a different picture. There were practically no foreign borrowings before 1894. For twenty-five or thirty years they played a part of some importance in creating the increased totals of foreign investment. Since then they have fallen off.

The facts for the last thirty years may be considered in more detail. Compare the index numbers given above with the corresponding ones for government obligations; 54.1 for 1902, 100 for 1914, and 135.1 for 1931.[2] It is plain that business investments and loans increased at about the same rate between 1902–1914. Between 1914–1931, however, business investments continued to grow at about the earlier rate while the increase in government obligations was much smaller.

[2] It is to be borne in mind that the Boxer indemnity is not included except for a small amount in 1931.

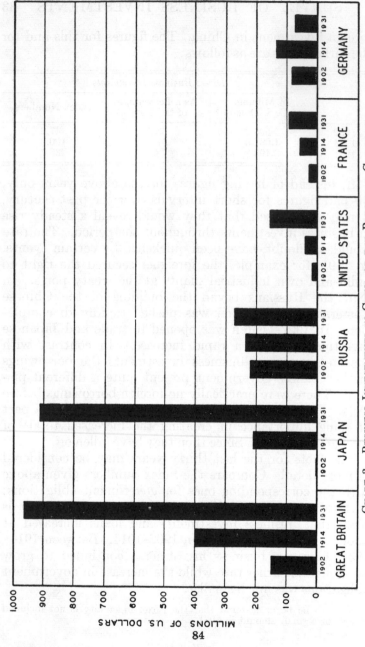

CHART 3.—BUSINESS INVESTMENTS IN CHINA OF THE PRINCIPAL COUNTRIES

Data in Table 13, p. 99

The totals of business investments which are presented above give some idea of the magnitude of the sums involved and of the steady increase throughout the period studied. The significance of such investments cannot be appreciated without further analysis, and such analysis is attempted in the pages which follow.

There is, however, one table which must be presented here. It shows the business investments in China of the nationals of each of the investing countries for which information is available, and for every country of importance, except, perhaps, Portugal. This table deserves special attention. It seems to be one which analyzes the total of U. S. $2,500 million for business investments in 1931. But it is more than an analysis, for it shows how the total was built up. It brings together the figures made available in the separate studies in Part II, and presents in the briefest space the results of the whole set of investigations of business investments.

TABLE 9

Business Investments in China, 1931

By Countries

	Millions of U. S. Dollars	Per Cent of Total
Great Britain	963.4	38.0
Japan	912.8	36.0
Russia	273.2	10.8
United States	155.1	6.1
France	95.0	3.8
Germany	75.0	3.0
Belgium	41.0	1.6
Netherlands	10.0	0.4
Italy	4.4	0.2
Scandinavian countries	2.0	0.1
	2,531.9	100.0

How the Business Investments Have Been Used

Business investments for four countries, Great Britain, Japan, Russia, and the United States, have been studied in sufficient detail to show the application of the funds in 1931. These four countries held direct investments to the value of U. S. $2,260.9 million which is about 90 per cent of all business investments. It is quite certain that the information for the other countries would not change the situation revealed in the accompanying table.

TABLE 10

DIRECT INVESTMENTS OF FOUR COUNTRIES, 1931

Distributed by the Nature of the Business

Figures in millions of U. S. dollars

	Great Britain	Japan	Russia	U. S. A.	Total	Per Cent of Total
Transportation	134.9	204.3	210.5	10.8	560.5	24.8
Public utilities	48.2	15.6		35.2	99.0	4.4
Mining	19.3	87.5	2.1	0.1	109.0	4.8
Manufacturing	173.4	165.6	12.8	20.5	372.3	16.5
Banking and finance	115.6	73.8		25.3	214.7	9.5
Real estate	202.3	73.0	32.5	8.5	316.3	14.0
Import and export	240.8	183.0	12.2	47.7	483.7	21.4
Miscellaneous	28.9	71.3	3.1	2.1	105.4	4.6
Total	963.4	874.1	273.2	150.2	2,260.9	100.0

The British and the Japanese are the most important holders of direct investments in every field except that of transportation where the Chinese Eastern Railway puts Russia first. The Americans are of importance in one field only, that of public utilities, and this is to be accounted for by their recent purchase of the electricity department of the Shanghai Municipal Council, now operated by the Shanghai Power Company, and by their recent acquisition of the interests of the former Shanghai Mutual Telephone Company.

DIRECT INVESTMENT IN TRANSPORTATION

Transportation accounts for a quarter of the direct investment of the four leading countries. In shipping we find one of the oldest forms of direct investment in

China. Most of the British total under transportation is in shipping and Japanese investment in this field comes to about U. S. $60 million, if we include, in addition to ships, the harbor works and wharves of the South Manchuria Railway Company. Total foreign investment in the coast and river shipping of China (including Hongkong shipping but excluding all shipping in the overseas trade) and in the facilities and equipment ashore is certainly in the neighborhood of U. S. $200 million. There is little doubt that over half the steam shipping in Chinese waters is owned by foreigners and under foreign flags. Domestic shipping in other countries is usually reserved to the nationals of the country. The unusual situation in China has its legal basis in treaty rights.[3] Its continuance has an economic basis and rests upon the effectiveness of the foreigner in the field. A Chinese corporation, the China Merchants Steam Navigation Company, entered the field at an early date with special privileges granted by the Chinese government. The Chinese company has not at any time however seriously threatened the continued success of the foreign companies.

The history of the China Merchants Steam Navigation Company illustrates many of the obstacles to investment in China through the Chinese corporation. It is a private enterprise inaugurated by officials with capital secured in part from public funds. It has borrowed from the government, made loans (some of them forced loans) to the government, and is now in process of being made entirely a state enterprise under the immediate control of the government at Nanking. The failure of domestic shipping to develop under this Chinese company is not held by the Chinese interested in this business to be due to foreign treaty rights.[4]

[3] For a brief historical summary see, Chamberlain, J. P., *Foreign Flags in China's Internal Navigation*, American Council, Institute of Pacific Relations, 1931, pp. 5–12.

[4] A brief history of the China Merchants Company is to be found in the *China Year Book*, 1931, pp. 107–9.

Direct investment in railways is the chief item under transportation. This occasions some astonishment. We have in direct investment a method which began in the treaty port and is adapted to the treaty port, and yet we find the largest investment to be in railways which cross great stretches of China. The legal basis of railway investment is to be found in the concession or grant by the Chinese government to a foreign corporation of the right to build and operate lines. The first concession was to the Russians in 1896.[5] Concessions of this sort in combination with the legal conditions which exist under extraterritoriality produce a situation more disturbing to the political security of China and to the possibility of national economic policy than the existence of direct investments at the treaty ports. The direct investment in the "concession" or "foreign" railways in China I find to be as follows for 1931 and to represent 15.8 per cent of the total direct investment in China.

	Millions of U. S. Dollars
Russian	
Chinese Eastern	210.5
Japanese	
South Manchuria (railway only)	138.3
Tientu Light Railway	2.2
Chinchow-Pitzuwo	2.0
British	
Canton-Kowloon, British section	7.8
French	
Yunnan Railway [6]	32.0
	392.8

In addition to railways and shipping there is a small investment in motor cars and equipment. Certain American corporations own plants for the assembling and repair of motor cars and for the building of automobile bodies. If foreign investment exists in cross-country transportation by motor car or bus it is so small as to be negligible.

[5] Russian Investments in China, p. 558.
[6] Not included in the direct investments distributed in Table 10.

The Interest of Foreign Governments in Direct Investments

It is necessary to point out a feature of special importance in connection with the "concession" railways. This is the extent of the interest of foreign governments in the corporations owning these railways.

When the proposal for the building of the Chinese Eastern Railway was first made there was Chinese objection to its ownership by the Russian government. To meet this objection a corporation was created, the whole of whose shares were purchased for the Russian government.[7] The complete ownership of the Chinese Eastern by this government has not been effectively questioned at any time. The statement is frequently made that the Chinese government is the owner of a half interest in this railway, but the agreements between the Chinese and the Soviet governments deal with the division of management and profits, not with ownership.[8] It has come about by the accidents of history that a communist government is the owner of a railway inside of the territory of another government. The political problems in the Russian case are much simplified by the fact that extraterritoriality is no longer in existence.

The South Manchuria Railway is the property of a corporation in which the Japanese government has always had a controlling interest as the owner of half of the capital stock. This company has been the owner not only of railways and workshops but also of capital equipment in a great variety of industries. Between 1925 and 1930 much of this property, aside from the railways themselves and certain mines, was turned over to a number of subsidiary corporations, in which the South Manchuria Company owns a controlling interest.[9] It is difficult to measure the total interest of the Japanese government. The railway company itself is the owner of busi-

[7] Russian Investments in China, p. 559.
[8] *Ibid.*, p. 615.
[9] Japanese Investments in China, pp. 474–77.

ness property valued at U. S. $318.9 million. In addition, its interest in its subsidiaries is about U. S. $28 million. It has made loans to the Chinese government upon Manchurian railways to the amount of about U. S. $25 million. If we were to add the total paid-up capital of the subsidiary companies, aside from that furnished by the South Manchuria, this would amount to nearly U. S. $50 million. The Japanese government controls by the familiar methods of corporate organization business holdings within Manchuria that reach a total of nearly U. S. $425 million. In the list below I have set down only the direct business holdings of the South Manchuria.

In the case of the Yunnan Railway we have a corporation in which the French government has always taken a keen interest. No less than 40 per cent of the capital invested in the railway in China has come from the colonial government of Indo-China. The control of this railway company may be said to lie with the French government.[10] The British section of the Canton-Kowloon Railway, that is the section inside of the leased area of Kowloon on the main line opposite Hongkong, was built by the government of the crown colony of Hongkong and is owned by that government.

We may draw up a total of direct business investments in China owned by foreign governments or by corporations in which foreign governments hold a controlling interest. The total investment of U. S. $569.2 million is

	Millions of U. S. Dollars
South Manchuria Railway	318.9
Chinese Eastern Railway	210.5
Canton-Kowloon Railway (British section)	7.8
Yunnan Railway	32.0
	569.2

no less than 22.5 per cent of the whole of foreign business investments in China. It is to be borne in mind that this total includes no holdings of property for administra-

[10] French Investments in China, p. 624.

tive or governmental purposes, such as consulates. If we were to add the capital of the subsidiaries of the South Manchuria we would find that foreign governments control about one-fourth of all the direct business investments in the country. Most of this sum represents holdings in Manchuria by the Japanese and Russian governments. The importance of the interests of foreign governments has been emphasized to guard against the assumption that business investments, as I report them, are entirely in the hands of private business organizations. The political significance of the extent of government control which has been revealed is obvious.

INVESTMENTS IN THE IMPORT AND EXPORT BUSINESS

The foreigner in China has at all times been a trader and the immediate interests of trade are the concern of the largest group in the foreign colonies outside of Manchuria. If the railways of Manchuria had been financed through the Chinese government, as have the railways south of the Great Wall, the import and export business and general trading would include, at the present day, a larger fraction of the total foreign investment in China than is to be found under any other heading in Table 10. Investments in this field include those which are associated with the importing of foreign goods, the exporting of Chinese products, and with wholesale and retail trade in the open ports of China. Such investments are reported for the four countries with which I am now dealing at U. S. $483.7 million. This is 21.4 per cent of the total.

The investments here include the great stocks of goods which are at all times held in such ports as Shanghai, Tientsin, and Dairen. They include the holdings of the great trading companies of the British, such as Jardine, Matheson & Company and Butterfield & Swire,[11] and

---

[11] The holdings of these companies and of the others mentioned have been separated as far as possible. The textile mills of Jardine, Matheson & Company are reported under manufacturing, and the shipping of Butter-

the great distributors of foreign commodities under the American and British flags, such as the Standard Oil Company, the Asiatic Petroleum Company, and the British-American Tobacco Company. The outstanding fact about the import and export trade is the existence of a relatively small number of great firms who control most of the capital invested.

In contrast to these great firms are the many small trading ventures of the chief treaty ports. Here we find hundreds of small companies or of individual traders who are engaged in importing and exporting on a small scale. In the American case it was found that half the firms have offices in Shanghai only and are unrepresented elsewhere. These small firms control no more than 5 per cent of the total American business investment in China. The same situation exists in the cases of Great Britain, Japan, and Russia.

The holdings of the retail dealers in the treaty ports are included under this heading also. We have here to do with such firms as Whiteaway, Laidlaw & Co., and Lane, Crawford & Co. at Shanghai, the Japanese department stores in Dairen, and Chourin & Company of Harbin. Certain great firms, owned by Chinese and incorporated under the laws of Hongkong, have in recent years proven to be powerful competitors of the foreign firms in this field. The best known of these Chinese firms are the Wing-On Company and the Sincere Company. The success of the Chinese in this field is to be contrasted with the failure of the China Merchants Steam Navigation Company in the field of shipping.

MANUFACTURING

Foreign investment in manufacturing covers 14 per cent of the total investment of the four countries. Jap-

field & Swire under transportation. The so-called "installations" of the great oil companies have been reported under this heading but their investments in shipping and in manufacturing have been separated.

anese investment in the textile industry at Shanghai and in the other treaty ports of China comes to about U. S. $100 million, that is to more than a fourth of the total investment in this field.[12]   The Japanese cotton mills provide a conspicuous and interesting case.   The textile industry was prosperous in Japan during the World War. This prosperity carried the industry to the treaty ports of China, where Japanese management has brought a considerable degree of success.   In the Japanese case investment in the expressing and marketing of bean and other vegetable oils comes second with a total investment of about U. S. $9.5 million.   The center of this industry is Dairen.

The importance of the Japanese cotton mills should not be allowed to obscure the fact that the total investment of the British in manufacturing is somewhat greater than is that of the Japanese.   The British were the pioneers in a great variety of manufacturing industries and own manufacturing plants in practically every important treaty port in China.

In manufacturing we have an industry which has brought directly into China capital equipment of a modern sort.   It has brought with it foreign management and foreign technical skill.   Direct investment in manufacturing has meant the immediate development of modern industry in China.

REAL ESTATE

Real estate holdings, at Shanghai particularly, have been an important form of foreign investment since the 'seventies of the last century.   The total holding for the whole of China for the four countries studied is U. S. $316.3 million.   This total is probably farther from the complete figure of foreign holdings than in the case of the other fields of investment.   Large land holdings by

[12] A detailed account of these investments is to be found in the chapter on Japanese Investments, pp. 495–99.

the French and Belgians must be added to reach a reasonably correct total. It is probable that the holdings of real estate for income and for residence, together with the investments in hotels and apartment houses, comes to a total of U. S. $400 million. This includes land holdings in Manchuria, as well as at the treaty ports of China. From the information provided in the individual studies it is possible that the foreign holding of real estate at Shanghai alone runs to a total of U. S. $225 million. It is quite obviously true, as Lieu points out,[13] that the market value of these holdings is much greater than the original cost to the present holders. It is true, also, that the inpayments into China were considerably less than these original costs. What is more, the income from land owned at the treaty ports of China is usually paid to persons living in China. Real estate holdings are an investment which brings out the importance of the concept of the foreign colony in China. A large fraction of the real estate is held by members of the foreign colony, has been purchased from income received within China, and brings into existence income which is expended in China. A study of foreign land holdings, in other words, involves little examination of factors which enter into China's balance of payments.

Land holding may be contrasted with manufacturing. It has little to do with the introduction of modern industrial methods into China. At the same time it is apparent that the other cities of China have learned and are learning about urban land utilization from the development of Shanghai.

Investments in Other Fields

Investment in banking and finance comes to U. S. $214.7 million, 9.5 per cent of the total. An attempt has been made to include in this total the actual physical property of the banking and financial corporations, to-

[13] Lieu, D. K., *Foreign Investments in China*, 1931, p. 12.

gether with advances to Chinese. The financing of China's foreign trade is carried very largely by banks outside of China. As soon as a bill in terms of a "gold" currency comes into existence, the financing is from abroad. Shanghai is the great financial center of China and it is cut off by the silver exchange and for other reasons from the use, on any considerable scale, of short-term loans from foreign money markets. The use of such funds was less than usual during the years 1930–1931. Silver stocks at Shanghai were unusually great and local funds were obtainable on easy terms. A number of foreign bankers in Chinese centers told me during the winter of 1930–1931 that they were provided with sufficient funds by their Chinese depositors so that it might be said that they had no investment in China at all. To this it may be replied that the foreign bank is an income-producing business enterprise and that the income goes to foreign owners who are usually outside of China. A capitalization of the net income earned through a period of years by certain banks has been used as a check upon my figures of investment in this field.

In the field of mining, U. S. $109 million, we have investments based upon the "concession," not the treaty port. In this field the Japanese lead and the Fushun mine alone has produced about a quarter of the coal mined in China in recent years. The percentage of the coal production of China which is from "foreign" mines is about 40 per cent.[14]

This is a high percentage yet it would be higher but for the failure of many projects through local opposition

[14] W. H. Wong presents the following figures for 1928 in the *China Year Book*, 1931, p. 325.

Produced by	Coal: Millions of Tons	Per Cent of Total Production
Japanese mines	7.6	30.5
British "	2.5	9.8
Russian "	.4	1.6
German "	.07	0.2

and for other reasons.[15]   The modern iron industry of China is largely in the hands of foreign corporations. Iron mining in Manchuria has been developed by the Japanese, who have interests in the Yangtze valley as well, including loans to the Hanyehping Company, the owner of the greatest mine. There is considerable foreign interest in gold mining but the antimony mines are in Chinese hands almost entirely. A great enterprise in this field is that of the Kailan Mining Administration with its head office at Tientsin. It is a partnership of a British and a Chinese corporation for which the British have provided the larger share of the joint capital. The Kailan mines produce more coal than any other group in China and the Kailan enterprise has been as successful financially as any "concession" in China outside of Manchuria.

In the field of public utilities we find British and American investments in the chief treaty ports and Japanese investments in Manchuria. This is the one field in which the Americans play a part of some importance. There has been a rapid development in this field since 1921. A recent writer lists some 500 electric light and power plants in China. Most of them are small and locally owned.[16]   There has been some foreign investment in this field by the provision of equipment on credit but, in general, we have here an example of the obstacles and difficulties of foreign investment in China.

The various fields of foreign investment have been listed in Table 10 with some attention to the extent in which they have brought modern industrial equipment into China. This has been important in transportation, public utilities, mining, and manufacturing. About half the investments, it may be estimated, have been connected with the process of industrialization. At the same

[15] That of the *Syndicat du Yunnan*, French and British capital, of the Eastern Pioneer Company in Szechuan, of the proposed joint enterprise of the Chinese government and the Standard Oil Company.
[16] Tsha Kyung-we, "Electric Light and Power Plants in China," *Chinese Economic Journal*, July, 1931, pp. 686–728.

time it is to be recorded that certain small investments, as in the lace and drawn-work industry of Swatow, have served to extend an older form of industrial organization. And it is to be noted once more that land holdings by foreigners at such centers as Shanghai do not directly stimulate the industrial modernization of the country.

THE GEOGRAPHICAL DISTRIBUTION OF THE DIRECT INVESTMENTS OF FOUR COUNTRIES

Nearly half of the direct investments of the important countries were found to be in Shanghai in 1931. Over a third were in Manchuria and about one-sixth in the rest of China. The figures are shown in the accompanying table. The investments in Manchuria are shown to be

TABLE 11

THE GEOGRAPHICAL DISTRIBUTION OF THE DIRECT BUSINESS INVESTMENTS OF FOUR COUNTRIES, 1931

Figures in millions of U. S. dollars

	Great Britain	Japan	Russia	U. S. A.	Total	Per Cent of Total
Shanghai	737.4	215.0	——	97.5	1,049.9	46.4
Manchuria	——	550.2	261.8	——	812.0	36.0
Rest of China (incl. Hongkong)	226.0	108.9	11.4	52.7	399.0	17.6
Total	963.4	874.1	273.2	150.2	2,260.9	100.0

those of the Japanese and the Russians only. If British and American investments in Manchuria were known, the Manchurian total would probably be increased by no more than U. S. $40 million. British investments at Shanghai must still be counted about as great as Japanese investments in Manchuria and Shanghai. It is shown in the Japanese study that Japanese investments at Shanghai increased at a more rapid rate between 1914 and 1931 than did Japanese investments in Manchuria.[17]   It is

[17] Japanese Investments in China, pp. 473–74.

shown, also, that Japanese exports of cotton manufactures to the rest of China have grown more rapidly since 1914 than exports to Manchuria.[18] Even from the Japanese point of view the importance of Shanghai is growing, how much the more from the point of view of other countries who have fewer interests elsewhere. I turn now to the business investments of the six countries of leading importance.

THE BUSINESS INVESTMENTS OF SIX COUNTRIES

Certain general conclusions of fundamental significance in understanding the Chinese situation are based upon a study of the three tables which follow. The first of these shows the percentage of the total which business investments have formed for each of six countries in 1902, 1914, and 1931. The total upon which the percentages are based includes in each case holdings by the particular country for the year in question of government obligations as well as business investments. This table brings out changes in the form which foreign investments have taken.

TABLE 12

BUSINESS INVESTMENTS AS A PERCENTAGE OF TOTAL INVESTMENTS
FOR SIX COUNTRIES

	1902	*1914*	*1931*
Great Britain	57.6	65.8	81.0
Japan	100.0	87.6	76.9
Russia	89.4	87.8	100.0
United States	88.8	85.2	78.8
France	32.5	35.0	49.4
Germany	51.7	51.6	86.2

The second table shows the percentage distribution of the business investments among the six countries. This table brings out the relative importance of the different countries over the period since 1900.

[18] Japanese Investments in China, p. 462.

TABLE 13

BUSINESS INVESTMENTS IN CHINA BY COUNTRIES, SHOWING PERCENTAGE
DISTRIBUTION

	1902		1914		1931	
	Millions of U. S. Dollars	Per Cent of Total	Millions of U. S. Dollars	Per Cent of Total	Millions of U. S. Dollars	Per Cent of Total
Great Britain	150.0	29.8	400.0	36.9	963.4	38.9
Japan	1.0	0.2	210.0	19.4	912.8	36.9
Russia	220.1	43.7	236.5	21.8	273.2	11.1
United States	17.5	3.5	42.0	3.9	155.1	6.3
France	29.6	5.9	60.0	5.5	95.0	3.8
Germany	85.0	16.9	136.0	12.5	75.0	3.0
	503.2	100.0	1,084.5	100.0	2,474.5	100.0

The third table provides index numbers showing business investments for each country as a percentage of the
total business holdings of that country for the year 1914.
This table brings out the rate of growth for each of the
countries over the period which has been studied.

TABLE 14

RELATIVES SHOWING BUSINESS INVESTMENTS BY COUNTRIES
Values for 1914 = 100

	1902	1914	1931
Great Britain	37.5	100.0	240.8
Japan	0.5	100.0	434.7
Russia	93.1	100.0	115.5
United States	41.7	100.0	369.3
France	49.3	100.0	158.3
Germany	62.5	100.0	55.1
Total	46.4	100.0	228.2

Only the briefest comment is required to bring out the
general changes revealed in the three tables. Consider,
first, the situation in 1914 as compared with 1902. British
investments showed an increase in the percentage which

business investments formed of the total, and for every other country the change was insignificant (Table 12). Great Britain showed a sharp increase in the percentage which she held of the total investments of the six countries (Table 13). Great Britain showed the most rapid rate of growth (Table 14). After 1902 Great Britain swung into a position of leadership which she maintained to the time of the World War. Japan's rise was remarkable but it brought her, by 1914, no further than among the countries of secondary importance. Russia fell from first place to take a place with Japan. There were no other outstanding changes.

Consider the changes between 1914–1931. For Japan and the United States there has been a decline in the proportion which business investments form of total investments. This means that they have tried the alternative form, loans to the Chinese government. But the significant point is brought out in Table 13, which shows that Japan and the United States each held a greater percentage of the total for the six countries in 1931 than in 1914. In Table 14 this is shown from another angle. Japanese investments were over four times as great in 1931 as in 1914 and American investments over three and one-half times. The investments of the Americans were, of course, relatively small in 1914 and their increase counted for a relatively small part of the total. It was Japan that rose from a secondary place to share first place with Great Britain. It was Japan alone whose business investments more than quadrupled.

On the other hand consider the decline in the case of Germany. Her investments in 1931 were mostly recent business investments, and they were little more than half of the 1914 total. The Russian situation was somewhat better than the German since Russia retained her ownership of the Chinese Eastern. France showed a sharp increase in the ratio of business investments to the total, but her business investments increased by only 60 per cent and she held a very modest percentage of the total in 1931.

Great Britain is the most difficult case to judge. The British continued to hold an increasing percentage of their total in the form of business investments. The British percentage of the total investments of all countries continued to grow and the value of British investments was almost two and a half times that of 1914. Great Britain seemed to hold a solid middle ground and to be in nearly as strong a position in 1931 as in 1914. It is true that the increases of the period went to Japan and the United States, but the British continued to stand first. It is by no means certain that the position was as favorable as it seems. Land holdings in Shanghai, and property acquired at an earlier time had increased its value. The British position in 1931 showed their business wisdom at an earlier date as well as some increase in new investments. The British were carried forward by the momentum of their remarkable development during the years before the war.

If the period from 1902 to 1914 belonged to Great Britain, the period from 1914 to 1931 belonged to Japan. It was the remarkable development of Shanghai that carried Great Britain on to 1931 as the leading country. It was the remarkable development of Manchuria and Shanghai that brought Japan up. The United States increased in importance but failed to show her new place in world economic affairs as clearly in China as she did elsewhere in the world.

The survey shows that transportation and the import and export trade are the important fields of foreign investment in China. Growth has probably been greatest in fields associated with Shanghai, such as manufacturing and real estate. Foreign business investments are in Shanghai and Manchuria with a remarkable recent growth in the importance of Shanghai. The investments belong to Great Britain and Japan. Russia was once in first place and Japan was once without much in the way of investments. The rise of Japan has been outstanding but the British still stood first as holders of business investments in China when the period which we have been considering was brought to a close by the events which began in Manchuria in September, 1931.

CHAPTER VII

THE SIGNIFICANCE OF BUSINESS INVESTMENTS

For the general explanation of the great importance of business investments among the foreign investments we must go back to the economic and political organization of traditional China. The Chinese economy has not reached out for capital no matter how badly it was needed or, to put it better, no matter how great the apparent opportunity for its effective use. One may say that China is "mediaeval" or "Asiatic." [1] I prefer the term "Eastern" but the name makes little difference so long as it is not accepted as a substitute for an appreciation of the actual complex situation. Since China did not go abroad for capital, she received only the capital which the foreigner brought in and to the introduction of this capital she offered the same passive resistance that she did to foreign trade and Western or modern economic concepts. Direct business investments were important because other forms of foreign investment were unimportant.

These other forms are foreign borrowing by the Chinese government and by the Chinese corporation. The obligations of the Chinese government are dealt with in the following chapter but the general picture presented above shows them to be much smaller than direct investments. The failure of the Chinese corporation to serve as a means for the introduction of foreign capital requires brief consideration.

---

[1] Wittvogel follows Marx in the use of this term. See his *Wirtschaft und Gesellschaft Chinas*, Leipzig, 1931, Ch. XV, p. 763.

103

Foreign Investment Through the Chinese Corporation

The Chinese economic organization had no business unit capable of borrowing abroad until the modern corporate form of organization was made available in 1903.[2] These regulations were somewhat modified and better adapted to Chinese conditions in 1914.[3] The latest form of Chinese company law was promulgated by the national government on December 26, 1929.[4] The number of corporations created under these laws is said to have increased in recent years. Nevertheless, the success of the corporate form has not been great up to the present time and it is probably true to say that no Chinese corporation exists whose bonds could be floated in a foreign money market. This is the chief reason for the failure to use this means of securing foreign capital.

Certain great corporations have been brought into existence in China by special act of the Chinese government. The China Merchants Steam Navigation Company, the original Chinese Engineering and Mining Company, and the Hanyehping Company are examples. Such companies have had official support and their obligations, when they have dealt with foreigners, have often become obligations of the Chinese government. The history of such enterprises affords few examples of successful foreign borrowing.[5] It is unlikely that any corporation could undertake to borrow abroad without official or government interest of some sort.[6]

[2] Laws were promulgated in this year as the result of the work of a committee of which Yuan Shih-kai and Wu Ting-fang were members.

[3] An English translation is to be found in the *Far Eastern Review*, vol. 12, no. 4, Sept., 1915, pp. 125–33.

[4] *The Nanking Government's Laws and Regulations Affecting Trade, Commerce, Finance, etc.*, British Chamber of Commerce, Shanghai, 1930, vol. 5, pp. 1–48.

[5] The obligations of the Hanyehping Company to Japanese lenders is about Yen 40 million. Japanese Investments in China, p. 510.

[6] The difficulty of foreign investment through the corporation was put in this way by a man of long experience in China. "The officials will always involve themselves in any successful venture. They will use their

There have been greater borrowings by the Chinese corporation than the figures given in the preceding chapter show, since such borrowing is opposed by popular prejudice in China and is, therefore, frequently kept secret.

The Japanese are, I believe, the only bankers and business men who have undertaken to deal with the Chinese corporation by accepting its obligations in exchange for advances made on familiar investment banking lines. I had an opportunity to discuss this matter at some length with a Japanese banker who regarded his company's ventures as a failure. The reasons for this failure he found in the lack of Chinese experience in the operation of industrial plants, in the fact that the Chinese corporation seldom borrows so long as the corporation is financially successful, and in the difficulty of handling any matter that goes before a Chinese court.[7] In the opinion of this man, his company would have done better if it had gone in for direct investment of the familiar sort. It is obvious that we have in the experience of this Japanese company a concrete example of the reasons for the importance of direct investments. The Japanese case may not be a fair test since popular prejudice may have tended to limit Japanese business to weak firms or to those in financial difficulties. On the other hand, the reasons for failure, set forth by the Japanese banker, are admitted by Chinese industrial leaders and bankers to have considerable weight.

Here we touch the field of policy. The Chinese corporation might become a means of bringing the capital of the foreign colony in China, or even capital from abroad, under Chinese law while still retaining some of the advantages of direct investment if foreign interests were permitted to hold a controlling interest in a Chinese

prerogatives to eliminate competition. They will then refuse to take the business and technical problems seriously and will ruin the enterprise."

[7] Japanese Investments in China, p. 413.

corporation.[8] This is not permitted and the explanation offered by the officials of the National government is the existence of extraterritoriality. The choice of the foreigner desiring to engage in business in China is either to use a foreign corporation—in certain cases one adapted to Chinese conditions under the laws of Hongkong or the China Trade Act—or to participate in a Chinese corporation in which he cannot own a controlling interest.

This is, however, a minor matter. The more important fact is that the Chinese corporation has not become a means of borrowing abroad. If China is to be developed by private enterprise, under what has been called group individualism, there must be a development of Chinese corporations or associations with the power to reach sources of capital abroad. The changes required for such a development are better dealt with when policy is being considered.

DIRECT INVESTMENTS AND EXTRATERRITORIALITY

When the great importance of direct investments is brought to the attention of Chinese and foreigners in China the usual explanation offered is the word, extraterritoriality, by which is meant the whole legal system under which the foreigner lives and carries on his business in the country. To be clear it ought to be called the system of extraterritoriality, treaty ports, and special concessions to foreign corporations. This explanation is, I believe, too easily accepted and I propose to examine it.

It is, of course, true that the foreign business man and the foreign corporation have rights granted by treaty or by decree of the Chinese government to own land at certain places, to own industrial plants, to carry on busi-

[8] The Company Law of 1929 does not prohibit a foreign controlling interest. A resolution of the Central Executive Committee passed at the 179th meeting of the Political Council and communicated to the Legislative Yuan on March 13, 1930, sets up the following conditions: Chinese shares shall be over 51 per cent, Chinese shall be in a majority on the Board of Directors, and the Chairman of the Board as well as the Manager shall be Chinese.

ness, and to remain under the jurisdiction of their own courts. Without the existence of arrangements of some sort which would have this effect the foreign colony and foreign direct investment would have no legal foundation at all. In this sense the extraterritorial system, if I may use the phrase to indicate the whole situation, is the basis of direct investment. The difficulty with this is that it proves too much. By this sort of reasoning everything in China's foreign relations may be explained as due to extraterritoriality.

The importance of direct investments reflects certain conditions which exist, which were not created by the system of extraterritoriality and whose removal does not depend upon treaty arrangements. The first of these is the immaturity of China as a borrower. The history of capital movements in the West shows that the direct investments of merchants engaged in foreign trade were the original form. There are examples of such investments in fairly recent times. The first railway in France was a direct investment by the British [9] and British corporations have played a considerable part in the development of Argentina and other South American countries. In India and Japan the very earliest investments were of this sort. It is, then, not unusual for direct investments to be important in the early years of capital import into a country. If China differs it is in the persistence of direct investments as the chief form. The Chinese economy failed to develop other forms even under the stimulus of considerable direct investments.

In the second place the Chinese have not easily adapted themselves to the technique of modern industry. Every doubt as to the technical effectiveness of Chinese control must serve to maintain the importance of direct investments. It is no matter for surprise that Chinese traditions of management and of industry make difficult the mastery

[9] Jenks, L. H., *The Migration of British Capital to 1875*, New York, 1927, p. 141.

of the technique of modern industry. The necessity for technical assistance from abroad is generally admitted in China. It is not so generally seen that technical processes have a sovereignty of their own with which there is no compromise. There is a discipline in machine industry which the Chinese are learning as are the Japanese, the Russians, the Indians and, for that matter, the peoples of the West.

A further reason for the importance of direct investments lies in the absence of certain concepts in the fields of law and accounting. One is driven to the use of words which indicate rather than describe the situation. Western business law and Western accounting, influenced by the rise of modern industry, have become more impersonal. In these matters the Chinese preserve a personal point of view which is not adapted to modern ways. The Chinese viewpoint tends to be that it is not quite respectable to to be governed by law and that there is a meanness about careful accounting.[10] In practice this means that business law does not set the enforced conditions of business competition and that accounting is not generally and impersonally accepted as an indicator of business policy.[11]

No better illustration of the difficulties in the field of investment which proceed from the absence of appropriate technical, legal, and accounting concepts may be offered than the discussion which developed during a conference with a group of Chinese bankers. The problem of foreign investment in China by the ordinary methods of private finance is the same as that faced by the modern banker of Shanghai in placing investments in the "interior." The modern Chinese banker occupies a position which enables him to see both the Western and the traditional point of view. These bankers of Shanghai form a group

[10] See the introductory section of chapter 5 in Hu, Shih, *The Development of Logical Method in Ancient China*, Shanghai, 1922.
[11] For a general discussion of the legal aspects see Ware, Edith E., *Business and Politics in the Far East*, New Haven, 1932, especially chapters II and III of Part II.

who see more clearly than any other in China the nature of the task of Chinese economic development by means of private enterprise.

At this conference in Shanghai the Chinese bankers were asked to consider the possibility of introducing foreign capital into China through a Chinese banking syndicate organized to borrow abroad and lend in China. Such a plan would avoid prejudice and politics since the only indebtedness abroad would be that of the Chinese syndicate at Shanghai. It would avoid the difficulties associated with extraterritoriality except as between the banking syndicate and the foreigner. The lending would be done by Chinese within China.

The bankers gave serious consideration to the proposal. Every doubt of its workability from the Chinese side was found in analysis to rest upon matters which have here been considered. There would be, it was maintained, difficulty in assuring technical effectiveness. The accounting methods of the Chinese business organization raised other difficulties. Cases were mentioned which illustrated the failure of the legal machinery to function impersonally and effectively. The Chinese bankers said many of the things that were said by the Japanese banker with whom I discussed investment through the Chinese corporation.

The existing conditions have been indicated. These conditions are changing under the influence of modern methods and the most active influence making for change is the modern banking system of China which is exerting from its center at Shanghai a pressure in the direction of impersonal, accounting controlled business. The final reason for the failure of China to borrow abroad is the absence of certain concepts. This is usually put more dramatically by the foreign business man in China who is frequently able to cite examples of the reasons for lack of confidence in the Chinese courts and of the ineffectiveness of Chinese management in some technical field. Until the appropriate concepts are created some form of direct investment will be important whether or not the system of extraterritoriality is still in existence.

THE TARIFF AND SILVER

A Chinese tariff succeeded the treaty tariff early in 1929. A new tariff came into effect on January 1, 1931. It is difficult to compare the rates since many of them are specific and the 1929 tariff was in silver, while the 1931 tariff is in terms of gold units.[12] The tariff of 1931 provides rates which are considerably higher than those of the conventional tariff and they mean moderate protection for certain industries. The *ad valorem* duties upon cotton piece goods, for example, run from 10 per cent to $12\frac{1}{2}$ per cent and on other forms of cotton manufactures from $7\frac{1}{2}$ per cent to 25 per cent. The duties upon woolen manufactures are as high as 40 per cent. The highest duties are evidently a tax upon imported luxuries but even among these there are some which bring a certain amount of protection.

A protective tariff has been adopted in some countries in part for the purpose of attracting foreign capital and it has worked that effect in others whether so designed or not.[13] There has been little time for the results of the 1931 tariffs to show such an effect. The evidence ought to be an increase in direct investments in the protected industries.

Such a result is more often viewed with fear than with satisfaction in China. A Chinese economist prepared a statement for me on the attitude toward foreign investment expressed in the Chinese language newspapers of Shanghai. He found many references to foreign, usually Japanese, evasion of the Chinese tariff by the building of

[12] The Customs gold unit equivalent to U. S. $.40 was proposed by the Kemmerer Financial Commission of 1929. A similar suggestion is said to have been made by Sir Robert Hart at an earlier time.

[13] Canada may be cited as an example of the first and the United States of the second.

factories in Shanghai and Tsingtao. The Chinese National Products Salvation Association proposed to check "this commercial invasion of the powerful foreign merchants" by the imposition of heavy taxation and other restrictions upon "foreign" factories. A serious effort was made, within the last three years, to bring about discrimination in freight rates on the Chinese railways against the products of certain "foreign" factories at the treaty ports. One familiar with the usual protectionist arguments finds it strange to encounter such proposals. They are evidently an interpretation of the principle in terms of protection against the foreign "colony" in China and its direct investments. Whatever may be the purpose of the leaders, that of the public is not, primarily, the economic development of the country but its development by Chinese.

Another matter about which there has been much talk is the effect of the rapid decline of silver since 1929 upon the industries in China. The reasoning is that a fall in the value of silver ought to stimulate local industries by making imported products more expensive in terms of silver. The recent fall of silver has gone with a general fall in the gold price of commodities outside of China. This accounts in large part for the failure of many of the predicted consequences to reveal themselves. Falling silver has kept funds in China but there is little evidence to show that it has attracted funds from abroad in any considerable amounts.[14] The rising tariff and falling silver may have stimulated direct investments somewhat. It is only in the Japanese case that evidence of this has been found.[15]

The Importance of Shanghai

The importance of Shanghai is such that no less than a third of the total foreign investment in China is to be

[14] Certain investments in Shanghai real estate may have been stimulated by falling silver.

[15] Japanese Investments in China, p. 498.

found there and nearly a half of the direct business investments. The general reasons for this are well enough known. They include the geographical position of Shanghai and its early opening to foreign trade and residence which have given it the impetus of an early start. The importance of the great stocks of goods held there may be mentioned. The increasing importance of Shanghai since 1914 is shown above in Table 6. This increase has been accelerated, I believe, since 1925. One bit of evidence is the rapid increase in the stock of silver held at Shanghai. The causes for this increased importance in recent years are in part a continuance of a vigorous and healthy growth. This has been both the cause and effect of the development in Shanghai of a point of view consistent with the rise of modern industry. The increase in Shanghai land values from 1929 to 1931 reflects this healthy growth and, in addition, the general economic troubles of China. There seems good reason to believe that the economic consequences of civil war in China began to make themselves felt after 1924. Among these consequences were the increased silver stocks mentioned above, low money rates, and rising land values.

Shanghai stands out as the great example of the economic development of a treaty port under the system which has prevailed in China. It is first in foreign trade, first in foreign population, if we exclude the Manchurian cities of Dairen and Harbin, and first in foreign investment even if we compare it with the whole of Manchuria. It is the greatest urban center of the Far East. It is the greatest industrial center of China and is the financial capital of the country. The future of the economic development of China under private enterprise is bound up with Shanghai and its influence upon the rest of China. Its position depends in part upon the existence of the foreign settlement and here the consequences of direct investment through the treaty port and foreign colony are working themselves out in ways that compel attention.

The Importance of Manchuria

Manchuria stands next to Shanghai as a field for direct investments. Here the railway concession rather than the treaty port has been the basis of foreign investment. The nature and extent of this development is set forth in the account of Japanese investments in Part II. The history of Manchuria may be contrasted with that of Shanghai. In Manchuria the political interest of the foreigner preceded his economic interest. Russia had no investments in Manchuria, or practically none, when she proposed and put through the building of the Chinese Eastern Railway. Investment followed the flag in the Russian case and found a railway "zone" ready to receive it. The chief direct investment, the railway itself, was hardly a business venture in the ordinary sense of the term. We have here to do with something quite different from the growth of Shanghai under private initiative as a business and financial center. It has been shown that Manchuria was in 1931 the site of the chief direct investments in China in which foreign governments own a controlling interest.

The Japanese interest in Manchuria, like the Russian, was political and strategic before it was economic. Japanese investment followed the other interests of the Japanese. The Japanese government has always played a part of first importance. The South Manchuria Railway Company has been a business success, but it has not been limited in its activities by a business point of view.

Direct investments combined with extraterritoriality seem to the Chinese to lead unavoidably to foreign political interference and to foreign political control within China. To the passive resistance of traditional China the rising nationalism of recent years has added a more active opposition. The opposition has directed its attention to Shanghai and Manchuria. The student may make distinctions and may attempt to show that direct investments in Manchuria followed an interest which was not directly and immediately economic. He may point out that direct investment need not lead to political complications and that it exists in every country in the world, that it is unusually great in Canada, and that some form of direct investment will, no doubt, continue to play an important part in China in the future. So long as the Manchurian question is unsettled or so long as Manchuria remains separated from China, the nationalist will continue to view direct investment and the conditions that are associated with it as a danger to China.

GREAT BRITAIN AND JAPAN

The survey of direct investments has brought out the continued importance of Great Britain and the rapid rise of Japan. Great Britain has continued to hold first place very largely as the result of an early and a successful start. The changes since the war seem to indicate that Great Britain may soon hold second place. But prediction is dangerous. It was freely predicted at the turn of the century that Russia was to supersede Great Britain in every aspect of China's foreign relations and there are those today who find in Russia the great influence of the future. Much depends upon one's analysis of the reasons for Japan's rapid rise to importance.

The rapid growth of Japanese business investments has depended upon her nearness to China. No country so close to China could develop as rapidly as has Japan without carrying her development into the parts of China open to her. It has depended also upon her earlier mastery of the technique of modern transportation and machine industry. It was greatly accelerated by the prosperity which came to Japan during the war and gave her exportable capital for the first time in her history. Direct investments bring into a country management as well as capital, and it is as entrepreneur that Japan has played her strongest economic rôle. But there are significant limitations which Japan faces. Japan has been, and is today, a country which is normally an importer of capital. Where is the capital to come from for the continued rapid development of Japanese direct investments in China?

The increased importance of the United States is not to be measured by index numbers only. American investments are on a much smaller scale than those of Great Britain and Japan. That the United States does not count for more in China needs explanation. It is to be found, I believe, in her preoccupation with Europe since the World War and in her nearness to the countries of Central and South America. The great increase in American investments has been in public utilities at Shanghai. The Americans count for most where a great capital outlay is combined with business management in a highly technical field. The new position of the United States as a capital exporter had not, in 1931, produced a great change in her economic relations with China, although there was evidence that a change was taking place.

Conclusion

Among the possibilities of economic organization for China, presented in an earlier chapter, were state socialism under official leadership and private enterprise adapted to the group individualism of China under the leadership of the business men. How far the Chinese government has succeeded in getting the foreign capital required for economic development is considered in the following chapter. Whatever may be the possibility for the future in the second form of economic organization, it has been found of little importance so far. Practically no foreign capital has entered China through the Chinese corporation.

The fact is that direct investment has at all times been of first importance. The capital which has come has been brought to China by the foreigner. It has come through the foreign "colony" and it has remained under the control and management of the foreigner. The attempt has been made to point out the significance of this situation. Viewed broadly it may be maintained that direct investment, treaty ports, and extraterritoriality rest upon the fact that China and the West are different. In this sense direct investments may be said to be connected with extraterritoriality. Extraterritoriality is inconsistent with the development of Chinese nationalism and will, no doubt, come to an end.

The importance of direct investment, in some form, may be expected to persist so long as the underlying economic conditions remain and so long as other channels of investment are closed.

CHAPTER VIII

THE FOREIGN OBLIGATIONS OF THE
CHINESE GOVERNMENT

China had, when she met the West, a government which took no practical interest in the economic state of the country. The Chinese economy had not developed public credit, and the government was slow to avail itself of the possibilities of foreign borrowing, even after it possessed, in the Chinese Maritime Customs, a revenue service under such control that it might have borrowed abroad.

At the same time, the economic condition of China was such that foreign capital had to be brought in swiftly and used with shrewdness and economy if China was to take her place with other nations, or move in the direction of a higher standard of living for the mass of the Chinese people. The one available means of rapid economic development under Chinese control seems to the student to have been the importation of foreign capital through the Chinese government. The whole weight of Chinese tradition was against this. The rulers and leaders of China seem to have had no power to see the country clearly in her true relation with other nations, nor do they seem to have appreciated the danger and weakness involved in the poverty of the Chinese people.

A fundamental problem in China today is the creation of a Chinese government which will provide the leadership for the economic development of the country either through its own borrowing and a wide extension of government ownership or by the establishment of the necessary conditions of successful private enterprise. So

117

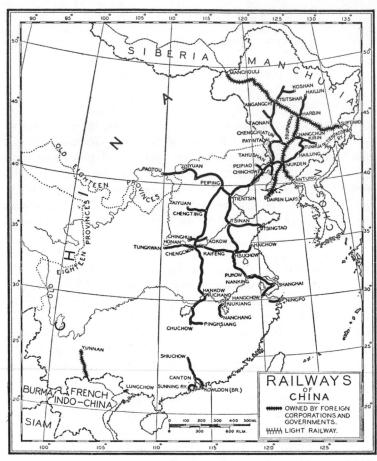

THE RAILWAYS OF CHINA, SEPTEMBER 1931: SHOWING CHINESE GOV-
ERNMENT RAILWAYS AND THOSE WHICH INVOLVE DIRECT FOREIGN IN-
VESTMENTS

much follows from the analysis of traditional China which I have offered above.

The increasing indebtedness of the Chinese government to foreigners is briefly analyzed in the following pages. This indebtedness has been associated with war, anti-foreign disturbances, civil strife, and political intrigue. The Chinese government has brought in some capital for railway construction, but this has not been great. The balances of international payments presented below show that, except for the briefest periods, there has not been a net inflow of funds into China as the result of government financing, taking into account payments on interest and principal. This means that the Chinese government has paid out to foreigners more than it has received. I am now interested, however, not in the flow of funds between China and foreign countries but in the analysis of the debt as it stands today and as it was at certain dates in the past.

The Obligations of the Chinese Government at the End of 1901

Before 1895 when the war with Japan came to an end the Chinese government showed no dependence on foreign banks or money markets. The foreign borrowings had been, to use a Chinese phrase, a few tens of millions. By the end of 1901 the indemnity loans had been made and the foreign obligations of the government stood at a total of U. S. $284.7 million. Since most of the loans were well known, there is little reason to doubt this total. It formed 36.1 per cent of the total foreign investment in China and may be compared with direct business investments of U. S. $503.2 million.

Obligations for railways were small, U. S. $35.3 million. They included loans from British sources for a part of the line which was known later as the Peking-Mukden and the original loan from a Belgian syndicate [1] for the

---

[1] "Which subsequent events showed to be a Franco-Belgian combina-

Peking-Hankow line. In addition to the railway obligations there were loans for communications other than railways to the amount of U. S. $1.2 million. These were for a cable to connect Shanghai and Tientsin. These loans for "productive" purposes were 12.8 per cent of the total outstanding at the end of 1901.

By far the largest part, U. S. $248.2, forming 87.2 per cent of the total, was for the general purposes of the Chinese government and the amount outstanding on the three great loans for the indemnity was no less than U. S. $219.9 million. The obligations of 1901 were largely to Great Britain, Germany, and France.[2] This statement is based on the known place of issue. It is probable that France held a considerable part of the bonds originally issued in Russia and that Great Britain held bonds of the various issues in other countries.

THE JAPANESE INDEMNITY LOANS

The treaty of peace which brought the Sino-Japanese War to an end carried with it an obligation on the part of the Chinese government to pay an indemnity of Kuping taels 200 million and a share of the expense of the Japanese occupation of Weihaiwei which was held as a guarantee. On the very day, as Joseph puts it, that the treaty was signed the Russians took steps to upset it.[3] The Japanese were advised by Russia, France, and Germany to refrain from taking possession of the Liaotung peninsula which had been ceded in the treaty of peace. The real negotiators of the final settlement of the war were not China and Japan but Japan and the three powers who

tion with Russian proclivities." Kent, P. H., *Railway Enterprise in China*, London, 1907, p. 97. The Americans and the Belgians were the chief competitors.

[2] Tables showing the geographical distribution for six countries are to be found below.

[3] Joseph, Philip, *Foreign Diplomacy in China, 1894–1900*, London, 1928, p. 124. Joseph's sixth chapter is an excellent account of the politics behind the first indemnity loan, based largely upon documents recently made available.

had intervened. The outcome on the financial side was an increase in the indemnity to taels 230 million, to which is to be added taels 1.5 million toward the expense of the Weihaiwei occupation.

The total sum was paid over in London to the Japanese government between October 31, 1895 and May 8, 1898. The payment was in English money at an agreed rate and came to U. S. $185.3 million.[4] This sum could not have been found by the Chinese government without borrowing abroad and Li Hung-chang expressed the opinion that it would lay an impossible burden on the Chinese government to meet interest payments, even if China did succeed in borrowing the necessary amount.[5] The loans involved bring out certain characteristics of Chinese government financing which deserve brief attention.

In the first place the new obligation was the result of compulsion. The initiative was not with the Chinese. The nature of the obligation makes this evident. It was quite beyond reasonable expectation that a government which took the first steps reluctantly and under compulsion could, or would, lead in the economic development of the country by means of foreign capital, even if the other conditions were favorable.

In the next place the indemnity loans were dominated by political considerations and were far from being an ordinary financial transaction. In the first loan, the so-called Franco-Russian,[6] the very importance of the Russians in the negotiations carries proof of this. Russia was a capital importing country and the Russian government a borrower abroad. The French provided a large

[4] Matsukata, M., *Report on the Adoption of the Gold Standard by Japan*, Tokyo, 1899, pp. 171–3. The sum in English money was £38,082,884.

[5] In a reply to the first draft of the peace treaty. "The amount demanded is beyond the ability of China to pay under her present system of taxation. To increase the internal or domestic taxes at this time would lead to great discontent and probably to insurrection." Quoted in Volpicelli, Zenone (pseud. Vladimir), *The China-Japan War*, London, 1896, p. 414.

[6] In the formal lists of loan obligations this is called the Chinese Imperial Government 4% Gold Loan of 1895. It was for francs 400 million (£15,820,000) for 36 years.

part of the funds under the terms of the loan contract and their whole share was, no doubt, considerably larger.[7] Why were the French willing to invest in China through the Russians? Why were the Russians able to secure French financial support for this and other ventures in China? The answer is to be found in the international political situation. The security for this first loan offers further proof. The loan was guaranteed by the Russian government, which is unusual,[8] and the Chinese government agreed in a separate protocol, in case the Russian government were called upon to make its guarantee good, to furnish the Russian government security beyond that upon the Maritime Customs revenue provided for in the contract. "The manner of such additional security will be made the subject of a special agreement to be established between the two governments by their plenipotentiaries at Peking." The British were not slow to see in these provisions an effort to weaken the position or remove the head of the Maritime Customs Service, who was a British citizen.[9] In the course of the negotiations for additional indemnity loans the British were assured that a British citizen would continue to be employed as inspector-general of the Maritime Customs so long as British trade was preponderant.[10] The loan agreements for the additional loans, the Anglo-German of 1896, and that of 1898, [11] carried the provision that the Customs Service was "to continue as at present" during the cur-

[7] Russian Investments in China, p. 556.

[8] Article 9 of the loan agreement, MacMurray, John V. A., *Treaties and Agreements With or Concerning China, 1894–1919*, vol. I, p. 37, and article 3 of the Protocol of July 6, 1895, p. 41.

[9] Joseph, Philip, *Foreign Diplomacy in China, 1894–1900*, London, 1928, p. 153. Upon British-Russian relations see the memorandum by J. A. C. Tilley in *British Documents on the Origins of the War, 1898–1914*, vol. 1, pp. 1–3.

[10] MacMurray, John V. A., *Treaties and Agreements With or Concerning China, 1894–1919*, vol. I, p. 105. For the provisions of the loan agreements, see pp. 57, 109.

[11] The Chinese Imperial Government 5 % Gold Loan of 1896 for £16 million and the 4½% Gold Loan of 1898 for £16 million. These loans were issued in equal portions in London and Berlin.

rency of the loans. In this struggle over the Customs
Service we may observe political features which go far
toward the explanation of the continued reluctance of
the Chinese government to borrow. Under such circumstances the avoidance of a loan came to be regarded by
the Chinese people, if not by the Chinese government itself, as a diplomatic victory.

A third feature of the indemnity loans is an important
consideration in China's balance of payments. The three
loans made available to the Chinese government a net
sum of about U. S. $213 million. The agreement with
Japan concerning payment brought it about that U. S.
$185.3 million were turned over to the Japanese in London.
The actual inpayment into China could not have been
more than U. S. $27.7 million. Here we have obligations
of a nominal value of U. S. $233 million which brought
payments to China of little more than one-tenth of this
amount. Borrowing abroad of this sort increased China's
obligation without in any way increasing her fiscal or
economic capacity to make payment.

These early loans provide concrete examples of the obstacles to effective and useful borrowing by the Chinese
government. The government did not borrow except
under compulsion. The negotiations were the occasion
for diplomatic quarrels among the creditor powers over
the conditions of the loans and they brought to China
practically no new funds. It has been a tradition since
these loans were made that political influence in China is
indicated, if not measured, by the amount of the obligations to a particular country.[12]

OBLIGATION OF THE CHINESE GOVERNMENT
AT THE END OF 1913

In 1902 the Japanese indemnity loans of a few years
before were followed by another of the great obligations

[12] This explains in part the preoccupation of the writers on China with
the obligations of the Chinese government and their neglect of business
investments in the country.

of the Chinese government, the Boxer indemnity. If the earlier loans brought little inpayment into China, the Boxer indemnity brought none at all; nor was it met by borrowing abroad. This obligation was not in existence at the end of 1901 and it appears in the figures for 1931 in a form so modified and so reduced that it amounts to a small part only of the total obligations. In view of these facts the Boxer indemnity has been eliminated for purposes of comparison.

Including the Boxer indemnity the total obligations of the Chinese government are found to have been U. S. $835 million at the end of 1913. The total outstanding on the Boxer indemnity at this date has been calculated at U. S. $309.2 million.[13] The amount outstanding on the Japanese indemnity loans was U. S. $174.6 at the end of 1913. Taking the two together we find that U. S. $483.8 million, or 57.9 per cent of the total obligations of China, were the result of these two indemnities. They took annually so large a fraction of the Customs revenue that the next great obligation, the Reorganization loan of 1913, was secured upon the salt revenue.

Eliminating the Boxer indemnity we find the obligations of the Chinese government to have been U. S. $525.8 million. This may be divided into obligations for the general purposes of the Chinese government (the Japanese indemnity loans are included here) of U. S. $330.3, which is 62.8 per cent of the total, and obligations for railways and communications of U. S. $195.5 million, 37.2 per cent of the total. The new obligations among those for the general purposes of the Chinese government arose from the efforts at financial reorganization during the early years of the republic. There was outstanding on the Crisp loan of 1912 and on the Reorganization loan of 1913 a total of U. S. $146 million. Railway obligations had increased greatly since 1902.

[13] The original obligation was 450 million taels at a fixed rate and came to U. S. $333.9 million.

Most of the railways now under the control of the Chinese government were built during the first decade of the century.

Great Britain, in 1913, was the chief country holding the obligations of the Chinese government. Her holdings, calculated on the place of issue, were U. S. $207.5 million, almost exactly 40 per cent of the total. Germany and France held somewhat more than U. S. $100 million each and were the only other countries of importance. The amounts actually in the possession of British and French nationals were, no doubt, somewhat greater than appears in these figures but no satisfactory estimate of the additional sums can be made.

THE REORGANIZATION LOAN

The third great obligation of the Chinese government, after the Japanese indemnity loans, and the Boxer indemnity, was the Reorganization loan of 1913. With it is associated certain other obligations of the early years of the republic, many of which now find a place among the "unsecured" obligations listed by the Financial Readjustment Commission of 1925. The Reorganization loan deserves brief comment. It throws the illuminating light of concrete illustration over the situation before the World War and enables one to estimate the significance of the changes since the negotiations of the late 'nineties over the Japanese indemnity loans.

The loan was negotiated by what is called the "old" Consortium. Its origin is to be found in a British, French, and German association during the early stages of the negotiation of the loan for the Hukuang railways. During the later stages the Americans insisted upon admission.[14] This four-power group began, late in 1911, the long and complicated series of discussions which ended with the signing of the Reorganization Loan Agreement on April 26, 1913.[15]

[14] American Investments in China, pp. 268–70.
[15] See MacMurray, John V. A., *Treaties and Agreements With or Con-*

The events which began with the outbreak of the revolution at Hankow on October 10, 1911, swept into control of China a government without funds and with increasing unpaid obligations. On its surface the Reorganization loan was a provision of funds by means of broad international co-operation for the financial support of the new Chinese government and to assist in creating the conditions for orderly progress under the new republic. What it was beneath the surface depends upon one's analysis of the course of events in China since 1913.

The Chinese government's need for money became pressing early in 1912. In February the Consortium representatives were asked for an immediate advance and they were given to understand that a loan for £60 million was being considered.[16] Certain advances were made and an assurance was given to the Consortium that it held an option on the proposed comprehensive loan for general reorganization purposes.[17] Within a few days the Chinese government undertook to conclude an agreement with a Belgian syndicate for a loan of £1 million secured upon the income and property of the Peking-Kalgan Railway. This brought about the first break in the negotiations. They were not resumed again until the Chinese government had agreed to cancel the Belgian loan contract. What seemed to the Consortium representatives "a clear breach of contract"[18] appeared to the Chinese and to the bankers outside the Consortium as an effort to break an attempt to monopolize the Chinese loan market.[19]

cerning China, 1894–1919, vol. II, pp. 1007–38 for the agreement with annexes.

[16] Field, Frederick V., American Participation in the China Consortiums, 1931, p. 73. The author was permitted by J. P. Morgan Company to see the correspondence.

[17] The letter from President Yuan Shih-kai is printed in MacMurray, John V. A., Treaties and Agreements With or Concerning China, 1894–1919, vol. I, p. 852.

[18] The quotation is from Willard Straight's comment. Quoted by Field, Frederick V., American Participation in the China Consortiums, 1931, p. 78.

[19] "The . . . Consortium would not tolerate this legitimate competition." From a vigorous denunciation in the Bulletin de la Société Belge d'Études Coloniales, May, 1912.

The admission of Japan and Russia into the Four-Power Consortium was a matter that required some months of discussion. The Americans had brought with them into the Consortium an agreement for currency reform and industrial development which had special application to Manchuria.[20] This loan agreement brought objection from both Japan and Russia. Negotiations to bring these two powers into the group were undertaken with the knowledge and consent of the Chinese government, and were successfully concluded in June, 1912. With the entrance of Japan and Russia we see the inclusion of groups from countries who were borrowers abroad, not lenders. As a matter of fact, when the loan was issued the whole of the Japanese share and a considerable part of the Russian were actually issued in the financial centers of western Europe.

The Reorganization loan was finally signed by a group whose common interest was in the international political problems of China rather than in the business of investment banking. This was, no doubt, unavoidable and it means that the Consortium is finally to be judged, not by its economic effect but by its political consequences.[21] Capital exports to China by countries which are normally capital importers present a problem the answer to which may not be in the political field but frequently is.[22]

Negotiations between the Chinese government and

[20] The "preliminary agreement" with the Americans is to be found in MacMurray, John V. A., *Treaties and Agreements With or Concerning China, 1894-1919*, vol. I, p. 851. This loan became a consortium loan but was never issued.

[21] The Consortium was vigorously attacked in London upon just this ground. *The Economist*, Sept. 21, 1912, p. 518, expressed the hope that Sir Edward Grey could "see the absurdity of Great Britain lending all the money, or nearly all, and getting one-sixth of the control." Hartley Withers, *International Finance*, New York, 1916, pp. 108-9, writes "the financial strength of England and France had to be shared, for political reasons, with powers which had, on purely financial grounds, no claim whatever to participate in the business of furnishing capital to China."

[22] A country which is normally a capital importer may undertake direct business investments abroad in fields in which its people are technically effective. Japanese cotton mills in China have an economic explanation. Japanese participation in the Reorganization loan does not.

the Six-Power Consortium were not smooth. The Chinese representatives objected to the provisions for the supervision of expenditure and to the terms of the loan as proposed by the banking group. It soon developed that the Chinese were undertaking to borrow elsewhere. On August 30, 1912, an agreement for a loan was signed in London between a representative of the Chinese government and the British firm, C. Birch Crisp and Company.[23] The history of this loan demonstrates the difficulty of securing the degree of unified action in the financial field necessary to success.

This time the independent bankers were of a country represented in the Consortium. Their act was in accordance with a tradition of independence of the government dear to the heart of the London "city." [24] The British Foreign Office had tried to stop the Crisp negotiations. It went so far as to tell Crisp that, although "His Majesty's Government were not in a position to put pressure on the syndicate interested in the loan, they could put considerable pressure on the Chinese government and would not hesitate to do so at once." [25] Here we have a situation which could probably not have arisen in any of the other countries of the Consortium group. The Japanese and Russian governments would have found it easy to deal with a banker who defied them. In France and Germany access to the money market could have been cut off. The American banking group was acting virtually at the request of the government.[26] In spite of the applause the Crisp loan was a failure. Only one-half of the £10 million was issued and the agreement was can-

---

[23] MacMurray, John V. A., *Treaties and Agreements With or Concerning China, 1894–1919*, vol. II, p. 967.

[24] The British newspapers supported Crisp partly because they disliked government control and partly because they failed to understand the nature of the political problems involved in the whole transaction.

[25] *China, No. 2, 1912*, p. 15.

[26] These differences in the power of the different governments over their bankers are briefly discussed by Feis, H., *Europe, the World's Banker*, New Haven, 1930, pp. 455–6.

celed December 23, 1912, on payment of £150,000 to the company.[27]

After the Crisp loan the negotiations dragged on. Early in 1913 it seemed that the loan was about to be signed when a new source of difficulty arose. This time it was the appointment of advisers. The French would not have a German and the Russians would have a Russian. This quarreling was carried to such a length that the Chinese Minister of Finance felt justified in delivering the bankers a lecture on their "succession of unreasonable delays."[28]

The American group now withdrew from the Consortium as the result of the refusal of the new American government under President Woodrow Wilson to request that they continue the negotiations.[29] This withdrawal was regarded by many Chinese as a friendly gesture and was viewed by many Americans with unreasonable alarm.[30] American withdrawal hastened the negotiations but they were probably more effectively hurried by the fear of additional independent loans. At the very last moment an alteration had to be made in the contract because the Chinese government had signed an Austrian loan within two weeks of the final signature. The final steps were hurried also by the convening of the National Assembly in Peking on April 8, 1913. The members of this body who belonged to the Kuomingtang vigorously opposed the signing of the contract. Their leader, Dr. Sun Yat-sen, appealed to the world to prevent the loan and charged President Yuan Shih-kai with plans to use the funds to destroy his opponents. His followers today point to one of the sentences of Dr. Sun's telegram as an embodiment of their point of view. "If the people are

[27] MacMurray, John V. A., *Treaties and Agreements With or Concerning China, 1894–1919*, vol. II, pp. 967, 1034.

[28] In a letter of March 11, 1913, *U. S. Foreign Relations*, 1913, p. 169. *China Year Book*, 1914.

[29] American Investments in China, p. 269.

[30] "The country that lends the money gets the trade," said one business man. "We have been set back half a century," said another. The *China Press*, Shanghai, April 18, 1913.

now forced into a life and death struggle for the preservation of the republic, not only will it entail terrible suffering to the masses, but it will inevitably adversely affect all foreign interests in China."[31] This was Dr. Sun's opinion of a transaction which was supported by the various foreign governments "under the conviction that the moment had come when it was politically expedient to strengthen the hands of the *de facto* administration in China against the forces of anarchy."[32]

A final point is to be made. The Reorganization loan brought more into China in the way of inpayments than did the Japanese indemnity loans but the amount was surprisingly small. The nominal amount of the loan was £25 million. The amount actually placed to the credit of the Chinese government was £21 million. About half of this amount was paid at once to foreigners to cover previous advances, obligations of the Chinese government in arrears, foreign loans to the provinces, and foreign claims arising out of the Chinese revolution.[33] A sum of £2 million was set aside for the reorganization of the salt administration. The remainder, £8.5 million, was available for the disbanding of troops and for the current expenses of the government.

Such was the stormy course of the Reorganization loan negotiations, marked by efforts to deal with independent competitors, by the entrance of Russia and Japan into the Consortium and the withdrawal of the United States, by the presence of representatives of countries who had no money to lend but had political interests to watch, by bickering over adviserships, by the resistance of the Chinese government to measures of control, and by the opposition of a strong group in China. The Chinese

[31] Printed in the *Times* (London), May 3, 1913, p. 7.
[32] *China*, No. 2, 1912, p. 4.
[33] The amount set aside for these claims was £2 million. It is said that the claims included estimated profits on goods left unsold on account of the revolution. Harvey, T. Edmund, "International Extortion in China," *Contemporary Review*, vol. 105, pp. 316–20.

government was as far from vigorous leadership in economic development as in 1895 and the foreign powers as little free from preoccupation with political considerations.

GOVERNMENT OBLIGATIONS IN 1931

The total foreign obligation of the Chinese government and of government institutions in China I find to be, at the end of 1930, between U. S. $700 million and U. S. $750 million. This invites comparison with the larger figures of recent studies but I propose to postpone such comparison until after the outline of the situation in 1931 has been presented. The tangled skein of Chinese government finance cannot be neatly unraveled and no figure may be given with assurance. The very reasons for the uncertainty help to reveal the situation and much may be learned from an analysis of the information which is available.

If the foreign obligations of the Chinese government are studied from the point of view of the loan contracts and other evidences of indebtedness, the result is a total which reaches U. S. $723.1 million. This total is, I believe, as near to the truth as one may come, but for purposes of analysis I am forced to use a somewhat smaller figure.

If we accept a total of U. S. $723.1 million and proceed next, still working on the basis of the loan contracts, to discover how much the Chinese government owes to the British or the Germans, the result is so seriously wrong that it cannot be accepted. To distribute the total of China's foreign obligations among the creditor countries on the basis of the place of issue has been the method employed for the earlier years. It cannot be used for 1931. Take, for instance, the Russian case. It can be shown on the principle of the place of issue that the Russians held Chinese bonds to the value of U. S. $13.9 million at the end of 1930. At the same time it is shown in the chapter on Russian investments that the Russians hold none. Or take the German case. It can be demonstrated on the principle of the place of issue that Germany held Chinese obligations to the amount of U. S. $82 million at the end of 1930. At the same time the German bankers and other informed persons maintain this to be quite impossible and put the figure at U. S. $10 or 12 million.

The difficulties might be presented at considerable length. Take the case of the railway obligations to Germany. A table which was prepared by the Ministry of Railways of the Chinese government to show the situation at the end of 1929 states the railway obligations of the Chinese government in the German case to be about U. S. $30 million. This is nearly three times the total obligations which the German bankers estimate to be in Germany. If the legal obligation or the place of issue is accepted as the basis of analysis, obvious absurdities result. There is still a legal obligation upon the Customs authorities to make payments on the Austro-Hungarian share of the Boxer indemnity which has been made the security for a domestic loan.[34] To count Austria-Hungary among China's creditors is no more unreasonable than to count Russia when it is known that Russians hold no such obligations.

The alternative was to secure the best estimate possible of the actual holding of Chinese securities and obligations within the different countries. In spite of the obvious difficulties this was attempted. The result of this method is a total of U. S. $696.4 million. In other words, it was possible to find in foreign countries obligations to the amount of U. S. $696.4 million and at the same time it could be demonstrated that obligations existed to the amount of U. S. $723.1 million.

The difference between these two figures, U. S. $26.7

[34] *Chinese Government Loan Issues and Obligations*, Bank of China, Shanghai, 1930, pp. 14, 100.

million, is more than accounted for. It is smaller than an estimate prepared for me in Shanghai of the holding within China of the bonds of China's foreign loans. Some of these bonds held within China are the property of "foreign" banks and financial institutions, others of Chinese banks.[35] The total holdings were estimated at U. S. $40 million. No attempt has been made to distribute the "foreign" holdings, estimated at U. S. $15 million, by countries or to deal with the problem presented by the fact that some of the Chinese holdings are in foreign financial centers and some in Shanghai. These bonds are the chief factor in the explanation of the fact that the obligations considered here are less than the known total of the foreign obligations of the Chinese government.

The obligations of the Chinese government are then accepted for purposes of analysis at U. S. $696.4 million. To this there is added the small sum of U. S. $14.2 million as the holding in Great Britain of the obligations of the Hongkong government, of the foreign municipality at Shanghai, and of the British Concession at Tientsin.[36] This makes a final total of U. S. $710.6 million. This total represents the known holdings abroad of the obligations of government institutions in China.

The nature of the obligations represented by this total is shown in the following list:

	Millions of U. S. Dollars	Per Cent of Total
General purposes of the Chinese government	427.6	60.2
Chinese government railway obligations	248.5	35.0
Chinese government obligations for communications other than railway	20.3	2.8
Obligations of foreign municipalities	14.2	2.0
	710.6	100.0

[35] In January, 1931, one French financial corporation held over £1 million of Reorganization bonds. The Chekiang Industrial Bank, a Chinese Corporation, held £300 in Reorganization bonds and U. S. $200,000 in bonds of the French Indemnity Loan of 1925.

[36] British Investments in China, pp. 278–79.

The increase in the obligations for the general purposes
of the Chinese government is the only notable change
from the situation in 1914 and it is to be accounted for
largely by a great increase in "unsecured" obligations to
Japan.

The chief new items in the obligations of the Chinese
government from the beginning have been the Japanese
indemnity loans of 1895, the Boxer indemnity of 1902,
the Reorganization loan of 1913, and the Japanese "unsecured" loans of the post-war years which are represented by the so-called "Nishihara" loans of 1918.[37] Two
of these sets of obligations, the indemnity loans by Russia,
Great Britain, and Germany and the Reorganization
loan by the five-power group have been considered at
some length.   They revealed a Chinese government ineffective as a capital importer and political conditions
which were highly unfavorable for any effective financing.   In the "Nishihara" loans we reach the lowest
point in the foreign financing of the Chinese government.
On the one hand we see a Chinese government pursuing
a policy which can only be described as the desperate
pawning of options upon future loans and on the other
a Japanese group willing to accept obligations, later
taken over by the Japanese government, in exchange for
funds to be used for civil war and political intrigue.   Here
we are about as far as it is possible to be from the importation of capital for economic development.

The creditor countries were led by Great Britain in
1931 as in 1902 and 1914, but Japan now shared the
first place.   France was the only other creditor of importance.   The total obligation is shown by countries in
the following list and represents the situation at the end
of the year 1930.

[37] A number of the loans are listed in the chapter on Japanese Investments in China, p. 539.   An account of the "Nishihara" loans is to be
found on pp. 540–45.

	Millions of U. S. Dollars	Per Cent of Total
Great Britain	225.8	31.8
Japan	224.1	31.5
France	97.4	13.7
Belgium	48.0	6.8
Italy	42.0	5.9
United States	41.7	5.9
Netherlands	18.7	2.6
Germany	12.0	1.7
Scandinavian countries	0.9	0.1
	710.6	100.0

The Years 1902, 1914, and 1931 Compared

The first comparison for the thirty-year period covers the use which has been made of the borrowings. This is shown in the accompanying table.[38] The only significant

TABLE 15

FOREIGN HOLDINGS OF GOVERNMENT OBLIGATIONS DISTRIBUTED BY THE USE OF THE FUNDS

	1902		1914		1931	
	Mills. U. S. Dollars	Per Cent of Total	Mills. U. S. Dollars	Per Cent of Total	Mills. U. S. Dollars	Per Cent of Total
General purposes	248.2	87.2	330.3	62.8	427.6	60.2
Railway obligations	35.3	12.4	192.3	36.6	248.5	35.0
Communications other than railway	1.2	0.4	3.2	0.6	20.3	2.8
Obligations of foreign municipalities					14.2	2.0
	284.7	100.0	525.8	100.0	710.6	100.0

change lies in the increase in railway obligations between 1902–1914. Another important change which is not shown lies in the increase in the "unsecured" loans which are included in the total for the general purposes of the Chinese government. The term is used to de-

[38] Boxer indemnity excluded.

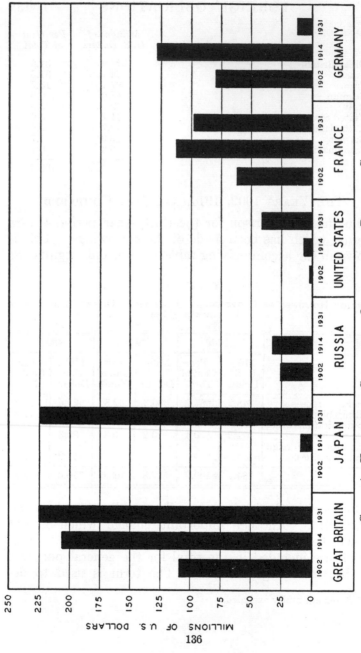

CHART 4.—HOLDINGS OF GOVERNMENT OBLIGATIONS BY PRINCIPAL COUNTRIES

Data in Table 16, p. 138 except British figure for 1931 on p. 135

scribe an assortment of obligations, including most of
the "Nishihara" loans, which have come into existence
since the revolution and are evidence of the disorganized
state of China's finances during most of the period.
These obligations were studied by the Financial Readjustment Commission of the Chinese government and a total
was reached for the year 1925.[39] This total was no less
than Chinese $407.2 million. At the end of 1927 these
loans were estimated at Chinese $475 million. The total
which enters into the above table is U. S. $189.2 million.
Of this total no less than U. S. $100 million is owed to
Japan. China agreed in May, 1930, to call a conference
for the consideration of these obligations and preliminary
steps toward such a conference were taken in November
of that year.[40]

A second comparison deals with the obligations of the
Chinese government only and with the importance of
the six chief countries, Great Britain, Japan, Russia, the
United States, France, and Germany. Two tables are
presented, which show the totals, the percentage distribution by countries and index numbers for the holdings of the different countries. These tables reveal the
fact that Great Britain was the chief creditor in 1902 and
in 1914. Her total was slightly smaller than that of
Japan in 1931. Between 1902–1914 the British percentage of the obligations of the Chinese government increased and British holdings grew at a more rapid rate
than those of any other country of importance. Japan
and the United States had, by 1914, done little more
than enter the field.

[39] The figures are to be found in a series of publications by the Commission. The two of chief importance from the present point of view are
"Tables of Inadequately Secured Foreign Loans of the Ministry of Finance" and "The Outstanding Debts of the Ministry of Communications." The first set of tables were brought down to 1927 in an unpublished document of the Ministry of Finance with the title (in Chinese)
Various Domestic and Foreign Loans and the Boxer Indemnity. Totals are
printed in Lieu, D. K., *Foreign Investments in China, 1929,* p. 37.
[40] Japanese Investments in China, p. 544.

TABLE 16

HOLDINGS OF CHINESE GOVERNMENT OBLIGATIONS BY COUNTRIES,
SHOWING PERCENTAGE DISTRIBUTION

	1902		1914		1931	
	Mills. U. S. Dollars	Per Cent of Total	Mills. U. S. Dollars	Per Cent of Total	Mills. U. S. Dollars	Per Cent of Total
Great Britain	110.3	39.4	207.5	41.8	211.6	36.1
Japan	0.0	0.0	9.6	1.9	224.1	38.2
Russia	26.4	9.4	32.8	6.6	0.0	0.0
United States	2.2	0.8	7.3	1.5	41.7	7.1
France	61.5	22.0	111.4	22.5	97.4	16.6
Germany	79.3	28.4	127.6	25.7	12.0	2.0
	279.7	100.0	496.2	100.0	586.8	100.0

TABLE 17

RELATIVES SHOWING HOLDINGS OF CHINESE GOVERNMENT
OBLIGATIONS BY COUNTRIES

Values for 1914 = 100

	1902	1914	1931
Great Britain	53.2	100.0	102.0
Japan	0.0	100.0	2334.4
Russia	80.5	100.0	0.0
United States	30.1	100.0	571.2
France	55.2	100.0	87.4
Germany	62.1	100.0	9.4
Total	56.4	100.0	118.3

Between 1914–1931 there were significant changes.
Japan now stood first. Her holdings of the obligations
of the Chinese government were now twenty-three times
as great as in 1914 and she held 38 per cent of the total
obligations. Great Britain shared first place with Japan
and the two were far ahead of all others. The United
States was the only other country to show a high rate of
increase but her holdings of the obligations of the Chinese
government were insignificant in 1931. The holdings
of the other countries declined; in the case of Germany

to less than a tenth of the earlier total, and in the case of Russia to nothing.

Between 1914–1931 China's foreign obligations increased. She did not borrow from Great Britain, although financial relations between the two countries were of long standing. The history of her borrowings made Great Britain the logical creditor. She did not borrow from the United States, although the United States was the world's great creditor nation during the period. The world situation made the United States the logical creditor. But most of the increase was in obligations held by the Japanese. There was some degree of logic, from the economic point of view, in Japan's advance, resting upon her nearness to China and her war-time prosperity. The chief explanation, however, lies in another field. A large part of the obligations consists of loans which no group of financiers would have undertaken without the assurance of political backing. Aside from the increase in the "unsecured" loans there was some increase in loans for railways in Manchuria. During the period, railway building in Manchuria was pushed by the Chinese when it meant possible political complications with Japan, by the Japanese when it meant possible political complications with both China and Russia. The methods of financing were such as to remove the transactions from the operations of the "New" Consortium, created between 1918–1920, and thus to bring it about that British and American capital was not employed. The new obligations of the Chinese government between 1914–1931 were dominated for political reasons by a country which has not been a capital exporter in the past, though the prosperity of the war made Japan a lender abroad for a time.

Foreign Capital in the Chinese Railways

China had about 200 miles of railway in 1894. No foreign loan which involved a loan contract had been undertaken and the foreign interest amounted to practically nothing.

In 1913 she had about 6,000 miles of railway. Of this, about 2,000 miles were owned by foreign corporations and the direct investment in these railways was U. S. $383 million. The other 4,000 miles was very largely in the hands of the Chinese government and there were outstanding government railway obligations to foreigners to the amount of U. S. $192.3 million. The total foreign interest in Chinese railways in 1913 was thus U. S. $575.3 million.

In 1931 there were about 10,000 miles of railway in the country. About 1,000 miles consisted of provincial railways and railways connected with mines and industrial plants, or in private hands. Over half of the increase since 1931 was in railways in Manchuria built after 1923. The lines in which there were direct investments were shorter than in 1913 by the 210 miles of the Shantung railway. The total foreign direct investment in these lines is found to have been U. S. $392.8 million at the end of 1930. The lines under the control of the Chinese government, about 7,000 miles, had outstanding against them obligations to the amount of U. S. $248.5 million. This makes a total of U. S. $641.3 million as the total foreign financial interest in railways in China in 1931.[41]

Separating the obligations of the Chinese government from other forms of investment in railways, we find them to be:

1902	U. S. $ 35.3 million
1914	U. S. 192.3 "
1931	U. S. 248.5 "

This shows the greatest increase to have taken place between 1902–1914. Most of the railways under the con-

[41] Laboulaye undertook to make a similar estimate for 1909 or 1910. He reached a total of U. S. $323 million as the total foreign interest. Laboulaye, Edouard de, *Les Chemins de Fer de Chine*, Paris, 1911, p. 333.

trol of the Chinese government in 1931 were built before the Chinese revolution. They include the Peiping-Hankow, the Peiping-Mukden, the Shanghai-Nanking, and the Tientsin-Pukow.

The history of the railway contracts which China has made with foreign interests shows a progressive increase in Chinese control until recent years. J. E. Baker has prepared a table [42] showing railways classified according to the degree of foreign participation which shows that the earlier contracts provided greater foreign supervision. This declined until we reach the Tientsin-Pukow contract which provided for foreign technical supervision only.[43] The recently built railways in Manchuria show a swing in the opposite direction, that is, toward extensive foreign supervision.

There is to be observed, also, in the history of Chinese railways an alternation in the making of contracts and the building of railways. Railway contracts have multiplied when the Chinese government has been weak. Consider the "battle of concessions" between 1895 and 1900. Consider the many contracts of the early years of the revolutionary period. As Lieu points out the "Lunghai, Tung-chen, Pukow-Hsinyang, Nanking-Changsha, Shasi-Shingyi, Chin-yu, Harbin-Blagoveschensk, Kirin-Changchun, Ssupingkai-Chenchiatun, and the Siems Carey 1,100-mile railway contracts" were all made within the space of four years.[44] On the other hand the actual building of railways has made progress when the

[42] Baker, J. E., "Transportation in China," *Annals of the American Academy of Political and Social Service*, Nov., 1930, p. 167.

[43] Tientsin-Pukow Terms were looked upon as marking a new era in railway contracts with the Chinese government. See Barry, A. J., "Railway Development in China," *Journal of the Royal Society of Arts*, vol. 57, p. 542. The terms of the contract with Pauling and Company of 1914 for the Shasi-Shingyi Railway marked a new stage. The foreign corporation was to be little more than a contractor. This railway has not been built. See Rhea, F., *Far Eastern Markets for Railway Materials*, Washington, 1919, p. 50.

[44] Lieu, D. K., *Foreign Investments in China, 1929*, p. 24. "What else," Lieu asks, "can we consider such loans except a scramble for concessions?"

Chinese government was relatively strong. Consider the actual construction during the years from 1902 to 1911 and the railway building in Manchuria during the years of peace there and from 1927 to 1931 when the power of the new nationalist government was growing.

In the present financial status of the railways there is ground for the opinion that the effects of civil war and disturbance in China did not make themselves felt until about 1924. Before this date the railways had been subjected to seizure and used for the transportation of troops but there was no major interference with their commercial operation. There were considerable obligations for materials and supplies but interest in foreign bonds was not generally in arrears. From 1924 to 1930 the effect of disturbance has been fully felt. The financing of civil war has been in considerable part from railway revenues or from exactions which the possession of the railway has enabled military leaders to collect. Commercial operation has been disrupted. Rolling stock has been destroyed or carried away and the permanent equipment of the railways has been damaged. The result has been a failure to meet the interest on foreign obligations which has become more general until, with the additional difficulties caused by the decline in silver, few, if any, of the Chinese railways are today without obligations in arrears.[45]

Recent events give some hope of financial rehabilitation. Sums remitted in the Boxer indemnities are to be used for the completion of the Canton-Hankow Railway and for equipment for other lines. There has been an attempt to bring the railways into some sort of financial order, passenger and freight rates have been raised [46]

[45] Interest has been in arrears since the following dates on these railways: Lunghai, 1925–1926; Honan Railway, 1926; Tientsin-Pukow (British issue), 1925–1926; Canton-Kowloon, 1925; Shantung, 1927: Details are given in the chapters on the investments of the various countries.

[46] The increase in rates is connected with the fall in silver. We see here that railway service within China may be similar to an import from a

but it will require a comprehensive plan of financing to meet the problem.

The railway obligations of China are held in the countries of chief importance as general creditors of the Chinese government. France held the greatest sum in 1902 with Great Britain a close second. In 1914 the obligations to Great Britain were about two-fifths of the total and were almost twice as great as those held in France. The known obligations for 1931 were as follows for the chief countries:

	Millions of U. S. Dollars
Japan	83.6
Great Britain	70.4
Belgium	37.5
Netherlands	18.2
United States	15.0
France	13.9 [47]

"The railway," says Max Weber, "is the most revolutionary instrumentality known to history." [48] Certainly no modern economic equipment introduced into China has produced a greater effect. The international relations of China between 1895–1900 were dominated by the politics of railway concessions. The railway was an instrument of imperialism from the first. The railway has exerted a profound influence upon the economics and politics of traditional China. Railways carry with them a demand for a national point of view and for an effective central government. This was perceived by the Manchus and the revolution of 1911 was precipitated by their effort to centralize the railways. Every new civil war in China drives this home. Revolutionary China faces this paradox that a rebellion against the Monarchy cannot be finally successful until a government exists able to do

"gold" country. For announcement of increases see the North China Daily News, April 9, 1931.

[47] But see the comment in the chapter on French Investments in China, p. 628.

[48] Weber, Max, General Economic History, translated by F. H. Knight, New York, 1927, p. 297.

that which the Monarchy was attacked for doing. The Chinese political organization is being built by efforts to deal with such problems as those presented by the railway.

Plans for a national railway system played a part in the negotiations which preceded the formation of the new Consortium in 1920. An effort on the part of the Chinese government to weaken the economic position of Russia and Japan in Manchuria, which depends upon railways, has had much to do with bringing on the Manchurian difficulties of recent years. Unpaid railway obligations and insistent foreign creditors are among the results of civil war. But railway problems are not to be avoided, for the railway is so effective a bit of modern equipment and so profitable that railways continue to spread and to attract a paying business when there is the slightest opportunity.

THE TOTALS OF OTHERS AND THE BOXER INDEMNITY

The total foreign obligations of the Chinese government have been estimated at about U. S. $725 million for 1931. This total is found to be small when it is compared with the results of other recent studies. An estimate for the end of 1926 has been made by A. G. Coons who arrives at a total of almost exactly U. S. $1,000 million. Lieu found the total at the end of 1928 to be about U. S. $810 million. The work of the Kemmerer Commission seems to have been carried on with the understanding that the distinction between foreign and domestic obligations was not to be emphasized. The detailed results of the Commission's work have not been made public but one may guess from the available totals that their estimate for 1929 comes to about U. S. $900 million.[49]

The chief difference between the total at which I have

[49] Coons, A. G., *The Foreign, Public Debt of China*, Philadelphia, 1930, pp. 101-2. Lieu, D. K., *Foreign Investments in China, 1929*, pp. 37-8. The early figures of the Kemmerer Commission are to be found in the *China Year Book*, 1931, pp. 346-7.

arrived and the larger totals lies in the amount set down as a foreign obligation under the Boxer indemnity. Coons, for example, gives the amount outstanding on the Boxer indemnity as U. S. $195 million.[50] The totals of the others must include nearly as much. The principle on which these totals have been reached seems to have been the legal obligation of the Chinese government to make payments in connection with obligations which were once to be made to foreign governments. This is, of course, quite reasonable if one's point of view is that of the fiscal problem which the Chinese government faces. The Boxer indemnity has a history which makes it a foreign obligation, it is bound up with legal arrangements in which foreign governments are involved, and it may as well, it has seemed to many students, be set down as foreign.

The fact is, however, that the Boxer indemnity has practically come to an end as a foreign obligation of such a sort as to permit any but an insignificant capital sum to be set down against it.[51] I have accepted as valid the principle that nothing is to be included as a capital sum unless it may reasonably be expected to bring about out-payments from China which are independent of equivalent inpayments. It could be successfully maintained that the only portion of the Boxer indemnity to be included in a total of China's foreign obligations consists of the shares due to Spain, Portugal, Norway, and Sweden. The capital sums for these countries come to about U. S. $160,000. This may be called the outstanding portion.

But there were at the end of 1930 two recent U. S. dollar loans which had been issued against the French and Belgian shares of the indemnity. The indemnity, as such, had in these cases come to an end. The payments which would have been made if the indemnity had been continued were made the basis of these two loans and the use of the

[50] That is, a round £40 million.
[51] Considerable payments, U. S. $7.8 million, according to my calculation, which may be regarded as outpayments from China were made in 1930 but under such circumstances as make any capital sum meaningless.

proceeds of the loans was agreed upon between the government concerned. These ought perhaps to be regarded as new obligations but, since they continue payments by the Chinese government which would have been made if the indemnity had not been "returned," they may be accepted as Boxer obligations. The amounts outstanding on these loans were about U. S. $40 million in the French case and U. S. $4 million in the Belgian.

Accepting these two loans and the outstanding portion, I have set down U. S. $45 million as the amount outstanding on the Boxer indemnity.[52] The remaining share of the Boxer indemnity I have omitted entirely. The reasons may be briefly indicated.[53] The German, Austro-Hungarian, and Russian portions were canceled as the result of the World War and the Russian revolution. The so-called international claim was involved in the liquidation of the Deutsch-Asiatische Bank and passed into the hands of the Chinese government, July, 1919.

The shares of the "Allied" powers were remitted for five years, beginning with December 1, 1917. When payment was resumed such steps were taken that the obligations may no longer be said to exist as foreign obligations. The British share was carried in a special account and the disposition of the funds provided for in the China Indemnity Application Act of 1931. The money will either be expended for supplies to be sent to China or placed at the disposal of trustees in China.[54] The Japanese share was dealt with by a law of March 30, 1923, which calls for payments to China approximately equivalent to the payments received by Japan.[55] The French

---

[52] The exact figure is U. S. $45,013,222 which enters into my total of U. S. $723.1 million and U. S. $44,880,850 which enters into my total of U. S. $696.4 million.

[53] The best history of the Boxer indemnity is that of Stanley F. Wright in his *The Collection and Disposal of the . . . Customs Revenue*, Shanghai, 1927, pp. 91–126.

[54] This bill became a law on March 17, 1931, and superseded the Act of June 30, 1925.

[55] Wright, S. F., *op. cit.*, p. 117.

and Belgian shares have become the basis of the loans mentioned above. The payments on the Italian share have, since July, 1930, been held by the Italian Bank for China, subject to final disposition in accordance with a plan which calls for their ultimate use for educational and philanthropic objects. Payments to Italy may be made in the future for materials but the original obligation no longer exists.[56]

The share of the United States, which was not remitted in 1908, was disposed of by a Joint Resolution of Congress, approved May 21, 1924.[57] Payments made to Chinese students in the United States and to the China Institute in America do not justify the setting down of any sum as a foreign obligation of China under the Boxer indemnity. The share of the Netherlands is to be used for a study of the Yellow River and the funds have been accumulating in China since January, 1926. There is no reason to suppose that the indemnity will call for payments to the Netherlands in the future except as new arrangements may be made.[58]

The discrepancy between my total and that of other recent studies is found to be relatively small after adjustment is made for the Boxer indemnity. Differences in the classification of items and in the handling of the "unsecured" obligations make further comparison difficult.

CONCLUSION

Our interest has been in a general view of the foreign obligations of the Chinese government. We found that they really began with the loans to meet the Japanese war indemnity, loans dominated by politics which brought little in the way of new funds into China. After the early railway concessions were granted the Chinese government

[56] For the details I am indebted to Comm. Marco Rosenthal who was in China in 1931 in connection with the arrangements.
[57] MacMurray, John V. A., *Treaties and Agreements With and Concerning China, 1894–1919*, Washington, 1929, vol. I, p. 132.
[58] *China Year Book*, 1929–1930, p. 669.

seems to have undertaken borrowing for railway purposes on what was for China a considerable scale. The result was an increase in foreign borrowings between 1902–1914 at about the rate of increase which we found in the case of direct business investments. The period came to an end with the new loans of the first years of the revolution. The borrowings had come from Great Britain and France, the two great capital exporting countries of the world. The Chinese government came nearer to being the means of capital import for the economic development of the country during the early years of the century than it has at any other time before or since.

Between 1914–1931 the increase in the obligations of the Chinese government was small and the increase in railway obligations still smaller. There was a relative decline both in the quantity and quality of the borrowings. China did not get much foreign capital for her economic development through the Chinese government and the capital which she did get did not come from the capital exporting countries of the West. The funds came from Japan and were associated with the political policy of the Japanese government.

It might have been said with some show of reason that the Chinese government was beginning, during the early years of the century, to shoulder the task of securing capital for the development of China. The course of events during later years has given little ground for such a statement. Since the rise of the nationalist government in China, that is, since 1928, foreign borrowing has not been attempted. If capital is to come through the Chinese government, to be used wisely and without serious international political complications, the Chinese government must solve problems which have defied solution in the past.

CHAPTER IX

FOREIGN INVESTMENTS AND THE BALANCE OF PAYMENTS

The Point of View

This and the following chapters are concerned with the baffling problem of China's balance of payments. The viewpoint is at once broader and narrower than that of the preceding chapters. It is broader since not only capital movements but every transaction which brings about a movement of funds into or out of China must be considered. It is narrower in that the attention is directed to the flow of funds only. Other aspects are given little attention.

The economic and political problems which arise because the foreigner is in China may now be disregarded. From our present point of view the foreign "colony" is within the area whose financial relations with the rest of the world we desire to examine. This area, which I shall call the Chinese economic area when clarity demands the term, includes the whole of the territory of China and Hongkong. I ask the reader to forget for the time any preoccupation with political and legal problems, to put aside any consideration of national policies, either foreign or Chinese, and to turn his attention to the one problem of the balance of payments. The question to be considered is this: How does China pay for what it gets from the world outside of China? Or, to put it in another way, what does China get from outside in return for the payments which it makes? The economic relations of the Chinese economic area with the rest of the world are to be examined in so far as these relations bring about a movement of funds.

149

An effort to make out a reasonable balance of payments for China is more than an exercise in mathematics. It brings to estimates in a variety of fields the acid test of consistency, a test which those who affect to look down upon figures often avoid. China, we are frequently told, is different. This is true and the differences between China and the West have been shown to be important. But China is not different in any such sense as enables her to receive an excess of imports year by year without paying for it. An attempt at a balance of payments has this further virtue that it demands an account which is inclusive and complete. A complete picture puts the emphasis where it belongs. It thrusts aside partial views. This is a service not to the student of China's economic problems only, but to every one who has decisions to make in the field of policy. In the field of capital movements policy which disregards the importance of direct investments is fatally weak; and so, in more general fields, is policy which disregards the position of the overseas Chinese, to mention but a single example. The balance-of-payments method makes for a consideration of all the factors, and a complete account is of general importance.

It must be added at once that a demand for a complete account is not easily supplied. All work in the field of China's balance of payments is pioneering and must be so judged. A certain amount of new material is presented in the chapters which follow and the whole subject has been re-examined. Although my conclusion can be only a rough approximation, I believe that my figures constitute a substantial advance. The importance of a complete picture seems to me to justify the attempt.

THE USE OF THE CHINESE DOLLAR

For the measurement of foreign investments I have used the U. S. dollar.[1] I propose to use the Chinese dollar

[1] The fact that the United States has been on the gold standard throughout the period made the American dollar a more convenient unit than the yen or the pound sterling.

for the balance of payments. A gold currency was used in the case of investments for a variety of reasons. The foreign obligations of the Chinese government are, almost without exception, payable in some gold currency, usually the English pound.[2] The investments of certain great corporations are made public in foreign currencies. The South Manchuria Railway is the outstanding example. The practice is general among Japanese corporations in the North but it is by no means confined to them. Foreign corporations with branches in China usually report their holdings in a foreign currency. Stocks of imports at Shanghai are usually replaceable only by purchase abroad and are usually valued in "gold." It was inconvenient to use silver and the reasonableness of valuation in "gold" was apparent.

The Chinese dollar has been chosen for the balance of payments because it is widely used in China and better known abroad than any other silver unit. The Haikwan tael would have been more convenient but it has the disadvantage of artificiality and it may be discarded by the Chinese government at any time.[3] The particular silver unit is unimportant but it is important that some silver unit be used. China finds the means of making her payments abroad in silver and she receives considerable quantities of silver which enter into bank reserves and currency. Taxes are collected in silver, or paper which calls for silver, and business profits come into existence as a result of silver transactions. A ship, or a cotton mill,

[2] Among the foreign obligations in silver are certain loans for the Lunghai railway and a part of the Peiping-Mukden Double-Track loan. The debentures of the Shanghai Municipal Council have often been in terms of silver. The Kemmerer Commission estimated that 75 per cent of the total obligations of the Chinese government, domestic and foreign, were in foreign currencies. *Project of a Law for the Gradual Introduction of a Gold-Standard Currency*, Chinese Government, Commission of Financial Experts, Nov. 11, 1929, p. 72.

[3] Chinese trade statistics are in Haikwan taels, a silver unit of account employed by the Customs. I have taken the Haikwan tael as equal to Chinese $1.50. A gold unit of account, the Customs Gold Unit, is now being introduced. It is the equivalent of U. S. $0.40, which is the weight of the "Sun" proposed as a gold-exchange unit by the Kemmerer Commission.

or a railway, may have been paid for in gold and may be carried in gold on the books of the owner, but in China it must earn its way in silver. The overseas Chinese thinks of his remittances in terms of silver and their amount is influenced by the exchange rate.[4] International payments stated in silver show the amount and direction of the pressure upon the exchanges. In short, China is a country in which prices and money incomes are in terms of silver and her international accounts are best stated in a silver unit.

THE METHOD OF PRESENTATION

In this chapter I deal with the inpayments into and the outpayments from China which are connected with government obligations and business investments. This is followed by a chapter on the remittances to China from Chinese overseas. The reasons for believing that exports from China are undervalued are then presented, together with an estimate of the necessary correction. After dealing with these items of chief importance the results are brought together in a general chapter on the balance of payments where estimates are presented, not of the chief items only, but of all the items for which information of any usable sort is available.

For the presentation of the chief items I have adopted the device of an average or representative year. The reader will find in Chapter XII figures showing the chief items for a representative year for the period 1902–1913 and for the period 1914–1931. All that can be discovered about trends and changes over the whole period of thirty years is brought out by comparing the figures for these two representative years.

The work that has been done in recent years enables annual figures to be presented for the years 1928, 1929,

---

[4] It was formerly said in Hongkong that remittances were made when the Hongkong dollar was worth less than U. S. $0.50 and funds held abroad when the dollar was higher. Recent rates have made this inapplicable. The Hongkong dollar was worth about U. S. $0.27 at the end of 1930.

and 1930. The figures for these years are discussed in the chapters on the chief items, but they are not brought together for final presentation until I reach Chapter XII. The plan is to discuss the chief items and show how great they were for a representative year in each of the two periods studied and to show all the items for these recent years.

The information which is available for most of the items consists of annual estimates which cannot be checked against cumulative totals of any sort. For the capital items it ought to be possible to check the results of the annual figures against the totals at the end of each period. We have as the result of our study presented in the earlier chapters and in Part II an inventory or "a census of foreign debts and investments." [5] If we had adequate annual figures we ought to be able to build up a cumulative total which would agree with the census or inventory. For China annual figures have been drawn up which show inpayments and outpayments in connection with the finances of the Chinese government. It is, therefore, possible to compare the debt of the Chinese government, as it stood in 1914 or 1931, with the international payments for the preceding years.

In the case of business investments, however, we have practically no information as to what has happened year by year. What we do have is a periodic inventory. In the case of business investments I have been rash enough to make annual estimates on the basis of the periodic totals. I recognize the dangers and uncertainties of this method but it was the only way forward in the field of greatest importance. The annual estimates, I may add, were not made without the use of whatever scraps of information were at hand.

With this introduction I turn to the international pay-

[5] I take the phrase from Lewis, Cleona, *The International Accounts*, New York, 1927, pp. 97–8, 108, where the relation between the annual figures and the periodic census is explained.

ments connected with Chinese government finance. I must, however, add a final warning to the reader that we are entering upon a difficult and uncertain path up a relatively unknown mountain side. If the climb can be made we shall gain a summit which offers a general view of the broad field of Chinese international financial and economic relations.

Inpayments and Government Borrowings

The first of the important items to be presented by periods is inpayment in connection with the borrowings of the Chinese government. This is a capital item and is so presented. Our information is insufficient to enable the corresponding outpayment for amortization to be segregated in spite of the fact that inpayments and outpayments on government account have been made the subject of a special study.[6]

This study makes it possible to say, with some degree of certainty, that the total inpayments into China for the years 1894–1901 were Chinese $170.2 million. It will be remembered that the foreign borrowing of the Chinese government amounted to little before 1894. The great loans of the years 1895, 1896, and 1898 were for the payment of the Japanese war indemnity. The payment to Japan was made in England and in pounds sterling. The actual payments to Japan did not at any time become an inpayment into China. We are, therefore, prepared to find that the inventory of debts at the end of 1901 shows a total much greater than can be accounted for by capital inpayments into China. The amount outstanding on government obligations was U. S. $284.7 million and at the average rate of exchange for the preceding eight years (U. S. $1.00 = Chinese $2.00) this comes to a total of Chinese $569.4 million. This was the sum of China's debts in 1902 and the creation of this debt

[6] The results of this study are in an appendix to this chapter.

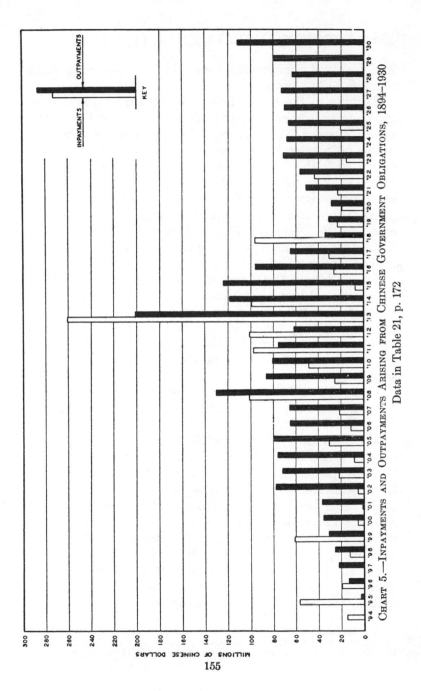

MILLIONS OF CHINESE DOLLARS

CHART 5.—INPAYMENTS AND OUTPAYMENTS ARISING FROM CHINESE GOVERNMENT OBLIGATIONS, 1894–1930

Data in Table 21, p. 172

had involved inpayments into China of no more than Chinese $170.2 million.[7]

Turning to the period from 1902 to 1913 we find total inpayments on government borrowing abroad to have been Chinese $731.8 million. These were years of considerable borrowing for railway construction and the period ended with the inpayments on the Reorganization loan of 1913. The figure of total inpayments is more nearly consistent with the total of the inventory than for the years before 1902. The total of foreign obligations outstanding on December 31, 1913, was U. S. $525.8 million. This is an increase during the period of U. S. $241.1 million and at the average rate for the period (U. S. $1.00 = Chinese $2.18) comes to Chinese $525.6 million. China received on capital account during the period over Chinese $700 million and her debt was greater at the end of the period by over Chinese $500 million. The difference is to be explained by the fact that outpayments for amortization reduced the total from what it would otherwise have been.

If the Boxer indemnity had been included among the outstanding obligations, the inventory at the end of 1913 would have shown an increase of U. S. $309.2 million in addition to the sum of U. S. $241.1 million shown above. This would mean a total increase in silver of Chinese 1,200 million for the period. The total debt would have been found once more to have grown faster than could have been supposed from a study of the inpayments. The explanation is the same as for the former period, but the new obligation of this period, the Boxer indemnity, brought no inpayments into China whatever.

For the years 1914–1931 we find that the total inpayments on government obligations was Chinese $404.4 million, according to the table presented in the appendix.

---

[7] The rates of exchange used are the Customs rates for Haikwan taels turned in a rate for Chinese dollars at Chinese $1.50 to Hk. Tls. 1.00. For the rates year by year see the table at the end of this chapter.

The total outstanding on government obligations we find to have been U. S. $723.1 million.[8] The difference between this total and that for 1914 is U. S. $197.3 million. At the average rate of exchange for the period (U. S. $1.00 = Chinese $1.92) the increase is Chinese $378.8 million. The total inpayments are little larger than the difference in the outstanding debt. Amortization payments abroad may be supposed to have been offset by an increase in the debt due to arrears in interest and other items which involved no inpayment into China.

The annual inpayments shown in the table in the Appendix are accepted for the building up of the balance of payments for a representative year in each of the two periods 1902–1913 and 1914–1931. The total inpayments for these periods and the annual average are shown below in millions of Chinese dollars:

	Total Inpayments	Annual Average
1902–1913	731.8	61.0
1914–1931	404.4	23.8

The annual inpayments on government borrowings bring out clearly the differences between the two periods before and after 1914 which have been noted in all the previous discussion of government obligations. Observing the inpayments only, we find a general upward trend from 1894 to 1913 and downward trend from 1914 to 1930. This difference has been sufficiently emphasized. If we look closer we find that years of unusually great inpayments occur at intervals of four years to 1903 and at intervals of five years to 1919. I have no explanation to offer for the astonishing regularity in the recurrence of these years of unusually great borrowings. It is improbable that these inpayments have ever dominated the international economic relations of China sufficiently

---

[8] I use here the results of the study of loan contracts which give the total outstanding and not the results of the estimates of the actual holdings abroad.

to repay closer investigation, except for the three years
1911, 1912, and 1913 when there was a continuous and
rising inpayment.   I can do no more in this exposition
than direct attention to the fact that China has borrowed
abroad at intervals of four or five years.

OUTPAYMENTS ON GOVERNMENT DEBT

The outpayments on government debt are put down
in my general figures for the two periods as current outpayments.   This is done in spite of the fact that they
include payments on principal.   It was practically impossible to make the necessary separation.   What is
more, it was felt that in the cases of the obligations for
the Japanese war indemnity loans and the Boxer indemnity a distinction between current and capital payments was pointless.

A general view of the outpayments on the government
debt shows a gradual increase in the annual sums to the
year 1913 with a drop during the first years of the revolution when the Chinese government failed to make certain of its payments.   The decline after 1913 was connected with the rise in silver during the war years.   Total
outpayments reached a low point in 1920, lower in fact
than for any year since 1898.   From 1920 to 1930 outpayments on government account increased and this increase was unusually great during the closing years.   In
1930 the Chinese government made payments abroad
greater than for any year since 1915.   These payments
were required in spite of the fact that the service on
most of the railway obligations and upon certain other
loans was not met.   The reason is to be found in the
sharp fall in silver which began in 1929 when the government was making strenuous efforts to meet its arrears
and put its finances into better order.

The payments upon the Crisp loan of 1912 illustrate
the unfortunate combination of circumstances.   The
Chinese government failed to make the annual payment

of £325,200 in 1928, the first year of control by the
Nationalist government.   To make this payment in
1928 would have required about Chinese $3,286,000. Un-
der the administration of the new government the arrears were made up in 1929 and 1930.[9] The exact dates
of the payments are not known but at the 1929 rate the
requirement was Chinese $3,680,000 and at the rate for
1930 Chinese $5,160,000. Arrears for 1928 on the Anglo-
French loan and the Hukuang Railways loan were made
up in the same way. Upon these three loans a delay of
about two years in payments cost the Chinese government a sum of about Chinese $2.5 million. This is one con-
crete illustration of the fiscal consequences of the decline in silver and explains the greater outpayments from
China during the three years 1928, 1929, and 1930.

For the years before 1902 the outpayments from China
on government debt were small since the debt had but
recently come into existence. The total and the annual
average for these early years and for the two periods
which are being examined are shown below in millions
of Chinese dollars:

	Total Outpayments	Annual Average
Before 1902	167.2	20.9
1902–1913	1,070.3	89.2
1914–1930	1,205.6	70.9

NET PAYMENTS ON GOVERNMENT ACCOUNT

The payments which have just been considered are
combined with others in a later chapter to show their
place in the balance of payments. It is desirable to bring
them together now in order to show the net movement
of funds into and out of China in connection with the
obligations of the Chinese government. The complete
table in the appendix to this chapter is the result of an
effort to determine the amount of such payments. The

[9] Statements of the Chinese Minister of Finance, *North China Daily News*
(Shanghai), October 1, 1930, and December 19, 1930.

payments have been calculated at varying exchange rates, taking into account all the known facts concerning amortization and arrears. Exactness is not claimed for these figures but they show the general course of events and I believe that they may be trusted to show changes year by year.

Consider, first, the changes which are revealed when the items are divided by periods. This is shown in the accompanying table. We find that the financial operations of the Chinese government brought into China the sum of Chinese $3 million during the years before 1902 but that since 1902 there has been a total net outpayment of Chinese $1,139.7 million. This was at the rate of Chinese $28.2 million a year for the earlier period and Chinese $47.1 million a year for the later. The net outpayment has been fairly large and it has been growing.

TABLE 18

INPAYMENTS AND OUTPAYMENTS ARISING FROM GOVERNMENT
OBLIGATIONS BY PERIODS

(All figures in millions of Chinese dollars)

Period	Total Inpay- ments	Total Outpay- ments	Average Annual Inpay- ment	Average Annual Outpay- ment	Total Net Inpay- ments	Total Net Outpay- ments	Average Annual Net In- payment	Average Annual Net Out- payment	Average Exchange Rate, U. S. Dollars to Ch. Dollars
1894– 1901	170.2	167.2	21.3	20.9	3.0	——	0.4	——	2.00
1902– 1913	731.8	1,070.3	61.0	89.2	——	338.5	——	28.2	2.18
1913– 1930	404.4	1,205.6	23.8	70.9	——	801.2	——	47.1	1.92

The years during which there has been a net flow of funds to China are few. They include 1894, 1895, 1896, and 1899, all in the first period. From 1902 to 1913 the years of net inpayment were 1911, 1912, and 1913 when the Reorganization loan was being negotiated to an accompaniment of advances from the Consortium and loans from independent bankers. In more recent years the one year 1918 shows net inpayments. This was the year of the "Nishihara" loans.

Net outpayments have been the rule. In 1902 the Boxer indemnity payments began and they called for annual outpayments of about U. S. $14 million a year until 1918. Net outpayments were unusually great in 1915 but this year was the first year of great net outpayments after some years of unusually great inpayments. It is when we come to the period since 1919 that we find the position growing steadily worse. The Chinese government, relieved of a large part of the Boxer obligation,[10] has remitted abroad increasing sums in silver at a time when she was not making interest payments on many railroad bonds and on certain other obligations. The burden of falling silver became greater through 1929 and 1930. The Chinese government entered upon the year 1931 with the unpleasant prospect of having to make greater net outpayments than at any time in its history. At rates of exchange which have prevailed in recent years any plan to meet the full service on all her foreign obligations, to pay off arrears of interest, to adjust and begin payments on the unsecured debt, calls for so great an annual expenditure in Chinese dollars that the Chinese government may be unable to find it.[11]

[10] The outpayments from China on the Boxer indemnity I calculate to have been as follows during recent years:

1918–1921	U. S. $	39,572
1922		318,061
1923		3,381,438
1924		3,361,876
1925		6,566,310
1926		7,856,233
1927		7,856,233
1928		7,350,800
1929		7,840,784
1930		7,840,757

[11] The events of 1931–1932 have made the financial task of the Chinese government more difficult. It is true that nearly half of the public revenue has been expended for military purposes in recent years (see the *Annual Reports of the Minister of Finance for 1928–1929 and 1929–1930*) but these

The capacity of the Chinese economy to make payments abroad is not involved in these comments and cannot be discussed without taking into account other items in the balance of payments. At the same time it is clear that the use which the Chinese government has made of the inpayments on government account has an effect upon both fiscal and economic capacity.

Certain of the obligations have carried with them a reorganization of revenue services.   The salt revenue service was brought under more effective control as a result of the Reorganization loan and funds were provided to bring this about.   The Boxer indemnity brought about a revision of the treaty tariff.   These were advantages to the Chinese government as a revenue collecting institution.

Some of the funds made available to China have been so used as to make the Chinese economy more capable of paying abroad.   Railways have been built and other means of communication provided.   The railways have brought an income to the Chinese government and have exercised a stimulating effect upon foreign trade.   But railway obligations are little more than a third of the total outstanding.

Obligations, such as the Japanese war indemnity loans and the Boxer indemnity, have been a burden upon an economic organization with no direct help toward the bearing of the burden. A large part of the Chinese government debt has at all times been of this sort.   In other words, the Chinese government has been an indemnity paying institution rather than a capital importing institution.

INPAYMENTS ON BUSINESS INVESTMENTS

I turn now to the estimating of the inpayments into China on account of business investments.   The method

expenditures cannot be cut off suddenly.   If the attempt were made it would probably raise other economic problems.

is to find the increase in the investment during each of the two periods under consideration, to determine how much of this increase was due to changes which involved no inpayments into China, to regard the remainder as having been remitted to China, and to determine from it the annual average inpayment.

The value of the foreign business investments in China was estimated at U. S. $503.2 million for 1902 and U. S. $1,084.5 million for 1914. This means an increase during the period of U. S. $581.3 million. How much was remitted to China to bring about this increase? How much of the increase was due to changes within the country?

There is little information by which to arrive at an answer to this question. We know that British land holdings at Shanghai were important throughout the period. They were estimated at U. S. $33.6 million for 1902 and U. S. $87 million for 1914. We know also that the price in silver of land in Shanghai in 1903 was about 40 per cent of its price in 1916.[12] The fact that the value of British land holdings increased at about the same rate as the value of the land is not proof but it certainly creates a strong presumption that remittances to China involved in this increase in the value of foreign investments was small.

Concerning the South Manchuria Railway it is known that its holdings were U. S. $105 million in 1914 and that there had actually been remitted to China practically the whole of the proceeds of the sale of debentures in London and the sale of new shares in Japan, say U. S. $65 million.[13] The history of the South Manchuria was

---

[12] The assessed value of land in the central and northern districts (whose area did not change) was as follows: (Figures from the *Feetham Report*, vol. 1, p. 346.)

Year	Thousands of Shanghai Tls.	Index Nos.
1903	39,801	40.1
1916	99,149	100.0
1927	229,140	231.1
1930	319,971	322.7

[13] For details see Japanese Investments in China, pp. 477–78.

too brief in 1914 to serve as reliable index, but it is significant that the value of the holdings in 1914 had meant remittances to China during the preceding period of about 60 per cent of the total.

Upon such information and by comparison with the conclusion for the later period for which the information is more adequate I conclude that remittances to China during the period 1902–1913 were half of the increase in the value of business investments. Half of U. S. $581.3 million is U. S. $290.7 million and at the average rate for the period (U. S. $1.00 = Chinese $2.18) this comes to Chinese $633.7 million which means an annual average inpayment on account of business investments of Chinese $52.8 million.

The increase in the value of business investments was from U. S. $1,084.5 million to U. S. $2,531.9 million between 1914–1931 or a total increase of U. S. $1,447.4 million. We must consider briefly the information upon which to base an estimate of the inpayments involved.

Land holdings in Shanghai were at the end of 1930 an important factor in British holdings and of some importance in the Japanese and American totals. The rise in the value of land in silver was at a higher rate than for the earlier period but this rise was most rapid during the closing years when silver was falling and the rise in terms of gold was not much greater. It was great enough, however, to be taken into account.

For the South Manchuria Railway we have estimates that show about half the total investment as it was in 1930 to be covered by remittances from Japan. The estimate of management of the railway bears this out.[14] If we take into account the holdings of the South Manchuria Railway Company in its subsidiaries we reach a somewhat smaller estimate, about 40 per cent. For

[14] In consulting the figures in the chapter on Japanese Investments, p. 480, it must be borne in mind that the borrowings from Great Britain were made during the earlier period.

Japanese holdings in Shanghai estimates of "50 per cent or less" were made by a banker and an official of the Japanese government.

American companies holding investments to the amount of U. S. $37,151,000 reported to me that these investments had involved remittances to China to the amount of U. S. $13,395,000; the remittances were about 36 per cent of the current value of the holdings. There were American firms, the whole of whose holdings represented remittances from the United States and others, who reported that they "started on a shoe string" or had been "built up from nothing."

In the Russian case it is known that the business property of the Russians who are permanent residents of China was worth about U. S. $60 million in 1931. It is shown in the chapter on Russian investments that this property, which was greater than the 1914 total by U. S. $13 million, involved practically no remittances to China. Russian refugees may have brought U. S. $2.5 million into the country in furs, gold, and jewels, and other portable property.

Taking the whole of the information I believe that the proportion of the increased value which called for inpayments was smaller than for the earlier period. I therefore offer an estimate of 45 per cent.

Taking 45 per cent of U. S. $1,447.4 million we find total inpayments on account of business investments to have been U. S. $651.3 million for the period 1914–1931. Converting this figure at the average rate for the period (U. S. $1.00 = Chinese $1.92) we reach a total of Chinese $1,250.5 million, which gives us an annual average inpayment of Chinese $73.6 million.

OUTPAYMENTS ON BUSINESS INVESTMENTS

The outpayments on business investments must be estimated from the information which has been discovered in arriving at the total business investments for the different countries.   In the American case there was sufficient information to enable an estimate of U. S. $5 to 10 million to be made as the remittance from China on business investments of U. S. $155 million.   Japanese remittances of business profits were estimated at about U. S. $37.5 million for recent years on a total business investment of U. S. $913 million.[15]   Remittances from China on the holdings of Russian business men were practically nothing and on the Soviet-owned Chinese Eastern Railway they were not much greater.   The discoverable outpayments were no more than U. S. $12.5 million.   Outpayments on British investments were estimated at from U. S. $25 to U. S. $50 million in recent years on total British holdings of U. S. $963 million.   The facts justify an estimated remittance from China on account of business investments at the rate of 4 per cent on the total value of the business investments.

The average total business investment for the period 1902–1913 was U. S. $793.9 million, a figure midway between the total at the beginning and at the end of the period.   Four per cent of this is U. S. $31.8 million which at the average rate of exchange for the period gives us Chinese $69.3 million as the average annual outpayment on business investments for the period 1902–1913.

By the same method of calculating we arrive at an annual outpayment of U. S. $72.3 million for the period 1914–1930.[16]   This at the average rate of exchange for the period comes to Chinese $138.8 million.   The figures for payments in and out of China, connected with business investments, are shown in the following table.

---

[15] This is borne out by the totals reported in the *Financial and Economic Annual of Japan*, 1931, p. 154.   After an item covering interest on foreign government securities as "other interest and dividends received from long-term capital investments abroad."   The figure for 1928 was yen 65.7 million and for 1929 it was 84.8 million.   A very large proportion of these investments was in China.

[16] Four per cent of U. S. $1,808.2 million which is midway between U. S. $1,084.5 million and U. S. $2,531.9 million.

TABLE 19

INPAYMENTS AND OUTPAYMENTS ARISING FROM BUSINESS INVESTMENTS
BY PERIODS

(All figures in millions)

Period	Total Increase in U.S. Dollars	Estimated Total Inpayments in U.S. Dollars	Estimated Total Inpayments in Ch. Dollars	Average Annual Inpayment in Ch. Dollars	Average Business Investment in U.S. Dollars	Average Annual Outpayment in U.S. Dollars	Average Annual Outpayment in Ch. Dollars	Equivalent of the U.S. Dollar in Ch. Dollars
1902–1913	581.3	290.7	633.7	52.8	793.9	31.8	69.3	2.18
1914–1930	1,447.4	651.3	1,250.5	73.6	1,808.2	72.3	138.8	1.92

FIGURES FOR THE THREE YEARS 1928, 1929, AND 1930

The three years at the end of the second period offer an opportunity to estimate the amount of the individual items directly. The studies of Part II required the assembling of information which is useful for this purpose and they made it possible to estimate minor items which were unimportant over the whole period.

It was found, for example, that new Japanese ventures in Manchuria during the years 1929 and 1930 included the building of a wharf at Newchwang for the handling of Fushun coal, the building of a coal pier at Dairen, the completion of the shale oil plant at the Fushun Collieries, and the construction of a new 500-ton blast furnace at the Anshan Iron Works. During the same years there was a sharp increase in American investments at Shanghai in local public utilities. New purchases of land in Shanghai by British interests were reported, also considerable building activity in which the British were interested. These developments account for the considerable inpayments on capital account shown under business investments.

There were no new borrowings abroad by the Chinese government, with the exception of one item of Chinese $4 million, which represents the sale outside of China, chiefly in the United States, of the bonds of a domestic loan issued in 1928. These bonds were issued after the troubles between China and Japan connected with the so-called Tsinanfu incident. My estimate is based upon reports from Chinese bankers in the United States.[17] The attitude of the Nationalist government toward new foreign financing has been expressed by T. V. Soong, Minister of Finance, in a recent report. "The suggestion has often been put forward that the Ministry should attempt to obtain financial assistance by means of foreign loans, but it has been its policy studiously to avoid even negotiations in this direction, until there was assurance that the terms and conditions which could be offered prospective foreign purchasers of our bonds would be such as could be accepted and yet which would not imperil China's financial integrity." [18]

Among the capital outpayments there is an item for each year which is headed, Purchase of Foreign Securities. There is a small holding of foreign securities in China and there has been, as I have pointed out elsewhere, some purchase of the foreign issues of Chinese government loans by banks and financial institutions in Shanghai. The outpayments I estimate to have been considerably greater in 1929 than for the other years.[19]

[17] It is generally true that overseas Chinese have purchased few of the securities of the Chinese government. In Amoy and Swatow, cities whose economic life is dominated by overseas Chinese, the bankers reported practically no dealings in Chinese government securities at a time when such dealings were important at Shanghai. This is true in spite of the fact that efforts have been made to promote such dealings by the modern Chinese banks.

[18] *Annual Report for the Fiscal Year, 1928–1929*, p. 7.

[19] The information that the officials of the Chinese government make large purchases of foreign securities was frequently reported to me in a loud whisper. I had an unusually good opportunity to secure information on the subject of Chinese purchases of foreign securities and I do not believe the total holding was over U. S. $4 or 5 million at the end of 1930, excluding the holdings of the foreign issue of the bonds of the Chinese government. The item is too uncertain to be entered in my totals. I found no evidence of great purchases which would justify the implication of the whisper. A number of Chinese, usually "returned students," maintain accounts with brokers in New York and foreign securities may be conveniently purchased in Shanghai, but the transactions seem to be small.

The current items include a small inpayment on the foreign securities held by Chinese but the important items are outpayments.   They include the payments abroad by the Chinese government which are found in the table in the Appendix. In addition there are remittances from China of income on business investments and business profits of all sorts which I estimate to have been considerably smaller in U. S. dollars for 1930 than for the earlier years. The fall in silver accounts for the fact that the item is as great as Chinese $200 million for 1930.   The figures for the three years are shown below.

TABLE 20

INPAYMENTS AND OUTPAYMENTS ON GOVERNMENT DEBT AND BUSINESS INVESTMENTS, 1928, 1929, 1930

(Figures in millions of Chinese dollars)

Capital Items
Inpayments

New business investments	100.0	190.0	210.0
Sale of government securities abroad	4.0	0.0	0.0

Outpayments

Purchase of securities abroad	4.0	20.0	8.0

Current Items
Inpayments

Interest on foreign securities	1.0	1.5	2.0

Outpayments

Interest and amortization on government loans	63.0	79.1	111.4
Profits on business investments	180.0	200.0	200.0

THE GENERAL RESULTS

Certain general results may be presented after this review of the relations between investments and the balance of payments.

Inpayments on capital account are shown below. They were smaller during the second period than during the first.   The decline has been in government borrowings. For the years 1929 and 1930 there were no inpayments at all under this heading.   Business investments have shown a persistent increase, which brought the figures for recent years well above the average. The figures are in millions of Chinese dollars.

	Inpayments on Capital Items		
	Government	Business	Total
Annual average 1902–1913	61.0	52.8	113.8
Annual average 1914–1930	23.8	73.6	97.4
1928	4.0	96.0	100.0
1929	0.0	170.0	170.0
1930	0.0	202.0	202.0

Outpayments on current account have increased throughout the period. Their increase was marked during the three years for which separate figures are given. The outpayments are shown below:

	Outpayments on Current Items		
	Government	Business	Total
Annual average 1902–1913	89.2	69.3	158.5
Annual average 1913–1930	70.9	138.8	209.7
1928	63.0	179.0	242.0
1929	79.1	198.5	277.6
1930	111.4	198.0	309.4

This enables us to show the net flow of funds from China on account of all payments connected with the obligations of the Chinese government and foreign business investments in the country.

NET OUTPAYMENTS CONNECTED WITH GOVERNMENT OBLIGATIONS AND
BUSINESS INVESTMENTS

(In millions of Chinese dollars)

Annual average 1902–1913	44.7
Annual average 1913–1930	112.3
1928	142.0
1929	107.6
1930	107.4

The preceding tables afford a general view of the results in the field of international payments of the transactions arising from government obligations and business investments.   The conclusion seems unavoidable that these transactions have brought about a net outflow of funds from China.   This must be emphasized for it is contrary to an idea which is widely held, namely, that China's excess of imports represents new borrowings abroad and new investments by foreign business men. The contrary conclusion that China has made greater payments on account of debt and investment than she has received seems to be established.   We must, therefore, turn to other items in her balance of international payments if we are to find a solution of the puzzle presented by China's great and growing excess of imports.

APPENDIX

TABLE OF INPAYMENTS AND OUTPAYMENTS ON GOVERNMENT ACCOUNT WITH EXPLANATORY NOTES

TABLE 21

INPAYMENTS AND OUTPAYMENTS ARISING FROM CHINESE GOVERNMENT OBLIGATIONS, 1894–1930

(In thousands of Chinese dollars)

Year	Total Inpayments	Total Outpayments	Net Inpayment	Net Outpayment	U. S. Dollar Equivalent to Ch. Dollars
1894	14,700		14,700		1.95
1895	56,740	2,600	44,140		1.88
1896	19,300	13,430	5,870		1.85
1897		22,000		22,000	2.08
1898	12,700	25,595		12,895	2.14
1899	61,200	30,894	30,306		2.05
1900	5,100	35,715		30,615	2.00
1901	480	36,980		36,500	2.08
1902	5,000	77,237		72,237	2.38
1903	21,283	71,870		50,587	2.34
1904	8,250	75,807		67,557	2.27
1905	30,595	79,046		48,451	2.05
1906	11,245	65,091		53,846	1.88
1907	21,471	65,468		43,997	1.90
1908	101,326	130,015		28,689	2.31
1909	25,414	86,019		60,605	2.38
1910	48,442	80,822		32,380	2.27
1911	97,451	75,940	21,511		2.31
1912	101,027	61,817	39,210		2.03
1913	260,325	201,198	59,127		2.05
1914	99,280	118,419		19,139	2.24
1915	7,443	123,799		116,356	2.42
1916	26,166	95,526		69,360	1.90
1917	30,375	64,878		34,503	1.46
1918	96,636	34,334	62,303		1.19
1919	23,004	30,719		7,715	1.08
1920	19,334	28,699		9,364	1.21
1921	22,964	51,101		28,137	1.97
1922	43,676	56,432		12,756	1.81
1923	15,264	70,994		55,730	1.88
1924		68,039		68,039	1.85
1925	20,293	66,301		46,008	1.79
1926		70,095		70,095	1.97
1927		72,767		72,767	2.17
1928		62,992		62,992	2.11
1929		79,067		79,067	2.34
1930		111,432		111,432	3.26

EXPLANATORY NOTES

The year-by-year inpayments and outpayments which have resulted from the obligations of the Chinese government cannot always be discovered either by consulting the official loan contracts or formal amortization tables. It has often been necessary to make use of other sources and occasionally to adopt certain arbitrary methods in determining the yearly amounts to be set down against certain loans. A short explanation of our handling of particular loans, together with a list of the sources we have employed in compiling the above table, is accordingly presented.

1. The inpayments arising from the construction expenses of the Canton-Hankow Railway, which amounted to U. S. $6,750,000, have been assigned to three years, namely an inpayment of Chinese $3,000,000 in 1900, an inpayment of Chinese $5,000,000 in 1902, and another of Chinese $5,000,000 in 1903.

2. In the case of the three early loans of the Chinese government associated with the payment of the Japanese indemnity, viz., the Franco-Russian loan of 1895, and the first and second Anglo-German loans of 1896 and 1898, only the differences between the proceeds of the loans and the payments to Japan have been entered as inpayments.

3. The contract for the construction of the Shanghai-Nanking Railway was concluded early in July, 1903, but various other preliminaries held up the actual issuance of bonds on the London market till July, 1904. However, since the total amount of the first issue (£2,250,000) was undoubtedly remitted over the period of the next three years, this amount has been broken up and entered as an inpayment of £750,000 in 1904, 1905, and 1906. The total amount of the second issue of Shanghai-Nanking Railway bonds (£650,000) has been entered as an inpayment in 1907, the year of issuance.

4. The loan agreements for the Pienlo Railway were officially concluded in 1903 and 1907 but the inpayments arising from this obligation have been distributed according to the dates of bond issuance reported by the Société Belge de Chemins de Fer en Chine, that is from 1905 through 1908.

5. The inpayments involved in the loans of various banks to

the Chinese government, which were dealt with in accordance with the Reorganization Loan Agreement, Annex B, have been broken up, one-third being arbitrarily assigned to each of the three years, 1910, 1911, and 1912.

6. The advances for the Grand Canal loan of U. S. $900,000 authorized in 1917 have been spread over four years, 1918–1921.

7. The advances of the South Manchuria Railway Company for the line running between Ssupinkai-Taonan amounted to approximately 32 million yen in 1925.[20] The amounts paid in during 1919 and 1920 may be fixed but the remainder of loan (over 5 million yen) was in the form of monthly advances about which there was no exact information. The method employed in this case has been the arbitrary assignment of one-fourth of this remainder to each of the four years (1920–1923) during which the railroad was under construction.

8. Outpayments on account of the Kirin-Changchun Railway loan of 1917 have covered only interest. Since the exact condition of this loan today is not known, these payments are considered to have lapsed after 1927.

9. For the Peking-Suiyuan Railway only one payment on principal has been made and that was in 1920. Partial interest was paid in 1921 but since that year no payments whatsoever have been made.

10. Of the inadequately secured loans of the Chinese government held by the Japanese, only the most important have been considered to have brought inpayments into China. These are the six loans in the Nishihara group, the second Arms loan, the Bureau of Engraving (Mitsui), and the Hankow Paper Mill loans.

11. The inpayments funded in the Japanese 96-million dollar loan of 1922 have, with the exception of the Flood Relief loan of 1917, been assigned arbitrarily in equal portions to the years 1918, 1919, 1920, and 1921.

12. Since it appears from the 1923 Document of the Ministry of Communications that two payments of £12,683 were made on the principal of the Taoching Railway loan of 1919 for the purchase of rolling stock, one in 1921 and one in 1923, the equivalents in Chinese dollars have been entered as outpayments in those years.

[20] See Japanese Investments in China, p. 524.

13. The last payment of interest on the Lunghai Railway loan bonds of 1913 is considered to have been made in 1925. No payments have ever been made on the principal.

14. The inpayments resulting from the Chinese Government 8% Treasury Notes of 1920 for the Lunghai Railway have been distributed to correspond to the dates when the bonds were issued in Brussels and Amsterdam. Following this procedure we obtain inpayments amounting approximately to Chinese $11,000,000 in 1920, Chinese $7,000,000 in 1921, and Chinese $14,000,000 in 1923.

15. Outpayments on the principal of the pound sterling share of the Peking-Mukden Double Track loan of 1921 have been assigned as follows: £50,000 in 1922, £90,000 in 1923, £120,000 in 1924, and £22,258 in 1925. No outpayments on the interest of this loan have been made.

16. In those cases where the banker's commissions on the loans have come to a significant amount, viz., in the cases of the loans for the Shanghai-Nanking Railway, the Hukuang Railways, the Shanghai-Fenching Railway (after 1925), and the Pienlo Railway, the commissions enter into our figure for outpayments from the Chinese economy.

17. The Chicago Bank loan of 1919 has not been considered as effecting an inpayment into China because it merely repaid an earlier loan of U. S. $5 million made in 1916.

18. The outpayments on the loans secured on salt revenue are considered to have been made according to the program announced by the Chinese government in 1929. For the Anglo-French loan of 1908 the outpayments have been entered as follows: £123,750 in interest during 1928, £362,500 in 1929 which covered the installment of principal due in 1928 together with the interest for 1929, and £351,250 in 1930 which covered the installment of principal due in 1929 together with the interest for 1930. No outpayments were made on the Crisp loan in 1928. However, in 1929 the payments of interest due in 1928 (£229,208) were paid and in 1930 all arrears of interest were wiped out by payment of the interest for 1929 and 1930. Outpayments arising from the Hukuang Railway Sinking Fund Gold loan of 1911 have been set at £131,899 for 1929 and £131,690 for 1930. The former payment covered coupon 31 of the American, British, and French shares and coupon 30 of

the German, while the latter disposed of coupon 32 of the American, British, and French shares and coupon 31 of the German.

Sources:

Matsukata, *Adoption of the Gold Standard in Japan*, for inpayments on indemnity loans, 1895, 1896, and 1898.

MacMurray, John V. A., *Treaties and Agreements With or Concerning China, 1894–1919*, 2 vols., Carnegie Endowment for International Peace, Washington, 1921, for various loan contracts.

Baylin, J. R., *Foreign Loan Obligations of China*, Tientsin, 1925, for amortization tables in case of most of the loans.

Kent, Percy H., *Railway Enterprise in China*, London, 1907, for dates of inpayments on early railway loans, e.g. Shanghai-Nanking Railway.

China Year Book, particularly Kann & Baylin, "Foreign Loans of China" in the 1931 issue.

Wright, Stanley F., *Collection and Disposal of Maritime and Native Customs Revenue since the Revolution of 1911*, Shanghai, 1927, for Boxer indemnity and early government loans.

1923 Document of the Ministry of Communications, for various railway loans.

Report of the Financial Readjustment Commission (1925), for inadequately secured loans.

Bank of China, *Chinese Government Loan Issues and Obligations*.

Information was supplied by the Ministry of Finance and the Ministry of Railways of the Chinese Government, J. P. Morgan & Company, The Hongkong and Shanghai Bank, the National City Bank, the Bank of China, the Bank of Japan, the Italian Bank for China, and others.

CHAPTER X

REMITTANCES FROM CHINESE OVERSEAS

The Chinese Overseas

In general, the East has differed from the West in that Easterners stay at home. The Chinese of the southeastern coast of China are an exception and their migration throughout the Pacific area is a fact of outstanding importance in every field of international relations. This migration has gone on under the surface of the political changes that make a stir in the world, but it is more significant than many of the alterations that change the color of the map. To deal adequately with the economic consequences of the spread of the Chinese abroad would be to write a large part of the economic history in recent centuries of such countries as Siam, the Philippines, and Netherlands India, or such cities as Singapore and San Francisco.

The consequence in which we are interested, that is, the flow of funds back to China from the Chinese abroad, is but poorly indicated by such a title as emigrant's remittances. It is true that some of the money sent back to China is from Chinese laborers. Chinese are employed, to mention a few of the places, on the rubber plantations of the Malay Peninsula, in the tin mines of the Dutch East Indies, and in the tobacco fields of the east coast of Sumatra. These Chinese send remittances back to China which are small in the individual case but which come to considerable sums in the aggregate.

The great sums are, I believe, remittances of business profits and of income from property holdings rather than savings from wages, though it is, of course, impossible to draw a sharp line of distinction between them. An ex-

177

ample or two will serve to show the nature of the payments I have in mind.

Near Amoy in a Chinese village of about one hundred families, I interviewed the head-master of a local school and the chairman of the board of trustees of this school. The funds for the school had come from the Philippines, and one-half of the board of trustees consists of persons living in the Philippines. Every family in this village, except two, had at least one of its members in the Philippines at the time of my visit. The remittances to the families in this village from their members abroad were estimated at about Chinese $600 a year for each family. This village is the Chinese home of a group of Chinese families who are the owners of a number of prosperous business organizations in an important city in the Philippines.

Consider the life history of a man in a village near Swatow which was told by one of his younger relatives. At the age of about seventeen he was taken to Siam by his father who, with his uncles, was in charge of the family's business there. After two years in Siam he was sent back to Swatow. Here his marriage took place and at the age of about twenty-two he returned to Siam. From this age until after his fiftieth year he spent three or four years in Siam for every one he spent in Swatow. When I heard his story he had retired and one of his sons had taken his place, carrying on the tradition. Here we have a Swatow family owning business property in Siam which is managed by a family whose home is in China. What shall we call the sums remitted to China from Siam in this case? They are business profits from an enterprise owned by a Chinese family. The amount of these remittances is more closely related to the size of the holdings of the family than to the number of persons who happen at any time to be in Siam.

The Chinese may be said to have invested a part of the family abroad, to have built up business holdings abroad through the family and to receive an income from

these holdings through the family.   Much has been said
in earlier chapters of the foreign "colony" in China; we
have now to deal with the Chinese "colony" abroad and
with the annual sums that are sent to China by such
colonies.   The Chinese have built up business investments
abroad with practically no outpayments from China.
These investments bring into China payments from outside which are of the greatest importance in her balance
of payments.

The Economic Position of the Chinese Abroad

The number of Chinese abroad has been estimated by
a considerable number of writers.   Figures for years since
1902 have usually been between seven and nine million.[1]
The lowest estimate which I have found is that of Wu
Cheng Ch'ao, who puts the total for about 1926 at 5.7
million.   The Chinese government has made efforts in recent years to arrive at a total.   The figures do not seem to
have been published, but there are frequent references
to a total of about nine million.[2]

Figures of population are useful to check the results of
estimates of remittances but they do not provide direct
evidence.   They include, for example, Chinese in Formosa
to the number of about four million, who are at home
there and are not to be included in any total in which

[1] Estimates by the following writers are listed with reference to the
sources in Remer, C. F., *The Foreign Trade of China*, Shanghai, 1922, p. 219.

Morse	1903	7.3 million
Gottwaldt	1903	7.6 "
Richard	1908	9.0 "
MacNair	1921	8.6 "

[2] Wu Cheng Ch'ao, " Chinese Immigration in the Pacific Area," *Chinese
Social & Political Science Review*, vol. 12, no. 4, pp. 543–60.   The progress
of an investigation by the Chinese Ministry of Foreign Affairs is indicated
in *Far Eastern Review*, vol. 23, p. 460, with a total estimate of 9.6 million.
The China Year Book, 1923, p. 143, gives an "official estimate" of 8.5
million and there have been recent references in the newspapers of the
China coast to an "official" figure of 9 million.   *China*, The China Society,
New York, April, 1927, vol. 3, no. 2.

we are interested. It seems certain, on the other hand, that there are Chinese who ought to be counted but who are omitted from the total. The number of Chinese in Siam is usually given at four hundred thousand to five hundred thousand. I have a report from a banker in Bangkok, who states it as his opinion, and one generally held in Siam, that the number of Chinese in the country is between one million and a half and two million. Official figures for French Indo-China put the Chinese population at about two hundred and thirty thousand, but the number is believed to be about five hundred thousand. The number of Chinese in the Philippines is usually put at about fifty thousand, but a Chinese consular official states the number of "persons of Chinese parentage" in the Philippines to be between one hundred and twenty thousand and one hundred and fifty thousand.[3] Against these figures we must put the number of Chinese who have lost touch with China and send no remittances. This is the case with a certain number in every country.

After a survey of the material I have reached the opinion that the number of Chinese who may send remittances to China is at any one time between three and four million. The greatest colonies of Chinese abroad are in British Malaya, the Dutch East Indies, Siam, French Indo-China, the Philippines, and the United States (including Hawaii).

In the countries to which they have gone the Chinese have achieved a high measure of economic success. In British Malaya they are the wealthiest group in the community and the leaders in trade and industry. Throughout southeastern Asia the Chinese are the great middlemen in foreign trade. Imports go through their hands on the way to the native consumers and exports are first bought by the Chinese who, in turn, sell them to the actual exporters. It is estimated that the Chinese control 90 per cent of the retail trade of the Philippines and a

[3] *China Weekly Review*, Dec.–Feb., 1927–1928, vol. 43, p. 2.

large part of the wholesale trade.[4] In the United States they are owners of restaurants, farmers, and laundrymen. In Hawaii they are among the wealthiest traders in the territory. They are important in the trade of Korea. In Siberia they have long held an important place and the power of the Chinese family system is seen in the fact that the Soviet government has made special arrangements to permit remittances to be sent back to China from Siberia.[5]

THE HONGKONG INVESTIGATION

My estimate of remittances to China is the result of an attempt to find out in Hongkong (in January and February, 1931) and in other cities of southern China how much was received from abroad during the years 1928, 1929, and 1930. As a check upon the results of this investigation I have obtained, from practically every American bank having relations with China, figures showing remittances to China by Chinese during 1930. There is information from other remitting countries, but it is not so complete.

Sixteen banks in Hongkong handle practically the whole of the remittance business. The number includes every "foreign" bank and a number of the modern Chinese banks. I was able to secure figures from eleven of these banks covering the years 1928, 1929, and 1930. Of the five who did not provide written reports two handle only a small amount of the business and were dropped from consideration. The managers of the other three were willing to give me information, so long as it was not in written form, and permitted me to interview staff members.

[4] Miller, Hugo H., *Economic Conditions in the Philippines*, Ginn and Co., Boston, 1920, pp. 419-21. The Chinese "have built up a large commercial organization consisting of importers, wholesalers, middlemen, and buyers and a credit system extending through all of these."

[5] These remittances come to about Chinese $1 million for sixteen months. Russian Investments in China, p. 607.

The chief difficulty in the Hongkong investigation proved to be the separation of remittances to pay for goods exported from China and the elimination of such payments from the total, leaving only remittances for families or for investment.   In the few cases in which the bankers themselves were unable to make this separation, I accepted 25 per cent of the remittances from the South Seas and 60 per cent of those from the United States as destined for families or for investment.   These percentages were arrived at after consultation with Chinese and foreign bank managers.   The result is shown in the table below.   The figures cover remittances received in Hongkong for the families of those remitting or for investment in the country.   They represent inpayments into the Chinese economy from outside independent of merchandise trade.

REMITTANCES FROM OVERSEAS CHINESE TO HONGKONG

	In millions of Hongkong Dollars	In Millions of Chinese Dollars
1928	217.3	228.2
1929	241.5	253.6
1930	272.7	286.3

Information from other important centers must now be considered.   It is probable that remittances directly to Canton amount to practically nothing.   The important banks at Canton have offices in Hongkong; business abroad is through these banks.   The Canton bankers were quite certain that direct remittances to Canton might be neglected.

For Swatow, after several conferences with the manager of the Kwong Yak Bank, the largest "letter hong" in the city, an estimate was made of the total remittances received from abroad.[6]   This estimate was confirmed in conferences with other bankers and with officials.   A

[6] I was assured in Swatow that the problem of separating remittances for goods does not arise. Remittances through the letter hong are for families, remittances for goods are handled quite differently.

"letter hong," it may be explained, is engaged in the business of receiving money abroad for payment within China. The name is common in the ports of the southern coast. The Chinese term which is so "translated" means a foreign bill or foreign exchange house. A letter accompanies remittances through the letter hong and the letter hong agrees to deliver the letter and a sum in Chinese dollars to the person to whom it is addressed,[7] even if this requires that an agent be sent to a remote village. An envelope for the receipt accompanies the letter and the whole transaction is ingeniously devised to prevent fraud or mistakes.

ESTIMATE OF OVERSEAS REMITTANCES RECEIVED IN SWATOW

In Millions of
Chinese Dollars

1928	27
1929	27
1930	30

Swatow is close to Hongkong and the letter hongs use the banks in that city for their foreign transactions. We may be fairly certain, then, that none of these sums come directly to Swatow. In other words, from Chinese $27 to 30 million of the funds remitted to Hongkong were really destined for Swatow.

In the case of Amoy conditions are somewhat different. The estimates of bankers and officials agree in the statement that half the remittances are through Hongkong and the other half direct. The total for Amoy is from estimates prepared by the local bankers' guild at the request of the American Consul-general. These estimates were considered in detail with a number of bankers. An independent estimate by the manager of the Ho Hong Bank put the total received in Amoy, for investment

---

[7] The charge to cover a remittance of Chinese $5.00 from Siam was, in February, 1931, 20 cents to cover postage and 25 cents for "making the payment."

ESTIMATE OF OVERSEAS REMITTANCES RECEIVED IN AMOY

*In Millions of
Chinese Dollars*

1927	51.8
1928	44.8
1929	54.2
1930	60.0

only, during the three years 1928–1930, at Chinese $40 million. We may deal with the Amoy figures by adding one-half the remittances to the Hongkong total to arrive at the China total. The other half serves to indicate how the distribution of the sums originally received in Hongkong has been made.

The total remittance to China was shown on the basis of the investigation at Hongkong and other important centers to be as follows:

TOTAL OVERSEAS REMITTANCES TO CHINA

	Hongkong	*Amoy (direct)*	*Total*
1928	228.2	22.4	250.6
1929	253.6	27.1	280.7
1930	286.3	30.0	316.3

THE AMERICAN INVESTIGATION

These totals seem to me large but I have been driven to accept them as the result of other work on the subject. An investigation carried on in the United States is first to be considered.

The figures provided by the Hongkong bankers made it possible, with some estimates, to arrive at the following conclusion as to the source of the remittances to Hongkong. I use the figures in Hongkong dollars as the more convenient.

During the spring of 1930 an effort was made to get a statement from the banks in the United States known to be interested in the sale of remittances to China.[8] Re-

[8] I wish to acknowledge the assistance of the late Mr. M. D. Currie of the Far Eastern Division of the National City Bank and Mr. G. B. Lau of the New York office of the Bank of Canton.

SOURCES OF REMITTANCES TO HONGKONG, 1930

	Millions of Hongkong Dollars
Canada	17.5
South America	4.2
United States	119.3
Straits Settlements	42.0
Dutch East Indies	29.4
Siam	20.0
Philippines	12.5
Australia	8.5
French Indo-China	5.0
India	4.3
Other sources	10.0
	272.7

plies were received from eleven banks. One bank, known to be important in this field, failed to send figures. Each bank was asked to give the amount in the most convenient currency of the total remittances to China for Chinese customers for the year 1929 or 1928. Most of the banks reported in Hongkong dollars and practically all of them reported for the year 1928.

Many of the banks indicated that remittances had been on a larger scale during 1930 on account of the fall in silver. "Many of our customers," one bank reports, "are now (i.e. in July, 1930) transferring funds which have been accumulating in this country for from ten to forty years."

There was general agreement that 80 per cent of the funds remitted from the eastern part of the United States were to families or for investment in China and that this percentage was smaller for remittances from the Pacific coast. The use of the letter of credit for trade purposes, the bankers point out, has been growing. It follows that a larger percentage of the remittances is for family and investment.

The total for the eleven banks, making the deductions which they indicate for remittances connected with the purchase of goods in China, that is, the total remittances to China for families and for investment during the year

1928, was Hongkong $84,366,000. The Hongkong dollar was worth almost exactly half an American dollar and this makes the total in U. S. $42.2 million.[9]

Here we have independently gathered information which corroborates the Hongkong investigation in so far as the great total for the United States is concerned. There is no doubt that a figure of Hongkong $84.4 million for 1928 is consistent with a figure of Hongkong $120 million for 1930, when the U. S. dollar total for 1928 at the 1930 exchange rate comes to Hongkong $125 million. The American investigation supports the results of the Hongkong study.

AMOY IN RECENT YEARS

Amoy offers further opportunity to test the reasonableness of the estimates of remittances. Amoy is a port whose export trade is small. Information made available to me from local Customs reports shows total exports from Amoy of Chinese $7.1 million for 1929.[10] During the same year there were merchandise imports of Chinese $46.7 million,[11] and in addition a net import of silver to the total of Chinese $4 million. During conferences in Amoy it was frequently said that net silver imports are about as great as the total merchandise exports from Amoy and that they have been known to be considerably greater.[12]

Until recently it has been the custom of overseas Chinese to invest in land in the villages near Amoy and even at some distance from the city. In recent years disturbed conditions and the spread of communism have made land an uncertain and undesirable investment. During the years when these conditions prevailed, the drop in silver

[9] The Hongkong dollar was equivalent to the following in U. S. dollars: 1928 $0.5007, 1929 $0.4717, 1930 $0.3385. *Commerce Year Book*, 1931, vol. 2, p. 518.
[10] Native produce of local origin exported to foreign countries Hk. Tls. 3,425,324 and to Chinese ports Hk. Tls. 1,332,267.
[11] Imported from foreign countries and Hongkong, Hk. Tls. 18,776,560 and "net total native imports."
[12] The net silver import into Amoy in 1930 was about Chinese $10 million.

brought unusually great remittances, many for the purpose of investment.   The result was a real estate boom in the city, the results of which were the subject of general comment in 1931.   Land was changing hands at three and four times its former value, projects for development were numerous, and there was an eager interest in rising prices on the part of bankers and business men.[13]

The explanation of the trade situation is at hand in the information about remittances and no other explanation can be discovered.   The land boom is consistent with the information concerning unusual remittances for investment.   The information given above concerning the remittances from the Philippines to one village near Amoy, the existence in the city of Amoy University supported by a man who has made a fortune in Singapore, all add to the convincingness of the picture.   We have in Amoy a city whose economic life is dominated by remittances from overseas Chinese.

The city of Toyshan in the Sunning district near Canton is another such city, according to information obtained at Canton and Hongkong.   The power of economic recovery which Canton has repeatedly shown in the past fifteen years has been due in no small part to the continued inflow of funds from abroad.   The life of the cities of China's southern coast bears witness to the powerful influence of the overseas Chinese in the economic life of their home country.

FINAL ESTIMATES

H. B. Morse estimated the remittances to China from overseas Chinese at Chinese $110 million for the year 1903 and raised his estimate to Chinese $150 million for 1906.[14]

[13] For comment on a similar land boom in Canton see *North China Daily News*, April 9, 1931.

[14] Morse, H. B., *An Inquiry into the Commercial Liabilities and Assets of China in International Trade*, Chinese Maritime Customs, Shanghai, 1904. For the later estimate see *China and the Far East*, Clark University Lectures, New York, 1910, p. 107.

C. S. See, who is himself a member of the Chinese colony in the Philippines, set the total at Chinese $115 million in 1913.[15] I have made an estimate of the annual average remittance for the years 1899–1913 at Chinese $105.[16] The present investigation seems to me to justify an estimate of Chinese $150 million as the annual average remittance for the years 1902–1913.

The results of the Hongkong investigation provide figures for the closing years of the period 1914–1930. The average of these figures is Chinese $282.5 million. It happens that these figures cover for the first year a period of unusual prosperity in the area from which the remittances came for the second and third years and a great decline in the gold price of silver. There is reason to believe that the remittances were unusually high. It is true also that the high price of silver during the war years reduced remittances for the early years of the period.

The estimates of others for the earlier years of the period 1914–1930 put the figure lower than the results of the present study would indicate. An unpublished estimate by a Japanese banker in Shanghai put the total at Chinese $150 million for 1926. Coons accepted an estimate of Chinese $150 million a year as reasonable for the years 1920–1923. My own estimate was Chinese $120 million for the years 1914–1921.[17]

Estimates for more recent years tend to support the results of the Hongkong investigation. D. K. Lieu has made available to me a study by a Hongkong banker for 1929 who reached a total of Chinese $345 million. Communications from China found in the files of the Department of Commerce at Washington give estimates by American observers of U. S. $90 million for 1928, of U. S.

[15] See, C. S., *The Foreign Trade of China*, New York, 1919, pp. 334–6.
[16] Remer, C. F., *Foreign Trade of China*, Shanghai, 1926, p. 221, for this estimate and one for 1914–1921.
[17] Coons, A. G., *The Foreign Public Debt of China*, Philadelphia, 1930, p. 183.

$100 million for 1929, and of Chinese $300 million for 1928. An investigation by an American broker in Shanghai for certain silver dealers in the United States resulted in an estimate of Chinese $250 million for a recent year. And we have as the highest estimate ever made, one of Chinese $400 million, reported by a Chinese news agency as from "official" sources.[18]

These are estimates which would have seemed unreasonable ten years ago. But it is beginning to be more generally appreciated that we have to do with returns from great business holdings as well as with remittances from the humble Chinese worker of the tin mines and the rubber plantations. In view of the facts revealed by the Hongkong study I propose to accept an annual average of Chinese $200 million for the years from 1914 to 1930.

I have on several occasions looked into the subject of remittances to China from Chinese abroad. Each time I have found it difficult to believe that the remittances could be as great as they seemed on examination to be. Each time I have become convinced by supporting evidence. After the present investigation in Hongkong, Amoy, and Swatow I found it impossible to resist the final conclusion that the figures for 1928, 1929, and 1930, which are found in the preceding pages, represent a close approximation to the facts.

[18] *Kuomin News Agency*, August 1, 1930.

CHAPTER XI

TRADE AND SPECIE MOVEMENTS

THE GENERAL FACTS [1]

The outstanding and the most widely recognized problem of China's international accounts is presented by the excess of imports over exports in her international trade. The Customs statistics have shown imports to exceed exports in value for every year except the first, 1864, for which they are available. It is true that the statistics are hardly to be relied upon before 1871 and that corrections were considered necessary by the Customs authorities themselves before 1903. What is more, there has been a tendency for these "unfavorable" balances to increase. It is true again that there have been interruptions in this upward trend, the most significant coming during the period of the European War when world trade was generally restricted and when the gold price of silver was high. The annual average net import of merchandise was Chinese $188.2 million during the years 1902–1913; it was Chinese $272 million during the years 1914–1930, which include the war years; it reached Chinese $622.4 million in 1930 and in 1931 it rose to no less a figure than Chinese $833.8 million. The general facts about the merchandise trade are clear enough, however puzzling the problems which they raise.

The movement of gold is a small item which we may accept as part of the merchandise trade. The Chinese see the gold price of silver as the silver price of gold and

---

[1] A table showing the merchandise trade since 1902 in Chinese dollars, and one showing the net movement of gold and silver is to be found in an appendix to this chapter. Net movement only is shown for gold and silver. Much of the gross movement is seasonal to and from Hongkong.

when its price is high (and silver is low) gold tends to move out of China, just as it tends to move in when the price is low (and silver is high). Gold movements often help to explain fluctuations but they have at no time played a part of major importance. There was a net import of gold during the years 1902–1913 but the annual average was less than Chinese $1 million. During the second period the excess of exports was at the annual rate of Chinese $3.3 million, which serves to reduce the average excess of imports by little more than one per cent.

With a large and increasing excess of imports in her merchandise trade, China has imported silver. This has been true generally for the whole period since 1899 when Customs statistics showing movements of "treasure" began. During the years 1902–1913 the net import of silver was at the average annual rate of Chinese $2.4 million. For the later period it was at the rate of Chinese $62.9 million per year. The net import for recent years, when the net import of merchandise was largest, has been at a rate never before equaled for a three-year period.

A general view of the two periods reveals these facts. During 1903–1913 the average excess of merchandise imports was Chinese $188.2 million, of gold imports Chinese $1 million, and of silver Chinese $2.4 million, making a total outpayment of Chinese $190.6 million. During 1914–1930 merchandise and gold, taken together, came to Chinese $268.7 million and silver to Chinese $62.9 million, making an average of Chinese $331.6 million as the outpayment called for by the three items.

The figures for the three years 1928–1930 bring total outpayments for these three items of no less than Chinese $475.6 million, Chinese $530.8 million, and Chinese $698 million. Increasing net merchandise and silver imports have gone together and were accompanied in 1928 by a net import of gold. The year 1930 is the only one during which there was a considerable net gold export.

These are the general facts. I propose to consider in

the following pages how far the figures may be accepted as showing the true situation.

The Customs Statistics

In 1903 and 1904 reforms were brought about in the returns of the Chinese Maritime Customs by H. B. Morse who was then statistical secretary. From this time on the figures were believed to show the whole of China's foreign trade and to show as accurately as was possible the true value of imports and exports.[2]

The methods of valuation employed by the Customs remained practically unchanged throughout the years 1902–1930. The object has at all times been to show in silver the value of the imports and exports at the boundary of China and at the moment of shipment or of landing.[3] Minor improvements were made in the handling of the trade across the land frontiers of the Manchurian provinces by the opening of additional Customs houses.

Any attempt to correct or to amend the figures of the Customs reports must rest upon evidence that they do not cover the whole of the trade or that the values are not beyond question.

Unrecorded Trade: Russia

The existence of unrecorded trade was recognized by Morse as early as 1904. In drawing up a balance of international payments to cover the year 1903, he entered an item to cover an excess of exports in such trade with Russia over the land frontiers of the northwest which he esti-

[2] Chinese Maritime Customs: *Report on the Trade of China*, 1904, pp. iii–iv. For a brief historical account of these and later changes see Otte, Fr., "Commercial Statistics in China," *Chinese Economic Monthly*, vol. 3, no. 9, Sept., 1926, pp. 368–70.

[3] In a communication from the National Tariff Commission of China I am informed that the value of imports subject to specific rates of duty is "c.i.f. invoice." In the case of imports subject to *ad valorem* rates it is "the wholesale market value less the duty and 7 per cent of the duty paying value derived in conformity with the formula stated in Rule I of the Import Tariff Provisional Rules." For exports "the Customs has always taken for returns purposes what is supposed to be the wholesale market value of local markets without deduction."

mated at Chinese $6 million.   Further study of Russian trade statistics led him to the conclusion that this trade was larger than he had supposed and his estimate for 1906 was Chinese $30 million.[4]   The evidence on which Morse relied was the fact that Russian statistics showed a much greater movement of goods from China than did the Chinese figures.

The corrections that Morse offered seem to have been taken over by other writers of the period before the Russian revolution.[5]   Coons has looked into the matter for later years and he estimated the annual average excess of exports for the period 1920–1923 at Chinese $10 million a year.[6]   A Russian writer upon the foreign trade of China made a detailed estimate for the year 1925 and reached the conclusion that "the volume of trade that escapes being recorded in the customs returns amounts in the aggregate to something like Chinese $60 million."[7]   Practically the whole of this trade he believed to be across the frontiers of Sinkiang and Mongolia.

The figures of Russian trade computed by the Birmingham Bureau of Research have been compared with Chinese trade statistics for the years 1926–1930.[8]   The comparison shows that the net movement of goods from China to Russia has usually been greater according to the Chinese statistics than according to the Russian statistics.   For 1930 we find that the Chinese statistics show a net movement of goods to Russia and the Russian statistics a net movement to China.

[4] *An Inquiry into the Commercial Liabilities and Assets of China in International Trade*, Shanghai, 1904, and *China and the Far East*, Clark University Lectures, New York, 1910, p. 107.

[5] See, C. S., *The Foreign Trade of China*, Studies in History, Economics and Public Law, Columbia University, Vol. LXXXVII, No. 199, 1919, p. 334, and Wagel, S. R., *Finance in China*, Shanghai, 1914, p. 473.

[6] Coons, A. G., *The Foreign Public Debt of China*, Philadelphia, 1926, p. 182.

[7] Marakueff, A. V., "China's Share in World Trade," *Capital and Trade*, Shanghai, August 12, 1927, p. 163.

[8] Birmingham Bureau of Research on Russian Economic Conditions, *Memorandum*, No. 2, Birmingham, 1931.

In view of the uncertainty of the figures I propose to disregard any unrecorded excess of exports across the land frontiers during the years 1914–1930, and to accept a figure of Chinese $20 million as the annual average for the years 1902–1913. The closeness of the relations between Mongolia and Russia in recent years takes away most of the significance for China of any trade which thus escapes attention.

Unrecorded Trade: Hongkong

Hongkong has long been a source of difficulty in dealing with Chinese trade statistics but the problem of unrecorded trade was of minor importance from 1889 to the enforcement of China's first national tariff in 1929. Higher rates than for 1929 came into effect in 1931, but the 1929 tariff was high enough to bring into existence a certain amount of smuggling. I found in Swatow in February, 1931, evidence that smuggling was important enough and efficient enough to have an effect upon legitimate business. No estimate can be made of the amount of this trade but it is safe to say that it reached a total by 1930 which must be measured in millions of Chinese dollars.

Among the unrecorded exports to Hongkong there is one item which may be estimated, the smuggling of gold from China. The Chinese government placed an embargo on the export of gold in May, 1930.[9] This was done during a period of falling silver. The history of China's trade shows that every considerable fall in silver, or rise in gold as the Chinese see it, has been accompanied by rapid increase in gold exports. The Chinese Customs statistics show an export of gold before the embargo to the value of about Chinese $25 million. The Hongkong statistics show a net export of gold to countries other than China to the value of Chinese $45 million for the period April to December, 1930, and an import of Chinese $50,000

[9] *Report on the Foreign Trade of China*, 1930, p. 73.

only from Chinese ports during the same period. How much of this gold came from China cannot be discovered but it is not unreasonable to suppose that it was at least half. Information secured at Swatow and at Amoy makes it certain that the total was by no means small. I propose to accept the sum of Chinese $22.5 million as an unrecorded export of gold in 1930.

The Valuation of Exports, 1928–1930

The next problem is the acceptability of the Customs figures showing the value in silver of the foreign trade of China. The conclusion, that exports from China are probably undervalued, rests upon the explanation, which I offer, of the facts first revealed by a study of the years 1928–1930. This explanation is, of course, tentative and subject to revision; but, if it is wrong, how are the facts to be explained?

The study of valuation during these recent years was undertaken because there is evidence, of a scattered and unrelated sort, that exports are undervalued. In 1913, while making inquiries at Tsingtao, I found a single firm that reported straw braid exports from Tsingtao in 1912 of a higher value than the total reported by the Customs on the whole trade of the port. At Swatow in February, 1931, the total export of oranges reported by the Customs was found to be quite inconsistent with information from the two Chinese firms of greatest importance in the trade with overseas Chinese. On both occasions I was informed that the Customs figures were far too small and that this is a matter of a common knowledge among the merchants. At Tientsin and in Manchuria furs are evidently either undervalued or unrecorded, or both.

Such information led to a series of conferences with officials of the Chinese National Tariff Commission at Shanghai. It was found impossible to test the valuation of the Customs by any general comparison with local market values. Price statistics are not available and there are numerous technical difficulties. The market makes distinctions of quality which are not to be found in the Customs reports. The units of measurement offer numerous difficulties. There was general agreement, however, that goods which pay specific duties are more likely to be incorrectly valued—which usually means undervalued, than those paying *ad valorem* duties, and it was found that a larger proportion of exports pay specific duties than of imports.[10]

The problem was then attacked by a different method. A comparison was undertaken of the total values of the goods entering into China's international trade as reported by the Chinese Customs and as reported in the official trade statistics of the chief foreign countries trading with China. The results of this method, applied to the three years 1928–1930, are the strongest reason for believing that Chinese Customs figures need correction.

The results of the comparison as applied to goods moving from China to foreign countries will be considered first. The figures for direct exports from China to the chief foreign countries were taken from the Chinese Customs reports and expressed in Chinese dollars. The imports from China into the various foreign countries were taken from the official trade reports of the various countries in foreign currencies and reduced to Chinese dollars.[11] Imports from Hongkong were excluded wherever possible, but this was not possible for Germany, France, and Italy. For goods moving from China the Chinese figure was taken as 100 and the foreign figures expressed as relatives,

[10] The imports and exports were distributed as follows in 1929:

Imports (Import tariff of 1929)		Exports (Export tariff of 1858)	
Duty free goods	8%	Duty free goods	2%
Specific duty goods	64%	Specific duty goods	81%
Ad valorem duty goods	28%	*Ad valorem* duty goods	17%
	100%		100%

[11] The exchange rates used were the equivalent of the Haikwan tael in foreign currencies, as reported by the Customs. The tael was taken at Chinese $1.50.

which will be referred to as the export indexes. The results for the three years are shown in the table which follows.

TABLE 22

EXPORT INDEXES FOR THE CHIEF COUNTRIES, 1928–1930

Direct Exports from China in Chinese Dollars = 100

	1928	1929	1930 *
Japan	110.0	106.6	142.0
United States	158.1	193.6	171.8
United Kingdom	132.1	123.4	166.9
British India	106.9	136.7	163.5
Germany	485.7	611.0	659.0
Dutch East Indies	89.9	95.2	133.5
France	129.0		143.1
Korea	109.1	133.3	149.8
Straits Settlements	123.2	154.1	
Italy	115.9	131.7	
French Indo-China	177.8	182.6	
Belgium	34.6		
Total	137.7	152.8	175.2

* Details for 1930 are shown in a table in the appendix to this chapter.

This means that for every Chinese $100 in goods which the Chinese statistics report as having been sent out, the foreign countries reported that they received Chinese $137.7 in 1928 and Chinese $175.2 in 1930. The figure for 1928 was high, this is one point; the percentage by which foreign values exceeded Chinese values doubled between 1928 and 1930, this is a second point. Concerning the first point, it may be said that an unknown amount of transit trade is involved, that is, trade through one country to another. This is obviously the case with Germany. But the general rise in the indexes over the three-year period is not easily explained away.

Further light is thrown on the situation by a study of the goods moving to China. The figures for the same countries have been dealt with in the same way, except that for goods moving to China the index numbers are based upon the foreign valuation which is taken as 100. The general import indexes for the three years are:

1928	104.7
1929	103.6
1930	97.2

This means that for every Chinese $100 which, according to foreign statistics, was sent to China in 1930, the Chinese report an import of Chinese $97.2, a relatively smaller import than for 1928. The import indexes are small and they have declined.

It is to be noted that the rise in the export index means that Chinese values declined in relation to foreign values over the three-year period. It is to be noted that the fall in the import index means, also, that Chinese values declined in relation to foreign valuation. In the case of exports the decline was many times as great but the direction was the same.

The outstanding general change of the period is the decline in silver. If the silver values reported by the Chinese Customs failed for any reason to change as silver fell, the result would be what we find. An export from China would then continue to be valued in silver at, say, Chinese $3 per unit by the Chinese Customs when, as a matter of fact, it entered the trade statistics of the United States at a higher value each year, taking into account the rise in the silver equivalent of the American dollar valuation.[12] An import into China would continue

---

[12] Chinese $3 happens to be about the price of marmot skins, an export to the United States. The Chinese valuation and the Chinese dollar equivalent of the American valuation were:

	Chinese Valuation	American Valuation
1928	2.67	3.86
1929	2.82	4.45
1930	2.16	3.39

In addition, the United States reported as imported from China in 1929 more marmot skins than China reported as exports to all countries. Among the imports into China from the United States, leaf tobacco may be mentioned as a commodity whose valuation per unit by the Chinese

to be valued at Chinese $100, when, as a matter of fact, its gold value called for a higher silver valuation. In such a lag of Chinese Customs valuations we have a possible explanation.

The more rapid rise in the export index is consistent with this explanation. The Customs valuation of Chinese commodities is more likely to be held stable of the inertia of custom than is the valuation of imports. There is also the fact that a larger proportion of exports pay specific duties.

THE VALUATION OF EXPORTS, 1902–1930

For the three years 1928–1930 we have found export indexes that run from 138 to 175, and import indexes that are around 100. Index numbers of the same sort have been calculated for the trade of China with three countries; Japan, the United Kingdom, and the United States, for the whole period from 1902 to 1930. These three countries account for about half of the foreign trade at all times during the period. The index numbers for exports are found, over this longer period, to be consistently higher than the corresponding import indexes. For the whole period the export index is 131.5, and the import index is 104.4. It is not unreasonable to find that the Chinese Customs statistics report Chinese $104 in goods as having been imported for every Chinese $100 which the other countries report as having been exported to China. The fact that Chinese exports of Chinese $100 can be reported by the receiving countries as imports of Chinese $131 requires explanation and is most readily explained by supposing that the Chinese figures undervalue exports from the country.

The uncertainties and possibilities of error in this method of testing Chinese valuations by foreign valuations are obviously great. The facts for the years 1928–

Customs rose less rapidly than did the silver equivalent of the American valuation.

1930 point so clearly to the necessity for correction that an attempt was not to be avoided. A direct comparison of Customs values of exports with market values in China could not be made.

The comparison of Chinese and foreign valuation was, therefore, carried back to 1902 with the result that we have further evidence consistent with the conclusion that exports are undervalued. This conclusion is supported by evidence from other fields and by opinions which are rather generally held by merchants in China.

In view of these facts I propose to make corrections of the export figures of the Chinese Customs reports by adding to the figures for the whole period 1902–1928, 5 per cent of the value of the exports, as reported. In view of the situation revealed by the study of the three years 1928–1930, the general correction is accepted for 1928, but it is increased for 1929 to 7½ per cent and for 1930 to 10 per cent. These corrections will, I believe, provide figures showing merchandise exports from China nearer than those of the Customs to the true value in silver of China's exports.

A NOTE ON EXPORT VALUES AND THE FALL OF SILVER

My object in this chapter has been to examine the Chinese trade statistics from the point of view of their acceptability in drawing up a balance of payments, I have not gone beyond this field but my results for the three years 1928–1930 lead to the conclusion that the undervaluation of Chinese exports was connected with the fall in silver during those years. We ought, if this is true, to find evidence of the same sort when we compare the export indexes for the period of high silver during the war with those for the period of declining silver since 1925. The gold price of silver, as is generally known, rose rapidly during the years 1916–1919 and the export index for the trade of the three countries, Japan, the

United Kingdom, and the United States, was as follows:

1916	112.5
1917	119.4
1918	116.2
1919	105.6

From 1925 to 1930 the fall in the gold price of silver was persistent and fairly rapid. Silver was worth U. S. $0.69 per ounce in 1925 and U. S. $0.38 per ounce in 1930. The export indexes for these years were as follows:

1925	125.5
1926	124.0
1927	143.6
1928	127.9
1929	134.9
1930	155.4

It is plain that the same difference which we found in the brief three-year period shows itself when we compare the war period with recent years. Foreign figures show a greater increase in exports from China, measured in silver dollars, than do the Chinese figures. If the explanation of this difference lies in the fact that the Chinese Customs valuations fail to adapt themselves to the true situation, then it follows that the exports from China, measured in silver, have increased more rapidly with falling silver than the Chinese figures indicate. This means that some of the effect of falling silver upon the foreign trade of China has been concealed by the Chinese Customs statistics.

If the foreign figures could be entirely trusted it could be demonstrated that in 1930 China exported as much as she imported. No such conclusion is tenable without convincing direct evidence. This problem must await an adequate examination of the relation between Customs valuations and the actual silver prices of export commodities in China. My work enables me to say no more than this, that the Chinese figures may conceal a stimulus to the Chinese export trade which has actually taken place.

APPENDIX

STATISTICS OF CHINESE TRADE

TABLE 23

THE MERCHANDISE TRADE OF CHINA

(In thousands of Chinese dollars)

The Haikwan tael is taken at Chinese $1.50

	Imports	Exports	Net Import
1902	473,046	321,273	151,773
1903	490,108	321,528	168,580
1904	516,091	359,230	156,861
1905	670,651	341,832	328,819
1906	615,405	354,685	260,720
1907	624,601	396,571	228,030
1908	591,757	414,990	176,767
1909	627,237	508,489	118,748
1910	694,447	571,249	123,198
1911	707,256	566,007	141,249
1912	709,645	555,780	153,865
1913	855,243	604,959	250,284
1914	853,861	534,340	319,521
1915	681,714	628,291	53,423
1916	774,407	722,695	51,712
1917	824,278	694,398	129,880
1918	832,339	728,824	103,515
1919	970,497	946,213	24,284
1920	1,143,375	812,446	330,929
1921	1,359,183	901,884	457,299
1922	1,417,575	982,338	435,237
1923	1,385,104	1,129,375	255,729
1924	1,527,316	1,157,676	369,640
1925	1,421,797	1,164,529	257,268
1926	1,686,331	1,296,442	389,889
1927	1,519,398	1,377,930	141,468
1928	1,793,953	1,487,032	306,921
1929	1,898,668	1,523,530	375,138
1930	1,964,634	1,342,264	622,370
1931	2,141,365	1,331,176	810,189
1932 (Jan.–May)	762,608	363,812	398,796

Average Annual Net Import for Periods

1902–1913			188,241
1914–1930			272,013

TABLE 24

NET MOVEMENT OF GOLD AND SILVER INTO AND OUT OF CHINA

(In thousands of Chinese dollars)

The Haikwan tael is taken at Chinese $1.50

	Gold		Silver	
	Net Import	Net Export	Net Import	Net Export
1902		14,115		20,766
1903	157			9,068
1904	12,669			20,414
1905	10,588			10,794
1906	5,760			28,016
1907	3,675			46,812
1908		17,276		18,400
1909		10,232	10,260	
1910		1,465	32,691	
1911	2,299		57,459	
1912	11,187		28,872	
1913		2,078	53,952	
1914		19,501		20,434
1915		26,088		27,573
1916	17,701			43,017
1917	13,270			31,474
1918		1,579	35,242	
1919	61,773		79,687	
1920		27,603	138,958	
1921		24,690	48,646	
1922	6,184		59,358	
1923		8,500	100,794	
1924		14,603	39,003	
1925		357	93,785	
1926		11,397	79,805	
1927		2,047	97,625	
1928	9,089		159,593	
1929		2,955	158,738	
1930		24,902	100,508	
1931		23,253	67,688	
1932 (Jan.–May)		22,973	22,043	

Annual Average Movement for Periods

	Gold		Silver	
1902–1913	97		2,413	
1914–1930		3,306	62,896	

TABLE 25

VALUES IN CHINESE AND FOREIGN TRADE STATISTICS OF GOODS MOVING
FROM CHINA TO FOREIGN COUNTRIES, 1930

Source: Official trade statistics and U. S. *Commerce Year Book*

(In millions)

Country	Chinese Statistics		Foreign Statistics			
	In Hk. Taels	In Ch. Dollars	In Foreign Currency	Equiva-lent of Foreign Unit, Ch. Dollars	In Ch. Dollars	Export Index. Ch. Figure = 100
Japan	216.6	324.8	Y. 283.1	1.63	461.4	142.0
United States	113.9	197.8	G. $104.3	3.26	339.9	171.8
Great Britain	62.7	94.0	£. 9.9	15.87	156.9	166.9
British India	17.0	25.5	G. $12.9	3.26	41.7	163.5
Germany	23.4	35.1	R. M. 297.7	0.78	231.3	659.0
Dutch E. Indies	11.7	17.6	Florins 18.0	1.31	23.5	133.5
France	42.7	64.0	G. $28.1	3.26	91.6	143.1
Korea	44.2	66.3	Y. 60.9	1.63	99.3	149.8
Totals	550.2	825.1			1,445.6	175.2

CHAPTER XII

THE CHINESE BALANCE OF PAYMENTS

The way has been cleared for a general statement of China's balance of international payments by the discussion of the major items in the preceding chapters. The general statement is now to be presented. The task must of necessity be somewhat complex and it may, therefore, be well to begin with a brief notice of what is to follow. In the first place, the major items in China's balance of payments are brought together to show a representative year for each of two periods, 1902–1913 and 1914–1930. This provides a broad view of the situation during the present century. It is followed by a presentation of the information concerning the minor items. They are known in detail for the three years 1928–1930 only, but all the information we have points to the conclusion that the minor items, taken together, have been important throughout the century. The next step is the presentation of all the available information for the three years 1928, 1929, and 1930. If China's international financial position is to be known, we cannot be satisfied with anything short of carefully compiled annual figures. In this study an attempt has been made to provide such figures. The detailed tables for the two periods since 1900 and for each of the three recent years are brought together in an appendix to this chapter where they may be consulted by those interested in knowing what lies behind the more general figures in the text. If this study may claim to have advanced our knowledge of China's balance of international payments, the claim rests chiefly upon the fact that business investments are given what is more nearly their rightful place and that an attempt has been made to separate the capital from the current items.

205

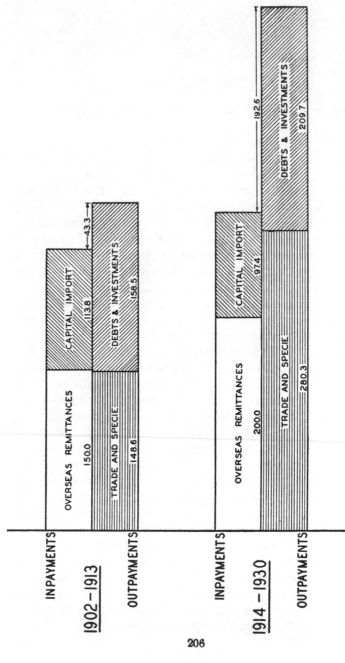

CHART 6.—MAJOR ITEMS IN THE CHINESE BALANCE OF INTERNATIONAL PAYMENTS BY PERIODS. THE FIGURES SHOW ANNUAL AVERAGES IN MILLIONS OF CHINESE DOLLARS

Data in Tables 27 and 28, pp. 220, 221

THE PERIOD 1902–1913 (TABLE 27)

The major items with which we have been concerned are: remittances from Chinese overseas, inpayments and outpayments on account of government debt and business investments and, finally, payments arising from merchandise trade and specie movements. Let us consider these items for a representative or average year during the period 1902–1913 without at the moment making any distinction between current and capital items. On the average, China received inpayments on account of overseas remittances at the rate of Chinese $150 million a year. She was required to pay out, on debt and investment, a net sum of Chinese $44.7 million a year and, in addition, a sum of Chinese $148.6 million on account of trade and specie movements. The outpayments for this first period were at the rate of Chinese $193.3 million and the inpayments at the rate of Chinese $150 million. This leaves what may be called an unexplained balance of Chinese $43.3 million on the outpayment side. How this was met we cannot say with any degree of certainty but our information concerning the minor items leads to the conclusion that they brought about a net inpayment.

Certain remittances to China from Japan and Russia in connection with the Russo-Japanese war are kept out of account. There is no doubt that the inpayments involved were fairly large but they came in under special circumstances and they may be neglected in an attempt to picture the general situation.

It is to be pointed out also that the movement of silver was toward China during this period, though it was extremely small. There was, indeed, a considerable period 1902–1908, during which the movement of silver was away from China (Table 24), but the net import during the later years was sufficiently large to bring an average net import of Chinese $2.4 million.

Let me now return to the major items for this early

period and present them in such a way as to bring out the place and importance of the capital items. China, it may be said, had current inpayments of $150 million coming in during the years 1902–1913 on remittances from Chinese overseas. She had, at the same time, to make current outpayments on loan service and business profits which our estimates put at Chinese $158.5 million a year. In addition, current outpayments were required to cover the net import of merchandise and specie at the rate of Chinese $148.6 million a year. Setting the current payments in and out against each other, we arrive at a net outpayment on current items of Chinese $157.1 million a year.

The Chinese economy had this net payment of Chinese $157.1 million to make for a representative year during the period 1902–1913. It is to be supposed that this sum indicates the rate at which the Chinese economy was going into debt or receiving payments from abroad on new business investments. When we turn to the capital items we find that there was a net inpayment at the average rate of Chinese $113.8 million. The current outpayments involved a capital import at this rate. But there remains the sum of Chinese $43.3 million, the unexplained difference, which was required each year and which was not covered by capital imports or by any other inpayments which are known. It is undoubtedly true that the unexplained difference would be considerably reduced if we had adequate information about the minor items in the balance of payments. Morse estimated for 1903 that the minor items brought a net inpayment and the estimates for the three years 1928–1930, which are presented below, lead to the same conclusion.

The Period 1914–1930 (Table 28)

During the more recent years of the second period we find the following situation. It is to be borne in mind that this first statement does not involve any distinction between capital and current items. China received from abroad inpayments of Chinese $200 million a year in the form of remittances from Chinese overseas. Net outpayments were required at the rate of Chinese $112.3 million on debts and investments and at the rate of Chinese $280.3 million on merchandise trade and specie. The unexplained difference thus comes to no less than Chinese $192.6 million a year.

A greater unexplained difference than for the earlier period did not, it is to be noted, involve any loss of silver. The flow of silver was toward China and at a much more rapid rate than during the earlier period. The annual average net import of silver was Chinese $62.9 million. What is more, an examination of the tables showing trade and specie movements (Tables 23 and 24) reveals the fact that silver frequently flowed toward China in unusual amounts during the very years when the excess of merchandise imports was greatest. The movement of silver offers no hope of an easy solution of the difficulties presented by the Chinese balance of international payments. There is reason to believe, as is pointed out below, that the years 1930 and 1931 show a change from the earlier situation.[1]

Let us turn to a re-examination of the situation during the years 1913–1930, applying now the distinction between current and capital items. The first of the major items, remittances from Chinese overseas, shows current inpayments to the amount of Chinese $200 million a year. Government obligations and investments required current outpayments to the amount of Chinese $209.7 million. On

[1] Two interesting comments on China's excess of imports are brought together in my *Readings in Economics for China*, Shanghai, 1926, pp. 389–90. A Chinese official of 1833 complained that the "treasure of the land" was flowing forth "to feed the cupidity of barbarians." The reformer Tan Sze-tong is reported to have said: "Though the balance of trade should be against China, it is still to her advantage to keep up the trade, for in that case the Westerners would supply economic wants which must be satisfied and would receive in return only money, which by itself cannot appease hunger nor quench thirst." As a matter of fact China receives both the goods and the silver.

merchandise trade and specie movements there was a current outpayment of Chinese $280.3 million for an average year. We find from these figures that the current items called for net outpayments from China at the rate of Chinese $290 million a year for the period now being considered.

We turn to the capital items to find that the average inpayments on this account were smaller than for the earlier period. They came to no more than Chinese $97.4 million a year. This brings us back once more to the unexplained difference of Chinese $192.6 million a year.

The estimates for the three years 1928–1930 enable us to say, as was said for the earlier period, that the minor items greatly reduce this unexplained difference. These minor items for the three recent years are dealt with in the section which follows. When the estimates of these minor items have been made and the more detailed balances of payments for these recent years have been presented, the discussion is brought back to the general problem presented by China's excess of imports.

The Minor Items

The first of the minor items is that of inpayments for military and naval purposes, that is, for the maintenance of foreign troops on Chinese soil and of foreign naval vessels in Chinese waters. My total of this item is considerably larger than is that of other students.[2] My figures are the result of an original estimate and a careful check after I found my figure to be high. The foreign troops in China in the spring of 1931 were: Japanese 12,600, British 7,150 (including Hongkong), American 2,800, French 1,950, Portuguese 1,500, and Italian 450. There were about the usual numbers between 1927 and the autumn of

---

[2] Morse estimated this item at Chinese $33.7 million in 1903, Wagel and See at Chinese $43.5 in 1912 and 1913 and Coons put the average at Chinese $53 million for 1920–1923, in studies which have been referred to above.

1931, and they are considerably higher than during the years before 1927. In addition the Japanese had 15,000 in Shantung between May and December, 1928, and, of these, 6,500 remained in China until May, 1929. For estimates as to the expenditure in China there was a considerable amount of information. The Japanese railway guards in Manchuria are reported to have cost the Japanese government from 6 to 11 million yen a year in recent years.[3] The British troops in China have involved expenditures of about £1.3 million.[4] The total expenditure by the American government cannot have been less than U. S. $2.5 million. The remaining troops probably involved expenditures no greater than the American.[5] The total must have been close to Chinese $45 million for 1930, and there must be additions to this total maintenance of a larger number of Japanese soldiers in 1928 and 1929.

The naval vessels of all sorts in Chinese waters, in the spring of 1931, included British 44 (about half at Hongkong), American 36, Japanese 20, and others 15. Careful estimates were made of the expenditure on the maintenance of selected British and American vessels. An allowance was made for the fact that additional vessels are usually in Chinese waters during the summer months. An estimate of Chinese $60 million was found reasonable for 1930. Taking military and naval expenditure together, my estimates are Chinese $139.7 million for 1928, Chinese $124 million for 1929, and Chinese $100 million for 1930.

The second item is an annual inpayment by mission societies and for philanthropic and educational purposes. The sum reported to me by the various American societies, as having been remitted to China for 1928, was U. S.

[3] Japanese Investments in China, pp. 487–88.
[4] North China Daily News, April 15, 1931. Pay is said to amount to half a million and some of this must be deducted.
[5] Half the French soldiers were natives of French Indo-China and a certain number of the Portuguese soldiers were from Africa.

$7,696,277.[6] Remittances to China by Catholic socie-
ties, and by the Propaganda Fidei, other than the direct
remittances of the American societies, I estimate to have
been Chinese $4 million in recent years.[7] Protestant so-
cieties in England and on the Continent of Europe account for at least Chinese $7 million. Certain Japanese
items have been estimated at Yen 6 million for recent
years, but Yen 4 million of this represents the contribution of the Japanese government to the funds of the local
government of the Kwantung leased area[8] and is included under remittances for diplomatic and consular
services. The Japanese remittances for cultural and philanthropic purposes I put at 2 or 3 million yen in recent
years. In addition the China International Famine Relief
Commission has reported to me donations from abroad to
the amount of Chinese $336,000 in 1928, Chinese $1,400,-
000 in 1929, and Chinese $1,430,000 in 1930. Allowance
must be made for the fall in silver, for the fact that remittances to China for mission purposes were below normal
in 1928, after the disturbances of 1927, and for the effects
of the world depression. Taking everything into account, I
arrive at an estimated inpayment for mission and philanthropic purposes of Chinese $25 million for 1928, Chinese
$30 million for 1929, and Chinese $40 million for 1930.

The remittances to China for tourists and travelers
was estimated after a study in Shanghai and after consultation with Japanese and American officials. I include
with this an estimate of the expenditure in China of the
crews of ocean-going merchant vessels and for repairs
to such vessels.[9] My totals for the three years come to

[6] American Investments in China, p. 307.
[7] It must be added that Catholic mission organizations have an income
from property owned in China which I estimate at twice the amount of
the remittances. In addition to the Propaganda Fidei, the chief remittances are through the Society of Peter the Apostle, and the Society of
the Blessed Infancy.
[8] Japanese Investments in China, p. 547.
[9] I exclude expenditures in connection with all ships reported under
business investments in China.

Chinese $25, 25, and 35 million. There is a final item for
diplomatic and consular offices in China which has been
estimated for me by a number of well-informed persons
working independently. My final estimates are Chinese
$30, 32, and 38 million under this heading.

Turning to outpayments I find the largest among the
minor items to be a net payment abroad for insurance
which was estimated by a number of men in this business in Shanghai to come to a net sum for the three years
of Chinese $15 million for the earlier years and Chinese
$20 million for 1930. Remittances for Chinese students
abroad and for Chinese travelers may be fairly closely
guessed. The number of such students on the average was
probably between 4,000 and 4,500. There were about
1,000 in Europe, 1,200 in the United States, and 2,000 in
Japan.[10] I estimate remittances for their use at Chinese
$6, 6, and 8 million. The Ministry of Foreign Affairs of the
Chinese government reported to me expenditures on Chinese consular and diplomatic offices abroad of Chinese
$4.4 million in 1929. I have accepted this sum for 1928 as
well, and increased it to Chinese $5 million for 1930. Re-
mittances by foreign professional men in China I was able
to estimate separately at Chinese $.5 million in 1928 and
1929 and at Chinese $1 million in 1930. Finally, there is
an item of Chinese $8 million, which is an estimate by
well-informed persons of the remittances from China of
motion picture royalties to the United States in 1930.

Taking the minor items together, we find them to be
as follows:[11]

	1928	1929	1930
Inpayments	224.7	216.0	218.0
Outpayments	25.9	25.9	42.0
Net Inpayments	198.8	190.1	176.0

[10] Reports from the Ministry of Education of the Chinese Government
(*North China Daily News*, Shanghai, April 12, 1931) from the World's
Chinese Students Federation, in Shanghai, and from the International
Institute of Education of New York, have been consulted.

[11] The details are shown in the tables for the three years in the appendix
to this chapter.

We are now prepared to turn to the examination of the international payments for the three years with estimates of the inpayments on minor items. Such estimates were not available when the totals for the two periods were presented.

THE BALANCE OF PAYMENTS FOR THE YEARS 1928, 1929, AND 1930

The three years 1928–1930 bring into sharp relief certain of the problems which China faces today and throw light upon the difficulties encountered in any effort to arrive at a satisfactory balance of payments for China. Leaving aside the details shown in the tables at the end of this chapter, I offer the following as a convenient condensed statement.

TABLE 26

CHINA'S BALANCE OF INTERNATIONAL PAYMENTS, 1928–1930

	1928	1929	1930
Current inpayments to China were:			
On overseas remittances	250.6	280.7	316.3
On minor items, as shown above	198.8	190.1	176.0
Current outpayments were required:			
On debts and investments	242.0	277.6	309.4
On trade and specie	401.3	416.6	541.2
Net outpayments on current items were thus:	193.9	223.4	358.3
Capital items brought:			
Inpayments on debt and investment	100.0	170.0	202.0
Leaving an unexplained difference of:	93.9	53.4	156.3

Here we have a more complete picture than it was possible to make of the whole period, but the broad outlines are the same. The chief current net inpayments into China were, as they have been since 1902, remittances from overseas Chinese. Every other item showing

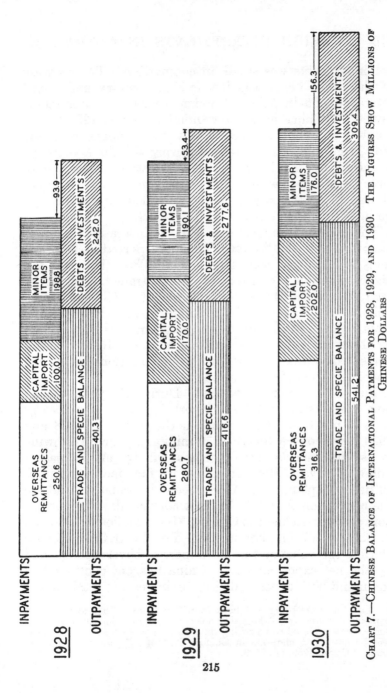

INPAYMENTS

1928

OVERSEAS REMITTANCES 250.6 | CAPITAL IMPORT 100.0 | MINOR ITEMS 198.8 | 93.9

OUTPAYMENTS

TRADE AND SPECIE BALANCE 401.3 | DEBTS & INVESTMENTS 242.0

INPAYMENTS

1929

OVERSEAS REMITTANCES 280.7 | CAPITAL IMPORT 170.0 | MINOR ITEMS 190.1 | 53.4

OUTPAYMENTS

TRADE AND SPECIE BALANCE 416.6 | DEBTS & INVESTMENTS 277.6

INPAYMENTS

1930

OVERSEAS REMITTANCES 316.3 | CAPITAL IMPORT 202.0 | MINOR ITEMS 176.0 | 156.3

OUTPAYMENTS

TRADE AND SPECIE BALANCE 541.2 | DEBTS & INVESTMENTS 309.4

CHART 7.—CHINESE BALANCE OF INTERNATIONAL PAYMENTS FOR 1928, 1929, AND 1930. THE FIGURES SHOW MILLIONS OF CHINESE DOLLARS

Data in Tables 29, 30, 31, pp. 221, 222

net inpayments was small in comparison. The greatest of the other items was for foreign military and naval establishments in China. Foreign troops have been maintained in China in greater numbers since 1927, as is pointed out above. The overseas remittances were not only large, but they increased during the three years, as is shown by the Hongkong investigation. There may have been a decline in remittances from Chinese laborers abroad in 1930 but remittances of business income and for investment increased.[12]

The excess of imports over exports increased. The net import of merchandise into China as reported by the Customs was Chinese $622.4 million in 1930. This was the highest figure in the history of China's trade but the figure for 1931 reached the remarkable height of Chinese $810.2 million. It may be that a complete knowledge of the facts would lead to a greater adjustment of this item than has been made in the preceding chapter. In any case I am satisfied that a part of the explanation lies in the undervaluation of China's exports.

But there is more to be said. During the years we are now considering, the net import of silver was greater than it has been at any time in the past. In 1928 and 1929 it was over Chinese $150 million a year. A growing excess of imports was accompanied by an increasing inflow of silver. Here, it seems, we face increasing difficulties of explanation. More recent information leads to the conclusion that this has not continued. The net import of silver declined to Chinese $100.5 million in 1930 and to Chinese $67.7 million in 1931. For the first five months of 1932 the value of the net import of silver was covered by the net export of gold. China has not continued to command both goods and silver in increasing total values.

---

[12] Laborers were being sent back from Singapore in 1930 and employment in Siam and Indo-China was not easily found. Chinese laborers in Borneo were reported to be asking the Chinese government for assistance. See the note on Emigration in Chinese Customs, *Report on the Foreign Trade of China*, 1930, pp. 75–6.

The outpayments to meet interest charges on the obligations of the Chinese government were undoubtedly growing. The information on this point must be accepted as quite certain. The current outpayments on business investments have increased somewhat in silver, which means a falling off in terms of gold currencies. These outpayments, it will be remembered, were found to be consistent with Japanese estimates of inpayments into Japan under this head.

The net inpayments on the various minor items have been large, but they have been found to decline over the three years. It may be that complete knowledge would increase the net inpayment somewhat, but the total error here cannot be large.

Looking back at Table 26 we see that the current payments in and out show an increasing deficit over the three years. Against these deficits we may set the inpayments which have resulted from the import of capital into China. They have been estimated at increasing amounts over the three years. In 1928 they covered over half the deficit on current account and in 1929 more than three-fourths.

The study of the three years, with the inclusion of the minor items, reduces the "unexplained difference" to modest proportions for the years 1928 and 1929. The year 1930, however, shows a great increase in outpayments on trade and specie, a resulting increase in net outpayments on current items, and a relatively small increase in inpayments on capital items. This means that the unexplained difference is much greater for 1930 than for 1929. The silver movement gives reason for believing that the situation changed in 1930; and all the known figures for 1931 lead to the conclusion that the excess of imports has been great enough to check the inflow of silver. No doubt the general explanation for the shift is to be found in the effects of the world depression.

Foodstuffs and raw materials have fallen in price during the depression more rapidly than have finished products. This means that the terms of trade have tended to move against the raw material producing countries.[13] China has been no exception and there is little doubt that she has given up an increasing quantity of her products for the same quantity of foreign goods.[14] A shift of this sort in the terms of trade helps to explain the fact that China has had greater outpayments to make in recent years, but it does not help to explain how she has made them, which is our immediate problem.

It is possible that the inpayments on capital account are too small. Japanese business investments in Manchuria during 1929 and 1930 may have been larger than they have been estimated, but it is difficult to believe that the error here has been great. It is the opinion of a foreign business man in China that most students have overlooked a considerable item among the inpayments indicated by the losses sustained by foreign business houses in China. There is no doubt that this item is of some significance, but it cannot be measured and does not assist in the explanation of the situation during 1930 and 1931.

It is more reasonable to look for an explanation in some factor which is directly associated with the fall in silver which has accompanied the increasing excess of imports of recent years. It has been suggested that the foreign firms with offices in China and abroad import goods into China when silver is falling, and that payment on these goods is postponed in the hope that silver will rise. This may be carried further. During a period of falling silver, outpayments, in general, tend to be postponed by the

[13] As is pointed out by Professor Ohlin in the *Course and Phases of the World Economic Depression*, Geneva, 1931, p. 82. See pp. 75–80 for the figures showing the price movements.
[14] Professor Franklin Ho has carried his calculations, published in *Problems of the Pacific, 1929*, to later years in a publication of the Nankai University Institute of Economics. J. B. Condliffe refers in his *China Today: Economic*, Boston, 1932, p. 185, to a similar calculation by W. L. Holland.

hope that silver will rise. I have found evidence of this in a variety of cases. Such postponements is really the creation of a short-term debt for speculative reasons. This means that something ought to be added to the inpayments for 1930 under such a heading as "short-term debts" or "deferred obligations in gold currencies." It is difficult to believe that such an item accounts for a large sum, but obligations which come into existence as the direct result of the fall in silver, may be larger than I have supposed them to be after some attempts to secure information. These are but suggestions as to the possible explanation of the situation year by year which has been made puzzling by the course of events in 1930 and 1931. No adequate account of the course of events over such short periods is possible without a study on a much more ambitious scale than the one I have been able to make. Without an adequate study of this sort, the current situation cannot be known.

Whatever difficulties may appear when we examine the changes year by year, it is nevertheless true that the study of the three years 1928–1930 makes the general situation more understandable. There is no doubt that the items, which have been grouped together as of minor importance, bring in current net inpayments on a considerable scale and carry us a considerable way toward our solution of the problem of China's balance of payments. If the earlier years are viewed after a study of the payments in and out, as they are shown for 1929, we do not seem far from a satisfactory answer. The true outlines of the picture are shown. China has depended upon remittances from abroad, upon new investments by foreigners, and upon a group of minor items to pay for her net imports of goods and silver.

The year 1930, and undoubtedly the year 1931 as well, show new difficulties. In part, these may be explained away as due to an undervaluation of exports. But they seem to show a real shift which has reduced the inflow of silver and, no doubt, they are evidence that the world depression made itself felt in China during these years.

APPENDIX

DETAILED TABLES SHOWING BALANCES OF INTERNATIONAL PAYMENTS FOR CHINA

TABLE 27

MAJOR ITEMS IN THE BALANCE OF PAYMENTS FOR THE PERIOD 1902–1913

(In millions of Chinese dollars)

Outpayments		Inpayments	
Current items		*Current items*	
Government debt	89.2	Overseas remittances	150.0
Business investments	69.3	Unrecorded land frontier	
Merchandise imports	631.3	trade	20.0
Gold and silver imports		Merchandise exports	443.0
(net)	2.5	Correction of exports (5%)	22.2
Total	792.3	Total	635.2
		Capital items	
		Loans of the Chinese government	61.0
		New business investments	52.8
		Total	113.8

Net outpayments on current items	157.1
Inpayments on capital items	113.8
Unexplained difference	43.3

TABLE 28

MAJOR ITEMS IN THE BALANCE OF PAYMENTS FOR THE PERIOD 1914–1930
(In millions of Chinese dollars)

Outpayments		Inpayments	
Current items		Current items	
Government debt	70.9	Overseas remittances	200.0
Business investments	138.8	Gold exports (net)	3.3
Merchandise imports	1,297.3	Merchandise exports	1,025.3
Silver imports (net)	62.9	Correction of exports (5%)	51.3
Total	1,569.9	Total	1,279.9
		Capital items	
		Loans of the Chinese government	23.8
		New business investments	73.6
		Total	97.4

Net outpayments on current items	290.0	
Inpayments on capital items	97.4	
Unexplained difference	192.6	

TABLE 29

BALANCE OF PAYMENTS, 1928
(In millions of Chinese dollars)

Outpayments		Inpayments	
Current items		Current items	
Government debt	63.0	Overseas remittances	250.6
Business investments	179.0	Merchandise exports	1,487.0
Merchandise imports	1,794.0	Correction of exports	74.4
Gold and silver imports (net)	168.7	Tourist trade	30.0
		Mission and philanthropic remittances	25.0
Travelers and students abroad	6.0	Diplomatic and consular offices in China	30.0
Diplomatic and consular offices abroad	4.4	Foreign military and naval establishments	139.7
Remittances by foreigners in China—professional classes	0.5	Total	2,036.7
Insurance	15.0	Capital items	
Total	2,230.6	Sale of domestic securities to Chinese overseas	4.0
		New business investments	96.0
		Total	100.0

Net outpayment on current items	193.9	
Inpayment on capital items	100.0	
Unexplained difference	93.9	

TABLE 30

BALANCE OF PAYMENTS, 1929

(In millions of Chinese dollars)

Outpayments		*Inpayments*	
Current items		*Current items*	
Government debt	79.1	Overseas remittances	280.7
Business investments	198.5	Gold exports (net)	3.0
Silver imports (net)	158.7	Merchandise exports	1,523.5
Merchandise imports	1,898.7	Correction of exports	
		(7½%)	114.3
Travelers and students		Tourist trade	30.0
abroad	6.0	Mission and philanthropic	
Diplomatic and consular		remittances	30.0
offices abroad	4.4	Diplomatic and consular	
Remittances by foreign-		offices in China	32.0
ers in China—profes-		Foreign military and na-	
sional classes	0.5	val establishments	124.0
Insurance	15.0	Total	2,137.5
Total	2,360.9		
		Capital items	
		New business investments	170.0

Net outpayments on current items	223.4
Inpayments on capital items	170.0
Unexplained difference	53.4

TABLE 31

BALANCE OF PAYMENTS, 1930

(In millions of Chinese dollars)

Outpayments		*Inpayments*	
Current items		*Current items*	
Government debt	111.4	Overseas remittances	316.3
Business investments	198.0	Gold exports (net re-	
Silver imports (net)	100.5	corded)	24.9
Merchandise imports	1,964.6	Unrecorded gold export	22.5
		Merchandise exports	1,342.3
Travelers and students		Correction of exports	
abroad	8.0	(10%)	134.2
Diplomatic and consular		Tourist trade	40.0
offices abroad	5.0	Mission and philanthropic	
Remittances by foreign-		remittances	40.0
ers in China—profes-		Diplomatic and consular	
sional classes	1.0	offices in China	38.0
Insurance	20.0	Foreign military and na-	
Motion picture royalties	8.0	val establishments	100.0
Total	2,416.5	Total	2,058.2
		Capital items	
		New business investments	202.0

Net outpayments on current items	358.3
Inpayments on capital items	202.0
Unexplained difference	156.3

CHAPTER XIII

THE INTERNATIONAL ECONOMIC POSITION
OF CHINA

Chinese Holdings Abroad and Foreign Investments in China

The international economic position of China may now be reviewed as it has been revealed in two connected, but different, sets of statistics. The whole of the second part of this work and a group of early chapters in this first part have been devoted to an estimate of the foreign obligations of the Chinese government and of the business investments of foreigners in China. This total of debt and investments was, of necessity, reached by methods which made it impossible to distinguish between holdings that bring about annual outpayments from China and those which do not. Now that the outpayments have been examined, it is possible to view these holdings somewhat differently and more nearly as they should be viewed, if China's international position is to be understood.

In the earlier chapters it was said that foreign investments in China came to certain totals in American dollars in 1902, 1914, and 1931. They are today about U. S. $3,300 million, and business investments account for about U. S. $2,500 million of the total. The business investments include, in so far as the total is correct, a fair valuation of all foreign holdings which may reasonably be put under this heading. In arriving at a total of business investments we used foreign ownership as our test. We are now in a position to view these foreign holdings as they are reflected in the current outpayments from

China. However much the foreigner may own in China, his effective holdings from the point of view of China's international position were such as to bring outpayments of Chinese $148.5 million, during an average year in the period 1902–1913, and outpayments at the rate of Chinese $209.7 million, during an average year in the period 1914–1930.

When foreign investment in China is viewed from this angle it becomes possible to make a comparison with the item which we have found to be of outstanding importance at all times among the inpayments, remittances from Chinese overseas. It is to be remembered, concerning these remittances, that they are in large part remittances resting upon business holdings abroad by Chinese families. It is true that remittances from laborers abroad play a part of some importance, but, generally speaking, remittances from overseas Chinese to China are income from property and the profits of going business concerns.

A complete total of Chinese holdings abroad has, no doubt, never been made, and, even if it could be made, it would be found to be less closely related to China's international payments than in the case of foreign holdings in China. There are foreign holdings in Harbin and in Shanghai which mean no outpayments at all from China, but the proportion of Chinese holdings in San Francisco or Rangoon, which mean outpayments to China, is probably smaller. I have undertaken to secure estimates from different centers as to the proportion of the Chinese residents whose connection with their homeland is such that funds are sent back. The Chinese in Formosa, as has been pointed out, are at home and make practically no remittances to China. Many Chinese in the United States no longer maintain close enough relations with China to bring about remittances. On the other hand, I have a report from a bank in Singapore which puts the proportion as high as 50 per cent of the Chinese in that community. A bank in the Philippines reports that 60 per cent of the Chinese send remittances. One bank in a small center reports a percentage as high as 95. We do not know the total of Chinese holdings abroad, but we do know that they were great enough, with remittances from Chinese laborers, to bring into China about Chinese $150 million a year during 1902–1913, and about Chinese $200 million a year during 1914–1930.

The sums which China has paid out on investments in China have been about equal to the sums which she has received in overseas remittances. Let us look at this more closely. Table 27 shows that China had current outpayments to make on business investments of Chinese $69.3 million during 1902–1913. On that part of the government debt which was for railways and communications, she had outpayments to make of about Chinese $33 million. Taking the two together, we find that China made outpayments on business investments and railway obligations to the amount of Chinese $102 million. During the same years she received remittances of Chinese $150 million from overseas. It is a guess, but one with some foundation, that property and business holdings abroad brought in two-thirds of this sum. By these steps we reach the conclusion that Chinese holdings abroad were of about the same magnitude as foreign holdings in China, counting, in both cases, only such holdings as occasioned in- and outpayments.

Consider the situation during the second period. We now find overseas remittances of Chinese $200 million a year. The business investments of foreigners in China brought outpayments from China of Chinese $138.8 million (Table 28). The outpayments on railway obligations were about Chinese $26 million on the average. We now find that the total for these two items was about Chinese $165 million. We may guess once more that remittances to China on Chinese business holdings abroad came to at least Chinese $133 million. The remittances cannot be capitalized, as this comparison may imply, but, if this could be done, we would find the Chinese to have holdings abroad as great as the foreign property which produced outpayments from China. It is not improbable that, on balance, China was a creditor country in the period before the World War, and it is quite certain that she is far from being a debtor country today to the extent that a total foreign investment of U. S. $3,300 million indicates.

Traditional China had in the family a powerful unit, and through the family the Chinese have built up a patrimony overseas which requires that we drastically alter the picture of China's international economic position derived from a study of foreign holdings within the country. The Chinese colony abroad must not be permitted to escape our general picture. It has many aspects of interest and importance. It presents racial and social, as well as economic, problems. With a rising nationalism in China and elsewhere in the East, it may be a political problem of the future. But the economic fact of the present is that the Chinese colony abroad brings into the Chinese economy about as much as the foreign colony in China with its investments causes to be sent out.

SOUTH CHINA, MANCHURIA, AND THE YANGTZE VALLEY

A single statement of China's net investment position is too simple to fit the complex facts. The area in China which is in touch with world trade and economic relations may be divided into three parts on the basis of the information concerning investments and overseas remittances. This division is supported and confirmed by the trade statistics of the three regions.

The first of these is South China, a creditor region. South China holds abroad greater sources of income than the foreigner holds within her territory. South China lives upon returns from foreign holdings as truly as does England. If the term *rentier* may be applied to any region in the world, it fits the coast of China, south of Foochow

and Amoy. The trade statistics show that the chief ports
of southern China have an excess of imports in recent
years in their direct trade with foreign countries of about
Chinese $50 million. In their total trade, both Chinese
and foreign, they have an excess of imports of about
Chinese $150 million. Remittances from overseas have
enabled them to pay for goods from abroad and from
elsewhere in China.

At the other extreme stands Manchuria, a debtor region
on a considerable scale. Into Manchuria have flowed
investments from Russia and Japan and in recent years a
stream of Chinese settlers from the great plain to the
south. Manchuria is a "new" country but her development has now gone so far that she shows an increasing
excess of exports in recent years. The total of this export
balance is about Chinese $100 million. The excess of
exports in the total trade of Manchuria including her
trade with the rest of China is about the same. In other
words, Manchuria's excess of exports goes abroad. It is
directly associated with the large foreign investments in
the region.

The region which lies between Manchuria and the
south occupies an intermediate position in the field of
trade, and in the field of investment also. The Yangtze
valley is of outstanding importance. Foreign investment
is greater in Shanghai than elsewhere in China, but the
resources and development of the Yangtze valley give
it sources of income which Manchuria does not have. The
Yangtze valley has, in recent years, had a great excess of
imports in its direct trade with foreign countries. For the
chief ports this has run as high as Chinese $300 million a
year. The statistics of the whole trade of these ports are
less significant for our purposes than for the other regions [1]
but they show a reduction in the excess of imports from

[1] I have used the Chinese Customs reports and have compared the
"value of the Direct Foreign Trade of Each Port" with the "value of the
whole Trade of Each Port" for selected ports. There is probably more
interport trade within the Yangtze valley than within the other regions.

Chinese $300 million to less than Chinese $100 million. The Yangtze valley has an excess of exports in its trade with the southern ports of China. By these currents of trade within China the sums remitted to the southern ports reach the Yangtze valley and become available to pay for its great excess of imports from abroad.

The trade statistics carry with them evidence that estimates of overseas remittances are not unreasonable and indicate that the effect of China's international economic relations may be traced in the trade balances of the chief geographical regions of the country.

CHAPTER XIV

CONCLUSION

Foreign investment in China has been examined in the preceding pages from a variety of angles. Familiar generalizations have been confirmed and some less familiar have been brought out. It is well known that foreign investment in China is recent; it is less well known that it was at a more rapid rate before the European war than in recent years. It is well known that Great Britain was of first importance in the early days; it is less well known that she stood above all others in 1914 and that she is still the holder of investments somewhat greater than those of the Japanese. The importance of Shanghai and Manchuria have been generally recognized, but it is not known that investment in Shanghai has been growing more rapidly in recent years, even from the point of view of the Japanese.

The importance of overseas remittances has been emphasized and they have been shown to be mainly returns upon Chinese business holdings abroad. The control by foreign governments of certain great corporations owning business investments in China has been observed. The railways of Manchuria are the outstanding example. It happens, also, in both the Japanese and Russian cases that funds were originally borrowed in third countries for investment in China.

The central economic problem of modern times for every country is the standard of living of its people. If this is true for countries in the West, it is doubly true for China. It seems to me no exaggeration to say that the most important economic problem of the world at the present time lies in the poverty of the mass of the Chinese

229

people. No one can doubt that it is China's chief problem. Its effects are felt, not only in the domestic affairs of China, but in her international relations as well. We may, whenever we face interrelated difficulties, adopt the device of the vicious circle. So we may point out, concerning China, that political security is not possible without economic, and that economic security, in turn, depends upon political.

Any rise in the standard of living of the mass of the Chinese people must be accompanied and supported by better and more plentiful capital equipment. The inadequacy of China's railway system is obvious and her industrial development is slight. It is not maintained that modern industry will bring an immediate rise in living standards. The population of China may have adapted itself so completely to a given economic situation that any change must mean loss and suffering for considerable groups. Nor do I suppose that capital equipment will raise standards of living without changes in other fields, of which the most important are the control of population, and the application of science to agriculture. But without modern capital equipment to support it, a rising standard of living in China is hardly possible.

This capital equipment cannot be provided by China. The available capital was, no doubt, insufficient before 1911, and the events since 1911 have destroyed capital equipment and have decreased any surplus at the disposal of the Chinese people. Here again it is necessary to qualify. The Chinese people themselves have capital which is not now made available, and railways under favorable conditions have provided considerable funds for extension and new construction. But the capital for the modern industrial equipment must come very largely from abroad.

The capital has been available in the capital exporting countries of the West throughout the century, except for the period of the World War. It has been available at rates well below the rates of interest that have prevailed in China. Why has it not gone to China? Why do we not find a Chinese economy which has been, or is being, made over more rapidly into an adequate means of livelihood for the Chinese people?

CAPACITY TO RECEIVE

The general answer to this question lies in the principle of capacity to receive. The flow of capital to a country in China's position depends upon the capacity of such a country to accept capital and put it to use. The checks and hindrances to the flow of capital lie in China rather than in the capital exporting countries. The effective limitations are on the demand rather than the supply side. It must be borne in mind that we are considering not funds for an impecunious general or for a weak and unpopular government, but for the economic development of the country.

The ultimate limitations upon the flow of capital to China may lie in the lack of natural resources in the country. The resources of China, as has been shown in an earlier chapter, are more modest than was supposed in the past, but they are great enough to support a considerable development. The reason for the inadequacy of China's transportation facilities, for example, does not lie in her lack of natural resources.

The limitations upon the movement of capital to China which lie in the social organization and the traditions of the Chinese people are of more immediate importance. China has offered a passive resistance to the penetration of foreign trade, foreign ideas, and foreign capital. These checks upon the flow of capital lie in the nature of the traditional organization of China which has been presented in an introductory chapter. The power of the family was such as to make it difficult to create other loyalties. The guild exercised a confining and narrowing influence upon industry. Banks were little concerned with the provision of capital for industrial activity. China was a series of peasant villages in which wealth was thought of in terms of land and consumers' goods. Into such a community modern capital can penetrate with the greatest difficulty.

BUSINESS INVESTMENTS AND GOVERNMENT BORROWINGS

Under the conditions which have existed in China the chief form of foreign investment has been direct investment by foreign firms and corporations. This form of investment is usually supposed to be completely dependent upon extraterritoriality and the whole set of legal arrangements under which the foreigner lives in China. I have undertaken to show that it rests also upon certain facts in the economic life and organization of China. The problems presented by this form of investment are separable from those of extraterritoriality and the existence of the two sets of problems should be recognized in the field of policy.

Direct business investment is investment by and through the foreign "colonies" in China, and it has carried with it the limitations set around these colonies. It has been confined to treaty ports òr has gone into the "interior" only as the result of special concessions by the Chinese government. In spite of the limitations upon this form, it has been the chief means of introducing foreign capital into the country, and business investments form about three-fourths of the foreign capital in China today.

A second means of securing foreign capital has been the Chinese government. The borrowings of the Chinese government have never been as great as new business investments, except for short periods. They have fallen off since 1914, and in recent years they have brought no flow of foreign funds into the country.

The decline in foreign borrowing by the Chinese government in recent years has rested, in part, upon the policy of the Chinese government, and, in part, upon the decline in the credit of that government abroad. Payments on loan service have frequently been in arrears, and the government faces the necessity of adjusting a mass of unsecured debts which have come into existence since 1918.

The Failure to Import Capital in the Past

The small flow of foreign capital to China, or to put it more carefully, the fact that the flow of capital has not been great enough to introduce fundamental economic changes must be set down to the traditional organization of China. But there have been a number of special circumstances which have played a part in this failure to develop China's capacity to receive.

The first of these lies in the political difficulties created by the ambition and jealousy of the foreign powers. These have been sufficiently dealt with in the discussion of the borrowings of the Chinese government. They have played a part in direct investments as well. The use of the Chinese Eastern Railway as a means of advancing the imperialistic policy of Russia is an example. The fear and distrust of the Chinese people, which was aroused by the course of events between 1894–1900, is powerful today and it has been reinforced by recent events. Since 1900 the Chinese people have been in the greatest danger of losing the very region in which direct business investments have been greatest. To point out that the economic development of Manchuria has been carried forward does not meet the issue, for no foreigner may determine for the Chinese people what weight they shall give to what they regard as threats against the political integrity of their country.

The second lies in the ineffectiveness of the Chinese government in the economic field. This is a legacy from traditional China. The Chinese government has in the past failed to provide either leadership or the indispensable conditions of progress. The point of view of the Chinese officials toward the business community has brought about a strong distrust of government activity in the economic field which is powerful today.

A third and important aspect of the matter lies in the failure of the Chinese economic and social organization to develop the concepts, in various fields, which are required for the importation and effective use of foreign capital. The concepts which are needed are those which will make for technical efficiency in handling modern capital equipment, will insure the impersonal enforcement of business law, and will develop the control of business operations through effective accounting.

Of the Chinese people it may be said that in the economic field they do well whatever can be done through the family; they do less well what must be done otherwise. The social organization resting upon the family is strong and tough and powerful, but it is not easily adapted to the conditions set by modern economic development.

The business corporation is new in China. While it is true that the corporation has not secured capital from abroad, it is also true that the checks, both actual and potential, upon investment by the other methods are powerful. There are good reasons for holding the position that there will be no great inflow of foreign capital into China and no great economic development in China until the Chinese are able to borrow abroad through the corporation or through some similar private group or business unit.

The Chinese have a group individualism which is illustrated in many fields. It is the private initiative and the group solidarity of the Chinese family which has made them successful in trade and industry around the Pacific. It is the same characteristic of Chinese life which makes them successful settlers in Manchuria. When groups of this sort are made effective in Chinese economic life, there is at hand in the modern Chinese bankers a means of securing capital from abroad.

An important step toward the economic development of China and toward the availability of foreign capital would be taken if the Chinese business community were completely convinced that the government intends to base its policy on private enterprise and to encourage private enterprise. This involves more than stability of government and freedom from extra-legal exactions on the part of military leaders pressed for funds. It means that a stable government must make known what is to be the field of private enterprise and what the field of government activity. The government ought perhaps to limit itself, if so broad a field can be called limitation, to planning and selecting and to the provision of the overhead conditions of industrial and business activity, such as railways, communications, and river conservancy.[1] It means, also, that a stable government must offer to business the security which Western business men find in a constitution or in other accepted limitations upon the acts of officials. I do not pretend to say how this may be done. It must fit the traditions of the Chinese people, but there must be security under generally accepted legal arrangements which are binding both upon the people and the officials of the government.

The capital which is required for the economic development of China will, no doubt, come in large part from the highly developed countries of the West. Before 1914 it came from western Europe, though not always directly. Some came through the Russian government, which borrowed in France to build the Chinese Eastern Railway, and some through the Japanese, who borrowed in England to reconstruct the South Manchuria Railway. For a time

[1] See the announcement of the creation of a National Economic Planning Commission for China by the Kuo Min News Agency, April 19, 1931, and the arrangements approved by the Council of the League of Nations in June, 1931, dealt with in a statement quoted in Condliffe, J. B., *China Today: Economic*, 1932, p. 141.

during and after the World War Japan was a capital
exporter to China on her own account. Since the war
there have been no borrowings by the Chinese government on any scale worth considering, and the direct
investments have been largely Japanese. The relations
between the Chinese borrower of the future and the
Western investor are likely to be of fundamental importance in the economic and political development of
China. The position of Japan will depend upon the part
which she plays in movement of capital to China from the
highly developed West. It is possible that Japan may
come to have some capital of her own to invest and it is
not to be forgotten that Russian success will offer an alternative to the Chinese.

The immediate situation is dominated by international
politics and the course of events in the economic and
financial field tends to be obscured. It is difficult to
suppose any revival of the international financial Consortium. It seems more likely that a new attempt at co-
operation, if it is made, will express itself through the
League of Nations.

Within China no statement is more frequently repeated
than this, that China wants and should have foreign
capital without political domination or economic exploitation. If this could be sincerely agreed to as desirable by all concerned, difficult problems would remain
to be faced. How are the political problems connected
with foreign capital to be dealt with? How is foreign
capital in China to be so controlled and directed as to be of
greatest effect in raising the standard of living of the
Chinese people? Solemn assertions and good intentions
are not enough. A concrete program is necessary, built
upon effective study and applied with common sense and
good will.

PART II
INDIVIDUAL STUDIES

CHAPTER XV

AMERICAN INVESTMENTS IN CHINA

INTRODUCTION: A BRIEF ESTIMATE OF AMERICAN INVESTMENTS

The briefest generalization on the subject of American investments in China is that they amount to about U. S. $200 million at the present time. A more careful statement is this: On the basis of such information as I have succeeded in collecting and as has been made available to me, I estimate that American investments in China, as of January 1, 1931, may be valued, with some show of reason, at U. S. $196,606,400. This and appropriate lesser totals have appeared in the general chapters on foreign investment in China. In these chapters it was necessary to deal in totals and summaries. In the account which follows I present matters in greater detail. Those who are particularly interested in the American aspect of China's international economic relations will find here as complete a picture as my information enables me to make. Those who doubt my totals—and I have my own doubts—may see how I arrived at them, and may judge for themselves whether or not I dealt adequately and reasonably with the many difficulties which arose.

Foreign investments in China—and this includes American investments—are presented under two headings, a division which is both convenient and significant. The two headings are: (1) American holdings of Chinese government securities and all other obligations of the Chinese government and of government institutions, and (2) American business investments in China. All investments in China fall into these two classes, and the separation may usually be made with little difficulty. There is overlapping when American firms in China have sold supplies to the government and to such government institutions as the railways and have not been paid, or when American firms hold other claims against the government. Such debts and claims have been counted as American holdings of the obligations of the Chinese government and not as business investments.

A third division, the property in China of American mission and philanthropic societies, has been employed in arriving at a total of all American holdings. I have included under this heading the property of certain educational and scientific institutions as well. All the holdings under this head have certain features in common. They have come into existence with no expectation of an income, or of a monetary return of any sort on the part of their owners, and they are held with no expectation that the funds which they represent will ever be withdrawn from China. These features seem to me to mark them as not being investments at all. Clarity of thought would be promoted and prejudice in some measure avoided if those who write about mission activities in China would dispense with the term mission "investments."

Although I do not regard mission property in China as an investment in any business or economic sense, it does not follow that such holdings may be left out of account. They reflect an American interest in China which is old and strong and important—one which may not be neglected without presenting a false picture.

Here too it must be recognized that no sharp and complete division can be made, for there is property held by mission societies in China from which a return is expected and received. Such holdings seem to me true investments and I have so regarded them. The problem need not concern us here since American mission and philanthropic societies hold practically no income-producing property in China.

From the point of view of China's international accounts the importance of mission activities is measured by the flow of funds which they bring about. The purchase of land in China, the erection and equipment of buildings for mission and educational purposes, and the maintenance in China of the persons engaged in these activities require fairly large remittances to the country from abroad, and an attempt has been made to measure them.

A final reason for the inclusion of information concerning mission holdings is that they are seldom excluded from other holdings in the earlier reports of American property which I have succeeded in finding. The inclusion of mission and philanthropic societies makes it possible to arrive at an estimate of the value of American property of every sort in China. This total is certainly not far from U. S. $250 million at the present time.

For the earliest estimate of American investments in China I go back one hundred years to Canton before the Treaty of Nanking and the opening of the five ports. This is followed by an estimate for the 'seventies of the last century, before the great decline in the importance of American shipping in Chinese waters. Estimates are made for about the year 1900, and for the years just before the beginning of the World War. Finally, I present the results for the year 1930 of a new study of American investments in China. This new study was my task in the international co-operation in the general study of foreign investments in China which is incorporated in this volume.

Canton, a Hundred Years Ago

It is well known that the trade of China before 1842 was practically confined to Canton and that it was carried on by foreign business men under unusual restrictions. These conditions of the early trade need not be dwelt upon here, but it is plain that they greatly limited the possibilities of foreign investment in China.

The trade of a century ago was small, and it was largely in the hands of the British who were represented in China by the British East India Company. Morse states that the annual average for the sixteen years ending 1833 was U. S. $48 million for the combined trade of Great Britain and the United States, of which the American share was about U. S. $12.5 million.[1] This sum of U. S. $12.5 million is considerably greater than the direct trade between China and the United States, for it includes non-American goods carried in American ships.[2] Throughout the early trade and until the 'seventies the importance of American shipping was an outstanding characteristic of American participation in the trade of China, and was out of proportion to other American interests. Morse gives the average number of American ships calling at Canton during the same sixteen years as 37 and of British ships as 56. No account of American shipping is taken in my figures of American investments, since ocean-going ships represent an investment in the carrying trade of the world and not an investment in China.

A census of foreigners and foreign firms for the year 1836 provides a certain amount of information about Canton in the days of the factories.[3] According to this census the total foreign population of Canton was 307 and the number of firms was 55. Of this number 44 persons and 9 firms were American. Among the nine American firms were Olyphant and Company, Russell and Company, and Wetmore and Company, three firms who were to be well known in the China trade for many years.[4]

The amount of property actually owned by Americans in Canton at this time is not easy to estimate. The foreign

---

[1] Morse, H. B., *The International Relations of the Chinese Empire*, 1918, vol. I, pp. 89–92.

[2] Statistics from American sources are brought together in a convenient table in Pan, S. L., *The Trade of the U. S. with China*, New York, 1924, p. 15.

[3] *Chinese Repository*, 1837, vol. V, pp. 426–32.

[4] It may be noted that 14 per cent of the population was American, and 16 per cent of the firms.

firms were not permitted to own either land or buildings; they hired buildings from the Chinese hong merchants at rates which were moderate.[5] There is no question, then, of holdings of real property. Other property was the subject of occasional comments in documents which are available. A young American, who was for a time a partner in Russell and Company at Canton, wrote home to his mother in 1835 giving her an account of a fire which had threatened the factories. He had found it necessary to place the goods of his company in a boat for safety. "We had," he says, "about $300,000 in our treasury, and perhaps $50,000 worth of goods in the house."[6] Another, and later, fire gives us additional information. During the events which led to the "Arrow" war, the Canton factories were completely destroyed in December, 1856. The claims of American firms for damages are to be found in an American government document.[7] The largest claim allowed we find to have been that of Purdon & Company for U. S. $111 thousand. Another firm was allowed U. S. $98 thousand. Russell and Company submitted various statements which show the property of the firm to have been valued at about U. S. $100 thousand. The total amount of damages paid for was Tls. 500 thousand (U. S. $735,239), a part of which was returned to the Chinese government at a later time.[8] The indemnity was for other losses than those by fire at Canton, but the information about individual firms gives some idea of

[5] MacNair, H. F., *Modern Chinese History—Selected Readings*, Shanghai, 1923, p. 27. MacNair has reprinted comment on the Canton factories from Hunter, W. C., *Bits of Old China*.

[6] Hughes, Sarah Forbes, *Letters and Recollections of John Murray Forbes*, New York, 1899, pp. 76–7. It is significant that Forbes, a New Englander, began his business career in the China trade and ended as Chairman of the board of an American railroad in the Middle West.

[7] *Message of the President of the United States Relative to the Execution of the Treaty with China for the Settlement of Claims*. 40th Cong., 3rd Sess., Ex. Doc. No. 29, Washington, 1869. A summary statement of claims is to be found on pp. 158–61.

[8] Foster, J. W., *American Diplomacy in the Orient*, Boston, 1903, p. 244. The sum paid over to the Chinese government in 1885 amounted, with accrued interest, to U. S. $453,400.

the value of the goods on hand. It is probable that the
silver had been removed from the buildings when the fire
took place.[9]

The amount of silver in hand at any one time was
large, especially before 1827. I have estimated elsewhere
that 60 per cent of the total value of the goods brought
to China by the Americans from about 1800 to 1834 was
in the form of silver.[10] From the evidence which we have
it is not unreasonable to suppose that the large amount
of silver which Russell and Company held in 1835 was
characteristic of American firms at Canton, and of foreign
firms in general.

There is, however, information to show that Americans,
in the early days of their trade, borrowed considerable
sums from the Chinese hong merchants at Canton.[11]
Some allowance must be made for this, though it is
probable that the Americans were trading upon their
own capital after the Napoleonic wars.

An unconsidered aspect of these early relations is
brought out in the correspondence of John Murray Forbes,
who mentions the fact that, after his return to the United
States, he had the management in America of "about
half a million of my friend Houqua's money." [12] This
money was invested, we are told, in American stocks. No
doubt it constituted an investment within America and
in American economic development much more truly
than American goods at Canton constituted an investment within China, and in Chinese economic development.

[9] This opinion is supported by Morse, H. B., *The International Relations
of the Chinese Empire*, vol. I, p. 435.

[10] Remer, C. F., *The Foreign Trade of China*, Shanghai, 1926, p. 24. The
decline in silver imports was closely connected with the increase in the
import of opium, pp. 25–6.

[11] Dennett, Tyler, *Americans in Eastern Asia*, New York, 1922, p. 52.

[12] Hughes, Sarah Forbes, *op. cit.*, p. 101. Houqua was the name by
which the wealthiest of the hong merchants was known to the foreign
merchants. Mr. W. Cameron Forbes, American Ambassador to Japan,
speaking of John Murray Forbes on Sept. 30th, 1930, is reported to have
said, "I have recently discovered a check signed by Houqua for $300,000,
which he sent my grandfather to invest for him in the United States and
a power of attorney as representative in his business."

For Houqua to invest in America required no more than
that he find the means of transmitting his money. For
Forbes to have invested his money in economic development within China required nothing less than a new
China.

The Americans brought to the trade on the confined
bit of Canton waterfront the silver and goods of America.
We may guess that they had in hand at any one time
during the years immediately after 1830 some half a
million dollars in goods, and about U. S. $2.5 million in
silver, say 3 million dollars altogether. In the language
which is used in the presentation of information for later
periods, the whole of the American investment was direct
business investment in the one port of Canton and in the
import and export trade.[13]

In the 'Seventies during the Last of the Old Days

American holdings in Canton in the 'thirties reflected
the importance in world trade of American ships and
American merchants. By the end of the 'seventies American shipping had suffered a decline and the American
trader—often a New Englander—was less in evidence on
the China coast. During the early 'seventies Americans
were still of first importance, and these years were often
referred to at a later time as the last of the "good old
days." I have, therefore, selected the early 'seventies for
my second estimate of American investments in China.

At about the same time there were important changes
in the general conditions of trade with China. By the
'seventies the Suez Canal had been opened, steam and
steel were making fundamental differences in the world's
shipping, and there was telegraphic communication between China and the West.

The trade of China in the 'seventies was on a far greater

---

[13] American mission societies held no property in China, I believe, until
after the opening of the five ports. The first American missionary is said
to have arrived in China in 1829.

scale than the earlier trade at Canton. The Chinese were beginning to accept certain of the newer commodities, such as cotton yarn and kerosene oil. The total trade, including both imports and exports, was about Hk. Tls. 140 million a year from 1871 to 1875.[14] The American share of this trade was about 7 per cent. At the rates of exchange of the time the trade with the United States was about U. S. $15 million. According to the figures of the United States government American trade with China was U. S. $15 million in 1875, and did not reach U. S. $20 million until 1880.[15]

The total number of foreign firms in China during the early 'seventies was about 350 and the foreign population about 3,500. Of the firms about 50 were American, and of the population about 500. The Americans, with 7 per cent of the trade, had over 14 per cent of the firms and of the population. In the case of the population the explanation is easily found. It lies in the great number of American missionaries. In the 'thirties there had been practically none, but by 1875 the number was over 200.[16]

In the case of the firms the explanation lies in the importance of American shipping. The total tonnage of shipping that came under the view of the Chinese Maritime Customs during the decade was from 8 to 12 millions. This includes river, coastwise, and ocean-going shipping. Of this total no less than 43 per cent was American in 1871. A French officer of the Chinese Customs said of the Americans in 1865 "it is impossible to compete with their steamers except by opposing them by others . . . built on the same model." Seven out of the nine steamers on the

[14] The Haikwan tael is a Customs unit of account used for Chinese trade statistics. It is roughly equivalent to $1.50 in Chinese silver currency. The Chinese silver dollar is ordinarily used in this volume but the Haikwan tael is convenient for trade figures.

[15] Statistics in taels are from the reports of the Chinese Maritime Customs and those in U. S. dollars from the *Statistical Abstract of the United States*.

[16] The figures of American population are from U. S. *Report upon the Commercial Relations of the U. S. . . . . 1875*, pp. 252–3.

Yangtze were American. An American boat, the *Suwon-ada*, "bears the palm for the rapidity of her coast voyages." [17] An American official, writing in the 'seventies, commented upon the persistent importance of American shipping "in the face of a small international commerce." He explained it as due "partly to the superiority of the models of our ships for certain branches of trade, as, for instance, river work, and partly to the enterprise and good fortune of a few of our citizens." [18]

Such was the situation in the early 'seventies. By 1876 the American percentage had declined to 24 and by 1877 to 5. This sudden drop from 2.5 million to .5 million tons was brought about by the sale of the entire fleet of the Shanghai Steam Navigation Company to the recently formed China Merchants Steam Navigation Company. [19] Russell and Company held the chief interest in the Shanghai Steam Navigation Company. The sum received for the ships was Tls. 2 million, but, in addition, the company retained its reserve, so the price actually came to Tls. 2.4 million. This amounted to the sum of U. S. $3 million at the time. [20] We may accept this sum as a large part of the American investment in shipping, and, indeed, of American investment in China for the years in which we are interested. [21]

Further information concerning American holdings is available from Shanghai. We are told in a document of 1856 that "property to the value of a million (U. S.) dollars

[17] Great Britain: *Reports from the Foreign Commissioners at the Various Ports in China for the Year 1865*, London, 1867, p. 137.

[18] U. S. *Commercial Relations, 1876*, p. 137.

[19] The founding of the China Merchants Company is dealt with in Pott, F. L. H., *A Short History of Shanghai*, Shanghai, 1928, p. 99, and in my own *Foreign Trade of China*, pp. 60–1. The history of the company illustrates many of the difficulties of modern industrial development under Chinese official leadership.

[20] U. S. *Foreign Relations*, 1877, pp. 87, 90, and *Commercial Relations*, p. 219.

[21] It happens that American shipping was further reduced by the sale of the steamers of the Pacific Mail Steamship Company to the Japanese at about the same time. Chinese Maritime Customs, *Reports on Trade*, 1878, p. 99.

is owned by Americans in Shanghai." [22] No doubt this
included both business and mission holdings. American
holdings at the time were largely in Hongkew, a part of
Shanghai lying north of Soochow Creek. The land in
Hongkew alone is reported to have been valued at almost
exactly Tls. 12 million in 1880.[23] We know also that a
local Chamber of Commerce at Shanghai estimated the
value of the land in the International Settlement and the
French Concession at Tls. 24 million in 1882, and the
stocks of merchandise in Shanghai at Tls. 32 million.[24]
It is the opinion of Shanghai business men that this estimate of 1882 may be relied upon.

Taking this information as a basis, I estimate that
American holdings of land in Shanghai were about U. S.
$2 million in 1875, that about half of this land was the
property of mission societies, and that Americans held
stocks of goods to the value of about U. S. $1 million.

By 1875 there had been no borrowing, I believe, on the
part of the Chinese government which involved the remitting of funds from abroad.[25] In any case it is quite
certain that there had been no borrowing from Americans. No other obligations of the Chinese government
to Americans are worth considering.

The estimates which I have made on the basis of the
available information are shown in the table on page 249.

American business investments in the early 'seventies
are estimated at U. S. $7 million. It may be said with

[22] U. S. government, *Report on the Commercial Relations of the U. S.* . . .
34th Cong., 1st Sess., Ex. Doc. No. 47, Washington, 1856, vol. 1, p. 257.
[23] *Chronicle and Directory for China, Japan, etc., for the Year 1899,*
The Daily Press, Hongkong, 1899, p. 138.
[24] *Chronicle and Directory . . . for the Year 1899,* p. 138. The exact
figures are, land Tls. 24,355,000, stocks of goods Tls. 32,645,000. The
following observation is added. "The settlement land was bought from
the original proprietors at about $50 per *mow*, which was at least twice
its then value. Some lots have since been sold at $10,000 to $16,000 per
mow" (p. 139).
[25] The Chinese government borrowed abroad through a British bank in
China in 1876 for the campaign against the Mohammedan rebels. Morse,
H. B., and MacNair, H. F., *Far Eastern International Relations*, Shanghai,
1928, p. 500.

TABLE 1

AMERICAN HOLDINGS IN CHINA, 1875

Business investments	U. S. $7 million
Securities and government obligations	U. S. $0 million
Mission property	U. S. $1 million
	U. S. $8 million

some confidence that about half of this total, U. S. $3.5 million, was in shipping. The other half was very largely in the import and export business or in general trading and in land holdings at Shanghai. Shipping, it may be remarked, was the first application of power-driven machinery to reach China. In 1875 practically all of the modern shipping in Chinese waters was in foreign hands. It may be estimated also that somewhat more than half the American business investment in 1875 was at Shanghai and the rest scattered among the chief open ports. In short, American business investments in China in the 'seventies were largely in shipping with Shanghai as the important center.

AMERICAN INTERESTS IN 1900: TRADE NOT INVESTMENT

The year of the Boxer uprising, 1900, is the middle year of the next period for which estimates of American holdings in China are presented. The whole period covers the years between the Sino-Japanese War and the Russo-Japanese War. After 1900, it may be said, economic relations with China were fundamentally altered by the growing importance of Japan.

Between the 'seventies and the end of the century trade had grown and the way had been opened up for the investment of foreign funds in the industrial development of China. But the actual investment had not yet taken place on any but the smallest scale. Politics, as is usual in China, had, by 1900, discounted all the railway development of the next quarter of a century.

The foreign trade of China reached a total in 1899 which was about three times that of the early 'seventies. Except for the Boxer year the trade did not again fall below Hk. Tls. 460 million.

The Americans' share of this trade was 6.2 per cent in 1898 and no less than 9.5 per cent in 1899, a higher percentage than for any year since 1871. The American statistics show the trade to have been about U. S. $30 million for these years. Imports from the United States, it may be remarked, had increased relatively to exports to the United States. The United States had taken its full share in the increased trade and certain imports, particularly kerosene oil, brought with them American business investments which are characteristic of the American position in China today.

Population and Firms

The Customs statistics show that Americans formed about the same percentage of the foreign population as in the 'seventies—and, it may be added, in the 'thirties. The percentage figures were these:

1898	15.2 per cent
1899	13.6 per cent
1900	11.3 per cent

The number of American firms had increased to 70 in 1899 and to 81 in 1900, but there was a considerable decline in the American percentage of total foreign firms, to about 8 per cent from as high as 15 per cent in the 'seventies. There are a number of reasons for this. The great American shipping companies had disappeared.[26] Many of the smaller American firms upon the China coast had gone with them. A number of the new arrivals were

[26] I quote from Dennett, Tyler, *Americans in Eastern Asia*, 1922, p. 529. ". . . the failure of Olyphant and Company in December, 1878, and of Russell and Company in June, 1891, eliminated two of the most famous of the older American firms, and surrendered to British and German competitors a prestige and commercial leadership in China which Americans have never regained."

great firms, such as the Standard Oil Company. The result of these changes was to make the American percentage of foreign firms in China about equal, in 1900, to the American percentage of the foreign trade.

The American share of the foreign population remained high. This is, no doubt, to be accounted for by the continued and rapid increase in the number of American missionaries sent out by the Protestant missionary societies. The number of societies increased from 15 in 1875 to 31 in 1900, and the number of missionaries from 200 in the earlier year to about 1,000.

Shipping

American shipping in Chinese waters continued to decline from the low point it reached in the late 'seventies. The American share of the tonnage recorded by the Chinese Customs authorities was no greater than about 1 per cent during the years under consideration and until the World War.[27]

Business Investments

The figures which have been given are no more than an indication of the position of Americans in the trade and economic life of China. The direct information about American investments is scattered and incomplete. We know that the 70 or 80 American firms included some of great importance. The Standard Oil Company must have had a considerable investment. In 1898 about 100 million gallons of kerosene were imported into China, one-half coming from the United States. A local directory lists two establishments at Shanghai having oil tanks and plants for the tinning of oil. One of these

[27] During the years 1884 and 1885 the percentage was higher, due to the fact that the fleet of China Merchants Steam Navigation Company was in the hands of Russell and Company while China was at war with France. On the decline of American shipping see Dennett, Tyler, *Americans in Eastern Asia*, 1922, p. 586.

was American property. An important American trading corporation was put down as controlling the Shanghai Rice Mill Company, the American Cigarette Company, and the Shanghai Pulp and Paper Company, but there is reason to believe that at least two of these corporations were financed in large part by Chinese.[28] The Americans played some part also in the early development of the textile industry in China. Foreigners secured the right to build and maintain industrial plants in China by the Treaty of Shimonoseki. This right brought a fairly rapid development between 1896 and 1900, which was followed by more than one failure and reorganization in the next few years. I find records which show that two of the nine or ten cotton mills in operation at Shanghai in 1900 had been established by American interests.[29] The total capital of the two American companies was probably about U. S. $1.2 million, some part of which was undoubtedly British and Chinese. By the end of 1901 one of these mills had failed.[30]

An incident in connection with this early industrial development shows the attitude of the American officials of the time. A group of Shanghai cotton mill owners drew up a report in 1897 in which they pointed out the desirability of freeing the infant cotton milling industry of China from taxation, and proposed other assistance to the industry, advancing familiar protectionist arguments. A copy of this report was sent to the American Minister at Peking by the interested American business men of Shanghai in the hope that the Minister would be willing to support them. The report was forwarded to Washington. "I am unable to see," said the Minister in his

[28] *Chronicle and Directory . . . for the Year 1899*, p. 147; *for the Year 1900*, pp. 168–9.

[29] By the American Trading Company and Fearon Daniel and Company, *Chronicle and Directory . . . for the Year 1900*, p. 168. The latter was said by Lord Charles Beresford to have been "half English." (*The Breakup of China*, New York, 1899, p. 94.)

[30] Chinese Maritime Customs, *Returns of Trade and Trade Reports*, 1901, p. 289.

covering letter, "how the interests of my own country are to be forwarded by fostering cotton manufacturing in China." The Secretary of State supported him, saying: "The report of the Committee is in favor of local manufactures (it matters not whether set up by Chinese or foreign capital) for the purpose of competing on a cheap labor basis with foreign importations. Our interest is to keep foreign markets open for our manufacture."[31]

Here was a clear answer. If the American Minister had been charged with inconsistency on the ground that he refused to "foster" American investment in cotton milling, while at the same time he was most anxious (as we shall see) to support American investment in Chinese railways, he would have found it easy to reply. In the case of railways he was helping to sell American railway equipment and so developing foreign markets for American manufactures. In the case of cotton milling it was plain that development within China, whether by Americans or others, would have the effect of cutting off the market for American goods. The American officials of the time thought in terms of trade and not in terms of investment. So much is relatively simple.

Behind the attitude of the American officials lay a variety of questions. What if it were a matter of selling cotton milling machinery? How direct must the favorable result of economic development be upon American exports to justify official support? Does not the export of capital or the opportunity for investment mean an American interest as well as the export of goods?

But there was a still more difficult question to answer from this point of view. The existence of extraterritoriality and the position of the foreigner in China gave an American citizen in Shanghai some show of right to support in any lawful undertaking. Was not an American cotton mill owner in Shanghai as much to be considered as an American cotton mill owner in New England?

[31] U. S. Foreign Relations, 1897, p. 92.

The American cotton mill owners at Shanghai might have pointed out also that Chinese support was not likely to be given them since the Chinese have usually taken a racial viewpoint in these matters as well as a political, refusing to encourage the foreigner under extraterritoriality in his business or industrial ventures in China.

One is surprised that there was not some consideration of the contending principles involved, for these conflicts are of fundamental importance in understanding the Chinese situation. It was only because the simple formula of direct stimulus to the American export trade could be applied to cotton mills and to railways that doubts do not seem to have arisen in the minds of officials who were warm in their support of American capital in one case and more than cool in the other.

I turn now to further information upon which an estimate of American investments in China at the beginning of the century may be based. The land in Shanghai was said, in 1900, to be worth about 50 million Shanghai taels and the stocks of goods in foreign hands 60 million taels.[32] My own estimate of the total value of the land is somewhat higher. The assessed value of the land under taxation in the Foreign Settlement was, according to the reports of the Shanghai Municipal Council, Tls. 44 million in 1900, and Tls. 60 million in 1903.[33] The standing instructions to assessors were, until 1907, to value land at 75 per cent of its market value. We may be certain, then, that the land within the Foreign Settlement was worth nearly Tls. 60 million in 1900. It is safe to add Tls. 15 million as the value of the land in the French Concession at the time. It is well known also that much land along the roads beyond the settlement boundaries was registered at the various foreign consulates in the names of their different nationals, but I make no attempt at

---

[32] *Chronicle and Directory . . . 1900*, p. 166.
[33] The figures are brought together in the *Feetham Report*, vol. 1, p. 346. For instructions to assessors, see p. 338.

a separate estimate of the value of such land. It is safe to say that the total value of the land in the Foreign Settlement, the External Roads areas, and in the French Concession at Shanghai, excluding such land as was known to be Chinese property, was worth Tls. 75 or 80 million in 1900. There is little doubt that by 1902 or 1903 this total had risen to Tls. 100 million. I shall accept the figure of Tls. 80 million for my further estimates.

Aside from the land excluded from the total as property known to be Chinese, a considerable fraction of the Tls. 80 million must be excluded as land which, while registered in foreign names, was really the property of Chinese.[34] There is a further complication here because land is held by corporations which are not Chinese, but in which Chinese own a large, or even the whole interest. But, making allowance for all the numerous difficulties, I estimate on the basis of information obtained in Shanghai and from the *Feetham Report*, that one-third of the land included in my total was land which ought not to be counted as foreign property in any sense of the word. Deducting this I reach a total of Tls. 55 million as the value of the land actually held by foreigners in Shanghai at about the year 1900. It is probable that Americans held somewhat more than 10 per cent of this land, say from Tls. 5.5 to Tls. 6 million, which at the rate of exchange of the time comes to U. S. $3.5 or 4 million.

So much may be regarded as fairly certain. I propose now to accept as applicable the percentages of American investment in land at Shanghai to total investments at Shanghai, and of American investments at Shanghai to total investments in China which are calculated from the returns of the investigation for the year 1930. Making these estimates I offer the sum of U. S. $10 million as a reasonable guess of the value of American business hold-

[34] Upon this subject, and for part of the information upon which my estimates are based, see *Feetham Report*, vol. 1, Pt. III, Chap. 5, and vol. 2, p. 170.

ings in Shanghai for the period under consideration, and the sum of U. S. $17.5 million for all American business investments in China.

Obligations of the Chinese Government

American holdings of the obligations of the Chinese government were, aside from one transaction, so small as to be negligible. This one transaction was a railway contract which the Americans held for a short time.

The period from 1895 to 1900 was one of fevered, if somewhat ineffectual, activity in the promotion of railway schemes in China. We are here concerned with the American efforts only and not with those of the other powers. The first American proposal, for the building of the Hankow-Peking line, came to nothing for reasons associated with international politics. It did not fail because of any lack of interest on the part of the American Minister, Charles Denby. Denby went so far as to call at the Foreign Office in Peking and demand that instructions be telegraphed to the Chinese negotiator at Shanghai to contract with the American company for the building of the line.[35] His interest was so keen and his action so vigorous that it seemed to him to need explaining. "I have not participated in the actual making of contracts," he said, in one of his letters to Washington, "though as an old lawyer I have confidentially advised applicants as to the measures to be adopted."

This case led to the formulation of instructions to Denby which may be taken as representing the attitude of the American government. He was told by the Secretary of State to "employ all proper methods for the extension of American commercial interests in China, while refraining from advocating the projects of any one firm to the exclusion of others." [36] These instructions, it is to be noticed, were based upon considerations arising

[35] *U. S. Foreign Relations,* 1897, pp. 57–8.
[36] *Ibid.,* p. 56.

from trade rather than from investment. It must have
been well known to the Secretary of State, however,
that the general interest in railway contracts in China
meant more than a desire to secure orders for rails and
railway equipment. Recent history offers no better example of the use of economic arrangements for political
purposes than railway contracts in China in the years
immediately before 1900.

It was not railway contracts alone around which the
battle of the concessions raged. There were leases of
ports, non-alienation agreements, and "spheres of influence" as well. John Hay's reassertion of the open door
policy in 1900 was called forth by the fact that partition
of China seemed highly probable and not very distant.
Again the consideration seemed to be trade and nothing
more. The Americans were after an agreement all around
that the right to trade would be respected, even if China
were divided. A strict constructionist may maintain
that there was nothing more than this in the doctrine
as it was stated in 1900. There is little doubt that more
than this was strongly implied, and that the implication
was a gesture of warning against actual steps toward the
partitioning of the country. In so far as Hay thought
of economic considerations, he had trade in mind, but
his main object was to secure a political result. He took
steps to prevent a political end, the means toward which
lay, in part, in the field of economics and, in so far as
they lay in this field, concerned trade rather than investment. The problem of an open door for investments
does not seem to have been attacked and the reason is,
no doubt, that Americans were little interested in foreign
investments in 1900.[37]

When the Americans lost the contract for the Peking-
Hankow, they were given to understand that the con-

[37] As Dennett says, ". . . there was not enough American money seeking investment to make it worth while to quarrel about the preferential
rights to construct railways or to operate mines which had already been
given to other powers." *Americans in Eastern Asia*, 1922, p. 648.

tract for the railway from Hankow to Canton would be given to them. This contract was signed on April 14, 1898. Here was the first concrete result of long effort and many proposals. It, too, came to nothing in the end. The Spanish-American War began within a few days of the final agreement and there was delay. A preliminary survey of the route was finally made and, as a result of this survey, a supplementary agreement was signed in July, 1900, increasing the sum of money to be paid for the construction of the line.[38] This supplementary agreement contained an article, the seventeenth, which provided that "the Americans cannot transfer the rights of these agreements to other nations or people of other nationality," and its inclusion was due to Chinese fears of the possible political consequences of foreign control of Chinese railways. They were particularly anxious to avoid control of the Hankow-Canton by the group who held the contract for the Peking-Hankow, or by a group of the same nation, Belgium.

When, by the purchase of the shares of the company in New York, a Belgian group acquired control of the American China Development Company, the Chinese demanded that the agreement be canceled.[39] There were other reasons behind the Chinese demand, such as the objections of provincial leaders, but there is little doubt that the important reason was the Belgian control of the company. J. P. Morgan and Company proceeded at once to purchase a controlling interest in the American China Development Company and the Chinese were informed that all the holdings were now American. The Chinese, however, persisted in their demand and finally

[38] Texts in Rockhill, W. W., *Treaties and Conventions*, Washington, 1904, pp. 252, 259. The agreement canceling the concession is in MacMurray, John V. A., *Treaties and Agreements With and Concerning China, 1894–1919*, vol. I, p. 519.
[39] The whole subject is dealt with in *U. S. Foreign Relations*, 1905, pp. 124–35. On the Chinese fear of foreign ownership and their feeling that Americans were least to be feared see Denby's letter of January 10, 1897. *U. S. Foreign Relations*, 1897, pp. 56–7.

bought out all the property and interest of the Company in China for the sum of U. S. $6,750,000. The American government informed the Chinese Minister in Washington on August 29, 1905, that it had withdrawn all objection to the cancellation of the contract and American interest in the railway came to an end. The sum paid over to the Americans was less than U. S. $6,750,000 by U. S. $2,222,000, the amount of the bonds already sold by the American China Development Company. These bonds represented an American holding of Chinese government securities until their retirement in 1911, in accordance with the provisions of the Hukuang loan agreement.[40]

Mission Property

Concerning American missionary activities in China at the beginning of the year 1900, we know that there were about 1,000 missionaries representing about 30 societies. This is to be compared with 210 representing 15 societies in 1875. There were about 60 American mission hospitals in China at the time, about half the total number. It is probable that about half of the mission educational institutions were American. The total number of "students in Christian schools" was reported to have been 10,000 in 1899 and about 30,000 in 1905.[41] American mission societies were awarded U. S. $570,983.75 in the Boxer settlement and "it is well known that only a small part of American mission property was destroyed or damaged."[42] The direct information available from

[40] See Article II of the Hukuang agreement in MacMurray, John V. A., *Treaties and Agreements With and Concerning China, 1894–1919*, vol. I, p. 866.

[41] *The Christian Occupation of China*, Shanghai, 1922, p. 346. My estimates are based upon this work and upon Beach, H. P., "China as a Mission Field," *Missionary Review of the World*, Feb., 1899, vol. 12, no. 2, pp. 86–98 and table on p. 93. And Dennis, J. S., "Missions in China," *Review of Reviews*, New York, Sept., 1900.

[42] Latourette, K. S., *A History of Christian Missions in China*, N. Y., 1929, p. 253. The amount awarded was more than half again as large as the claims of the societies.

my investigation of 1930 is for only 6 of the possible total of 30 societies. These 6 societies had property which they valued at U. S. $660,174. I have information concerning remittances from 13 societies showing a total of U. S. $638,989 from American protestants. The 6 societies from whom I have information do not include certain missions with large holdings. Making the best estimate possible on the basis of all available information, I estimate that American mission societies had property to the value of about U. S. $5 million around the year 1900.

The estimates for the period are shown in the following table.

TABLE 2

AMERICAN HOLDINGS IN CHINA, 1900

(In millions of U. S. dollars)

Business investments	U. S. $17.5
Securities and government obligations	U. S. $ 2.2
Mission property	U. S. $ 5.0
	U. S. $24.7

No attempt can be made to estimate the business investments according to the nature of the business. There was, however, a great decline in the importance of shipping. It is probable that there were no American ships in the river and coastwise trade of China in 1900. The geographical distribution of these investments cannot be determined from the information of the time. It may be estimated at U. S. $10 million for Shanghai and U. S. $7.5 million for the rest of China. Leaving mission property out of account American investments may be said to have increased from U. S. $7 million in 1875 to about U. S. $20 million in the year 1900.

AMERICAN INTERESTS IN 1914: GROWTH OF TRADE—
EFFORTS IN THE FIELD OF FINANCE

Background

Between 1900 and 1914 important changes took place in China. The Russian advance in the north was checked and Japan took the place of Russia in southern Manchuria after the Russo-Japanese War. Both of these countries played an important part in China's international economic relations during the period. American and British policy was modified by this change. Chinese domestic political changes were rapid. The Chinese revolution had begun by 1914 but it had not yet produced the confusion of its later stages. The China of 1913 and 1914 may be said to have been China before the revolution, as the world was still the world before the war.

The foreign trade of China on the eve of the World War was twice as great as it had been at the turn of the century. The increase was from about Hk. Tls. 400 million to over Hk. Tls. 900 million. The American share of this increased trade was about what it had been in 1900. As a matter of fact the American share in the foreign trade of China varied between 5 and 10 per cent throughout the whole period from 1871 to 1915 with the exception of a few years around 1905.[43]

The movement of goods from China to the United States was still somewhat greater than the movement in the opposite direction. When we consider the figures provided by the United States government in U. S. dollars and take into account American trade with Hongkong, there is evidence that the year 1897 marked a change in American trade relations with China. In 1897, and from that year on, American exports to China and Hongkong were about equal to American imports from China and Hongkong. This increase in the importance of American exports to China was, in part, the result of the further development of American organization for sales in China and for the distribution of American goods in that country. It may be assumed that increasing American exports to China meant an even greater relative increase in American business investments in that country.

[43] In 1905 it was 15 per cent and in 1915 it was 11.4 per cent. Calculations based upon Chinese Customs statistics.

Population and Firms

The American population in China continued to grow, as did the number of firms. The number of firms was now above 130 and the number of Americans around 5,000.[44] It is when we turn to the percentage of the totals that we encounter a great difference from the situation in 1900. In 1899 the Americans formed 13.6 per cent of the foreigners in China, and in 1913 no more than 3.2 per cent; American firms 7 per cent in 1899 and 3.4 per cent in 1913. The reason lies in the increase in the numbers of Japanese and Russians. There had been no important change in the American position in relation to the western European nations.

Shipping

Throughout the years from 1900 to 1918 American shipping formed no more than about 1 per cent of the total shipping in the foreign and domestic trade of China. An exception must be made, as in the case of trade, for the years of the Russo-Japanese War, but during these years it was no more than 2 per cent.

Business Investments

The American position in Shanghai provides information of first importance in estimating American business holdings in China. The foreign population of the Foreign Settlement was almost three times as great in 1915 as it had been in 1900; and the American percentage of this population was almost exactly the same, 7 per cent. The American population increased from 562 to 1,307. The Americans in the French Concession did not materially increase the percentage of Americans in the whole of Shanghai beyond this figure of 7 per cent.

[44] A table showing comparable figures is to be found at the end of this chapter.

The value of the land under taxation in the Foreign Settlement was assessed at Shanghai at Tls. 142 million in 1911 and at Sh. Tls. 163 million in 1916. I estimate that it was Sh.Tls. 155 million in 1914.[45] The French Concession was extended in 1914 to include an additional area of 15,150 *mow* (2,167 acres). The value of the land in the French Concession I estimate to have been one-third of that in the Foreign Settlement, that is about Sh. Tls. 55 million. The value of the land registered at the various consulates in the area covered by the external roads at the time was at least Sh. Tls. 20 million. If Sh. Tls. 20 million is added as the probable undervaluation of the land under taxation within the Foreign Settlement, a total of Sh. Tls. 250 million is arrived at as the total value of the land held in the name of foreign persons or corporations in the whole of Shanghai in 1914.

From this total I deduct Sh. Tls. 80 million as the probable value of the land which was held in foreign names but really belonged to Chinese, leaving a total of Sh. Tls. 170 million as the value of the land actually in the possession of foreigners. American holdings come to Sh. Tls. 17 million if the percentage for both earlier and later years may be accepted as giving some indication of the American proportion.

If the value of American land holdings was about U. S. $10 million (taking the average rate of exchange for 1914) in 1914, the total American investment in Shanghai may be guessed by this method at U. S. $30 million, and the total American business investment in China at about U. S. $50 million.

These calculations are based upon such information as the estimates by the same method for the year 1900. They establish, it seems to me, the upper limit of the possible total of American investments. The direct information which is available seems to point to a lower figure than U. S. $50 million.

[45] *Feetham Report*, vol. 1, p. 346.

An American Chamber of Commerce was organized at Shanghai in 1915 with a membership of 32 firms.[46] There was an American bank in China in 1914, the International Banking Corporation, with an office at Shanghai and four other branches in the country. When this bank was taken over by the National City Bank of New York in 1916, it had capital, surplus, and undivided profits of about U. S. $8 million, but it must be borne in mind that it had branches in Europe and South America as well as in the Far East.[47] The National City Bank was the first to enter China after the restrictions upon national banks were removed by the Federal Reserve Act and certain supplementary acts.

My investigation brought replies as to the date of entrance into China from 130 American firms. I find that 22 of these firms were in existence before 1914 and 25 before 1915. In the 22 are included five of the largest American corporations in China today. In almost every case my returns show that the investment of the company in 1913 is not known today, or that it cannot be calculated without great difficulty. I did, however, secure estimates from a number of these firms, or from men formerly associated with them. I find that the eight largest of them had investments in China to the amount of U. S. $30.5 million in 1914. The number of American firms in China cannot be closely estimated. The Customs statistics make the number too large, for they count every branch at every port to arrive at a total. My estimate is that the 130 firms in the Chinese Customs reports represent about 75 separate American business houses. I know that the largest of these firms are included in my estimate of U. S. $30 million and it is unlikely that the

[46] "Annual Report of the President," *Millard's* (now *China Weekly Review*), June 19, 1920, vol. XIII, no. 3, p. 119. This was said at the time to be the first American Chamber of Commerce outside the United States.

[47] Lee, Frederic E., *Currency, Banking and Finance in China*, Washington, 1926, p. 94. Bennett, C. R., "American Banks Taking Their Place in China," *Millard's* (now *China Weekly Review*), June 19, 1920, vol. XIII, no: 3, p. 119.

others had investments of more than U. S. $10 or U. S. $12 million.

I have arrived by one method at an estimate for American business investments of U. S. $50 million and by another at U. S. $40–42 million. The second method is more direct, and is based upon information about a considerable number of individual firms. It seems to me reasonable to accept the total arrived at by the second method and to set down American business investments for 1914 at about U. S. $42 million.

Obligations of the Chinese Government

American holdings of Chinese government securities may be estimated fairly exactly for the year 1914. A comparison of the figures for 1900 and for 1914 does not, however, bring out the significant facts concerning American relations to Chinese government finance. The course of events leads from an American interest in Manchuria to a dramatic entrance upon the main stage of Chinese finance in 1911, and, finally, to a dramatic withdrawal in 1913 in the midst of the exciting preliminaries to the signing of the contract for the Reorganization loan.

The period from 1900 to the beginning of the World War saw many adventures in which Americans were interested come to nothing. The Canton-Hankow Railway project has been dealt with above. Other plans which would have involved Americans and American capital, if they had been successful, were associated with Manchuria, the area which the Chinese call the Three Eastern Provinces. The reasons for American interest in Manchuria are not easy to find in the simple theory that capital follows trade. In fact, no American economic interest in existence serves to explain the Manchurian proposals. No doubt the explanation is that Russian ambitions in Manchuria drew the attention of Americans to this region and that the continued centering of international politics in the Far East upon Manchuria served to keep it there. It was a political problem which called for financial measures among others. This is said without raising the question as to how far Russian and Japanese interest in Manchuria may have an economic explanation.

The Russian reply to the American note of 1899 on the subject of the open door was less definite than that of any of the other powers.[48] The continued presence of Russian troops in China and in Manchuria after the suppression of the Boxers, the signing of the Anglo-Japanese alliance in 1902, and the course of events leading to the Russo-Japanese War kept up the interest of the United States in Manchuria.[49] The effect of these factors was reinforced by the part which President Roosevelt played in the bringing of the war to an end. American attention was fixed upon Manchuria in 1905 as it was upon Shantung in 1919.

The first proposal involving possible American investment in Manchuria was Mr. E. H. Harriman's plan to secure the Manchurian railways, or their use, as a part of a round-the-world system of transportation. This would have involved a considerable business investment but it came to nothing. This was followed, in part, because of the ambition and energy of Willard Straight, by an attempt to put through a joint British-American project for a railroad from Hsinmintun to Aigun. The British contract for the line from Hsinmintun to Fakumen was signed in 1907 and it was for a railway which was specifically mentioned as a British project in a supplementary letter to the exchange of notes between Great Britain and Russia in 1899, concerning "spheres" for

[48] MacMurray, John V. A., *Treaties and Agreements With and Concerning China, 1894–1919*, vol. I, pp. 234–5. The Russian reply did not deal directly and completely with any one of the "three principles" set forth in the American communication.

[49] "At no time since 1905 has Manchuria been so nearly on the verge of practical absorption as during the closing years of the Russian period before 1905," Young, C. W., *The International Relations of Manchuria*, Chicago, 1929, p. 7.

railway concessions.[50]   Nevertheless, the Japanese prevented the contract from being carried out, relying upon certain secret "protocols" connected with the Sino-Japanese Treaty of December, 1905, in which China gave her consent, in so far as was necessary, to the provisions of the Treaty of Portsmouth.[51] The British government did not desire to press the matter.   The same short stretch of railway from Hsinmintun to Fakumen played a part in the proposal for the construction of a line from Chinchow to Aigun.

This line from Chinchow to Aigun was designed to be the contribution of the Americans and the British to the pooling and "neutralizing" of all Manchurian railways which was proposed by the American Secretary of State in 1909 and known as the "Knox plan." [52]   The Knox plan was for a loan to the Chinese government to enable this government to buy all the railways in Manchuria, including the Chinese Eastern and the South Manchuria.   The Knox plan, which would have meant a considerable advance of American funds to the Chinese government, was opposed by both Russia and Japan. These two governments regarded the plan as contrary to their political and economic interests.   They joined in notifying the Chinese government that they were to be consulted first if capital required was for railway development in Manchuria.   This communication was regarded, and probably rightly, as a joint assertion of opposition to any future proposals of a nature similar to the Knox plan.[53]   The Canton-Hankow project failed

[50] MacMurray, John V. A., *Treaties and Agreements With and Concerning China, 1894–1919*, vol. I, pp. 204–5.

[51] "The alleged secret protocols" are printed in MacMurray, John V. A., *Treaties and Agreements With and Concerning China, 1894–1919*, vol. I, pp. 554–5. In Young, W. C., *The International Relations of Manchuria*, Appendix B, there will be found an examination of the evidence for the existence of these protocols.

[52] Both are dealt with in Secretary Knox's letter of Nov., 1909, to the British government. *U. S. Foreign Relations*, 1910, p. 234.

[53] *U. S. Foreign Relations*, 1910, p. 257. MacMurray, John V. A., *Treaties and Agreements*, vol. I, pp. 803–4. See also Hornbeck, S. K., *Contemporary*

very largely because the required capital was not available in the United States at the time. In some part it failed because the Americans did not appreciate or chose to disregard the political considerations which have at all times given railway projects in China a greater importance than business or economic considerations would justify. The failure of the Knox plan, and the proposals associated with it, was in all probability not due to a lack of available funds. It was due, rather, to political ambitions, which the United States was now willing to oppose. In this opposition the United States was not successful. The international political situation at the time brought support to the Japanese and Russians from Great Britain and France, leaving Germany the only government willing to support the United States. As a well-informed American has said, "In the light of what is now known regarding the arrangements existing among the powers at the time, it is evident that this plan never had any prospect of success."[54]

The Manchurian efforts of the United States led, on the one hand, to American entrance into the three-power group which was interested in the Hukuang railways, and, on the other, to the signing of a preliminary agreement for a loan for currency reform and for certain industrial enterprises in Manchuria. The latter loan, when it was finally signed in 1911, became a four-power group loan. The Americans had now effectively entered the association of national banking groups which had come to be known as the Consortium.

The Hukuang railways include the section of the Can-

Politics in the Far East, N. Y., 1916, pp. 259–60. The whole chapter deals with the proposals under discussion.

[54] MacMurray, John V. A., "Problems of Foreign Capital in China," Foreign Affairs, N. Y., vol. III, no. 3. Reprinted in Arnold, Julean, China, A Commercial and Industrial Handbook, Washington, 1926, p. 306. Hornbeck has put the reasons for this failure thus: "We had not sufficient economic anchorage in the region concerned; we had no intention of using or threatening to use force; we were left in the lurch diplomatically in quarters where we had been led to believe we would have support." Proceedings of the Academy of Political Science, N. Y., July, 1917, vol. VII, p. 89.

ton-Hankow which lies in the province of Hunan and the section of the Hankow-Ichang Railway which lies in the province of Hupeh. During the negotiations for the contract for these railways President Taft sent a personal telegram to the Chinese ruler in which he requested "equal participation by American capital in the present railway loan." [55] This loan contract, into which the forceful measures of President Taft brought the Americans, was signed on May 20, 1911. It was, in 1914, the only outstanding Chinese government loan with direct American participation.

These events of 1911, and especially the signing by the four-power group of the currency reform and industrial development loan which involved Manchuria, led to successful efforts on the part of Japan and Russia to enter the Consortium.[56] A six-power group took the place of the four-power group. The negotiations for the Reorganization loan were now carried on by this larger group, but a change of administration in the United States brought about the withdrawal of the American banks before the signing of the contract in April, 1913.

It is worth while to consider briefly the explanation of the entrance and withdrawal of the American banks in so short a time. In a statement to the press concerning President Taft's Hukuang loan telegram, the Secretary of State gave as one reason for American insistence the fact that the Hukuang loan was different from earlier railway loans in that it involved the general revenues of the central government of China. It was important, he maintained, that the United States participate, for important general questions might arise as a result of the nature of the revenues pledged.[57] So much con-

---

[55] The telegram is reprinted in Willoughby, W. W., *Foreign Rights and Interests in China*, Baltimore, 1920, p. 551.

[56] Agreement of June 18, 1912. MacMurray, John V. A., *Treaties and Agreements*, vol. II, p. 1021.

[57] The statement is reprinted in Willoughby, W. W., *Foreign Rights and Interests in China*, 1920, pp. 551–2.

cerning American entrance. American withdrawal from
the six-power group followed a reply from the American
government to the American banking group's request
for continued support. In its reply, March 18, 1913, the
government pointed out that certain general Chinese
revenues are pledged, and under such conditions as to
"touch very nearly the administrative independence of
China."[58] The same conclusion as to the facts, namely,
that the loan touched general revenues and carried with
it general political possibilities, led to quite different
conclusions as to policy. To the Taft administration it
meant that America ought to insist on participation;
to the Wilson administration that the United States
ought to withdraw. Here was a difference resting upon a
divergence of views as to American policy in China, and
as to the means of giving effect to it. The divergence of
views was not fundamental, however, for within a few
years the United States took the initiative in bringing
into existence the so-called New Consortium.

The interest in Manchuria, which carried the United
States into full participation in the so-called Old Consortium, is best seen from the American viewpoint as
an effort to apply the open door principle to the provision of capital for China through the Chinese government.
It is true that documents of the time may be cited which
repeat the old formula: trade not investment; but the
problem of an open door for investment was emerging
as a separate one.

The American attack upon this problem through the
Old Consortium was bound to fail for the simple reason
that the Consortium did not provide an effective instrument. So long as an open door for investment was a political problem it could not be solved by an agreement
among financiers to conduct themselves as if the political problem did not exist, or to conduct themselves as

[58] Text in MacMurray, John V. A., *Treaties and Agreements*, vol. II,
p. 1025. See also *U. S. Foreign Relations*, 1913, p. 171.

if the political problem lay in administrative loans to China and not in railway loans.

Consider the course of events. The Old Consortium became by the inclusion of the United States, Japan, and Russia a group whose existence can be explained only on political grounds. Japan and Russia were both importers of capital and the United States was a relatively unimportant exporter. The six-power group had behind it political reasons for its existence. During the same period of expansion in membership the Consortium came to adopt the policy that it was interested in administrative loans only and not in industrial loans—railway loans being included among the industrial.

American interest throughout the period from the Russo-Japanese War to 1913 was quite rightly centered upon Manchuria. The test of the open door for investment lay in Manchuria and in Manchurian railways. The means of getting forward with this problem was at hand in the six-power Consortium if the Consortium could be brought to deal with railway contracts in the Three Eastern Provinces. When, however, railway contracts seemed to be excluded from the field of Consortium operations, the possible effectiveness of the Consortium was in a large measure destroyed.

An open door for trade was regarded by the Americans as having been won by an agreement which avoided political issues. An open door for investment could not, it seems, be isolated from politics and dealt with as an economic problem. In any case it could not be so handled by a group including Japan and Russia so long as that group failed to meet the issue presented by the Manchurian railways.

The Reorganization loan of 1913 carried provision for the repayment of advances made against the Currency Reform loan of 1911, and others made by the six-power group while the loan was under negotiation. The Americans had participated in these advances. They had taken part also in a loan of Sh. Tls. 3 million to the Shanghai Taotai in 1910, and in a loan of Hankow Tls. 2 million to the Hupeh provincial government. All of these obligations were wiped out with the proceeds of the Reorganization loan, leaving the Americans with no known investment except in the Hukuang Railways loan.[59] No new loans were made during the remaining months of 1913, for, as a Chinese student of the subject remarks, American finance in China reached "a period of total stagnation" after American withdrawal from the Consortium.[60]

The Hukuang loan was for £6 million and it was shared equally among the four interested countries. It provided for the retirement of the bonds which remained in American hands after the cancellation of the contract of the American China Development Company, U. S. $2,222,-000.[61] The total holdings of Chinese government securities was, in 1914, the American share of the Hukuang loan and the amount outstanding was U. S. $7,299,000. There may have been small American holdings of Chinese securities issued in Europe but I am informed by American bankers that such holdings were negligible before 1919. No obligations for the year 1913 of the Chinese government to American business firms have been reported to me.

Mission Property

The property in China of American mission and philanthropic societies may be estimated from published information and from the returns received in the course of my study. American missionaries in China numbered about 2,500 in 1914, some 40 per cent of the total Ameri-

[59] The repayments are listed in Annexes A and B to the loan agreement. MacMurray, John V. A., *Treaties and Agreements*, vol. II, p. 1018. A list of the American group's claims is to be found in *U. S. Foreign Relations*, 1913, p. 172.

[60] Tan, S. H., *The Diplomacy of American Investments in China.* An unpublished dissertation of 1927 in the library of the University of Chicago.

[61] MacMurray, John V. A., *Treaties and Agreements*, vol. 1, p. 866.

can population.[62] The number of missionaries was two and one-half times that of 1900. The number of hospitals maintained by American Protestants had increased from about 60 to about 140. The number of schools was probably three times the number in 1900. An estimate for 1914 of the value of the plant and equipment of five important institutions for higher education put the total at U. S. $1.5 million.[63] The property of the American Y.M.C.A. was reported at about the same time to have been U. S. $1 million.[64] The total number of societies was about 45 in 1914 as compared with about 30 in 1900. I have returns from 19 societies showing that these 19 had property to the value of U. S. $4.7 million in 1913. Certain important societies, such as the Y.M.C.A., did not report to me the value of their property in 1913. The societies for whom I do not have reports for 1913 and who had over U. S. $1 million in 1930 number five who were, to my knowledge, established in China before 1913. It is to be mentioned also that the value of certain property held for educational purposes may not have been included. I estimate that the property of American mission and philanthropic societies was at least U. S. $8 million and could not have been over U. S. $12 million. I set down U. S. $10 million as a reasonable estimate. Remittances from the United States for mission and philanthropic purposes are shown in my returns for 25 societies and the total reported for 1913 was U. S. $2 million. The total for all mission societies may well have been U. S. $3 or U. S. $3.5 million. Estimates made shortly after 1914 include one of U. S. $3.5 million for all mission remittances and one of U. S. $1.8 million for four important societies.[65] My estimate of the

[62] Estimates of 2,309 and 2,858 for 1915 and 1916 are to be found in Arnold, Julean, *Commercial Handbook of China*, Washington, 1919, vol. 1, p. 423 and vol. 2, p. 288.
[63] Arnold, Julean, *Commercial Handbook of China*, 1919, vol. 2, p. 429.
[64] *Ibid.*, vol. I, p. 288.
[65] *China Mission Year Book*, 1919, p. 297. *Commercial Handbook of China*, 1919, vol. 1, p. 287; vol. 2, p. 423. The last reference is to an es-

value of the property of mission and philanthropic societies enters into the table below, in which I offer a summary of the estimates I have made for the last year before the World War.

TABLE 3

AMERICAN HOLDINGS IN CHINA, 1914

Business investments	U. S. $42,000,000
Securities and government obligations	U. S. $ 7,299,000
Mission property	U. S. $10,000,000
	U. S. $59,299,000

The result of these estimates for the period immediately
before the war is a total of American investments in
China of U. S. $49,299,000, or nearly $50 million, which
is to be compared with a total of about U. S. $20 million
for the beginning of the century.

AMERICAN INTERESTS IN 1930: A NEW ESTIMATE OF AMERICAN INVESTMENTS

The results of a new study of American holdings in
China are presented in the following pages. It must
not be forgotten that this American study is part of a
general examination of China's international relations
which has included an estimate of the investments in
China of the citizens of every country which it is important to consider. Since many countries were involved,
it was necessary to set up a plan which would, so far as
possible, make the results for the different countries comparable. This will help to explain the fact that certain
investigations for a particular country were not carried
as far as the reader interested in that particular country
may desire. The view of American investments is presented here independently of the others. It was not
planned independently and cannot be so judged.

timate by Dr. Frank Rawlinson of $3,572,780 for 1916 which was based on
an investigation in Shanghai. See also Sammons, Thomas, "American
Missions in China," *Millard's Review* (later *China Weekly Review*), July 7th,
1917, vol. I, no. 5, pp. 120–1.

There are, of course, important facts about American investments in China which lie outside the estimation and analysis of American holdings in China. Among them the China Trade Act and the American initiative in the creation of the so-called New Consortium may be mentioned for the period between 1914–1930. Such matters are dealt with after the figures have been presented. My immediate task is to present the totals of American holdings in China and such analysis of the figures as may be made.

Business Investments

American business investments in China will be considered first. The total of American business investments I find to be U. S. $155,112,778. This implies a degree of precision which cannot, as a matter of fact, exist. It does, however, give a figure which has been built up carefully, and which can be defended. I will do my best to explain how it was reached. In doing so certain figures will be dealt with which are included in the total but which cannot be made the subject of further analysis. When these have been disposed of, the analysis will be presented.

It must be remembered at all times that my information has come largely from the business firms themselves and under conditions which limit the possibility of analysis. It must be borne in mind, also, that information was frequently given in such a way as to make it necessary for me either to make statements as if from my own knowledge, or to make use of the phraseology of anonymity which every investigator learns early to suspect. I must ask the reader to believe that every specific statement is made as the result of information given to me by persons who had either direct knowledge or that kind of indirect knowledge which the lawyer, banker, and official has. I had, during the investigation, no connection with any government or with any business organization.

My results are in many ways unsatisfactory and inadequate, for direct business investments are not easily discovered or measured. In one case, for example, property to the value of U. S. $250,000 was found to be held in trust for Americans living in the United States to whom the income is regularly remitted. It happens that this holding was unknown to the local American officials. I have no doubt that there are other cases of the same sort and, on the other hand, an equal number which I have failed to include. But, when the property is known, the problem of valuation remains to be solved.

Business assets ought, when international economic relations are being considered, to be valued in relation to the flow of funds which they occasion. American business investments in China ought to be valued in accordance with the cost of their acquisition in terms of remittances to China, or at a capitalization of the flow of funds out of China which they bring about. What, for example, is the value to be placed on an American-owned factory in China? It may be valued at what it cost in outpayments from the United States, or it may be valued at a reasonable capitalization of the inpayments into the United States, which it brings about. From the point of view of international economic relations, its value must have some relation to an item or a series of items in the international accounts or the international balances of payments of the two countries concerned.

But in the difficult field of American business investments in China the investigator finds himself a beggar who cannot be a chooser upon these high grounds of theory. My request was for information as to, (1) the value of the physical property of the firm in China, (2) the value of the other assets owned by the firms in China. The value of the physical property has been, in practically all cases, the approximate market value of land holdings, equipment, and stocks of goods. The "other assets" have been watched carefully and only such assets have been included as may be reasonably expected to produce a net income for the business. Goodwill has not been entered. Claims against the Chinese government have not been included at all. I find the total reported to me by 213 firms, as the value of physical property, to be U. S. $106,736,855, and of other assets U. S. $43,591,123.

The total which I have is, then, a total value of active business assets in China, exclusive of good-will. The problem of the remittance to China, which has been required to build up this business investment, and of the remittance to America, which it brings about, I leave at the moment for future consideration.

These business investments I have valued in U. S. dollars, but they are actually in a country which uses silver. How, then, secure a value in U. S. dollars? The method has been to take the average rate of exchange for the period and to ask the business man to do so. Investigation revealed that business holdings in China are of two sorts, those whose basic value is a silver value, and those whose basic value is in gold or is strongly affected by valuation in a gold currency. The owner of a piece of land at a treaty port has in his possession a source of silver income and the basic value of the land must be considered to be its silver value. A fall in the value of silver means a fall, in so far as this is the only change, in the value of land. Consider, however, the owner of a stock of goods which must be imported, such, for example, as motor trucks or American tobacco. A fall in silver will be reflected in some rise in the value of his stocks, for in this case the basic value may be regarded as a gold value. Those who reported to me have, in many cases, which have been called to my attention, taken this into account. The valuation of American investments is, then, a gold dollar value, supplied by the business man himself, or calculated at current rates, taking into account the fact that basic valuation is sometimes the value in gold dollars and sometimes the value in silver dollars.[66]

The total value of business investments included, as I have said, certain items which are not further analyzed. The first of these is the value of the property of clubs and similar organizations, and the value of the property of Americans at the various mountain and seaside resorts in China.[67] This property is like business property since it is held by individuals, is bought and sold, and since a money income is sometimes derived from it. It is not like business property since it consists largely of durable consumers' goods held by the consumers themselves. Such holdings are for the recreation and health of Americans living in China. I find the total value of such property from which a business income is not normally derived to be U. S. $1,590,000. Of this total about U. S. $500,000 is the value of American clubs at Shanghai, and U. S. $1,000,000 the value of holdings at Peitaiho, Kuling, Chikungshan, Mokanshan, Tsingtao, and similar places, not including schools for American children or churches for the American or foreign community.

The next item which is excluded from the analysis is the property of Americans in the various professions in China. I include under this heading doctors of medicine, lawyers, dentists, architects, brokers, etc. I have received reports from 18 Americans in the various professions and these reports enable me to estimate the total holdings under this heading at U. S. $1,194,800. The reports enable me to separate investments in connection with their professional activities, U. S. $133,100, from their other investments in China, U. S. $1,061,700.[68] It may be noted also that the

[66] The importance of this consideration is increased by the fact that values reported for 1928 in silver had to be recalculated, in terms of 1930, in gold. In the important cases this was done after consultation with the business men in China. In some cases the value for 1928 had to be accepted.

[67] I have not included as business investments schools and churches for the American community in China. These are dealt with under mission and philanthropic holdings below.

[68] The counting of this sum in my total may involve some duplication

total amount remitted from China by these professional men amounted to no more than U. S. $69,400 for the year 1929. Most of this was for payment of insurance premiums. The total of the above two items, eliminated from further analysis, is U. S. $2,784,800.

I turn now to a brief statement of the results of my inquiries in connection with the study. It brings out, among other things, the reason for a further elimination of a relatively small sum. The investigation of American business investments in China involved the sending out of 611 inquiries.

Sixty-seven firms reported "no business in China" or business carried on in such a way as to require no investment. In 132 cases it was found that there was no American interest in the firm or, more often, that the firm was no longer in existence in China. In these 199 cases no inquiry would have been made if the facts had been known in advance. It was somewhat surprising, however, to find no American interest whatever in firms incorporated under the China Trade Act.

Another group of firms not included consists of 11 owned by Philippine Chinese. These firms were omitted because it was impossible to measure the investments of the numerous and important Chinese firms in a similar position in the Dutch East Indies and other parts of the South Seas. The whole subject is considered elsewhere in connection with remittances to China from Chinese overseas. Two of the 11 firms, considerably larger than the others, have total holdings in China and the Philippines of more than U. S. $1,000,000 each, according to information secured in Amoy.

Deducting the firms dealt with in the preceding paragraphs there remain 401 American firms having investments of some sort in China. The efforts to secure in-

since some of the "other investments" are in American companies dealt with below. The amount is not great however. Much of the "other investment" consists of residences.

formation from them brought the following results. In four cases information was refused and I could not secure from other sources information which enabled an estimate to be made. In 140 cases I found the firm to be in active business in China but too small to justify the spending of time in an effort to secure sufficient information to enter into analysis. The holdings of these firms I estimated at U. S. $15,000 each after consultation with officials in local Chambers of Commerce and with others who knew the American business communities in China. There were found to be 44 special cases which are not entered in my final total. These 44 include five firms whose only assets in China consist of claims against the Chinese government for supplies and equipment furnished in the past. There is included also in these special cases a considerable number of firms which have not been dealt with separately because they are closely allied with or subsidiaries of firms which have been counted.

This leaves a total of 213 firms and of these it may be said that satisfactory information was secured. In most cases the information was secured from the firms themselves, though in a few cases it was secured from others who knew the facts directly. This final group includes, I am fairly certain, every important American firm in China or with interests in China. The results of my questionnaires are shown in the following table:

TABLE 4

THE NUMBER OF INQUIRIES MADE AND THE RESULTS

Total number of inquiries made	611
Eliminated for reasons stated above	210
American firms having investments in China	401
Information refused, no estimate made	4
Found to be small, investment estimated	140
Special cases	44
Satisfactory information secured	213
	401

It is the estimated investment of U. S. $2,100,000 of the 140 small firms which is the next and last item to be deducted before the study of American business investments is carried further. The facts are shown below:

TABLE 5

BUSINESS INVESTMENTS TO BE ANALYZED

	U. S. Dollars
Total business investments	155,112,778
Deduct:	
Property from which business income is not ordinarily derived	1,590,000
Investments of professional men	1,194,000
Investments of 140 small firms	2,100,000
Leaving:	
Investments of 213 firms	150,227,987

According to size of firm: The classification of these firms, according to size, involves the small firms and it is the only classification which does. The outstanding fact about the size is that there are a few firms with great holdings. There are, in fact, 17 firms with investments of over U. S. $1,000,000 each and these 17 hold no less than 82 per cent of the investments. Many of these firms are banks, and a number of them are the great trading firms who have a long history in China, such as the Standard Oil Company and Andersen Meyer & Company. Certain of the firms are recent, however, and are in manufacturing and in the field of public utilities.

TABLE 6

AMERICAN FIRMS IN CHINA CLASSIFIED ACCORDING TO SIZE

	No. of Firms	Per Cent of Total	Investment in U. S. Dollars	Per Cent of Total	Avg. Investment in U. S. Dollars
Small	140	39.7	2,100,000	1.4	15,000
Medium	196	55.5	25,359,828	16.6	129,387
Large	17	4.8	124,868,150	82.0	7,345,185
	353	100.0	152,327,978	100.0	431,524

The average investment of the 213 firms is U. S. $705,296.

The analysis of the investment of the 213 firms is presented in such a way as to make possible some degree of comparability with the information which has been brought together about Japanese and British business investments. Some care has been taken, also, to present totals which completely preserve the anonymity of the firms who have been sufficiently interested in this study to provide information.

According to geographical distribution: The geographical distribution of the investments of the 213 firms is shown in the following table:

TABLE 7

GEOGRAPHICAL DISTRIBUTION OF AMERICAN BUSINESS INVESTMENTS

	In U. S. Dollars	Per Cent of Total
In Shanghai	97,495,917	64.9
Outside Shanghai	50,567,803	33.7
In Hongkong	2,164,978	1.4
	150,227,978	100.0

This table shows that about 65 per cent of American business investments in China are in the single port of Shanghai and 35 per cent in the rest of China, including Hongkong.

Other information of importance is shown by the distribution of the firms. The information which I have enables a clear picture to be presented of the importance of Shanghai and other ports as independent centers of American business activity. Of the 213 firms, 146 have offices in Shanghai. In practically every case the chief office is in Shanghai and in 105 cases the only office is in Shanghai. In other words, 65 per cent of the capital invested by business firms is in Shanghai and 68.5 per cent of the firms have offices there. Of the other centers Tientsin is by far the most important. This is shown in the following table which gives information about American firms with one office only in China. It will be seen that Tientsin is not only second in importance to Shanghai but also that it is the only center with any degree of independence of Shanghai.

TABLE 8

AMERICAN BUSINESS INVESTMENTS. DISTRIBUTION OF FIRMS WITH ONE OFFICE ONLY, ACCORDING TO THE LOCATION OF THAT OFFICE

Place	No. of Firms
Shanghai	105
Tientsin	33
Hongkong	6
Peiping	5
Canton	4
Harbin	3
Hankow	3
Six others	8

This table may be supplemented by information which shows the investment, in the three important centers, of the firms with a single office. The figures are as follows:

	U. S. Dollars
Shanghai	59,821,975
Tientsin	2,644,600
Hongkong and Canton	606,978

These figures bring out the fact that about 50 per cent of the firms studied are firms with one office only and that office at Shanghai. Such firms do not hold more than about 40 per cent of the total investment of American firms in China. This concentration of firms with a single office in Shanghai must be considered in connection with the distribution of capital according to the nature of the trade or business which is dealt with below.

According to the time of establishment of firm: The number of years the firm has been in business in China is reported in 130 cases out of the 213. The firms may be classified in various ways. In the first place we may divide them as follows:

Firms who entered China before 1900	4
From 1900 to the end of 1913	18
From 1914 to the end of 1930	108

We may also divide them thus:

Firms in China before the World War	22
Those who entered during the war	18
Those who entered after the war	90

A classification by years, not shown here, reveals that, at the end of 1930, the largest group, 18, was but one year old and the next largest group, 10, was eleven years old. There is a high rate of infant mortality among American firms in China. Nevertheless 10 firms of the year 1919 and 9 firms of the year 1920 have survived through 1930. In order to bring this about there must have been an entrance into China of many times this number. It is not unreasonable to suppose, when we consider the Customs figures which are presented later, that new American companies to the number of nearly 150 ventured into China during the years 1919 and 1920. It may be stated, also, as quite certain that at any particular time a majority of the American firms in China have been there for less than ten years.

According to nature of business: I turn next to a classification of American business investments in China according to the nature of the business. The classification is made in such a way as to facilitate comparison with other countries and to enable investments through borrowing by the Chinese government to be added. The table presented on page 285 requires little in the way of explanation. The fractions are the result of the fact that certain firms have been divided for the purpose of this classification. A firm may be in shipping and in the import and export business, and sufficient information may have been provided to enable its investment to be divided between the two. Such a division was undertaken in only two cases.

Import and Export: It is seen from these tables that the import and export trade is of first importance. About 100 of the firms are engaged in it and they own about 32 per cent of the capital invested by all American firms. Consider in this connection the facts brought out in Table 10. Of the 100 American firms engaged in import and export, no fewer than 48 are firms who have but a single office in China and that office in Shanghai. About

TABLE 9

AMERICAN BUSINESS INVESTMENTS IN CHINA CLASSIFIED ACCORDING TO
THE NATURE OF THE BUSINESS

Nature of Business	Firms		Investments	
	No. of Firms	Per Cent of Total	Investment in U. S. Dollars	Per Cent of Total
1. Transportation				
a) Aviation, railway equipment, etc.	2		810,000	
b) Motor cars and accessories	19		3,790,298	
c) Shipping	5⅚		6,199,620	
d) Total	26⅚	12.6	*10,799,918*	7.2
2. Public utilities	2	0.9	35,200,000	23.4
3. Mining	½	0.2	104,500	0.1
4. Manufacturing				
a) Textiles	9			
b) Others	19⅓			
c) Total	28⅓	13.3	*20,509,095*	13.7
5. Banking and finance	9	4.2	25,320,280	16.8
6. Real estate	10	4.7	8,478,550	5.6
7. Import and export	99⅓	46.7	47,748,240	31.8
8. Miscellaneous	37	17.4	2,067,395	1.4
	213	100.0	150,227,978	100.0

TABLE 10

AMERICAN FIRMS WITH ONE OFFICE AND IN SHANGHAI ONLY, CLASSIFIED
ACCORDING TO THE NATURE OF THE BUSINESS

Nature of Business	Firms			Investments		
	No. in China	In Shanghai Only	Per Cent in Shanghai Only	In China U. S. Dollars	In Shanghai Only U. S. Dollars	Per Cent in Shanghai Only
1. Transportation	26⅚	10	37.0	10,799,918	2,252,750	20.9
2. Public utilities	2	2	100.0	35,200,000	35,200,000	100.0
3. Mining	½	0	0.0	104,500	0	0.0
4. Manufacturing	28⅓	16	56.5	20,509,095	11,012,550	53.7
5. Banking and finance	9	2	22.2	25,320,280	762,930	3.0
6. Real estate	10	5	50.0	8,478,550	5,084,050	60.0
7. Import and export	99⅓	48	48.3	47,748,240	3,984,500	8.3
8. Miscellaneous	37	22	59.5	2,067,395	1,525,195	73.8
	213	105	49.3	150,227,978	59,821,975	39.8

one-fourth of the American firms studied were found to be in the import and export business and unrepresented outside of Shanghai. But we must look further. The 48 firms we are now considering hold no more than about U. S. $4 million of a total American investment of U. S. $150 million. Of the 213 firms which have been studied, over 22 per cent are firms with one office at Shanghai, and they have less than 3 per cent of the total American investment in China. It is to be observed also that a large number of the firms classified as miscellaneous are small firms at Shanghai only. When it is remembered that the 140 firms excluded from the analysis are all small and that many of them are at Shanghai only, a guess of the following sort may be ventured. About half the American firms in China are firms with one office, at Shanghai only, very largely in the import and export business, and so small as to control no more than 5 per cent of the total American business investment in China. The larger firms in the import and export business bring the total capital in this field up to nearly 32 per cent.

Public Utilities: Public utilities come next in importance. The two firms provide a contrast with those in importing and exporting. Here we have firms with but one office and at Shanghai, but they are among the greatest from the point of view of investment. Both of these firms entered China since the beginning of 1929. They constitute the largest recent addition to American business investment in China. In each case an American corporation acquired property in China or a controlling interest in property in China. In each case the management of the business passed to American hands. The management was imported with the capital as is characteristic of direct business investments.

The more important of the two public utility corporations is the Shanghai Power Company. This company has been organized to hold and operate the plant formerly held by the Municipal Council of the Foreign Settlement of Shanghai. The Municipal Council had purchased the plant of a local electric light and power company in 1893. The early years of municipal operation did not give satisfaction and in 1899 the Municipal Council advertised for tenders with the intention of selling the plant to a private corporation.[69] After the failure to sell, the Municipality undertook to develop the plant and it met with considerable success. At the end of 1928 there was in existence a plant which was carried on the books at Sh. Tls. 39,410,422.16.[70] The capital outlay for the undertaking was, we are told, Tls. 34,905,961, excluding appropriations for land.

It was not financial difficulties which lay behind the sale of this plant in 1929 to the American and Foreign Power Company. We may suppose that possible future political difficulties played a part in the willingness of the Council to consider a sale and that the possibility of further ventures in China played a part in the willingness of the three groups to make an offer. In any case offers were made and, on April 17, 1929, the Shanghai rate-payers passed a resolution authorizing the sale of the plant to the American and Foreign Power Company at the price which it offered, Sh. Tls. 81 million.[71] The Company purchased the plant subject to a franchise giving a monopoly in the Foreign Settlement for forty years.[72] Dividends above 10 per cent are to be divided into two parts, one of which is to bring about reduction in rates. The Council reserves the right to repurchase at the end of forty years. There were other conditions, among them one which provided that local firms and residents were to be given an opportunity to invest in the company.

The plant was actually turned over to the Shanghai Power Company on August 9, 1929.[73] By the end of 1930

---

[69] *Chronicle and Directory* . . . *1900*, p. 166.
[70] *Shanghai Municipal Gazette*, August 10, 1929; March 28, 1929.
[71] *Shanghai Municipal Gazette*, April 17, 1929.
[72] Franchise printed in the *Shanghai Municipal Gazette*, March 28, 1929.
[73] *Shanghai Municipal Gazette*, August 16, 1929.

the Company had made payments to the Municipal Council on the purchase price. Of the funds so paid, Sh. Tls. 17.5 million were raised locally, and the balance was remitted from the United States. The Company had by the same date made additions and improvements which are estimated at Sh. Tls. 5 million.

This company illustrates the difficulty of classifying direct investments by nationality. The purchase was made, we are told, by the Shanghai Power Company "and British associates." [74] The shares of the company are held by British, Chinese, and Japanese as well as by Americans who own a controlling interest. Legally the company is American. The Shanghai Telephone Company, the other public utility corporation reported in the preceding tables, presents a similar problem. There are minority shareholders of many nationalities but the company is legally American and Americans own a controlling interest. In both cases the whole investment has been regarded as American. It was found impossible to go behind the legal status of the corporation and distribute the actual holding by nationality. The source of the funds in both of the above cases is known and the error involved in classifying the whole investment as American is slight.

The entrance of American corporations into public utilities in Shanghai has increased the proportion of American investments in that city as compared with the rest of China by adding two firms with great holdings who have offices in Shanghai only. In the American case there has been this special reason for the increase in the relative importance of Shanghai which has been the general result of the unsettled state of the country and the rise of Chinese nationalism.

Banking and Finance: Banking and Finance is next in importance in percentage of total investment. The chief item under this heading is the investment of the four

[74] *Shanghai Municipal Gazette,* March 28, 1929.

American banks in China. The National City Bank (9 offices), the American Express Company (4 offices), the Equitable Eastern Banking Corporation (2 offices), and the American Oriental Banking Corporation (2 offices with its head office at Shanghai). The problem of estimating investment from the banks presented difficulties which were solved in consultation with the late Mr. M. D. Currie of the National City Bank. The investment was taken to be the physical property of the bank and the total of the amount outstanding in loans to Chinese. Loans to Americans and other foreigners in China were excluded since this would involve the duplication of items already reported by business firms, as, for example, a stock of goods upon which an importing firm had secured an advance. The total arrived at by the above method has been checked against a capitalization of the net income from the operations of the bank in China, made after consultation with the bankers.

Manufacturing: Manufacturing, 13.7 per cent of the total business investment, has been divided so as to show textile manufacturing separately. Practically the whole of this investment is in the manufacture of Chinese carpets in Tientsin and Peking. The other manufacturing plants turn out electrical equipment, wood products, shipping containers, egg products, cigarettes, and other articles. The 16 firms, which are reported in Table 10 as having offices in Shanghai only, do not own any of the plants which are reported under textiles.[75]

The only other field of importance is that of the im-

[75] A recent investigation of the Department of Commerce of the U. S. government (*American Direct Investments in Foreign Countries*, Washington, 1930, p. 26) shows 15 firms engaged in manufacturing in China having investments of U. S. $10,221,000. The smallness of this figure is to be explained by the fact that holdings of Americans resident in China and of American firms incorporated under the China Trade Act are excluded. The Department of Commerce was interested in the value of properties situated abroad and owned by residents of the United States. This explains its definition of direct investments. My totals show the property in China of American citizens and corporations, wherever domiciled.

porting, assembling, and operating of motor cars. These activities are all included under the term "motor cars and accessories."

The automobile business is more concentrated in Shanghai than one would suppose from the figures for transportation in general. Of the 19 firms concerned with motor cars, 9 have offices in Shanghai only, and these nine hold U. S. $1,602,750 of the investments. A number of the other 10 firms have offices in Shanghai as well.

American corporations are of first importance in real estate, especially in Shanghai. In mining American capital is so small as to be negligible.

Remittances to and from China: Certain additional information of value in arriving at estimates of the remittance to and from China in connection with American business investments will be presented next. Chinese participation in the ownership of the 213 firms will be dealt with first. Chinese participation was reported in no more than 22 cases.

Four of the 22 are special cases which may be eliminated from further consideration. In three of the four the Chinese participation was reported to be over 50 per cent and in one it was just under 50 per cent. In each case the sum which enters my total of American business investments is the American share of these joint ventures. In two of the cases the Chinese government or some government institution has undertaken an enterprise in which it has entered into an agreement with an American corporation. I have dealt with the American corporation in these cases and I have entered its investment only. I have handled the other two cases in the same way, although they are with private Chinese interests and not with the Chinese government. In these four cases I have entered only such sums as Americans have actually invested and no adjustment or correction need be made.

In the other 18 cases Chinese own some share in an American corporation and the total holdings of the corporation have been entered in my figures. Some part of the profits in these cases is paid over to Chinese in China and does not enter into any estimated sum of profits remitted from China. In the 18 cases the Chinese participation varied from 2.8 per cent to 50 per cent. The average was almost exactly 20 per cent. Let me state the matter in other words. In a total of 213 cases it was found that Chinese held some share of the ownership of 18 American firms and the average Chinese ownership was 20 per cent.[76]

These figures seemed to me surprisingly small and not consistent with statements made to me in various Chinese cities on the subject of Chinese participation. I spent some time in talking this matter over with American business men and, while I do not suppose that I have a true total of Chinese participation in American business ventures in China, nevertheless I am convinced that it is much less general and much smaller than is generally supposed. I was frequently told, for example, that Chinese ownership of the Shanghai Telephone Company was above 50 per cent. I do not know what it may have been in the past but I found it to be actually 23.2 per cent. In a considerable number of successful American corporations I found Chinese participation in the ownership to be non-existent or negligible.

A second matter upon which a small amount of information is available is the remittance to China from the United States for the building up of the investments which are now in the possession of the American firms. The nature of the business is an important consideration. An import and export firm usually has in its possession assets which have been paid for entirely by remittances from the United States. The firm in China may be a branch of the firm in the United States and the Ameri-

[76] It does not, of course, follow that profits not paid to Chinese in China are sent out of the country. They may be paid to Americans or to other nationals in China.

can company may be the owner of all the assets in China. Many firms exporting embroideries from Swatow and many exporting furs from Tientsin report that such exports are entirely for their own account. Other aspects of these property holdings will be dealt with later; at present I wish to emphasize the fact that such holdings have usually been paid for entirely by remittances from the United States.

At the other extreme are firms who have property in China for which nothing at all has been remitted from the United States. Several firms have reported to me that their holdings, which now amount to a considerable sum, were "built up from nothing" or that they "started on a shoe string." But it is not only such firms who have remitted little or nothing to China. There are important corporations in Shanghai owning property worth millions of dollars who report to me that the whole of their financing has been done locally. Such firms in China are, upon the territorial principle and from the point of view of international payments not "foreign" firms at all but domestic firms. Yet, because of extraterritoriality and the Chinese emphasis upon the racial or family principle, they are regarded as "foreign" both by the Chinese and by the Americans resident in China. Such is the situation in China that a firm financed entirely by funds within China and paying no dividends out of China is "foreign" if it happens to be owned by someone who is not Chinese. At the same time a firm financed entirely from outside of China and remitting profits from China is regarded as "Chinese" if the owners, as in the case of the Philippine Chinese firms at Amoy, are of Chinese blood. If I may use the word colony as a purely descriptive term, the situation may be made clear by saying that there is a foreign political colony inside the Chinese economy and that in various places outside of China there is a Chinese racial colony inside the particular foreign economy.

The information concerning the remittances to China for the building up of American holdings within the country is presented with a full appreciation of the difficulties. In the cases in which such remittances have been reported to me I find that a total remittance of U. S. $13,395,000 has been made by firms who, at the end of 1930, had investments within China to the amount of U. S. $37,151,000. This shows remittances of about 36 per cent of the current value of business holdings. How far such a ratio may be applied in general is a question of judgment which is considered in connection with the international payments into and out of China.

Information touching profits and dividend payments is available in some form from about 50 of the 213 firms. A study of the returns shows that a distinction must be made between firms in the import and export group and all other firms. I have returns from about 20 firms in this group showing profits that vary from nothing to over 300 per cent of the reported investment in China. The information in this field reinforces the conclusion which I have reached on other grounds, that the holdings of import and export firms in China are to be regarded differently from other investments within the country. They are usually investments in a trade which is international—involving four or five countries in some cases. Its spread depends upon the location of raw materials, upon localized skill, and upon the nature of the market. Consider the case of a great "department store" in an American city, which has agents in China who receive linen purchased in Ireland, supervise its handling in China, and ship the finished linen products to America. Here they are sold at retail. The profit in such a case can have little relation to the investment in China which happens to be involved in that part of the work taking place there. Consider again the purchase in China of raw furs which have been brought from Mongolia by a firm operating for its own account. The furs are prepared and shipped to New York where they are made up into garments for wholesale or retail sale in the American market. Here again there is no point in attempting to relate profits to the part of the investment which happens to be in China. Other products such as bristles, hides, and wood oil can be named. The importer is more likely to be able to answer whether or not he has made money on his China business than is the exporter, but in this case also there are difficulties. Overhead charges are frequently met in America and not charged against Chinese business, stocks may be shipped from China if prospects seem good elsewhere, turnover may be slow or rapid and so make holdings large or small in relation to volume of business. For these reasons it has seemed best to eliminate the import and export firm altogether from my calculations of remittances from China of profits upon American capital.

Putting aside the firms in the import and export business, I find that reports from about 30 firms show results that run from considerable losses to profits as high as 50 per cent in their investment. When there are any profits they are usually between 10 per cent and 25 per cent of the investment. The reports in most cases are from 1924 to 1928 and in a few cases from 1924 to 1930. In general it may be said that profits were greater in 1928 and during the preceding years than they have been since 1928. The evidence seems to show that in years of ordinary prosperity American investments in China bring in a return of from 10 per cent to 20 per cent. It is probable that there must be an expectation of profit which runs above 10 per cent to bring about investment. The total American investment outside of the import and export business was U. S. $102.5 million in 1930. This means a profit of at least U. S. $10 million in ordinary years and it may well run to U. S. $15 or 20 million in good years. Some such sum as this seems to me to represent the upper limit of possible remittance to the United States in this connection. But all the evidence seems to show that profits which are earned in China or dividends which are paid by American corporations in China do not go to the United States in any large proportion. When account is taken of the fact that profits have been smaller in 1929 and 1930 than they were in 1928, the opinion may be ventured that remittances to the United States from China of returns from the holdings we have been considering cannot have been over U. S. $10 million in 1928 and were probably no more than half of this sum in 1930.

I must add the estimate of a well-informed man of the royalties paid to American moving picture corporations. It is his opinion that the total receipts from the showing of such films in China came to at least silver $20 million in 1930 and that the remittance to the United States on account of royalties was U. S. $2 million during the same year. It will be remembered that remittances to America from China by persons in the professions came to U. S. $69,400 for the year 1929. The total of remittances from China connected with returns from American business ventures of all sorts cannot have been more than about U. S. $15 million in 1928 and were probably not over U. S. $7 or 8 million in 1930.

Securities and Obligations of the Chinese Government

In addition to business investments in China Americans hold certain obligations which are most accurately described as Chinese government securities and obligations of the Chinese government and of government institutions. These items are now more numerous than the single one reported for 1914.

The only American issue of Chinese government securities is still the issue of one-fourth of the Hukuang Railway loan of 1911. This was a 5 per cent loan for £6 million. It is usually listed as a loan secured upon salt revenues but the Ministry of Finance of the Chinese government accepts the payment of only one of the two annual coupons as a charge upon the salt revenues of the central government. The amount of the principal outstanding in this loan on January 1, 1931, was £5,645,-258.[77] The arrears of interest were on January 1, 1931, £1,030,278 but they include arrears which need be considered only in arriving at the obligation involved in the German issue. The arrears shared among the four banking groups came to £914,514. This makes the total obligation, U. S. $31,976,662, deducting the amount due on the German bonds only. The American share of this comes to U. S. $7,994,165.

Two loans, which are ordinarily known as the Chicago Bank loan and the Pacific Development loan, are nominally secured upon the revenues of the Chinese government from the taxation of wine and tobacco. As a matter of fact both of these obligations are included in a list of "inadequately secured foreign loans of the Ministry of Finance," prepared by the Financial Readjustment Commission in 1925.[78]

The first of these loans was originally a loan for U. S. $5,000,000 for which a contract was signed in Washington on November 16, 1916, between the Chinese government and the Continental and Commercial Trust and Savings Bank of Chicago.[79] This contract was for a loan of 6 per cent at 91 and for three years. The security was said to be revenues derived from the "tobacco and wine public sales tax." In a supplementary agreement of May, 1917, the security was made certain provincial "goods taxes" in order to provide security "which is entirely free from any conflicting claims of any sort." This loan was repaid in 1919 from the proceeds of a loan for

[77] It is assumed that bonds to the face value of £381,640 turned over to the Chinese government in connection with the Sino-German agreement of June, 1924, were disposed of outside of China.

[78] Printed by the Commission and issued at Peking in November of that year.

[79] The contract is printed in MacMurray, John V. A., *Treaties and Agreements*, vol. II, p. 1337, and the supplementary agreement on p. 1343.

U. S. $5,500,000, the contract for which was signed in October of that year,[80] and the security for which was the same as for the earlier loan. No payments of principal or interest have ever been made upon this loan. The amount of this loan outstanding at the end of the year 1930 was U. S. $9,130,000.[81]

The second is a loan for which a contract was signed with the Pacific Development Corporation on November 26, 1919,[82] the sum of U. S. $5,500,000 at 91. The rate of interest was 6 per cent and the Treasury Notes to be issued were payable in two years. The loan was a charge upon the wine and tobacco administration and carried with it a proposal for the appointment of an American adviser. This came to nothing. No payment of principal or interest had been made when this loan fell due in 1921. The loan was extended at 8 per cent by supplementary agreements, but no payments have been made since. The amount outstanding on this loan at the end of 1930 was U. S. $9,969,666.[83]

The next item among the loans with inadequate security is the result of advances by an American corporation in connection with a contract for engineering operations on the Grand Canal. It is usually called the Grand Canal Conservancy loan. Five advances were made upon this loan at various dates from May, 1918, to June, 1921, amounting altogether to U. S. $905,000.[84] The ob-

[80] Printed as Annex V to the *List of Contracts of American Nationals*, Washington, 1925. This list was submitted in pursuance of Resolution 11 of the Conference on Limitation of Armaments. Printed also in *Treaties and Agreements With and Concerning China, 1919–1929*, Washington, 1929, p. 1.

[81] If the figures of the Financial Readjustment Commission are accepted as of December 31, 1925, the amount as of December 31, 1930, becomes U. S. $9,125,738.03.

[82] Printed as Annex VI to the *List of Contracts of American Nationals*, Washington, 1925. Printed also in *Treaties and Agreements With and Concerning China, 1919–1929*, Washington, 1929, p. 11. The supplementary agreements are to be found in the same place.

[83] The figure of the Financial Readjustment Commission for December 31, 1925, brought down to date.

[84] Annex IV of the *List of Contracts of American Nationals*, Washington, 1925.

ligation of the Chinese government has been arrived at
by accepting the total reported by the Financial Readjustment Commission of 1925 and adding interest to
the end of 1930. The amount outstanding at the end of
1930 is found by this method to be U. S. $1,656,000.

Certain additional loans, without specific security,
are listed by the Financial Readjustment Commission
in its reports for the end of the year 1925, and in a schedule of obligations to Americans drawn up by the Chinese
Ministry of Finance to show the situation at the end of
1927. These loans are from American banks for expenses
connected with Chinese students in the United States.
The outstanding amount of these loans was at the end
of 1930, according to my calculations, U. S. $146,593.

There are, finally, obligations of the Chinese government to American firms. Lists of such obligations were
drawn up in connection with the work of preparation
for the Conference on the Chinese Customs Tariff (October, 1925–April, 1926). The lists for these earlier years
are now out of date. The obligation, for example, of the
Chinese government to the American Trading Company
for materials and equipment for the Shanghai Mint,
reported in 1925 at about U. S. $765,000, has been ad-
justed as the result of recent negotiations. The Chinese
government has recently appointed a "Commission for
the Consolidation of Foreign and Domestic Obligations."
This Commission is the successor to the Financial Readjustment Commission of 1925 whose work has been
referred to above. The work of this commission will bring
into existence a new estimate of the total obligations of
the Chinese government which are unsecured or inadequately secured. At the same time the various foreign
governments are taking steps to arrive at new estimates
as a result of proposals put before a meeting of foreign
diplomatic representatives called together in Nanking on
November 15, 1930. These new lists of obligations are
not yet in existence and they may alter the total which

I report below. What I have done in the American case
is to accept without alteration the sums reported to me
by the various American firms as due to them from the
Chinese government for supplies and materials and claims
against the Chinese government for actual goods and
property seized or destroyed. A large part of the obligations are debts due to American firms for equipment and
supplies for the Chinese government railways.

My list is by no means complete. It includes no claims
of missionaries or mission organizations. I know of claims
which amount to hundreds of thousands of dollars which
are not entered because the firms preferred to report such
debts to no one but the American government so long as
negotiations were in progress. In general it may be said
that practically every important American firm in China,
and many that are unimportant, hold unpaid obligations
of the Chinese government. It is well known in China
that the financial difficulties of certain American firms
during the last ten or more years are due to the failure
of the Chinese government to meet its obligations. I
have pointed out above that five American firms have
reported to me that they have no other interest in China
than their claims against the Chinese government. In
four of these cases the firms were actually represented
in China in the past and have withdrawn.

The only sum in my total below which has been reported in other lists of obligations is one which represents
an advance by an American firm, Siems and Carey, on
a contract for the construction of the Chuchow-Ching-
chow Railway in Hunan province. The American International Corporation is the successor to the rights and
obligations of Siems and Carey. I include the sum in my
total since it was reported to me in the same way as the
other debts of the Chinese government to American firms.
It may be said also that the total under this heading has
been reported in some cases for the end of the year 1928
and in others for 1929 and 1930. The total under this

heading, that is, debts of the Chinese government and of government institutions to American firms at the end of 1930 I find to be U. S. $11,814,922.

The items listed above reach a total of U. S. $40,711,346 and this total is the American holding of Chinese government obligations calculated on the principle of the place of issue. The total based on the actual holding of such securities is the one presented below. In order to arrive at this total it is necessary to estimate the movement of Chinese securities into or out of the United States. The only issue which may have moved out of the United States is the American share of the Hukuang loan. J. P. Morgan and Company, who are in charge of the service of the bonds in America, have been good enough to prepare a statement showing the number of coupons of the American issue received from abroad and the number of coupons of the European issues presented for payment in New York. This statement shows that the number of Hukuang bonds of the American issue held abroad is almost exactly equal to the number of bonds of the European issues which have been imported. The conclusion is that the total arrived at on the principle of the place of issue is substantially the correct total on the principle of the place of actual holding.

There are, however, certain bonds of other loans in which the United States did not participate which have been imported into the United States. These bonds are very largely Chinese sterling bonds and they moved to America with other sterling securities in the period immediately after the war. The importation of such securities represents not an importation of Chinese securities as such but an importation of sterling securities some of which happened to be bonds of Chinese loans. Many of these bonds were of the Chinese Imperial Government Gold loan of 1895. This loan was issued in French francs at a fixed rate of exchange for payment of both interest and principal in pounds sterling. A representative of the chief importer of these bonds, a brokerage house in New York, has provided information which enables an estimate to be made that the American holding of these bonds amounted to about U. S. $2,000,000 in 1925 and to no more than about U. S. $250,000 in 1930. The chief reason for this decline is the retirement of the loan. The funds made available have not been reinvested in Chinese securities.

Information concerning other European issues of Chinese government securities makes it possible to estimate that the holding of such securities in the United States was perhaps U. S. $750,000. This includes a small holding of the Berlin, London, and Paris series of the Reorganization loan of 1913. The total American holding of Chinese securities not issued in the United States I estimate to have been about U. S. $1,000,000 in 1930.[85]

A total of American holdings of Chinese government securities and other obligations of the Chinese government may now be presented. It must be borne in mind in making comparisons that it represents an estimate on the principle of place of actual holding though the difference between the two is no more than U. S. $1,000,000 in the case of the United States.

TABLE 11

AMERICAN HOLDINGS OF SECURITIES AND OBLIGATIONS OF THE CHINESE
GOVERNMENT

Hukuang loan	U. S. $ 7,994,165
Chicago Bank loan	9,130,000
Pacific Development loan	9,969,666
Grand Canal loan	1,656,000
Other unsecured loans	146,593
Obligations of the Chinese govt. to American firms	11,814,922
American purchase of bonds issued elsewhere	1,000,000
Total	U. S. $41,711,346

[85] It ought to be mentioned that there are in the United States certain bonds, to the face value of about U. S. $2.5 million of the original Russian series of the Reorganization loan of 1913. It seems that the subscribers to the original Russian series, many of whom were in France, received receipts for their payments and scrip which called for the delivery of the definitive

The Property of American Mission and Philanthropic Societies

Information concerning the property in China of American mission and philanthropic societies and the annual remittances of these societies to China is presented as it has been reported to me in the course of my study. The studies and estimates of others are not considered for the moment nor is any attempt made to allow for the obvious fact that I have not received reports from every American society. I deal with mission and philanthropic holdings as I did with business investments. The purpose is to bring together for convenience of reference all the facts revealed by the 1930 study.

The first sum I present is the value in U. S. dollars of the property such as that of the American schools and churches devoted primarily or exclusively to the service of the American community in China. Such property is certainly not a business investment. It differs also from the other holdings presented under this heading since it is not for the service of the Chinese people. The value of such property in China I find to be U. S. $1,166,300. This includes the American school and the community church at Shanghai and the American schools at Peiping, Kuling, and Chikungshan. It includes also the property of the Young Men's Christian Association in China which is for the service of the foreign community. The annual remittances from the United States in connection with this property have not been reported to me. It is probable that very little is remitted directly from America for the

bonds. Before the bonds were delivered the war began and the bonds were allowed to remain with the participating bank in Russia. These bonds were seized by the Soviet government after the Russian revolution and their sale in London was permitted. It is some of these bonds which are now in the United States. The Chinese government issued new "Green" bonds, and these have been exchanged for the scrip. I have not included the American holding of the original bonds in my total since the Chinese government does not recognize its obligation to make payments upon them. I make no comment on the legal and political questions involved.

support of these institutions. It may help to remove misunderstanding if it is made clear that this property has been secured entirely from voluntary contributions. The American government has not appropriated money toward the building or support of the American schools in China.

The property in China of American mission and philanthropic societies, devoted principally or exclusively to the service of the Chinese people, which has been reported to me is valued at U. S. $41,904,889. I have reports from forty Protestant societies, nine Catholic societies or orders, and ten educational, medical, and philanthropic institutions. The total number of Protestant societies may be sixty. The twenty from whom I do not have information are small except in one or, at most, two cases. There are two or three Catholic societies who have not reported but the number is not great. I am satisfied that I have as good a total as may be arrived at for educational and other institutions, though the property of some institutions is held as a part of the general property of the mission societies interested and cannot be clearly separated. These comments give some idea of the extent of the holdings which are not covered by my returns.

Dividing the property as I have indicated in the preceding paragraph, the following table may be presented.

TABLE 12

AMERICAN MISSION AND PHILANTHROPIC SOCIETIES—VALUE OF THE PROPERTY IN U. S. DOLLARS IN 1929 AND 1930

Protestant societies	U. S. $27,355,720
Catholic societies	1,022,422
Philanthropic and educational institutions	13,526,747
Total	U. S. $41,904,889

The information concerning the Protestant societies enables further study to be made. Of the forty societies reporting for 1929 and 1930, the number reporting for 1913 was eighteen with property valued at U. S. $4,425,-

981. Of these eighteen only six reported for 1900 and the value of the property so reported was U. S. $660,174. These totals cannot, of course, be compared but it may be worth while to present the facts in a somewhat different way. The six societies reporting for 1900 had property valued at U. S. $660,174; the same six societies had, in 1913, property valued at U. S. $1,977,430, and in 1929 property valued at U. S. $7,715,671. The eighteen societies reporting for 1913 had property valued at U. S. $4,425,981; the same eighteen had in 1929 property to the value of U. S. $15,439,729. These are the older and the larger societies and they show the continued and vigorous growth of their holdings in China.

An attempt was made to discover the amount of property held by the mission societies for the purpose of securing an income and not directly used for the work of the society. Such property was reported in the case of only three societies over the whole field of American mission and philanthropic holdings, and the amount was U. S. $156,078. Most of this property is in the hands of the societies as a result of changes in plans for the use of land purchased in the past. It may be stated as a general fact that American societies held no property in China for the purpose of securing an income. Endowment funds are usually held abroad.

The societies were asked also to report the value of the property "which has been turned over to Chinese religious, educational societies . . . either without payment or with nominal payment." Two societies reported that property to the value of U. S. $1,432,100 had been turned over and three others reported that property had been so turned over at various times in the past but that no figures could be given. This is wholly inadequate as an indication of contributions which have been made toward the securing of land and buildings now entirely out of the hands of the mission societies.

It is well known that missionaries have the right to

hold real property outside the treaty ports and that business firms do not. The geographical distribution of the holdings of American Protestant societies is given below. The total value of the property which my reports enable me to distribute is U. S. $16,070,819.

TABLE 13

GEOGRAPHICAL DISTRIBUTION OF PROPERTY OF PROTESTANT SOCIETIES

	U. S. Dollars	Per Cent of Total
Shanghai	3,596,983	22.3
Other treaty ports	3,522,625	22.0
Outside of treaty ports	8,951,211	55.7

It is to be noted that no more than 22.3 per cent of the holdings of American Protestant societies is in Shanghai as compared with a figure of 65 per cent in the case of American business investments. It may be pointed out also that southern China has a much larger percentage of mission property than it has of business property. Mission activity has tended to develop where it got a start and its development has been more nearly under the same control. This greater continuity is shown by the fact that, of the mission societies studied, 50 per cent were in China before 1914 and, of the business firms, about 30 per cent. There are, of course, other reasons for the distribution of mission holdings.

I am able to present also the distribution of mission property to the value of U. S. $19,052,149 according to the nature of the work. This table shows property of Protestant societies only. If the property of the philanthropic and educational societies is added, the percentages are considerably altered. If we take medical and educational work together, the accompanying table shows that 52.9 per cent of mission property is so used. Adding the property of the China Medical Board as both medical and educational at the same time, the figure becomes about 70 per cent as the share of the property devoted to medical and educational work. If the whole of the facts were known, this percentage would probably not be far from correct for the whole of the property in this field.

TABLE 14

DISTRIBUTION OF MISSION PROPERTY ACCORDING TO THE NATURE OF THE WORK

	In U. S. Dollars	Per Cent of Total
Medical	2,786,836	14.7
Educational	7,277,504	38.2
Evangelization and organized religious work	8,987,809	47.1

I do not wish to emphasize unduly the comparison of American business and mission activity, but one more comment may be made. From the facts brought out concerning geographical distribution and the nature of the work or business, it may be said that the "typical" American in mission or philanthropic work is a teacher or doctor away from a treaty port while the "typical" American business man is in the import and export business in Shanghai. This helps to explain the differences which frequently reveal themselves in the attitude and point of view of the two groups.

Concerning the number of persons engaged in mission and philanthropic work this study does not give complete figures since some societies did not report. Those who did report give a total of 2,200 persons. The societies were asked to give, also, the total number of Americans in their service on December 31, 1925. The number for the Protestant societies only was 2,548 for 1925 and 2,024 for the end of 1928, a decline of about 20 per cent.

I turn next to the annual remittances to China for the purpose of maintaining this mission and philanthropic work. The facts for the year 1928 are found in the table on page 307.

In the case of the Protestant societies the returns are from forty-two, that is, two in addition to the number who reported property holdings. The number under the two other headings who reported remittances is the same as the number reporting property holdings. It must be pointed out again that this total is the sum actually reported to me as having been sent to China. The whole sum sent was, of course, larger. This total is a factor of some importance in China's international accounts. It is an index of the most general American interest in China which expresses itself in tangible form.

TABLE 15

REMITTANCES TO CHINA FROM THE UNITED STATES IN 1928 BY MISSION AND PHILANTHROPIC SOCIETIES

	In U. S. Dollars
Protestant societies	5,607,319
Catholic societies	221,564
Philanthropic and educational institutions	1,867,394
	7,696,277

The change in the ratio of remittances to property holdings since 1900 is a matter to which attention should be drawn. I have calculated the ratio for the six societies for which I have information about both property holdings and remittances. I find that for every $100 in property these societies sent to China $46 in remittances in 1900, $29 in 1913, and $15 in 1929. My totals for 1929 show that for every $100 in property the American societies as a whole sent $20 in remittances. There is little room for doubt that the ratio of remittances to property holdings was greater in the past and may have been more than twice as great in 1900. The chief reason for this is, no doubt, the more valuable and more extensive equipment which is now required for this work and the larger number of Chinese whose services are enlisted. A modern mission hospital is a much more expensive plant than was the hospital of 1900. An institution for higher education represents a greater outlay today than it did in 1900. There is no doubt that the ratio of remittances to property holdings was greater in the past in the American case;

there is, I believe, little doubt that the ratio is higher for other countries than for the United States. The statistical information seems to carry proof of a significant change in mission and philanthropic work in the past twenty-five years, a change which is, no doubt, still going on.

The totals for this study of the property in China of American mission and philanthropic societies is presented in the following table.

TABLE 16

PROPERTY IN CHINA OF AMERICAN MISSION AND PHILANTHROPIC SOCIETIES

	U. S. Dollars
American community property	1,166,300
Protestant and Catholic societies	28,378,142
Philanthropic and educational institutions	13,526,747
	43,071,189

Estimate of American Holdings in 1930

The totals for the study of the American holdings in China for 1930 are presented in the table below. It must be remembered that the property of mission and philanthropic societies is not regarded as an investment. This information, which has been supplied to me by the various firms and societies, brings the total of American holdings in China to U. S. $239,895,313, and the total American investment in China to the sum of U. S. $196,824,124.

TABLE 17

AMERICAN HOLDINGS IN CHINA, 1930

	U. S. Dollars
Business investments	155,112,778
Securities and obligations of the Chinese government	41,711,346
Property of American missions and philanthropic societies	43,071,189
Total	239,895,313

Other Recent Estimates Reviewed

The totals in my final table (Table 17) may be compared with the results of other recent investigations of

American holdings in China. The number of such investigations has not been large. I shall refer to four, no one of which covers all of the three divisions which appear in my table.

An estimate of American "direct" investments abroad was made for the year 1929 by Paul D. Dickens of the Department of Commerce of the United States government.[86] By "direct" investments Mr. Dickens means "commercial and industrial properties situated abroad and belonging to residents of the United States and its territories from which a return is normally expected." [87] He specifically excludes "the investments outside the United States of American citizens domiciled in foreign countries.[88] Without undertaking to deal here with all the problems involved, I may say that my estimate of American business investments in China includes all the holdings in that country by American business men or business corporations, no matter where domiciled. It would have been highly inconvenient, if not impossible, to have undertaken my investigation on Mr. Dickens' principle. He has excluded, as he points out, China Trade Act corporations, which are American corporations created especially for China and holding a considerable fraction of the total American business investments in that country. He must have excluded also the holdings of other American corporations, created under the laws of various states, whose entire business is in China.

The Department of Commerce was undoubtedly interested in a total of American foreign investments which would give some indication of the annual return coming into the United States from abroad upon these holdings. I have done my best to estimate this for American busi-

---

[86] *American Direct Investments in Foreign Countries*, U. S. Dept. of Commerce, Trade Information Bulletin, No. 767, Washington, 1930.

[87] *Op. cit.* He distinguishes "direct" from "portfolio" investments, the latter being such investments as cause an international movement of securities (p. 1).

[88] *Op. cit.* His study excluded also mission and philanthropic holdings (p. 3).

ness holdings in China. In order to do this I found it necessary to make a separate estimate. From this estimate of annual remittance to the United States I can arrive at some guess as to the total of American holdings in China which are significant in that they bring about such annual payments. I do not believe it would have been possible, in the Chinese case, to arrive at this significant total directly, though I have little doubt that the domicile of the real owner would be of first importance if such a direct attempt were made.

The figures for China which Mr. Dickens arrives at are as follows:

TABLE 18

AMERICAN "DIRECT" INVESTMENTS IN CHINA

Department of Commerce Figures for 1929

	Number	Value in U. S. Dollars
Manufacturing	15	10,221,000
Selling	25	6,973,000
Petroleum	6	42,839,000
Miscellaneous	29	53,721,000
Total	75	113,754,000

This total cannot be directly compared with mine for the reasons which have been stated, and it is not necessary to undertake such a comparison for there is a later figure available as the result of Mr. Dickens' work. In an estimate of American investments abroad at the end of 1930 he gives, without details, a figure for direct investments in China which reaches a total of U. S. $129.8 million.[89] When it is borne in mind that Mr. Dickens has omitted China Trade Act companies whose total capitalization is, as he says, "between $20 and $30 million and is very largely owned by American citizens residing in China," it is plain that the difference between his estimate and mine is small.

Comparing the items shown in Table 18 with my own

[89] Dickens, Paul D., *A New Estimate of American Investments Abroad*, Trade Information Bulletin No. 767, Washington, 1931, p. 20.

figures I find that the differences are due in large part to exclusions from the Department of Commerce estimate which are easily explained. I find, for example, that we are in substantial agreement in the case of companies having to do with petroleum. These are all large companies whose chief offices are in the United States. In the field of manufacturing my figures show almost twice as many firms as are shown in the report of the Department of Commerce and investments of U. S. $20.5 million, as against U. S. $10.2 million. The chief offices of many of these firms are in China, some of them are China Trade Act companies and many are small. These facts are quite consistent with the general differences between the two studies.

My conclusion is that Mr. Dickens' figures support the reasonableness of my own. His definitions, set up to measure and classify American direct investment throughout the world, do not fit the Chinese case. My study was probably more complete for China since my attention was confined to that one country. These are the general reasons for the differences in the items shown above. When the total at the end of 1930 is considered, the differences in large part disappear. The figures of the Department of Commerce which Mr. Dickens has brought together are, I believe, more nearly correct for American business investments in China than are the figures of any other study. They are independent evidence that my emphasis upon "direct" investments in China is justified.

The second of the four recent estimates of American investments in China was made by Frederic E. Lee, who visited China during the years 1921 and 1922 as a special agent of the Department of State for the purpose of studying Chinese currency and banking. His report appeared as a publication of the Department of Commerce in 1926.[90] The total American investment in China was

[90] Lee, Frederic E., *Currency, Banking, and Finance in China*, Washington, 1926. For the estimate of American investments in China see pp. 122-3.

estimated in this study at U. S. $69.3 million. The property of American mission and philanthropic societies was entirely omitted. The four classes of American investment which were included are shown in the following table.

TABLE 19

AMERICAN INVESTMENTS IN CHINA

Frederic E. Lee's Estimate for 1924

		U. S. Dollars
Class 1.	Bonds and other government securities	20,000,000
Class 2.	Railway bonds and advances	9,300,000
Class 3.	Long-term credits by American concerns	10,000,000
Class 4.	Investments in lands, buildings, etc.	30,000,000
		69,300,000

This total of about U. S. $70 million is to be compared with my total of about U. S. $200 million for American business investments and American holdings of the securities and obligations of the Chinese government. I have pointed out that American investments have probably not grown rapidly since 1928 and that the rate of growth was rapid during the war and the years immediately following. Only a small part of this great discrepancy, therefore, is to be accounted for by the increase in investments since 1924.

The total obligations of the Chinese government to Americans, shown in Classes 1, 2, and 3 of Lee's estimate, is U. S. $39.3 million. This is to be compared with my total of U. S. $41.7 million. Here the discrepancy is very small. When it is born in mind that I have added interest for these six years since 1924, the very smallness of the discrepancy requires explanation. The explanation is to be found in the difference in American holdings of Chinese securities issued in Europe. Lee's estimate of this total for 1924 was U. S. $9 million. My estimate for 1930 is U. S. $1 million. He includes U. S. $2.5 million of the Russian series of the Chinese Government Reorganization loan of 1913. I included nothing under this head. Other differences are explained in my comments in the preceding pages. Mr. Lee has been kind enough to discuss his estimates with me and I have consulted American investment houses from whom he secured information. There is little doubt that American investments under this heading are much smaller than they were in 1924. Differences between Lee's estimate and my own for all other government obligations may be explained by my addition of interest in arrears, or are so small that comment is not called for.

American business investments find a place in Class 4 of Lee's estimate and the total is U. S. $30 million. My total, it will be remembered, is U. S. $155 million. Here lies the outstanding difference which needs explanation. The first step in this explanation is to point out that Lee omitted entirely from his estimates stocks of goods in the possession of American firms in China. He undertook to estimate the value of lands, buildings, and other capital equipment. Estimates of the value of stocks of goods on hand in the past and my own study of American business investments make it a reasonable guess that stocks of goods are worth from 75 to 100 per cent of the value of lands, buildings, and equipment. Taking the larger of these figures, that is doubling Lee's estimate to allow for his omissions, I arrive at an estimate of U. S. $60 million which is to be compared with my estimate of U. S. $155 million. It is to be pointed out, also, that certain important investments have been made since 1924, as in public utilities in Shanghai, but making allowance for these, there is still a considerable discrepancy.

This discrepancy rests finally upon the fact that my study shows American investments to be considerably larger than Lee's 1924 estimate. The reasonableness of my larger figure is supported by the recent investigation of the State Department, which is presented below. It must be borne in mind that the 1924 estimate was incidental to a study of Chinese currency and banking and was not the result of direct investigation.

A third study in the field of American investments in China was made by the Department of State in 1927 and 1928. The State Department dealt with two of the three fields into which I have divided my work. The results of this third investigation, in so far as they have been made public, are found in the following table. The title of the Department's announcement is retained.

TABLE 20

AMERICAN FINANCIAL INVESTMENTS IN CHINA, INCLUDING HONGKONG AND DAIREN, BASED ON REPORTS RECEIVED FROM AMERICAN CONSULAR OFFICERS UP TO SEPTEMBER 25, 1928 *

(Figures are in United States currency)

Business investments		$ 95,352,836
Philanthropic and mission investments		
In open ports	$26,902,861	
In interior	25,206,212	52,109,073
		$147,461,909

* The business investment does not include the obligations due American firms by the Chinese government or its branches or by individual Chinese, and claims of American citizens or firms against the Chinese government for injuries or losses. The value of the investments by Americans in non-American enterprises in China is also not included.

The philanthropic and mission investment does not include Chinese property, the funds for which came partly or wholly from the United States.

The State Department made no estimate of the obligations of the Chinese government to Americans. In this field no comparison is possible. The value of business investments, U. S. $95.4 million, is to be compared with my estimate of U. S. $155.1 million only after certain observations have been made. The State Department was interested in securing the total value of physical property which carried with it a claim to American protection or a possible claim for damages in case of loss. The Department, therefore, included in its totals stocks of goods as well as lands, buildings, and equipment. It did not include the non-physical property which I have reported as "other assets" and which I find in the case of the 213 firms studied to be valued at U. S. $43.6 million. A considerable part of these "other assets" consists of American banking capital in China. Another item of some importance among my "other assets" consists of sums due to American firms from Chinese firms, often for industrial equipment. My own estimate of physical property of the 213 firms is U. S. $106.7 million and it is this sum which, with certain additions for firms that did not report, is to be compared with the State Department total. This leaves no great discrepancy to be explained. I believe, however, that my figure of U. S. $155.1 million is much closer to the business investment in China upon which Americans expect a return than is the State Department's total of U. S. $95.4 million.

The fourth estimate to which I wish to draw attention is an estimate of the property of American mission and philanthropic societies made by A. L. Warnshuis. It is introduced here because it is my desire to bring together this estimate and that of the State Department in the same field for comparison with my own. The estimate by Warnshuis was published in 1927 and his total is the round number of U. S. $80 million, which he himself says is approximate.[91]

This estimate might have been dismissed as a rough approximation if I had not been informed that it was made after some investigation. It is to be compared with the State Department's total of U. S. $52.1 million and my own total of U. S. $43 million. I believe that the U. S. $80 million estimate is too great. It seems to me greater than could by any possibility be the case if all property were included. I account for this large estimate as due to the high price of silver when it was made and to the further fact that there was probably some influence

[91] Warnshuis, A. L., "Christian Missions and the Situation in China," *Annals of the American Academy of Political and Social Science*, July, 1927, vol. CXXXII, July, 1927, p. 81.

of the still higher price of silver during the World War and the years immediately following. If the Chinese dollar totals behind the three estimates were known, there would probably be a smaller discrepancy than appears in the totals as they are given.

There remains for consideration the difference of about U. S. $10 million between the State Department's total and my own. I have pointed out above that my reports cover forty out of a possible sixty Protestant societies and that there are two or three Catholic societies who have not reported to me. The twenty Protestant societies are small. The largest estimate that may be reasonably made of the omissions from my total would hardly bring the figure to U. S. $50 million. Here too, it is probable that the conversion of Chinese dollars into American dollars accounts for most of the difference between the State Department's total and my own.

The estimates which have been considered are brought together in the following table, which is to be seen in the light of the comments of the preceding pages.

TABLE 21

RECENT ESTIMATES OF AMERICAN HOLDINGS IN CHINA

(In millions of U. S. dollars)

	Business Investments	Securities and Obligations of the Chinese Government	Property of Mission and Philanthropic Societies
Warnshuis—1924 (?)			80.0
Lee—1924	30.0	39.3	
State Dept.—1928	95.4		52.1
Dickens—1929	113.8		
Remer—1930	155.1	41.7	43.0

The China Trade Act

Recent American policy in the field of investment in China has been expressed in the China Trade Act and in the initiative of the American government in creating the so-called New Consortium. In both cases the policy of the government is most easily explainable as direct encouragement to American investment. The China Trade Act seems a direct stimulus to business investment, and the Consortium to investment in the obligations of the Chinese government. In both cases, however, the reasons for action made public at the time emphasize trade and political policy rather than investment. I have yet to find a strong statement by a responsible American political leader advocating the encouragement of American investment in China on the ground that it is desirable in itself for economic reasons. Assistance to the export trade and support of political policy seem more natural to Americans in public office. It is significant, however, that investment has been given a place of increasing importance as a means toward the desired ends in the fields of trade and international politics.

The China Trade Act of 1922, as amended in 1925, provides for the federal incorporation of American companies engaged in business within China and for certain exemptions from federal taxation. Federal incorporation is not, I believe, provided for any other private business ventures except national banks. Exemption from federal taxation is most unusual. To understand the significance of the Act it must be seen in its historical setting.

So long ago as 1868 an American official in China pointed out that "persons desirous of uniting in joint stock enterprises in China and Japan labor under the disadvantage that there is no way in which they can form the necessary corporation on the spot." [92] The desire for a local means of incorporation available to the American business community in China was the earliest

[92] *Report on the Commercial Relations of the United States with Foreign Countries for the Year 1875*, Government Printing Office, Washington, p. 267.

of the needs which were finally satisfied by the China Trade Act.

The inconvenience involved in a lack of a means of incorporation "on the spot" was felt generally in the foreign business community in China at the time, for the tradition of solidarity was still strong. The inconvenience was in large part removed by the growth of the general practice of incorporating in Hongkong under the liberal laws of the Crown Colony.[93] The foreign business man in China who was not British accepted incorporation under the Hongkong Ordinances with little question, and the British authorities, in turn, set up no restrictions on grounds of nationality. The desire for a local means of incorporation was not a matter of concern to the Americans until after 1914.

A British Order in Council was promulgated in 1915 which changed the local situation and proved to be the first step toward further changes.[94]   The law was so altered as to require that the majority of the directors of a China company be British subjects, that the auditor of such a company be a British subject, and that no one but a British subject be appointed as liquidator of such a company. In addition, provision was made for greatly increased control over such companies by the British Minister to China.[95] In 1919 other restrictions were added. It was now ordered that no person other than a British subject shall act as managing director or exercise general or substantial control.[96]

[93] The Hongkong and Shanghai Banking Corporation was incorporated under a Hongkong ordinance in 1866. *Encyclopaedia Sinica*, Shanghai, 1917, p. 236.

[94] The China (Companies) Order in Council, 1915.   Reprinted in the *China Year Book*, 1919, pp. 647–51.

[95] For example, "No China Company limited by guarantee shall be allowed to operate in China without the consent of the Minister. As a condition of this consent the Minister may require that no person other than a British subject shall be a member of the company." *China Year Book*, 1919, p. 650.

[96] Mounsey, K. W., *Guide to the Ordinance Law of China Companies and the Orders in Council Relative Thereto*, Tientsin, 1922, p. 19.   For the order now in force see *China: Order in Council of March 17, 1925*, H. M.

The reason for the change in British policy was plain. "With the outbreak of the war," we are told, "the incongruity of a non-British company doing business as a British corporation in China became so conspicuous that it was found necessary to deal with the problem." [97] The new orders were not directed against Americans but their effect upon Americans was great enough to bring a protest from the American business community and to be reported in an American periodical in Shanghai under the heading: "New British Companies' Order Produces Shanghai Sensation." [98]   The new British policy brought to an end the possibility of local incorporation in China by Americans who desired to retain control of such locally created companies.

A local means of incorporation under American law was made available shortly after the new British law became effective. It is impossible to say whether American policy was in any way an answer to British.   In March, 1917, American officials in China granted a charter under the Alaskan Code to a local company, and the applicability of this code was sustained in June, 1917, by the United States Court for China. [99]   Incorporation under the Alaskan Code was available until July 5, 1924, when it was ended in effect by an order of the United States Court for China. [100]   Under the Alaskan Code one

Stationery Office; London, 1926, pp. 51–6.   For a brief history from the legal point of view see Théry, François, *Les Sociétés de Commerce en Chine*, Tientsin, 1919, pp. 305–25.

[97] *China Year Book*, 1919, p. 647.

[98] *Millard's* (later *China Weekly*) *Review*, Dec. 27, 1919, p. 191.   For comment on the protest see the *Review* for Feb. 7, 1920, p. 462.   In editorial comment on Jan. 3, 1920, p. 198.   "The chief companies in Shanghai containing an American interest that are affected by this act are in the following lines; life insurance, real estate, hotels, shipping, manufacturing, and lumber.   Although their number is not large, their business in China is extensive, in some cases the most extensive in China."

[99] In the case of U. S. Ex rel. Raven v. Paul McRae, *Millard's* (later *China Weekly*) *Review*, vol. 1, no. 1, June 9, 1917, p. 7.   See also Smith, Viola, "Incorporation of American Firms in China" in Arnold, Julean, *Commercial Handbook of China*, Washington, 1926, pp. 143–4.

[100] An amendment to the China Trade Act, February, 1925, made this act the sole means of local incorporation available to Americans in China. Smith, Viola, *op. cit.*, p. 144.

hundred sixty-three corporations were created and the American business community in China had at its disposal an effective means for local incorporation.

In spite of the fact that local incorporation was made possible by the use of the Alaskan Code, there developed in China a growing demand for federal incorporation. Such incorporation, it was felt, offered important advantages other than local facilities. Most of the American corporations doing business in China were not local but were created under the laws of the various American states. Much was made of the argument that it would give greater dignity, especially in the eyes of the Chinese, to American companies if they were the creatures of the national government of the United States. It was pointed out that under extraterritoriality the Chinese plaintiff in suits against a number of American corporations may find himself involved in American legal inconsistencies. These statements were usually unaccompanied by examples or cases. Nevertheless there is some weight to the argument on the ground of dignity.

An important reason for the increased vigor of the agitation which finally led to the China Trade Act is to be found in the field of taxation. It is well known that American federal taxation became heavier during and immediately after the World War. In 1917 taxation upon excess profits was introduced and in 1918 the corporate income tax rate was raised from 2 per cent to 12 per cent. Taxation by other governments was not so new, and in the case of the British China companies particularly there was a relatively small increase. The American business man now desired to be relieved of some or all of this taxation on the ground that he was of service to American business and industry and that he ought not to be subjected to heavier taxation than his competitors. These things could hardly be brought about without action by Congress, and such action was already associated in his mind with federal incorporation. That which had begun as a desire for a local means of incorporation became during the closing years of the World War a desire for American federal incorporation with tax exemption.

The first bill along these lines was introduced in the Senate in December, 1918. It died in committee. A second bill was introduced by Representative L. C. Dyer in July, 1919. This bill failed to return from committee, as did a similar bill introduced in the Senate in December, 1920. It was not until four other efforts had been made that Mr. Dyer finally introduced a bill in April, 1921, which, after being fundamentally altered in the Senate, finally passed both houses, received executive approval on September 19, 1922, and became the China Trade Act.

The China Trade Act differed from the earlier bills which failed, in two respects. In the first place its provisions for continued American control were less stringent. The requirements were that a majority of the board of directors and two of the three chief officers be American citizens. There was no requirement that a majority of the shares be owned by American citizens as had been the case in earlier bills.[101] In the second place the China Trade Act was much less satisfactory, to the business men concerned, in the matter of tax exemption than the earlier bills. In fact these provisions were so unsatisfactory as to cause the Act to fail of its purpose if its success may be judged by the number of corporations created. During the years 1922, 1923, and 1924, only 10 charters were granted.

The tax exemption provisions of the earlier bills failed to remain in the bill in their original form because of opposition which developed in the Senate. In a conference report submitted to the Senate in April, 1922, the tax provisions of the China Trade Act, 1922, first appear.

[101] For example, the bill introduced by Senator Fletcher, Dec. 14, 1918 (S. 51924), reprinted in the *Bulletin of the American Asiatic Association*, Feb. 15, 1919, and the bill introduced by Mr. Dyer July 11, 1919 (H. R. 7204).

The conference committee had before it a House bill which provided total exemption for the corporations in question from corporation income tax and excess profits tax unless it derived 5 per cent or more of its gross income from sources within the United States, and a Senate amendment which provided no exemption at all from federal taxation.[102]

The tax provisions agreed to, gave no exemption except from the corporate income tax upon business done in China. The essential point in determining exemption was the residence of the stockholder. There was no exemption for capital put into business in China by Americans residing in the United States or by an American corporation domiciled in the United States.[103] The result was that an American corporation was, in effect, penalized if it undertook to bring into existence a subsidiary under the China Trade Act to carry on its Chinese business. The net income of the China Trade Act corporation was subject to the federal income tax and the parent corporation was subjected to federal income tax upon its net income, including that from its China Trade Act subsidiary.[104]

The changes made in the final draft seem to be based upon the principle that the American "colony" in China, as I have used the term, was to be encouraged to procure Chinese capital and engage in business in China. This would explain the more liberal provisions concerning stock ownership and the emphasis upon the residence of stockholders in determining tax exemption. The China Trade Act was skillfully drawn up if its purpose was to enable the American business "colony" in China to employ local capital for business within the country under

[102] Mr. Volstead's comment on the conference report, *Congressional Record*, 67th Cong., 2nd Sess., pp. 5962-3.

[103] See the comment in Shoop, Max, "The China Trade Act—A Stepping Stone Only," *China Weekly Review*, November 18, 1922, p. 402.

[104] This was pointed out by a number of persons at a hearing in January, 1924, on a bill to amend the China Trade Act. *Hearing Before the Committee on the Judiciary, House of Representatives, 68th Cong., 1st Sess. on H. J. Res. 149*, pp. 12-3, 18-9.

a charter from the national government. The facts concerning Chinese participation in American corporations which I have presented above show such participation to be relatively small. The China Trade Act unamended had a narrow field of applicability but it was logically drawn to cover that field.

In so far as the purpose behind the act was to encourage American trade with China and the investment in China of capital owned in the United States by giving either exemption from American federal taxation or equality in taxation with other nationals in China, it failed. Its failure in these respects brought prompt agitation for its amendment.

Amendments were proposed as early as February, 1923, in a bill introduced by Mr. Volstead which was not acted upon. The bill which was finally passed was introduced by Mr. Dyer on February 21, 1924, and received executive approval on February 26, 1925. The China Trade Act as amended presents changes in the same two respects which have been dealt with above.[105]

In the matter of American control the amended act provides that the president and the treasurer shall be American citizens, resident in China. In the matter of federal taxation the changes are more significant. The important consideration in the determination of exemption is no longer the fact of residence in China. It is now the fact of American or Chinese citizenship. The exemption is in proportion to the amount of stock owned by persons resident in China, the United States or its possessions, and by individual citizens of the United States or China wherever they reside. It is no longer the American business "colony" in China which receives exemption in so far as it provides its own capital or secures Chinese capital for the business of a China Trade Act

[105] The amended act is reprinted in Arnold, Julean, *Commercial Handbook of China*, Washington, 1926, pp. 783–92, together with the regulations approved by the Secretary of Commerce.

corporation. American citizens, wherever they reside, may now invest in China Trade Act corporations or join with Chinese in doing so without making the corporations in which they invest liable to American federal taxation. Americans and Chinese are offered an opportunity to form China Trade Act corporations and these corporations are practically free of American taxation. Equality in this respect is now assured in so far as it may be assured by American legislation. It is American capital which is now offered exemption from taxation rather than the American "colony" in China.[106]

The course of events has now been followed from the early desire for a means of incorporation in China through the steps which lead to the desire for American incorporation, to federal incorporation, and to federal incorporation with exemption from federal taxation. The use which has been made of the facilities offered is shown in the table on page 325. It must be borne in mind that the amended act came into force early in 1925 and that the figures for 1930 cover only the first five months of the year.

It is highly probable that the China Trade Act would not have been proposed if extraterritoriality had not been in existence. In so far as this is true the China Trade Act may be said to depend upon extraterritoriality. At the same time it may be pointed out that the provisions of the Act in the field of taxation are a reconciliation in advance with the tax policy of the Chinese government under conditions which will obtain after the surrender of extraterritoriality. The avoidance of double taxation would, if there were no extraterritoriality, call for the exemptions which are now found in the China Trade Act. In this respect the future of the China Trade Act is not bound up with the future of extraterritoriality, though certain administrative provisions may well be.

[106] The U. S. Treasury Department in *Statistics of Income for 1930* (Preliminary Report), p. 16, shows returns of 61 China Trade Act corporations with a total net income of U. S. $908,487 and no payment of corporation income tax.

TABLE 21

STATUS OF CHINA TRADE ACT CORPORATIONS AS OF MAY 1, 1930

	Charters Granted	Authorized Capital Stock	Dissolved
1922	2	U. S. $ 2,250,000	
1923	6	1,304,600	
1924	2	156,000	1
1925	14	5,941,000	2
1926	25	5,121,500	1
1927	5	6,295,000	1
1928	18	3,582,000	8
1929	24	4,874,500	2
1930	4	205,000	4
	100	29,730,600	19
Dissolved or pending dissolution	26	6,074,100	
Active	74	23,656,500	

There were 8 charters pending for corporations with authorized capital stock of U. S. $649,500.

Much may be said for federal incorporation, even compulsory federal incorporation, for all American companies owning "direct" investments outside of the United States. Where business investments of the sort which Americans have in China are under consideration, the necessity for protection by the national government and for some degree of supervision by the national government makes it not unreasonable that the corporations involved should be the creatures of the national government. The future of the China Trade Act may be determined by American policy in the field of "direct" foreign investment.

The attitude of the Chinese government toward the China Trade Act and toward other legislation of a similar sort rests in part upon the attitude toward extraterritoriality of which it is held to be a sign. In so far as the China Trade Act may be regarded as undesirable for reasons other than those touching extraterritoriality in general they must rest upon the provisions for tax exemption. Where these provisions apply to American capital in

China they may be regarded as provision in advance, as I have said, for the avoidance of double taxation. The Act can hardly be regarded as carrying any injury to China. If, indeed, the Chinese government were desirous of encouraging American-owned capital to unite with Chinese-owned capital under Chinese law the China Trade Act might be regarded as an obstacle to Chinese policy. The policy of the Chinese government has not in recent years been favorable to this. Any change in Chinese policy in this respect will undoubtedly exert a prompt effect upon the usefulness of the China Trade Act to American business men interested in China.

In so far as the provisions of the China Trade Act apply to Chinese capital in American corporations created under the Act, the Chinese government may be said to have a grievance which requires further examination. The argument from the Chinese point of view has been well put by S. L. Pan.[107] The argument is twofold; in the first place it is maintained that the China Trade Act is an injustice to China in that it deprives China of the power "to tax her own capital within her own territory," in the second place it diverts Chinese capital into the hands of Americans and thus enables such American and Chinese capital to compete unfairly with business still remaining in the hands of Chinese.

Concerning the first it may be pointed out that the argument depends for its force upon how far extraterritoriality does actually carry with it exemption from Chinese taxation and how difficult it is for the Chinese government to reach the income or property in other ways. To put my conclusions briefly I may say that extraterritoriality has been less important as a means of avoiding taxation in recent years than it was formerly. It may be said also that it carries little protection against extra-legal exactions on the part of local authorities. The Chinese

107 Pan, S. L., *The Trade of the United States with China*, New York, 1924, pp. 296–7.

government has the power to tax the income of Chinese citizens from China Trade Act corporations or to reach Chinese holdings in other ways. But more important is the fact that Chinese participation in American firms has been shown above to be no more than about 20 per cent and, in a number of cases, to be participation by the Chinese government itself. The unfairness to China, which may be shown by legal logic to exist, is in practice of relatively small importance. It is one aspect of the general subject of extraterritoriality and, in the American case, it is not an important aspect.

The second charge is that exemption from taxation gives to China Trade Act corporations an unfair competitive advantage. This charge I have investigated on the spot and I find that the Chinese business man seldom makes it. A considerable part of the manufacture of Chinese carpets for export is in the hands of Americans. In Tientsin and elsewhere in north China I interviewed Chinese carpet manufacturers. In no case was the charge made that extraterritoriality gives the American an unfair advantage, and the largest Chinese manufacturer specifically denied the charge. American capital and management is of some importance in the manufacture of cigarettes. Here the charge was sometimes made but the advantage of the foreign manufacturer was found to rest upon other advantages than those conferred by extraterritoriality or by the provisions of the China Trade Act. I may say once more that the important aspect of this matter was often found to be the avoidance of extralegal local exactions and, it may be added, location within a settlement or concession is more important in this connection than is extraterritoriality. This second charge proved upon investigation to be of less practical significance than one who had not investigated the facts might suppose.

The future of the China Trade Act corporations is in part bound up with that of extraterritoriality. I have

ventured the opinion that the Act may serve as a model
for federal incorporation of companies engaged in foreign business. If extraterritoriality were abolished there
would be certain advantages in having the Act. A more
important consideration is the attitude of the Chinese
government toward the creation of corporations under
Chinese law in which the foreigner owns the sole or a
controlling interest. The present policy of the Chinese
government prevents this. A change in this respect,—the
inauguration of a liberal policy—will, no doubt, make
incorporation under Chinese law the usual procedure for
the local business community. Whatever the future may
be, the solid fact at the present time is that a means of
federal incorporation under American law exists, that
under it there are now about 75 corporations with an
authorized capitalization of about U. S. $24 million, and
that it is regarded as fair and usable by the American
business man in China.

The New Consortium

American entrance into and withdrawal from the Old
Consortium has been dealt with. It is to be remembered
that the initiative was with the American government
rather than with the American group of bankers. At as
late a date as June, 1917, the State Department was
little interested in proposals for the re-entrance of the
American group.[108] Within six months the State Department telegraphed to the American Minister to China
that American participation in the Consortium was being favorably considered and that steps would probably
be taken to organize a new American group at once.[109]
By July, 1918, a new American banking group was ready
to consider a loan to China if international co-operation

---

[108] *U. S. Foreign Relations*, 1917, p. 134. Secretary Lansing found it
"impossible to make a definite statement" on account of the disturbed
state of China. See p. 126 for the letter of the Group.
[109] *U. S. Foreign Relations*, 1917, p. 153.

could be secured and if the American government agreed
to state when the loan was issued that it had been undertaken at the suggestion of the government.[110] The French,
British, and Japanese governments were now approached
and long negotiations led finally to the signing of the
China Consortium Agreement in October, 1920.[111]

Considering these events from the American point of
view, the first question is: Why did the attitude of the
American government change?   The chief reason is to
be found in the new position of Japan in the Far East
after the first years of the World War.   In the political
field the Twenty-One Demands were the first evidence
of this new position.   In the financial field the so-called
Nishihara loans are well known.   These loans were in themselves an indication that the Old Consortium agreement
was no longer powerful.   In August, 1917, the Chinese
government took steps toward securing new and additional loans.   If China persisted, the loans would be, in
fact and in practical effect, Japanese loans.   The American government faced a situation which called for independent loans to China by American bankers or for
American entrance into the old or a new Consortium.
It is highly probable that this was the immediate cause
of the change in American policy.   The general cause for
this and other changes in policy was the new position of
Japan in Far Eastern and in world affairs.[112]

After the negotiations which led to the New Consortium began, additional reasons for American interest appeared.   The new position of the United States in world
finance played a part, as did also the course of events in
Paris during the discussions which preceded the Ver-

[110] *The Consortium*, Carnegie Endowment, Washington, 1921, pp. 3–6.
[111] For the text see *The Consortium*, pp. 67–72.
[112] *U. S. Foreign Relations*, 1917, p. 142.   The Secretary of State commented on September 20, 1917: "The loan to China now under consideration by the American government is intended as a substitute for the Consortium loan now under consideration in Peking. . . . If the Consortium
loan should be made, Japan would be the lender and would have the backing of the Allied group.   This is undesirable."

sailles Treaty.[113] The course of events which led in the political field to the Washington Conference of 1921–1922 led in the financial field to the creation of the New Consortium. In both cases the new position of the United States placed the initiative with the Americans; in both cases the new position of Japan constituted the major problem.

The important difficulties of the formation of the New Consortium were two. The first of these was the problem of the relation of the governments to their banking groups. This difficulty was largely British and, to a lesser extent, French. In the American case it did not exist, for American newness in the field and the importance of the political aspect made the American government the leader.

The second difficulty was that of securing the consent of Japan to a Consortium agreement which covered the whole of China including Manchuria. This difficulty was not resolved without months of negotiation during which an American banker representing the American group visited Japan. After certain railway projects in Manchuria were placed outside of the sphere of Consortium activities, and after the Japanese government was assured that the powers concerned would refuse to sanction any enterprise inimical to the security of the economic life and national defense of Japan, the agreement of the Japanese group was secured.

The importance of this second difficulty demonstrates that the New Consortium represented a more realistic approach to the problems involved than did the Old Consortium. The New Consortium included in its scope from the beginning industrial as well as administrative loans. Industrial loans, in so far as the creation of the Consortium was concerned, meant railway loans; and railway loans meant loans for Manchurian railways. An

[113] For a full account of the formation of the New Consortium see Field, Frederick V., *American Participation in the China Consortiums*, American Council Institute of Pacific Relations, 1931, Chap. X.

agreement which the Japanese and the other groups could sign seemed to offer the hope that the political problem had been set aside, for the time at least, in favor of the economic and financial. This hope seemed the more reasonable after the Washington Conference.

The Consortium has not been accepted by the Chinese government or by Chinese political leaders. They have regarded it as carrying the threat of international control of Chinese finance, and frequently mention Egypt in discussing the matter. It has been opposed on the ground that it is a monopoly or an attempted monopoly of Chinese government borrowings abroad. It is quite usual for a Chinese in discussing the Consortium to express a vague fear, and a conviction that his government ought to have nothing to do with it.

With the success of the Nationalist movement since 1925 a group has been brought into power who give great weight to the political significance of financial relations. The Nationalist movement attained power when Chinese credit was at a low point. What is more, the Nationalists were accustomed to depend upon domestic loans. The result has been to carry the Chinese government further from dependence upon the Consortium.

The attitude of the American group in the Consortium is that the Consortium stands ready to negotiate with China when the initiative is taken by the Chinese government.[114] To the Chinese who say, in effect, that they will have nothing to do with the Consortium, the reply of the Consortium is that the Chinese government must take effective steps to meet her obligations before she can borrow. The New Consortium, which was expected to increase the American holding of Chinese government securities, has had no such effect. The Consortium has done no more than to prevent certain loans. It has main-

[114] Speech by Thomas W. Lamont at the annual dinner of the China Society on November 9, 1928, and at the Amsterdam meeting of the International Chamber of Commerce on July 10, 1929.

tained some solidarity among possible lenders to China. It is the answer of the foreign financial and political leaders to the difficult problem presented by Chinese government borrowing in the past. The American government, after rejecting it in 1913, returned to the principle of the Consortium in 1918. The reason for the Consortium lies in the actual situation in China and in the experience of the foreign financial groups with China, with each other, and with the international political situation in the Far East.

CONCLUSION

American holdings in China during the past century have been estimated and the results presented in the preceding pages. They are brought together in the following table. In 1835 and in 1875 conditions differed

TABLE 22

AMERICAN HOLDINGS IN CHINA, 1830–1930

(In millions of U. S. dollars)

1835	3.0
1875	8.0
1900	24.7
1914	59.3
1930	239.9

so greatly from those of the period since 1900 that only the roughest comparison may be made. After 1900 sufficient information has been available to make it possible to present the totals under the three headings, business investments, securities and obligations of the Chinese government, and the property of mission and philanthropic societies. These are shown in Table 23 with relatives which show the rate of growth in each case. The figures for 1930, it is to be borne in mind, are the result of a new and direct investigation which was completed in China.

TABLE 23

AMERICAN HOLDINGS IN CHINA, 1900–1930 WITH RELATIVES

(In millions of U. S. dollars)

	Business Investments		Government Obligations		Mission Property	
1900	17.5	42	2.2	33	5.0	50
1914	42.0	100	7.3	100	10.0	100
1930	155.1	369	41.7	571	43.1	431

The holdings of property by mission and philanthropic societies reveal a continued American interest, and the rate of growth of these holdings is due in part to the increased equipment required for modern education and for modern medicine.

Business investments and loans to the Chinese government taken together constitute American investments in that country. The fact that there are no American holdings of the securities of Chinese business corporations is significant. China has failed to develop this means of securing foreign capital.

The relative importance, at each date, of the two forms which American investment in China has taken is shown in the following table. The outstanding fact is the over-

TABLE 24

AMERICAN BUSINESS INVESTMENTS IN CHINA, 1900–1930

Percentage Distribution by Classes

	Business Investments		Government Obligations		Total	
	Millions of U. S. Dollars	Per Cent of Total	Millions of U. S. Dollars	Per Cent of Total	Millions of U. S. Dollars	Per Cent of Total
1900	17.5	88.8	2.2	11.2	19.7	100.0
1914	42.0	85.2	7.3	14.8	49.3	100.0
1930	155.1	78.8	41.7	21.2	196.8	100.0

whelming importance of business investments. Certain conclusions concerning this will be presented after consideration has been given to American holdings of government obligations.

In Tables 23 and 24 it is shown that American holdings of Chinese government securities have increased more rapidly since 1900 than have business investments. The sums involved were small in the earlier years. The fact that American investment through the Chinese government was in 1930 no less than nineteen times as great as it had been in 1900, while business investments were about nine times as great, means no more than that the United States was late in entering the field. Not only have Americans been late; it may be said also that they have been either unsuccessful or unfortunate, or both. Table 11 shows that a large fraction of the total government obligations is to American firms, usually for railway equipment. These obligations are entirely unsecured. In fact, the Americans hold but one loan (a part of the Hukuang loan) which may be regarded as a secured loan. Of this loan it must be said that there are payments in arrears. Americans hold no directly acquired obligation of the Chinese government of any appreciable size on which all payments are being made. These statements must be taken as showing the financial difficulties of the Chinese government rather than any discrimination against American holders.

It may be said also that American investment in Chinese government securities has never reached beyond the international political problems involved to the economic development of China. It is the importance of the political aspect which explains many things in this field. It explains the initiative of the State Department in American financial ventures in China. I believe it fair to say that American government initiative is not so usual in any other field. The importance of the political explains also the changes in policy which have taken place. The United States forced its way into the Consortium, withdrew from the Consortium, and took steps to create a new Consortium for political reasons and not for financial or economic reasons. The center of American financial interest has been Manchuria. American investments in Manchuria are small. No American economic interest explains the recurring attention to Manchuria in American loan negotiations. It is adequately explained on political grounds. Manchuria has been the chief international political problem in the Far East since the end of the Sino-Japanese War. The United States has shown a keen interest in Manchuria railways because the solution of the railway problem promised a solution of the political problem. This is said without raising the question as to whether Japanese and Russian activities in Manchuria have an economic explanation. It seems to me that here, as elsewhere, we move from financial problems to political, and from political problems to the underlying economic problems.

If the center of political and financial interest has been Manchuria, the center of American business investment has been Shanghai. It has been shown in Tables 7 and 8 that 65 per cent of American business investment in China is in Shanghai, and that about half of the American firms studied have offices in Shanghai and nowhere else in China. The business investments are in a variety of fields, of which the most important is the import and export trade. In this Shanghai plays an important part. The second field is that of public utilities. More than 20 per cent of the total American business investment in China is in two public utilities in the foreign settlement at Shanghai.

The importance of American business investments has played a large part in bringing the China Trade Act into existence. This Act embodies two unusual features: it provides federal incorporation for private business ventures, and it practically exempts the corporations so created from American federal taxation. It may be regarded as an encouragement to "direct" business investments in China.

American business investments, along with other such foreign investments, are direct, in the sense in which I use the term, that is, to mean business holdings in China by corporations and individuals not Chinese. These investments take the form they do because of the existence of extraterritoriality, but behind extraterritoriality lie the many differences between China and the economically developed countries of the West. So long as these differences are great enough, business investment in China will continue to have many of the present features of direct investment.

Efforts have been made to estimate the flow of funds to and from China occasioned by American business investments. If generalization is possible on the available information, it may be estimated that $100 in American business investment has brought about a remittance to China of $30 to $40 in the past, and that it brings about an annual remittance from China to the United States of $10 to $15 in prosperous times. No attempt has been made to estimate remittances to the United States for the service of government loans.

The World War brought changes which are of the greatest significance to China, in the international economic relations of the United States and of Japan. The evidence of this change in the case of Japanese interests in China is abundant. It has been mentioned in connection with the New Consortium. In the case of the United States the evidence is hard to find. Capital has flowed out of the United States since the World War at a rate which reached a billion American dollars a year for a time. During the same years American business investments in China increased by no more than about U. S. $60 million, and American loans to China by about U. S. $15 million. Since 1928 American investment in Shanghai has been considerable, but the new international position of the United States has not noticeably increased American investment in China. The investments which have been made have been in large part Japanese. Investment in China has, on the whole, been small. If it had been great the United States would no doubt have played a more important part.

The underlying cause for the smallness of recent foreign investment is no doubt China's narrow capacity to receive foreign capital and put it to effective use. The more immediate causes are the increasing disturbance and unrest in China, and the success of the Nationalist movement.

The success of the Nationalist movement in China since 1925 aroused a lively interest in China's economic relations. Dr. Sun Yat Sen during the closing years of his life dwelt much upon the position of the foreigner in China, the significance of China's trade balance, the meaning of foreign settlements and concessions, and the problem of foreign investment. These aspects were emphasized by the Russian advisers of the Nationalists who brought familiar Soviet doctrines to bear. Therefore it happened that as the United States became a great lender, a socialist analysis gave an economic turn to the Chinese Nationalists' suspicion of the foreigner in China.

There can be little doubt that the economic reconstruction of China will require capital from abroad. Chinese business and political leaders are convinced of this. The United States must, it would seem, be an important source of this capital. With proper allowance for the importance of Japan and Russia, the opinion may be ventured that the immediate future of China's economic development depends upon the relations between the Chinese Nationalist and the American investor.

The following table shows the position of the United States in various fields of China's international economic relations since 1900. A similar table for each of the six important countries is to be found at the end of the chapter dealing with that country.

TABLE 25

THE POSITION OF THE UNITED STATES IN CHINA'S INTERNATIONAL
ECONOMIC RELATIONS

Customs Statistics except for Investments

TRADE	Direct Trade Mills Hk. Tls.	Relatives	Per Cent of China's Total Trade
1899	43.7	59	9.5
1913	73.0	100	7.5
1930	364.3	499	16.5
POPULATION	American Population in China	Relatives	Per Cent of Total Foreign Population in China
1899	2,335	44	13.6
1913	5,340	100	3.6
1930	6,875	129	1.9
FIRMS	American Firms	Relatives	Per Cent of Total Foreign Firms in China
1899	70	53	7.5
1913	131	100	3.4
1930	566	432	6.8
SHIPPING	American Tonnage in Millions	Relatives	Per Cent of Total Chinese and Foreign Shipping
1899	0.3	33	0.7
1913	0.9	100	0.9
1930	6.5	722	4.2
INVESTMENT	American Investment Millions U. S. Dollars	Relatives	Per Cent of Total Foreign Investment
1900	19.7	40	2.5
1914	49.3	100	3.1
1930	196.8	399	6.1

CHAPTER XVI

BRITISH INVESTMENTS IN CHINA

INTRODUCTION

The Early Importance of British Interests in China

Throughout the nineteenth century Great Britain was the foreign power of greatest importance in China. Every available index of comparative importance in China's international economic relations shows the predominance of the British, a predominance which in most fields did not persist beyond 1900. It is not to be supposed that British trade with China and British shipping in Chinese waters and other evidences of British economic activity actually declined as we approach the present day; it is the British share which declined. It was hardly to be expected that the British should continue to hold an increasing share of a growing Chinese trade and industry. It is remarkable that Great Britain succeeded in doing this as long as she did.

British investments in China do not seem to have been estimated until after 1900. It is, therefore, not possible to offer direct evidence of British holdings, but the overwhelming importance of Great Britain and of the British Empire must be appreciated if recent developments are to be understood.

The trade at Canton in the days of the East India Company was largely in the hands of British merchants, the cargoes were carried in British ships, and the European market for the goods was London. A census of the Canton factories, taken in 1836 shortly after the East India Company lost its monopoly of British trade, showed that over half of the residents were British and that three-fourths of the foreign firms, excluding the Indian, were British.[1] Probably half the ships that called at Canton between 1818–1833 were under the British flag and more than half the trade was with Great Britain.[2]

The available evidence shows an increase in the predominance of Great Britain after the opening of the five ports and the British acquisition of Hongkong. In the field of foreign population in China we find that the British formed over 50 per cent of this population, as reported by the Chinese Customs, until after 1880. By 1899 the British percentage had dropped to 32 and the decline continued. In 1865 the British population of Shanghai was 60 per cent of the total foreign population; in 1900 it was 40 per cent.[3] Again it may be said that the decline has been fairly continuous throughout the following years. If we were able to add the figures for Hongkong they would make little change. It is fairly certain that over half the foreign residents of China were British until about 1875. After this date the change was gradual until the entrance of Russia and Japan into Manchuria.

The trade statistics show that the direct trade of China with Great Britain was over 40 per cent of China's total from the beginning of the records in the 'sixties to 1874, above 30 per cent to 1877, above 20 per cent to 1889, and about 12 per cent at the end of the century. Such figures are inadequate, however. We must see the foreign trade of China with the British Empire or, better, as with and through two great distributing centers under the British flag, London and Hongkong. In the 'seventies of the last century no less than 90 per cent of China's imports came from Hongkong, India, and Great Britain, and they received about 70 per cent of her exports.

---

[1] *Chinese Repository*, 1837, vol. V, pp. 426–32.
[2] Morse, H. B., *The International Relations of the Chinese Empire*, vol. 1, pp. 89–92.
[3] The actual numbers were 1,372 in 1865 and 2,691 in 1900. The figures are those of the Shanghai Municipal Council. *Feetham Report*, vol. 1, pp. 51–2.

The importance of Hongkong as a distributing center increased until after 1900. The statistical information concerning trade with Hongkong is unsatisfactory for the earlier years, but from 1887 to 1902 over 40 per cent of the total trade of China passed through this British port.[4] After 1902 the trade with Hongkong declined with the growing importance of Shanghai and, later, Dairen.

The British have a long record as the leading foreigners in shipping both in the foreign trade and in the coastal and internal trade of China. If we consider the figures of total tonnage in the whole of the Chinese trade, including that with foreign countries and between the treaty ports of China, we find the British tonnage was above 60 per cent until 1899 and that it has not been as high as 60 per cent for any year since 1899. If we eliminate the foreign trade and consider shipping along the coast and on the rivers of China we find the predominance of the British more striking. The great foreign shipping companies in China were all British from the decline of American interests in the 'seventies to the rise of Japanese interests after 1900.

In 1865 a British company undertook to run vessels between Hongkong, Canton, and Macao. In 1873 the China Navigation Company started its shipping on the coast and rivers of China. In 1881 the Indo-China Steam Navigation Company took over the ships of Jardine, Matheson and Company, one of the great British trading firms, and developed important lines. These are but the chief examples. A British official was able to report in 1897 that "Great Britain carries 82 per cent of the total trade under foreign flags and pays 76 per cent of the dues and duties collected in that trade."[5]

In view of the predominance of British interests and the

---

[4] For the changes in the returns of the Chinese Customs in 1887 see Remer, C. F., *The Foreign Trade of China*, p. 75.

[5] *Board of Trade Journal*, vol. 24, Jan.–June, 1898, p. 150.

commercial importance of Hongkong it is not surprising to find the British of first importance in the financial field and the chief British bank, the Hongkong and Shanghai Banking Corporation, the first to undertake loans to the Chinese government. This bank, incorporated in 1866 under the Hongkong government, began business with a paid-up capital of silver \$2.5 million. By the end of the century this had been increased to silver \$10 million. In 1898 this bank, with Jardine, Matheson and Company, formed the British and Chinese Corporation for the purpose of railway building and industrial development in China.

The earliest borrowings of the Chinese government were from this British bank, which has been called the "unofficial Master of the Mint" for the colony of Hongkong.[6] A loan of taels 1,720,000 (£540,000) was made to the authorities at Foochow in 1875.[7] A second loan for about £1,600,000 was undertaken by the bank in 1877. The price to the public was 98 and the rate of interest 8 per cent. This loan began the connection between war and foreign borrowing. It was for the support of the campaign against the Mohammedan rebels in western China.[8] During the years which preceded the war with Japan, the Hongkong and Shanghai Bank continued to play a leading rôle and, during the war, undertook certain loans though not on the scale of the loans of 1895 to 1898. In so far as they were outstanding, these loans enter the estimate below of British obligations of the Chinese government at the end of 1901.

The estimate of British investments in China at the end of the century has been undertaken, although the in-

[6] Hinton, W. J., "A Note on Some Anomalies in the Currency of Hongkong," *Indian Journal of Economics*, vol. 2, p. 3, Dec., 1918.

[7] "History of the Hongkong and Shanghai Banking Corporation," *Encyclopaedia Sinica*, Shanghai, 1917, pp. 235-7. Reprinted in Remer, C. F., *Readings in Economics for China*, pp. 371-7.

[8] U. S. Government, Department of State, *Report on the Commercial Relations of the U. S. with Foreign Countries for the Year 1878*, Washington, 1879, p. 225.

formation is in many respects inadequate, because it was
plainly necessary to arrive at an approximate total of the
interests which, in the light of the above facts, were far
greater than those of any other nation or national group
in China.

Loans to the Chinese Government, 1902

British investments in China at the end of the century
are estimated under the two headings generally used,
business investments and obligations of the Chinese government. The estimate of the government obligations is
based upon the available published information which is
fairly adequate.

The early loans by the Hongkong and Shanghai Banking Corporation have been mentioned above.   It has
seemed best to disregard these early loans in making an
estimate for 1902 for it may be safely assumed that they
were repaid by this date.[9] There is little doubt that these
early loans were in large part advances of funds from a
bank within the economic, if not the political, boundaries
of China and that they involved little, if any, remittances
of funds from Great Britain.

The first of the loans to be considered was a 7 per
cent loan of 1894 for Sh. Tls. 10.9 million,[10] from the
Hongkong and Shanghai Banking Corporation.   The
amount outstanding on this loan on December 31, 1901,
at the rate of exchange of the time was U. S. $6,540,000.
This loan was followed in 1895 by a 6 per cent sterling
loan from the same bank to the nominal amount of £3
million. The amount of the second loan outstanding at the
end of 1901 was U. S. $12,652,900.

These two loans were for expenses connected with the

---

[9] With the exception of the so-called 7 per cent silver loan of 1886 which
was originally for less than a million Shanghai taels. Wright, S. F., *The
Collection and Disposal of the* . . . *Customs Revenue*, Shanghai, 1927,
p. 61. See also Lieu, D. K., *Foreign Investments in China*, Shanghai, 1929,
pp. 12–5.

[10] Kuping Tls. 10 million.

Japanese war and were secured upon the revenue of the
Chinese Customs. The earlier loan went far in the direction of specific security for it authorized the bank or
its agents to collect at any treaty port or ports the
amount required to meet any default upon the loan. The
financial arrangements connected with these loans may be
regarded as generous to the issuing bank but hardly as
unfair.

A third loan for £1 million was made in 1895 by the
Chartered Bank of India, Australia, and China.[11] This
loan was for 20 years at 6 per cent, and was secured upon
the Customs revenue. The sum to be received by the
Chinese government was fixed at 95½ per cent but, as a
matter of fact, the bonds were sold to the British public
at the price of 106.[12] This represented an unusual profit
to the bankers. The amount outstanding on this loan at
the end of 1901 was U. S. $4,542,391.[13]

The three loans considered above were small when they
are compared with the loans made to enable China to meet
the indemnity payments to Japan at the close of the war.
With the first of the indemnity loans the British were not
concerned, except as they undertook to prevent it. It was,
in fact, evidence of Russian political influence which
threatened the position of Great Britain in China.[14] The
Franco-Russian loan of 1895 was followed in 1896 and in
1898 by two loans by an Anglo-German syndicate in which
the British representative was the Hongkong and Shanghai
Banking Corporation. The loans were for £16 million
each and they were both secured upon the Maritime

[11] Usually referred to as the Cassel loan after the name of the British
signer.
[12] Wright, S. F., *The Collection and Disposal of the . . . Customs Revenue*, Shanghai, 1927, p. 66.
[13] For the loan contracts see MacMurray, John V. A., *Treaties and Agreements*, vol. I, pp. 11, 15, 35.
[14] The British and German governments joined in an effort to get the
Chinese government to accept a loan from an Anglo-German syndicate.
British Documents on the Origins of the War, vol. 1, p. 328, Memorandum
of J. A. C. Tilley.

Customs revenue. A stipulation in both loan contracts was that there could be no conversion or redemption of the loan except as provided for in the agreement. This must be taken in connection with the provision that "the administration of the Imperial Maritime Customs shall continue as at present" during the currency of the loan.[15] It is to be noted that before the second loan was signed the Chinese government declared that a British subject would be employed as chief of the Customs service so long as British trade predominates.[16]

The loan of 1896 was at 5 per cent for 36 years. It was issued in two portions, £10 million in March, 1896, at $98\frac{3}{4}$ and £6 million in September, 1896, at 99. The price to the loan syndicate was 94. The amount outstanding on this loan on December 31, 1901, was U. S. $73,374,654 of which the British share was 50 per cent or U. S. $36,687,-327.

The loan of 1898 was at $4\frac{1}{2}$ per cent for 45 years. The price to the public was 90 and the price to the bankers, 83. In addition, there was provision for a commission of one-fourth of one per cent on the annual loan service undertaken by the banks.[17] The amount outstanding on this loan at the end of 1901 was U. S. $76,104,882, of which the British share was 50 per cent or U. S. $38,052,441.

British interest in railways in China goes back to the earliest proposals. The first railway in China, from Shanghai to Woosung, was a direct investment by a British company. It was not, however, until the problem

[15] Article 7 of the loan agreement of 1896 and Article 6 of the loan agreement of 1898. MacMurray, John V. A., *Treaties and Agreements*, vol. I, pp. 57, 109.

[16] MacMurray, John V. A., *Treaties and Agreements*, vol. I, p. 104.

[17] For the loan contracts see MacMurray, John V. A., *Treaties and Agreements*, vol. I, pp. 55, 107. For further details see Wright, S. F., *Collection and Disposal of the . . . Customs Revenue*, pp. 67–9. For amortization tables see Baylin, J. R., *Foreign Loan Obligations of China*, Tientsin, 1925, pp. 8, 10.

of transporting coal from the Kaiping mines, north of Tientsin, to the sea presented itself for solution that railway construction was seriously undertaken. When it became necessary to secure foreign capital the Chinese government borrowed abroad. The loan, called the 5 per cent gold loan for the Imperial Railways of North China, was for £2.3 million, to run for 45 years, and was secured upon the property and earnings of the railway. The stipulation that the railway was to be under Chinese control "so long as the principal and interest of this loan are regularly paid" was noted in the agreement as different from the provisions of other contracts and as a mark of friendly relations.[18] The whole amount of this loan was outstanding on December 31, 1901, that is, U. S. $11,192,950.

In addition to this railway loan there were two loans which may be classified as for communications other than railways. These loans were for a cable from Shanghai to Taku (the seaport of Tientsin) via Chefoo. The first of these was the subject of an agreement of August 4, 1900, and the second of an agreement of December 21, 1900. In both cases the loan was at 5 per cent and was to terminate on September 30, 1930. These loans were made by the Eastern Extension Telegraph Company, a British corporation, and the Great Northern Telegraph Company, a Danish corporation. Half of the loan in each case is taken as British. The amount outstanding on December 31, 1901, on the Shanghai-Taku New Cable loan was U. S. $1,006,747 and on the Duplicate Taku-Chefoo Cable loan U. S. $233,592. The British share was U. S. $503,373 and U. S. $116,796.

The following is a summary of the known obligations of the Chinese government which must be entered in a total of British investments for the date under consideration.

[18] MacMurray, John V. A., *Treaties and Agreements*, vol. I, p. 175.

TABLE 1

BRITISH OBLIGATIONS OF THE CHINESE GOVERNMENT AS OF
DECEMBER 31, 1901

	U. S. Dollars	
General purposes of the Chinese government:		
7% Loan of 1894	6,540,000	
6% Sterling Loan of 1895	12,652,900	
Cassel Loan	4,542,391	
5% Gold Loan of 1896	36,687,327	
4½% Gold Loan of 1898	38,052,441	
		98,475,059
Railways:		
Chinese Imperial Railway 5% Gold Loan		11,192,950
Communications other than railways:		
Shanghai-Taku New Cable loan	503,373	
Duplicate Taku-Chefoo Cable loan	116,796	
		620,169
Total		110,288,178

Business Investments at the Beginning of the Century

In the case of British loans to the Chinese government
at this time the information is fairly complete; in the case
of British business investments it is neither complete nor
exact. A reasonable guess of the total value of the business
investments is all that can be offered. It is necessary,
however, to make this guess, for the investments under
this heading were certainly a large part of the total of
British investments and the grand total of all foreign investments in the country. I propose to establish first a
lower limit under this heading, then an upper limit, and to
arrive at an acceptable estimate between these limits on
the basis of the discoverable information.

An anonymous writer in the *Quarterly Review* for July,
1907, presented estimates of British foreign investments
for the year in which he wrote and, to facilitate comparison, for the year 1897.[19] He relied upon the publications of

[19] "British Investments Abroad," *Quarterly Review*, vol. 207, no. 412,
July, 1907, pp. 245–72.

the London Stock Exchange and of other stock exchanges in the United Kingdom. He brought together information concerning "all companies, home and foreign, whose shares are dealt with in any of the stock exchanges of the United Kingdom." The *Quarterly Review* total for British business investments in China for 1897 is £14.3 million or U. S. $69.6 million. For 1907 it is £22.5 million or U. S. $109.5 million. It may be supposed that the figure for 1902 would have been about U. S. $90 million. It is, of course, well known that British business investments in China included more than could possibly have been included in any study based upon securities sold in the United Kingdom. It seems reasonable, therefore, to regard U. S. $90 million as the lower limit.

In order to establish the upper limit it is necessary to estimate first the value of British land holdings in Shanghai. It has been shown in the discussion of American holdings for 1900 that the total value of the land held under foreign registry at Shanghai was probably Sh. Tls. 100 million by the year 1902. A generous estimate of the proportion of this land which was actually the property of Chinese would put it at one-third. Of the land actually held by foreigners no less than 78 per cent was British owned in 1930 and it is highly probable that 90 per cent was so owned in 1901 and 1902. The British land holdings for the years with which we are now concerned may be estimated at Sh. Tls. 60 million, which, at the exchange rate of the time, comes to £7 million or U. S. $33.6 million.[20]

In the American case it was found that American holdings in Shanghai were about three times the total of land holdings. This is supported by evidence that certain Shanghai Chamber of Commerce estimates of stocks of goods and equipment come to about the value of the land and that the value of the improvements upon the land

[20] Figures based upon the *Feetham Report*, vol. 1, p. 323, vol. 2, p. 170, and upon information secured in Shanghai.

were also about equal to its value.[21] If this is applied to the British case we reach U. S. $100 million as an estimate of British investments in Shanghai. These investments were certainly half of the total British holdings in China, even if we include Hongkong. We come, then, to an estimate of U. S. $200 million as the upper limit of British business investments in China.

In order to determine where, between U. S. $90 million and U. S. $200 million, a final estimate ought to fall, I propose to consider very briefly the actual available information in various fields.

British direct investments in the field of transportation were almost entirely in shipping. There were important British shipping lines with headquarters at Hongkong. "The coasting trade radiating from Shanghai," we are told, was "almost entirely in the hands of three companies," two of them British, the Indo-China Steam Navigation Company and the China Navigation Company, whose joint fleets amounted to over seventy ocean-going and river steamers.[22] The directories of the time carried lists of coast and river steamers and it may be said with some confidence that the British owned 80 or 85 boats permanently in Chinese waters and engaged in commerce. The average tonnage of these boats was about 1,500 and they may be valued at about U. S. $50 per ton. This gives a total of about U. S. $6.5 million as the value of the British coast and river steamers. Taking into account the facilities on shore, wharves, warehouses, docks, and offices in the possession of the steamship companies it may be maintained that a reasonable total of the total British investment in shipping was U. S. $10 million.[23]

The Shanghai Mutual Telephone Company, a British corporation formed in Shanghai took over the telephones

[21] *Chronicle and Directory for China . . . 1899*, Hongkong, 1899, p. 138.
[22] British Government, Diplomatic and Consular Reports, *Report for the Year 1900 on the Trade of Shanghai*, p. 11.
[23] Ships engaged in the foreign trade are excluded in this case as in the others.

of the city in 1899 and completed important new construction by August, 1900. At about the same time the authorities of the International Settlement granted a franchise for the operation of a local street car system but neither the French Concession nor the International Settlement had street cars until after 1902. Water, gas, and electricity [24] were provided by private corporations. In Hongkong and Tientsin the British had investments in public utilities. No estimate can be made, but U. S. $2 million is not unreasonable.

Mining ventures of later importance go back to 1900 but there was little investment in this field until after the final settlement of the Boxer troubles in 1901. In manufacturing the British from the beginning played an important part. Before 1900 Hongkong had three large sugar refineries, two or three engineering works, a rope factory, steam saw mills, and plants for the manufacture of glass, matches, soap, and ice. All these were owned or controlled by the British. After the treaty of Shimonoseki, British corporations or individuals at Shanghai undertook to build cotton mills, to build or acquire silk filatures, and a considerable variety of industrial plants. The British firm of Jardine, Matheson and Company were the owners, either directly or through subsidiaries, of a cotton mill, a large modern silk filature, and a silk spinning, weaving, and dyeing plant. The same firm held a considerable interest in the Shanghai and Hongkong Wharf Company, and in a number of insurance companies incorporated under the laws of Hongkong. These are but examples to show that British interests were large. No estimate of British holdings is available but it must have been at least U. S. $20 million.

In the field of banking there was the important Hongkong and Shanghai Banking Corporation with a paid-

---

[24] Until 1893 when the Council of the International Settlement took over the entire plant of the company paying Sh. Tls. 66,100. Pott, F. L. H., *A Short History of Shanghai*, Shanghai, 1928, p. 111.

up capital of U. S. $5 million. Two other British banks had interests of some importance, the Chartered Bank of India, Australia, and China, and the Mercantile Bank of India.

The investment of British firms in the import and export business was greater by far than in any other field. Tea, silk, strawbraid, and beans were purchased and exported in a large measure by British firms. The import of cotton textiles was almost entirely in British hands until the late 'nineties when British merchants noted the rise of American and Japanese competition. The *Decennial Report* of the Chinese Maritime Customs provides statistics of foreign population for 29 treaty ports. The British outnumbered the nationals of any other country in 17 of these ports, including Shanghai, Hankow, Tientsin, Foochow, Swatow, and Chingkiang.[25] It is by no means unreasonable to guess the total of British investment in the import and export business at about U. S. $40 million.

If we add a reasonable estimate of real estate holdings, and allow for property which escapes notice in so brief a review, it is not difficult to account for more than U. S. $100 million. Much of this property did not, we may be certain, serve as a basis for securities sold on the stock exchanges of the United Kingdom. I am inclined to put the estimate of British business holdings in China for about the end of 1901 at U. S. $150 million and to maintain as fairly certain that it was between U. S. $100 million and U. S. $200 million.

Summary of British Investments, 1902

The following summary of British investments for the beginning of the century is offered. It is to be repeated that the total business investments is a guess but a guess which rests upon considerable information. Obligations

[25] Chinese Maritime Customs, *Decennial Report, 1892–1901*, vol. II, pp. xi ff.

TABLE 2

BRITISH INVESTMENTS IN CHINA, 1902

	Millions of U. S. Dollars
Business investments	150.0
Obligations of the Chinese government	110.3
	260.3

of the Chinese government formed 42.4 per cent of the total, and business investments no more than 57.6 per cent. This, it is to be remembered, was at a time when British business investments were of outstanding and predominant importance.

BRITISH INTERESTS IN 1914

The estimate to be presented next is that of British investments in China on the eve of the World War. The information concerning these investments is similar to that for the earlier year; it is fairly easy to estimate British loans to the Chinese government and extremely difficult to arrive at a total for business investments. The outstanding importance of British business investments is again my reason for making an estimate in spite of the difficulties.

Certain indicators of the importance of British interests in China are presented first. I shall deal briefly with British population, trade, and shipping in China.

Population and Firms

The British population of the treaty ports of China was reported by the Maritime Customs at 8,966 for 1913. This was a considerable increase over the total of 5,562 for 1899. It does not include the British population of Hongkong which must have been about 5,000,[26] mak-

---

[26] The non-Chinese civilian population of Hongkong was 12,075 in 1913. About half consisted of Portugese, Indians, and other non-Chinese

ing a total of about 14,000 for China and Hongkong. The number of British citizens at Shanghai increased from 2,691 in 1900 to 4,822 in 1915.

It is when we turn to the British percentage of the total population that we see a sharp difference from the situation as it was at the beginning of the century. In 1899 the British constituted 32.4 per cent of the foreign population reported by the Customs; in 1913 no more than 5.4 per cent. This decline reflects the increase in the number of Russians and Japanese in Manchuria. The decline in the case of Shanghai, for example, was much smaller, that is, from 39.7 per cent in 1900 to 26 per cent in 1915. Further indication is to be found in the number of treaty ports in which the British population exceeded that of any other nationality. In 1901 the Customs report covered 29 ports and in 17 the British population was first. The 17 ports included Shanghai, Tientsin, Hankow, and Foochow, practically every port of outstanding importance. In 1911 the Customs report covered 45 ports. British population was first in only 14 and, among them, Canton was the only city of importance.[27] In general it may be said that in the trading centers of China British population showed a considerable increase and a decline in relative importance which was not startling. In the whole of China, however, a fundamental change had been brought about by the entrance of Russia and Japan into Manchuria.

The information concerning British firms is less to be trusted than is the information concerning population. The number of British firms reported by the Customs was 401 in 1899 and 590 in 1913. Accepting the totals shown in the Customs statistics, we find that 43 per cent of the foreign firms were British in 1899 and 15 per cent in 1913.

natives of Asia. British Government Colonial Reports—Annual, no. 814, *Hongkong, 1913*, p. 27.

[27] These figures are from the *Decennial Reports* of the Chinese Maritime Customs for 1892–1901 and 1902–1911.

Trade

The share of the United Kingdom in the direct trade of China was almost exactly the same in 1899 and in 1913. The figures were for 1899 11.8 per cent (Hk. Tls. 54 million) and for 1913 11.6 per cent (Hk. Tls. 113 million). There was, nevertheless, a decline in the relative importance of the British Empire in the trade of China. It will be remembered that the share of the British Empire, including Hongkong, had declined from more than 80 per cent of China's total trade in the early 'seventies to about 60 per cent at the end of the century. This decline continued and by 1913 the share of the British Empire was less than half.

The British colony of Hongkong accounted for no less than 40 per cent of China's foreign trade in the late 'nineties. By 1913 this had fallen to 30 per cent. With the continued rise in the importance of Shanghai and, after 1907, of Dairen, Hongkong was no longer the chief gateway and warehouse of China.

The United Kingdom continued throughout the period 1899–1913 to be of greater importance in China's import than in her export trade. Fifteen per cent of China's imports came from Great Britain in 1899 and 17 per cent in 1913. On the other hand, only 7 per cent of China's exports went to Great Britain in 1899 and 4 per cent in 1913. We do not know enough about the trade of Hongkong to be certain of the meaning of these figures. It may be that Hongkong played a larger part in the handling of goods moving from China to Great Britain than in the handling of goods moving the other way. Figures from British sources, however, corroborate the Chinese figures, showing exports from the United Kingdom to China and Hongkong several times as great as the imports. The United Kingdom was in 1913 a great manufacturer of goods, especially cotton textiles for Chinese consumption; London was not in 1913 as great a European market for

Chinese goods as she had been during the earlier days of the trade.

It is to be noted, also, that the direct trade of China with the United Kingdom was about equal to her direct trade with Japan in 1899. By 1913 the Japanese share of this trade was 19 per cent and the British share practically unchanged. The rise of Japan dates from the opening up of Dairen and other ports in Manchuria in 1907 and in the following years.

The changes shown in the position of the United Kingdom in the trade of China during the years from 1900 to 1913 were such as to foreshadow the changes of a later time. The chief exception to this lies in the position of the United States, for there was little indication in 1913 of its later rise to importance. At the beginning of the World War Great Britain was probably still as important in the trade of China as Japan and the British Empire accounted for about half of the total trade.

Shipping

The only satisfactory general figures of shipping are those which show the total tonnage in the foreign trade of China and in the trade between the open ports. The British share of this shipping was about 60 per cent until 1899 when it fell to 59 per cent. In 1913 it was 41 per cent. In other words two-fifths of all the modern shipping, both Chinese and foreign, in the whole of China's trade was under the British flag in 1913.

If we turn to what may be called the coast trade of China and eliminate from our calculations the Chinese tonnage, we find that over 50 per cent of this shipping was British in 1913 and that British ships carried over 60 per cent of the total value of the cargoes.

To complete the picture we must add shipping under "inland steam navigation rules." This is shipping from a treaty port to places which are not treaty ports. The information concerning this shipping, which is compiled by the Customs, shows the total number of foreign vessels registered at the various ports under steam navigation rules to have been 194 in 1913, 17.2 per cent of the total registrations. The figures of entrances and clearances for the various treaty ports on the other hand show foreign shipping to have been 31 per cent of the total. If again we eliminate Chinese tonnage, we find that British vessels account for 23.9 per cent of the foreign tonnage involved.

The information concerning shipping may be briefly recapitulated. The British share in the foreign and coast trade was 41 per cent. The British share of the foreign shipping in the coast trade alone was over 50 per cent and the British share in the inland waters navigation was about 25 per cent. An estimate of the value of British shipping in Chinese waters appears below.

Obligations of the Chinese Government

The obligations of the Chinese government to the British is shown in the following list. This list is divided according to the classification adopted for Chinese obligations in general. There is added the outstanding obligation to Great Britain on the Boxer indemnity which stands by itself and for which no sum is set down in the estimates for 1931. A brief title is given for each loan and in practically every case the date of issue is given also. The percentage of the British share of the total loan is shown and in every case the amounts are in U. S. dollars at $4.8665 to the £. The calculation of the amount outstanding on December 31, 1913 has been made according to amortization tables to be found in the works of Baylin, Wright, MacMurray, and Lieu.[28] The items are numbered for convenience of reference. It is to be emphasized that the principle of the place of issue has been accepted. This means that an issue of bonds in London is accepted as

[28] Baylin, J. R., *Foreign Loan Obligations of China;* MacMurray, John V. A., *Treaties and Agreements;* Wright, Stanley F., *The Collection and Disposal of the Maritime and Native Customs Revenue since the Revolution of 1911;* Lieu, D. K., *Foreign Investments in China, 1929.*

TABLE 3
British Share of the Obligations of the Chinese Government, 1914

	Outstanding Dec. 31, 1913	British Share	
	(U. S. Dollars)	Per Cent	(In U. S. Dollars)
General purposes of the Chinese government:			
1. 5% Gold Loan of 1896	56,869,554	50	28,434,777
2. 4½% Gold Loan of 1898	66,208,732	50	33,104,366
3. 6% Gold Loan—Arnold-Karberg (Nanking) loan—1895	973,300	100	973,300
4. 6% Gold Loan (Cassel loan), 1895	649,191	100	649,191
5. 5% Gold Loan of 1912 (Crisp loan)	24,332,500	100	24,332,500
6. 5% Reorganization Gold Loan of 1913	121,662,500	29.7	36,093,273
Subtotal			123,587,407
Railway Obligations:			
7. Chinese Imperial Ry. 5% Gold Loan (Imperial Rys. of N. China), 1899	8,674,536	100	8,674,536
8. Shanghai-Nanking Ry. Loan, 1903	14,112,850	100	14,112,850
9. 5% Honan Ry. Gold Loan of 1905	3,893,200	100	3,893,200
10. Canton-Hankow Ry. Loan of 1905	1,070,630	100	1,070,630
11. 5% Canton-Kowloon Ry. Loan of 1907	7,299,750	100	7,299,750
12. 5% Tientsin-Pukow Ry. Loan of 1908	24,332,500	37	9,003,025
13. 5% Shanghai-Hangchow-Ningpo Ry. Loan of 1908	7,299,750	100	7,299,750
14. 7% Peking-Hankow Redemption Loan of 1908	2,189,925	100	2,189,925
15. City Safe Deposit Co. Loan on Peking-Hankow Redemption Bonds of 1908	729,975	100	729,975
16. 5% Tientsin-Pukow Ry. Supplementary Loan of 1910	14,599,500	37	5,401,815
17. Tientsin-Pukow Advance, 1912	1,459,950	100	1,459,950
18. Shanghai-Nanking Ry. 6% Land Bonds of 1913	729,975	100	729,975
19. Pukow-Sinyang Ry. Advance of 1913	1,008,611	100	1,008,611
20. 5% Gold Loan of 1908 (Anglo-French)	24,332,500	50	12,166,250
21. 5% Hukuang Rys. Sinking Fund Gold Loan of 1911	29,199,000	25	7,299,750
Subtotal			82,330,002
Communications other than railways:			
22. Shanghai-Taku New Cable Loan, 1900	751,329	50	375,665
23. Duplicate Taku-Chefoo Cable Loan, 1900	174,333	50	87,166
24. Telegraph Charges Advance, 1911	2,324,425	50	1,162,213
Subtotal			1,625,044
Total			207,552,443
British share of the amount outstanding on the Boxer indemnity			34,608,000

357

a British obligation. No attempt has been made to estimate the obligations on the principle of the place of actual holding. It may well be that the British were the holders of some bonds issued elsewhere but it is impossible now to discover such holdings as they were in 1914, and it is not probable that such holdings were large.

Business Investments

British business investments in China were estimated for 1907, by the author of the *Quarterly Review* article referred to above, at U. S. $109.5 million. No additional estimate of the period before the war has been discovered.[29] It is not possible, therefore, to establish a lower limit based on securities dealt with in Great Britain.

We may turn to land values at Shanghai for some indication of an upper limit. The total value of the land at Shanghai which was held under foreign registry has been estimated in the American chapter at Sh. Tls. 250 million, and the total value of the land actually owned by foreigners at Tls. 170 million. Of the land actually in the possession of foreigners it may be estimated that 80 per cent was owned by British citizens. This makes the total of British land holdings Tls. 136 million or about U. S. $87 million (taking the Shanghai tael at U. S. $0.64). If we estimate the whole of British investments at Shanghai at three times this value of the land holdings we arrive at a total of U. S. $261. It is highly probable that British investments in the whole of China, including Hongkong, were not in 1914 twice the Shanghai total. If, however, we hold to this figure we come out with a possible total of U. S. $522 million for British business investments in China.

[29] It is true that Sir George Paish published an estimate of "Great Britain's Capital Investments in Individual Colonial and Foreign Countries" in the *Journal of the Royal Statistical Society*, January, 1911, vol. 74, part 2, but this estimate, which ought, as J. M. Keynes remarks (p. 195) to have been called an estimate of capital subscribed in London, puts the total for China, aside from government obligations, at the unbelievably small sum of £4,332,000, about U. S. $21 million.

It is impossible to check this total against information concerning more than a few of the fields of investment. I offer briefly certain information which I have been able to secure.

In the field of transportation we have, in the first place, the British section of the Canton-Kowloon Railway which was built by the Hongkong government. The total expended upon the construction of the British section at the end of 1913 was Hongkong $13,521,231, that is, about U. S. $6.7 million.[30]

In the same field we have, in the second place, British investments in shipping in the coast and river trade of China. The number of British ships was now about 100 and the tonnage about 170,000. The ships were larger than in 1900 and the value per ton was somewhat greater. In addition there had been a considerable expansion in shipbuilding and repairing. There were turned out by engineering and shipbuilding plants "under European management" at Hongkong in 1913 a total of 59 vessels of over 12,000 gross tons.[31] The three important companies engaged in this industry were very largely British owned. An estimate arrived at after consultation in Shanghai put the total British investment in shipping, excluding entirely ships in the foreign trade beyond Hongkong, at about U. S. $40 million.

Investments in public utilities which may be accounted for by the paid-up capital and surplus of companies for which information could be secured must have reached U. S. $20 million. The companies include the Shanghai Gas Company, the Shanghai Mutual Telephone Company, the Shanghai Electric Construction Company, the Hongkong Tramway Company, and the Hongkong and China Gas Company.

Mining accounts for certainly no less than U. S. $15

[30] British Government: Colonial Reports—Annual, no. 814, *Hongkong, 1913*, p. 5.
[31] *Ibid*, p. 14.

million. The investment of the British participant in the Kailan Mining Administration was £2.2 million.[32] The Peking Syndicate had interests in Honan which are difficult to estimate but which must have involved an investment of £500,000. There was, in addition, the Tung Hsing Sino-Foreign Coal Mining Company, Ltd., owners of a colliery at Mentoukou, about sixteen miles from Peking. The British investment in this venture was Tls. 500,000.[33]

British holdings in the field of manufacturing included three cotton mills at Shanghai (107,000 spindles) and one at Hongkong (45,000 spindles), three sugar refineries at Hongkong and one at Swatow, the factories of the British American Tobacco Company at Hankow, Newchwang, Mukden, and Shanghai, silk filatures at Shanghai, a rope factory at Canton, oil mills at Newchwang and Shanghai, a cement factory at Hongkong, and a great variety of smaller industrial plants. It is not unreasonable to estimate investments in this field at U. S. $100 million.

Real estate holdings at Shanghai have been estimated at U. S. $87 million and to this must be added holdings elsewhere. These holdings are, in part, devoted to industrial and business uses and, in so far as this is the case, they are included under the appropriate headings.

In the field of importing, exporting, and general trading it is not difficult to account for a sum that reaches a total of U. S. $100 million. A list of British Chambers of Commerce in China, drawn up in 1917, included Chambers at 15 Chinese ports.[34] The chief traders at most of the ports of China were British firms, the chief foreign land

[32] For an account of the financing connected with the creation of the Kailan Mining Administration see *The Economist* (London), June 8, 1912, pp. 1322–4.

[33] *China Year Book,* 1919, p. 69.

[34] *List of the Principal Foreign and Chinese Industrial Enterprises in China and Hongkong,* Kelley and Walsh, Shanghai, 1918. The list was compiled by the British Commercial Attaché.

holders at practically every port outside of Manchuria were British citizens.

When investments in the field of banking and finance are considered in addition to those enumerated, it is plain that a total in the neighborhood of U. S. $400 million can be shown to be fairly conservative, and I propose to adopt this estimate for British business investments at the beginning of the World War.

This estimate of U. S. $400 million for 1914 is, of course, a guess and this fact must be borne in mind when comparison is made with the estimate of business investments for 1931 which rests upon a series of new investigations. But it is a guess based upon wide information and upon conferences with a considerable number of British business men and officials in China.

Summary of British Investments, 1914

The total of British investments in China arrived at in the preceding estimates is shown in the following table.

TABLE 4

BRITISH INVESTMENTS IN CHINA, 1914

	Millions of U. S. Dollars	Per Cent
Business investments	400.0	65.8
Obligations of the Chinese government	207.5	34.2
	607.5	100.0

Comparisons are deferred until the figures for recent years have been presented. It may be worth while, however, to point out that the percentage of the total formed by the obligations of the Chinese government was considerably smaller in 1914 than it had been in 1902. It is not to be forgotten that the British share of the Boxer indemnity is excluded, but, even if it were included, the percentage formed by government obligations would be no more in 1914 than 37.7 per cent, as compared with 42.4 per cent at the end of 1901.

The preceding account of British investments and of Great Britain's relative importance in the international economic relations of China is quite obviously incomplete. One reason is the lack of adequate information, as in the case of business investments. I have considered it necessary to attempt estimates in this field because otherwise comparisons with other countries would be misleading and general totals difficult to interpret.

A second reason lies in the overwhelming importance of Great Britain in every field before the year 1900. Any general account of China's international economic relations in the nineteenth century is very largely an account of her relations with Great Britain. In certain fields a decline in the relative importance of the British began with the penetration of Russia and Japan into Manchuria. It is true, also, that the closing years of the nineteenth and the opening years of the present century witnessed a general increase in international competition involving most of the powers interested in China. The early importance of Great Britain must not be forgotten as we approach the present situation.

BRITISH INTERESTS IN 1931

Population

I turn now to the nature and extent of British interests in China of a tangible and measurable sort, as they are at the present time. Population, trade, and shipping will be dealt with briefly and I shall then undertake to present an estimate of British investments based upon new material.

Figures of British population in China are of two sorts: those which may be compared with the figures for earlier years and a new estimate of the actual number of British citizens in the whole Chinese area, including Hongkong.

The comparable figures of population are those from the Maritime Customs Reports. The number of British citizens was reported as 13,015 at the end of 1930. This was an increase of about 45 per cent over 1913. The decline in the relative importance of the British continued and they formed no more than 3.6 per cent of the total foreign population of China in 1930.

The British population in the International Settlement at Shanghai was 6,221 in 1930, according to the figures of the Shanghai Municipal Council. The British percentage of the total foreign population of Shanghai dropped from 26 per cent in 1915 to 17 per cent in 1930. At the end of 1930 there was probably no open port at which the British were in the majority and there was certainly none among the larger ports.

If we examine the Customs figures more closely we find the British population declined somewhat during the World War, reaching a low point (7,935) in 1918. After the war there was an increase to a high point of over 15,000 in 1925. After 1925 there was a general decline in foreign population in China which is shown in the British figures also. At the end of 1930 the British figures were still somewhat below those of 1925.

In short, British population in China, as reported by the Maritime Customs, showed a fairly continuous increase in actual numbers from 1900 to 1930 and a decrease in relative importance. The explanation lies in the increase in Japanese and Russian population, particularly in Manchuria.

British firms in China numbered 645 in 1929 and 1,027 in 1930, according to the Customs statistics. Such a change is unexplainable and adds to one's doubts as to the reliability of the Customs figures. It is fairly certain, however, that the number of British firms varied with the British population and that the relative importance of the British did not decline to as low a percentage in the case of firms as of population. Of the foreign firms 12.4 per cent were British in 1930 and 7.8 per cent—undoubtedly more correct than the larger figure—were British in 1930. The British percentage of firms is more than twice as great as the British percentage of population. We shall find the same thing to be true when we compare population with trade and shipping.

To arrive at an estimate of the actual number of British citizens in China at the end of 1930 requires that we go outside of the figures of the Maritime Customs. The Customs reported 13,015. The census of the Shanghai Municipal Council stated the British population of the International Settlement and the external roads area contiguous to the Settlement to be 6,221.[35] The British population of the French Concession at Shanghai was 2,219 in 1930.[36] According to the authorities of the municipality of Greater Shanghai there were 891 British nationals in the parts of Shanghai entirely under Chinese political control. From these sources we arrive at a total British population of 9,331 for the whole of the Shanghai area.

The non-Chinese civilian population of Hongkong was 18,150 in 1930. It may be estimated that a third of this population, about 6,000, consisted of persons of British nationality from outside of Asia.

If we accept the Customs figures for British population outside of Shanghai, add the Shanghai figures given above, and the estimated British population of Hongkong, we arrive at a total of at least 20,000. This figure is to be compared with the estimate of 140,000 for the Russian population and, at the highest, 280,000 for the Japanese population in 1931.

Trade

The best comparable index of British trade with China is to be found in the reports of the Chinese Maritime Customs, and I turn first to their figures. After this an

---

[35] *Feetham Report*, vol. 1, p. 51.
[36] Census of April, 1930. *China Year Book*, 1931, p. 694. The figures of the Municipality of Greater Shanghai are reprinted on the same page.

estimate is presented of the whole of British trade with China, including Hongkong.

The direct trade of the United Kingdom with China (excluding Hongkong), as reported by the Maritime Customs, amounted to 11.4 per cent of China's total foreign trade in 1913. The British share had remained at about this level since the beginning of the century. In 1930 it was only 7.8 per cent. In Haikwan taels British trade was 113 million in 1913 and 171 million in 1930. The low point for the whole period was, as might have been expected, during the last year of the war. In 1918 the figure was no more than Hk. Tls. 75 million, 7.2 per cent of China's total trade. The outstanding fact was the decline in the relative importance of Great Britain over the whole period.

The share of Hongkong (dealt with as a foreign country in the Chinese statistics) continued to decline. From about 40 per cent in 1900 it had dropped to about 30 per cent in 1913. In 1930 it was 17 per cent. The figure was as low as 11 per cent in 1926, when the full effect of the anti-British boycott was being felt.

Taking into account the same British countries as entered into the earlier figure, we may say that the British Empire, including Hongkong, accounted for less than one-third of China's trade in 1930. In 1913 it had accounted for almost half. The drop, it may be repeated, was from about 85 per cent in the late 'seventies of the last century.[37]

The following tables show the importance of the United Kingdom in the foreign trade of China and the importance of China in the foreign trade of the United Kingdom. These tables bring together statistics from Chinese and

---

[37] The figures given above are for Great Britain, British India, and Hongkong. These countries have formed the British Empire in the Chinese trade statistics of the past. The percentage for the whole British Empire, including Hongkong, was really 32.3 per cent in 1929. Department of Overseas Trade, *Economic Conditions in China, to August 30, 1930*, London, 1930, p. 72.

from British sources.   I am not now interested in the discrepancies in these tables but in the general changes which are shown in both.

TABLE 5

The Importance of the United Kingdom in the Foreign Trade of China

Chinese Statistics

(Figures of value are in millions of Haikwan taels)

	Imports from United Kingdom	Per Cent of China's Total Imports	Exports to United Kingdom	Per Cent of China's Total Exports	Total Trade	Per Cent of China's Total Foreign Trade
1899	40.2	15.2	13.9	7.1	54.1	11.8
1913	96.9	17.0	16.3	4.1	113.2	11.6
1929	119.2	9.4	74.3	7.3	193.5	8.5
1930	108.3	8.3	62.7	7.0	171.0	7.8

TABLE 6

The Importance of China in the Foreign Trade of the United Kingdom

British Statistics

(Figures of value are in millions of pounds sterling)

	Exports to China	Per Cent of Total Exports of United Kingdom	Imports from China	Per Cent of Total Imports into United Kingdom	Total Trade	Per Cent of Total Trade of United Kingdom
1913	14.8	2.8	2.9	0.4	17.7	1.5
1929	14.0	1.9	9.7	0.9	23.7	1.9
1930	8.6	1.5	8.2	0.9	16.8	1.1

Between 1900 and 1913 the British share of China's trade hardly changed but there was a noticeable fall in the percentage of China's exports going to Great Britain and a slight rise in the case of imports.   The decline from 7.1 per cent to 4.1 per cent in percentage of exports going to Great Britain was the result of increased exports to Japan and of a decline in the importance of London as a market for Chinese goods on their way to the continent of Europe. The slight rise in the case of imports reflects the fact that Great Britain held first place as the source of cotton manufactures for the Chinese market. So far as the finer grades of cotton goods are concerned, it may be said that before 1914 no country seriously threatened the supremacy of Great Britain.[38]

Between 1913 and 1930 the decline in the importance of Great Britain in China's foreign trade was marked. Again, the import and export trade offer a contrast, for the percentage of China's exports going to Great Britain nearly doubled. It is not surprising that this happened during and immediately after the war.[39] Foodstuffs and raw materials were then in great demand. Great Britain continued after the war to take a larger percentage of China's exports than during the years 1908–1913 and in 1929 the figure was higher than at any time since 1899, excepting the war period. There was a notable increase in the case of eggs and egg products. In 1913 China sent the bulk of her egg products to Germany and only 1.4 per cent (Hk. Tls. 79,586) to Great Britain; in 1929 [40] Great Britain took no less than 47.8 per cent (Hk. Tls. 24,742,165). There was a great increase in the case of soya beans and bean oil, from Hk. Tls. 2.2 million to 19.7 million. Other increases, as in furs, were smaller. It was not in goods moving from China that the British decline took place.

[38] I quote from a recent address in London by Sir Kenneth Stewart (*British Chamber of Commerce Journal*, Shanghai, September, 1930, p. 254): "In 1913 the situation had arisen that the coarse yarns for hand-loom work were being supplied by mills on Chinese territory, the coarser machine-made cloth was being supplied by Japan, and Great Britain supplied the rest. In fact after India, China was our greatest market in the world. It is true it was a long way after India."

[39] In 1919, for example, 9.1 per cent of China's exports went to the United Kingdom.

[40] Figures for 1929 are used here to represent the situation before the world depression.

When we turn to goods moving to China we find a drop in the British share from 17 per cent in 1913 to 9.4 per cent in 1929 and to 8.3 per cent in 1930. Again it is to be noted that there was a sharp drop during the war, to 9 per cent in 1918. There was a rapid recovery after the war, from 9.9 per cent in 1919 to no less than 17.3 per cent in 1920. Since 1920 the British share in the import trade of China has been steadily declining and in 1930 it was smaller than in any other year for which we have records. [41]

The decline in British imports into China has been the subject of much comment in Great Britain and in the British community in China. It has been a matter for official and unofficial investigation and report. "If the 1929 figures for imports from Great Britain into China [I quote from a recent report] are reduced to the basis of 1913 values, the magnitude of the decline in the volume of British trade to the China market becomes apparent. It amounts to over 30 per cent." [42]

There is general agreement that the decline has been very largely in the British export to China of cotton textiles. The British cotton industry differs from that of other countries in its dependence upon exporting. It has been estimated that about one-fifth of the world's production of cotton piece goods passes into international trade, but that about 80 per cent of British production in 1924 was exported. [43] India is, of course, the greatest market [44] taking from five to ten times as much as China

[41] With the exception of 1927 when the British share was 7.4 per cent. This is explained, in part at least, by the success of the Nationalist movement and the continued anti-British boycott.

[42] Conclusions and Recommendations of the British Economic Mission to the Far East, *Board of Trade Journal*, May 14, 1931, p. 627.

[43] British Census of Production of 1924 quoted in the final sections of the report of the Cotton Mission to the Far East, *Board of Trade Journal*, April 16, 1931, p. 482.

[44] India took about 40 per cent of the export of cotton piece goods from the United Kingdom in 1909–1913, and about 30 per cent in 1929 and 1930. See *The Cotton Industry Since the War*, issued for private circulation by the Cotton Trade Statistical Bureau, Manchester, 1931.

which has long held second place. This British export
trade, as is well known, has not prospered since the war
and the export declined fairly rapidly from 1925 to 1930.
The industry is peculiarly vulnerable. It is among the
first to be undertaken in undeveloped countries, the product is not easily sheltered from competition, and it is
highly boycottable.

The importance of Japanese competition is another
point upon which there is general agreement. "In the
period 1909 to 1913 Great Britain held between 60 and
65 per cent of the total world export trade and Japan less
than 3 per cent. Britain's share fell by 1929 to 45 per
cent and Japan's share had increased to 17 per cent.
Great Britain exported to China and Hongkong in the
years 1909 to 1913 an average of 587 million linear yards,
in 1929, 210 million, in 1930 only 69 million. In 1913
Britain's exports to China and Hongkong were four times
the value of those of Japan, but in 1930 they were only
one-sixth part of the value of Japan's." [45] In 1913 no
less than 85 per cent of the "grey shirtings" imported
into China came from Great Britain, in 1930, 73 per cent
of the "grey shirtings and sheetings" came from Japan.
In the import of printed and finer goods Great Britain
was still important in 1929 and 1930, but even here the
Japanese supplied more than half.

The proportion of China's import of piece goods coming from Great Britain and Japan has fluctuated under
the influence of a succession of Chinese boycotts. The
anti-British boycott of 1925–1927 brought imports from
Great Britain down to a low figure in 1927. There was
a rapid rise during the next year when an anti-Japanese
boycott followed the so-called Tsinanfu affair. The figures for 1931 and 1932 will, no doubt, show a rise in the
proportion of piece goods coming from Great Britain.
The boycott has played a part of some importance but

[45] "Conclusions and Recommendations of the Cotton Mission," *Board
of Trade Journal*, April 16, 1931, p. 482.

the persistent downward trend in the British share of the Chinese import of cotton goods is an underlying fact.

British business men and officials are by no means agreed upon the explanation and there is little doubt that it is due to a variety of causes. Some of these lie in Lancashire and London. The industry is said to be over-capitalized and to be so organized as to make it difficult for producers to co-operate. The recent Cotton Mission gave much weight to the necessity for "a radical improvement in our methods of exporting and marketing Lancashire goods." [46] The greatest importance is usually given to other factors, however, with special emphasis upon two. The first of these is the Japanese advantage in competition resting upon effective combination and upon low wages. [47] The second is stated in a variety of ways. China, we are told, is essentially a price market. The Chinese cannot afford to buy goods which are high in quality and high in price. The analysis of such statements usually leads back to the fields of production and marketing. The competition of Japanese and Chinese mills has been more successful in the low priced field and it follows that the British goods still in the field are high in price and quality. British marketing methods in the absence of co-operation give an exaggerated importance to standards. [48] The success of these methods depends

[46] *Board of Trade Journal*, April 16, 1931, p. 484.

[47] It is significant that the British Cotton Mission of 1931 and A. S. Pearse (*The Cotton Industry of Japan and China*, Manchester, 1929) who visited the Far East in 1929, agree, as do other observers, that low wages in Japan are not counterbalanced by inefficiency. The Cotton Mission made this direct statement: "The Japanese spinner employs no more operatives than would be employed in a similar Lancashire mill, the wages per head are lower, the hours worked are longer, and the output per operative per hour appeared to be as high as at home." *Board of Trade Journal*, April 16, 1931, p. 483.

[48] Sir Ernest Thompson, Chairman of the British Cotton Mission speaking at a dinner in Shanghai on Dec. 8, 1930, said: "I have just returned from Japan . . . and I can state quite definitely that much of the cloth I saw being woven and at least half the goods I saw being packed would be rejected in Manchester as being definitely unfit for shipment to China. I can further vouch for the fact that if we had shipped such goods to China you would have rejected them on this side. I ask you . . . to realize

also either upon the word of dealers or upon the strict enforcement of contracts by the courts. In the disturbed state of China the advantage has gone to the importer with a highly organized marketing system, the British American Tobacco Company or the Asiatic Petroleum Company, and not to the importer who has depended upon the enforceability of contracts made in an open market.

The traditions of Lancashire, the marketing methods in the trade in cotton goods, Japanese competition, the rise of the Chinese cotton milling industry, the high degree of boycottability in the case of cotton goods have all played a part in the decline in the British share of this trade and in the British share of China's import trade in general. There are fields in which the British have held their own, in machinery, for example, but the outstanding difference between 1913 and 1930 lies in the field of cotton textiles.

I turn now to an estimate of the total British trade with China, including Hongkong, for the year 1930. The total British trade with China, not including Hongkong, was Hk. Tls. 171 million, 7.8 per cent of China's trade. The Hongkong government began the publication of trade returns in April, 1930. Upon the basis of the Hongkong figures for nine months of the year, 1930, I have calculated the total trade for China including Hongkong.[49] This total I find to have been Hk.Tls. 2,320.1 million, and the British share I find to have been, not Hk. Tls. 171 million and 7.8 per cent, but Hk. Tls. 216.3 million and 9.3 per cent. The inclusion of Hongkong gives a clearer picture of China's total trade and it is significant that it makes the British percentage considerably higher.

what a great advantage it is to a competitor if he trades under a system which relieves him of the necessity of complying as strictly with the precise details of an order as we are forced to do." *British Chamber of Commerce Journal* (Shanghai), Dec., 1930, p. 345.

[49] *Hongkong Trade and Shipping Returns*, December, 1930. The rate for conversion to Haikwan taels accepted for 1930 is Hk. Tls. 1 = Hongkong $1.36.

TABLE 7

BRITISH TRADE WITH CHINA AND WITH CHINA AND HONGKONG, 1930

	Trade with China	Trade with China and Hongkong
Imports from United Kingdom	Hk. Tls. 108.3 million	Hk. Tls. 150.7 million
Imports as a per cent of the total imports	8.3	10.6
Exports to United Kingdom	Hk. Tls. 62.7 million	Hk. Tls. 65.6 million
Exports as a per cent of the total exports	7.0	7.3
British total	Hk. Tls. 170.9 million	Hk. Tls. 216.3 million
As a per cent of the general total	7.8	9.3

Shipping

The general figures, showing the total tonnage, both Chinese and foreign, in the foreign trade of China and in the trade between the open ports, for the year 1913 gave the British flag 41 per cent. In 1930 the British percentage was about 37. The British held a larger percentage than did any other nation (the Japanese percentage was 29.3) of the modern shipping in the whole of China's trade.

If we turn to what is called the coast trade, that is, the trade between the open ports, we find, leaving the Chinese tonnage in, that the British flag accounted for 38 per cent of the tonnage and carried 42 per cent of the value of the total cargoes. If the Chinese tonnage is taken out, we find the British share of the foreign shipping in the coast trade to be 50 per cent.

The shipping "under inland steam navigation rules," frequently called the river shipping, includes all vessels engaged in trade between the open ports and places which are not open. The number of foreign vessels registered under these rules was 544, 20.3 per cent of the total, at the end of 1930. The Customs reports provide no information as to the nationality of the vessels so registered. They do,

however, provide information as to the tonnage of entrances and clearances at the various treaty ports by
flags. From these reports we find that the foreign share of
this river shipping was not 20.3 per cent, as shown by the
number of ships, but 11.7 per cent. The British share of
the total, including Chinese tonnage, was 1.8 per cent and
the British share of the foreign tonnage was 15.8 per cent.
The Chinese share of shipping under inland steam navigation rules had increased so greatly by 1930 as to take much
of the significance from these percentages.

It may be estimated from these figures that about one-
fifth of the steam shipping in the domestic trade, that is,
in the coast and river trade of China, was under the British
flag at the end of 1930 and that two-fifths of the foreign
shipping was British. These conclusions are borne out by
information provided in Shanghai, the source of which I
am not at liberty to quote. These figures show that British
companies carried 42 per cent of the cargo in the coast and
river trade, including the trade between China and Hongkong as coast trade, and about the same percentage of the
passengers. It is safe to assume that the British share of
the tonnage, which I have estimated at 20 per cent, carries
with it a considerably larger fraction of the business. The
Japanese share of the domestic shipping of China has
grown since 1913, but at the end of 1930 the British were
the leading foreign nation in this field.

Investments: Three Estimates

Three unpublished estimates are of basic importance in
arriving at my final figures of British investments in
China. These three estimates provide the only available
information over most of the field of business investments
and they have been used to supplement the published
material on the foreign obligations of the Chinese government.

The first estimate is by a committee of the Royal Institute of International Affairs of London.[50]   This committee drew up a report which was presented at the Kyoto Conference of the Institute of Pacific Relations.   The Royal Institute of International Affairs has been good enough to make this study available to me, after including in the totals all returns received to July, 1931.   The classification of business investments which was found best after a study of the Japanese and American estimates differed from that which had been originally adopted by the British Committee.   The Honorable H. A. Wyndham and the members of the staff of the Royal Institute took the trouble to go over the returns and assist me in bringing them into a form which made comparison possible with the results of the other investigations.[51]   The figures arrived at as the result of this investigation by the Royal Institute of International Affairs will appear in the pages which follow.   For the present it is sufficient to point out that the report of the British Committee reaches a figure for total British interests in China, excluding good-will, which may, they say, be put down at roughly £260 million (U. S. $1,260 million).

The second estimate is that of Mr. D. K. Lieu, based upon returns from 414 British firms in China.   I shall include with this an estimate of the British obligations of the Chinese government, as of December 31, 1929, by Mr. C. Sun of the Bureau of Statistics of the Legislative Yuan of the Chinese government.[52]   The two taken together form what I shall refer to as the Chinese estimate of British investments in China.   Mr. Lieu's returns were originally published in his *Foreign Investments in China, 1929*.   A more recent compilation, which includes information received to April, 1931, has been drawn up.

[50] The signers of the letter which was sent, early in 1929, to British firms with interests in China were: C. S. Addis, K. D. Stewart, A. Brooke Smith, Th. Gregory, and Dennis Robertson.

[51] I am particularly indebted to Miss Margaret E. Cleeve, Secretary for Library and Publications.

[52] The Bureau is now, I believe, under the direct supervision of the Chairman of the National Government.

Although Mr. Lieu's returns give him a figure of more than Chinese $1,500 million, he has reached the conclusion that British business investments may be reasonably estimated at Chinese $1,000 million. He took as the exchange rate for his calculations Chinese $10.70 to the pound sterling. Accepting Chinese $2 to U. S. $1 as roughly equivalent, we find Mr. Lieu's estimate to come to U. S. $500 million for business investments. To this I add U. S. $184 million, Mr. Sun's estimate of government obligations and the result is a Chinese estimate of British investments which is no more than U. S. $684 million.

The third estimate is that of the British Chamber of Commerce of Shanghai. This estimate is the result of work which extended over a period of two years commencing in 1926. The attempt was made to arrive at what was called British assets in China. The results of the actual returns from the direct inquiry show a total under business investments and mission property holdings of £185,453,-485. The figures supplied by the various firms were regarded as conservative in 1927 when the compilation was made. The secretary of the Chamber undertook to make, on his knowledge of the percentage of returns and of the increase in holdings and in their value since 1927, a guess at the total value of British interests in China, including British holdings of the obligations of the Chinese government and including Hongkong, and this total he put at between £350 million and £400 million. Taking the lower of these figures we find the estimate of the British Chamber of Commerce at Shanghai to be £350 million or U. S. $1,700 million.

The above are the important facts about the three estimates which must serve as the basis for a final estimate. The total for each of the three has been given with no intention of creating the impression that these totals may be compared, as they stand. The differences are in part due to the fact that different things are included and that the same terms have different meanings.

After a critical examination of the three I will present an estimate which is my own, since I must take the responsibility for it, but one which includes practically no figures which have not been taken from one or the other of these estimates.

Holdings of Government Obligations: The Three Estimates

The estimate of the Royal Institute of International Affairs contains the following items under this heading. The British share only is shown:

Secured loans (including the Boxer indemnity)	£31,500,000
Unsecured loans	2,400,000
Railways in which the interest is solely British	11,500,000
Railways in which the interest is a joint one	7,500,000
Debts due from the Chinese government to British firms	1,718,000
Debentures of the foreign municipalities in China	4,000,000
Total	£58,618,000

In American dollars the total of the British Committee's estimate comes to U. S. $285,264,497.

The Chinese estimate of British holdings is confined to those of the Chinese government and shows these obligations as of December 31, 1929, or at the beginning of 1930. The classification shows the method by which Mr. Sun arrived at his total.

Obligations of the Ministry of Finance:		
Secured loans	£17,776,397	
Unsecured loans	6,150,222	£23,926,619
Obligations of the Ministry of Railways:		
Secured and unsecured obligations		£13,866,294
Total		£37,792,913

In American dollars this estimate comes to U. S. $183,919,211.

The estimate of the British Chamber of Commerce does not deal separately with the obligations of the Chinese government and need not be considered in this connection.

Loans for the General Purposes of the Chinese Government: The first step in arriving at a final estimate of British investments is to present the amount outstanding as of December 31, 1930 on the secured loans for the

Chinese government, excluding railway loans.   The amounts shown have been arrived at on the principle of the place of issue, no account being taken for the present of the fact that bonds issued elsewhere are now held in England.   Such a list may be made from published information and, with two exceptions, it is the same as the list shown in Table 3 above.

TABLE 8

BRITISH SHARE OF LOANS FOR THE GENERAL PURPOSES OF THE CHINESE
GOVERNMENT, 1931

	Outstanding Dec. 31, 1930	British Share	
	U. S. Dollars	Per Cent	In U. S. Dollars
5% Gold Loan of 1896	8,749,724	50	4,374,862
4½% Gold Loan of 1898	39,304,885	50	19,652,443
5% Gold Loan of 1912 (Crisp loan)	22,308,800	100	22,308,800
5% Reorganization Loan of 1913	111,915,776	29.7	33,238,985
			79,575,090

The total of these loans I find to have been U. S. $79,575,090 or about £16,350,000 at the end of 1930.   The loans included here are those which the Chinese Committee lists as secured obligations of the Ministry of Finance with a total of £17,776,397.   The difference here is entirely accounted for as due to amortization payments during the year 1930.[53]   My total is the same as that of the Chinese estimate.

The Royal Institute of International Affairs, however, sets down a total of £31.5 million or U. S. $153.3 million. This includes a capital sum for the Boxer indemnity which I do not include, and U. S. $21,880,000 may be deducted for this, leaving a sum of U. S. $131,420,000 to be compared with my total of about U. S. $80 million. The explanation of the discrepancy does not lie in the

[53] No such payments on the Crisp loan were made in 1930.

fact that the British Committee includes estimates of British purchases of Chinese bonds issued elsewhere. In part, it lies, I have good reason to believe, in the fact that a total for a much earlier date was taken over by the British Committee without adjustment for payments on principal.   In part, the discrepancy may be due to the inclusion of loans under this head which I have put elsewhere.   I propose my figure under this heading as the best obtainable.

Debentures of the Foreign Municipalities in China: The sum set down against this by the British Committee is £4 million.   It is entirely omitted from the Chinese estimate and no separate estimate is made by the British Chamber of Commerce.   There is no doubt that this item ought to be included in a total of British investments in China.   In so far as these debentures are held in Great Britain the service upon them constitutes an outpayment from China.   In so far as they are held by British citizens in China, they constitute a part of the holdings of the British "colony" within the country.

The amount of such obligations is not easily determined.   The sum of £4 million is reported by the British Committee as the obligations of the International Settlement at Shanghai.   These obligations were much reduced by payments from the Shanghai Power Company, an American corporation which took over the electricity department of the Shanghai Municipal Council under an agreement dated August 8, 1929.   The total outstanding loans of the International Settlement were reported at Sh. Tls. 38,242,300 for 1930.[54]   This makes a total (at Sh. Tls. 12 to the pound sterling) of £3,186,858. The British Committee undoubtedly had in mind the situation as it was before the sale of the municipal electricity plant, when the loans outstanding were about £6 million.   It is reasonable to assume, as the British

[54] *Annual Report of the Shanghai Municipal Council for the Year 1930,* Part 2, pp. 372 and 433.

Committee undoubtedly did, that two-thirds of these obligations were in British hands. This makes £2 million a reasonable estimate of the British holding of debentures of the Shanghai International Settlement at the end of 1930.[55]

The public debt of the colony of Hongkong, which was probably in British hands, was estimated by bankers in that city at about £800,000. This makes allowance for sinking funds and for the fact that the 6 per cent public works loan of 1927 was repayable in 1932.[56] The outstanding debentures of the British Concession at Tientsin came to Tientsin Tls. 2,278,800 at the end of December, 1929. These debentures are more largely in Chinese hands than are the debentures of the International Settlement at Shanghai. The total in British hands was estimated at Tientsin in 1931 at about £125,000. British holdings of the debentures of other municipalities were so small as not to merit consideration. It may be added that the local governments of Chinese municipalities have not undertaken to borrow abroad or from foreign financial institutions within China.

The total of the above estimates comes to £2,925,000, which I take to be a reasonable estimate of British holdings of the long-term obligations of local governments in China in which the foreigners have some degree of political control. This sum comes to U. S. $14,235,000.

Chinese Government Railways: The estimate of the Royal Institute of International Affairs sets the total under this heading higher than any other responsible estimate of recent years. Railway investments are put at £19 million or U. S. $92.5 million. To this there must be added a part of the sum of £1,718,000 set down as debts due from the Chinese government to British firms.

---

[55] D. K. Lieu, *Foreign Investments in China, 1929,* Shanghai, 1929, App. A, p. 125, "the annual report of the Shanghai Municipal Council shows that no more than 10% of the debentures were in Chinese hands in 1927."

[56] British Government Colonial Reports, *Hongkong,* Report for 1928, p. 5.

This estimate, no doubt, includes loans which appear in my list as for communications other than railways. The chief reason for the high figure is, no doubt, the fact that the estimate is for an earlier year than in the case of the estimates dealt with below.

The British Chamber of Commerce does not include an estimate which gives separate figures for the railways and it may be eliminated from our consideration.

The Chinese estimate contains a list of railway obligations drawn up by Mr. Sun which is the result of a careful survey and which I propose to accept as my final estimate of British investments. It is to be compared with two other estimates, one of them a recent one and the other for the year 1923. The estimate for 1923 is from a document drawn up by the Ministry of Communications, as it was then known, of the Chinese government [57] of the time. The obligations to Great Britain, shown in this document, amount to Chinese $167,537,538 or (at the rate of U. S. $1 = Chinese $2 which was employed) U. S. $83,768,769.

The recent estimate is one which was drawn up for me by the Ministry of Railways of the Chinese government in 1931. It shows the railway obligations distributed by nationality as they were on December 31, 1929. The available details are shown in the table on page 381.

I return to the estimate of Mr. Sun, whose work was carried on in conjunction with that of Mr. D. K. Lieu and who had access to the materials used in drawing up the 1929 table of the Ministry of Railways. It is this estimate which I have accepted and the total which enters my final table of British investments is U. S. $67,948,613. If a later estimate were available it would differ from this estimate only by the addition of further arrears of interest and by the addition of such new obligations for ma-

[57] With the title, *Tables Showing Various Obligations of the Ministry of Communications, Calculated up to January 31, 1923.* Printed by the Ministry of Communications.

TABLE 9

BRITISH OBLIGATIONS OF THE CHINESE GOVERNMENT RAILWAY AS OF
DECEMBER 31, 1929

Source: Ministry of Railways of the Chinese Government

	Rate	U. S. Dollars	
Secured:			
£11,629,334	4.8665	56,594,154	
Ch. $ 635,969	2.50	254,388	
			56,848,542
Unsecured			
£ 636,725	4.8665	3,098,622	
U. S. $ 21,100		21,100	
Ch. $ 1,664,625	2.50	665,850	
Tls. 5,384,315	1.80	2,991,286	
			6,776,858
Total			63,625,400

terials and supplies as may emerge from the work of the Commission for the Consolidation of Foreign and Domestic Obligations. We may accept U. S. $68 million as the British total. The details are shown in the table on pages 382 and 383.

Communications Other than Railways: Obligations in this field are not separately estimated in either of the British sources. They are so listed by Lieu who does not, however, undertake to make a separate total for Great Britain. The list below undertakes to show the amount outstanding on December 31, 1930, upon the various loans. It is to be noted that the single addition to the list, as it appeared for 1914, is the so-called Marconi Telegraph Advance made in accordance with an agreement of October, 1918.[58] Other advances by the Marconi Company, Ltd., are among the unsecured loans dealt with in another section.

The original cable contracts, in which British participation was through the Eastern Extension Telegraph Com-

[58] Baylin, J. R., *Foreign Loan Obligations of China*, p. 78, and the *China Year Book*, 1931, p. 365.

TABLE 10

Amounts are shown in the original currency except that obligations in
Taels are converted into Chinese dollars

	Principal Outstanding	Interest in Arrears	Total
I. Peiping-Hankow Railway:			
Anglo-French Loan	£1,250,000	———	1,250,000
Advances by Chartered Bank	Ch. $ 200,780	25,310	226,090
Sundry Obligations on Materials	{ £ 6,348	5,817	12,165
	{ Ch. $ 332,400	196,983	529,383
Total	£1,256,348	5,817	1,262,165
	Ch. $ 533,180	222,293	755,473
II. Peiping-Mukden Railway:			
Chinese Imperial Ry. Loan	£ 862,500	———	862,500
Double Track Loan	£ 217,743	208,848	426,590
Whitall Co. (for cost of rolling stock supplies)	£ 424,537	231,131	655,669
Total	£1,504,780	439,979	1,944,759
III. Tientsin-Pukow Railway:			
Original Loan from Chinese Central Ry. Co.	£1,156,250	232,406	1,388,656
Supplementary Loan from same	£ 888,000	199,800	1,087,800
Sundry Obligations on Materials	{ £ 79,489	74,077	153,565
	{ Ch. $ 766,021	573,392	1,339,413
Total	£2,123,739	506,283	2,630,021
	Ch. $ 766,021	573,392	1,339,413
IV. Peiping-Suiyuan Railway:			
Loan from Anglo-Chinese Coal Mining Co. for Peiping-Mentoukou Branch	Ch. $ 300,000	139,623	439,623
	{ £ 19,293	15,124	34,417
Sundry Obligations on Materials	{ U. S. $ 12,205	6,480	18,685
	{ Ch. $ 59,306	49,577	108,883
	£ 19,293	15,124	34,417
Total	U. S. $ 12,205	6,480	18,685
	Ch. $ 359,306	189,200	548,506
V. Shanghai-Nanking Railway:			
S. N. Railway Loan	£2,784,000	———	2,784,000
S. N. Ry. Rolling Stock Loan	£ 156,000	———	156,000
Total	£2,940,000	———	2,940,000
VI. Shanghai-Hangchow-Ningpo Railway:			
S. H. N. Railway Loan	£ 637,500	———	637,500
Total	£ 637,500	———	637,500

TABLE 10—*Continued*

STATEMENT OF THE BRITISH SHARE OF THE OBLIGATIONS OF THE CHINESE
GOVERNMENT RAILWAYS AS OF DECEMBER 31, 1929

Amounts are shown in the original currency except that obligations in
Taels are converted into Chinese dollars

	Principal Outstanding	Interest in Arrears	Total
VII. Taokow-Chinhua Railway:			
Taokow-Chinhua Ry. Loan	£ 495,700	86,747	582,447
T. C. Ry. Rolling Stock Loan	£ 63,419	25,159	88,578
Advances for Chinghua-Menhsien Branch	£ 87,301	57,128	144,429
Total	£ 646,420	169,034	815,454
VIII. Hankow-Canton Railway (Hupeh-Hunan Section):			
Hukuang Railway Loan	£1,402,660	210,399	1,613,059
Sundry Obligations on Materials {	£ 91,234	80,770	172,004
	Ch. $ 9,402	214	9,616
Total	£1,493,894	291,169	1,785,063
	Ch. $ 9,402	214	9,616
IX. Canton-Kowloon Railway:			
Canton-Kowloon Ry. Loan	£1,111,500	250,088	1,361,588
Advance from British Chinese Corporation	£ 4,505	1,970	6,476
Advance from British Chinese Corporation	Ch. $ 216,293	116,436	332,729
Commission due to same Corp.	£ 5,000	1,201	6,201
Total	£1,121,005	253,259	1,374,265
	Ch. $ 216,293	116,436	332,729
X. Pukow-Sinyang Ry. (Projected):			
6% Advance	£ 198,792	78,376	277,168
7% Advance	£ 8,464	3,995	12,459
Total	£ 207,256	82,371	289,627

Grand Total:	£13,713,271	U. S. $66,735,633
	U. S. $ 18,685	18,685
	Ch. $ 2,985,737	1,194,295
		U. S. $67,948,613
Loan obligations		U. S. $62,133,124
Obligations for materials		5,815,489
		U. S. $67,948,613

pany, were to come to an end on December 31, 1930. Since payments were to be completed at that date, the whole of the amount still due, as shown below, may be regarded as in arrears. The new contract with the British and Danish companies, which is for a further period of fourteen years, was negotiated only after agreement seemed hopeless,[59] and did not, I am informed, involve any payments by the Chinese government which would reduce the obligations shown below.

Of the obligations listed below all but the last are usually regarded as "secured." This last one, the Marconi Wireless advance, has, however, not been included in the obligations considered by the Financial Readjustment Commission of 1925 nor is it listed in the 1927 document of the Ministry of Finance which lists the so-called unsecured loans. The existence of a definite agreement and the history of the obligation make it reasonable to list it here and not to place it among the unsecured obligations when that term is used to cover the obligations which have been reserved for special consideration since 1925.

TABLE 11

BRITISH OBLIGATIONS FOR COMMUNICATIONS OTHER
THAN RAILWAYS—1931

	Outstanding Dec. 31, 1930	British Share	
	U. S. Dollars	Per Cent	U. S. Dollars
Shanghai-Taku New Cable Loan, 1900	604,278	50	302,139
Duplicate Taku-Chefoo Cable Loan, 1900	140,175	50	70,087
Telegraph Charges Advance, 1911	500,086	50	250,043
Marconi Wireless Telegraph Advance, 1918	1,338,565	100	1,338,565
			1,960,834

[59] For the published terms of the agreement see *China Year Book*, 1931, p. 364. The financial settlement has not been made public.

The "Unsecured" Loans: The set of obligations to be considered here does not include all of the loans of the Chinese government which may be regarded as unsecured, for there are railway obligations listed above which may be so described. The obligations included here are, in general, the unsecured and inadequately secured loans of the Ministry of Finance, but I include also other inadequately secured loans which have not been listed under the other headings.

The Chinese government has made only one real attempt to arrive at a total of these obligations. This was made by the Financial Readjustment Commission whose final report gives the total loans outstanding on December 31, 1925. The Commission secured figures from the creditors as well as from the records of the Chinese government. In the British case the difference between the two totals was no more than Chinese $2 million, and the figures of the Commission for obligations to Great Britain came to a total of Chinese $40,684,504.[60] The figures of the Financial Readjustment Commission were brought down to the end of 1927 in a report drawn up by the Ministry of Finance at Peking in 1928. This report, which is in Chinese, I shall refer to as the 1927 document. In the British case it includes one railway loan, which is listed above. Making a deduction for this loan, the British total from the 1927 document is found to be U. S. $20,-093,515.

A new examination of China's unsecured obligations is being undertaken by a Commission on the Consolidation of Foreign and Domestic Obligations which began its work after a conference between the Chinese government and the representatives of the chief creditor powers on November 15, 1930. No results of its work are available. One can do no more than guess that the new Commission will arrive at figures somewhat larger than those of the 1927 document. In view of the circumstances surround-

[60] Lieu, D. K., *Foreign Investments in China*, Shanghai, 1929, p. 37.

ing these obligations, it seems best to accept the figures of the 1927 document, which means a British total of about U. S. $20 million.

The largest items in this list are an obligation to the Vickers Company, Ltd., for aëroplanes, and two to the Marconi Company for wireless equipment. The obligation to the Vickers Company was originally for the nominal amount of £1,803,200. The actual value received was to have been £1,650,000.[61] This sum was for the purpose of aëroplanes and was a part of a project for the development of aviation in China which involved the purchase, we are told, of six Handley-Page passenger planes, 40 Vickers-Vimy commercial planes, 40 Vimy training machines, and 65 Avro planes.[62] Elaborate plans were drawn up for the development of commercial aviation and assurance was given that the equipment would not be used for military purposes. Most of these planes were seized by military leaders during the year 1920 and the whole development came to nothing. The 1927 document states the amount of this one obligation as £2,632,573 at the end of 1927. It is difficult to believe that such transactions did not involve the unofficial knowledge on both sides that the equipment would probably be used for military purposes. This is but one example of the nature of the unsecured obligations which have been more fully examined in the Japanese case. It is not to be supposed that all of the obligations to the British were of this sort. They include, for example, a small sum advanced by the Westminster Bank for Chinese students in Great Britain and indemnities due to British shipping companies.

Summary of Holdings of Government Obligations, 1931

The following table shows the summary of British investments as presented in the preceding pages.

[61] C. C. S. and H. K. L., *Notes on the Inadequately Secured Loans of China*, Peking, 1926, p. 16.
[62] *China Year Book*, 1929–1930, p. 484.

TABLE 12
BRITISH HOLDINGS OF GOVERNMENT OBLIGATIONS, 1931
In U. S. dollars to the nearest thousand

	U. S. Dollars	
General purposes of the Chinese government	79,575,000	
Chinese government railways	67,949,000	
Communications other than railways	1,961,000	
Unsecured loans	20,094,000	
		169,579,000
Obligations of foreign municipalities in China		14,235,000
Total		183,814,000

Purchases of Chinese Bonds Issued Elsewhere

I have arrived at the above total on the principle of the place of issue. It shows obligations to Great Britain as they would be if the securities issued in Great Britain had remained there and if no securities issued elsewhere had been purchased by the British. It is well known, however, that other issues have moved to Great Britain. When, for example, payment on the service of the German issue of the 5 per cent Gold Loan of 1896 was held up, owing to a dispute with the Deutsch-Asiatische Bank, the London *Times* observed that "many, if not the bulk, of the bonds of the German issue have in recent years been sold to British investors." [63]

Figures made available to me by bankers in London show the following holdings in London of German and Russian issues on December 31, 1930:

5% Gold Loan of 1896:		
German issue	£ 165,000	U. S. $ 802,972
4½% Gold Loan of 1898:		
German issue	£ 590,000	U. S. $ 2,871,235
5% Reorganization Gold Loan of 1913:		
German issue	£ 870,000	U. S. $ 4,233,855
Russian issue	£ 650,000	U. S. $ 3,163,225
Total	£2,275,000	U. S. $11,071,287

[63] London *Times*, April 6, 1927.

This makes a total of £2,275,000 or about U. S. $11 million. There are included here only such bonds as are definitely known to the bankers to be in Great Britain. There is no doubt that the total holding was considerably larger. It may have been twice as large. I believe that it is not unreasonable to estimate the British holding at U. S. $20 million.

Concerning British purchases of bonds issued in France we have definite information also. The bankers provided the following information:

5% Gold Loan of 1908 (Anglo-French):		
French issue	£ 500,000	U. S. $ 2,433,250
5% Reorganization Gold Loan of 1913:		
French issue	£3,600,000	U. S. $17,519,400
Total	£4,100,000	U. S. $19,952,650

In 1931 the British held £4.1 million, about U. S. $20 million, of Chinese bonds originally issued in France. It is believed by the bankers that the total holding of French issues is not much greater than this amount. Taking the two together we reach a total of U. S. $40 million and, if all the facts were known, it may have reached U. S. $45 million. I propose to take U. S. $42 million as a reasonable estimate.

The total Chinese government obligations reported above on the principle of the place of issue was U. S. $169,-579,000. The new total arrived at on what may be called the principle of actual holding requires the addition of the U. S. $42 million, and gives us a total of U. S. $211,-579,000. To this must be added for our final total on the principle of the place of actual holding the obligations of foreign municipalities in China, which gives us a final total of U. S. $225,814,000 as the total British holding of the obligations of government organizations in China.

Further evidence concerning the total British holding of Chinese government securities is to be found in the Annual Reports of the Commissioner of Inland Revenue.

The income from Chinese government securities reported under Schedule C of the income tax [64] amounted for the year 1927–1928 to £2,017,245 and for the year 1928–1929 to £1,827,639. At 5 per cent the income reported would account for holdings of U. S. $196 million for the earlier year and U. S. $178 million for the later year.

It must be borne in mind that payments on certain loans were not made during 1928, for example, the Crisp loan, and the Hukuang loan, and that payments on other loans, as, for example, the Anglo-French, were made only in part. It must be borne in mind, also, that no payments were made on the unsecured loans during these years. In view of these facts it may be said with some confidence that the income reported would support a total estimate larger than that at which I have arrived.[65]

Business Investments: Three Estimates

The first task under this heading is to present as briefly and clearly as possible the results of the three estimates referred to above. The British committee presents two sums which, taken together, show their estimate of business investments. In the first place they report a sum of £71,377,700, arrived at from the answers to the questionnaire which they sent out. This sum they report as follows:

---

[64] Schedule C covers "income from British Dominion and Foreign Government securities where such income is taxed by deduction at the source." The figures given are to be found in the *72nd Report of the Commissioners of His Majesty's Inland Revenue for the year ending March 31, 1929*, p. 81, and in the *73rd Report*, p. 75.

[65] Mr. Robert Anthony Eden, Under-Secretary of State in the House of Commons, on November 23, 1931, "so far as I am able to ascertain the nominal amount of Chinese government securities in which British subjects are primarily interested, and which were in varying degrees in default on the 31st of December, 1930, in respect of contractual obligations for sinking fund or interest, or both, was approximately £18,000,000 at that date. It would require further investigation to enable me to state whether all the loans in question were in the technical sense floated on the London market." *Parliamentary Debates*, Official Report, 5th Series, vol. 260, col. 12.

Hongkong	£14,520,300
Shanghai	38,497,400
Rest of China	13,690,000
Shipping [66]	4,670,000
	£71,377,700

The second sum is arrived at by estimating certain items which do not appear in the answers to the questionnaire but which the British committee felt justified in adding as the result of estimates made in London. These additions are:

1. Land (not reported above)	£47,500,000
2. Private mortgages (Shanghai only)	3,500,000
3. Recent loans made by British firms	2,500,000
4. Mines (not reported above)	2,100,000
	£55,600,000

Taking the two sums together we find the amount reported by the British committee to be £126,977,700. It is to be remembered that roughly 60 per cent of the firms responded. The committee suggests the addition of £10 to 20 million to cover banking investment not otherwise reported, and a sum of £4 million to cover dwelling houses omitted from the returns which they received. While the British committee reports £127 million, it is plain that they believe the real total of British business investments in China and Hongkong to have been at least £140 million.

Mr. D. K. Lieu presents his latest results in a pamphlet prepared for the 1931 Conference of the Institute of Pacific Relations.[67] His reports were from 414 British firms and he takes occasion to thank the British business men in China for their co-operation. I deduct from Lieu's original total the sum reported for rubber estates, since these investments are entirely outside of China. His total is, then, Chinese $1,501,397,750 for the end of 1928. At the rate of exchange which he used (Chinese $10.70

---

[66] This represents an addition for coast and river shipping not reported under the other headings.

[67] Referred to as *Foreign Investments in China, 1931*, Shanghai, 1931.

to the pound sterling), his total comes to £140,317,546. This is remarkably close to the figure of the British committee, but it must be added at once that Lieu believes this figure to be entirely too large. This opinion rests upon the following considerations. His total shows the paid-up capital of the firms reporting to him. He finds the paid-up capital of the insurance companies to include over £30 million reported in English currency. This, he believes, represents almost entirely holdings outside of China. He finds, also, that under manufacturing a total of £29.9 million is reported in sterling. "We find," he says, "that in Hongkong there are a great many British manufacturing concerns whose sphere of business is in their own country and whose capital is in sterling, but they are registered with the Hongkong government for the special purpose of promoting the sales of their products in China." [68] I am willing to concede that his case is a good one in these two fields, but I do not believe that it is reasonable to go so far as he does when he concludes that business investments reported in sterling are outside of China. He arrives at his final estimate by taking as British business investments, first, the total reported in Chinese currency, Chinese $595.8 million, and, secondly, one-fourth of the total reported in British and other non-Chinese currencies. This gives him a final sum of Chinese $870 million. To this Lieu is willing to add, as the result of additional information, a sum which brings his final total to Chinese $1,000 million, or roughly £100 million. It is this sum which must be compared with the total of the British committee.

The report of the British Chamber of Commerce at Shanghai contains figures of business investments which they specifically state to be based on actual returns. These returns include mission property and certain sums which I report under British holdings of government obligations, such as, for example, the debentures of the Shanghai Mu-

[68] Lieu, D. K., *Foreign Investments in China, 1931*, p. 10.

nicipal Council. Making deductions for these known items I find the report of the British Chamber of Commerce to be as follows:

Shanghai	£164,272,504
Tientsin	8,000,000
Hankow	3,734,145
Canton	3,000,000
Peking	500,000
Total	£179,506,649

This total the Secretary of the British Chamber of Commerce at Shanghai believes to be too small and he points out that it does not include investments at Hongkong. In his opinion the total for 1927 must have been at least £200 million, and he believes that a further addition must be made to represent the situation as it was at the end of March, 1931.

We have, then, three estimates of British business investments which run from £100 million to £200 million and the problem is to reduce them to a single reasonable total.

A Final Estimate of Business Investments

In arriving at a final total of British business investments I depend very largely upon the fact that each of the three estimates presented above is built upon actual returns received in response to separate inquiries. In each case these actual returns have been reported.

Consider, first, British business investments in Hongkong. The British committee gives us a total of £14,520,-300. To this I add one-half of the sum of £4,670,000 set down for coast and river shipping not reported elsewhere by the British committee, that is £2,335,000. I add, also, the sum of £1.6 million to represent the investment of the Hongkong government in the British section of the Canton-Kowloon Railway. This railway, while it is the property of the government of Hongkong, represents a business investment in the same way as the South Manchuria Railway or the Chinese Eastern.[69] Taking these sums together I find the total for Hongkong to be £18,-455,300.

I turn next to British investments in the rest of China outside of Shanghai. The British committee reports £13,690,000 as the total from their returns. They state that they received replies from 64 per cent of their inquiries. The British committee is of the opinion that British land holdings in China outside of Shanghai come to a total of £15 million. Of this sum £2,811,000 were reported in their returns. To include total land holdings we must add £12,879,000 to the amount reported in the questionnaire. The British committee estimates the total British investment in mining at £3.3 million. Of this, £1.2 million are included in the answers to the questionnaire. We must, therefore, add for mining interests not included £2.1 million. The total of these items, that is the total British holdings in China outside of Shanghai and Hongkong, comes to £27,979,000. This sum I accept as the best possible estimate from the available information. The total for the rest of China, reported by the British Chamber of Commerce, comes to about £15.2 million, which seems to me entirely too small.

We come finally to the most difficult task, namely, the estimating of British investments in Shanghai. It is here that the greatest difference appears between the report of the British committee of the Royal Institute and that of the British Chamber of Commerce. The British committee's total from its returns is £38,497,400. If we add to this one-half of the separate item for shipping it comes to £40,832,400.

The British committee reports land holdings in Shanghai of £16,337,000. They estimate elsewhere that total holdings in Shanghai come to £55 million. My own estimate of the value of British land holdings in Shanghai

[69] Investment in this railway is not included in the sum reported above as British investment in the debentures of the colony of Hongkong.

is derived from information published by the Shanghai Municipal Council. I find the assessed valuation of land registered in British names to have been Sh. Tls. 300,195,125.[70] In 1926 we are told that the total value of land in the Foreign Settlement registered in the British consulate in the name of British subjects was Tls. 282.9 million and that, of this total, Tls. 103.3 million was the value of land registered in the name of British subjects but owned by those who were not British.[71] I estimate from this that one-third of the land of British registry was owned by Chinese. Applying this to the figure for 1929 I reach Sh. Tls. 200 million as the value of land actually owned by British subjects in the Foreign Settlement.

Something must be added for the undervaluation of this land by the assessors and we must add, also, the value of British-owned land outside of the settlement, largely in the French Concession. It is highly probable that the value of British-owned land in Shanghai reached a total of Tls. 300 million in 1929.[72] At Tls. 8.6 to the pound sterling, this comes to about £35 million. I am, therefore, obliged to conclude that the holding reported by the British committee is too high for 1929, though I am willing to concede that the total may have been as high as £40 million.

If the total of the British committee is altered to include land holdings of £40 million, we come to a new total of £64,495,400.

The British Chamber of Commerce, however, reports British investments at Shanghai as £164,272,504. Concerning this total I know that it includes holdings outside of Shanghai. I am informed, for example, that certain great corporations reported their entire holdings through the Shanghai office and that they were, therefore, credited

---

[70] This is on the basis of a land tax of Tls. 2,401,561 at eight-tenths of one per cent. *Feetham Report*, vol. 2, p. 170.

[71] *Feetham Report*, vol. 1, p. 323.

[72] It was probably nearer Tls. 500 million at the prices prevailing in 1931.

to Shanghai. It is unreasonable, also, to find that the
British Chamber of Commerce report gives a total for the
rest of China which is much smaller than the total of the
committee of the Royal Institute when the general total
of the British Chamber is so much larger. What we need,
then, is a method by which to correct the total of the
British Chamber for Shanghai.

A correction which may certainly be made is to take
from the British Chamber's total for Shanghai the difference between the British committee's figure for the rest of
China, £27,979,000, and the British Chamber's figure for
the rest of China, £15,234,000. Making this deduction we
find the corrected figure to be £151,527,500.

I have presented a corrected total for Shanghai by the
committee of the Royal Institute which comes to £64
million and a corrected total for the British Chamber of
Commerce which comes to £151 million. It is certain
that the former figure is too small. I am, therefore,
obliged to accept the larger figure. I am convinced, however, that this figure ought to be further corrected in such
a way as to make the total outside of Shanghai larger and
the total within Shanghai smaller.[73] Since the information
for further correction is not available, I accept the following as my total of British business investments in China
on the basis of the information provided in the three
available estimates.

TABLE 13

BRITISH BUSINESS INVESTMENTS IN CHINA, 1929

	Pounds	U. S. Dollars	Per Cent of Total
Shanghai	151,527,500	737,408,000	76.6
Hongkong	18,455,300	89,812,000	9.3
Rest of China	27,979,000	136,160,000	14.1
	197,961,800	963,380,000	100.0

[73] My own guess would be about as follows:

Shanghai	£130 million
Hongkong	35 million
Rest of China	30 million

Fields of British Investment

The geographical distribution of British business investments is shown, so far as information is available, in the preceding table. The preponderance of Shanghai, and its increasing preponderance, as the scene of these investments is hardly to be doubted. What seems to me doubtful, as I have indicated, is that Shanghai's preponderance is as great as this table shows.

The distribution of business investments according to the nature of the business is shown in the table which follows. This table rests upon a study of the returns received by the British committee and the results of the Chinese study.

In the case of the British returns an effort was made to classify the results on the plan generally adopted. Reported investments of 110 firms to the value of nearly £70 million were so classified. It was found that shipping alone accounted for about one-third and that the import and export trade accounted for nearly another third. It is difficult to believe that this is true and it is easy to explain the overweighting of these items in the case of an investigation carried on in London.

In the case of the Chinese investigation the returns have been printed.[74] These returns were first corrected, on the basis of Lieu's comments, in the cases of insurance and manufacturing. The corrected total, distributed according to the generally used classification, showed such a preponderance in the case of manufacturing, about 45 per cent, and so small a percentage for the import and export category, about 10 per cent, as to lead to doubts. In this case, too, it was easy to explain the overweighting in the case of manufacturing since it usually involves the existence of a considerable plant.[75]

[74] Lieu, D. K., *Foreign Investments in China, 1931*, Shanghai, 1931, p. 9.
[75] Lieu's statement that some Hongkong companies own plants outside of China and Hongkong is to be borne in mind.

The method finally adopted for the distribution of British investments was to arrive at a percentage distribution on the basis of the British and the Chinese studies. This percentage distribution was then applied to the total estimate of British business investments with the results shown in the following table.

TABLE 14

DISTRIBUTION OF BRITISH BUSINESS INVESTMENTS IN CHINA ACCORDING TO THE NATURE OF THE BUSINESS

	Investment in Pounds	Investment in U. S. Dollars	Per Cent of Total
1. Transportation	27.7	134.9	14
2. Public utilities	9.9	48.2	5
3. Mining	4.0	19.3	2
4. Manufacturing	35.6	173.4	18
5. Banking and finance	23.7	115.6	12
6. Real estate	41.6	202.3	21
7. Import and export and general trading	49.5	240.8	25
8. Miscellaneous	5.9	28.9	3
	197.9	963.4	100

Concerning the individual items in this table there is a considerable amount of scattered information which serves to do no more than corroborate the estimates at which I have arrived.

In the field of transportation shipping is of outstanding importance. A recent account of shipping in the coast and river trade put the number of British ships at 148 and the tonnage at 284,909. One corporation, the China Navigation Company, affiliated with Butterfield & Swire, one of the greatest British firms in China, held 87 of these ships with a tonnage of 161,440.[76] Lieu reported a total investment in shipping of Chinese $160 million and $29 million for dock, engineering, and shipbuilding, all of which are included in my estimate of shipping. The

[76] *China Year Book*, 1931, Chap. 5, pp. 95–118.

British committee reported investments in shipping alone at U. S. $130 million, but this included certain ocean shipping which ought not to be considered an investment in China.

Under railways the one item was for the British section of the Canton-Kowloon Railway. The grant of the Hongkong government toward the building of this railway is reported at Hongkong $20.4 million and the cost of construction to the end of 1928 at Hongkong $28.5 million. Interest on the government investment was Hongkong $498,571 for the same year which is nearly 5 per cent.[77] I have taken £1.6 million as the investment in this railway.

British investment in mining is chiefly through three companies. The Chinese Engineering and Mining Company, Ltd., British participant in the Kailan Mining Administration, had a share capital of £1 million and 6 per cent debentures outstanding in 1930 to the amount of £792,000. Dividends of 25 per cent and 20 per cent were paid in 1928 and 1929, and 9 per cent in 1930. The dividend for the year ending June 30, 1931 was $2\frac{1}{2}$ per cent.[78] The Peking Syndicate, which owns mines in Honan province, has a paid-up capital of £1,242,822 and owns a half interest in a selling company known as the Fu Chung Corporation (capital Chinese $1 million). It reported property holding of £865,899 for a recent year. The Company has paid no dividends in recent years.[79] In 1927 the mining properties were seized by General Feng Yu-hsiang, who is said to have secured a considerable revenue from their operation. No recent information is available concerning the Tung Hsing Sino-Foreign Coal Mining Company, owners of the Mentoukou Colliery,

[77] Maguire, C. R., *The China Stock and Share Handbook, 1930*, Shanghai, 1930, p. 270.
[78] *Economist* (London), December 20, 1930, p. 1196. The property account was reported at £1,836,163. *North China Herald* (Shanghai), December 31, 1931, p. 455.
[79] Maguire, C. R., *China Stock and Share Handbook, 1930*, p. 198. *Shanghai Evening Post*, Jan. 18, 1931.

in which the British interest is half, that is, Tls. 500,000.
It may be remarked that Lieu reports British investments
in mining at Chinese $27 million.

The larger public utilities in which there are British
investments are well known. They include the Shanghai
Gas Company, the Shanghai Waterworks Company, the
China General Omnibus Company, the Hongkong Electric
Company, the Shanghai Electric Construction Company,
the Hongkong Tramway Company, the Peak Tramways
Company, and electric companies at Peiping, Chinkiang,
Hankow, Kowloon, and Kulangsu (Amoy).[80] Dividends
for the important utility companies were reported at
from 7 to 25 per cent for the years 1925–1929. In more
recent years there has been a decline. The Shanghai
Waterworks Company, for example, undertook to increase
its rates in 1931, giving as its chief reason the increased
expenditure in silver to meet overhead charges in sterling
and to buy equipment abroad. Lieu's total for this item
is Chinese $25.8 million to which he added Hongkong
$15 million to cover known utility companies who failed
to report.

Under manufacturing, we have the Ewo Cotton Mills,
Ltd., the owner of the three British mills at Shanghai.
This company with a paid-up capital of Sh. Tls. 5.4
million holds land and buildings valued at Tls. 5.2 million
in 1929 and stocks of goods to the average value of Tls.
4 million in recent years. It paid dividends of 12, 40, and
15 per cent on its ordinary shares for the years 1928–1930.
This company illustrates a common difficulty in dealing
with foreign investments. It is affiliated with Jardine,
Matheson and Company, and British interests are in
control. At the same time the so-called "Consulting
Committee" of the company has three Chinese members.
Chinese ownership means payment of dividends within
China. British ownership may mean the payment of
dividends in China or in England. It is highly probable

[80] Lieu, D. K., *Foreign Investments in China, 1929*, pp. 71–2.

that income which is the result of its operations reaches England through the parent company.

Important British (and some American) investments in the field of manufacturing are through the British American Tobacco Company. This company and its subsidiary, the British Cigarette Company, own factories at Shanghai, Hankow, Tientsin, Mukden, and Harbin. Chinese participation in this company is through the British American (China) Tobacco Securities Company, Ltd., of Shanghai. Funds invested in this company are reinvested in the shares of British-American (China) Tobacco Company, and the Securities Company reported in January, 1930, investments of only Chinese $9.8 million. Chinese participation in the great holdings of the parent company must, therefore, be small.[81]

Other British manufacturing establishments are found in a wide variety of fields. They include: cement, chemicals, bean oil, flour, ice, printing, rope, lumber, soap, and candles. There are plants, also, which prepare products for export, such as skins, furs, bristles, and wool.

Banking and finance offered difficulties to the British committee who undertook to guess British investments at from £10 to £20 million. The total reported to Lieu for banks, financial syndicates, and insurance (deducting sums reported in sterling in the last case) was about Chinese $90 million. This is undoubtedly far too small. Information about individual banking and insurance corporations seems to me to justify my total. The Hongkong and Shanghai Banking Corporation had paid-up capital and reserves reported at about £8 million on December 31, 1930.[82] It has paid to its shareholders in recent years £7 or 8 per share. The shares (160,000) have a nominal value of Hongkong $125 and were sold at as high as Chinese $2,300 at Shanghai during the year 1931. It is frequently

---

[81] Lieu, D. K., *Foreign Investment in China, 1929*, pp. 81–2.
[82] *The Economist* (London), in its "Annual Banking Supplement," publishes a digest of the annual report of this bank. See October 10, 1931, p. 58.

pointed out that such foreign banks receive deposits from Chinese and that they invest in foreign securities and keep reserves abroad.   They are, it is maintained, a means by which Chinese funds are invested abroad. This is quite true but it does not alter the fact that such a bank is income-yielding property in the legal possession of a British corporation and, in so far as they are British, of British shareholders.   Nor does it alter the fact that such a bank yields an income which is paid, in part, out of China (and Hongkong) and into Great Britain.   The Hongkong and Shanghai Bank is but one of six banks in Lieu's list and he lists, also, three financial syndicates and a number of insurance companies.

British real estate companies include the Shanghai Land Investment Company with a paid-up capital and funded indebtedness of Chinese $18 million and with real estate holdings of Chinese $22 millions in 1930. This is but the largest of a number of British companies at Shanghai and there are British companies in the same field in Tientsin and Hongkong.   The Hongkong and Shanghai Hotels, Ltd. is the most important foreign corporation in this field.   It holds property valued at about Chinese $25 million in 1930.   The company controls nine hotels in Hongkong and the chief treaty ports of China.   The real estate companies have made unusual profits in recent years.   Dividends of from 15 to 18 per cent have been common.   Here again it may be pointed out that local ownership, foreign and Chinese, is a factor of considerable importance.

Concerning investments in the import and export business and in general trading, it may be said that the British Committee reported a total of nearly £25 million and Lieu Chinese $108 million.   It may be remarked that British-owned "department stores" and shops have not been profitable in recent years.   Chinese competition has been severe and a number of shops, long familiar to old residents of Shanghai, have disappeared.   It is true that the successful competitors have often been Chinese-owned companies registered in Hongkong. The changes in the import and export field have been away from the great, locally controlled establishments and toward manufacturer's representatives.[83]

The few comments upon the different fields which I have been able to offer are not the foundation for my estimate of British investments which is laid in the three independent estimates to which I have made frequent reference. They serve to show some of the details of the picture and to give an idea of the rates of return upon the investments.

International Payments and British Business Investments

In discussing the American study, the opinion was ventured that it requires an expectation of a return of 10 per cent to bring about business investment in China. The Japanese study seems to justify the guess that a business investment of a certain amount has involved the remittance to China of 50 per cent of that amount in the past. These conclusions were put before persons who know British business in China. It was their general opinion that the rate of return suggested was perhaps true for 1930 but that higher returns were both expected and received in the earlier days of the trade and until, say, 1910. The remittances from abroad involved in building up the present business investments were probably not as high as 50 per cent of the present value in the British case, though they may have been for Japan and the United States. One British banker of long experience spoke at some length of the enormous profits of the early days and stated it as quite certain that much more than half of the value of present British holdings represent reinvested profits and appreciation in the value of land.

[83] As is pointed out in my *Foreign Trade of China*, pp. 130–1.

Any attempt to arrive at annual outpayments from China and Hongkong to Great Britain on account of profits and dividends meets a variety of difficulties. If the rate of return is about 10 per cent and if this is applied, as in the American case, to all investments except those in the import and export business, we have a figure which is still far too large. We must deduct for Chinese participation and we must recognize the fact that the British "colony" in China is older and has been more permanent than any other. A considerable part of the income from much business property is paid to British citizens resident in China and does not enter into international payments.

There is the further fact to be considered that 1928 was the last normal year. Profits were less in 1929, and in 1930 they were much less in practically every line.

It may be guessed that business investments of U. S. $963.4 million have meant about U. S. $400 million in remittances to China. An allowance for losses which have now disappeared may make this higher but I found no one willing to venture an opinion on this matter of losses. It may be guessed, also, that the remittance of income from China on these business holdings may have been U. S. $50 million in 1928 but was probably no more than U. S. $25 million in 1930.

Summary of British Investments, 1931

The following table brings together the estimates of British business investments for recent years. In the case of government obligations, most of the figures are for the end of 1930; in the case of business investments, for different years between 1927 and 1930.

TABLE 15

SUMMARY OF BRITISH INVESTMENTS IN CHINA, 1931

	Pounds	U. S. Dollars
Business investments	197,961,800	963,380,000
Government obligations	46,400,000	225,814,000
	244,361,800	1,189,194,000

Property of Mission Societies

The nature of the information concerning British holdings in China has not made it possible to estimate separately the property from which no income is expected. This includes the property of clubs, societies, and religious organizations devoted to the service of the British community or of the foreign community in China, in general. It includes, also, British holdings at the mountain and seaside summer resorts in China. The secretary of the Kuling Estate has been good enough to estimate British holdings and his figure is Chinese $1 million for the end of 1930. This is the largest British holding at any one summer resort in China.

Estimates of the property of British mission societies are difficult to make. The committee of the Royal Institute of International Affairs and the British Chamber of Commerce at Shanghai both tried to secure information. The former estimated the holdings of mission societies at £1.5 million, specifically excluding the property of Roman Catholic missions. The British Chamber of Commerce offered the same estimate. Property actually reported to the British Chamber reached a total of £746,-836 but these reports did not cover Hongkong, Tientsin, Shanghai, Hankow, and Canton. It is probable, however, that land holdings by mission societies in these centers did get into the general figures. I propose to allow the figure of £1.5 million to stand for the holdings of the mission societies and add £500,000 for philanthropic and educational institutions not held by mission societies. I believe that this is too small an estimate, but I hesitate to set down a larger figure than that reported in the two British investigations. The total for British mission and philanthropic societies is, then, £2 million or about U. S. $9.7 million.

CONCLUSION

British investments in China have now been presented. I am satisfied that the information concerning British

holdings of government obligations may be trusted.   In
the more important field of business investments I have
had to rely upon the best estimates I could make for the
two earlier years 1902 and 1914.   For 1930 I have relied
upon the work of my British and Chinese collaborators
and that of the British Chamber of Commerce at Shanghai.   I am satisfied that the true outlines of the picture
have been sketched in, but it is after all a sketch.

What are the outstanding facts?   British investments
in China began early.   They had reached a total of about
a quarter of a billion U. S. dollars as long ago as 1902
and they are well over a billion dollars today.   These
totals are shown in the final column of the table below.
British investments more than doubled between 1902
and 1914, and they almost doubled between 1914 and
1930.   When the rate of growth of business investments

TABLE 16

British Investments in China, 1900–1930

By Chief Divisions with Relatives

Values shown in millions of U. S. dollars

	Business Investments	Rela- tives	Government Obligations	Rela- tives	Total	Rela- tives
1902	150.0	37.5	110.3	53.2	260.3	42.8
1914	400.0	100.0	207.5	100.0	607.5	100.0
1930	963.4	240.8	225.8	108.8	1,189.2	195.8

and of loans to governmental institutions is observed the
pre-war and the post-war periods stand in sharp contrast.
During the earlier period the two grew together; during
the later period business investments have increased and
loans have not.

Business investments have at all times been greater
than holdings of government obligations, and the proportion of business investments has grown steadily.   This
is brought out by the percentage distribution in my second
general table.   I do not propose to make comparisons

with other countries at this time nor to offer explanations. There can be no doubt of the fact, however, that direct business investments formed a much larger part of the British total in 1930 than in 1902.

TABLE 17

BRITISH INVESTMENTS IN CHINA, 1900–1931

Percentage Distribution by Chief Divisions

Values shown in millions of U. S. dollars

	Business Investments		Government Obligations		Total	
	Dollars	Per Cent	Dollars	Per Cent	Dollars	Per Cent
1902	150.0	57.6	110.3	42.4	260.3	100
1914	400.0	65.8	207.5	34.2	607.5	100
1930	963.4	81.0	225.8	19.0	1,189.2	100

If it had been possible to present estimates for any year before the close of the war between China and Japan, business investments would, no doubt, have formed a larger percentage than in 1902. The course of events was this. Throughout the nineteenth century British investments were largely direct business investments. When, at the end of the century, the Chinese government undertook to borrow abroad, British investments came to be nearly equally divided between the two forms. From about 1902 business investments have grown in importance and today about 80 per cent of British investments are accounted for by holdings which are the property of British individuals, firms, and corporations.

The overwhelming importance of British investments, especially in the earlier years, points to my final observation, namely, that the history of British investments in China is the history of Chinese capital imports. The study of China's international economic relations meant until but yesterday the study of British trade, British shipping, the British business community, and British investments in China.

TABLE 18

THE POSITION OF GREAT BRITAIN IN CHINA'S INTERNATIONAL ECONOMIC
RELATIONS

Customs Statistics for All Items except Investments

TRADE	Direct Trade Mills. Hk. Tls.	Relatives	Per Cent of China's Total Trade
1899	53.9	47.6	11.7
1913	113.3	100.0	11.4
1930	170.9	150.8	7.8
POPULATION	British Population in China	Relatives	Per Cent of Total Foreign Population in China
1899	5,562	62.0	32.4
1913	8,966	100.0	5.4
1930	13,015	145.6	3.6
FIRMS	British Firms	Relatives	Per Cent of Total Foreign Firms in China
1899	401	68.0	43.0
1913	590	100.0	15.0
1930	1,027	174.1	12.4
SHIPPING	British Tonnage in Millions	Relatives	Per Cent of Total Chinese and Foreign Shipping
1899	23.3	61.2	59.4
1913	38.1	100.0	40.8
1930	57.2	150.1	36.8
INVESTMENT	British Investment Millions U. S. Dollars	Relatives	Per Cent of Total Foreign Investment
1902	260.3	42.8	33.0
1914	607.5	100.0	37.7
1930	1,189.2	195.8	36.7

CHAPTER XVII

JAPANESE INVESTMENTS IN CHINA

INTRODUCTION

The Japanese Study

The estimates of Japanese investments in China which are presented in the following pages were made by a committee appointed by the Japanese Council of the Institute of Pacific Relations in 1928. The work of this committee was completed during the summer of 1930. It was the subject of discussion at a number of conferences in Tokyo during the month of August. The manuscript in Japanese and English was taken to China and the estimates were critically examined by a number of Japanese bankers and business men during the winter of 1930–1931. It was not until after consultations in Manchuria during June, 1931, that the estimates may be said to have taken their final form.

The figures are those of this Japanese committee with some minor changes, but the order and arrangement have been altered and additional material has been added. I wish to accept the responsibility for the editing and so for the results as they appear, while at the same time I give the credit for the long and difficult task to the committee of the Japanese Council of the Institute.[1] The manuscript of this committee is the basis of my whole report on Japanese investments.

The available results of the work of the Japanese committee were presented by Mr. M. Odagiri at the Kyoto

[1] And especially to Mr. Shizuo Hirai of that Committee, who went over the whole report with me in Tokyo, explaining it and adding important supplementary information.

Conference of the Institute of Pacific Relations in 1929 and printed as one of the documents of the Japanese council under the title, *Japanese Investments in China*. The final report is found in the following pages.

The Classification of Japanese Investments

Japanese investments in China are diverse and varied. They range from those of the South Manchuria Railway Company with its apparently endless ramifications to those of a small retailer or restaurant owner in Shanghai. They have offered the greatest obstacles to classification, and certain modifications of the classification generally adopted by the collaborators in this study have been found necessary in the Japanese case.

The major divisions in the accepted classification are: (1) business investments or, more accurately, direct business investments, that is the property and assets in China of Japanese corporations, firms, or individuals and (2) Japanese loans to the Chinese government and holdings of the obligations of the Chinese government or of government institutions. It must be understood that this classification, which was in part suggested by the study of the Japanese case, covers a very large proportion of the Japanese investments. The necessary modifications are of minor importance.

Some information is available, also, under the heading, The Property in China of Japanese Philanthropic and Cultural Institutions. This heading is different from the similar one in the American case, but is intended, as in that case, to include the foreign-owned property in China from which no income is derived or expected. In dealing with Japan important holdings are omitted unless we include property devoted to administrative and similar purposes. The heading has, therefore, been modified to include administrative holdings along with property used for philanthropic and cultural purposes. This seems a satisfactory solution of a problem which presents many difficulties. Administrative property is usually entirely in the hands of a government but in the Japanese case the South Manchuria Railway owns property used for administrative purposes. Property devoted to philanthropic purposes is usually not in the possession of a business corporation but the South Manchuria Railway is the owner of schools, hospitals, and museums. Governments do not ordinarily own important business investments in China but the Japanese government owns a half interest in this railway. The difficulties have been met by separating the property of the railway which is devoted to administrative purposes and that for philanthropic and cultural purposes from the business investment, and putting it under the heading now being considered.

In general in this study the administrative property of foreign governments in China has been found negligible. In the Japanese case, however, the government owns—aside from its interest in the South Manchuria Railway—public property in the leased area in Southern Manchuria which is called Kwantung. The value of this public property is not known and no attempt has been made to estimate it. A figure as high as Yen 234 million is often seen but this is a cumulative total of all expenditure for public purposes.[2]

The heading now being considered, Japanese Administrative and Philanthropic Holdings in China, covers property which is not investment at all, the term investment being reserved for property and assets from which an income is derived or expected. Nevertheless, information under this heading is desirable since it helps to make the account of foreign property within China more complete and provides estimates of inpayments into China from abroad which are important in the drawing up of China's balance of international payments. The modifica-

---

[2] *Japanese Investments and Expenditures in Manchuria*, South Manchuria Railway Company, New York, 1929, pp. 3, 4.

tion of this heading in the Japanese case to include public property shows that Japanese non-income-producing property in China is largely in the possession of the Japanese government. In the American case such property is largely in the possession of mission societies and educational institutions.

A more important modification of the accepted classification remains to be considered. It is, in fact, so important that a separate heading is given to it, namely, Japanese Investment in Chinese Corporations. This heading is given third place in the tables and discussion below. It must be pointed out, however, that there are investments, in the Japanese and in other cases, which seem to come under this heading but really do not.

Foreign advances to Chinese corporations, for example, are often made in connection with the purchase of industrial machinery or equipment. A Chinese cotton mill frequently makes such arrangements for the purchase of machinery on the installment plan. These arrangements are usually made with the local agent in China of the manufacturer of the machinery and the legal title to the machinery remains with the foreigner until payment has been made. In 1929 the known obligations of Chinese cotton mills to Japanese amounted to Yen 7,988,000. In this and in similar cases it is best to classify such advances as direct business investments on the part of the foreigner. They are not investments in Chinese corporations as the term is here used.

Another fairly common case is that of foreign participation in corporations in which the Chinese government or one of its departments has a substantial or a controlling interest. A foreign corporation and the Chinese government enter into a sort of partnership and the foreign participation usually takes a form which amounts to an advance to the government. This usually becomes clear when financial difficulties arise, if not before. Investment of this sort is classified usually as an obligation of the Chinese government. In some cases when the circumstances are known it is set down as a direct investment of the foreign corporation. In general it may be said that there seem to be few Chinese corporations important enough to borrow from foreigners in which the Chinese government does not have an interest of some sort.

The Japanese have tried many forms of joint enterprise with the Chinese. Among them are a considerable number created in accordance with the provisions of the Japanese Commercial Code. In these cases the proportion of Chinese and Japanese investment is determined in advance by the articles of incorporation. The Japanese share is classified as a direct business investment. Among the mining and lumbering enterprises there are some whose organization is determined by special agreement. The principle is usually that of equal division of investment and control. In many of these cases the investment of the Japanese is known and it is regarded as a direct business investment.

When every effort has been made to look into the underlying state of affairs there are found to be Japanese investments in Chinese corporations which cannot be classified either as direct investments or as advances to the Chinese government. This has made the new heading necessary.

Japanese Investment in Chinese Corporations

Under this heading are included advances to Chinese companies by financial corporations in Japan, Japanese holdings of the securities of Chinese corporations, and in general such investment as may be contrasted with the more common direct business investment. This sort of investment in China is unusual but the Japanese have made an effort to use it. The development of any form of indirect investment is of such importance for the future that it is worth while to consider the efforts of the Japanese.

A well-informed Japanese banker told me at some length of the experience of his own corporation in this field. His company has borrowed in Japan and advanced funds to Chinese corporations. These transactions were not associated with the purchase of materials or with corporations in which the Chinese government is interested; they were purely financial or banking transactions and similar in essentials to British investment in the securities of American corporations. This business has not been a success and his company would have done better, in his opinion, if it had gone in for direct investment in China of the usual sort. He would not undertake to estimate the amount of such loans outstanding and he believed it impossible to secure the information. Among the transactions of his own company he mentioned loans to electric light and power companies and to corporations owning cotton mills.

Their failure in this field of investment is explained by the Japanese as due to one or more of the following causes. In the first place, they maintain that the Chinese lack the experience which would enable them to operate industrial plants successfully. A second and closely related reason is that the management of a Chinese corporation seldom undertakes to borrow so long as the corporation is successful and does so, in the usual case, only after financial difficulties are expected. A third and important point is the difficulty of handling any matter that goes before a Chinese court. "There is little confidence in the Chinese courts," said one banker, "when a debt due to a foreigner is to be collected, though I must admit that in one case a Japanese firm did succeed in securing the repayment of Yen 1.25 million from a Chinese electric light company by this means."

Estimates of Japanese investment in Chinese corporations are difficult and uncertain. It is hard to separate such investments from the other forms of Japanese investment. Enough has been said to make this clear. It

is impossible to tell how many investments of the sort
have been omitted. It has been found difficult to check
such investments in China. Popular feeling in China
during the past seventeen years has been such as to make
Chinese business men unwilling to admit that advances
have been received from Japanese sources. It is probable
that charges of accepting such advances have at times
been made by Chinese for the purpose of injuring business competitors. What is to be done when loans are
said by Japanese firms to have been made and are em-
phatically denied by the supposed borrowers? In spite
of the many difficulties, estimates of such investments
have been attempted and they are presented in the following pages.

Japan's Entrance, 1897–1900

Japanese consular officials in China reported to the
Foreign Office on Japanese interests in China in 1897. A
compilation of these reports was made public in 1915,
together with similar reports for 1913, under a title which
may be translated "The Development of the Japanese in
China." [3] This report for 1897 gives us the earliest information available from Japanese sources.

Before 1897 Japanese investments in China amounted
to practically nothing. The Chinese Customs reports
show that there were fewer than fifty Japanese firms in
China and that the number of Japanese residents in the
country was usually under a thousand. Less than 2 per
cent of the total shipping in the Chinese trade in 1897 was
Japanese and at the same time the Japanese tonnage was
considerably greater than it had been earlier in the decade.
It is not surprising, therefore, to find but few evidences of
Japanese interests in China in the Foreign Office report
for 1897.

The Japanese committee, relying upon the 1897 document, reports no business investments under the headings:

[3] A second edition was published in 1919.

agriculture, mining, power, and insurance. Under transportation, shipping to the amount of 800,000 tons was reported as calling at six Chinese ports. Under manufacturing the only venture was the operation, under joint ownership with Chinese, of a cotton gin at Shanghai valued at Chinese $140,000. In the commercial field, ten Japanese were reported in business in Tientsin, all of whom were small retailers. The Shanghai consulate estimated that Japanese merchants handled exports to Japan worth about Chinese $5 million. There was but one Japanese bank in China, the Yokohama Specie Bank, with branches at Shanghai and Hongkong. There were in 1897 no Japanese loans to the Chinese government or to government institutions. Under cultural enterprises, the Japanese committee reports a school in Shanghai (50 students) under a Japanese Buddhist society and Tung Wen College (80 students) which was moved in 1900 from Nanking to Shanghai.

Between 1897–1900 the increase in Japanese investments must have been considerable. The Customs figures show a fairly rapid growth in trade and foreign business in China during these years and we find that the Japanese share in almost every case grew to a significant proportion. In shipping the Japanese percentage increased from 2 in 1897 to 9 in 1900. When it comes to Japanese firms and population in China the changes are shown in the following table to mark a transition from a China in which the Japanese did not count to one in which they did.

TABLE 1

JAPANESE IN CHINA, 1897–1901

	Japanese Firms	Per Cent of Total Foreign Firms	Japanese Population	Per Cent of Total Foreign Population
1897	44	6.9	1,106	9.5
1898	114	14.7	1,694	12.6
1899	195	20.9	2,440	14.2
1900	212	21.1	2,900	17.2
1901	289	26.2	4,170	21.8

The industrial development of Japan during these years lay behind this increase in Japanese interests in China. The years immediately following the Sino-Japanese War saw the first fruits of the economic policy that may be said to have begun with the restoration in 1868. There was a great increase in foreign trade and a remarkable increase in the population of Japanese cities.[4] Japanese ocean shipping more than doubled between 1894–1896 as a direct result of the war with China and this was followed by further rapid increases. The number of power-driven cotton spindles in Japan reached a total of a million about the year 1898 and the growth after 1895 had been at a rapid rate. Imports of cotton yarn into China from Japan were no less than eight times as great in 1899 as in 1896.[5] In practically every field of industry and international economic relations Japan reached a new and higher level during the years that followed the war with China.

The movement of capital associated with these changes was toward Japan, if we may regard the payment of the Chinese indemnity as a capital movement. There was a great excess of imports into Japan during these years but the deficits in this and in other less important accounts was more than covered by the Chinese indemnity,[6] which was not remitted from China but from London to Japan. It is Moulton's opinion that Japan reached the year 1898 "square with the outside world" in the field of international debts and investments.[7]

Here we have a set of phenomena which are undoubtedly interrelated: war, an upswing in foreign trade, a sharp increase in shipping, a boom in industry and especially in

[4] Ogawa, *Conscription System in Japan*, New York, 1921. One of the Japanese monographs of the Carnegie Endowment. The author is Y. Tokata as Professor Ogawa himself points out in his preface. A table on p. 175 shows the yearly increase in population in cities (above 10,000) over the year before. The first year of increase at a new and more rapid rate was 1898. This the author connects with a great increase in foreign trade.

[5] Remer, C. F., *The Foreign Trade of China*, Shanghai, 1928, p. 93.

[6] As is pointed out by Moulton, H. G., *Japan: An Economic and Financial Appraisal*, Washington, 1931, pp. 497–9.

[7] Moulton, H. G., *ibid.*, p. 500.

cotton milling, and a shift to an adverse trade balance without an increase in indebtedness. What the nature of the interrelation may be, what the sequence of events in fact and in logic, it is impossible to say. One is tempted to give considerable importance to the leadership and the activity of the Japanese government and to believe that war may have been the immediate cause of the series of events. In any case it is significant that many of the events are directly connected with China. The war was with China, the increased trade was, to a considerable extent, with China, the output of the cotton mills was for the increased Chinese trade, and the new international credits were from the Chinese indemnity. Japan could not develop her international economic relations without changes of fundamental importance in her relations with China.

Japanese investments in China were still in the future. The Japanese committee did not venture any estimate of the value of Japanese holdings in 1897. Mr. Shizuo Hirai of this committee considered the possibility of a valuation at a series of conferences in Tokyo in August, 1930, and ventured a guess of about U. S. $150,000 for business investments.

For 1900 our information is not much more satisfactory. The growth of Japanese business investments must be estimated from such evidence as has been set forth concerning Japanese firms, population, shipping, and trade. The Japanese committee reports that branches of the Yokohama Specie Bank were opened in Tientsin and Newchwang between 1897–1900, giving this bank four branches in China at the later date. The Bank of Taiwan (Formosa) opened a branch at Amoy during the same period. The increased importance of Japanese shipping has been pointed out. Of the great Japanese companies, the Nippon Yusen Kaisha increased its fleet tonnage to 135,000 in 1895 (from 64,000 in 1893) and to 205,000 in 1900. Every one of its principal routes touched one or more Chinese ports. The Osaka Shosen Kaisha was organized in 1898 and, with a government subsidy, began the operation of a route to the Yalu River in Manchuria. With a subsidy from the government of Formosa it opened a South China route in 1899.

Upon such information as is available the extent of Japanese holdings in China may be guessed as between half a million and a million U. S. dollars in 1900.

The distribution of Japanese firms and residents in China as shown in the reports of the Chinese Customs for 1901 is brought together in the accompanying table.

TABLE 2

GEOGRAPHICAL DISTRIBUTION OF JAPANESE FIRMS AND POPULATION IN CHINA, 1901

Decennial Report of the Chinese Customs, 1892–1901

	Firms	Population
Newchwang	8	92
Tientsin	8	1,210
Chefoo	10	128
Hankow	6	74
Shanghai	78	1,477
Foochow	42	127
Amoy	126	920
Other ports	11	142
Total	289	4,170

The importance of Shanghai makes it reasonable to suppose that Japanese business investments at this early date were distributed in much the same fashion as the business investments of Great Britain and the United States. The importance of Amoy is probably to be explained by Japanese political control in Formosa. Here, as in later cases, Japanese business investments followed, and did not precede, political changes with which they were associated.

In general, it may be said that Japan entered into the international economic relations of China immediately after the Sino-Japanese War of 1894–1895. In 1897, however, Japanese business investments amounted to practically nothing.   Between 1897–1900 there was a vigorous development of Japanese interests in a wide variety of fields.   In Japan, itself, there was, during the same years, strong evidence that a new commercial and industrial era had begun.   This was reflected in many aspects of Chinese relations and the immediate cause may well have been the Chinese war.   Investment in China, while it increased remarkably after 1897, was still so small in 1900 as to be negligible.   The total of business investments may have been U. S. $1 million.   There were no obligations of the Chinese government to Japan or Japanese which were the result of loans.   Japanese cultural and philanthropic activities amounted to little.   The public property of the Japanese government was too small to be worth considering.   Japanese investment in Chinese corporations had not been attempted at so early a date.   A table based upon the slight information available concerning Japanese investments in China in 1900 is added for convenient reference.

TABLE 3

JAPANESE INVESTMENTS IN CHINA, 1900

Business investments	U. S. $1,000,000
Government obligations	none
Total	U. S. $1,000,000

JAPANESE INTERESTS IN 1914

Investments

Japanese investments and other interests in China were negligible in 1900; they were of real importance in 1914.   This change was brought about by a vigorous growth in business investments and by the rapid rise of Japanese interests in southern Manchuria after 1905.   An estimate of Japanese investments in 1914 is presented in the following pages.   Some attention is given to the course of events during the years from 1900 to 1914.   It must be remembered, however, that the method generally adopted for this study calls for estimates at certain points in time rather than for the tracing of the changes through the intervening years.

For the 1914 estimate the chief reliance is, of course, upon the report of the committee of the Japanese Council of the Institute of Pacific Relations. The Japanese committee relied, in turn, upon the same document as for their 1897 estimate. This, it may be repeated, was a report of the Japanese foreign office published in 1915, containing the results of the 1897 investigation and of a new investigation for 1914 which had but recently been completed. It was not until 1924 that another estimate was undertaken by a reliable Japanese authority. Information to supplement that brought together by the Japanese committee is from a variety of sources, the chief being the reports of the Chinese Maritime Customs.

Population

There is no better single index of the change in Japanese interests in China during the years from 1900 to 1914 than the figures of the Japanese population. The increase in the number of Japanese was from two or three thousand to no less than a hundred thousand. In 1900 less than a fifth of the foreigners in China were Japanese; in 1914 the Japanese were equal in numbers to all other foreigners in China taken together. In the recent history of China there has been no increase to be compared with this except that of the Russians during the construction of the Chinese Eastern Railway. In both cases the immediate explanation lies in Manchurian developments.

The rapid increase in the number of Japanese in China, shown in Table 4, is obviously connected with the Russo-Japanese War which began in 1904 and with the opening to foreign trade of Dairen and other less important cities in southern Manchuria which occurred in 1907. The statistics of the Chinese Customs provide further informa-

TABLE 4

JAPANESE IN CHINA, 1900–1914

	Japanese Committee Figures *	Chinese Customs Figures **		
		Firms	Population	Population as a Per Cent of Total Foreign Population in China
1900	———	212	2,900	17.1
1901	4,739	289	4,170	21.8
1902	5,306	317	5,020	26.4
1903	8,914	361	5,287	25.9
1904	8,908	650	9,139	33.5
1905	16,175	729	16,910	44.4
1906	27,891	739	15,548	40.2
1907	32,956	1,416	45,610	65.2
1908	40,119	1,149	44,143	56.6
1909	76,116	1,492	55,401	62.7
1910	76,678	1,601	65,434	46.1
1911	51,794	1,283	78,306	51.0
1912	97,384	733	75,210	51.9
1913	107,732	1,269	80,219	48.9
1914	———	955	84,948	51.5

* Including Hongkong and Macao.
** Exclusive of Koreans and of Hongkong and Macao. The figures for firms are much less reliable than for persons. Firms in Dairen, for example, are not included.

tion. In 1901 only 2 per cent of the Japanese in China were in Manchuria; the figure was 68 per cent for 1911.[8] Comparable figures from the same source are not available for 1914. The Japanese in China numbered about 100,000 at the end of 1913. It may be accepted as certain that 80 per cent were in Manchuria. The outstanding fact in the increase in the number of Japanese in China is the opening of Manchuria.

The matter may be pushed further. It is certain, also, that about 95 per cent of the Japanese in Manchuria in 1914 were in the Kwantung leased area and the South Manchuria Railway zone. Information is available con-

[8] *Chinese Maritime Customs:* Decennial Report 1902–1911, vol. 2, pp. 354–5. This is the source for all figures for the year 1911.

cerning the occupational distribution of the Japanese in Manchuria and, when this is compared with figures showing the number employed by the South Manchuria Railway and the Kwantung government, the conclusion is unavoidable that about 50 per cent of the Japanese in Manchuria in 1914 were either so employed or were the dependents of such employees.[9] In 1914 and from the earliest considerable increase in the number of Japanese in China, most of the Japanese have been in Manchuria in territory under the administrative control of Japan, and many of them have been directly dependent upon two great institutions under the Japanese government.

The importance of Manchuria must not be permitted to obscure the fact that the Japanese population of other centers increased greatly during the years under consideration. If we leave Manchuria out of account, we find that the distribution of the Japanese was like that of the other foreigners in China. Shanghai was the city of first importance. There were about ten times as many Japanese in Shanghai in 1915 as in 1900, and in 1915 the Japanese formed the largest national group. In 1910 the largest group had been British. The other centers in which the Japanese population reached a thousand or

TABLE 5

JAPANESE AT SHANGHAI, 1900–1915, ACCORDING TO THE CENSUS FIGURES OF THE SHANGHAI MUNICIPAL COUNCIL COVERING THE FOREIGN SETTLEMENT AND THE EXTERNAL ROADS AREA, BUT NOT INCLUDING THE FRENCH CONCESSION

Feetham Report, vol. 1, pp. 51–2

	Population	Per Cent of the Total Foreign Population
1900	736	11
1905	22,157	19
1910	3,361	25
1915	7,169	39

[9] Published figures support these statements. Hsiao, Chu, "Manchuria: A Statistical Survey" in *Problems of the Pacific, 1929*, pp. 413, 416, and 417. Royama, M., "Japan's Position in Manchuria," *Problems of the Pacific, 1929*, pp. 573, 574.

more in 1911 were Tientsin (2,970), Amoy (1,231), and Hankow (1,227). At Amoy the Japanese outnumbered all other foreigners taken together. The increase at Shanghai and other ports was significant but the fundamental difference between 1900 and 1914 was in Manchuria.

Trade and Shipping

The increase in the number of Japanese in China between 1900–1914 was so remarkable that it has been presented in some detail. Other indices of the growing importance of Japan are to be found in the foreign trade of China and in foreign shipping. Since the results of an investigation of Japanese investments are available, trade and shipping require only the briefest comment.

The trade of China was about twice as great in 1913 as in 1899.[10] The share of Japan in this total trade was 11.5 per cent in 1899 and 20.9 per cent in 1913. The growing importance of Japan is shown in Table 6. China exported to Japan increasing quantities and values and an increasing proportion of her beans and bean products, raw cotton, and cereals. The increase in exports to Japan was in part the result of the opening up of Manchuria. About 90 per cent of the soya beans, an export that showed

TABLE 6

THE IMPORTANCE OF JAPAN IN THE TRADE OF CHINA, 1899–1913

Chinese Customs Statistics. Figures of Value in Millions of Hk. Tls.

	Total Trade	With Japan	Per Cent with Japan
1899	460.5	53.1	11.5
1913	973.5	184.9	19.0
	Exports	To Japan	Per Cent to Japan
1899	195.8	17.3	8.8
1913	403.3	65.5	16.2
	Imports	From Japan	Per Cent from Japan
1899	264.7	35.9	13.5
1913	570.2	119.3	20.9

[10] These years are selected rather than 1900 and 1914 to avoid the consequences of the Boxer uprising and the outbreak of the World War.

a phenomenal growth after 1908, came from the Manchurian provinces. China imported from Japan increasing quantities and values of a variety of relatively unimportant commodities. The significant increase was in cotton textiles and cotton yarn. The plain cotton fabrics imported into China from Japan were as follows: 1.4 million pieces in 1909, 2.4 in 1910, 2.8 in 1911, 3 in 1912, and 5.7 in 1913.[11] Before 1900 the great increase had been in cotton yarn; after 1900 it was in cotton piece goods. Japan, in a large measure, displaced the United States in the Manchurian market and her sales of piece goods in China increased more rapidly than did the sales of British goods.

The increasing importance of Japan in China's trade was not matched during the years under consideration by a similar increase in the importance of China in Japanese trade. This is to be explained in part by the fact that the trade of Japan increased more rapidly than did the trade of China. A smaller percentage of Japan's trade formed a larger percentage of China's. But the significant point is that Japan's trade with certain other

TABLE 7

THE IMPORTANCE OF CHINA IN THE TRADE OF JAPAN, 1899–1913

Japanese Statistics. Figures of Value in Millions of Yen

(China includes Kwantung and Hongkong)

	Total Trade	With China	Per Cent with China
1899	431.9	110.6	25.6
1913	1,361.9	311.5	22.9
	Exports	To China	Per Cent to China
1899	211.5	74.5	35.2
1913	632.5	218.1	34.5
	Imports	From China	Per Cent from China
1899	220.4	36.0	16.3
1913	729.4	93.4	12.8

[11] Chinese Maritime Customs: *Report on the Foreign Trade of China, 1913,* p. 10.

countries increased more rapidly than did her trade with China. Among these other countries were the Dutch East Indies, Australia, British India, and the United States, though in the case of the United States the increase was only slightly greater than in the case of China. Japanese trade with China was about equal to her trade with the United States in 1899 and in 1913, and the two together accounted for about half of Japan's foreign trade. Their Chinese trade was for the Japanese of great importance throughout the period but not of increasing importance. Japan was making a place for herself in world trade during these years, her trade expansion involved an increasing trade with China but it carried her beyond China into many parts of the Pacific and of the East.

Statistics of shipping in China show the total tonnage coming under the view of the Chinese Customs in the foreign and domestic trade of the country. These figures include practically the whole of the steam shipping calling at each of the Chinese ports, taking ocean-going, coastwise, and river vessels together. The tables include tonnage under the Chinese flag as well as that under foreign flags. Figures of total tonnage mean little, but changes in the percentage distribution are significant. In 1899 Japanese tonnage was 7 per cent of the total and in 1913 no less than 25 per cent. The Customs statistics show also the share taken by each nationality in the carrying trade between the open ports of China. This is not an entirely satisfactory index of foreign interest in China's domestic shipping because of the position of Hongkong. In this trade 5 per cent of the tonnage was under the Japanese flag in 1899 and 24.6 per cent in 1913.[12]

The available figures for population, trade, and shipping have been reviewed. Substantial increases in Japanese interests in China are indicated by trade and shipping figures. Figures for population show a remarkable increase. The estimates of Japanese investments in China

[12] The figures are based upon outward tonnage only.

in 1913 or 1914, now to be presented, are to be viewed in the light of the preceding discussion.

Direct Business Investments

The direct business investments of the Japanese in China reached a total of about U. S. $190 million in 1914. The total for 1914 is to be compared with that for 1900, when such investments were certainly no greater than U. S. $1 million, and with that for 1897, when Japanese investments of all sorts amounted to practically nothing. In 1914 Japanese business investments in China were great enough to give Japan third place, following Great Britain and Russia.

Direct investments are from their very nature closely associated with foreign residence in China. We have found that, in 1914, 80 per cent of the Japanese in China were in Manchuria. The figures now to be considered show that almost 70 per cent of the business investment was in Manchuria.

TABLE 18

THE GEOGRAPHICAL DISTRIBUTION OF JAPANESE BUSINESS
INVESTMENTS IN CHINA, 1914 *

	Millions of U. S. Dollars	Per Cent of Total
In Manchuria	132.6	68.9
In the rest of China	59.9	31.1
	192.5	100.0

* Investment at Shanghai estimated at U. S. $30 million.

The geographical distribution of investments is, in general, such as was to be expected. If there is anything requiring comment, it is that the Japanese population outside of Manchuria carried with it so large a share of the investment. This is brought out in the case of Shanghai, which was the location of about 7 per cent of the Japanese population and no less than 15 per cent of the Japanese investment. The explanation of the difference between Shanghai and Manchuria lies in the fact that the characteristic Japanese of Shanghai was a business man or a banker, while the characteristic Japanese of southern Manchuria was an official or an employee of the South Manchuria Railway.

When we consider the situation outside of Manchuria we find that we have to do with business investments of U. S. $59.9 million. Almost exactly half of these investments were at Shanghai. The chief centers outside of Shanghai were Tientsin, Hankow, and Amoy. What we know of the distribution of Japanese investments in 1914 leads to the conclusion that, outside of Manchuria, this distribution was similar to that of American or of British business investments for the whole of China. A similar statement has been made concerning the distribution of population.

The South Manchuria Railway Company offers further evidence of the importance of Manchuria and of the difference between Japanese interests there and in the rest of China. From the organization of the railway company in 1906 the Japanese government has been the owner of half of its capital stock. This company owned no less than U. S. $105 million (79.2 per cent) of a total business investment of U. S. $132.6 million in Manchuria. In fact, about 55 per cent of the whole of Japanese business investments in China consisted of property owned by the South Manchuria. In addition, as will appear, the railway company had advanced more than U. S. $1 million to the Chinese government for railway construction in Manchuria. What is more, it was the owner of a large part of the Japanese property devoted to administrative and cultural purposes. It is difficult to overemphasize the importance in 1914 of the South Manchuria Railway Company among Japanese interests in China.

The place of the Southern Manchuria Railway Company is more fully dealt with below when investments in 1930 are considered. There is, however, a further fact to be noted here. Between 1907–1911 the railway company borrowed in London a total of £14 million. Of this sum £2 million, borrowed in 1908 for three years, was repaid in 1911, but there were still outstanding obligations to the amount of £12 million (Yen 117,156,000) in 1914.[13] No account of this is taken in the tables which follow, but it is to be borne in mind that the South Manchuria Railway and its property as it stood in 1914 represented a considerable investment of British capital. It is to be borne in mind, also, that the railway was originally constructed by the Russians with French capital.

TABLE 9

THE INVESTMENT OF THE SOUTH MANCHURIA RAILWAY COMPANY, 1914

The first column shows the value set upon the property turned over by the Japanese government to the company on its organization. The second column shows the sums carried "on capital account" on March 31, 1914. Figures in Yen.

Railways	25,719,896	97,967,268
Workshops	332,216	6,397,048
Vessels	———	4,892,636
Harbor works	6,209,134	17,175,110
Mines	46,013,892	58,261,041
Electricity and gas	367,232	6,803,942
Hotels	13,539	1,630,763
Local institutions	313,441	4,145,441
Lands	6,043,944	15,815,819
Buildings	7,770,685	18,321,882
	92,783,978	231,410,950

The last three items taken together, Yen 38.3 million, have been divided as follows:

Business investments	Yen 17.0 million
Administrative and cultural	Yen 21.3 million

Under "administrative and cultural" is included Yen 6 million in schools and hospitals.

Direct business investments are shown in the next table classified according to the nature of the business. The Japanese case is the only one in which such details are available for so early a date as 1914. It has been made

[13] For the details of these loans see *Economic History of Manchuria*, Bank of Chosen Seoul, 1920, pp. 95–6. There were two loans at 5% for 25 years and one at 4½% for 29 years. The issue price was 97 and 98.

possible by the work of the Japanese committee and by the report for 1914 of the Japanese foreign office.

The importance of the investment in the import and export trade is outstanding. It formed over 22 per cent of the total in 1914. This, however, marks a decline from 1900 when the import and export trade accounted for almost 100 per cent of Japanese investments. This decline indicates the development and diversification of Japanese business activities in China. Between 1900–1914 the Japanese entered new fields. The most important of these was transportation, 35.5 per cent of the total investment in 1914. In addition to railways, this includes river and coastwise shipping. Mining was of second importance, 15.1 per cent, the whole investment being in the hands of the South Manchuria Railway Company. There was also a Japanese investment in the Hanyehping Company, a Chinese company owning iron mines, blast furnaces, and a steel mill, which is reported under Japanese investments in Chinese corporations. Manufacturing was of minor importance, but it is to be noted that in 1914 the Japanese owned three cotton mills at Shanghai valued at Yen 7.8 million. When the way was opened, by their new place in Manchuria and by their success in modern industry at home, the Japanese entered a variety of industries in China.

TABLE 10

JAPANESE BUSINESS INVESTMENTS CLASSIFIED BY THE NATURE OF THE
BUSINESS

	Thousands of Yen	Per Cent of Total
1. Transportation	136,664	35.5
2. Public utilities	6,840	1.8
3. Mining	58,261	15.1
4. Manufacturing	21,175	5.5
5. Banking and finance	12,650	3.3
6. Real estate	16,967	4.4
7. Import and export	85,162	22.1
8. Miscellaneous	47,300	12.3
	385,019	100.0

The following, and the final table under this heading, shows the totals which have entered into the general statements concerning business investments in 1914. The geographical location of the investments is given as it is shown in the report of the Japanese committee. The territorial division is roughly this: North China includes Tsingtao and all ports in Shantung and farther north, Central China means the Yangtze valley, South China includes Foochow and all ports farther south. When the number of plants, establishments, or firms is known, this is indicated. The whole table puts into an abbreviated form the chief facts that are known about Japanese direct business investments in China in 1914.

TABLE 11

JAPANESE DIRECT BUSINESS INVESTMENTS IN CHINA IN 1914

A table showing details as to the nature of the business and the geographical location of the investments. The figures in parentheses show the number of plants or firms. Figures of value are shown in thousands of yen.

1. Transportation		
a. In Manchuria		
So. Manchuria Ry. railway investment	97,967	
So. Manchuria Ry. repair shops	6,397	
Other railway and horse-car lines	162	
So. Manchuria Ry. investment in shipping	4,893	
So. Manchuria Ry. investment in harbor works	17,175	
Steamship companies in Dairen	1,970	
b. In the rest of China		
Yangtze shipping—Central China	8,100	136,664
2. Public utilities		
a. In Manchuria		
So. Manchuria Ry. electricity and gas plants	6,804	
b. In the rest of China		
Light and power plants—Central China (1)	36	6,840
3. Mining		
a. In Manchuria		
So. Manchuria Ry. investment in mines	58,261	58,261

TABLE 11—*Continued*

JAPANESE DIRECT BUSINESS INVESTMENTS IN CHINA IN 1914

4. Manufacturing			
a. In Manchuria			
Oil mills	(3)	830	
Flour mills	(3)	2,500	
Matches	(2)	495	
Tobacco	(4)	3,200	
Other	(19)	389	
b. In the rest of China			
Cotton mills—Central China	(3)	7,800	
Oil mills—Central China	(4)	2,000	
Flour mills—Central China	(2)	2,920	
Matches—North, Central and South			
China	(3)	212	
Other—North, Central and South			
China	(20)	829	21,175
5. Banking and finance			
a. In Manchuria			
Japanese		4,850	
Japanese interests in Sino-Japanese banks		2,500	
b. In the rest of China			
Banks with chief offices in Japan		5,300	12,650
6. Real estate			
a. In Manchuria			
So. Manchuria Ry. investment in hotels		1,631	
So. Manchuria Ry. land and buildings			
(est.)		15,000	
Agricultural holdings	(3,668)	336	16,967
7. Import and export			
a. In Manchuria			
Known investment of 23 firms and esti-			
mates for others		10,000	
b. In the rest of China			
Known and estimated investment		75,162	85,162
8. Miscellaneous			
a. In Manchuria			
Reported under So. Manchuria Railway		2,000	
Outside So. Manchuria Railway		500	
Originally reported under General Trading		27,300	
b. In the rest of China			
Reported under General Trading, probably			
includes certain land holdings in Shang-			
hai		17,500	47,300
Total			385,019

Obligations of the Chinese Government

The obligations of the Chinese government to Japanese, which are listed below, include only Japanese loans to the Chinese government. The varied and complicated claims of a later time did not exist in 1914. There are, however, certain obligations that require separate comment before the loans are considered.

The first of these is the Japanese share of the Boxer indemnity. The principal of the Boxer indemnity obligation to Japan was U. S. $24.5 million on January 1, 1902, before payments began. It involved an annual payment to Japan of about U. S. $1 million from 1902 to 1910. From 1911 to 1913 the payment was slightly higher.[14] The principal outstanding on January 1, 1914, was U. S. $23.9 million. The Boxer indemnity involved, of course, no original payment *to* China and it was so altered after 1917 that no real net payment *from* China need be considered. For 1913 it is to be noted as an obligation of China to Japan, greater than the whole of the Japanese loans to the Chinese government.

The second obligation requiring separate comment is that which resulted from the signing of the Reorganization loan contract in April, 1913. The Yokohama Specie Bank was the Japanese agency and the loan was from the so-called five-power group which included British, German, French, and Russian agencies. Article 18 of the loan contract states that the five banks "shall take the loan in equal shares and without responsibility for each other." [15] This is reinforced by Article 10 in which the Chinese government agrees to make payments for interest and amortization "in equal shares to the Banks."

[14] It was made an obligation in pounds sterling early in 1906. Wright, S. F., *The Collection and Disposal of the Maritime and Native Customs Revenue*, Shanghai, 1927, p. 218. The amount payable in 1913 was £221,-732.

[15] MacMurray, John V. A., *Treaties and Agreements With or Concerning China, 1894–1919*, Shanghai, vol. II, p. 1014.

The nominal amount of the loan was £25 million, making the Japanese share £5 million or about Yen 50 million. This sum, or a sum near to it, usually appears in lists of Japanese loans to the Chinese government; it is, therefore, necessary to state the grounds for its omission here.

While it is true that the legal obligation to make payment to the Yokohama Specie Bank exists, it is also true that the whole of the Japanese share of the Reorganization loan was issued outside of Japan.[16] It is unusual, even in the complications of Chinese finance, for a legal obligation to exist to pay a bank in one country when the whole of the funds have come from investors in other countries, though Russia provides earlier examples. The explanation for such transactions lies in the political field. Concerning the Japanese share of the Reorganization loan, the fact is that the funds came from England, France, and Germany, and that the payments of the service of the loan were made through the Yokohama Specie Bank and through the banks in these European centers to investors in England and on the continent of Europe. Upon the principle of the place of issue the Japanese had no share in the loan. Efforts to secure information as to the actual holding of Reorganization loan bonds in Japan in 1914 support the conclusion that no such bonds were in Japan at this time. In view of these facts the Reorganization loan is excluded from the list of Japanese loans to China.

As a matter of fact the financial transactions connected with the Reorganization loan probably meant a transfer of funds from Europe to Japan rather than from Japan to China. This conclusion rests upon the fact that the schedules of payments to be made by the Chinese government from the proceeds of the loan included the repayment to the Yokohama Specie Bank of certain provincial

---

[16] For place and amount of issue see Baylin, J. R., *Foreign Loan Obligations of China*, Tientsin, 1925, p. 16. This agrees with the schedules of payments in the hands of the bankers which have been consulted.

loans and of a loan to the Chinese Ministry of Communications, amounting in all to about Yen 10 million.[17]

The first Japanese loan to the Chinese government, of which there is record, was made in 1909. It was from the South Manchuria Railway for the rebuilding of the eastern part of the Hsinmintun-Mukden Railway which had been purchased from the Japanese government.[18] The original loan was for Yen 320,000 at 93, and was to run for eighteen years. It carried with it some degree of Japanese interest which was fortified by the provision that "no repayment in full . . . shall be allowed before the expiration of the period named." [19] The original convention concerning the purchase of this railway and the building of the Kirin-Changchun was signed on April 15, 1907; a supplementary agreement was signed on November 12, 1908; and a detailed agreement on August 18, 1909.

The thirty-six miles of this line were the last link in the railway between Tientsin and Mukden and the Chinese were most anxious to acquire it. It was under effective control by the Chinese late in 1907, as may be judged from the fact that a rate war with the South Manchuria was reported toward the end of the year.[20]

The second loan was also from the South Manchuria Railway Company for the building of the Kirin-Changchun Railway. The preliminary agreements for this loan were made in connection with those for the Hsinmin-Mukden. This railway from the northern terminus of the South Manchuria east to the capital of Kirin province had been the subject of an agreement with Russia in 1902.[21] The Japanese were particularly desirous of

[17] MacMurray, J. V. A., *Treaties and Agreements*, vol. II, p. 1018.
[18] *Ibid.*, vol. I, p. 627. The purchase price was Yen 1,660,000.
[19] *Ibid.*, vol. I, p. 627.
[20] *Far Eastern Review*, November, 1907, p. 186.
[21] MacMurray, J. V. A., *Treaties and Agreements*, vol. I, pp. 629–31, prints a translation of the Chinese text of the original agreement. It was planned as a part of the Chinese Eastern and the conditions of Chinese acquisition were the same as for the main railway.

building this line since it was in the direction of the Korean border. The amount of the loan was Yen 2,150,000 and the whole of this amount was outstanding at the end of 1913. The agreements provided that this line (and the Hsinmin-Mukden) "must connect with the South Manchuria Railway line" and that the building of branches or an extension "shall rest of right with the Chinese government, but, if there should be a lack of capital, application shall be made to the South Manchuria Railway Company."[22] The provisions for the control of this line were such as to leave it entirely in the hands of the Chinese except that the traffic receipts were to be deposited with the local offices of the Yokohama Specie Bank. The Kirin-Changchun was completed in October, 1912, but it was run at a loss. Arrears in payments and proposals for the extension of the line toward the Korean boundary made it the subject of controversy between the Chinese and the Japanese.[23]

In the third place there were two loans made by the Yokohama Specie Bank to the Ministry of Communications of the Chinese government. One of these was a purchase of Chinese silver dollar bonds of a domestic loan to assist in the redemption of the Peking-Hankow Railway under such conditions as to make the transaction a loan of Yen 2.2 million to the Chinese government. The other was a loan of Yen 10 million known as the Yuchuanpu loan.[24] This loan was made in March, 1911, and was said to be for the provision of funds for railway administration. It undoubtedly had to do with the policy of centralization of control over the railways which was vigorously pushed by Sheng Hsüan-hwai, who became Minister of Communications in January. Sheng was

[22] MacMurray, J. V. A., *Treaties and Agreements*, vol. I, p. 628.
[23] See Article 6 of the Agreement relating to the Chientao region of September 4, 1909. MacMurray, J. V. A., *Treaties and Agreements*, vol. I, p. 797. Other agreements later than 1914 are referred to below.
[24] Yuchuanpu is the Romanization of the Chinese for Ministry of Communications.

energetic, unpopular, and generally held to be corrupt on a magnificent scale. His policy of central control of railways played an important part in bringing on the revolution of 1911.[25] This loan was issued at 95, at 5 per cent, for twenty-five years and it involved an immediate advance of Yen 2 million. The whole sum was outstanding at the end of 1913.[26]

Within a few months of the outbreak of the revolution in 1911 certain sums were borrowed from Japan which are not listed. In January, 1912, the Okura Company made a loan of Yen 3 million to the provisional government at Nanking. The provisions for the security of this loan, by a mortgage on a section of the Shanghai-Hangchow-Ningpo railway, were in direct conflict with the loan agreement of March, 1908, for the construction of the line. The difficulties which resulted were settled by the repayment of the Okura Company from the proceeds of a loan from the British and Chinese Corporation, the contract for which was signed in February, 1914.[27] This loan is omitted because it was the subject of protest at the end of 1913 and was repaid from a British loan early in 1914. A second loan is reported to have been made by the Mitsui Company in February, 1912. This loan was for Yen 1.5 million at 7 per cent. The company is said to have accepted treasury notes and the purpose of the loan was to meet expenses of the Nanking provisional government.[28] This loan is among the unsecured loans of the Chinese government in the totals for 1930.

There is, finally, a loan of Yen 3 million which was originally made to the Shensi provincial government mint

[25] MacNair, H. F., *China in Revolution*, Chicago, 1931, p. 28, and Wagel, S. R., *Finance in China*, Shanghai, 1914, pp. 48-9.

[26] The loan contracts for these two loans are to be found in MacMurray, J. V. A., *Treaties and Agreements*, vol. I, pp. 757, 835.

[27] MacMurray, J. V. A., *Treaties and Agreements*, vol. I, p. 713.

[28] The comment on this from a generally reliable source is, "The Treasury notes carried interest originally at 7% per annum. From Feb. 6, 1920, the rate was changed to 10% and the Ministry of Finance agreed to pay compound interest." C. C. S. and H. K. L., *Notes on the Inadequately Secured Loans of China*, Peking, 1926, p. 15.

by the East Asia Industrial Company, often referred to as the Toa Company. The exact date of this loan is unknown but it was in existence in 1913 and it was taken over by the central government in 1920.[29] This loan is to be found among the unsecured loans outstanding in 1930.

The following table provides a convenient summary of the Japanese loans to China outstanding at the end of 1913, including only those which are known and accepted. The total of these loans is U. S. $7,350,000. If we add the Mitsui loan of 1912 and the Shensi Mint loan, U. S. $2,250,000, the total of Japanese loans to the Chinese government becomes U. S. $9.6 million. It is this sum which may be accepted for purposes of comparison with other countries and with similar obligations for a later time.

The principal of the Japanese share of the Boxer indemnity was U. S. $23.9 million at the end of 1913. The addition of this sum would show the total obligations of the Chinese government to Japan and Japanese nationals to be U. S. $33.4 million. If we were to include the Japanese share of the Reorganization loan we would have a total of Chinese government obligations of no less than about U. S. $58 million. It is not probable that the loans from the South Manchuria Railway Company for the two Manchurian railways called for any transfer of funds from Japan. If we suppose that the other loans involved such transfers, we arrive at the astonishing result that Chinese government obligations to Japan were U. S. $58 million in 1914 and that the total inpayments into China involved in the creation of these obligations was about U. S. $8 million.

It seems more reasonable to accept as the total of Japanese loans to China the sum of U. S. $9.6 million, to point out that a capital sum of U. S. $23.9 was outstanding on the indemnity, and to leave the Reorganization loan out of consideration altogether.

[29] The rate is reported to have been changed from 8 to 10 per cent.

TABLE 12

JAPANESE LOANS TO THE CHINESE GOVERNMENT AS OF DECEMBER 31, 1913

Date of Issue	Term in Years	Denomination of Loan	Per Cent	Japanese Agency	Total Loan. Original Currency Yen	Amount Outstanding U. S. Dollars
1909	18	Hsinmintun-Mukden Railway loan	5	So. Manchuria Railway Co.	360,000	125,000
1909	25	Kirin-Changchun Railway loan	5	So. Manchuria Railway Co.	2,250,000	1,125,000
1910	12	Peking-Hankow Redemption loan bonds	7	Yokohama Specie Bank	2,200,000	1,100,000
1911	25	Yuchuanpu loan	5	Yokohama Specie Bank	10,000,000	5,000,000
						7,350,000

Shensi Copper Mint Loan (East Asia Ind. Co.)	1,500,000
Treasury notes of the Nanking gov't (Mitsui Co.)	750,000
	2,250,000
Grand Total	9,600,000
Principal of the Boxer indemnity outstanding on January 1, 1914	U. S. $23,891,262.

Investments in Chinese Corporations

In view of the investments to be recorded here it is desirable to repeat the statement that Chinese corporations important enough to borrow abroad usually have fairly close relations with the government or with government officials. There is not in China or in Japan the sharp legal distinction between publicly-owned and privately-owned corporations to which Westerners are accustomed, especially those Westerners who live under English or American law. Extraterritoriality and the treaties which set limits upon the activities of foreigners in China further complicate the problem. A mortgage held by foreigners upon a Chinese industrial plant away from a treaty port offers possibilities of complications which create an interest on the part of the Chinese government in such a transaction. In spite of the uncertainties it is probably best to classify the loans dealt with below as investments in Chinese corporations; they are neither direct investments nor the obligations of the Chinese government.

The first case is that of a series of loans made by the Yokohama Specie Bank to the Hanyehping Corporation, China's greatest producer of iron and steel and the owner of coal and iron mines in the Yangtze valley. The history of this corporation need not be dealt with here. German loans to the amount of 4 million marks were made against its property as early as 1902.[30] The German loans were followed by a Japanese loan. It was not until later (1908) that a series of advances from the Yokohama Specie Bank began. These loans usually took the form of payment in advance for iron ore and pig iron to be turned over to the Yawata Iron Works of the Japanese government. In the agreement of December 2, 1913, covering total obligations of Yen 12 million, it was stipulated that payments for pig iron and iron ore by the Japanese Iron Works were to be made to the Yokohama Specie Bank. The Bank was, in turn, to make "payments of principal and interest due on all old and new obligations of the company."[31] The Company was to have at its disposal only the balance remaining to its credit. In a supplementary agreement the Company undertook to employ Japanese financial and engineering advisers and to borrow from the bank if funds were to be procured from non-Chinese sources.

Under financial arrangements of this sort it is not easy to determine the amount of the Company's indebtedness to the bank at any one time. Several lists of loans are available which are quite inconsistent in details.[32] We may accept as reliable the report of a committee appointed by the Ministry of Mines and Agriculture of

[30] MacMurray, J. V. A., *Treaties and Agreements*, vol. II, pp. 1083–4.
[31] *Ibid.*, p. 1079. The supplementary agreements follow.
[32] Lieu, D. K., *Foreign Investments in China, 1929*, p. 95, prints a table from Ku, Lang, "Ten Large Mines in China" (in Chinese). The table of the Ministry of Mines and Agriculture for 1924 is given on p. 96.

the Chinese government in 1927 which drew up a list of the obligations of the Hanyehping Company to Japanese creditors as of December 31, 1924. This list shows total Japanese advances of Yen 29,754,736 and Tls. 2.5 million at the end of 1913. Ku Lang made the total Yen 27,811,-390 and Tls. 120,000 for the same date. In the newspapers of the time the total after the agreement of December, 1913, was usually stated to be about Yen 30 million.[33] In view of the agreement as to the total we may set down the amount of the Japanese investment in the Hanyehping Company at U. S. $15 million at the beginning of 1914.

The second case is that of the Kiangsi Railway Company, frequently referred to as the Nanchang-Kiukiang Railway or the Nanshun Railway.[34] This railway illustrates perfectly the difficulty of the distinction between privately-owned and publicly-owned corporations in China. It was undertaken by a group of officials and merchants in Kiangsi province. They memorialized the Imperial government in 1904 and received permission to proceed. The funds were to be procured by subscription and the sale of lottery tickets. There was at the same time a guarantee resting upon an increase in the provincial salt tax. A contract for the construction of part of the line was entered into with a Japanese Company (Okura) in 1907. By 1910 some twenty-three miles had been built when the Company determined to employ only Chinese. By 1912 the line reached Teanhsien (thirty-

---

[33] *North China Herald*, March 14, 1914, p. 759. "The Company has for long been in such a bad way that the Japanese have had to pay the monthly wages bill in order to keep the business going." The writer believed the Chinese were getting "not a bad price" for this iron ore. It was stated to be Yen 27 a ton f.o.b. *China Year Book*, 1919, p. 357. Japanese loans to the Hanyehping Corporation "are said to be Yen 31 million."

[34] Information is from a report on Chinese railways issued by the South Manchuria Railway Company and from the following: Rhea, Frank, *Far Eastern Markets for Railway Materials, Equipment and Supplies*, Washington, 1919, pp. 122–3; Kent, P. H., *Railway Enterprise in China*, London, 1907, pp. 180–1; Hsu, M. C., *Railway Problems in China*, New York, 1915, pp. 93–4.

four miles from Kiukiang).   Continued financial difficulties led to borrowing from the East Asia Development Company.[35]   This company advanced Yen 5 million in 1912, a part of which was used to meet an earlier obligation arising out of the original Japanese contract.   There is little doubt that this sum represented the total obligations of the railway company to Japanese at the end of 1913.   The fact that the source of these funds was the Deposit Bureau of the Department of Finance of the Japanese government, which controls the investment of postal savings bank and other funds, is evidence of government interest from the Japanese side.   While there was official knowledge of this loan and some degree of official interest on both sides, the loan was from a Japanese financial institution to a Chinese railway corporation and it is so classified here.

There is little doubt that other investments were in existence at the end of 1913 which ought to be included here.   They must have been small and it is probable that most of them were in southern Manchuria.   The known investments reached a total of U. S. $17.5 million.

TABLE 13

JAPANESE INVESTMENTS IN CHINESE CORPORATIONS, 1914

	U. S. Dollars
Loans from the Yokohama Specie Bank to the Hanyehping Corporation	15,000,000
Loans from the East Asia Development Co. to the Kiangsi Railway Company	2,500,000
Total	17,500,000

Administrative, Cultural, and Philanthropic Holdings

The total value of the Japanese property devoted to cultural, philanthropic, and administrative purposes cannot be satisfactorily estimated, although there is fairly accurate information concerning some parts of it.   It may

[35] Sometimes called the Oriental Enterprise Company.   The Japanese name is *Toa Kogyo Kaisha*.   It may also be translated Oriental Development Company.

be estimated, for example, that the South Manchuria Railway Company, in 1914, owned schools and hospitals to the value of Yen 6 million and that the property of the railway used for general administrative purposes (exclusive of the administration of the railway itself) was Yen 15,283,000. The administrative property of the Kwantung government must have been greater than that of the Railway Company. In addition to its general administrative property the Kwantung government owned telephone and telegraph equipment. For the financial year 1913–1914 it reported revenue from public undertakings and state property at about Yen 1.5 million, but this was net revenue and the expenditure cannot be determined.[36] The annual grant from the Japanese National Treasury to the Kwantung government was Yen 3,122,150 for the year 1913–1914 and it was on the average about Yen 3 million beginning with 1907–1908.

The following table shows the chief institutions supported by the Japanese in China, together with their location. This shows that 63 per cent of these institutions were in Manchuria. Many of these institutions were, of course, for the service of the Japanese population, as is indicated by their geographical distribution, but it is also true that many were at the service of the Chinese as well.

TABLE 14

JAPANESE CULTURAL AND PHILANTHROPIC INSTITUTIONS
IN CHINA, 1914

	Schools	Hospitals	Buddhist Temples	Christian Churches
Manchuria	51	36	27	3
North China	3	2	3	1
Central China	7	32	4	2
South China	7	7	1	0
	68	77	35	6

[36] *Financial and Economic Annual of Japan, 1913*, Appendix, pp. 1–2. The special account of the Kwantung government included expenses for guarding the Antung-Mukden line.

It is probable that the total value of the property here being considered was about Yen 25 million aside from that of the Kwantung government which was certainly worth more. No closer approach to a definite estimate can be made on the available information.

Expenditures of the Japanese Government in China to 1914

The expenditures of the Japanese government in China during the period under consideration were of some importance in China's balance of international payments. The greatest payments were, of course, those connected with the Russo-Japanese War. The Manchurian provinces were the scene of the war. Of the Japanese land forces that took part in the war, 1,088,996, all except a few divisions went to Manchuria.[37] The total expenditures for the war, some part of which may have gone to Manchuria, were about Yen 1,730 million. Certain information is available as to the amount which was actually expended in China.

For many local expenditures in Manchuria the Japanese government authorized its military authorities to issue "war tickets." These were issued in denominations that ran from 10 yen to as small an amount as 10 sen. The redemption of these was arranged for in various ways through Japanese banks in Manchurian cities and in Tientsin and Chefoo. The total amount expended in the redemption of the "war tickets" to July, 1906, was Yen 191,145,455. It is fairly certain that the whole of this amount was remitted to China.[38] It is known also that the so-called administrative expenditures of the war in-

[37] Ogawa, G., *Expenditures of the Russo-Japanese War*, New York, 1923, p. 29. The author of the book is H. Oyama, as stated in the preface. See p. 107 for figures of total expenditure for the war.

[38] *Ibid.*, pp. 105–6. The total amount issued in war tickets was Yen 206,398,813. Some of the tickets were redeemed by the issue of notes of the Yokohama Specie Bank.

clude an item of about Yen 2 million, set down as expenditures of the Kwantung governor-general's office. There is, finally, a series of items for transportation which include expenditures for the construction of the Antung-Mukden and Fushun-Tiehling railways and for certain changes and additions in the case of the Russian Railway. These were reported to have reached a total of Yen 58 million by June, 1906, with an appropriation of over Yen 23 million still to be expended.[39] It may be safely estimated that the Japanese government expended in China in connection with the Russo-Japanese War a total which was certainly no less than Yen 250 million and may have been considerably greater.

Other expenditures of the Japanese government in China may be estimated from scattered information. The payments for the deficits of the Kwantung government were, as has been said, about 3 million yen each year beginning with 1907–1908. Ono states the total for the period in which we are interested at Yen 21.8 million.[40] The Japanese military forces in China were increased to one infantry corps in 1903. After the Russo-Japanese War this corps was stationed in the Kwantung leased area.[41] In addition there were in 1913 about 1,700 Japanese soldiers in northern China. This was in accordance with the Boxer agreement and with arrangements among the powers after the outbreak of the revolution in 1911.[42] In addition there were in southern Manchuria railway guards stationed along the South Manchuria Railway. The number of such guards has been maintained at about 10,000 since the withdrawal of Japanese troops from Manchuria at the close of the Russo-Japanese War. The annual expense of maintaining these guards has been

[39] Ono, G., War and Armament Expenditures of Japan, New York, 1922, p. 87. Far Eastern Review, June, 1906, p. 18.
[40] Ono, G., War and Armament Expenditures of Japan, New York, 1922, p. 148.
[41] Ogawa, G., The Conscription System in Japan, New York, 1923, pp. 47, 54.
[42] China Year Book, 1919, pp. 332–3.

from Yen 6 to Yen 11 million.[43]   The expenditure for
these troops and guards must have reached a total of
12 million yen on the average for the period beginning in
1907–1908.

If the information is to be trusted, there is good ground
for believing that the total expenditure of the Japanese
government in China, including Manchuria, for the
whole period under consideration was probably not less
than Yen 300 million.   Practically the whole of this was
expended in connection with the Russo-Japanese War
or with the Japanese interests in Manchuria.   Expenditure of this sort is probably never to be regarded as an
investment.   In this case, however, the Japanese government did secure control of the South Manchuria railway
and capital stock in the railway to the nominal value of
Yen 100 million.[44]

Summary of Japanese Investments in China—1914

Before the World War and its important changes in the
political and financial position of Japan in the Far East
and in China, the investments of Japan in China reached
a total of about U. S. $220 million.   The change in the
situation between 1900 and 1914 was remarkable and is
to be explained largely by the growth of Japanese interests
in Manchuria after the Russo-Japanese War.   Of the total
business investments, U. S. $132.6 million were in Man-
churia and, of the loans to the Chinese government, U. S.
$1.2 million were for Manchurian railways.   Of all Japa-
nese investments in China 60 per cent were in Manchuria
in 1914.   This growth in Manchurian interests was the result of a war, it was accompanied by political control over
a leased area and a railway zone, and by a great growth

[43] South Manchuria Railway, *Report on Progress in Manchuria, 1907–
1928*, p. 60.   It is possible, but unlikely, that some of this expense may have
been charged to the Kwantung government.
[44] The income of the Japanese government upon its holdings was about
Yen 10 million during the years 1909–1914.

in Japanese population in the areas so controlled. The acquisition of these interests had been costly to the Japanese government and they required a net annual expenditure of at least U. S. $5 million at the close of the period.

Outside of Manchuria Japan's investments were in trade, shipping, and manufacturing and centered in Shanghai. Loans to the Chinese government were outstanding in 1914 to the amount of about U. S. $10 million, largely in government railways. The Japanese had taken part in the greatest of general loans to the Chinese government, the Reorganization loan of 1913, but her part in this was dictated by political considerations, for the whole of the Japanese share of the bonds was issued in Europe. The Japanese undertook in two important cases to invest in Chinese corporations but this effort in a new field of foreign investment in China was hardly a success. The following table shows a summary of Japanese investments in China. No attempt has been made to estimate the value of the property used for administrative, philanthropic, and cultural purposes which was shown to be worth at least U. S. $12.5 million.

TABLE 15

JAPANESE INVESTMENTS IN CHINA, 1914

	U. S. Dollars
Direct business investments	192,510,000
Loans to the Chinese government	9,600,000
Investments in Chinese corporations	17,500,000
Total	219,610,000

JAPANESE INTERESTS IN 1930

General

Japanese investments in China have been presented as they were at their beginning in the late 'nineties of the last century and in 1914, that is, early in the Chinese revolution and before the World War. Japan had advanced by 1914 to a position of some importance among the holders of Chinese investments but there were other national groups whose holdings were greater. By 1930 the situation had changed. Japanese holdings were now greater than those of any other country except Great Britain. Japan, with Great Britain, is today of outstanding importance. It is this continued rise in Japanese interests which is now to be examined.

The chief reliance for estimates of Japanese investments at the present time or for recent years is upon the work of the committee of the Japanese Council of the Institute of Pacific Relations. This committee did not have at its disposal a report of the Japanese government as it had for 1897 and 1914. It, therefore, undertook a new and independent investigation, the results of which are the basis of the estimates in the following pages. This investigation was pushed through to a successful conclusion in spite of the numerous difficulties encountered. At the same time the Japanese committee had for reference and comparison a considerable number of complete or partial investigations of Japanese investments in China which are listed below.

A second important source of new information is an investigation carried on in China by Mr. D. K. Lieu in co-operation with this general study of foreign investments in China. Lieu's results were first made public in a report presented by the China Council of the Institute of Pacific Relations at the Kyoto Conference of the Institute, under the title *Foreign Investments in China* (referred to as *Foreign Investments in China, 1929*). Further study of the material was presented in a publication of the China Council for the Shanghai Conference of 1931 under the same title (referred to as *Foreign Investments in China, 1931*). Lieu's purpose was to collect and present the material available in China in the investments of the various countries. His work is a valuable check on that of others who have worked outside of China. The new material presented here is that of Lieu and of the Japanese Committee.

Japanese Estimates

There has been an increasing Japanese interest during the past ten years in the foreign holdings of the Japanese. This is due, in part, to the great importance of China in Japanese affairs and, in part, to the general recognition in Japan of the importance of her international financial and economic position. This interest has led to numerous attempts to estimate Japanese investments abroad and especially in China. The more important of these estimates are listed below. Many are referred to later.

1. The first is that of Junnosuke Inouye for 1924. This is to be found in the author's *Present Condition and Methods of Improvement of Our International Financial Relations,* published in Tokyo in 1926. His estimate of the total of Japanese foreign investments at the end of 1924 was Yen 1,811,719,000. Of this total he estimated investment in China to be Yen 1,385,800,000.

2. The second is an estimate for the year 1927 by the Japanese Ministry of Commerce and Industries. It was published in 1929 in a pamphlet in the Japanese language. The title is *Overseas Investments of the Principal Japanese Companies.* The report contains a note stating that returns are included from eighty-nine companies, that loans are excluded, and that there are no returns from companies in finance, shipping, and insurance. The total for these companies was Yen 1,036,500,000. Of this, Yen 926 million was reported as in China, Yen 760.3 million in Manchuria and Yen 165.7 in the rest of China.[45]

3. A third estimate is that of the South Manchuria Railway Company for Manchuria only. This estimate is really a series of estimates, which began with the one for 1924. This has been published by the Railway Company. The total for 1924 was Yen 1,402,034,685. The Company has issued other estimates in which the total for "loans"

[45] D. K. Lieu had access to these figures before the report was in its final form. They are given in his *Foreign Investments in China, 1929,* p. 120, Estimate B.

is always the same, Yen 171,691,196. The total for other (largely business) investments was as follows:

	Yen
1924	1,230,343,489
1926	1,335,708,268
1929	1,468,405,831

The figures for 1926 were published in the United States by the New York office of the South Manchuria Railway Company under the title *Japanese Investments and Expenditures in Manchuria*, dated February, 1929.[46]

4. There is next the estimate of the Japan-China Industrial Association for the year 1926. This estimate was originally made public in a small leaflet issued in Tokyo. It is for business investments only. This estimate appeared, with more detailed information than is to be found in the leaflet, in a work by Akira Nagano, *The Capital War of the Powers with China as the Stage*, which was published in 1928 at Tokyo by the Society for the Study of Chinese Problems. A translation of a part of this work has been made for this study by Susumu Kobe. The estimate of the Japan-China Industrial Association was Yen 1,859 million, in Manchuria Yen 1,237 million and in the rest of China Yen 522 million. This estimate was pronounced by a number of the business men and bankers with whom I talked in Japan in 1930 as the best estimate that had been made. They had not at the time seen the estimate of the Committee of the Institute of Pacific Relations.

5. Finally there is an estimate by M. Odagiri which was printed as a paper of the Japanese Council of the Institute of Pacific Relations and presented at the Kyoto Conference of the Institute. For this estimate the material of the Japan-China Industrial Association was employed and material on Japanese loans to China available at the Tokyo office of the Yokohama Specie Bank.

---

[46] The table for 1924 is to be found in Lieu's *Foreign Investments in China 1929*, p. 122, Estimate D.

As a matter of fact, the estimate of the Japan-China Industrial Association was made in close co-operation with the Bank. Odagiri's chief totals are: Loans Yen 730,477,-000, Business Investments 1,809,154,000, making a total of Yen 2,539,631,000. This total was for 1927 or 1928. This estimate by Odagiri has been given a separate place because the author had access to the materials of the Yokohama Specie Bank and because it contains his judgment as a reasonable total of Japanese loans to China. There is no Japanese student of the subject better able to speak with authority.

Population

There were in 1930 between 260,000 and 280,000 Japanese in China. They were at once the largest foreign "colony" in China and the largest group of Japanese in any one country outside of Japan.[47] The increase was from three or four thousand in 1900, to about 100,000 in 1914, to about 270,000 in 1930. The Customs figures show that the Japanese comprised no less than 70 per cent of the foreigners in China in 1930. Some modification of the Customs figures may be made on the basis of the reports of those who have collaborated in this study. But the fact stands out that the Japanese were predominant in numbers in 1930. The significance of the increase in their actual and relative numbers requires examination.

The first point to be noted is that the increase from 1914 to 1930 did not involve a fundamental change in the geographical distribution of Japanese population in China as did the increase between 1900–1914. It will be remembered that only 2 per cent of the Japanese in China were in Manchuria in 1901, 68 per cent in 1911, and about 80 per cent in 1914. In 1930 the percentage was the same as in 1914. The opening of Manchuria and its development attracted Japanese in greatly increasing numbers

[47] Of the Japanese residing outside of Japan about 34 per cent were in China.

TABLE 16

JAPANESE POPULATION IN CHINA, 1914–1930

	Japanese Committee Figures*	Chinese Customs Figures**		
		Firms	Population	Population as a Per Cent of Total Foreign Population in China
1914		955	84,948	51.5
1915	120,994	2,189	101,589	55.1
1916	141,175	1,858	104,275	56.1
1917	162,329	2,818	144,492	65.5
1918	178,347	4,483	159,950	65.4
1919	242,092	4,878	171,485	48.8
1920	239,944	4,278	153,918	47.2
1921		6,141	144,434	59.9
1922	230,030	3,940	152,848	55.6
1923	222,743	4,067	201,704	62.0
1924	226,401	4,278	198,206	61.7
1925	241,205	4,708	218,351	64.8
1926	242,103	4,446	235,339	67.8
1927	251,957	4,848	201,721	66.7
1928	261,153	8,926	239,180	68.3
1929	270,717	4,792	245,634	68.9
1930		4,633	255,686	70.6

* Including Hongkong and Macao.
** Exclusive of Hongkong and Macao. Koreans not included. Figures for firms much less reliable than for persons. Firms in Dairen not included.

during the early years. By 1914 this came to an end and since 1914 the increase in Japanese population in Manchuria has been relatively no greater than the increase in Shanghai or elsewhere in China. In 1914 one might have supposed that a migration of Japanese to China was taking place, but by 1930 it was plain that it was not.

The statement is often made that the Japanese hoped to find in Manchuria an opportunity for great numbers of settlers, that Manchuria was in the opinion of the Japanese to be the home of a new Japan which would absorb such numbers as to count in the solving of the population question. It is to be doubted that such opinions were held by responsible and well-informed men. There was in the first place the legal difficulty. The Japanese did not have the right, outside the small leased territory and

railway zone, to acquire land and engage in agriculture
or trade. The rights which they did have to engage in
mining and lumbering were not general and the limitations
were effective. Any general immigration of Japanese
to Manchuria was out of the question under the situation before 1915. In 1915, after the prolonged negotiations concerning what are commonly known as the
"Twenty-one Demands," a treaty was signed which was
to give the Japanese additional rights. The Chinese,
however, resisted the proposal that Japanese subjects
be permitted to own land. They "may," it was agreed,
"lease land necessary for erecting suitable buildings for
trade and manufacture or for prosecuting agricultural
enterprises." Japanese subjects were also to be "free to
reside and travel in South Manchuria and to engage in
business and manufacture of any kind whatsoever." [48]
These rights were granted subject to the acceptance of
Chinese taxation and police regulations. The date of
their coming into force was postponed by an exchange of
notes of the same date as the treaty. Detailed regulations
for the leasing of land have never been made public. The
comment of the Japanese committee is that "the object
for which this treaty was made has not been realized to
this day." So much for the legal obstacles to free Japanese
migration to Manchuria. Plans for the settling of a million Japanese in Manchuria or for the creation of a great
colony on the plain of the Sungari River, such as one
sees in print occasionally, required important changes in
the legal position of the Japanese. [49]

If the only obstacle, or the chief one, had been legal, it

[48] Articles 2 and 3 of the Treaty of May 25, 1915, respecting South Manchuria and Eastern Inner Mongolia. MacMurray, J. V. A., *Treaties and
Agreements*, vol. II, p. 1220.

[49] A list of "instances of China's violation of treaties and agreements"
compiled by the Research Office of the South Manchuria Railway Company (dated October 20, 1931) contains the following statement concerning
Article 2 of the treaty mentioned above: "Although request was made repeatedly by Japan to reach a detailed agreement in this connection, China
refuses to pay any attention." There are allegations concerning Article 3
also.

would, no doubt, have been removed. There were other obstacles of greater and more enduring importance. The climate of Manchuria, where the winters are severe, is a barrier. In Japan itself the northern island of Hokkaido has a greater proportion of uncultivated arable land than any other region.[50] Japanese clothing, house construction, and food are for a temperate climate.

The important obstacles, however, to Japanese migration to Manchuria are economic and social. It is difficult for the Japanese farmer to compete with the Chinese. This rests in part upon the willingness of the Chinese to live upon a lower standard of living; it rests also upon the fact that the Chinese have in their family system, as it has developed in China, a relatively adaptable as well as a strong organization. The family has some of the adaptability of individualism and the strength of unity. The Japanese in Manchuria have relied very largely upon the state, a more powerful and less adaptable organization than the family. The result is that the political control of Manchuria may be more easily taken over by the Japanese than may the cultivation of the soil and the operation of agriculture. The Chinese have the economic and social strength and the political weakness of their reliance upon the family.

One may speculate upon the situation which would arise if Japanese farmers were in Manchuria in sufficient numbers to justify on economic grounds the setting up of organizations for the scientific study of agricultural problems and the control of marketing. It might then be possible for the Japanese to maintain a higher standard of living and at the same time to compete with the Chinese. Such arrangements would probably make the railway and trading operations less profitable. It is pointless, however, to pursue this further. It is sufficient to

---

[50] Nasu, S., *Land Utilization in Japan*, Japanese Council of the Institute of Pacific Relations, Tokyo, 1929, p. 128. It is not to be supposed that the only explanation of the slow settlement of Hokkaido is its climate.

point out that competition is not merely a matter of living standards, it depends upon economic, social, and political organization as well.

That the advantage is with the Chinese is shown by the fact that Japanese farmers have not gone to the leased area in South Manchuria which has been entirely under Japanese political control since the Russo-Japanese War. There were in 1927 only 195 Japanese households in Kwantung whose main occupation was agriculture. In southern Manchuria outside of the leased area there were at the same time less than 700 such households. These figures speak for themselves.

Turning from the small Japanese leased area to the great stretches of the three Eastern provinces, one sees the outstanding fact to be that the population is overwhelmingly Chinese. The beans which are Manchuria's chief export are carried on Japanese, or Russian, railways and they are shipped on Japanese boats, but they are planted and harvested by Chinese farmers. This has been true since Newchwang was opened to foreign trade in 1864. Since 1923 the Chinese have migrated to Manchuria in greater numbers than in the past. It has been estimated that more than 5 million have become permanent residents in the last eight years.[51] The statistics of Manchurian population, which are at best careful estimates, show a Chinese population of at least 25 million in 1930. The migration to Manchuria has been Chinese and not Japanese. This situation has been accepted by Japanese political leaders and students. No Japanese to whom I talked in Japan or China expressed the opinion that Manchuria would be the future home of a great Japanese colony.[52]

[51] Young's estimate was 4 million for the years 1924–1928. The chief studies of this immigration are Young, C. W., *Chinese Colonization and the Development of Manchuria*, Honolulu, 1929, and Ho, Franklin, *Population Movement to the Northeastern Frontier in China*, Peiping, 1931. The publications of the South Manchuria Railway have dealt with the same subject.

[52] Orchard, J. E., *Japan's Economic Position*, pp. 43, 46, brings together a number of published statements by Japanese leaders. General conclu-

Having considered the possibilities of a great migration to China, I return to the actual situation. Eighty per cent of the Japanese in China were in Manchuria in 1930 (and in 1914), that is, about 215,000. Of this number no less than 199,500, 92.8 per cent, were in the Kwantung area and the South Manchuria Railway zone. In 1914 the percentage had been 95. In 1930, as in 1914, three-fourths of the Japanese in China were within territory directly under the control of their own authorities. This is sufficient demonstration, perhaps, that there was little change in the distribution of the Japanese population in China between the two dates, but there is more to be said.

For 1914 it was estimated that those in the service of railway or government with their dependents constituted about half of the Japanese in Manchuria. A recent study shows that about 40 per cent of the Japanese in Manchuria are dependent upon transportation, public service, and the professions for a living.[53] The number engaged in commerce was about 23 per cent of the total. Practically all of those engaged in transportation were with the South Manchuria Railway and a very large percentage of those in public service and the professions were with the Kwantung government. The figure for 1930 shows a somewhat greater diversification of occupation with the development of the territory. But it could still be said of the Japanese in China in 1930 that most of them were in Manchuria in territory under Japanese control and that many of them were directly dependent upon two great institutions under the Japanese government.

The Japanese population of Shanghai continued to increase. In 1930 there were more than 18,000 Japanese in the Foreign Settlement and the external roads area and 318

sions in substantial agreement are expressed by Orchard and in another recent study to which reference has already been made, Moulton, H. G., *Japan: An Economic and Financial Appraisal*, p. 394.

[53] Royama, Masamichi, "Japan's Position in Manchuria," *Problems of the Pacific, 1929*, p. 574.

in the French Concession. The Japanese in 1930 for the first time formed more than 50 per cent of the total number of foreigners in the Settlement. Taking into account the total foreign population for the whole of Shanghai, 48,806, the Japanese, 18,796, formed 38.5 per cent.

TABLE 17

JAPANESE AT SHANGHAI, 1915–1930, ACCORDING TO THE CENSUS FIGURES OF THE SHANGHAI MUNICIPAL COUNCIL COVERING THE FOREIGN SETTLE-MENT AND THE EXTERNAL ROADS AREA BUT NOT INCLUDING THE FRENCH CONCESSION *

	Population	Per Cent of the Total Foreign Population
1915	7,169	39
1920	10,215	44
1925	13,804	46
1930	18,478	51

* Feetham Report, vol. 1, pp. 51–2.

The events of the period under consideration brought a great many Japanese to Tsingtao. The former German leased area was in Japanese hands from 1914 to 1922. The Chinese Customs statistics show the number of Japanese at Tsingtao to have been 21,609 in 1921,[54] when the Tsingtao-Tsinanfu Railway was under Japanese manage-ment and there was a Japanese civil administration in the former German area. Japanese figures for 1925 put the number at 11,046. There have been larger estimates for later years, one for 1927, for example, of 13,294.[55] The number of Japanese in Tsingtao in 1930 was probably about 12,000. The situation may be compared to that in Manchuria. It was an interest in which the Japanese government was the leader which brought large numbers of Japanese to Tsingtao. Their numbers have declined somewhat in recent years. In 1930 Tsingtao was second to Shanghai in Japanese population.

Tientsin (5,168), Hankow (2,501), Amoy, and Foochow

[54] Chinese Maritime Customs, *Decennial Report, 1912–21*, vol. 2, pp. 450–1. A German census in 1913 gave the Japanese population as 316.
[55] *Japan Year Book*, 1929, p. 46.

each had a Japanese population above a thousand in 1921. In 1930 the Japanese population of Tientsin was estimated by local Japanese authorities at about 5,000 and there were more than a thousand Japanese resident at each of the following cities, outside of the Manchurian provinces: Tsinan, Hankow, Peiping, Amoy, and probably Foochow. There were few trading centers in China at which the Japanese population was not almost as great as the population of all other foreigners taken together.

For certain general statements I turn from the figures of the Chinese Customs to those which seem to me reasonable on the basis of the reports which have been made in connection with this study. I include Hongkong and Macao with China. Taking the whole area into account it may be estimated that the foreign population in 1930 was about 475,000. Of this total foreign population the Japanese constituted about 60 per cent. Of the total foreign population in China, the Japanese in Manchuria formed about 45 per cent. Of the total foreign population in Manchuria, the Japanese formed nearly 70 per cent. Taking into account the foreign population of China (and Hongkong) outside of Manchuria, it may be said that nearly half (45 per cent) was Japanese.

The difference between the situation in 1900 and 1914 lay in the opening of Manchuria. There were fundamental changes in the relative numbers and the distribution of the Japanese in China between 1900–1914. Between 1914–1930 there was a great increase in the number of Japanese residents in China but this increase was not accompanied by any significant change in distribution except, perhaps, the increase at Tsingtao. Their relative importance was greater in 1930 than in 1914. Looking at the whole period it may be said that the Japanese advanced from an unimportant place in 1900 to one, in 1914, of predominance in Manchuria and of importance everywhere else. In 1930 they held their predominant place in Manchuria and led all other foreign groups elsewhere with the one exception of Hongkong. It remains to be seen how far this predominance in numbers carried with it a predominance in trade and in investments.

Trade

During the years immediately before the World War Japan's share in the foreign trade of China increased from a sixth to a fifth of the Chinese total. The present situation is that the Japanese share is a fourth. Japan took an increasing share in a growing trade, for the trade of China more than doubled between 1914–1930.

But the history of the intervening years makes so simple a statement unsatisfactory. For the three years 1917–1919 the average share of Japan in China's trade was above a third. Japan added no less than 5 per cent of China's total trade to her share each year from 1916 to 1918. During the next three years 1919–1921 Japan's share declined by about 4 per cent of the total each year. In 1921 the Japanese share was about 25 per cent. There was an increase in 1925 and a decline after 1926 to about 25 per cent in 1930. The years 1925 and 1926 were the last years of normal trade relations between Japan and China. Further details are shown in Table 18.

When it is said that a fourth of China's trade was with Japan in 1930 it is to be borne in mind that the trade of the Kwantung leased area is included and that the trade of Hongkong is excluded from the total. Efforts have been made to include Hongkong within the territory considered. The result is an estimate of 26.4 per cent as Japan's share of the total trade of China-and-Hongkong in 1930. It is well known that goods from the United States and Canada enter China through Japan and that Chinese exports to these countries go through Japan. Not enough is known about this trade to enable a close estimate to be made.[56] It is fairly

[56] Japan's re-exports of foreign goods have been about 80 million yen annually for recent years. Chinese statistics show imports of motor cars

TABLE 18

THE IMPORTANCE OF JAPAN IN THE FOREIGN TRADE OF CHINA, 1913–1930

Chinese Customs Statistics

(Figures showing value in millions of Haikwan Taels)

	Total Trade with Japan	Per Cent of Total Foreign Trade of China	Imports from Japan	Per Cent of Total Imports into China	Exports to Japan	Per Cent of Total Exports from China
1913	184.9	19.0	119.3	20.9	65.5	16.3
1914	191.7	20.7	127.1	22.3	64.6	18.1
1915	197.9	22.7	120.2	26.5	77.7	18.5
1916	273.4	27.4	160.5	31.1	112.9	23.4
1917	327.4	32.3	221.7	40.3	105.8	22.8
1918	402.3	38.6	238.9	43.0	163.4	33.6
1919	441.9	34.6	246.9	38.2	195.0	30.9
1920	371.1	28.5	229.1	30.1	141.9	26.2
1921	382.5	25.4	210.4	23.2	172.1	28.6
1922	391.2	24.4	231.4	24.5	159.8	24.4
1923	409.5	24.4	211.0	22.9	198.5	26.4
1924	435.9	24.4	234.8	23.1	201.2	26.1
1925	486.1	28.2	299.8	31.6	186.3	24.0
1926	548.7	27.6	336.9	30.0	211.7	24.5
1927	502.6	26.0	293.8	29.0	208.8	22.7
1928	547.9	25.0	319.3	26.7	228.6	23.1
1929	579.6	25.4	323.1	25.5	256.4	25.2
1930	543.7	24.7	327.2	25.0	216.6	24.2

certain that the smallest reasonable reduction on this account will bring Japan's share of the trade down to about 25 per cent.

Turning to the Japanese figures we find, as we did for the earlier period, that the increase in the Japanese share in the trade of China was not accompanied by any increase in the share of China in the trade of Japan. The share of Japan's total trade which was with China was 22.9 per cent in 1913, 25.9 per cent in 1914, and, for recent years, 20.8 per cent in 1929 and 22.8 per cent in 1930. There was a sharp decline during the early years of the war and an equally rapid rise during the later years to

as follows: in 1929 from Japan Hk. Tls. 4.2 million, from U. S. A. 5.3 million; in 1930 from Japan Hk. Tls. 2.6 million, from the U. S. A. 2.9 million. No motor cars are manufactured in Japan. American cars are assembled there.

26.7 per cent in 1919. The difference in the figures is to be explained by the fact that Japanese trade showed a greater and more widely distributed increase. The share of Japan's trade which was with the United States, for example, increased from 22.5 per cent in 1913, when it was about equal to the Chinese figure, to 33.8 per cent in 1921, 35.9 per cent in 1929, and 31.4 per cent in 1930. The Japanese figures show that it was only during the years just before the war and in 1918 and 1919 that Chinese trade was as important to Japan as it had been in 1899 and during the first years of the century. These figures reflect so vigorous a growth in Japanese trade that Japan's large share of China's trade was a smaller share of Japanese foreign trade in general.

TABLE 19

The Importance of China (Including Kwantung and Hongkong) in the Foreign Trade of Japan, 1913–1930

Japanese Statistics

(Figures showing value in millions of Yen)

	Total Trade with China	Per Cent of Total Foreign Trade of Japan	Imports from China	Per Cent of Total Imports into Japan	Exports to China	Per Cent of Total Exports from Japan
1913	311.5	22.9	93.4	12.8	218.1	34.5
1914	308.4	25.9	90.5	15.2	217.9	36.9
1915	306.0	14.7	115.3	21.6	190.7	26.9
1916	408.4	11.7	143.6	19.0	264.8	23.5
1917	629.5	23.9	188.3	18.2	441.3	27.5
1918	922.3	25.4	383.1	23.0	539.2	27.5
1919	1,142.4	26.7	486.0	22.4	656.3	31.3
1920	1,015.2	23.7	417.2	17.9	598.0	30.7
1921	728.7	25.4	304.6	18.9	424.1	33.9
1922	788.4	22.3	317.6	16.8	470.8	28.8
1923	750.5	21.9	355.1	17.9	395.4	27.3
1924	914.4	21.5	414.4	16.9	500.0	27.7
1925	1,035.4	21.2	391.7	15.2	643.7	27.9
1926	972.3	21.9	397.9	16.7	574.4	28.1
1927	852.1	20.4	360.1	16.5	492.0	24.7
1928	925.7	22.2	386.1	17.6	539.5	27.4
1929	909.1	20.8	376.9	17.0	532.2	24.8
1930	686.9	22.8	283.6	18.3	403.3	27.4

A separate examination of imports and exports in China's trade with Japan must be made to show the significance of the changes in Japan's position. An outstanding fact is that the Japanese share in China's exports has grown more steadily and more continuously than has the Japanese share in China's imports. This is an important difference for Japan requires a steady market for her exports, especially of manufactured goods. The reasons for the difference lie in two fields.

In the first place Manchuria plays a much greater and more important part in Japanese imports than in Japanese exports and Manchurian trade with Japan has been more stable than the trade of the rest of China. In 1926, for example, 19 per cent of Japan's exports to China went to Dairen (Kwantung) and in 1929 about 26 per cent. On the other hand, about 40 per cent of her imports from China came from Dairen in 1926 and about 44 per cent in 1929. The greater stability in the Manchurian trade gives Japan the assurance of a steady supply of certain raw materials and foodstuffs; it fails to give her assurance of a steady market for her manufactured goods.

This brings out the second reason for the greater stability in imports from China than in exports to China. Each aspect of Japan's trade with China is dominated by a single commodity or group of commodities. On the import side it is beans and bean products. Since 1900 beans and bean products have formed about a third of all Japanese imports from China, and practically the whole supply comes from the Manchurian provinces. Manchurian beans and Manchurian bean cake are of outstanding importance, as has frequently been pointed out by writers upon Sino-Japanese relations. But there is more to be said. While nearly 100 per cent of the imports of beans into Japan came from Manchuria, Japan takes no more than about two-thirds of the total Manchurian export to foreign countries. Japan may, then, buy all the beans and bean cake she desires in an open market in Manchuria which supplies the whole world. Japan's increased imports from China reflect her growing need for foodstuffs, raw materials, and fertilizers.

The export side of the trade, from the Japanese point of view, is dominated by cotton manufactures of all sorts. Cotton goods and cotton yarn together have formed about a third of Japan's exports to China throughout the years since 1900. In 1913 exports of cotton manufactures were 33.9 per cent of Japanese exports to China and 11.7 per cent of the total exports of Japan. In 1926 the percentages were 45 and 12.6 and in 1929 they were 37.4 and 9.3. The importance of cotton goods is quite obvious. A significant change in the trade is shown in the figures of Table 20. Yarn is one-seventh as important today as it was in 1913 and tissues about six times as im-

TABLE 20

EXPORTS OF COTTON MANUFACTURES, INCLUDING YARN, FROM JAPAN TO CHINA INCLUDING HONGKONG, SHOWING EXPORTS TO KWANTUNG AND THE REST OF CHINA

(Figures in thousands of Yen)

		To China	To Kwantung	Per Cent	Rest of China	Per Cent
1913	Yarn	69,301	3,458		65,843	
	Tissues	29,217	9,109		20,108	
		98,518	12,567	12.8	85,951	87.2
1918	Yarn	115,618	5,779		109,839	
	Tissues	112,477	20,823		91,654	
		228,095	26,602	11.6	201.493	88.4
1926	Yarn	34,988	1,190		33,798	
	Tissues	220,842	16,042		204,800	
		255,830	17,232	6.7	238,598	93.3
1929	Yarn	9,453	682		8,771	
	Tissues	186,259	15,358		170,901	
		195,712	16,040	8.2	179,672	91.8

portant. These figures reflect the industrial development
of Japan and of China, and the success of the Japanese
in competition with the British in the piece-goods market
of China. The development of the Chinese industry is
in part due to the increase in Japanese-owned mills within
the country.

Japan's chief import from China comes wholly from
Manchuria, as has been pointed out. Her chief export to
China goes very largely, not to Manchuria, but to the
rest of China. The figures for Kwantung may be accepted
as indicating the situation fairly well. Over the period since
1913 we find that the percentage of cotton goods and
yarn sent from Japan to Kwantung has declined. The
rest of China took 87.2 per cent of these Japanese goods
in 1913 and no less than 93.3 per cent in 1926. Manchuria
is much less important than the rest of China, and this
importance was declining until the year 1926, that is,
until the last year of normal trade before the series of
boycotts which began in 1927.

The difference in rate of growth is to be observed. Japanese exports of cotton manufactures to the rest of China
were three times as great in 1926 as in 1913; to Kwantung the increase was only from 12.5 to 17 million yen.[57]
The decline in the export of yarn was at about the same
rate for Manchuria and the rest of China. The significant fact is that Japanese exports of cotton tissues to
Kwantung failed to increase much between 1913–1930.
It is, of course, true that Japanese piece goods reach
Manchuria through other ports (chiefly Antung) and
that a small part of the import into Tientsin is for the
Manchurian market, but the figures given indicate the
fact, borne out by the Chinese statistics, that the great

[57] It is to be borne in mind that all imports into China from Japan, according to Chinese statistics, were 2.8 times as great in 1926 as in 1913,
and that imports into Manchuria from Japan were almost 5 times as great.
The exact figure is 4.8, see I. D. and A. P., *The Foreign Trade of Manchuria*, Manchurian Monitor, 1931, no. 5, p. 32 ff. Harbin, 1931. (In
Russian.)

increase in the consumption of Japanese piece goods in China has been elsewhere in China and not in Manchuria.

This is to be explained in part by increased imports into Manchuria of cotton goods manufactured in Shanghai, Tsingtao, and Tientsin. About a third of the import into Dairen comes from within China and the fraction is even larger for Newchwang.[58] The increase in the output of Manchurian mills is to be considered also. In addition there is reason to believe that the Japanese-owned mills of Central China have sent a larger part of their output to Manchuria since 1927. Whatever may be the explanation, the fact remains that China, outside of Manchuria, is the great market for Japan's cotton goods. The relative stability of political conditions in Manchuria, until September, 1931, did not, for this reason, have any great effect upon the import of cotton textiles.

There are further reasons for the fluctuations in imports into China from Japan. The fact that British goods have only recently been displaced in the Chinese market by Japanese goods means that an alternative source of supply is at hand in England and indicates that a rapid change may be rapidly reversed. Moreover, cotton piece goods are a finished product and do not enter into industrial processes difficult to change. They are, therefore, more easily boycotted than most goods. From the 'seventies of the last century cotton goods have been a large factor in the fluctuations of imports into China. They are sensitive to changes in the gold price of silver and in general economic conditions in China.[59] There is the further fact that cotton milling is developing in China. Taken together these considerations serve to explain the fluctuations in imports of cotton goods and so, in general, imports into China from Japan. They show the preca-

[58] For comments on the increasing use of Chinese and of Manchurian piece goods, see the *Report on the Foreign Trade of China* of the Chinese Customs for 1928, pp. 5–6.

[59] Remer, C. F., *The Foreign Trade of China*, pp. 153, 196.

riousness of Japanese dependence upon the Chinese market
for cotton goods.

The contrast between bean products and cotton goods,
between Japan's chief import from and her chief export
to China, between a raw material from Manchuria and a
finished product for sale in the Yangtze valley throws
light upon the economic and political policy of Japan in
China.

Japanese imports from China include other important
raw materials.   In recent years China has exported to
Japan raw cotton to the value of 40 or 50 million yen,
6 per cent of Japan's total raw cotton import in 1929.
She has also sent to Japan other vegetable fibers, such as
ramie, to the value of an additional 8 or 10 million yen.
None of these come from Manchuria.

Chinese iron ore and pig iron are seen to be of minor
importance to Japan when the total Japanese consumption is considered.   Variations in the importance of China
may be noted.   Imports from China played a part of some
significance in the early iron and steel industry of Japan.
During the war Japan's dependence on China became
greater.   In 1918, for example, ore to the value of Yen
9.6 million (99 per cent of the total import from foreign
countries) and iron and steel in crude forms to the value
of Yen 50.2 million (78 per cent of the total import) came
from China.   In 1913 none of these products had come
from Manchuria, but 13 per cent of the crude iron and
steel was imported from Kwantung in 1918.[60]   Since the
war Japan has developed other sources of these products.
This is due to the failure of Japanese interests to secure
the expected results from investments in China and to the
availability of cheaper supplies of iron ore in the Malay
States and of pig iron in India.[61]

[60] The figures of the war period are brought together in *The Foreign Trade
of Japan,* U. S. Tariff Commission, Washington, 1922, pp. 157–67.   Of the
fabricated iron and steel, 95 per cent came from the United States in 1918.
The chief source before the war was Europe.
[61] Orchard, J. E., *Japan's Economic Position,* pp. 332–7, gives an ac-

This is clearly shown in the trade statistics. In 1929 and 1930 Japan imported iron ore and pig iron to the value of Yen 54.3 million and Yen 39.8 million. About one-tenth of the iron ore and over one-third of the pig iron came from China. The iron ore was from the Yangtze valley and the pig iron largely from Manchuria where Japanese interests own plants at Anshan and Penhsihu. At the same time Japan's import of pig iron from India was greater than her import from China, twice as great in 1929. Japan, it may be said, has searched the Far East for iron ore and crude iron. Her early dependence was upon China. As her needs have grown she has gone elsewhere for her supplies.

Japan is both an importer and an exporter of coal. In 1913 her exports were about five times as great as her imports. During the war imports increased and in 1927 for the first time Japan became a net importer of coal. She has remained a net importer. In 1930 Japan sent to China coal to the value of Yen 12.5 million (over half her export) and imported from China coal to the value of Yen 26.6 million (over three-fourths of her import). The explanation lies in the fact that her imports come from Manchuria and her exports go to Shanghai and the southern ports of China.

Wool is the only other major import into Japan in which China takes any share and this share is so small as not to be worth considering. Other imports into Japan from China include a wide variety of raw materials and food products: timber, wild raw silk, bristles, hides, peanuts, and fresh eggs.

Among the exports from China in recent years the Chinese Customs authorities have given a special place to Chinese factory products. The products of the textile industry are of first importance among these Chinese exports and it is interesting to observe that cotton yarn has been moving from China to Japan in small but in-

count of the increasing imports of iron ore from the Bukit Medan Mine in the Malay States and from other Far Eastern countries.

creasing amounts in recent years, though the total value was no more than about Yen 5 million in 1929.

The goods that move from Japan to China, other than cotton manufactures, are of the widest variety. They include refined sugar to the value of Yen 25.2 million in 1930. Two-thirds of China's imports of this commodity came from Japan. They include also "aquatic products," chiefly sea-food, to the value of about Yen 10 million. Among the manufactures are to be found paper, electrical materials, galvanized iron sheets, clothing, rubber boots and shoes, chemicals, medical preparations, cement, and different sorts of machinery.

In short, Japan exports to China the products of her textile industry and a great variety of manufactured goods. These things are sold throughout China. Japan imports from China beans, bean products, and a wide variety of raw materials and food products. As a source of raw materials Manchuria counts for more than she does as a market for finished goods. Japanese exports to China fluctuate more than do Japanese imports from China. Japan may provide an example of a general proposition, that dependence upon textile exports is precarious. Efforts on the part of Japan to secure from China any great share of her necessary supplies of iron ore and pig iron have not met with much success, but both coal and iron now come more largely from Manchuria than in the past. Japan has become of greater importance in the trade of China since 1913; China, on the other hand, is no more important in the trade of Japan than in 1913 or, for that matter, in 1900.

Observing the value of the goods moving in both directions between Japan and China, we find that Japanese exports to China increased more rapidly between 1900–1914, and that Chinese exports to Japan increased more rapidly between 1914–1926. It is to be borne in mind that China is the chief market for Japan's textile products and for a variety of other manufactured goods.

TABLE 21

JAPANESE TRADE WITH THE UNITED STATES, INDIA, AND CHINA, 1913–1930

	Millions of Yen			Relatives (1913 = 100)		
	1913	1926	1930	1913	1926	1930
United States						
Imports from U. S.	122.4	680.2	442.9	100	556	362
Exports to U. S.	184.4	860.9	506.1	100	467	274
Total	306.8	1,541.1	949.0	100	502	309
India						
Imports from India	173.2	391.1	180.4	100	226	104
Exports to India	29.9	156.0	129.3	100	522	432
Total	303.1	547.1	309.7	100	181	192
China						
Imports from China	93.4	397.8	283.6	100	426	304
Exports to China	218.1	574.4	403.3	100	263	185
Total	311.5	972.2	686.9	100	312	221

Certain international comparisons may be made. The leading countries in the trade of Japan are the United States, China, and India. Japanese trade with the United States increased more rapidly between 1913–1930 than did Japanese trade with China. The importance to Japan of her exports has been pointed out, and it is to be observed that Japanese exports to both the United States and India increased more rapidly between 1913–1930 than did Japanese exports to China. China and India are the chief markets for Japanese cotton textiles. Since 1913 Japan has increased her export of cotton goods to India more rapidly than to China. Japan imports more pig iron from India than she does from China and this trade has grown rapidly. It is true that Japanese trade with China has increased greatly, but it has not increased as rapidly as has the total trade of Japan. Chinese trade throughout the last hundred years has disappointed many who hoped great things from its growth. Since the war Japan has continued to hold first place in the trade of China but many aspects of her Chinese trade were unsatisfactory in 1930.

Shipping

The Japanese share in shipping in Chinese waters has shown a steady and fairly continuous growth since 1900. The most general figures are those of the Chinese Customs which show the total tonnage in "the carrying trade from and to foreign countries and between the open ports" of China. These figures are properly considered in relation to the foreign trade of China. The more detailed information is dealt with in connection with investments in the following pages. Taking into account the whole of the shipping, both Chinese and foreign, which came under the view of the Chinese Customs we find the Japanese percentage to have been 25 per cent in 1913, 31 per cent in 1918, and 29 per cent in 1930. During the early years of the period under consideration the tonnage of Japanese and Chinese shipping was about equal, but in recent years Japanese tonnage has been greater. Ships under the British flag have been first throughout the whole period for which information is available. In 1930, however, Japanese tonnage in this combined foreign and domestic trade was more nearly equal to British tonnage than it has been at any time in the past except for a brief period during the World War. The figure of 29 per cent may be taken to represent the Japanese share in the modern shipping in the whole of China's trade.

Direct Business Investments, 1930

The direct business investments of the Japanese in China are estimated to have been Yen 1,748 million at the end of 1930. This may be accepted as showing the situation when Japanese troops advanced into Manchuria in the autumn of 1931 from the area under Japanese control. Direct investments, it will be remembered, are the business holdings in China of Japanese corporations

or Japanese individuals from which an income is derived
or expected. These investments consist of property under
the control and management of Japanese, and they include
practically the whole of such property.

It is believed that the significant facts will be most
clearly established by dealing first with the situation as it
was in 1930. An attempt will be made to state the outstanding generalizations briefly. This is followed by a
more detailed account in which special attention is given
to the differences between the situation in 1914 and in
1930. The observer, looking at 1930, sees things which
cannot be understood without a glance at the developments and changes of the past fifteen years.

The first of the outstanding generalizations is that
direct business investments were about three-fourths
(76.9 per cent) of the total Japanese investments in China
in 1930. In other words, property under the legal control
and the management of the Japanese in China constituted
a very large fraction of the Japanese total.

A second fact of outstanding importance is the proportion of Japanese direct investments which were in Manchuria. The distribution of the total direct investment of
Yen 1,748 million is found to have been as follows:

	Yen	Per Cent
In Manchuria	1,100.4 million	62.9
In the rest of China	647.8 million	37.1

Over 60 per cent of the direct business investments were
in Manchuria at the end of 1930.

A third point is the great importance of the South
Manchuria Railway Company. The total business holdings of the railway company itself were found to be
Yen 637.8 million. To this must be added the investments of the subsidiaries of the railway company and the
holdings of the company in the corporations which it
has brought into existence. This sum is at least Yen

56 million.[62] Taking the two together we see that in 1930 more than 60 per cent of the Japanese direct investments in Manchuria were those of the South Manchuria Railway Company. This one company's holdings constituted about 40 per cent of all Japanese business investments in the whole of China.

It is to be pointed out, in the next place, that one-half of the shares of the South Manchuria Railway Company are the property of the Japanese government. The Japanese government was the direct owner of a controlling interest in this company which, in turn, held two-fifths of the direct business investments of the Japanese.

The last of these general statements concerns the importance of Shanghai. Direct investments in China, outside of Manchuria, were found to be Yen 647.8 million. Of this total Yen 430.1 million, or two-thirds, were in Shanghai. Of the total direct investments in the whole of China, about one-fourth (24.6 per cent) was in Shanghai.

Such is the general picture revealed by the investigation of 1930. Direct investments were of overwhelming importance; a large part of these investments were in Manchuria; the South Manchuria Railway Company alone held more than half of the investments in Manchuria which were thus under the direct control of the Japanese government; and about one-fourth of the investments were in Shanghai.

Direct Investments in 1914 and 1930

Direct investments were found to be Yen 1,748 million in 1931 and this sum was 76.9 per cent of Japanese investments of all sorts. In 1914 they were Yen 385 million, almost 98 per cent of the total. In 1900 direct investments were 100 per cent of the total. The outstanding impor-

[62] The general balance sheet of the Company, March 31, 1931, reports Yen 88 million as "stocks of subsidiary companies and other Bonds, Stocks, etc." A list of "collateral companies," 54 in all, is given by Royama in *Problems of the Pacific, 1929*, pp. 571–2. The South Manchuria Railway Company investment in these companies is stated to be Yen 52.8 million.

tance of this form of investment is a characteristic of
the Chinese situation and Japanese investments do not
differ in this respect from the investments of other nationals. It is to be noted, however, that the relative importance of this form declined considerably between
1914–1931.

The direct investments of the Japanese were about
four and a half times as great in 1931 as they had been
in 1914. In only one other case, that of the Americans,
was the rate of increase great enough to suggest comparison and American business investments were somewhat
less than four times as great in 1930 as in 1914.

If we turn to other indexes of the economic position
of Japan in China for comparison, we find that direct
business investments increased at a more rapid rate than
did Japanese trade with China, Japanese shipping in
Chinese waters, or Japanese population in China. At
the same time it is to be observed that the Japanese, in
the field of direct investments, did not hold a position of
such outstanding importance as in foreign trade or in
the total foreign population in China. The figures are
shown in Table 22 below. The Japanese took first place
in the foreign population in China shortly after the opening of Manchuria in 1907. They took first place in the
foreign trade of China during the World War. In the
field of business investments they had second place in
1931.

Direct Investments in Manchuria and Shanghai

The importance of Manchuria in this field needs no
further emphasis; 63 per cent of the direct investments
were in Manchuria in 1931. There is more to be said
about this matter, however. Significant facts are brought
out by a more detailed examination of the geographical
distribution of the direct investments. Consider, first,
the differences between 1914–1931. In 1914 the percen-

tage of direct investments in Manchuria was 68.9; in
1931 it was 62.9. The increase in these investments outside of Manchuria was especially great in Shanghai. The
accompanying table shows that investments in Manchuria were about four times as great at the later date
and the investments in Shanghai no less than seven times.

TABLE 22

DIRECT INVESTMENTS 1914 AND 1930 IN MILLIONS OF YEN WITH
RELATIVES

	1914		1930	
In Manchuria	265.2	100	1,100.4	415
In the rest of China	119.8	100	647.8	541
In Shanghai	60.0	100	430.1	717

We may compare the geographical distribution of
Japanese population with that of Japanese direct investments. Eighty per cent of the Japanese population in
China was in Manchuria in 1914 and 68.9 per cent of the
direct investment. In 1930 the percentage of the population was the same, but the percentage of the investment
had fallen from 68.9 to 62.9. This may be more clearly
stated by putting it in terms of China outside of Manchuria, where 20 per cent of the Japanese population was
found in 1914 and in 1930, and where 31.1 per cent of the
investment was found in 1914 and 37.1 per cent in 1930.
The contrast is sharper if Shanghai is compared with
Manchuria. About 7 per cent of the Japanese population in China was at Shanghai in 1914 and in 1930; but
the percentage of Japan's total business investment which
was at Shanghai increased from 7.8 per cent to 24.6 per
cent. The Japanese population in Manchuria represented
in 1930 a per capita investment of Yen 5,100; the Japanese in Shanghai represented a per capita investment of
Yen 23,000. Between 1914–1930 the importance of Manchuria in the field of population remained the same, but
the importance of Manchuria as a field for Japanese
business investments declined. With the development

of Shanghai as an industrial and trading center there were increased opportunities for Japanese capital and for Japanese management. The laborers were, at all times, the Chinese. In Manchuria, on the other hand, economic development failed to maintain the rate set during the early years. The Japanese population of Manchuria consisted, in a fairly large measure, of employees and of those engaged in administrative activities. In Shanghai the Japanese were those concerned with trade, banking, and the management of cotton mills and other manufacturing plants. It may be repeated that the overwhelming importance of Manchuria must not be permitted to obscure the fact that Japanese business investments in Shanghai grew more rapidly between 1914–1931 than did Japanese investments in Manchuria.

The South Manchuria Railway Company's Investments

The South Manchuria Railway Company was in 1914 the owner of business property valued at Yen 210 million, about 55 per cent of Japanese direct investments in China, and nearly 80 per cent of such investments in Manchuria. The comparable figures for 1931 have been given. They show that the railway company was the owner of business property and paid-up interest in other companies in Manchuria to the value of at least Yen 690.8 million. This sum represents 39.5 per cent of the direct investments of the Japanese in China and 63 per cent of the investment in Manchuria. This seems to indicate a substantial decline in the relative importance of the company.

The decline was real in so far as it resulted from the increase in Japanese investments in Shanghai and elsewhere in China. A smaller percentage of Japanese investments in the whole of China were under the control of the South Manchuria Railway Company. How far there was a real decline in the proportion of business investments under the railway company's control in Manchuria is not easily determined. If there was a decline at all it was certainly not as great as the drop from 80 to 63 per cent indicates. The change was in the form of ownership and control rather than in the substance.

In 1914 the South Manchuria Railway Company owned, in addition to its railway and repair shops, a great variety of business property. Many forms of such property were no longer carried on its books in 1931. In 1914 the company owned ships, electric light and power plants, gas works, and hotels to the value of Yen 13.3 million; in 1931 none of these items appear. The shipping is now owned by the Dairen Steamship Company, organized in 1915, with a capital of Yen 25 million, over half of which is owned by the South Manchuria Railway Company. The hotels are now owned by the South Manchuria Hotel Company organized in 1928, with a paid-up capital of Yen 3.9 million held by the railway company, which thus owns a controlling interest. The electric light and power plants are now owned by the South Manchuria Electric Company with a capital of Yen 25 million. Of this, Yen 22 million is paid up and the whole of the paid-up capital is owned by the railway company. The gas plants are now owned by the South Manchuria Gas Company, organized in 1925 with a capital of Yen 10 million, of which 9.3 million was paid up. The whole of the paid-up capital was held by the railway company.[63]

In some of these cases it is known that the property and equipment of the railway company was turned over to the new corporation in exchange for paid-up capital stock to the value of the property as it had been carried on the books of the railway company. It is safe to assume that this was the general practice wherever extensive capital equipment was involved. In these cases it is plain that the only change has been in the form of owner-

[63] *Report on Progress in Manchuria, 1907–1928*, pp. 97, 98, 99. *Second Report on Progress in Manchuria to 1930*, p. 132.

ship. A group of subsidiary corporations, owned by the parent company, has been set up.

In addition to such corporations as have been mentioned there is a large number of others in which the South Manchuria Railway Company owns an interest which varies from 100 per cent to less than 1 per cent. A list of over fifty such corporations is provided by Royama.[64] Most of them appear under the heading "assisted companies" which indicates clearly enough the relation to the railway company. Among the companies in which the railway company owns either a half interest or more, are the following:

Dairen Ceramic Work Company
Mukden Exchange Trust Company
Ssupingkai Electric Company
Liao Yang Electric Company
Tiehling Electric Company
Yingkow Water and Electric Company
Manchuria Dock Company
Fuku Shoka Industrial Company
South Manchuria Mining Company
Manchuria Daily News Company

The total paid-up capital in the hands of the South Manchuria Railway Company for the subsidiaries and the "assisted" companies comes to a total of Yen 56.6 million and the total capitalization of these companies to Yen 146.3 million. In addition, the railway company has made investments which it reports at about Yen 50 million in railways which are closely related to the South Manchuria, though they were in the hands of the Chinese government until September, 1931. Taking all of these facts into account it may be estimated that the effective control of the South Manchuria Railway Company over Japanese business investments in Manchuria represented as great a percentage of the total of such investments at the end of 1930 as it did in 1914.

[64] *Problems of the Pacific, 1929*, pp. 571-2.

Financial History of the South Manchuria Railway Company

The financial history of the company goes back to its formation by the Imperial Ordinance in 1906.[65] The authorized capital of the company was made Yen 200 million. One-half of the shares were given to the Japanese government in exchange for the railway lines and other property which the government turned over to the company. The property thus turned over was set down in the books of the company at a value of Yen 92.8 million.[66] This property is best regarded as having been won by the Japanese in the war. As a matter of fact the expenditures of the Japanese government upon Manchurian railways during the war may have reached Yen 80 million but this expenditure ought to be charged to the prosecution of the war. If this is done it may be said that the Japanese government turned over to the company railway lines and equipment which had been paid for by the Russians from funds borrowed in France.[67]

The other Yen 100 million in shares were issued under the condition that they might be subscribed for by the Chinese government or by Chinese and Japanese citizens. The Chinese government took none of these shares. Chinese citizens have never owned any of the shares of the company with the exception, we are told by one writer, of "a few shares held by Chinese employees." [68] The first offer of any of these shares to the Japanese public was made shortly after the organization of the company. Shares to the value of Yen 20 million were subscribed for, of which only Yen 2 million was called in.

[65] MacMurray, J. V. A., *Treaties and Agreements*, vol. I, pp. 557–8. The articles of incorporation are to be found on pp. 559–63.

[66] I am informed that an independent appraisal of the value of the property was made.

[67] The Japanese took over 515 miles out of a total of 1,596 miles of railway. The Russian expenditure on the portion turned over is estimated to have been 81 million rubles, about Yen 81 million. The section turned over had been, in part, destroyed by the Russians for military reasons.

[68] Kinney, H. W., *Manchuria Today*, Dairen, 1930, p. 37.

It is fairly certain that the total investment of the Japanese public amounted to Yen 24 million by the end of 1914.

It is plain that the funds required for the rehabilitation of the railway came neither from the Chinese nor the Japanese. The company secured these funds by borrowing in London. Debentures were offered in London in 1907, 1908, and 1911 to the amount of £14 million. Allowing for refunding, there were outstanding in 1914 £12 million.[69] The obligation involved was about Yen 120 million and the actual net receipts from the loans Yen 108,640,241.[70] By the end of 1914, then, the company had received new funds to the amount of about Yen 134 million. The new capital expenditure of the company to March 31, 1914, was Yen 138.6 million. The South Manchuria Railway Company at the end of 1914 held business investments in China to the amount of Yen 210 million. The total investment of Japanese funds in this property was Yen 24 million.

The annual dividend paid to the Japanese government by the South Manchuria Railway Company was Yen 2.5 million for the year ending March 31, 1914. The shareholders, other than the government, received 6 per cent to the year 1912. By 1914 the rate was 8 per cent. We may, therefore, estimate the amount paid as dividends to Japanese shareholders for 1914 at Yen 1.9 million. The annual payment to the holders of the debentures issued in England was about Yen 5.7 million.

Between 1914–1930 important changes took place in the finances of the company. In the first place the debentures issued in England were taken over by the Japanese government in 1920. In exchange for the taking over of this obligation the government received additional shares in the company to the amount of Yen 120 million.[71] In

[69] £6 million in 5% bonds issued at 97, and £6 million in 4½% bonds issued at 98.
[70] *South Manchuria Railway, Its Origin and Development,* June, 1917, p. 12.
[71] The government was credited with Yen 117,156,000 as paid up, leaving

1931, then, the Japanese government held capital stock to the value of Yen 220 million. The share of the government was still one-half, since the total capitalization is now, or was in 1931, Yen 440 million.

By 1914, as has been said above, the Japanese public had paid up Yen 24 million on a total issue of shares to the amount of Yen 40 million. By March, 1920, the Japanese public held Yen 60 million in shares which had been fully paid up. In 1920 an additional Yen 120 million was brought into existence. By March 31, 1931, the total amount paid up on the new shares and on the old was Yen 170 million, leaving Yen 50 million uncalled. The situation in 1931 was that the Japanese government held shares to the amount of Yen 220 million. For these it had turned over the original property and had assumed the obligation on the early debenture issues in London. The Japanese public held shares to the nominal amount of Yen 220 million of which Yen 170 million had actually been paid up.

There were in existence, also, bonds to the amount of about Yen 40 million (Yen 39,052,000) as the result of new borrowings in London, and bonds to the amount of Yen 257.5 million issued and held in Japan. There are, in addition, reserves of Yen 188.6 million which have been built up out of the profits of the company.

The total investment in the South Manchuria Railway in 1931 represented a larger proportion of funds actually remitted from Japan than in 1914. The items dealt with above may be grouped into those which are known not to have involved outpayments and those which have, in all probability, involved such payments. The original shares of the Japanese government and the borrowings in London make a total of about Yen 260 million which has not involved the transfer of funds from Japan. The long-term investment, represented by reserves, of Yen

Yen 2,844,000 unpaid. *Second Report on Progress in Manchuria to 1930*, p. 102.

188.6 million may be said with some assurance to consist almost entirely of reinvested profits. On the other hand, outpayments from Japan were involved in the case of the paid-up capital stock held by the Japanese public and of the bonds issued in Japan, a total of Yen 444.7 million.

The problem of calculating the actual outpayments from Japan on account of the South Manchuria Railway Company was considered at a conference with the manager of the Tokyo office of the company in August, 1930. It was the estimate of the manager that the total so remitted had been about Yen 440 million since the company commenced operations in April, 1907. In the case of this company, which represents no less than 40 per cent of Japanese business investments in China, we may be fairly certain that business holdings which have been estimated at Yen 690.8 million, property devoted to administrative and cultural purposes estimated at Yen 104.5 million, and loans to the Chinese government of Yen 50.7 million, a total, that is, of Yen 846 million has required a remittance from Japan of Yen 440 or 450 million.

The manager of the Tokyo office of the company put the matter thus. The assets of the company were, he said, about one billion yen. About one-half had been actually remitted from Japan; about one-quarter was accounted for by the borrowings in London and the original property received from the Japanese government; and about one-quarter represented reserves which had been set aside from the profits and other smaller items.

The annual remittances to Japan consist, in the first place, of dividends paid to the Japanese government. These were at the rate of 5.3 per cent for the years ending March 31, 1929 and 1930, and 4.3 per cent for 1931. The actual amount was Yen 11,509,268 for the earlier years and 9,337,708 for 1931. It is to be borne in mind that the government must, in its turn, meet a charge of about Yen 5.7 million on the sterling debentures it has taken over.[72]   In the second place there is the dividend on the stock held by the public, 11 per cent in 1929 and 1930, and 8 per cent in 1931.   The actual amount was Yen 18.7 million for the earlier years and Yen 13.6 million for 1931.   The interest on the bonds held in Japan was about Yen 12.5 million a year for the past three years and about Yen 2 million on the bonds held in Great Britain.   This means that remittances from China came to a total of Yen 44.7 million for the earlier years and Yen 37.4 million for 1931, and that the remittances retained in Japan were Yen 37 million and Yen 29.7 million.

The remittance to Japan was considerably less in 1931 than in the earlier years.   This is to be accounted for chiefly as the result of the decline in railway revenues.   The net revenue from the railway was Yen 82 million in 1930 and Yen 61 million in 1931.   From the mining operations it was Yen 18 million in 1929, Yen 15.8 million in 1930, and Yen 4.6 million in 1931.   The iron works at Anshan showed a net income (Yen 1.6 million) for the first time in 1929; it was slightly smaller in 1930 and for 1931 there was practically no net income.   The net profit of the whole enterprise was reported as Yen 45.5 million in 1929 and Yen 42.5 million in 1930; by 1931 it had declined to Yen 21.7 million.

The world-wide depression in 1931 accounts for much of this decline.   The Manchurian exports are raw materials and foodstuffs, the products of agriculture, and the prices of such products dropped further than did the prices of industrial products.   In part the decline was due to the fall in the gold price of silver in 1930 and 1931.   The South Manchuria Railway owns property which it carries on its books at a value in a gold currency which was at about mint par in 1930.   This property is in a silver using country and it competes with railways owned by the Chinese

---

[72] The whole amount of Yen 117,156,000 was reported as outstanding in 1931. *Financial and Economic Annual of Japan, 1931,* p. 59.

government whose rates are in silver.   This competition
was of such growing importance that the South Manchuria Railway Company announced rates in silver currency in 1931.[73] There is little doubt that the losses which
resulted from the silver rates increased the Japanese dis-
satisfaction with the course of recent events in Manchuria.

The South Manchuria Railway Company's financial
organization may be described thus.   The Japanese government holds the common stock and the control; the
Japanese public holds shares which are in effect preferred
stock upon which a return of 6 per cent is guaranteed.[74]
Bonds are held in Japan and in Great Britain.   The
Japanese had actually remitted no more than Yen 24
million from Japan for the building up of the enterprise
by 1914, but by 1931 the Japanese remittance was about
Yen 440 million.   The enterprise has been a fair financial
success.   If its success had been great, the Japanese government would hardly have taken over fixed-interest-
bearing obligations in exchange for common stock.   The
railway has always been the chief source of net revenue.
The mines have paid.   The iron works have not, and there
has been a considerable net expenditure for local administration.   The company suffered a considerable reduction in net revenue for the year ending in March, 1931,
due in part to the fact that it is a property whose value
is carried in a gold currency and whose earnings are in
a silver using country.

Japan has been a borrowing country during most of
her recent history.   How, one may ask, does a borrowing
country succeed in making investments abroad on the
scale required for such an enterprise as the South Manchuria Railway?   The answer is to be found in the analysis

[73] This announcement reported in the newspapers of China in June,
1931, has recently been confirmed by a personal letter from the New York
office of the railway.

[74] "The majority of shares, other than those held by the government are
in the hands of a small number of Japanese capitalists." Royama, Masamichi, *Problems of the Pacific, 1929*, p. 567.

which has been made of the situation in 1914. The Japanese government at that time had a controlling interest in a corporation which held property paid for almost entirely by British and French funds. By 1931 the actual investment of the Japanese was much greater but a considerable fraction of the capital equipment had now been purchased out of reinvested profits of the enterprise. The company had, by 1931, brought into existence a considerable number of subsidiary corporations whose capital consisted of equipment turned over by the South Manchuria. The South Manchuria Railway Company's financial history shows it to have been, until after the World War, a means of exporting from Japan to China entrepreneurial ability which required capital rather than a means of exporting funds seeking investment.

The South Manchuria Railway Company and the Japanese Government

In the political situation which has existed in Manchuria the entrepreneurial ability has been obliged to meet political as well as economic problems. The chief stockholder in the enterprise has always been the Japanese government. It was able in the early and critical years to guarantee the political conditions which made financial success highly probable and created the basis for borrowing outside of Japan.

Japanese writers have, at times, affected to ignore this aspect. The writer of the *Economic History of Manchuria* [75] spends several pages in an attempt to demonstrate that the South Manchuria Railway Company is purely an economic enterprise. This is hardly a tenable position in view of the fact that the Japanese government owns a controlling interest in the company, that its principal officers are appointed by the Japanese government, that it has administrative powers including the power to collect taxes within the railway zone and to carry on local gov-

[75] Published by the Bank of Chosen, Seoul, 1920, pp. 91-2.

ernment in the urban areas. Its administrative and
political powers have at times brought about conflict
with the other Japanese political authorities with jurisdiction in all or part of the same area, the other authorities being the government of the Kwantung leased area
and the Japanese consular authorities in southern Manchuria.[76] In fact, an important problem which the Japanese government has faced throughout the history of its
interest in Manchuria has been that of making harmonious
use of its various means of giving effect to its political
and economic policy.

For a time (1914–1919) the presidency of the South
Manchuria Railway Company and the governor-general-
ship of Kwantung were held by the same person. When it
is remembered that, until 1919 the governor-general was a
military officer of high rank, it will be seen that matters
were under a unified supervision. Since 1914 the governor
of the leased area has been a civil official, the chief military
official has been the commander of the Kwantung Garrison, and the chief consular official, namely, the Japanese
consul-general at Mukden, has been given an appointment
as "secretary" in the Kwantung government. The presidency of the South Manchuria Railway has usually not
been the same official as the governor but the governor
has at all times had power to "supervise" the business
of the South Manchuria Railway Company, and the
commander of the Kwantung Garrison has had control
of the railway guards who have been soldiers.[77]

It is plain from this brief statement that the Japanese
government has faced legal difficulties in working out a
satisfactory arrangement for the administrative control of

[76] "This triple form of government has evoked much criticism as hinder-
ing Japanese activity in Manchuria as a whole. They were often divided
among themselves when united action would have produced a better
result." *Economic History of Manchuria*, p. 66.

[77] A clear and concise account of the history of the administrative or-
ganization is to be found in Young, C. W., *The International Relations of
Manchuria*, pp. 61–7, 148–50. See also Royama, M., "Japan's Position in
Manchuria," *Problems of the Pacific, 1929*, pp. 540–50.

Japanese interests in southern Manchuria. To give effect to Japanese policy by means within the treaties has been increasingly difficult. The point to be emphasized is that the South Manchuria Railway Company has been dealt with, at all times, by the Japanese government, as one of the means of giving effect to its policy in Manchuria. It has given attention to the economic field but it has not been regarded as an independent business corporation pursuing its own business advantage. Japanese policy has called for a division of labor and certain tasks have been assigned to the South Manchuria Railway Company. It is important for the student of these matters in America or western Europe to see that the railway company has at once an independent legal existence and at the same time a complete subordination to the policies of the Japanese government.

The functions of the railway company were diverse and varied from the beginning. Since 1925 the company has tended to discharge these functions, not directly, but by setting up subsidiary and affiliated companies. The direct field of its activities is narrower today than it was in 1914, but its effective influence is probably wider. "It is," says Royama, "not only the controlling body of a whole chain of industrial enterprises, but is also the central financial institution in the territory." [78]

Japanese business men with whom I talked in Shanghai expressed the opinion that the power of the South Manchuria Railway Company tended to stifle individual initiative in Manchuria. The same criticism, I am assured, has been expressed from time to time in Japan and it may, indeed, be directed against the whole plan of direct encouragement of business enterprises by the Japanese government. Without raising the question as to the wisdom of the policy, one may say that the policy or an important part of the policy of the Japanese government has been the economic development of Manchuria under

[78] *Problems of the Pacific, 1929,* p. 570.

Japanese control. This policy had to be worked out by the government of a country which has been an importer of capital throughout its recent history, except during a few years of war prosperity. This required borrowing abroad on a considerable scale in the beginning. It required that a fairly extensive railway be developed under a unified management. It required a point of view which the small Japanese trader of the early days did not have.[79] These requirements the Japanese government met by bringing into existence the railway corporation, by guaranteeing its borrowings in Japan and abroad, and by entrusting to it, in a way which Japanese traditions make possible, the supervision of the economic development of Manchuria in so far as this could be brought about by a foreign corporation in China. The result was that in 1931 the Japanese government owned a controlling interest in a company which held no less than 40 per cent of all Japanese business investments in China and over 60 per cent of such investments in Manchuria.

Manchuria in the Finances of the Japanese Government

According to the calculations for the period before 1914, the Japanese government expended in Manchuria a net total of about Yen 225 million after the outbreak of the Russo-Japanese War. Estimates for the period since 1914 are made in the following paragraphs.

The government's share in the South Manchuria Railway Company was its only source of revenue in Manchuria. The dividends which were paid to it for each year ending March 31 of each date, were in yen:

1915	2,500,000	1919	3,500,000
1916	2,500,000	1920	3,500,000
1917	2,500,000	1921	9,337,708
1918	3,500,000	1922	9,337,708

[79] For the comments of a Japanese observer see the *Economic History of Manchuria*, p. 122. "A conglomeration of small traders, retail shops, barbers, restaurants, and photographers would never have made Manchuria what it is." For the comments of a disinterested foreign observer see Christie, Dugald, *Thirty Years in Moukden*, London, 1914, pp. 194–5.

1923	9,337,708	1928	9,337,708
1924	9,337,708	1929	11,509,268
1925	9,337,708	1930	11,509,268
1926	9,337,708	1931	9,337,708
1927	9,337,708		

The total for the whole period was Yen 125 million. The sharp rise in 1921 was due to the increase in the government's holding of the stock of the company. It involved a much smaller increase in the government's net income than is shown since the government now became responsible for the interest payments on the early borrowings in London. The amount of these payments was about Yen 5.7 million for each year, or a total of Yen 62.7 million. About one-half of the government's receipts consisted of sums really destined for British bond-holders.

There continued to be an annual deficit in the accounts of the Kwantung government which was met by the home government. The grants from the home government were as follows, again for the year ending March 31, in each case:

1915	2,233,000	1924	4,000,000
1916	1,937,000	1925	4,000,000
1917	2,007,000	1926	3,000,000
1918	2,007,000	1927	3,000,000
1919	2,103,000	1928	4,000,000
1920	3,000,000	1929	4,000,000
1921	3,250,000	1930	4,550,000
1922	4,000,000	1931	5,000,000
1923	4,300,000		

The total of these amounts comes to about Yen 56 million. It happens that these grants and the interest payments on the British bonds make a total of payments about equal to the total receipts in the way of dividends from the railway company.

This leaves as net remittances to Manchuria by the Japanese government the sums required for the upkeep of consular establishments in Manchuria and of the military forces. The total for the military, that is, for the garrison and the railway guards comes to about Yen 11

million a year on the average for the years 1915–1931.[80]
The total expenditure on this account has been about
Yen 190 million during the years 1915–1930. A complete
account would include additional sums, for we are told
that "in cases where peace and order in Manchuria have
been threatened by civil war or other disturbance on a
large scale, the army authorities have incurred much
additional expense," and again that "keeping peace and
order in the leased territory and railway zone in Manchuria
is indeed costly to Japan." [81] Without attempting to
present details for such additional expenditure or for the
maintenance of consular officials, one may offer the guess
that it brings the total to Yen 250 million for the whole
period. In view of the facts already set forth this total
may be accepted as the total net remittance to Manchuria
by the Japanese government for the period which is being
considered.

Direct Investments in Transportation, 1930

The details of Japanese business investments are considered under separate headings in the following pages
and the information is brought together in Tables 24, 25,
26, and 29 below. The first heading to be considered is
transportation.

Investment in railways is estimated at Yen 285,324,000.
Of this total the investment of the South Manchuria
Railway Company was Yen 276,696,000 at the end of
1930. The other direct investments in railways included
the following: 1. Japanese interest of Yen 4,458,000 in
the Tien-Tu Light Railway Company, a Sino-Japanese
enterprise. The line covers a distance of about ninety

---

[80] "For the maintenance of railway guards the Japanese Army Department of the Home government has spent 6 to 11 million yen annually." *Report on Progress in Manchuria, 1907–1928*, p. 60. "For the
maintenance of the Kwantung area and railway guards the Japanese Army
Department of the Home government has spent from 7 to 16 million yen
annually in recent years." *Second Report on Progress in Manchuria to 1930*,
p. 92.

[81] *Report on Progress in Manchuria, 1907–1928*, p. 60.

miles from mines at Tienpaoshan to Tumenkiang.[82] This line was begun in 1919. After some delay it was completed in 1926. 2. The investment in the Chinchou-Pitzuwu (or Chengtzetuan) Railway of Yen 4 million. This railway of sixty-three and four-tenths miles lies entirely within the Kwantung leased area. The company is reported to be Sino-Japanese but the only available information is that there are "some Chinese shareholders." [83] It may be regarded as a Japanese enterprise. 3. An investment of Yen 170,000 in a railway which has never been entirely completed. Of this sum 70 per cent was from the South Manchuria Railway Company and 30 per cent from the Penhsihu Coal and Iron Company. Fourteen miles of this railway, from Penhsihu to Niuhsintai, both in the Manchurian province of Liaoning or Fengtien, have been completed. This covers the whole of the direct investment in railways.[84] There were no such investments in China outside of Manchuria.

The second heading under transportation is shipping. Only such shipping interests are included as are entirely within China, engaged in the coastwise or river trade. The first item is the investment of the Dairen Kisen Kaisha. This company in 1913 took over certain of the shipping interests of the South Manchuria Railway Company and in 1928 it took over the South China route of the same company. It now has a variety of shipping including the outright ownership of 40 vessels with a tonnage of 112,000. The investment of the company is taken to be Yen 20 million. The second company of importance is the Nishin Kisen Kaisha which took over the Yangtze River shipping of four companies in 1907. This company owned twenty-seven ships in 1930 of about 50,000 tons and its total paid-up capital was Yen

[82] Hsiao reports it to be 69 miles in length. *Problems of the Pacific, 1929*, table opposite p. 406.
[83] *China Year Book*, 1928, p. 357.
[84] Five miles of light railway between Miaoerhkou and Nanfen owned by a Sino-Japanese corporation are omitted. No details are available.

10,125,000. In addition there were smaller investments in shipping to a total which is estimated at Yen 10,000,000.

There is included under transportation the investment of the South Manchuria Railway Company in harbor works and wharves. This was reported by the company to have been Yen 83.2 million at the end of March, 1931.

Direct Investments in Public Utilities, 1930

Such investments are entirely in Manchuria. There are Japanese investments in public utilities elsewhere in China but they are through Chinese companies and are reported under that heading. Here we are concerned with Japanese corporations, and chiefly with two such corporations, the South Manchuria Electric Company and the South Manchuria Gas Company. The South Manchuria Electric Company has taken over many of the plants formerly owned by the South Manchuria Railway. Twelve such plants were reported as having been built between 1914 and the creation of the South Manchuria Electric Company in 1926. The South Manchuria Gas Company now owns plants which were formerly the property of the railway company at Dairen, Anshan, Mukden, and Antung. The plant at Fushun is still the property of the railway company and is so reported. The total investment in public utilities was found to be Yen 31.3 million.

Direct Investments in Mining, 1930

In this field the greatest investment is that of the South Manchuria Railway Company. The railway company owns coal mines at Fushun and Yentai. The Yentai mine produced about 150,000 tons of coal in 1930. The Fushun mine, frequently referred to as the greatest open cut coal mine in the world, produced 7.4 million tons in 1930. The railway company's investment in coal mines was Yen 117,872,000 in 1931. The Fushun mine produces much of the coal that is exported from Dairen to Japan and the coal mines have shown a profit throughout the period.

The blast furnaces and iron works at Anshan, which are the property of the railway company, are included here at Yen 27,717,000. This plant is of unusual importance for it represents an effort to secure in Manchuria a raw material much needed in Japan. The total capital expenditure on this plant has been over Yen 50 million since May, 1917, when construction began. It has presented technical difficulties upon which a committee of American mining engineers was consulted in 1922.[85] The ore requires concentration and such ore will not be commonly used, in the opinion of engineers, so long as ores are available which do not require treatment. It is improbable that better ores will be found in southern Manchuria. In spite of the technical problems the plant has been extended until, with the opening of the latest blast furnace on March 9, 1930, its capacity is well above the 210 thousand tons of pig iron which were turned out in 1929–1930. Increasing quantities of pig iron have gone to Japan in recent years. The operations of the iron works have not, however, been financially successful. The plant showed a net income on the books of the company for the first time in 1929, and the figures for the last three years have been

1928–1929	1,649,000
1929–1930	1,213,000
1930–1931	76,000

These figures make no allowance for depreciation which was Yen 809,000 for the latest year.

One other investment of the railway company is included here; that of Yen 8,824,000 in an oil distillating

[85] Bain, H. F., *Ores and Industry in the Far East*, p. 89. "In 1922 a commission of mining engineers and geologists consisting of Messrs. W. R. Appleby, W. J. Mead, W. H. Crago, and Frank Hutchinson studied the iron ore problems of the Anshan plant . . . while no report has been published it is generally understood that they pointed out areas for prospecting with the hope that sufficient high grade ores might be found to supply the works."

plant completed in November, 1929, at a cost of Yen 9 million.[86] The introduction of this plant followed a number of years of experiment and the accounts of the company show a small net income for the year ending March 31, 1931. The Japanese navy has taken an interest in this project from the beginning. The capacity of the plant, 70,000 tons of fuel oil a year, is not great enough to supply more than a tenth of Japan's import. There is no reason, it may be added, to feel assurance that the plant will be a financial success. Oil shale distillation has usually turned out a dearer product than fuel oil from wells.[87]

The largest Japanese mining venture, not in the hands of the South Manchuria Railway Company, is that at Penhsihu on the Mukden-Antung Railway about fifty miles from Mukden. It began with coal mining by a Sino-Japanese company, known as the Penhsihu Coal Mining Company, created by an agreement between the Chinese government, through the local provincial authorities, and the Japanese firm of Okura and Company.[88] By this agreement the capitalization of the company was made Chinese $2 million. The contribution of the Chinese government was the mine itself and Chinese $650,000 in cash; the contribution of Okura and Company was equipment and buildings valued at Chinese $1 million.[89] In 1911 it was agreed that the iron mine at Miaoerhkou should be operated by the same company and the capital of the company was increased by Chinese $2 million. In 1914 the capital was again increased by Chinese $3 million to the present total of Chinese $7 million. "All

[86] *Second Report on Progress in Manchuria to 1930*, p. 122.

[87] Orchard, J. E., *Japan's Economic Position*, New York, 1931, p. 310. Orchard points out that shale in Scotland is distilled only when the price of petroleum is high.

[88] MacMurray, J. V. A., *Treaties and Agreements*, vol. I, pp. 793–5.

[89] Lieu in his *Foreign Investments in China, 1929*, p. 65, says: "Careful investigation and evaluation in 1909 showed that the Japanese investments in the mine thus far amounted only to Tls. 454,843, yet the Japanese company demanded much more and as a compromise they were put at Ch. $1 million."

the shares of Fengtien province in the Penhsihu Iron Works" became a part of the security offered for a loan from Okura and Company in 1916. "All the shares held by Fengtien province in the Penhsihu Collicry Company" became the security for a loan from the Bank of Chosen in 1918.[90] From this it is probably safe to conclude that the whole enterprise has passed into the hands of the Japanese, and the whole investment may be set down as Yen 7 million. The output of coal has been from 400,000 to 500,000 tons per year in recent years; it was 521,000 tons in 1929. The output of pig iron has been about 60,000 tons. The Penhsihu enterprise is reported to have been a financial success during the World War and to have had financial difficulties since 1921. The difficulty was represented to me in Manchuria as one of price. It goes back, of course, to other things, such as the poor quality of the ore most readily available, the distance from Penhsihu to the sea which makes an expensive railroad haul necessary, a method of turning out coke which makes it dear.[91] A recent German commission to China which gave particular attention to coal and iron found the Penhsihu venture unpromising. It is highly improbable that this venture has paid its owners since 1929.

Other Japanese mining ventures in Manchuria are estimated by the Japanese committee to have represented an investment of Yen 3.8 million in 1929. This includes coal mines at various places in Liaoning (Fengtien) province, silver and copper mines at Tienpaoshan in Kirin province, and zinc mines in Liaoning (Fengtien) province. Lieu lists twelve mining ventures in addition to those mentioned above.[92]

[90] MacMurray, J. V. A., *Treaties and Agreements*, vol. II, pp. 1336, 1417.
[91] The difficulties are set forth by Tegengren, F. R., *The Iron Ores and Iron Industry of China*, p. 390. See also *Bericht der China-Studienkommission des Reichsverbandes der deutschen Industrie*, Berlin, 1930, pp. 176–7.
[92] *Foreign Investments in China, 1929*, pp. 67–8. Royama states that, excepting those of the South Manchuria Railway Company, there are nineteen mining operations with a total paid-up capital of Yen 2.3 million. *Problems of the Pacific, 1929*, p. 577.

Investments in mining outside of Manchuria include, first, certain mines in Shantung province, formerly operated by German interests.[93] The mines were occupied by the Japanese when they took the German leased area in Shantung province in 1914. At the Washington Conference of 1921–1922 these mining interests were discussed and it was agreed that they should be handed over to a Sino-Japanese corporation in which Japanese participation should not be greater than Chinese.[94] As a result of this agreement the Lu Ta Mining Company was formed in April, 1923, and took possession of the properties at Fangtze, Tzechuan, and Chinglingchen in August. Lieu reports that the Japanese investment in equipment was Yen 5 million before the formation of the Lu Ta Company, and this sum may be accepted as the Japanese investment at the end of 1930. The coal production of the company has averaged about 700,000 tons during recent years; figures showing iron ore production at Chinglingchen are not available.[95]

The second venture in which the Japanese are interested is an iron mine at Taochung in the province of Anhwei. The mine is the property of the Yu Fan Company which has borrowed from the Chunichi Jitsugyo Kaisha (Central Japanese Commercial Company). The Japanese investment is estimated by the Japanese committee to have been Yen 4,147,000 at the end of 1926 and this is accepted for 1930. A third Japanese interest is in coal mines in the province of Jehol. The particulars available indicate that the Japanese investment is Yen 570,000. There are, no doubt, other ventures [96] but it is believed

[93] Until 1913 the Schantung Bergbau Gesellschaft, after 1913 the Schantung Eisenbahn Gesellschaft.

[94] Willoughby, W. W., *China at the Conference*, Baltimore, 1922, p. 308.

[95] Iron ore production declined from 179,000 metric tons in 1919 to 8,000 in 1924. *Commercial Handbook of China*, 1926, p. 740, *China Year Book*, 1929–1930, p. 54.

[96] Certain ventures have, of course, failed. An example is that of the Yi Hwa Company in the Yangtze valley. *Commercial Handbook of China*, 1926, p. 710.

that the Japanese investment is not far from the total of the above, that is, Yen 174,930,000. The coal mines mentioned as Japanese or Sino-Japanese have in recent years turned out over half of the production of the mines with modern equipment in China. In the field of iron mining and pig iron production Japanese control reaches three-fourths, taking into account the Hanyehping Company dealt with below.

Direct Investment in Manufacturing, Cotton Mills

Cotton spinning and weaving, Yen 195,653,000, represents almost a third of the total Japanese investment in manufacturing in China. The estimate of Yen 195.7 million is considerably smaller than the total reported by the Japanese committee. The reason for adopting the smaller figure is the unanimous testimony of the Japanese business men in Shanghai that the original figure of the Japanese committee which came to about Yen 200 per spindle was too large. The estimate accepted by Mr. Odagiri came to about Yen 150 per spindle. Mr. K. Uchida of the Tokyo office of the East Asia Industrial Company was critical of both of these estimates and stated it as his opinion that Yen 100 was more nearly correct.[97] Professor Zenichi Itani who has recently given attention to the subject accepted Yen 65 per spindle and Yen 450 per loom.[98] The estimate at which I have arrived after consultation in Shanghai comes to about Yen 100 per spindle.

The Japanese investment in cotton milling in China is very largely outside of Manchuria. The total for Manchuria is only Yen 12,331,000 and for the rest of China Yen 183,322,000. This means that Shanghai is the center of the industry, the total for that one port being Yen 144 million. Cotton milling stands in sharp contrast to the geographical distribution of Japanese business invest-

[97] In an interview on August 27, 1930.
[98] The Export of Capital to China, Tokyo, 1931, p. 13.

ments in general. Here we have a large factor in the relative increase in Japanese investments in Shanghai since 1914. The overwhelming importance of Shanghai, with three-fourths (73.6 per cent) of the investment, is the first general statement concerning cotton milling.

A second is the fact, pointed out by the Japanese committee, that practically the whole of the Japanese interest in the industry in China is "a branch of that industry in Japan and accurately reflects the condition of the industry in Japan." The Naigai Wata Kaisha, the Japan and Shanghai Spinning & Weaving Company, the Dai Nippon Spinning Company, and the Toyo Company are all large concerns having mills in both Japan and China. The industry is an example of a development in Japan in which the Japanese have shown themselves effective, which has, one may say, overflowed to China. The cotton spinning industry of Japan grew remarkably during the years 1916 to 1921 and again during the years 1924 to 1929.[99] It was, in general, during these years that the great increase in the number of Japanese-owned spindles in China took place. It is to be noted, however, that the increase in China was not checked from 1921 to 1924 as it seems to have been in Japan. In fact, the period 1918 to 1923 saw the most rapid growth. This is to be explained, in part, by the effective financing of the Japanese which enabled them to take over the mills of certain Chinese and foreign companies which suffered reverses during the post-war depression. In part, it is due to the adoption of different tariff rates for the various grades of cotton yarn at the Shanghai Tariff Conference of 1918.[100] The accompanying table shows that the Japanese share of the spindles in China was about 16 or 17 per cent of the total during the years before the war and probably to 1918. By 1919 or 1920 the Japanese percentage had increased

[99] See Moulton, H. G., *Japan: An Economic and Financial Appraisal,* pp. 554–5 for tables.

[100] King and Lieu, "China's Cotton Industry," *Problems of the Pacific, 1929,* p. 264.

to 22 per cent and by 1929 or 1930 it was about 40 per cent.

TABLE 23

THE NUMBER OF COTTON SPINDLES IN CHINA AND THE PERCENTAGE OWNED BY JAPANESE

	Total Spindles in China	Japanese-Owned	Percentage Owned by Japanese
1909 [1]	721,674	98,928	13.7
1912 [6]	831,946	95,872	11.5
1914 [7]	865,788	105,952	12.2
1919 [1]	1,513,964	333,012	22.0
1927 [4]	3,612,606	1,351,704	37.4
1928 [5]	3,850,016	1,514,816	39.3
1930 [2]	4,222,956	1,673,844	39.6
1931 [3]	4,210,338	1,630,436	38.7
1931 [8]	4,497,902	1,821,280	40.5

Source:

[1] *Textile Manufacturers' Handbook and Directory*, Shanghai, 1920 (in Chinese).
[2] *Nankai Weekly Statistical Service*, Feb. 23, 1931.
[3] Itani, *Export of Japanese Capital to China*, p. 4.
[4] *British Chamber of Commerce Journal*, May, 1928.
[5] King and Lieu, *Problems of the Pacific, 1929*, p. 272.
[6] Nagano, *Foreign Investment in China*, translation by Susumu Kobe.
[7] *North-China Herald*, March 7, 1914, p. 692.
[8] *Chinese Economic Journal*, Dec., 1931, p. 1289.

The effectiveness of the Japanese in this industry is admitted by the Chinese mill owners and managers. It is borne out by the available statistical information. We are informed by the Nankai Statistical Service that the Japanese mills in China employ 30.6 per cent of the workers in the cotton milling industry of China, turn out 35 per cent of the yarn and thread, and weave 55.2 per cent of the cloth. "If we remember that, in the first place, the Japanese mills weave more cloth than the Chinese and therefore require more workers and, secondly, that the yarns and threads spun by the Japanese mills are of much higher count than those by the Chinese mills, we get a very strong contrast of labor efficiency against the Chinese mills and in favor of the Japanese mills." [101]

[101] *Nankai Weekly Statistical Service*, Feb. 23, 1931.

The legal basis of the Japanese industry in China goes back to the Treaty of Shimonoseki by which the Japanese —and all foreigners—secured the right to own and operate industrial establishments in China. This brought a few cotton mills to Shanghai but they were very largely in other than Japanese hands. Tariff rates adopted by international agreement in 1918 have been mentioned above but, so long as China was under a conventional tariff, fundamental changes could not take place. The so-called national tariff which came into force February 1, 1929, placed a duty of about $7\frac{1}{2}$ per cent *ad valorem* on cotton manufactures and the new tariff which came into force on the first day of January, 1931, increased this duty to about $12\frac{1}{2}$ per cent. These tariff changes have played some part in the increase in the number of Japanese-owned spindles in China in the last two years. The number of looms has increased also and many of the Japanese companies in China were planning for additional looms in 1931.[102] The development of the last two years has probably been stimulated by the rapid decline in the gold price of silver. It has not been connected with any unusual prosperity of the industry in Japan.

The importance of political and racial considerations in the Chinese viewpoint is illustrated in the comment upon this recent increase in Japanese spindles which was frequently made to me in Shanghai. The Japanese, it was said, by establishing mills in China were defeating the very purpose of the tariff. Such development is rather generally held by Chinese to be undesirable when the industrial establishments are owned by those who are not Chinese and when they are under the political control which extraterritoriality gives to foreigners.

In conclusion it may be said that the Japanese-owned cotton milling industry in China provides an illustration of certain characteristics of direct investments in China. It was developed under the treaty port extraterritorial-

[102] Itani, Zenichi, *Export of Japanese Capital to China*, Tokyo, p. 10.

ity system. It is an industry which was growing in Japan and which the Japanese had learned to handle effectively. The Japanese brought to China the skill of the entrepreneur and manager. It was not until the closing years of the World War that the prosperity of the industry in Japan provided the capital for Japanese mills in China. This capital cannot easily be traced since most of the Japanese mills in China belong to corporations owning mills in both countries. Efforts to secure information as to the profits and dividends of the investments in cotton mills have produced meager results. The estimate of the Japanese Ministry of Commerce and Industry for 1927 showed a profit of Yen 8.4 million on an investment of 153.6 million, which comes to 5.5 per cent.[103] Profits were greater during 1917–1920. The industry has not, however, lived up to expectations. "The development," says Nagano, "of Japanese investment in the cotton spinning industry in China for some time to come can hardly be expected to parallel the development up to the present time. The future of the mills already in existence in China is itself problematical." [104]

Direct Investment in Manufacturing (continued)

Investment in oil, that is in the expressing of vegetable oil and its marketing, is estimated at Yen 19,183,000. Oil from the soya bean has long been extracted in Manchuria by means of household equipment. The first stimulus to this industry was given by the increased demand for bean cake for fertilizer in Japan. Later the oil was exported in increasing quantities. The Japanese investment began in 1909 with a mill at Yingkow. The center of the industry is now Dairen. The chief Japanese companies are the Kodera Oil Company, the Sino-Japanese Oil Company, the Santai Oil Company, and the Suzuki

[103] The returns were from 89 companies only.
[104] Nagano, Akira, *Foreign Investment in China*, Kobe translation.

Oil Company which, in 1915, took over a plant operated until that time by the South Manchuria Railway Company. About 75 plants in Manchuria are owned by Japanese. In addition there are seven plants at Tsingtao for the expressing of peanut oil.

Flour milling accounts for an investment of Yen 3,565,-000. The oldest flour mill in China is probably the Japanese Mitsui mill at Shanghai.[105] The industry is now principally in Manchuria, and the development has been very largely due to the Russians. Japanese interest began in 1906 with the establishment of the South Manchuria Milling Company at Tiehling. There are now Japanese mills at a number of important centers.

In tobacco manufacturing the Japanese investment is Yen 8,170,000. Most of this is the East Asia Tobacco Company which operates in the Kwantung leased area by permission of the Tobacco Monopoly Bureau of the Japanese government. This company alone is capitalized at Yen 10 million.

The manufacture of paper, in which the Japanese investment is Yen 3,309,000, is confined to Manchuria and it is chiefly along the Yalu river.

Saw mills and woodworking plants, entirely in Manchuria, account for an investment of Yen 6,497,000. The manufacture of matches, Yen 5,192,000, is largely in Manchuria.

In addition there is a great variety of other manufacturing which cannot conveniently be classified. There are included here everything from the Manchurian Woollen Company of Mukden with a capital of Yen 10 million to small establishments at Shanghai engaged in the greatest variety of activities. The total in this miscellaneous group has been somewhat arbitrarily divided between Manchuria and the rest of China but this has not been done without consultation with Japanese business men and officials in China.

[105] *China Year Book*, 1931, p. 133.

Banking and Finance

The total under this heading is estimated to be Yen 147,614,000. This includes an investment of Yen 825,000 in insurance. The South Manchuria Railway Company is interested in insurance companies to the amount of Yen 184,000.

The Japanese investment in banking has been difficult to estimate. Banking in China is carried on principally by the so-called "Special banking institutions," the Yokohama Specie Bank, the Bank of Taiwan (or Formosa), and the Bank of Chosen. These banks are not interested principally in China, and certain estimates of Japanese investments err by including the whole of the capital of these banks.

In making the estimate which follows I had the assistance of certain Japanese bankers in Shanghai. The estimate of the Japanese committee of the paid-up capital of the banks definitely within China, Yen 36,789,000, was accepted. Estimates of the outstanding advances to Chinese were Yen 60 million for Manchuria and Yen 50 million for the rest of China. In making the estimate of the distribution of the investment between Manchuria and the rest of China a list was drawn up which showed 122 separate offices or branches of Japanese banks in China. Sixty per cent of these were in Manchuria and 40 per cent elsewhere in China. The number of Japanese banks in Shanghai was found to be about 10.

Information is available concerning banks having their headquarters in China and was taken into account in arriving at the final estimate. This shows that there were in China 27 main offices and branches of such banks in 1916 and 55 in 1925. The capital of these banks was reported to be Yen 5.8 million in 1916, and Yen 77.5 million in 1925; deposits Yen 10.9 million in 1916 and Yen 73.5 million in 1925; and loans Yen 12.5 million in 1916 and Yen 148.7 million in 1925. The net profits reported by these banks, that is Japanese banks with headquarters in China, was in millions of yen:

1916	0.6	1921	5.4
1917	0.6	1922	5.7
1918	1.7	1923	5.1
1919	2.7	1924	3.0
1920	2.8	1925	1.2

Since it is estimated that these banks with head offices in China account for about half of the Japanese banking in the country, we have here some indication of the totals which are involved, but only the most general indication.

Concerning insurance, it may be added that the available information [106] makes it possible to present the following index numbers of insurance premiums collected in Manchuria by Japanese companies:

1914	100	1922	700
1920	600	1923	650
1921	550	1924	600

The total Japanese investment in banking and insurance has been estimated at Yen 82,568,000 for Manchuria and at Yen 65,046,000 for the rest of China.

Real Estate, Agriculture, and Forestry

The total under this heading, Yen 145,990,000, is entirely in Manchuria. It is not, therefore, a good indication of the total land holdings of the Japanese in China. The real estate at the various treaty ports owned by Japanese is estimated by Nagano at Yen 100 million.[107] It has been found impossible to separate these holdings from the other investments in the various fields. The total is to be regarded as showing certain identifiable land holdings in Manchuria and investment in industries in which land plays a part of great importance.

[106] From the *History of Twenty Years of the Kwantung Government* (in Japanese).
[107] Nagano, A., *Foreign Investment in China*, Kobe translation, p. 19.

The holdings of the South Manchuria Railway Company reported under this heading are: office buildings Yen 4,262,000, employees' dwellings Yen 37,547,000, and land Yen 46,458,000. In addition there is included the investment in hotels which were turned over to the South Manchuria Hotel Company by the railway company in 1928.[108] The hotels were valued by the railway company at Yen 3,880,000.

The total reported as the Japanese investment in agriculture by the Japanese committee was Yen 21,005,000. The statistics of the government of the Kwantung leased area show the investment in agricultural enterprises within the leased territory to be Yen 7,928,000. They show, also, that the total number of Japanese families whose main occupation was agriculture was 195 in a recent year. Elsewhere in southern Manchuria there were 666 Japanese families so engaged. Efforts made by the Kwantung government, we are told, and by the South Manchuria Railway Company to encourage the migration of Japanese farmers to the area under Japanese control have not met with much success.

The total investment in forestry is estimated to be Yen 31,338,000. The creation of a Sino-Japanese company, the Yalu Timber Company, was the subject of an agreement between China and Japan in May, 1908.[109] This agreement established a concession and brought into existence a company with a capital of Chinese $3 million of which China and Japan were each to contribute half. The difficulty of making an estimate is illustrated by the fact that one of the largest companies, the Cha Mien Lumber Company with a capital of Yen 6 million, is a joint enterprise which brings together Chinese, Japanese, and Russians.

There is, it may be added, a small Japanese investment in fishing which has its center at Dairen.

[108] *Report on Progress in Manchuria, 1907–1928*, p. 99.
[109] MacMurray, J. V. A., *Treaties and Agreements*, vol. I, p. 731.

Import and Export and General Trading

This is the only field, aside from manufacturing, in which well over half of the total investment, Yen 365,-927,000 is outside of Manchuria. The investment in Manchuria is Yen 117,758,000. This is close to the estimate of the Japan-China Industrial Association, listed above as the fourth Japanese estimate, which put the total for Manchuria at Yen 115 million.

The total for the rest of China is put at Yen 248,169,000. Here I must record another difference between the estimate finally accepted and that which was arrived at by the Japanese committee. The Japanese committee's total under this heading was Yen 166 million. At the same time the committee accepted as reasonable the total of Yen 118 million for Manchuria alone, leaving the estimate for the rest of China about Yen 48 million. It was difficult to believe that investments in general trading were greater in Manchuria than in the rest of China and that they were less than Yen 50 million. At Shanghai it was discovered that a committee of the local Japanese Chamber of Commerce had undertaken to make an estimate of Japanese holdings in 1926 and had arrived at a figure of Yen 519 million for companies engaged in the import and export trade at that port alone. The figures of the committee of the Japanese Chamber of Commerce show obvious inconsistencies with other Japanese estimates and the classification adopted makes certain that more is included under importing and exporting than ought to be put there. After consultation with Japanese bankers, business men, and officials at Shanghai a total was arrived at which was generally accepted as satisfactory.

The total for the import and export business and for general trading arrived at in Shanghai came to Yen 365,927,000 for the whole of China, divided into Yen 117,758,000 for Manchuria and Yen 248,169,000 for the rest of China. The investment outside of Manchuria was estimated to be so distributed as to make the total for Shanghai Yen 148,901,000 and Yen 99,268,000 for other centers outside of Manchuria and Shanghai. The total for Shanghai includes holdings of land and buildings devoted to trading as well as stocks of goods in the legal possession of Japanese importers and exporters. The distinction between this category and manufacturing was at times difficult to draw. In general, if the business required only the assembling and preparation of goods for export, the investment was set down here. If, on the other hand, it required that the goods be carried through an industrial process, that a plant be erected, and workmen employed at other tasks than sorting and packing, the investment was set down as manufacturing.

The figures which are presented here are, of course, estimates but they are estimates which were worked out with some care and with an examination of the grounds for disagreement among the lists and totals which were available.

TABLE 24

JAPANESE DIRECT BUSINESS INVESTMENTS IN CHINA DISTRIBUTED BY THE NATURE OF THE BUSINESS

	Thousands of Yen	Per Cent of Total
1. Transportation	408,649	23.4
2. Public utilities	31,300	1.8
3. Mining	174,930	10.0
4. Manufacturing	331,299	18.9
5. Banking and finance	147,614	8.4
6. Real estate	145,990	8.4
7. Import and export	365,927	20.9
8. Miscellaneous	142,550	8.2
	1,748,259	100.0

There is a final heading, miscellaneous, with a total of Yen 142,550,000, about equally divided between Manchuria and the rest of China. The Manchurian total includes the following holdings of the South Manchuria Railway Company: Yen 35,197,000 reported by the com-

TABLE 25

DIRECT BUSINESS INVESTMENTS IN MANCHURIA AND THE REST OF CHINA
DISTRIBUTED ACCORDING TO THE NATURE OF THE BUSINESS

(In thousands of yen)

	Manchuria	Per Cent of Total for Manchuria	Rest of China	Per Cent of Total for Rest of China
1. Transportation	388,524	35.4	20,125	3.1
2. Public utilities	31,300	2.8	——	——
3. Mining	165,213	15.0	9,717	1.5
4. Manufacturing	98,602	8.9	232,697	36.0
5. Banking and finance	82,568	7.5	65,046	10.0
6. Real estate	145,990	13.3	——	——
7. Import and export	117,758	10.7	248,169	38.3
8. Miscellaneous	70,445	6.4	72,105	11.1
	1,100,400	100.0	647,859	100.0

TABLE 26

DIRECT BUSINESS INVESTMENTS SHOWING THE PERCENTAGE DISTRIBUTION
OF EACH CLASS

(In thousands of yen)

	Per Cent in Manchuria	Per Cent in the Rest of China
1. Transportation	95.1	4.9
2. Public utilities	100.0	——
3. Mining	94.4	5.6
4. Manufacturing	29.8	70.2
5. Banking and finance	55.9	44.1
6. Real estate	100.0	——
7. Import and export	32.2	67.8
8. Miscellaneous	49.4	50.6

TABLE 27

DIRECT BUSINESS INVESTMENT, 1930: GEOGRAPHICAL DISTRIBUTION

	Thousands of Yen	Per Cent of Total
In Manchuria	1,100,400	62.9
In Shanghai	430,125	24.6
Elsewhere in China	217,734	12.5
	1,748,259	100.0

pany under a similar heading, and Yen 51,000 reported
by the company as the value of a fertilizer plant which it
owns.   The other items under miscellaneous are those
reported by the Japanese committee with a deduction for
items removed from the committee's list and placed under
general trading.

Japanese Investments in Chinese Corporations, 1930

Japanese loans to Chinese corporations were estimated
at Yen 35 million for 1914.   Two Chinese corporations
only were reported as having borrowed from Japanese
sources.   The first of these corporations, the Hanyehping
Company, leads the list at the end of 1930.   Japanese
loans to this company were estimated to have reached a
total of Yen 30 million in 1914.   By the agreements in
force at that time the company was under such obligations
to the Japanese as to give them a considerable degree of
control, which was exercised through the Yokohama
Specie Bank.

The relations of the Japanese to the Hanyehping
Company were dealt with in the "Twenty-one Demands."
The original proposal of the Japanese reveals the fears
which they entertained.   It was proposed: that the company "be made a joint concern of the two nations,"
this to be done "when the opportune moment arrives";
that no disposal of the rights or property in the company
be permitted without the consent of the Japanese government; that no mines in the neighborhood of those of the
company be permitted to be worked without the consent
of the company; and that no other measure be taken
which may "affect the interests of the said company
directly or indirectly" without its consent.[110]   The sweeping nature of these demands was somewhat modified in
the course of the negotiations.   In the final exchange of
notes the Chinese government agreed: to give permission
if the Hanyehping Company and Japanese capitalists

[110] MacMurray, J. V. A., *Treaties and Agreements*, vol. II, pp. 1232-3.

agree upon co-operation; to refrain from confiscating the company or from converting it into a state enterprise; to refrain also from causing the company to borrow foreign capital other than Japanese.[111]

In the agreement of 1913 the Hanyehping Company had undertaken to provide the Japanese Government Iron Works with 17 million tons of iron ore and 8 million of crude iron during a period of forty years in addition to such sales of iron ore and pig iron as were made to meet the obligations created by the loan agreement of the same date. This represents more than half of the reserves, according to some estimates of ore reserves,[112] and the whole of the reserves, according to others. The company delivered increasing quantities of iron ore and pig iron to the Japanese through the war years and until the depression of 1921. The price of these deliveries was a subject of frequent dispute between the Chinese and Japanese during these years and the Chinese succeeded in getting some increase.[113] Since 1921 the Hanyehping enterprise has suffered a decline. In 1922 the steel plant was closed down. This plant had turned out a costly product and was equipped with obsolete machinery. It was the first department to feel the results of the post-war depression and it has not been reopened. The pig iron production fell off in 1923 on account of the general depression and particularly on account of the effect of the depression in Japan. Production of pig iron had varied from 130,000 tons to 166,000 tons between 1914–1922. In 1923 it fell to 73,000 tons and by 1927 to practically nothing. Since 1928 the iron works, both at Hanyang and Tayeh, have been idle and the company has been almost completely disorganized. The only depart-

[111] MacMurray, J. V. A., *Treaties and Agreements*, vol. II, pp. 1229–30.
[112] Bain, H. F., *Ores and Industry in the Far East*, pp. 94–5. *China Year Book*, 1919, p. 74. Bain gives a number of estimates including that of Tegengren, 32 million tons gross and 19.3 million tons net above sea level. T. T. Read's estimate of 50 million tons is to be found in the *China Year Book*.
[113] Lieu, D. K., *Foreign Investments in China, 1929*, p. 98.

ment in operation has been the Tayeh iron mine. This mine has continued to turn out ore for delivery in Japan. The iron ore production was about 500,000 tons in 1914. By 1920 it reached a total of about 825,000 tons. There was a steady decline to 1926 when the production was no more than 70,000 tons. These fluctuations are to be explained, in part, by the course of business activity in Japan. They reflect, also, the state of affairs within China and particularly in the Yangtze valley. There is little doubt that Chinese-Japanese relations have played a part also. Since 1926 the production of iron ore has increased. It was over 400,000 tons in 1928 and somewhat less in 1930. The whole of this production has gone to Japan.

During the years 1914–1930 the Hanyehping Company has borrowed further sums in Japan. A loan of Yen 8.5 million made in 1924 is to be found in the list of obligations prepared by the Ministry of Mines and Agriculture of the Nationalist government of China in 1927 and in a footnote we are told that there was another loan of Yen 2 million in 1926. This loan is said to have brought greater Japanese control over the business of the company.[114] The total obligation of the company is said by Lieu to be Yen 50 million. On June 1, 1930, the whole of these loans, which were originally advances secured from the Savings Deposit Department of the Japanese government and from the Bank of Japan, were transferred to the financial department of the Japanese Government Iron Works. The amount involved was certainly above Yen 37 million and may have been as high as Yen 49 million.[115]

The report of the Japanese committee shows a total Japanese investment of Yen 35,153,185 in the Hanyeh-

[114] Lieu, D. K., *Foreign Investments in China, 1929,* p. 96.
[115] Go, Toshi, *A Brief History of Japanese Investments in China,* p. 7, states the amount to have been Yen 37 million. Orchard, John E., *Japan's Economic Position,* found the newspapers of the time in Japan to have put the total at Yen 49 million.

ping Company at the end of 1926. Chinese sources show additional obligations of Yen 10.5 million for the period 1914–1930. Adding this to the investment reported above for 1914 we reach a total of Yen 40.5 million. It seems reasonable to conclude that the Japanese investment in the Hanyehping Company at the end of 1930 was Yen 40 million. What was at the beginning a venture in which the Chinese were in control has by successive steps become in effect Japanese. Behind this change lies the desire of the Japanese to be assured of a supply of iron ore and pig iron. As a result of the Chinese attitude toward the "Twenty-one Demands," of the post-war depression, of civil war in China, and as an indirect consequence of the repeated boycotts of recent years, the Hanyehping corporation has suffered a progressive disintegration. In 1931 its only activity was the provision of iron ore for export to Japan. Investment through a Chinese corporation was not fairly tested in this case, since both governments were involved, but in so far as it was a test it must be regarded as a failure.

The second example in 1914 of Japanese investment in a Chinese corporation was that in the Nanchang-Kiukiang Railway with outstanding loans of Yen 5 million. During the period since 1914 there have been additional loans. The company borrowed Yen 2.5 million from the East Asia Enterprise Company in 1914, Yen 679,650 in 1918, and Yen 2.5 million in 1922. In addition there was a loan of Yen 80,768 in 1915 from the Mitsui Company for the purchase of cars. About Yen 60,000 of this is reported as still outstanding. The total for the period comes to Yen 5,739,650 and this, with the amount for 1914, which is still outstanding, comes to a total of Yen 10,739,650 as the Japanese investment in this Chinese railway corporation. This railway is now under the supervision of the Chinese government, according to information supplied by the Ministry of Railways in April, 1931, but the obligations of the company are not accepted as government obligations since it is regarded as a private enterprise. Investment in this company is hardly to be regarded as an example of success. The Japanese committee reports that no repayment has ever been made except of a small amount to the Mitsui Company. It is to be noted, also, that Yen 7.5 million of the outstanding amount has been advanced from the Deposit Department of the Japanese government. In this enterprise, as in the Hanyehping Company, the interest of the two governments lies just beneath the surface.

Other investments under this heading are loans from Japanese sources to local public utilities in China. A characteristic example are loans to the Chapei Electric & Water Company by Okura & Company and loans to the Hankow Electric Company from the East Asia Industrial Company. A long list of such loans might be made up. Lieu provides such a list and refers to one drawn up in 1922 by the Chinese Government Bureau of Economic Information. No accurate total of the amounts involved is to be arrived at. I have taken the chief items reported by Lieu and reported by the Japanese Committee. The total of these items I find to be Yen 18.7 million and this may be accepted as the loans under this heading outstanding at the end of 1930.[116] It is the general opinion among the Chinese and Japanese who have been interested in this financing that the obligations of the Chinese public utilities have been met with some regularity. At the office of the East Asia Industrial Company in Tokyo this statement was agreed to but at the same time it was maintained that the policy of financing Chinese corporations had not been a success.

A final item under this heading consists of loans to Chinese corporations engaged in cotton spinning and

[116] Lieu, D. K., *Foreign Investments in China, 1929*, pp. 98–100. Lieu gives the total arrived at by the Bureau of Economic Information at Chinese $44.3 million but this includes loans to the Nanchang-Kiukiang Railway.

weaving. This matter was given particular study by Mr. Shizuo Hirai of the Japanese committee. He reports the amount outstanding in 1930 to have been Yen 7,988,000. These are loans not made for the purchase of equipment. They represent either long-term advances to the Chinese companies or participation in the business.

Concerning investments of this sort in general I must refer again to the opinions of a well-informed Japanese banker and business man. His company, he said, would be better off if it had not advanced funds to Chinese corporations but had instead gone in for direct business investments in China. So long, he maintained, as direct investments are more successful than investments through Chinese corporations extraterritoriality will be and ought to be continued. He recognized the fact that direct investment under extraterritoriality offers only limited possibilities. Investments through Chinese corporations will in the future bring the chief movement of capital toward China. We must wait, he said, for the Chinese to develop the handling of industry and the corporation. If extraterritoriality is abolished soon for political reasons, its abolition may stimulate Japanese participation in Chinese corporations.

The estimates under this heading are summarized in the following table.

TABLE 28

JAPANESE INVESTMENT IN CHINESE CORPORATIONS, 1930

	Yen
Hanyehping Company	40,000,000
Nanchang-Kiukiang Railway Company	10,739,650
Local public utilities	18,700,000
Loans to cotton milling companies	7,988,000
Total	77,427,650

In order to facilitate comparison with the investments of other countries the following table is presented, which shows distribution of the direct business investments of the Japanese and their investments in Chinese corporations according to the nature of the business. The items in the following table have been arrived at by adding the amounts shown in the preceding table to the amounts shown in Table 24. This table includes all Japanese business investments in China of every sort.

TABLE 29

DIRECT BUSINESS INVESTMENTS AND INVESTMENTS IN CHINESE CORPORATIONS DISTRIBUTED ACCORDING TO THE NATURE OF THE BUSINESS

	Thousands of Yen	Per Cent of Total
1. Transportation	419,389	23.0
2. Public utilities	50,000	2.7
3. Mining	214,930	11.8
4. Manufacturing	339,287	18.6
5. Banking and finance	147,614	8.1
6. Real estate	145,990	8.0
7. Imports and exports	365,927	20.0
8. Miscellaneous	142,550	7.8
	1,825,687	100.0

Japanese Loans to the Chinese Government: Certain Omissions

In addition to Japanese loans to the Chinese government there are included here all Japanese holdings of the obligations of the Chinese government or of government departments and institutions. To arrive at a total under this heading has required so frequent an exercise of judgment that different totals, arrived at by different persons, may well be defended. My task is to show how the total which I offer has been built up.

In the first place certain items have been omitted. These include the Japanese share of the Boxer indemnity, and the obligations created by the final settlement of questions relative to Shantung.[117] The Shantung set-

[117] *Treaties and Agreements With and Concerning China, 1919–1929,* pp. 80–8.

tlement involved the handing over to the Japanese government of treasury notes to the value of Yen 14 million for public properties and salt interests at Tsingtao and of treasury notes to the value of Yen 40 million in compensation for the return to China of the Tsingtao-Tsinanfu Railway. These obligations came into existence at the end of 1922.[118] Boxer indemnity payments were deferred for five years from December 1, 1917, as a result of China's decision to declare war upon Germany.[119]   In thus deferring payments Japan joined the other Allied powers and in the Japanese case the deferment covered the whole of the sums to be paid. Toward the end of the five-year period China proposed a further deferment of two years. This was not agreed to and payment to Japan was resumed from December 1, 1922.

These payments, which were to begin at the end of 1922, were dealt with in a law, known as the Law of the Cultural Works Special Account, promulgated on March 30, 1923. The payments were to be made into an account set aside for cultural and educational purposes. These include a research institute for the study of literature and the social sciences, a research institute for the study of the natural sciences, grants to Chinese students for study in Japan, to educational institutions, and to hospitals run by Japanese in China.[120]

The annual sum paid by China to Japan on the Boxer and Shantung obligations comes to about Yen 4 million for 1930. The total disbursement for cultural enterprises—the sum paid by Japan to China—reported by the Japanese committee for 1928 was Yen 3,143,854. In view of the approximate equality of inpayments and outpayments it seems evident that the obligations, whatever their legal form, cannot be regarded, from an economic viewpoint, as if they were still in existence. They have, in

---

[118] Baylin, J. R., *Foreign Loan Obligations of China*, pp. 27, 68.
[119] Wright, S. F., *Collection and Disposal of Customs Revenue*, p. 111.
[120] *Ibid.*, pp. 117–8.

effect, been wiped out and it is best to recognize this fact by omitting them from any list of Japanese holdings of the obligations of the Chinese government. In doing this I follow Mr. M. Odagiri and the Japanese Committee of the local Council of the Institute of Pacific Relations.

Another omission is the Japanese share of the Reorganization loan of 1913. In this I disagree with my Japanese collaborators and with others who have undertaken to draw up lists of China's obligations to Japan. The reasons for the omission have been set forth in the discussion of Japanese loans as they were in 1914. A legal obligation to pay a Japanese bank exists in this case but the real payment is to security holders who are not in Japan.

Japanese Share of the General Secured Loans

In the sections which follow there is presented in detail an explanation of the way in which the sums assigned to Japan were arrived at. This involves the following classification of the obligations of the Chinese government: the general secured loans, railway obligations, obligations for communications other than railways, and the so-called unsecured loans. The first question to be answered is: what was the Japanese share of the general secured loans at the end of 1930.

The Japanese took practically no part in the provision of funds for the general purposes of the Chinese government before the Chinese revolution and the World War. During the early years of the revolution, under Yuan Shih-kai, funds were secured from Europe. The Japanese participated in the Reorganization loan of 1913 but, as has been pointed out above, no funds came from Japan. After the death of Yuan Shih-kai in 1916 the government depended upon short-term loans from domestic sources and from every available foreign source. An attempt was made in 1920 and 1921 to refund certain of these short-term obligations, especially those which carried with

them some claim to the revenues from the Government
Salt Service which remained after the service of the Reorganization loan had been met. This revenue is ordinarily referred to as the salt surplus. Among these short-
term obligations were loans from the following Japanese
sources: the Industrial Bank of China, the Bank of Taiwan, Okura and Company, the East Asia Development
Company, the Exchange Bank of China, and the China
& Japan Industrial Company. They included the Flood
Relief loan of Yen 5 million, made in 1917.[121] The refunding was accomplished by issuing bonds for Yen 39,-
608,700 at 8 per cent, payable in six and one-half years, and
secured on the salt surplus. They are generally known as
the Japanese share of the $96 million loan. The payments
on the principal have been in default since January 1,
1924, and the payments on the interest since July 31,
1925.[122] Nothing was paid on this loan during the years
1928, 1929, and 1930. The principal outstanding on
January 1, 1931, was Yen 32,478,400 and the arrears of
interest amounted to Yen 12,991,360. The total amount
outstanding on January 1, 1931, was, taking the Yen at
U. S. $.50, U. S. $22,734,880. This is the only obligation
to Japan among the general secured loans.

Japanese Share of the Railway Obligations of the Chinese Government

Japanese investments in railways in China have been
presented under direct investments—the South Manchuria Railway—and under investments in Chinese corporations—the Nanchang-Kiukiang. The railways to be
considered here are those in which the Chinese government and the Japanese have a joint interest, that
is those over which the Chinese government has some

---

[121] For a list, together with the loan agreement, see *Treaties and Agreements
With and Concerning China, 1919–1929*, pp. 61–69.
[122] *China Year Book*, 1931, p. 354.

recognized claim and in which the Japanese have, at the same time, some investment.

Certain totals are presented first. They are derived from Chinese and Japanese sources and are to be regarded as establishing a reasonable indication of the magnitude of Japanese investment. This is important since it is impossible to arrive at an exact figure, because the amount of certain items is a matter of judgment and because the accounts of certain railways have been in a state of confusion brought on by civil war.

The first estimate is one which is derived from a list of Chinese government obligations to Japan and to Japanese nationals drawn up by the Bank of Japan to show the situation at the end of 1925.[123] The Bank of Japan list shows total railway obligations of Yen 117,729,200. The information given enables a division to be made which shows obligations of the Manchurian railways at Yen 78,696,812 (66.8 per cent of the total) and obligations of the railways outside of Manchuria at Yen 39,-032,388 (33.2 per cent of the total).[124]

The second estimate is that of Mr. M. Odagiri.[125] This estimate was accepted by the Japanese Committee who collaborated in this study. Odagiri's estimate shows railway obligations which reach a total, at the end of 1928, of Yen 155,976,000. Further examination of Odagiri's items reveals two important differences between himself and the Bank of Japan. In the first case his total of the amount outstanding of the loan known as that for "Four Railways in Manchuria and Mongolia" exceeds the Bank of Japan total by an unexplainable difference of about Yen 25 million (Yen 24,746,745). In the next

[123] This list is printed in Moulton, H. G., *Japan: An Economic and Financial Appraisal*, pp. 534–7. Moulton excludes certain obligations for interest installments found in the original table.

[124] In this and the other cases the single loan (of Yen 10 million) which is a general obligation of the Ministry of Communications is taken as "outside of Manchuria."

[125] Presented with other loans and claims in his *Japanese Investments in China*, p. 12.

case his total for Japanese obligations of the Peking-Suiyuan Railway shows a difference of about Yen 9 million. This can probably be explained by the omission from the list of the Bank of Japan of obligations for materials and supplies. Allowing for these and smaller differences, I find Odagiri's total to be reduced to Yen 124.9 million which, under the circumstances, brings the two Japanese totals into substantial agreement.   Odagiri's figures show the following percentage distribution:

In Manchuria	64 per cent
In the rest of China	36 per cent

The third total is derived from the lists presented by D. K. Lieu.[126]   These lists do not ordinarily allow for arrears of interest and this must be borne in mind in making comparison.   Lieu's total for the end of 1928 is Yen 115.3 million. He is in substantial agreement with the Bank of Japan on the amount outstanding on the loan for "Four Railways in Manchuria and Mongolia." The obligations of the Manchurian railways to Japan he shows to be Yen 77.1 million (66.9 per cent) and the obligations of the railways in the rest of China to be Yen 38.2 million (33.1 per cent).

The fourth total is from a table drawn up, at my request, by the Ministry of Railways of the Chinese government [127] to show the total foreign obligations of the government railways as of December 31, 1929. The obligations to Japan are shown in the following table.   In this and the other estimates presented, I have omitted the obligation of Yen 40 million connected with the Tsingtao-Tsinan Railway. The reasons for this omission have been explained above.

---

[126] In his *Foreign Investments in China, 1929.*
[127] That is of the government established at Nanking in 1928.   The Ministry of Railways differs from the Ministry of Communications of the former Peking government in that it has supervision of the railways alone and not of communications other than railways.

TABLE 30

JAPANESE OBLIGATIONS OF THE CHINESE GOVERNMENT RAILWAYS AS OF
DECEMBER 31, 1929, ACCORDING TO THE MINISTRY OF RAILWAYS

Original Currency		Rate	U. S. Dollars
Secured obligations			
Yen	133,477,330	2.0	66,738,665
Ch. $	65,093	3.5	18,598
			66,757,263
Unsecured obligations			
Yen	2,247,740	2.0	1,123,870
Tls.	15,094	2.5	6,038
Ch. $	2,968,542	3.5	771,012
U. S. $	578,330		578,330
			2,479,250
Total *			69,236,513

* The total in Japanese currency is Yen 138,473,026.

The total of the Ministry of Railways, Yen 138.5 million, is more recent and more complete than the others. It includes obligations for materials and supplies which the others omit. If we may calculate further arrears of interest for the year 1930 at 7 per cent of the total—certainly not too high a rate in the Japanese case—and add them we reach a final estimate of Yen 148.2 million as the adjusted outstanding railway obligations of the Chinese government to the Japanese at the end of 1930, based upon the table of the Ministry of Railways.

The following pages contain a new estimate of Japanese investments in Chinese railways which was not completed in its details until it became clear that this new estimate would show a total considerably larger than that of the Ministry of Railways. The examination of the obligations offers, at the same time, information touching the economic and political aspects of the Japanese interest in Chinese railways, especially in Manchuria.

*Japanese Investment in Chinese Government Railways
in Manchuria*

The Kirin-Changchun is the first of these railways. There was outstanding against it at the end of 1913 [128]

[128] See Table 12 above.

the sum of Yen 2,250,000. It is the first section of a line designed to connect the South Manchuria at Changchun with the Korean border to the east and with a seaport in Korea. Its political and strategic importance is obvious. In the "Twenty-one Demands," as they were originally presented, the Japanese government asked for the control and management of this railway for ninety-nine years.[129] In its final form this became an agreement "speedily to make a fundamental revision" of the loan agreement.

This was done in October, 1917. The loan was from the South Manchuria Railway Company for Yen 6.5 million to run for thirty years at 5 per cent and was secured on the property and receipts of the railway. There was, in addition, a provision that 20 per cent of the profits be reserved for the loan and a guarantee by the Chinese government. This transaction involved the refunding of the original loan. Japanese management and control was provided for by the appointment of three Japanese directors and there was a further provision that redemption of the loan was not permitted until the expiration of the full period.

The 1923 document of the Ministry of Communications lists a further advance of Yen 500,000 from the South Manchuria Railway Company on October 1, 1922, for two years at 9.5 per cent. In 1925 this became an obligation of Yen 1 million at 9 per cent.[130] The amount outstanding on the original loan on Jan. 1, 1931, was Yen 5,525,000, and it is to be supposed that an obligation of Yen 1.4 million is connected with the advance reported above.[131] The obligations for materials were reported at Yen 907,697.[132] The total obligations of

---

[129] MacMurray, J. V. A., *Treaties and Agreements*, vol. II, p. 1232.

[130] Lieu, D. K., *Foreign Investments in China*, p. 35.

[131] Kann and Baylin, *China Year Book*, 1931, p. 359. *China Year Book*, 1931, p. 200.

[132] *China Year Book*, 1931, p. 200. "On April 6, 1928, the above sum was borrowed from the South Manchuria Railway Company for purchasing 80-pound steel rails."

this railway to Japanese, which means to the South Manchuria Railway Company, were, at the end of 1930, Yen 7,832,697.

The Kirin-Tunhua Railway, completed October 10, 1928, carries the line from Changchun to Kirin on toward the Korean border. On June 18, 1918, three Japanese banks made a preliminary agreement for the building of a line from Kirin to Hueining.[133] The agreement called for "an advance of (Chinese) $10 million in full without any deduction for commission." Advances of a similar sort were made in connection with other agreements. They are separated in the general comments below from the funds actually invested in the construction of railways. It is, therefore, desirable to scrutinize this advance carefully. The agreement [134] with the three banks calls in its first article for an outline of the amount of funds required for the construction of the contemplated line and for the issue of bonds in accordance with the amount of funds which should prove to be required. This seems quite inconsistent with an immediate advance. We have, in the next place, a statement of the Chinese Minister of Communications at the time, Tsao Ju-lin, who is reported to have said that $10 million was paid into the Tokyo office of the Sino-Japanese Exchange Bank on the nineteenth of June to the credit of the Peking government "who are at liberty to use it without condition." [135] He then goes on to state, apparently recognizing a difference in the transaction, that the actual amount for the construction of the railway is to be determined in the future. This makes it doubtful whether the advance was for the purpose of building the railway at all. The doubt is confirmed by the 1923 document of the Ministry of Communications

---

[133] Young, C. W., *The International Relations of Manchuria*, p. 213. The three banks were the Industrial Bank of Japan, the Bank of Chosen, and the Bank of Taiwan. This contract had behind it the convention of April 15, 1907, concerning the Hsinmintun-Mukden and Kirin-Changchun Railways and the Chientao agreement of September 4, 1909.

[134] MacMurray, J. V. A., *Treaties and Agreements*, vol. II, pp. 1430-2.

[135] *Ibid.*, p. 1432.

in which we are told, concerning this advance, that it "was, heretofore, arranged and managed by the Ministry of Finance and our Ministry had no knowledge about its interest." The list of outstanding debts of the Ministry of Communications, drawn up by the Financial Readjustment Commission of 1925, specifically excludes this advance, which it states to have been Yen 10 million, from its list and puts it among the loans which are to be included in the consolidation plan of the Ministry of Finance.[136] The evidence seems sufficient to exclude this and other similar advances from funds used for railways. They may be regarded as obligations of the railways, if they are so accepted now or in the future, but, as a matter of fact, they were funds provided for what may be called the general purposes of the Chinese government.   The use of the funds will probably never be determined.[137]

The actual contract for the building of the Kirin-Tunhua Railway was signed by the South Manchuria Railway Company on October 24, 1925.[138] It called for the advance of Yen 18 million which was later increased to Yen 24 million. This sum was to be used for the construction of the railway and the line was to be transferred to Chinese management upon its completion. If payment in full was not made within one year of transference, the obligation of the Chinese government was to become a loan for thirty years at 9 per cent, secured upon the revenues of the line. Permission was given for the earlier redemption of the line but, during the life of the loan, Japanese were to be employed as chief and assistant accountants. The sum of Yen 24 million may be accepted as the obligation of this railway to the Japanese at the

[136] Financial Readjustment Commission, *Outstanding Debts of the Ministry of Communications*, p. 3.

[137] "The sum of Yen 10,000,000," says Young, "was given to the military clique in Peking to use for such purposes as they saw fit." Young, C. W., *Japan's Special Position in Manchuria*, p. 248.

[138] Young, C. W., *International Relations of Manchuria*, p. 213. The text of the agreement was communicated to the author by the head office of the South Manchuria Railway Company.

end of 1930. This sum does not, so far as is known, include the earlier advance of Yen ($?) 10 million.

Since the completion of the Kirin-Tunhua the Japanese have pressed for further construction in the direction of Hueining. Newspaper reports have from time to time mentioned alleged agreements for such construction.[139] It is improbable that a definite agreement existed in September, 1931, when Japanese troops advanced into Manchuria. It is to be noted that the Tien-Tu Light Railway, mentioned above as a direct investment, extends from the Korean border in the direction of Tunhua and that this leaves a gap of no more than sixty miles in a series of lines from Changchun to the sea. The bridging of this gap, we are told by a Chinese writer, has involved "one of the bitterest struggles between Japan and China." [140]

The Kirin-Tunhua is one of the two important railways financed by the Japanese in Manchuria since the creation of the New Consortium and the Washington Conference. The method adopted was, in both cases, an advance for construction not based upon a formal loan agreement. The formal loan was to be made later. The Japanese sought to exclude the whole Kirin-Hueining project from the scope of the Consortium. The specific exclusion of this project was not conceded by the other powers concerned and it is a common opinion that the method of financing adopted was, in part, for the purpose of avoiding the possible difficulties of a formal loan under the circumstances.

We have next to consider the Japanese interest in certain lines west of the South Manchuria. A convenient division is into lines south of Taonan, namely the Ssuping-kai-Chenchiatun, the Chenchiatun-Taonan, and the Chen-

---

[139] Young, C. W., *International Relations of Manchuria*, p. 215, footnote. Lin, T. C., "Political Aspects of Japanese Railway Enterprises in Manchuria," *Chinese Social and Political Science Review*, vol. 14, no. 2, p. 248.

[140] Lin, T. C., "Political Aspects of Japanese Railway Enterprises in Manchuria," *Chinese Social and Political Science Review*, vol. 14, no. 2, p. 248.

chiatun-Paiyintalai, and a single line north of Taonan, that is the Taonan-Angangki. The first of the lines south of Taonan, the Ssupingkai-Chenchiatun, was the subject of a loan contract signed by the Yokohama Specie Bank in December, 1915.[141] There lay behind this contract the secret exchange of notes between Japan and China on October 5, 1913, usually referred to as that concerning Five Railways in Manchuria, and the Chinese agreement in connection with the settlement of the "Twenty-one Demands" in May, 1915, to negotiate with Japanese capitalists first if foreign capital were required "for building necessary railways" in south Manchuria and eastern Inner Mongolia.[142] The contract with the Yokohama Specie Bank involved a loan of Yen 5 million at 5 per cent for forty years, secured on the property of the railway. Upon this loan there was outstanding on January 1, 1931, the sum of Yen 4,694,000.

Additional obligations of this line concern the other lines south of Taonan as well. In 1925 the South Manchuria Railway Company held an obligation of Yen 32 million. This covered earlier advances, such as an advance of Yen 13.7 million in May, 1922, an advance of Yen 3 million in October, 1922, and certain monthly advances. According to Lieu, Yen 10 million had been advanced in 1919 at 9 per cent in connection with a projected loan of Yen 45 million at 5 per cent.[143] This financing presumably covered the whole line from Ssupingkai to Taonan, actually opened to traffic on November 1, 1923, and the line from Chenchiatun to Paiyintalai, opened to traffic November 5, 1921, which is regarded as a branch line. No separate information is available concerning the financing of this branch and it may be supposed to be included with the Ssupingkai-Taonan. The amount outstanding, due to the South Manchuria Railway

[141] MacMurray, J. V. A., *Treaties and Agreements*, vol. II, p. 1249.
[142] *Ibid.*, pp. 1054, 1225.
[143] Lieu, D. K., *Foreign Investments in China, 1929*, p. 28.

Company, was on December 31, 1930, about Yen 47 million.[144] This total outstanding may include a principal sum in addition to the Yen 32 million, but there is no evidence that it does. The Japanese investment in the lines south of Taonan on December 31, 1930, may be estimated at about Yen 51,517,000.

The single line in northern Manchuria, the Taonan-Angangki, is one of the five railways of the 1913 agreement. The contract of December 27, 1915, permitted the Yokohama Specie Bank to finance such a loan. The Taonan-Angangki contract was signed at Mukden on September 3, 1924, by the Mukden government and the South Manchuria Railway.[145] It is really a construction contract. The contractors were to advance the construction cost and the entire sum so advanced was to be repaid within six months of the completion and transference of the line to the Chinese authorities. Failing payment, the obligation was to be converted into a loan at 9 per cent for thirty years. A Japanese advisor was to be engaged during the life of the loan. The railway was completed December 1, 1926, and covers a distance of 142 miles. The advance upon this railway came to Yen 12,920,000. It included a charge for the lease of rolling stock from the South Manchuria Railway.

The terms under which this line was built are similar to those in the case of the Kirin-Tunhua, for which they probably served as a model. The Taonan-Angangki is the second of the railways built by the Japanese in Manchuria since the creation of the New Consortium and the Washington Conference. It touches more closely the rights and interests of other nationals than does the Kirin-Tunhua. In the first place it traverses a part of the line covered by the Chinchow-Aigun Railway project of 1909 embodied

---

[144] *China Year Book*, 1931, p. 205, gives Yen 13,012,669 as of December 31, 1929.

[145] The text was communicated to C. W. Young by the Railway Company and is summarized in his *International Relations of Manchuria*, pp. 210–1.

in the preliminary agreement on the part of British and American interests with the Chinese government.[146]   In the next place the question of the exclusion of this railway from the scope of the New Consortium was, as Young says, the outstanding issue in the Consortium negotiations during 1920.[147] It was not specifically excluded. Whether or not it was excluded in effect, the financing of such a railway by a formal loan contract without reference to the Consortium might have raised questions. It is probable that such considerations influenced the financial arrangements and at the beginning of 1931 it remained to be seen whether a formal loan contract would be entered into by the Japanese without consultation with the other members of the New Consortium. This railway was actively opposed by the Russians. Treaty relations between China and Soviet Russia had but lately been resumed when the Taonan-Angangki contract was signed.[148]   This contract carried Japanese interests into the Russian sphere beyond the boundary set by the Russo-Japanese Secret Treaty of 1907, reaffirmed in the Secret Treaty of 1910, and reaffirmed once more in the Secret Treaty of 1912.[149] The attitude of the Soviet government in this matter was subjected to its first test by the proposal to carry a railway, financed by Japan, north to the Chinese Eastern. The difficulty was made more acute by the fact that the Russian railway has a wider gauge (5′) than the Taonan-Angangki (4′ 8½″). The new railway with its narrower gauge gave the Japanese a possible military advantage and was another step toward the "supremacy" of Dairen. The Soviet government opposed this line and entered a formal protest against its construction.[150] The only suc-

[146] MacMurray, J. V. A., *Treaties and Agreements*, vol. I, p. 800.
[147] Young, C. W., *International Relations of Manchuria*, p. 161.
[148] By the agreement of May 31, 1924.
[149] Young, C. W., *International Relations of Manchuria*, pp. 119–23. Young accepts the authenticity of these treaties and presents the evidence in Appendix C, pp. 266–9.
[150] Blakeslee, George H., *The Pacific Area*, p. 101. Young, C. W., "Economic Bases for New Railways in Manchuria," *Chinese Economic Journal*,

cess which attended this was the halting of Japanese interest in the line at Angangki. The extension of the line beyond Angangki is supposed to carry with it no Japanese interest.[151]

Without being certain that every obligation is known, we may say that Japanese interest in the Taonan-Angangki on December 31, 1930, was at least Yen 12,920,000. The whole of this sum had been advanced by the South Manchuria Railway.

There remains for final mention a preliminary agreement for certain railways in Manchuria and Mongolia signed on September 28, 1918, by the Industrial Bank of Japan for a syndicate representing itself, the Bank of Taiwan, and the Bank of Chosen.[152] This agreement is commonly called that for the Four Railways in Manchuria. None of these railways has been built.[153] The agreement is vague in the commitment of the Chinese government which is to "permit" the banks to raise the required funds. It is vague, also, as to financial arrangements. An advance of Yen 20 million was made upon this agreement. The conditions of this advance were the same as in the case of the advance upon the Kirin-Hueining contract. The 1923 document of the Ministry of Communications repeats its statement that the loan "was, heretofore, arranged and managed by the Ministry of Finance and our Ministry had no knowledge about its interest." In both cases we have to do with a so-called "Nishihara" loan and in this case we may be certain that the funds were not used for railway construction.

The Japanese interest in the various railways has now

April, 1927. Reprinted in the *Far Eastern Review*, May, 1927. The reference to Russian objections is on p. 206.

[151] This explains the importance attached to the advance of Japanese troops north of Angangki in November, 1931.

[152] MacMurray, J. V. A., *Treaties and Agreements*, vol. II, p. 1448.

[153] They are (1) the Kaiyuan-Heilung-Kirin Railway, (2) the Changchun-Taonan Railway, (3) the Taonan-Jehol Railway, (4) a line from the Taonan-Jehol to the sea.

been presented. It is seen to involve economic, political, and strategic problems of general international importance. From the point of view of Japanese investment in China, the facts may be summarized. The Japanese on January 1, 1931, held the following obligations connected with Manchurian railways or railway projects:

	Yen
Kirin-Changchun	7,832,697
Kirin-Tunhua	24,000,000
Ssupingkai-Taonan and branches	51,517,000
Taonan-Angangki	12,920,000
Kirin-Hueining	10,000,000
Four railways	20,000,000
	126,269,697

The total sum actually devoted to the construction of railways in Manchuria (with arrears of interest) was, on the same date, Yen 96,269,697. The presentation of a true picture requires that the other Yen 30 million be charged to the general purposes of the Chinese government.

The total sum which actually came from Japanese sources, either in Manchuria or in Japan, may be estimated at Yen 81,447,000, making a deduction of Yen 14,823,000 for arrears of interest included in the above total. Of the Yen 81,447,000, no less than Yen 76,752,000 came from the South Manchuria Railway Company. If we may suppose that the source of these funds was the same as that of the investment in the South Manchuria in general, we may make the further estimate that one-half of the South Manchuria Railway Company's investment involved a transfer of funds from Japan. The total funds transferred from Japan for the actual construction of railways may be estimated at Yen 43,071,000 and the funds so transferred in connection with all of the transactions here considered may be estimated, by adding the Yen 30 million referred to above, at about Yen 73 million.

A final summary of the Manchurian obligations at the end of 1930 may be offered.   Of the Yen 126,270,000, the obligation to the South Manchuria Railway Company was Yen 91,576,000 and to other Japanese creditors Yen 34,694,000.

Japanese Interest in Chinese Government Railways Outside of Manchuria

We have here to do with a very few loan contracts, for the Japanese interest in Chinese railways may be said to have followed other interests rather than to have preceded them.   We find, therefore, that outside of Manchuria the Japanese have taken an interest chiefly in the railways of Shantung province.   The obligation for Yen 40 million, which exists by reason of the turning over of the Tsingtao-Tsinan Railway to the Chinese government, is omitted from my list because, as I have pointed out, while it is a legal obligation of the railway it involved no net inpayment from Japan to China for its creation and it involves no net outpayment from China.

Two proposed railways in Shantung formed the basis of an advance.   These lines were originally arranged for in an exchange of notes between Germany and China on December 31, 1913, and the German rights may be held to have been transferred to Japan by the treaty of May 25, 1915, respecting the province of Shantung.[154]   The agreement with Japan is in important respects similar to the agreements referred to above for the Kirin-Hueining Railway and for Four Railways in Manchuria.   It provides for a future bond issue for the building of the lines and provides further for possible changes in the routes selected.   There was to be an advance of Yen 20 million at 8 per cent "furnished by means of discounting Treasury certificates" which were to be renewed every six

[154] MacMurray, J. V. A., *Treaties and Agreements*, vol. II, pp. 1094–1216. The agreement with Japan, p. 1450.

months. In a supplementary exchange of notes the two
lines are stated to be (1) between Tsinan and Shunte
and (2) between Kaomi and Hsuchow. Concerning this
advance, the 1923 document of the Ministry of Communications repeats its formula that the arrangement was
with the Ministry of Finance without the knowledge of
the Ministry of Communications. This loan is another
of the so-called "Nishihara" loans, to be regarded for the
general purposes of the Chinese government. It is included
among the unsecured loans and dealt with below.

A loan of Yen 10 million to the Ministry of Communications is included in the list of Japanese loans outstanding on December 31, 1913.[155] The amount of this loan
outstanding on January 1, 1931 was Yen 9,340,000. In
addition there were arrears of interest from June 1, 1922
amounting to Yen 2,554,500,[156] making a total obligation of Yen 11,894,500. This is accepted as a general
obligation of the Chinese Ministry of Railways but the
circumstances are held to justify its inclusion in this list
of loans for railways outside of Manchuria.

Japanese loans, reported as "obligations with securities," have been made in connection with the financing
of the Peking-Suiyuan Railway now called the Peiping-
Suiyuan or the Peiping-Paotouchen. These loans were
originally one of Yen 3 million for five years at 9 per cent
made in 1918 and one for Yen 3 million for four years
at 10 per cent made in 1921. The security consisted in
each case of debentures of the railway to the nominal
value of Chinese $3.5 million. There was outstanding on
these obligations on December 31, 1925, the last date
for which information is available, the sum of Yen 5.2
million, and arrears of interest of Yen 2,127,000.[157]
These obligations may be held to represent a total of
about Yen 9 million on December 31, 1930. There were,

[155] See Table 12 above. The loan is there called the Yuchuanpu loan.
[156] Kann and Baylin, *China Year Book*, 1931, p. 358.
[157] Financial Readjustment Commission, *Outstanding Debts of the Ministry of Communications*.

in addition, obligations for materials and supplies of an unknown amount. The Japanese obligation of this railway is stated by Odagiri to have been Yen 17,871,000 at the end of 1928.

The sum of these items is as follows:

	Yen
Advance on two railways in Shantung	20,000,000
The Yuchuanpu loan	11,894,500
Peiping-Suiyuan	9,000,000
	40,894,500

Concerning these obligations it may be pointed out that Yen 20,894,500 is connected with the railways and that Yen 20 million is regarded as not so connected and as having been used for the general purposes of the Chinese government. It may be pointed out, also, that these obligations have involved a remittance of funds from Japan to the amount of Yen 36 million. Of this sum 16 million was for the actual financing or construction of railways.

Total Obligations of the Government Railways to Japan

The total railway obligation of the Chinese government to Japan, distributed between Manchuria and the rest of China, is shown in the following table. This is followed by a table showing the estimates of others and the percentage in Manchuria in each case in which it is known.

TABLE 31

TOTAL OBLIGATION OF THE CHINESE GOVERNMENT RAILWAYS TO JAPAN, AS OF DECEMBER 31, 1930

	Yen	*Per Cent of Total*
In Manchuria	126,270,000	75.5
In the rest of China	40,894,500	24.5
	167,164,500	100.0

TABLE 32

ESTIMATES OF TOTAL OBLIGATIONS OF THE CHINESE GOVERNMENT
RAILWAYS TO JAPAN

	Year	Yen	Per Cent in Manchuria	Per Cent in Rest of China
Bank of Japan	1925	117,729,200	66.8	33.2
Odagiri	1928	155,976,000	64.0	36.0
D. K. Lieu	1928	115,300,000	66.9	33.1
Ministry of Railways	1929	138,473,000		
From preceding table	1930	167,164,500	75.5	24.5

The increase in the Manchurian percentage of Japanese railway obligations is an outstanding fact. If there is deducted from the total the amount of the advances for the general purposes of the Chinese government, the investment in Chinese government railways in Manchuria is found to be 82.2 per cent of the total and the investment in the rest of China 17.8 per cent. This is what, on general grounds, we should expect to find. Japan has not been an exporter of capital except for a few years immediately after the war. The funds for railway construction under the Chinese government have not come from Japanese sources except in the case of the Manchurian railways. The building of the Manchurian railways is to be regarded as an extension of Japanese direct investments in Manchuria. The Japanese, it may be said, have been business men extending their holdings rather than bankers and investors seeking opportunities abroad for Japanese capital. This is an additional illustration of Japan's position as entrepreneur rather than investor.

The estimates of remittances of funds from Japan in connection with this railway financing may be summarized. The remittance in connection with the Manchurian railways considered was estimated at Yen 73 million and that for railways outside of Manchuria at Yen 36 million. This means a total remittance of Yen 109 million. It must be borne in mind that Yen 50 million of this sum has been for other than railway purposes. It may, therefore, be estimated that funds to the amount of Yen 59 million have actually been transferred from Japan to China for the building and equipment of railway lines both in and out of Manchuria.

Japanese Investments in Communications Other Than Railways

The Japanese have taken a relatively small share in the development of telegraph, radio, and telephone communication in China. The three obligations listed below include all of the definitely recognized long-term obligations in this field. There are obligations for materials and supplies to Japanese which cannot be estimated. The 1923 document of the Ministry of Communications shows such obligations to the amount of Yen 10,859,000. D. K. Lieu's lists show such obligations to the amount of about Yen 14 million.

In this field, also, there is a loan which belongs to the Nishihara group. It involved an advance of Yen 20 million from the Exchange Bank of China in accordance with an agreement signed April 30, 1918.[158] The loan was for five years at 8 per cent and was to be "delivered without any discount." The security was sweepingly inclusive, if it was not specific, covering "all the property and revenue of the telegraph lines throughout the Republic of China," though it did take into account certain other contracts. This loan is mentioned here to make the list as complete as possible. It is not included in the total of the obligations now being considered but is placed with the unsecured loans.

The first obligation is the result of a contract concluded between the Chinese Ministry of the Navy and Mitsui & Company on February 21, 1918.[159] This contract was for the construction of a wireless telegraph station in

[158] MacMurray, J. V. A., *Treaties and Agreements*, vol. II, p. 1424.
[159] *Ibid.*, p. 1519.

China capable of direct communication with Japan, America, and Europe. Mitsui & Company were to control this station for thirty years, at the end of which time it was to be turned over unconditionally to the Chinese government. The Japanese company agreed, also, to respect other engagements concerning telegraphs entered into with Danish and British companies. A provision in a declaration dated March 5, 1918, contains the statement that "it is mutually agreed by both parties that during the term of thirty years no other party shall be allowed to erect a similar wireless telegraph station." This provision was the foundation for the Japanese claim that the later contract with the Federal Telegraph Company of the United States (January 8, 1921) was in violation of the terms of this agreement.

The obligation created by the Mitsui wireless agreement was £536,267. This may be accepted as the amount outstanding on January 1, 1931. It comes to a total of Yen 5,219,486.

The second of the loans to be listed here is the so-called Telephone Extension loan of October 25, 1918. It was for Yen 10 million at 8 per cent and was to run for three years.[160] The details of the loan contract were made public for the first time by Frederic E. Lee.[161] The security for this loan, as Lee points out, was not only the property and revenue of the then existing Chinese government telephones but it included operating rights and telephone developments in the future. Further security offered covered six wireless stations in China and treasury notes to the value of Yen 5 million. Lee was able to secure, also, a statement of the application of the funds made available by this loan. They include expenditures by the Ministry of Communications to the amount of about Yen 6.6 million and expenditures by the Ministry of Finance to

[160] Baylin, J. R., *Foreign Loan Obligations of China*, p. 79.
[161] *Currency, Banking, and Finance in China*, Washington, 1926, pp. 216-8, where it is referred to as the Chuijitzu Telephone loan.

the amount of about Yen 1.4 million. The loan may be accepted as having been used in part, at least, for the purposes now being considered. The payment of principal was not made at the end of three years and there are arrears of interest which bring the amount outstanding on January 1, 1931, to Yen 19,894,000.

The third loan is the so-called Telegraph Improvement loan entered into on February 10, 1920. The agreement was for a loan of Yen 15 million. Of this, Yen 6 million had actually been advanced. The term of the loan was for thirteen years and the rate of interest 9 per cent. The contract was with the East Asia Industrial Company. The agreement for this loan was made public by Lee [162] who states that Yen 2,730,000 of this loan was converted into Chinese dollars through the Exchange Bank of China and the Bank of Communications, and amounted to the sum of Chinese $1,132,950. The amount outstanding on this loan on January 1, 1931, is estimated to be Yen 10,320,000.

The total of the loans here considered is as follows:

	Yen
The Mitsui Wireless loan	5,219,486
Telephone Extension loan	19,894,000
Telegraph Improvement loan	10,320,000
	35,433,486

This total of about Yen 35.4 million called for remittances from Japan to China which cannot have been greater than Yen 21.2 million.

Japanese Share of the "Unsecured" Loans to the Chinese Government

The last set of obligations to be considered includes the whole series of items which are usually referred to as the "unsecured and inadequately secured" debts of the Chinese government. They include both domestic and

[162] *Currency, Banking, and Finance in China* pp. 219–20.

foreign obligations and they have come into existence very largely since the death of President Yuan Shih-kai. The Japanese are the largest holders of the foreign share of these obligations and a very large part of the Japanese share came into existence during the years 1917 and 1918 when war prosperity reached its height in Japan. The factors that brought about the situation in this field, so far as Japan is concerned, were the World War, the Chinese government's inability to borrow in Europe after the death of Yuan, the funds available in Japan during the late years of the war, and the China policy of the Japanese government, particularly under the Ministry of Premier Count Terauchi (1916–1918).

The first, and the last, adequate study of these obligations as a whole was that made by the so-called Financial Readjustment Commission which came into existence in August, 1923. The results of the work of this commission were made public in reports which show the various items as of September 31, 1925. The final report brings the figures down to December 31, 1925. It was the purpose of the Financial Readjustment Commission to offer a plan for the readjustment and refunding of the unsecured obligations. The commission, therefore, rejected certain items from the lists which were prepared for it by the creditors. In the case of Japan, for example, a loan of Yen 2 million to the provincial administration of Fukien province was omitted by the commission on the ground that it was not a claim against the central government of China. The total of the Japanese obligations listed by the Financial Readjustment Commission as of December 31, 1925, was Yen 254,993,960.[163] The figures presented by the Japanese creditors came to a total of Yen 330,614,405.[164] The difference between these figures is explained in part by such omissions as have

[163] The rate of exchange originally adopted by the Commission took 1 yen at Chinese $.76. In its later calculations the yen was taken as equal to the Chinese dollar.

[164] Lieu, D. K., *Foreign Investments in China, 1929*, p. 37.

been indicated, in part by different methods of calculating interest in arrears, and finally upon differences of opinion as to facts. A complete list of exclusions with the reasons in each case was drawn up at the time by the Financial Readjustment Commission, but this list has not been made public.

The work of the Financial Readjustment Commission was behind the figures of the Kemmerer Commission which have been made public.[165] It was, no doubt, impossible for the Kemmerer Commission to make a new and independent study of these obligations, particularly in the Japanese case. The figures of the Financial Readjustment Commission were carried down to the end of 1927 in a report drawn up by the Ministry of Finance of the Peking government shortly before the success of the Nationalists in 1928. This report is in Chinese and has the title "Various Domestic and Foreign Loans and the Boxer Indemnity." It will be referred to as the 1927 document. In this 1927 document the total of the unsecured and inadequately secured debts due to Japanese is Yen (or Chinese dollars) 298,391,632. The increase in this total over that of the Financial Readjustment Commission is to be accounted for almost entirely as due to interest charges. No important item is to be found in the 1927 document which was not in the Financial Readjustment Commission's report. What is more, we may be quite certain that practically no payments had been made on any of these loans by the end of 1930. The total from the 1927 document must be accepted as the only one available.

It is necessary to make certain modifications and adjustments in the total as it is given in the 1927 document. The first of these is the deduction of the sums which I have excluded entirely from my list of China's foreign debts. This means a single item of Yen 14 million issued for the payment to the Japanese on public property at

[165] *China Year Book*, 1931, p. 347.

Tsingtao. The amount under this item in the 1927 document is Chinese $15,609,836. There are to be deducted, also, the various loans which have been set down as obligations of the Ministry of Railways and which appear in the 1927 document also. These items are the advance on the Kirin-Hueining Railway, the advance for the construction of Four Railways in Manchuria and Mongolia, and the advance for the construction of Two Railways in Shantung. The total to be deducted on these advances of Yen 50 million is Chinese $83,945,874. After making this and certain minor adjustments, I arrive at a total of Chinese $200,087,492. Taking into account the fact that these obligations were almost entirely in yen and considering, for the few which were not in yen, the rate of exchange at the time, I reach the conclusion that the unsecured debts of the Chinese government to Japan amounted to Yen 200,087,492 at the end of the year 1927.

It has been found impossible to discover what additions ought to be made to this total in order to represent the situation at the end of 1930. It would not be unreasonable to add a round sum for the arrears of interest which have accrued during these three years. When one considers, however, the circumstances surrounding the creation of these obligations, it seems best not to undertake any such calculation and I have, therefore, allowed this total of about Yen 200 million to stand as the best estimate of the present obligation that can be made.

The following list of obligations, included in the 1927 document, has been drawn up to show, in the first place, something of the nature of the loans. This is indicated in the abbreviated titles given. The second purpose is to show the dates of the loans and particularly to show the number made during the year 1918. In the third place, the amount involved in the original transaction is given, in so far as it is known, in order to indicate the remittances from Japan which may have been, and probably were, involved in the creation of these obligations.

TABLE 33

THE CHIEF UNSECURED OBLIGATIONS FROM THE 1927 DOCUMENT OF THE
FORMER MINISTRY OF FINANCE

Date	Denomination of Loan	Rate of Interest	Nominal Amount	Actually Paid Over	Outstanding 12-31-27
			Yen	Yen	Ch. Dollars
2-15-12	Nanking Provisional Government	7-10%	2,000,000	1,950,000	3,427,277
5-12-16	Okura and Co.—Huaning notes	8%	1,000,000	990,000	2,455,957
11-19-17	Tai Hei Co.—First Arms Loan	7%	18,716,421	17,014,597	53,983,562
7-31-18	Tai Hei Co.—Second Arms Loan	7%	13,365,127	10,877,112	
1- 5-18	Mitsui—Bureau of Printing	8-10%	2,000,000	2,000,000	3,822,393
4-30-18	Exchange Bank—Telegraph Loan	8-9%	20,000,000	19,671,233	23,780,026
8- 2-18	Exchange Bank—Gold Mines and Forests	7.5%	30,000,000	29,001,370	34,666,576
	Advance Interest— Gold Mines Loan	14.4%	1,125,000		1,673,742
	Interest advances on Gold Mines and Telegraph Loans	14.4%	19,386,916		27,352,896
6-18-18	Industrial Bank— Kirin-Hueining Ry.	7.5%	10,000,000	9,625,000	11,617,454
9-28-18	Industrial Bank— 4 rys. in Manchuria	8%	20,000,000	19,200,000	23,848,448
9-28-18	Industrial Bank— 2 rys. in Shantung	8%	20,000,000	19,200,000	23,848,448
	Int. advances on the 3 railway loans above	9.5%	18,583,902		23,631,523
9-28-18	War Participation Loan	7%	20,000,000	18,400,000	
	Advance Int. above loan	8%	Principal	and Interest	36,039,294
6-30-19	Tai Hei Co.—Arms for War Participation Bureau	8%	1,069,985	1,060,085	1,583,839
10-15-25	Advance for Hankow Paper Mill	12%	1,000,000	1,000,000	1,294,038
			198,247,351	149,999,297	273,025,473

It is to be observed that loans to the nominal amount of about Yen 200 million brought remittances from Japan to China which may be estimated at almost exactly Yen 150 million. The rates of interest run from 7 to 14.4 per

cent a year. The total obligations created by these transactions are set forth in the 1927 document as about
Chinese $275 million.

The sum under the heading of unsecured loans, which
I have accepted for inclusion in my total of Japanese
obligations, is about Yen 200 million. This is smaller
than the total in the above table since the table includes
railway loans which I have listed with the railway obligations. By simple proportion I arrive at a probable remittance from Japan in connection with the smaller total,
that is, Yen 200 million, of about Yen 110 million.

The nature of the loans is to some extent indicated
by the names which appear in the table. Loans to the
nominal amount of Yen 120 million are dealt with separately in the next section. It is sufficient to remark
here that the chief use of the funds procured by the unsecured loans not dealt with below was for the purchase
of munitions.

The "Nishihara" Loans

Six of the obligations listed above were negotiated
with the same Japanese group and during the same year.
Three are reported by the Financial Readjustment Commission as having been created on the same day. The
total amount involved in the six was Yen 120 million,
which more than doubled the outstanding debts of the
Chinese government to Japan. In addition to the magnitude and rapidity of the transactions, there were other
unusual features which make them a remarkable venture
in the financing of the Chinese government.

It is difficult to find a name for these transactions.
They were hardly investments in any usual meaning of
the word. In attempting to state their nature carefully
and accurately, one might say this: they were a series
of payments of Japanese funds to a group of Chinese
officials then in power in exchange for agreements which

gave Japanese interests certain claims, particularly in Manchuria, and so advanced the policy of the Japanese government.

These loans, together with certain others, are usually referred to as the "Nishihara" loans,[166] since they were negotiated by Mr. K. Nishihara, once a member of the board of directors of the Bank of Chosen and at the time the personal representative in China of Premier Count Terauchi of Japan.[167] He seems to have acted quite independently of the official representative of the Japanese banking group in the Old Consortium, the Yokohama Specie Bank, and of the Japanese Legation at Peking. In any case the Yokohama Specie Bank joined other Consortium banks in protesting certain results of Mr. Nishihara's activities and the Japanese legation "on several occasions denied the progress of any negotiations, even after the time when (as subsequently appeared) those negotiations had led to an agreement." [168] The secrecy which surrounded Mr. Nishihara's negotiations was a matter of general comment in China at the time and we are told that the Chinese official with whom he negotiated, Mr. Ts'ao Ju-lin, acted "in most cases without the knowledge even of the subordinates in his own ministries," that is, the Ministries of Communications and of Finance.[169] The secrecy was enforced by a newspaper censorship. The American Minister to China (Mr. Reinsch) telegraphed to his government at the height of the negotiations that eight newspapers in

[166] The others included one of April 22, 1918, for Yen 3 million to the provincial government at Mukden which was stated to be for the readjustment of the reserves of the provincial bank. A translation of the text is to be found in MacMurray, *Treaties and Agreements*, vol. II, p. 1416. It brought about what was in effect a discrimination against non-Japanese business in Mukden according to American diplomatic officials in Peking. *U. S. Foreign Relations, 1918*, p. 133. Baylin lists a loan of Yen 20 million to the Bank of Communications as a "Nishihara" loan. *Foreign Loan Obligations of China*, p. 84.

[167] Young, C. W., *Japan's Special Position in Manchuria*, p. 239. *U. S. Foreign Relations, 1918*, p. 122. Young's chapter provides an excellent brief account of the loans, especially those connected with Manchuria.

[168] *U. S. Foreign Relations*, 1918, p. 122.

[169] *Ibid.*, p. 123.

Peking had recently been closed for printing the details of the loan contracts.[170]

The preparation for the "Nishihara" loans, according to a Japanese source,[171] involved the placing of restrictions upon the activities of the Yokohama Specie Bank, the granting of new rights to the Bank of Chosen, and the reorganization of the Industrial Bank of Japan whose debentures were guaranteed by the Japanese government. It involved, also, the creation of a new Exchange Bank of China, a Sino-Japanese enterprise.

It has already been observed that the railway loan contracts included among the "Nishihara" loans were unusual in many of their provisions. This is true of the contracts for loans for other purposes also. The financial details ordinarily to be found in such contracts were either entirely missing or extraordinarily brief. There was no provision in the contracts for any assurance that the funds were actually to be used for the ostensible purposes. On the contrary there were express stipulations that funds were to be placed at the disposal of the government of China in Tokyo without any discount.[172]

Reasons have been given for holding that the funds were not used for the purposes for which the loans were supposed to be intended. Mr. J. V. A. MacMurray, reporting from Peking at the time, states that the funds were actually used to meet the demands of military officials for expenses. Concerning the various projects in the industrial field, he remarks that "the contemplated industrial development has made no progress towards a beginning." [173]

[170] *U. S. Foreign Relations*, 1918, p. 112.

[171] Information from "General Outline of a Policy for Sino-Japanese Friendship and Economic Co-operation," published by the Japanese Ministry of Finance, June, 1918 (in Japanese) has been made available by C. W. Young, *Japan's Special Position in Manchuria*, pp. 242–4.

[172] In the case of the Kirin-Hueining Agreement, of the Gold Mine and Forestry Agreement, and of the Agreement for the Two Railways in Shantung.

[173] *U. S. Foreign Relations*, 1918, p. 123.

One of these loans, that for gold mining and forestry in the provinces of Heilungkiang and Kirin, aroused so great a storm of indignation that documents which were not supposed to reach the public were made available in the Chinese newspapers. If we may believe one such document published in Peking, Mr. Ts'ao Ju-lin in a memorandum submitted to the Chinese Cabinet in connection with the "gold mines and forests" loan stated that the loan was made because the Chinese government needed the money and that to get the money "he had been compelled to adopt the subterfuge of making a loan for nominally industrial purposes . . . inasmuch as the avowal of the fact that the money was for political purposes would lead to difficulties with the Consortium and with the foreign governments interested." [174]

The direct interest of the Japanese government hardly needs further proof in the light of the circumstances which have been described. Such further proof is available, however, for the Japanese government in 1926 decided to take over from the Japanese creditors their claims against the Chinese government and gave the creditors Japanese government bonds.[175] Bonds to the value of Yen 82,902,550 were delivered in 1927, Yen 52,036,325 in 1928, and Yen 21,091,850 in 1930, making a total of Yen 156,000,725. This transaction was brought to the attention of informed Japanese in Tokyo during the summer of 1930. Japanese creditors hold unpaid Russian obligations to the amount of about Yen 260 million. There has been some effort on the part of the holders of Russian obligations to secure Japanese government bonds but this has not been successful. The explanation offered of this difference between the Chinese and the Russian cases' was that the Chinese case involved political considerations.

[174] *U. S. Foreign Relations*, 1918, p. 131.
[175] This transaction is mentioned by Coons, A. G., *The Foreign Public Debt of China*, p. 92; by Young, C. W., *Japan's Special Position in Manchuria*, p. 256 footnote, and by Moulton, H. G., *Japan*, pp. 210, 580.

The Japanese with whom I have discussed the "Nishihara" loans fall into two groups. The bankers and business men in Japan who were not immediately interested in China were inclined to the opinion that the whole series of advances, made in the midst of the period of war prosperity, were to be accepted as losses. My attention was called on more than one occasion to the statements of Mr. Junnosuke Inouye concerning these loans. Their tenor is sufficiently indicated by the following: "These investments with the central and provincial governments of China—investments running to several hundred million yen—resulted in a dead loss, and today Japan can recover neither the capital which she thus locked up nor one penny of interest on it. To put the matter in a nutshell I would say that foreign investment was not practised by this country and that such trifling investments as were effected might just as well have been thrown into the sea." [176]

Those Japanese, on the contrary, who were closely in touch with China, either for business or official reasons, took the viewpoint that the "Nishihara" loans represent obligations on the part of the Chinese government which must be insisted upon. This attitude was behind an exchange of notes in connection with the Customs Agreement of May 6, 1930, between China and Japan in which the Japanese government asked for a "speedy consolidation" of the unsecured and inadequately secured obligations of China due to Japanese creditors. The Chinese government, in turn, stated its intention to call a conference of creditors by October 1, 1930. [177] On November 15, 1930, further steps were taken toward the calling of such a conference and toward the creation, on the part of the Chinese government, of its commission for the

[176] Quoted by Moulton, H. G., *Japan: An Economic and Financial Appraisal*, p. 284.

[177] Chinese Government Ministry of Foreign Affairs: *Agreement Concluded between the Republic of China and the Empire of Japan*, Nanking, May 14, 1930, pp. 22, 24.

Consolidation of Foreign and Domestic Obligations. Japanese policy has been indicated more recently by the reply of the Japanese Foreign Minister to an interpellation in the Upper House on March 9, 1931. The Minister, Baron Shidehara, is reported to have said that "Japan will never consent to China's demand for . . . cancellation." [178]

"Nishihara" loans to the amount of Yen 120 million have entered into my totals of railway obligations and of unsecured loans. Taking them together—and I have no doubt failed to include some—these loans brought payments into China to the amount of Yen 114,997,603, according to the reports of the Financial Readjustment Commission of 1925. They are the basis of obligations which the 1927 document of the Ministry of Finance sets down, as of December 31, 1927, at Chinese $206,458,-407. The calculations of the 1927 document took the yen and the Chinese dollar as equal. If we were to take into account further arrears of interest and the rate of exchange (about Chinese $2 for 1 yen) which obtained at the end of 1930 and in 1931, we might by such a method arrive at the fantastic sum of about Chinese $1,000 million as the amount due in 1931 on this one series of transactions. To state this figure is for all practical purposes to demonstrate the necessity for its modification. Such is the heritage left by what have been called the "unconscionable activities of one Mr. K. Nishihara." [179]

Summary of Japanese Holdings of Government Obligations

The following table brings together the results of the examination of Japanese holdings of the obligations of the Chinese government. It is to be borne in mind that no attempt has been made to arrive at a total of such loans as may have been made by Japanese to the provincial

[178] *North China Daily News* (Shanghai), March 10, 1931.
[179] Young, C. W., *Japan's Special Position in Manchuria*, p. 239.

and other local governments of China. The provincial
loans were estimated by Lieu at Yen 59.6 million at the
end of 1928.[180] The Bank of Japan included in its list
for the end of 1925 the sum of Yen 60 million under the
heading "Other Government Loans." How far they include the loans listed by Lieu cannot be determined.
Certain of the loans listed by the Japanese as loans to the
central government are placed by Chinese students among
provincial loans. As a matter of fact loans actually made
to provincial authorities are frequently accepted by the
central government as its obligations.   It has seemed
best to make no attempt to estimate provincial loans
separately and to point out that they have been omitted.
In the second place no success has attended an effort
to discover the total of "unsecured" obligations which
may have come into existence since the end of 1927. It
may be said with some confidence that the total is small.
I repeat, in the third place, that arrears of interest on
the "unsecured" loans have not been calculated since
the end of 1927. It has seemed best to accept the figures
of the latest available compilation by Chinese authorities.

TABLE 34

JAPANESE HOLDINGS OF THE OBLIGATIONS OF THE CHINESE GOVERNMENT
AS OF DECEMBER 31, 1930

	Yen	U. S. Dollars
General secured loans	45,469,760	22,734,880
Railway obligations	167,164,500	83,582,250
Obligations for communications other than railways	35,433,486	17,716,743
Unsecured loans	200,087,492	100,043,746
	448,155,238	224,077,619

Administrative, Cultural, and Philanthropic Holdings

It is impossible to arrive at an accurate estimate for
1931 of Japanese holdings of property in China devoted
to administrative, cultural, and philanthropic purposes.

[180] Lieu, D. K., *Foreign Investments in China, 1929*, p. 43.

Certain items are fairly well known, however. The South Manchuria Railway Company reported, on March 31, 1931, that it held schools and hospitals which it carried on its books at Yen 37,787,000. Land and other holdings which the railway company used for purposes of civil administration is estimated at Yen 66,458,000. These items make a total of Yen 104,245,000.

The Japanese committee reports two Japanese societies with important holdings. The first of these, the Toa Dobun Kai,[181] operated schools open to Chinese in Shanghai, Tientsin, and Hankow. The endowment of the society is reported to have been Yen 1,382,000 in 1928. The value of its property may be estimated at Yen 500,-000. Its expenditure came to Yen 657,000 in 1928. A second society, the Dojin Kai (Benevolence Association) operated four hospitals in China in 1930, one in each of the following cities: Peiping, Hankow, Tsinan, and Tsingtao. The operating expenses of this society was Yen 365,-000 in 1928.

Finally there was the capital sum in the so-called Cultural Works Special Account which may be estimated in various ways. The Japanese committee arrived at a total of Yen 59,270,000. Disbursements of Yen 800,000 were reported for the Science Institutes and Libraries in Peiping and Shanghai.

Upon such information we may estimate the total holdings of property devoted to the purposes here being considered at, say, Yen 115 million. This leaves out of account the administrative holdings of the government of the Kwantung leased area.

The annual remittance to China from Japan for these purposes is not easily arrived at. There is, in the first place, the annual grant to the government of the Kwantung leased area from the Japanese government. This came to Yen 4.5 million in 1930, as is shown above. The sums involved in payments under the Cultural Works

[181] Translated by Odagiri as the East Asia Common Script Association.

Special Account are omitted here since they do not constitute a remittance of Japanese funds, but a return to China of Chinese funds. We have to consider expenditures by the two societies mentioned above which were about Yen 1 million in 1928. If we leave out of account the sums which may have been raised in China, we arrive at a total of about Yen 6 million. No closer estimate of the annual remittances for these purposes can be made.

SUMMARY AND CONCLUSION

The investments of the Japanese in China, as they were at the end of 1930, have now been presented. There was no change worth considering in the situation during the following months and the total shown in the following table may be taken as showing the situation when Japanese troops advanced into Manchuria beyond the leased area and railway zone in September, 1931.

TABLE 35

JAPANESE INVESTMENTS IN CHINA AT THE END OF 1930

	Yen	U. S. Dollars
Direct business investments	1,748,259,000	874,129,500
Investments in Chinese corporations	77,428,000	38,714,000
Obligations of the Chinese government	448,155,000	224,077,500
	2,273,842,000	1,136,921,000

This brings to an end the series of estimates of Japanese investments. Certain conclusions may be shown by bringing together the figures for the selected years into general tables. The first of these shows total Japanese investments of all sorts for the three years. It will be remembered that there were practically no investments in 1897. The whole of the Japanese investment in China has been made during the present century. The increase was so great between 1900 and 1914 as to make comparison pointless and the whole of the small investment in 1900 was in business. In the following tables, therefore, figures for 1900 are not presented. The Japanese entry into Manchuria after the Russo-Japanese War so changed the situation that the earlier years may, for most purposes, be disregarded.

TABLE 36

JAPANESE INVESTMENTS IN CHINA, 1900–1930, IN MILLIONS OF U. S. DOLLARS, WITH RELATIVES

1900	1.0	0.5
1914	219.6	100.0
1930	1,136.9	517.7

The increase in Japanese investments under each of the main divisions is shown next. The table shows the totals and the rate of increase for direct business investments, investments in Chinese corporations, and in the obligations of the Chinese government. The outstanding fact is the remarkable increase in the Japanese investment in government obligations. A very large part of this increase took place during the war and post-war prosperity in Japan and a considerable part represents obligations which were brought into existence for political reasons. Some part consists of advances not from Japan but from the earnings of the South Manchuria Railway within China. Whatever comments and explanations may be necessary, the fact remains that the obligations of the Chinese government to Japanese were twenty-three times as great in 1931 as in 1914.

TABLE 37

JAPANESE INVESTMENTS, 1914–1930, BY MAIN DIVISIONS

(In millions of U. S. dollars with relatives)

	Business Investments		In Chinese Corporations		In Government Obligations	
1914	192.5	100	17.5	100	9.6	100
1930	874.1	454	38.7	221	224.1	2334

The changes in the percentage distribution of these investments among the main divisions is shown in the following table.

TABLE 38

JAPANESE INVESTMENTS IN CHINA, 1914–1930

Percentage Distribution by Main Divisions
(Values shown in millions of U. S. Dollars)

	Business Investments		In Chinese Corporations		In Government Obligations	
		Per Cent of Total		Per Cent of Total		Per Cent of Total
1914	192.5	87.6	17.5	9.6	9.6	4.4
1930	874.1	76.9	38.7	3.8	224.1	19.7

In 1900 business investments were 100 per cent of the total. This had fallen to 87.6 per cent in 1914 and to 76.9 per cent in 1930. The overwhelming importance of direct business investments needs no more emphasis. The decline in the relative importance of this form of investment would have been more significant if it had been brought about by an increase in investment in Chinese corporations rather than in the obligations of the Chinese government. Investment in Chinese corporations was a new field but the Japanese have not succeeded in its cultivation. Japanese investments in government obligations are such as to make it quite certain that in the Japanese case direct business investments are the only form which has brought funds to China on any considerable scale.

How much actual remittance of funds from Japan has accompanied the building up of Japanese holdings in China may be only roughly estimated. Accepting the results established in the case of the South Manchuria Railway Company as a basis for all business investments and adding what is fairly well known concerning the other fields, we arrive at a total of about U. S. $600 million. The remittance from Japan for investment in China has almost certainly been no greater than this sum.

The estimate of remittances to Japan from China is equally difficult to make. It is known that the Japanese obligations of the Chinese government have brought practically no outpayments from China in recent years. It is known that the South Manchuria Railway Company made such payments to a sum which was about Yen 36.5 million in 1930.[182] The profits paid to Japan on textile mills were at the modest rate of about 5.5 per cent in 1927. Dividends have not been much greater since 1927. Taking into account the information concerning other industries, secured in China, it may be estimated that the total of outpayments from China in connection with Japanese investments in the country was, in recent years, about Yen 75 million. The figure arrived at by this method is quite consistent with the reports of the Ministry of Finance of the Japanese government. These reports show Yen 80.6 million as "net profits of business enterprises abroad." [183] The average for the five years 1925–1929 was about Yen 75 million.[184]

In the preceding pages the results of a new study of Japanese investments in China have been stated. It is, of course, true that no complete and accurate account is possible. Nevertheless, figures may be offered with some degree of confidence. Japanese investments in China in 1931 reached a total of about U. S. $1,137 million. These investments have occasioned a remittance to China of about U. S. $600 million. They have, in recent years, brought remittances from China at an average rate of about U. S. $37.5 million. This summarizes the financial aspect of the matter.

Beyond the financial field lie the fields of trade and

---

[182] Not all of this was a net outpayment from China nor was it all a net inpayment into Japan. See the section above on Manchuria in the finances of the Japanese government.

[183] Moulton, H. G., *Japan: An Economic and Financial Appraisal*, p. 530.

[184] This includes the return on direct business investments in the South Seas, Siberia, and elsewhere, but this is hardly more than Yen 200 million while the total for China is Yen 1,748 million.

economic relations and that of general Japanese policy in China. In these fields the importance of Manchuria is, of course, outstanding. Manchuria is the source of important raw materials and the scene of a growing trade. It is the greatest single field of Japanese investment outside of Japan. It has afforded an opportunity for Japanese ability in the field of management and organization. The satisfaction that has gone with successful expansion is not to be measured in dollars and cents, or even in terms of trade and raw materials. It is important to point this out, for the preceding pages have shown that the economic importance of Manchuria to Japan may easily be overrated.

It is to be noted, also, that Japanese investments in Shanghai have grown since 1914 at a more rapid rate than Japanese holdings in Manchuria. This increase at Shanghai is consistent with trends which we have found in Japanese trade and with the direction of growth which is to be observed in the investments of other countries. How far it may modify Japanese policy remains to be seen. The great importance of the Japanese government as a holder of direct investments in China has been brought out. Fully half of these investments consist of holdings of the Japanese government or of corporations in which the Japanese government retains a controlling interest. The position of the Japanese government as the effective owner of business property in China is a feature of the situation which must not be forgotten.

The Japanese are relatively new in the field of foreign investment. They have, in the past, had relatively little capital to invest. The period of war prosperity gave them surplus funds and brought about such diverse developments as the great increase in Japanese cotton mills in Shanghai on the one hand and the "Nishihara" loans on the other. Japanese political policy seems to be based upon a determination to play an important rôle on the continent of Asia. This seems to mean—in the economic field to which attention is here confined—the provision of capital for the development of China and leads to these questions: Will Japan have capital of her own to invest in China in the near future? If not, what part will she take in the movement of capital to China?

TABLE 39

THE POSITION OF JAPAN IN CHINA'S INTERNATIONAL ECONOMIC RELATIONS

Customs Statistics except for Investments

TRADE	Direct Trade Mills Hk. Tls.	Relatives	Per Cent of China's Total Trade
1899	53.1	28.6	11.5
1913	184.9	100.0	19.0
1930	543.7	294.1	24.7
POPULATION	Japanese Population in China	Relatives	Per Cent of Total Foreign Population in China
1899	2,440	3.0	14.2
1913	80,219	100.0	48.9
1930	255,686	318.7	70.6
FIRMS	Japanese Firms	Relatives	Per Cent of Total Foreign Firms in China
1899	195	15.3	20.9
1913	1,269	100.0	33.3
1930	4,633	365.1	55.9
SHIPPING	Japanese Tonnage in Millions	Relatives	Per Cent of Total Chinese and Foreign Shipping
1899	2.8	11.9	7.2
1913	23.4	100.0	25.0
1930	45.6	194.9	29.3
INVESTMENT	Japanese Investment Millions U. S. Dollars	Relatives	Per Cent of Total Foreign Investment
1900	1.0	0.5	0.1
1914	219.6	100.0	13.6
1931	1,136.9	517.7	35.1

CHAPTER XVIII

RUSSIAN INVESTMENTS IN CHINA *

Introduction

Early Trade Relations

Russian trade relations with China began in the seventeenth century but the trade was insignificant. This early trade was conducted by overland routes and flowed through certain frontier cities. The chief of these was Kiakhta, situated on the Siberian-Mongolian border and reached through Urga and the Chinese trading center Maimaichen.

At the time of the opening of the five Chinese ports to European trade in the middle of the nineteenth century, Russo-Chinese trade amounted to about U. S. $10 million. The chief Chinese export to Russia was tea. Shortly after 1860 the export of Chinese tea through Kiakhta began to grow rapidly. At about the same time the shipment of tea to Russia by the sea route began and this gave a further impetus to the trade. The tea trade at Kiakhta brought about the accumulation of considerable wealth on the part of the local Russian merchants. Some of these traders and certain merchants from European Russia transferred their activities to Chinese territory. In the 'seventies certain Russian tea firms established themselves at Foochow and for two decades they continued their activities there with a large measure of success. In the 'eighties there were Russian tea traders in Szechuan province and by the beginning of the 'nineties they began to settle in Hankow. In 1896 the Russian government acquired a

* The estimate of Russian investments is the work of Mr. J. J. Serebrennikov and it is given practically as he wrote it. Important additions or modifications are indicated in footnotes with the initials C. F. R.

concession in Hankow, the first of the Russian concessions in China. In the course of time Hankow became the center of the Russian trade with China.

The tea trade was the earliest cause of Russian investment in China. The Russian tea merchants built tea factories and acquired landed property in China. Russians, interested chiefly in this trade, began to appear in certain cities of northern China, such as Tientsin and Kalgan, through which tea passed on its way to Kiakhta.

After 1860 there was a considerable increase in trade between Russia and China in the Amur region, which had been ceded to Russia in the treaties of 1858 and 1860. Russian settlements were made in this region and many of the centers became prosperous as gold mining developed along the banks of the Amur and its tributaries. The Chinese supplied many of the needs of the Russian population and a local trade across the international boundary grew up.

RUSSIAN INTERESTS IN 1904

The Early Interest of the Russian Government

In the course of time the Asiatic possessions of Russia began to attract the attention of the Russian government. The chief result of this was the construction of the great Trans-Siberian Railway which was begun in 1891. This railway made a fundamental change in the position of Russia on the Asiatic continent and brought a great increase in Russian political and economic influence in the Far East. This influence was clearly manifested at the time of the Sino-Japanese War of 1894–1895.

The war ended disastrously for China and in the Treaty of Shimonoseki, April 17, 1895, she was compelled to cede to Japan the southern end of the Liaotung peninsula. Russia, supported by France and Germany, entered a strong protest against this treaty, and Japan was compelled to abandon her territorial ambitions on the continent, receiving, in return, an increase in the war indemnity. In order to meet this indemnity China was obliged to borrow abroad.

The loan was successfully concluded in a short time with the assistance of Count Witte who was then Russian Minister of Finance. This loan appears in the lists as the Chinese Imperial Government 4% Gold Loan of 1895. It was for French francs 400 million or £15,820,000. The loan was secured upon Customs revenues and had this unusual feature, that it was guaranteed by the Russian government. It was for thirty-six years and was retired in 1931.

This, the first great Chinese loan, is sometimes referred to as the French and sometimes as the Franco-Russian loan. The latter name is the more correct, since both French and Russian banks participated. The four Russian banks taking part were: the International Bank of Commerce of St. Petersburg, the Russian Bank for Foreign Trade, the St. Petersburg Discount Bank, and the Volga-Kama Commercial Bank. The Russian share of the loan was French francs 150 million and the French share francs 250 million.[1]

At the time of the negotiation of this loan in St. Petersburg it was thought that the time had come to establish a special Russian bank for eastern Asia with the widest powers and under the protection of the Russian government. This was done in the same year that the loan was made. The Russo-Chinese Bank was the result. The establishment of this bank involved the following French and Russian banks:

French
   M. M. Hottinger and Company
   Paris Netherlands Bank
   Le Crédit Lyonnais
   Le Comptoir National d'Escompte de Paris

[1] Wright, S. F., *The Collection and Disposal of the . . . Customs Revenue*, p. 66. MacMurray, J. V. A., *Treaties and Agreements*, vol. I, p. 39.

Russian

The International Bank of Commerce of St. Petersburg.[2]

The capital of the new Russo-Chinese Bank was rubles 6 million.[3] Of this sum three-eighths was subscribed in Russia and five-eighths in France. It is an interesting fact that the proportions were reversed in representation on the board of directors, for here there were five Russian members and three French.[4] The statutes governing the Russo-Chinese Bank were drawn up in St. Petersburg and signed by the French and Russian representatives at the Russian Embassy in Paris on November 23, 1895. The approval of the Russian government was made formal on December 10.[5]

According to the statutes the bank enjoyed the widest powers. These included the financing of commercial undertakings, the issue of bank notes, the minting of local currency, the obtaining of concessions for the construction of railways and telegraph lines, the purchase and sale of goods on its own account, the purchase and sale of immovable property for the account of others, the general insurance business and the forwarding of goods.

With its many privileges and under the protection of the Russian government, the Russo-Chinese Bank developed rapidly. Its activities were the main factor in the growing Russian influence in Far Eastern affairs. In 1896 the Chinese government was permitted to deposit Kuping taels 5 million and to share in the profits of the bank.[6] By the year 1899 there had been issued a total of

---

[2] Wright, S. F., *The Collection and Disposal of the . . . Customs Revenue*, p. 66, points out that this bank "was obliged to move its headquarters to Paris" after the Russian revolution.

[3] Here and elsewhere the ruble referred to is the so-called gold ruble taken as equal to U. S. $0.513.

[4] Russia, it may be remarked, contributed the political influence and France the funds. The control seems to have gone with the political influence.

[5] Romanov, B. A., *Russia in Manchuria, 1892–1906*, Leningrad, 1928, p. 91.

[6] Lieu, D. K., *Foreign Investments in China, 1929*, pp. 50–1, states his conclusion that this agreement to advance a sum of Kuping taels 5 million

60,000 shares in this bank, of which the Russian government owned 16,200.[7] The capital of the bank at this date may be estimated at rubles 20 million.

In 1903 the Russo-Chinese Bank had branches at the following places in China: Harbin, Kirin, Hailar, Mukden, Tiehling, Port Arthur, Yingkow, Tientsin, Peking, Shanghai, Hankow, Hongkong, Kalgan, Urga, and Uliassutai (Mongolia).

The Chinese Eastern Railway Agreements

The question of building a railway through Manchuria to shorten the distance between Chita and Vladivostok arose at about the time that the Russo-Chinese Bank was established. To make this matter clear Russia entered into negotiations with China after the Sino-Japanese War. China was inclined to meet Russia's wishes and to rely upon her as an ally. The negotiations were accelerated by the arrival in Russia of China's special envoy, Li Hung-Chang, who was sent to represent his country at the coronation ceremonies. On May 22, 1896, a secret treaty was signed between Russia and China.[8]

By this treaty China consented to give the Russo-

taken with the agreement in the actual railway contract by which the Bank undertook to pay over this same sum to the Chinese government upon the opening of the Chinese Eastern Railway to traffic, mean that there was no actual cash payment by the Chinese government. This is borne out by a letter from Mr. Percy Chu of the "General Liquidation Office of the Russo-Asiatic Bank" in Shanghai to Mr. George E. Sokolsky on August 21, 1929. The letter is printed as an appendix (p. 66) in Sokolsky, George E., *The Story of the Chinese Eastern Railway*, Shanghai, 1929. In this letter Mr. Chu states that "the Chinese government paid nothing in the form of actual cash." He points out, also, that on August 12, 1911, when the Russo-Asiatic Bank was formed, the share of Tls. 5 million owned by the Chinese government was reduced to Tls. 3,500,000. The Kuping tael, it is to be noted was equal to about Chinese $1.50. The agreements are printed in MacMurray, *Treaties and Agreements*, pp. 78, 74. (C. F. R.)

[7] Romanov, B. A., *op. cit.*, p. 236.

[8] A brief account of the circumstances surrounding the signing of this treaty is given in Young, C. W., *The International Relations of Manchuria*, App. A, pp. 253–7. In Article 4 of this treaty the Chinese government consented to the construction of a railway across northern Manchuria in the direction of Vladivostock. (C. F. R.)

Chinese Bank a concession for the construction and exploitation of a railway in Manchuria. This railway concession was regarded as the necessary basis of a defensive alliance between China and Russia against Japan. At an earlier date, that is on May 18, 1896, an understanding had been arrived at between the Russian Imperial government and the Russo-Chinese Bank for the formation of a company to be called the "Chinese Eastern Railway Company" empowered to construct and exploit a railway through Manchuria. The Russian government in this way secured complete control of this railway across Manchuria, making Russian influence and prestige predominant there.

The Russo-Chinese Bank was compelled to subscribe to the whole of the capital stock of the railway company which was in turn handed over to the Russian government. The object of this was to make it appear to the Chinese that the railway was a private enterprise whereas it was, in fact, a government concern. This was necessary since Li Hung-Chang objected to the existence of the railway as a government concern and preferred that it be purely a private commercial undertaking.

The terms of the agreement between the Chinese government and the Russo-Chinese Bank for the building of the Chinese Eastern Railway were drawn up by P. M. Romanov, an assistant Minister of Finance in St. Petersburg, and by the Chinese diplomat, Hsu Ching-cheng, who was at the time acting in the dual capacity of Minister to St. Petersburg and Berlin. The agreement was signed in Berlin on September 8, 1896. On December 4 the statutes of the Chinese Eastern Railway Company were confirmed and on December 17, 1896, the subscription list was opened to the public. This subscription was fictitious and was closed a few minutes after it was opened.[9]

The Chinese Eastern Railway Company may be said to have come into existence in December, 1896. Among

[9] Romanov, B. A., *op. cit.*, p. 121.

the stipulations in the statutes of the company was one which provided that the construction of the line was to be started not later than August 16, 1897. The gauge was to be the wide, five-foot gauge of the Russian state railway system. At the expiration of thirty-six years from the completion of the line and its opening to traffic, the Chinese government had the right of redemption by the repayment of the capital and the debts incurred for the upkeep of the road, together with accrued interest. At the end of a period of eighty years China was to have the right to take possession of the railway with all its appurtenances free of charge. The management of the affairs of the company was entrusted to a board of directors composed of the president and nine members. The president was to be appointed by the Chinese government and to be the intermediary between the Chinese government and the railway company. The nine members of the board were to be elected by the shareholders. The immediate management of affairs was in the hands of the vice-president elected from the members of the board. The head office of the company was established in St. Petersburg with a branch office in Peking.

In the beginning of April, 1897, the first group of engineers was sent out and on their arrival in Vladivostok they commenced the surveys and preliminary work required for the construction of the railway. On August 16 of the same year a formal inauguration of the construction took place at the Cossack village of Poltavskaia in the southern Ussuri region near the Siberian-Manchurian border.[10] The progress was so rapid that in 1898 the town of Harbin was founded on the site of a small Chinese village where the present railway line crosses the Sungari River. This town grew rapidly and before long it became the center of Russian activities in Manchuria.

In the agreement between China and Russia for a

[10] *Guide to the Great Siberian Railway*, published by the Ministry of Communications, St. Petersburg, 1900, p. 494.

twenty-five-year lease of Port Arthur and Talienwan (March 27, 1898) and in a later agreement (July 6, 1898) the Chinese government granted to the Chinese Eastern Railway Company the right to build a railway from a station on the main line to Port Arthur.[11] On the conclusion of these treaties, the company began the survey and the construction of the South Manchurian line of the Chinese Eastern. In 1899 the building of railways in Manchuria was in full swing and gave employment to tens of thousands of Chinese workers. At about this time the Trans-Siberian Railway was opened to traffic. Trains were running on the whole of the line with the exception of a short section around Lake Baikal.

The Completion of the Chinese Eastern

The Boxer uprising of 1900 temporarily impeded the construction of the Chinese Eastern Railway. The damage and loss were enormous. The uprising occurred when the work of construction was being vigorously pressed.[12] The work was being pushed simultaneously from five points: from Harbin to the south, the east, and the west, from the eastern border of Manchuria toward Harbin, and from Port Arthur in the south toward Harbin. During the summer of 1900 work was proceeding on no less than 2,300 kilometers of the road-bed of the railway. Shipping facilities on the Sungari River were provided in order to transport materials by water. The bridge across the Sungari at Harbin was undertaken during the same year. The railway company owned thirteen sea-

[11] MacMurray, *Treaties and Agreements*, vol. I, pp. 119, 154. The territory covered by the lease was in 1931 the Kwantung leased area. Talien was called Dalny by the Russians. It is now known as Dairen. (C. F. R.)

[12] On July 3, 1900, missionaries and their converts were killed in Mukden and this was followed by attacks upon Russians in Mukden and elsewhere in Manchuria. There was a massacre of Chinese in the Russian border city of Blagovestchensk later in July. The Russians made the Boxer uprising a sufficient reason for the occupation of the whole of Manchuria including the railway between Shanhaikwan and Hsinmintun which was in 1931 a part of the Peiping (Peking)-Mukden line. (C. F. R.)

going steamers and began the construction of the port and town of Dalny. The development of mining enterprises in the Yentai and Wafangtien coal fields was taken in hand.[13]

Having helped in suppressing the Boxer rebellion, Russia temporarily occupied Manchuria and stationed troops along the railway from Shanhaikwan northward. The expense incurred by the Russian government for the military expedition is estimated to have been rubles 100 million; the loss and damage to the Chinese Eastern Railway, rubles 70 million.[14] When the Protocol of September, 1901, was signed, the indemnity claimed by the foreign powers was taels 450 million, of which the Russian share was about taels 130 million. In rubles the sum came to 184,084,021. The Russian share of the indemnity (almost exactly 29 per cent) was greater than the share of any other of the powers.[15]

During the years 1901 and 1902 expenditure on the construction of the Chinese Eastern continued, though the whole line was in existence in an unfinished state early in 1902. On July 1, 1903, the railway was opened to the general public for goods and passenger traffic. The operation of the railway was turned over to the proper department for the company by those who had been in charge of construction. From this date in the middle of 1903 it may be said that China and the Far East have been in railway connection with Russia and Europe.

The Chinese Eastern Railway and the Russian Government

From official estimates made in 1903 by the Russian Ministry of Finance, the expenditures on the construction of the Chinese Eastern Railway and on the port and

[13] Both of these mines were among those turned over to the South Manchuria Railway Company by the Japanese government in 1907. The mine near Wafangtien is of little importance. (C. F. R.)

[14] Romanov, B. A., *op. cit.*, p. 262.

[15] Baylin, J. R., *Foreign Loan Obligations of China*, p. 2.

town of Dalny for the period 1897–1902 are known. These expenditures, practically the whole capital expenditure of the railway company, are shown in the following table.

TABLE 1

EXPENDITURE IN MANCHURIA, 1897–1902, AS ESTIMATED BY THE MINISTRY OF FINANCE OF THE RUSSIAN GOVERNMENT *

(Figures in rubles)

	Railway	Steamships	Port of Dalny	Town of Dalny	Total
1897	5,000,000				5,000,000
1898	26,300,000				26,300,000
1899	62,700,000	3,500,000	3,000,000		69,200,000
1900	76,160,000	4,340,000	2,150,000	1,850,000	84,500,000
1901	64,111,750	3,547,430	3,827,970	1,624,430	73,111,580
1902	67,975,000	942,979	500,000		69,417,979
	302,246,750	12,330,409	9,477,970	3,474,430	327,529,559

* Source: Romanov, B. A., *Russia in Manchuria*, p. 44.

These figures do not include the whole of the expenditure of the period by the Russian government. In addition to expenditures shown in the table, borne by the Russian Ministry of Finance, there were expenditures borne by the Ministry of War, such as those for the building of fortifications at Port Arthur.

The total cost of the Chinese Eastern Railway to the time of the opening of the road to traffic on July 1, 1903, was, according to certain published data, rubles 375 million.[16] Although the line was open, construction was continued and the expenditures for the second half of 1903 and the two following years were as follows:[17]

	Rubles
1903, second half	31,000,000
1904	35,000,000
1905	6,000,000
Total	72,000,000

[16] More exactly: gold rubles 374,955,598.12. *Historical Review of the Chinese Eastern Railway, 1896–1923*, Harbin, 1923, p. 123.

[17] Steinfeld, N., *Russian Activity in Manchuria*, Harbin, 1910, pp. 53–4. *Statistical Yearbook of the C. E. R., 1923*, Harbin, 1923, p. 5.

From these figures we reach the conclusion that the total cost of construction of the Chinese Eastern Railway on January 1, 1904, that is, one month before the beginning of the Russo-Japanese War, was rubles 406 million.[18] This may be taken as a rather accurate estimate.

The expenditure on the construction of the port and city of Dalny, to the year 1904, amounted to rubles 30 million and of the "European" city of Port Arthur to rubles 12 million.[19] The expenditures on the fortification of Port Arthur are omitted since they may be considered as purely politico-military.

After the Boxer trouble, Russian troops were for a time along the railways of southern Manchuria and of the northern part of Chihli province. The Russian military authorities spent about rubles 1 million on the repair and reconstruction of these railways.[20] This sum must be taken into account in any summary of the total remittance of funds to China by the Russian government for the period before the Russo-Japanese War.

It is estimated, also, that the expenditure of the Russian government in connection with the acquisition of the Russian Concessions in Hankow in 1896 and in Tientsin in 1901 came to about rubles 1 million.

The expenditures on the Chinese Eastern Railway were closely related to the expenditures of the Russian government. It is necessary to make a separate estimate later of the sum which may be set down as the investment of the railway which may be regarded as more nearly like a business corporation during the years after the Russo-Japanese War. It will be convenient, before taking up the estimate of business investments, to set down in a table the total known Russian government expenditures in China during the years which preceded the Russo-Japanese War. These figures serve to show the magnitude

[18] Arrived at by adding rubles 31 million to rubles 375 million.
[19] *Northern Manchuria and the Chinese Eastern Railway*, Harbin, 1922, p. 478. See also *Economic History of Manchuria*, Seoul, 1921, pp. 46–7.
[20] Romanov, B. A., *op. cit.*, p. 314.

of the politico-economic venture. They include, of course, some expenditures which appear later as investments and others which do not. The table follows and it must be pointed out again that the expenditure of the Russian Ministry of War for the fortification of Port Arthur is excluded since the amount is not known.

TABLE 2

EXPENDITURES OF THE RUSSIAN GOVERNMENT IN CHINA TO THE
END OF 1903

	Rubles
Construction of the Chinese Eastern	406,000,000
Port and town of Dalny	30,000,000
Town of Port Arthur	12,000,000
Military expenditures (Boxer)	100,000,000
Repair of railways (Boxer)	1,000,000
Concessions in Hankow and Tientsin	1,000,000
	550,000,000

Business Investments, excluding the Chinese Eastern

No investigation of Russian business investments is available for the period which ended with the outbreak of the Russo-Japanese War in 1904. It is, therefore, necessary to present the information that can now be brought together in spite of the difficulties. The result is no better than an approximation. It will be convenient to consider the following regions separately: China proper, Outer Mongolia and Chinese Turkestan (Sinkiang), and Manchuria.

In China Proper: Tea was the chief article of the trade between Russia and China proper. Most of the private business investments of the Russians were connected with the trade in this product and centered in Hankow. In 1904 there were eight large Russian tea firms. Four of these may be reckoned as most important, as their turnover ran into many millions. At the beginning of the century the export of tea from China to Siberia and European Russia amounted to about 74 million Russian pounds [21] and to Mongolia about 9 million pounds. The average annual export of tea from China to Russia for the ten years, 1892–1901, came to Hk. Tls. 10,177,000 or rubles 16,182,000.[22]   In addition to Hankow, other important centers of the tea trade were Kiukiang and Foochow.   In these three cities Russian tea merchants owned land, tea factories, and warehouses, the estimated value of which was about rubles 4 million, according to our own inquiry.

The Russian representatives at Tientsin and Kalgan interested in the tea trade and transportation were the firms of Startzev and Bataniev.   These merchants and others, after accumulating fortunes, invested their wealth in the purchase of land and in the building of warehouses and residences to be leased.   Old Russian residents in Tientsin remember well the large investments of these firms in Tientsin, Tangku, and Peitaiho, and estimate them to have been not less than rubles 1 million.   The total Russian business investments in China proper must have been about rubles 5 million at the beginning of 1904.

In Mongolia: The investment of Russian capital in Outer Mongolia may be estimated from the end of the last century.   In 1897, in close co-operation with the Russo-Chinese Bank, a group of Russian financiers formed a financial syndicate, for the purpose of exploiting the mineral wealth of China, capitalized at rubles 500,000. In 1900 this syndicate was reorganized and a joint-stock mining enterprise came into existence, known as the "Mongolor" Company, which was to engage in mining in certain districts of Outer Mongolia.[23]   The capital of the company was fixed at rubles 3 million, divided into 12,000 shares, the paid-up capital being rubles 1.8 mil-

[21] 40 Russian pounds equal 36 English pounds (avoirdupois).

[22] Torgashev, B. P., "China as Supplier of Tea for Russia," *Manchuria Monitor*, Harbin, 1925, pp. 167–8.

[23] The official name of the company was the "Joint-Stock Company for Mining Enterprise in the Tushetu Khan and the Tsetsen Khan Aimak of Mongolia." Aimak is the name of a territorial division or district.

lion. This company undertook the exploitation of gold fields in Mongolia on a concession acquired in 1896 by a Russian, named von Grot, in the Chinese Customs service. During the years 1900–1903 the Mongolor Company invested about rubles 1 million in the equipping of the gold mines with machinery and buildings, and the purchase of small steamers to navigate the Orkhon River. Another rubles 500,000 was expended on the building of houses in Urga, the capital of Outer Mongolia. The total gold production of the Mongolor Company, from 1901 to 1903 inclusive, was 9,367 Troy ounces, having a total value of rubles 337,000. The venture was not a success and in 1905 the question of liquidating the enterprise was being considered.[24]

The number of Russians in Outer Mongolia in 1892 was about two hundred, not including the Uriankhai region,[25] and by 1900 their number had increased to four hundred. The first Russian firm was established at Urga in 1860. It was quickly followed by others. In 1885 there were ten fairly large firms there and at other centers. In 1903 the number of Russian firms had increased to fifteen, including two that were well known, Kokovin and Bossov, and Stooken and Company. Russian capital reached Mongolia by two routes, through Kiakhta on the eastern Siberian-Mongolian border and through Biisk in the Altai region in midwestern Siberia.

There is practically no information regarding the amount of Russian trade with Mongolia and Chinese Turkestan for the years 1895–1903. The investment of

[24] Romanov, B. A., *op. cit.*, pp. 599–605. Lieu, D. K., *Foreign Investments in China, 1929*, states that 15 per cent of the product of the company was to be turned over to the Chinese government as a royalty. The mines were leased for a time to an American firm, the Mongolia Trading Company at Urga. There is also a report by Mills and Manning, mining engineers, on the Mongolor concession to the Peking-Mongolor Mining Company. The latter company is said to. have acquired the concession by lease from the American firm.

[25] This region is now known to the Russians as the Tanna Tuva Republic and it is regarded as closer to Russia than Mongolia in general, of which it forms the northwestern part. (C. F. R.)

the firms must be estimated. There were some in the import and export trade and from the data presented above regarding Mongolia, it is safe to assume that the investment of these trading firms, together with that of the Mongolor Company, was about rubles 3 million. A more correct figure is perhaps unattainable today.

In Manchuria: The expenditure of vast sums of money by the Russian government on the construction of the Chinese Eastern brought a large influx of Russians into Manchuria. There were officials and workmen of the railway, military guards, and men engaged in business and commerce. In 1902 the number of Russians was about thirty thousand.[26] There were in Harbin a number of Russian trading firms, and Russians owned such industrial establishments as saw mills, flour mills, and distilleries. Many of these business holdings were created locally, built up and financed by those who had accumulated their wealth in Harbin or Manchuria. As the city grew, Harbin attracted the attention of merchants and traders in Siberia and European Russia. This brought additional investment in Harbin and in northern Manchuria generally. The Russians were the first to establish in this region manufacturing and mechanical industries based upon modern methods. In short, it is quite correct to say that Manchuria was opened up by Russians with Russian capital.

A flour mill was erected at Harbin in 1900 by a Russian firm, the First Manchurian Flour Mill Company, with a capital of rubles 400,000. The second flour mill was built by the Chinese Eastern Railway Company; in 1902 this flour mill was sold to a private company, the Sungari Mills Company, which became the largest owner of flour mills in northern Manchuria. In 1902 a flour mill was established in Fuchiatien, a Chinese city which is prac-

[26] The figures of the Decennial Report of the Chinese Maritime Customs, 1892–1901, do not show the facts. The only "treaty port" in Manchuria was then Newchwang with four firms and 1,150 residents according to the Customs. (C. F. R.)

tically a part of Harbin. In 1903 four Russian flour mills were built, two in Harbin, one in Changchun and one at Imienpo, an important station on the Chinese Eastern Railway east of Harbin. The first distilleries were built when the construction of the Chinese Eastern Railway began. A large distillery was built at Ninguta in 1900 and another in Harbin. During the next three years two Russian distilleries were started: one at Harbin and one at Fulaerhtze, a station on the Chinese Eastern.[27]

During the years 1897–1903 steps were taken toward the development of a timber industry in the zone of the Chinese Eastern Railway. The Chinese government granted timber concessions in the railway area. The largest of these concessions were obtained by two Russian firms, that of Skidelsky and of Kovalsky. Russian capital was invested in Harbin real estate and in a variety of commercial undertakings. The year 1898 saw the establishment of the great Russian commercial firm of Chourin and Company.

The Russian government took an interest in obtaining for Russians a number of mining concessions in Manchuria. In 1902 the Manchurian Mining Company was established with a capital of rubles 1 million and during the next few years prospecting was undertaken. At about the same time the Russian Gold Mining Company entered the field along with certain smaller Russian gold mining enterprises.

In southern Manchuria a Russian firm undertook to operate the well-known Bezobrazov concession. This company, the Russian Timber Company, was capitalized at rubles 2 million. It held a lease of forest lands on both banks of the Yalu River and certain other concessions, such as that for the development of the Fushun coal field, for steam navigation on the Liao River, and for an electric plant at Mukden. In 1902 the Russo-Chinese Bank held

[27] Sourin, V. I., *The Manufacturing Industry of Northern Manchuria and Harbin,* Harbin, 1928, p. 55.

a large interest in two Chinese enterprises in the province of Fengtien (Liaoning). The first company (Hua Hsin Li) was established for the development of the western part of the Fushun coal field and was capitalized at taels 160,000 of which the Russo-Chinese bank held taels 60,000 and the Manchurian Mining Company taels 54,700. The second enterprise (I Sheng King) was known as the Mukden Mining Company. It was founded for the development of coal and other mines in the province and was capitalized at taels 400,000, of which the Russo-Chinese Bank held taels 150,000.[23]

Taking into consideration the information which has been presented it may be taken as certain that the private investment of Russian capital in Manchuria at the end of 1903 came to at least rubles 15 million.

The following summary of the private investment of Russians is offered:

	Rubles
China proper	5,000,000
Mongolia	3,000,000
Manchuria	15,000,000
	23,000,000

Obligations of the Chinese Government

Russian participation with the French in the 4% Gold Loan of 1895 has been mentioned. The other Russian loans of the period were the result of the activities of the Russo-Chinese Bank. In negotiations between Russia and China in 1897 for the extension of the Shanhaikwan Railway northward the Russo-Chinese Bank advanced the Chinese government taels 600,000, or about rubles 1 million.[29]

[28] Romanov, B. A., *op. cit.*, p. 381.
[29] Romanov, B. A., *op. cit.*, p. 210. Mr. Serebrennikov does not here refer to the whole series of negotiations in connection with this advance and its repayment. Russian ambitions in Manchuria which carried them from the loan of July 6, 1895, to the building of the Chinese Eastern Railway, and the control of the southern end of the Liaotung peninsula, found unpleasant the existence of a railway built with British capital and by

In 1902 a loan of francs 40 million (rubles 16 million) was arranged in a contract between the Chinese government and the Russo-Chinese Bank for the building of a railway from Chengtingfu to Taiyuanfu, the capital of Shansi province. The railway is usually referred to as the Shansi or the Cheng-Tai Railway. The loan was issued in Paris on December 14, 1903. The French group in the Russo-Chinese Bank accepted the responsibility for this contract and the operation of the railway was turned over later to the "Société Française de Construction et d'Exploitation de chemins de fer en Chine." The loan may be regarded as entirely French on the principle of the place of issue and on the basis of all the information about it.[30]

Mission Property

Concerning the value of the property of the Russian .Orthodox Mission no statistics are available. It is, of course, well known that the Mission has existed in China for more than two centuries and that the converts have not been numerous. Before the outbreak of the Russo-Japanese War the Mission had landed property and buildings in Peking (Peiping), Tientsin, Peitaiho, Shanghai, Hankow, Dalny (Dairen), Harbin, Manchouli, and in a

British engineers which had reached Shanhaikwan from Tientsin and Peking by 1895 and which was to be pushed on toward Mukden. When it was proposed in 1897 to carry this line beyond Shanhaikwan (or Chunghouso) the Russians attempted to prevent its construction. (Kent, P. H., *Railway Enterprise in China*, pp. 53–6.) In the contract for a loan for the extension of the line there was provision for the repayment of certain loans. These, according to a statement issued at the time, included two from the Russo-Chinese Bank making a total of taels 600,000. The discussion raised by this loan contract led to the exchange of notes between Great Britain and Russia in April, 1899, concerning railway interests. Great Britain agreed not to seek railway concessions north of the Great Wall and Russia not to seek them in the Yangtze valley. (MacMurray, J. V. A., *Treatie and Agreements*, vol. I, pp. 179, 181, 204.) It is to be supposed that the obligation of 600,000 was paid from the funds made available under the final contract of October 10, 1898, and was not outstanding at the end of 1903. (C. F. R.)

[30] Romanov, B. A., *op. cit.*, pp. 215–6. Concerning the French interest see MacMurray, J. V. A., *Treaties and Agreements*, p. 369, and Baylin, J. R., *Foreign Loan Obligations of China*, p. 31.

few small towns and villages in the interior. The value of all of these buildings cannot have been more than one million rubles.

Summary of Russian Investments, 1904 [31]

At the end of 1903 Russia was a capital importing country which had but recently undertaken ventures in China calling for the export of capital. The initiative in these ventures was with the government and the government procured the necessary funds in France. The chief undertaking was the Chinese Eastern Railway. The Russian government found it expedient to create a corporation to hold and to operate this railway. We may, therefore, regard the Chinese Eastern Railway Company as a business corporation and set down its holdings as direct business investments in China. The Chinese Eastern was more completely owned and as completely controlled by the Russian government as was the South Manchuria Railway Company, after its creation, by the Japanese government. In both cases the railway companies may be set down as business corporations only after explanation.

It must be remembered that the Chinese Eastern was not fully constructed by 1904 and that it failed to meet the demands made upon it for the transportation of large bodies of troops during the war. The construction of the tunnel through the Khingan mountains in the western section had not been completed. It was opened in May, 1904. The railway workshops in Harbin were but partially complete. According to official estimates in January, 1904, the sum of rubles 57 million remained to be spent.[32] During the war rubles 41 million was spent in general improvement and in new construction. The total cost of

---

[31] This section has been altered from the original in such a way as to present totals more nearly comparable with the other studies. (C. F. R.)

[32] Romanov, B. A., *op. cit.*, p. 367.

construction of the whole railway to the beginning of 1906 came to rubles 447 million, including the cost of the South Manchuria line.

In addition to the Chinese Eastern Railway, which may with some show of reason be counted a business corporation, there were other expenditures of the Russian government in Manchuria which can hardly be termed business investments. They include rubles 30 million spent in the improvement of the port and town of Dalny and 12 million on the town of Port Arthur.

The total Russian investment in China is found to have been rubles 479,616,000. Of this total at the end of 1903 business investments were found to form 89.4 per cent and Russian holdings of Chinese government securities 10.6 per cent.

Concerning the geographical distribution of the total Russian investments, it may be said that 88.4 per cent were definitely assignable to Manchuria and Mongolia, and of the business investments no less than 98.8 per cent were so assignable.

The following table shows the totals with some detail, so that the share of the Chinese Eastern may be seen.

TABLE 3

RUSSIAN INVESTMENTS IN CHINA, 1904, AT THE END OF 1903

	Rubles	U. S. Dollars
Business investments		
In Manchuria and Mongolia		
Chinese Eastern Railway	406,000,000	208,278,000
Commercial investment (Manchuria)	15,000,000	7,695,000
Commercial investment (Mongolia)	3,000,000	1,539,000
In the rest of China		
Commercial investment	5,000,000	2,565,000
Obligations of the Chinese government		
Outstanding Russian share of the 4%		
Gold Loan of 1895	50,616,000	25,966,000
	479,616,000	246,043,000

RUSSIAN INTERESTS IN 1914

The Chinese Eastern Railway, 1904–1914

After the Treaty of Portsmouth (September 3, 1905) the following sections of the Chinese Eastern Railway were turned over to the Japanese: (1) the trunk line between Changchun and Dairen (Dalny), 437 miles, (2) the Port Arthur branch line, 28 miles, (3) the Yingkow branch line, 9 miles, (4) the Yentai branch line, 9 miles, and (5) the Fushun branch line, 28 miles. These make a total of 515 miles. The expenditure on these sections is estimated to have been rubles 81 million.[33] Japan received, also, the towns of Dalny and Port Arthur and the whole of the leased territory on the Liaotung peninsula, now known as Kwantung.

At the beginning of 1906 the total value of the Chinese Eastern Railway, excluding the sections ceded to Japan, was rubles 366 million. After the Russo-Japanese War and during the ensuing years of peace, 1906–1913, the investment of Russian capital in improvements was small and may be taken in round numbers at rubles 3 million. It will be seen from this that the total set down for the railway in 1914 was rubles 369 million. The new investments for the whole period 1904–1913 may be taken at rubles 44 million.

It is necessary to point out once more that this does not include the whole of the expenditure incurred by the Russian government in connection with the railway. The government was compelled to meet all deficits in connection with the operation of the railway. These deficits were as follows:

---

[33] The expenditure on the railway was compiled by the Economic Bureau of the Chinese Eastern Railway as of January 1, 1917, and published in the *Statistical Year Book* of the Railway for 1923, Harbin, 1923.

	Rubles
1903 (second half)	4,517,000
1904–1906	86,321,000
1907	21,252,000
1908	15,607,000
1909	12,653,000
1910	10,329,000
1911	9,470,000
1912	7,984,000
1913	5,934,000
	174,067,000 [34]

In a private Russian publication of the time the total expenditure of the Russian government in the railway was stated to have reached a total of rubles 662 million by the year 1910. The estimate was for the years 1897–1909 and was made up as follows:

	Rubles
Shares not guaranteed, 1897	5,000,000
Guaranteed 4% debentures and loans 1897–1904	366,976,000
Amount assigned to war purpose, 1904–1906	98,451,000
For losses and damages during the Boxer rebellion, 1900	65,975,000
Payments to cover deficits	97,351,000
Interest and refunds	28,645,000
	662,398,000 [35]

In conclusion it may be stated that the total indebtedness of the Chinese Eastern Railway to the Russian government was held to be no less than about rubles 900 million at the beginning of the year 1914.

Business Investments

In China Proper: The tea trade continued to be of the greatest importance. Its rapid growth is illustrated by the following.

[34] *Statistical Year Book of the C. E. R., 1923*, Harbin, 1923, lists these deficits under the heading "Deficit caused by extra expenditures incurred in the running and upkeep of the line due to special conditions."

[35] *The Russian Exchequer and the Chinese Eastern Railway*, St. Petersburg, 1910, p. 7.

TABLE 4

EXPORT OF TEA FROM CHINA TO RUSSIA, 1904–1913 *

	Piculs
1904	424,156
1905	600,599
1906	939,181
1907	988,711
1908	965,032
1909	917,317
1910	974,295
1911	826,841
1912	839,689
1913	905,716
	8,381,537

* Data from Torgashev, B. P., "China as Supplier of Tea for Russia," *Manchuria Monitor*, 1925, p. 167.

This comes to a yearly average of piculs 838,000, Russian poods 3,100,000 or English pounds 111.7 million with a total value of about rubles 25 million. Some of the Russian tea merchants extended their activities during the period. The well-known firm of Goubkin, Kouznetzov and Company, for example, had offices in Java and India and other important tea centers. This firm is reported to have had a turnover of rubles 40 million.

According to our own inquiry it may be safely supposed that, during the decade 1904–1913, Russian tea traders in Hankow added to their previous investments about rubles 3 million in land, buildings, and factories.

In 1913 there was in Tientsin a Russian population of about one hundred forty persons. Many of these Russian residents made new investments in land and buildings within the Russian and the other foreign concessions at Tientsin. Certain Russian trading firms of repute established themselves in Tientsin during the decade which ended in 1913. Among them were the firms of Tsindel and Morozov. It may be accepted that rubles 1 million was added during the period to Russian business holdings in Tientsin.

From the above we reach an estimate of rubles 4 million as the amount to be added for the period now under consideration to the commercial investment of Russians in China proper. The total under this heading was rubles 5 million at the end of 1903 and it is taken as 9 million for the end of 1913.

In Mongolia and Sinkiang: During the decade great changes took place in Outer Mongolia. These changes followed the Chinese revolution of 1911. Mongolia became politically separated from China and declared her independence. This was followed by a great increase in Russian political and economic influence in the region. Russian colonists in ever increasing numbers began to settle in Mongolia, particularly on the route from Kiakhta to Urga and in the Uriankhai region. In the latter region purely Russian settlements began to spring up and towns with Russian names, such as Bielotzarsk, came into existence. As Russian settlers and traders became more numerous there was some inflow of Russian capital, but this was not so great as might be expected.

The Mongolor Company continued to operate. Its profits came chiefly from leasing its gold mining areas to enterprising individuals, some of whom were fairly successful. The output of gold from the gold fields of the Mongolor Company during the years 1904–1913 came to a total of 266,575 troy ounces with a value of rubles 9.6 million.

GOLD PRODUCTION OF THE MONGOLOR COMPANY, 1904–1913
IN TROY OUNCES

1904–1905	4,632
1905–1906	6,407
1906–1907	9,944
1907–1908	10,352
1908–1909	37,810
1910	63,469
1911	63,381
1912	47,026
1913	23,554
	266,575

In 1912 the capital of the Mongolor Company was
increased from rubles 1.8 million to 3 million. During the
same year another Russian gold mining company was
formed,[36] and permission to mine iron ore was granted
by the Mongolian government to a Russian, Baron Fitting-
hoff, a well-known business man in Mongolia.[37]

It is estimated that there were in 1912 Russians to the
number of nine thousand in Outer Mongolia. Of these
seven thousand were in the Uriankhai region and two
thousand were elsewhere in Outer Mongolia. The number of Russian firms in Urga was estimated at twenty-five,
in Uliassutai, eleven, and in Kogdo, thirteen. These
figures do not include smaller firms in the various smaller
centers of trade.[38]

In Chinese Turkestan (Sinkiang) with a native population of about 2.5 million there were Russian firms at
various towns such as Kuldja, Urumchi, Chuguchak, and
Kashgar. Russian trade connections with this region go
back to 1860. In the course of time this trade became so
important that the attention of the Russian government
was drawn to it, consuls were appointed for the principal
centers, and postal and telegraphic communication was
established.[39] The trade between Russia and Sinkiang
was greatly stimulated by the building of the Tashkent
Railway in Russian Turkestan in 1904–1905. This trade
was chiefly in the hands of Russian subjects of Turkish
blood.

There is no exact information as to the amount of new
investment in Outer Mongolia and Chinese Turkestan
during the years 1904–1913 but it may be estimated at
about rubles 5 million. This figure can hardly be regarded
as too high considering the new Russian trading firms
who entered the region. Some of these firms held a large
capital. There were the Shoetzov firm, 1911, with a cap-

[36] Nemchinov, Sinitsin and Company.
[37] Karamisheff, W., *Mongolia and Western China*, Tientsin, 1925, p. 107.
[38] Maisky, J., *Present Day Mongolia*, Irkutsk, 1921, pp. 87, 88, 201.
[39] Karamisheff, W., *op. cit.*, p. 293.

ital of rubles 1 million, Biederman (1909), Jacob Zergagen, Noskov, and others.

It may be noted also that a small loan of rubles 100,000 was advanced to the Mongolian government by Russia for the reorganization of the Mongolian army. This loan was without interest and for a period of ten years.[40]

In Manchuria: The years 1904–1913 were dominated by the Russo-Japanese War and its consequences. The war made a fundamental change in the situation in Manchuria. We may consider first the cost of the war together with certain military expenditures which may be set down as due to preparation for the war. The cost to Russia from 1903 to 1906 was as follows:

	Rubles
1903	10,650,000
1904	9,000,000
1904 (after the war began)	657,191,000
1905	985,349,000
1906	415,587,000
	2,077,777,000 [41]

If we take into account the fact that Manchuria was the scene of the war and that local supplies were used, so far as possible, for the vast Russian army, we may get some idea of the large amount in gold funds that must have flowed in from Russia. This flow of funds benefited northern Manchuria and particularly the Chinese Eastern Railway zone. The growth of Harbin during the war was extraordinary. It was the principal base from which the Russian armies were supplied. Into it streamed by the thousands Russian traders, speculators, and adventurers. The Russian civil population of Harbin rose with startling rapidity to more than one hundred thousand.

[40] Maisky, J., *op. cit.*, p. 279.
[41] Romanov, B. A., *op. cit.*, p. 466. It may be added that Apostol, Paul N., in *Russian Public Finance during the War*, New Haven, 1928, p. 235, makes the following statement. "The cost of the war with Japan was 2,295 million rubles, including 2,113 million rubles spent in the years 1904 to 1906, and 182 million rubles spent in the succeeding years."

After having made their money, many of these speculators and adventurers disappeared from the Manchurian
horizon at the end of the war. After the war the older
residents and the newcomers who remained set about the
further building up of Harbin and the expansion of Russian
trade in Manchuria.[42]

After 1906 when peace again prevailed and the Chinese
Eastern was ready to resume its normal activities, the
trade and industry of northern Manchuria went through
a period of severe depression. A revival of business followed shortly. By 1910 the trade of Harbin reached a
total of rubles 35 million and rubles 17 million must be
added for other trading centers on the railway.

During the years 1904–1906 six Russian-owned flour
mills were established in the railway area, so that by 1910
there were fourteen Russian mills altogether. There
were additional breweries, distilleries, and soap factories
as well. In 1909 a sugar refinery was established at Ashiho
which was owned by a joint-stock company.[43] The output
of these industrial establishments at Harbin alone is estimated to have reached a total value of about rubles
12 million. Flour milling was the chief industry. The
expressing of bean oil, which had become of some importance in southern Manchuria by 1914, was beginning
to be introduced, but there were no more than three
modern bean mills in the Harbin district at the end of
1913.[44]

After the Russo-Japanese War the trade of Harbin
and northern Manchuria grew rapidly. The foreign trade
of the region doubled between 1908–1914.[45] In this trade

[42] Mr. Serebrennikov does not undertake to estimate the remittances
to China which were brought about by the Russian expenditures for the
Russo-Japanese War. They were considerably greater than the Japanese
remittances which have been estimated elsewhere at Yen 250 million.
(C. F. R.)

[43] Ashiho is on the railway about twenty-five miles east of Harbin.

[44] *North Manchuria and the Chinese Eastern Railway*, Harbin, 1924,
p. 248.

[45] *Ibid.*, p. 272.

Russian firms took an important share. Harbin saw the establishment of many new Russian trading firms, some banks, insurance companies, and forwarding companies. The building of office buildings and residences proceeded as did, also, the purchase of landed property by Russians.

It is difficult to estimate accurately the amount of private Russian investment in Manchuria for the period. By taking into account the new investments of the large and well-known firms and so constructing an estimate, we arrive at a total of rubles 60 million to be added to the investment of rubles 15 million reported for the year 1904.

Obligations of the Chinese Government

The war with Japan dealt a heavy blow to the Russo-Chinese Bank from which it did not recover until 1910 when it was merged with the Banque du Nord and was renamed the Russo-Asiatic Bank.[46] The Banque du Nord was a Russian bank with its head office in Russia but it was closely affiliated with the "Société Générale pour favoriser le Developement du Commerce et de l'Industrie en France." At the time of the amalgamation the capital of the Russo-Chinese Bank was rubles 23 million. This was increased to rubles 35 million after the amalgamation and at a later time to rubles 55 million. The bank was interested in commercial and industrial ventures but these have been taken into account in the total of business investments.[47]

Shortly after the Russo-Asiatic Bank was created Russian interest was shown in possible participation in the negotiations for the Hukuang Railway loan, signed May 20, 1911.[48] This interest was, no doubt, closely related to

[46] Usually called the Banque Russo-Asiatique.

[47] The Bank was the largest shareholder in the Amur Steamship and Trading Company, paid-up capital rubles 2,333,000, which was interested in the shipment of beans from the Sungari region to Europe by the Amur River route, that is, through Nikolaievsk.

[48] The inquiries of Russian interests are noted in Field, F. V., *American Participation in the China Consortiums*, p. 102, with a reference to *U. S. Foreign Relations, 1909*, pp. 183, 197, 203. (C. F. R.)

the loan, signed in April, 1911, for "currency reform and industrial development" in Manchuria.   Russian policy in Manchuria—and Japanese policy as well—was such that loans by others could not be viewed with indifference. Under the circumstances the Russians had two courses of action open to them; they could undertake to enter the Consortium and hope to guard what they considered to be their special interests from within, or they could remain outside and oppose the policy of the Consortium where it was felt to be contrary to their interests.   The fact that the Russians would work for the destruction of the Consortium if they were not admitted was a consideration in favor of admitting them.   At the same time the admission of Russia (and Japan) on terms of equality with the others was regarded by some of the others involved as a victory for the Consortium.

The long negotiations which preceded the signing of the Reorganization Loan Agreement included the entrance of Russia, and Japan, into the so-called Old Consortium.[49]   It was a six-power group from June 18, 1912, when the inter-bank agreement was signed, until the American withdrawal in March, 1913.   Among the four powers who had signed the Hukuang Loan contract and the contract for the Manchurian currency reform loan, that is, France, Germany, Great Britain, and the United States, there was general agreement as to the desirability of admitting Russia and Japan.   This agreement was based on a desire to secure "the broadest possible internationalization" in the financing of China, as an American official put it.[50]   In the language of a British official the British government was "animated by the desire to prevent a return to the previous policy of unprofitable competition in China." [51]   The approval of the French and

[49] The New Consortium was created as the result of negotiations begun by the American government in July, 1918.

[50] *U. S. Foreign Relations, 1912*, p. 110.   The acting Secretary of State to the American Minister at Peking.

[51] *U. S. Foreign Relations, 1912*, p. 110.   The Ambassador of Great

the German governments was expressed at the same time. In the Russian case the problem of entrance into the Consortium turned upon two matters, one of which was more immediately the concern of the Russian government and the other of the bankers.

The Russian government was interested in securing, if possible, some recognition that its position in Manchuria was different from the position of the other governments, with the exception of the Japanese. The outcome of the negotiations upon this point was the following paragraph in the minutes of the inter-bank meeting of June 19, 1912.

In the event of the Russian or Japanese groups disapproving of any object for which any advance or loan under the agreement shall be intended to be made then, if such advance or loan shall be concluded by the other groups or any of them and the Russian Government or the Japanese Government shall notify the other Governments concerned that the business proposed is contrary to the interests of Russia or Japan as the case may be, the Russian group or the Japanese group as the case may be shall be entitled to withdraw from the agreement, but the retiring group will remain bound by all financial engagements which it shall have entered into prior to such withdrawal. The withdrawal of the Russian group or the Japanese group shall not affect the rights or liabilities of the other groups under the agreement.[52]

The Russian bankers undertook to secure the right of the Russian representative, namely the Russo-Asiatic Bank, to issue some part of the Russian participation in whatever loans might be made in money markets outside of Russia and through representatives chosen by the bank itself. This would have meant the independent operation of the Russo-Asiatic Bank in the British and French money markets in possible competition with the

Britain at Washington to the Acting Secretary of State of the United States.

[52] MacMurray, J. V. A., *Treaties and Agreements*, vol. II, p. 1024.

Consortium representatives in those markets. The interbank agreement, by which bankers in one country were allowed to issue in other countries through the members of the Consortium, was, the bankers may well have said, a sufficient intrusion of political considerations. It gave Russia and Japan political influence based upon the existence of loanable funds in other countries. It was held by the other bankers that the Russian proposal to operate in other markets through their own agents was quite inconsistent with the principle on which the Consortium was based.[53]

After the admission of Russia and Japan a single loan agreement was entered into with China before the end of 1913. This was the so-called Reorganization loan which was issued on May 21, 1913. The bankers of the five countries involved accepted responsibility for equal participation. The £5 million of the Russian share were issued in St. Petersburg, Brussels, London, and Paris. The Russian issue was £2,777,780, which is taken as the Russian share. The amount outstanding at the end of 1913 was in £2,777,780, in rubles 26,305,577, and in U. S. $13,416,677.

Russian participation in the 4% Gold Loan of 1895 has been dealt with above. The amount outstanding upon the Russian share of this loan at the end of 1913 was rubles 37,601,525 or U. S. $19,320,910. The totals are brought together in the following table which includes the small loan to Mongolia mentioned above.

TABLE 5

RUSSIAN OBLIGATIONS OF THE CHINESE GOVERNMENT AT THE
END OF 1913

	Rubles	U. S. Dollars
Reorganization loan of 1913	26,305,577	13,416,677
4% Gold Loan of 1895	37,601,525	19,320,910
Mongolian loan	100,000	51,300
	64,007,102	32,788,887

[53] Field, F. V., *American Participation in the China Consortium*, p. 107.

Mission Property

The value of the property of the Russian Orthodox Mission is the chief item to be reported. This amounted to rubles one million in 1904. There must be added here the sum of approximately rubles 500,000 to cover additions to the property of the Russian Orthodox Mission during the years 1904–1913 and to cover some other Russian religious and philanthropic institutions in China. The total mission and philanthropic holdings in 1914 may be estimated at rubles 1.5 million.

Summary of Russian Investments, 1914 [54]

A summary of Russian investments in China in 1914 is shown in the table below. This summary does not include the whole of Russian expenditures in China. It has been shown above that expenditures in connection with the Chinese Eastern Railway were considerably greater than the amount set down against the railway. The effort has been made to include only holdings upon which a business return was normally to be expected.

Certain outstanding facts may be briefly presented at the risk of repeating what has been said above. In the first place the importance of Manchuria and Mongolia as a field for Russian investment was overwhelming in 1914 as it had been in 1904. The percentage of the total Russian investment in China definitely assignable to Manchuria and Mongolia was 88.4 per cent in 1904 and 86.1 per cent in 1914. Turning to direct business investments, that is eliminating obligations of the Chinese government from our calculations, we find the percentage in Manchuria and Mongolia to be 98.8 for 1904 and 98 for 1914. It is not far from the truth to say that the whole of Russian business investments in China in the days before the World War were in these two regions.

---

[54] This section has been altered to present totals and percentages more nearly comparable with those of the other studies. (C. F. R.)

A second outstanding fact is the importance of the Chinese Eastern Railway but it is to be observed, also, that this importance declined somewhat during the years 1904–1914. The estimates show that the Chinese Eastern Railway represented 94.6 per cent of Russian business investments in 1904 and 80 per cent in 1914.[55] This decline in the relative importance of the Chinese Eastern Railway was due chiefly to the industrial and commercial development of Harbin and of a few other centers in northern Manchuria. It was not due to the spread of Russian commerce and industry to other parts of China.

Russian holdings of the obligations of the Chinese government formed 10.6 per cent of Russian investments in 1904 and 12.2 per cent in 1914. The Russian case is similar to the others in showing a great preponderance of direct business investments over loans to the Chinese government. In 1914 the Russians had participated in two important loans to China. In both cases political interest prompted Russian participation. Russia was normally a capital importing country and it required a political interest and the consequent prompting of the Russian government to bring about these results in the financial field.

In general it may be said that the Russian government, working through the Chinese Eastern Railway, was the dominant factor in Russian business investments in China and that the Russian government, working through a Russian bank with French connections, was the dominant factor in Russian participation in loans to the Chinese government. An attempt has been made to separate the Russian funds from those of the French and others in the case of loans to the government. In the case of the railway it may be said that the funds came in a large measure from France. The similarity between the Russian situation and the Japanese in 1914 is to be noted. In both

[55] The Chinese Eastern Railway represented 84.6 per cent of total Russian investments in 1904 and 70.3 per cent in 1914.

cases the government of a borrowing country took an active interest in the promotion of foreign investments.

TABLE 6

RUSSIAN INVESTMENTS IN CHINA, 1914, AT THE END OF 1913

	Rubles	U. S. Dollars
Business investments		
In Manchuria and Mongolia		
Chinese Eastern Railway	369,000,000	189,297,000
Commercial investment (Manchuria)	75,000,000	38,475,000
Commercial investment (Mongolia)	8,000,000	4,104,000
In the rest of China		
Commercial investment	9,000,000	4,617,000
Obligations of the Chinese government	64,007,102	32,788,887
	525,007,102	269,281,887

RUSSIAN INTERESTS IN 1930

The Chinese Eastern Railway Since 1914

We must now turn our attention to the changes in the economic relations between Russia and China in recent times. This means that special attention must be given to two important events, the World War of 1914–1918 and the Russian revolution of 1917.

During the first years of the World War the earnings of the Chinese Eastern Railway increased rapidly. There were greatly increased demands for the transportation of manufactured goods from abroad to Russia. These goods, as well as railway and war materials, came through the port of Vladivostok. The result was that in 1915 the railway made a net profit (rubles 12,700,000) for the first time in its history.

The total cost of the railway to January 1, 1917 (one month before the revolution), amounted to rubles 370 million. The debt due to the Russian government to cover deficits was rubles 178.6 million.[56] The latter figure excludes interest upon the amounts reported as deficits.

The Russian revolution, after the success of the Bolsheviks in October, 1917, radically changed every aspect of Russian economic relations with China and of the economic condition of the Russians in the Far East. During the years 1918–1919 the railway was in an uncertain and difficult position.

There was, for a time, a continuation of the control over the railway by the officials of the former Russian government. It was suggested in 1918 that the Chinese government take over the control and the policing of the line. To this there was Japanese opposition[57] which brought about joint policing of the railway by Chinese and Japanese troops. The military problems led to inter-allied control of the line from 1919 to 1922. Inter-allied control, which was referred to as "trusteeship" at the Washington Conference was regarded as temporary and as having no effect upon the ownership.[58]

During this same period there was an assertion of some degree of proprietary interests in the line on the part of the Russo-Asiatic Bank. This bank was reorganized in Paris after the success of the Bolshevik revolution. After about a year of some participation by the Russo-Asiatic Bank in the affairs of the railway, the Chinese government took steps in 1920 toward the removal of General Horvath as manager and the appointment of additional Chinese members of the board of directors. This caused a storm of protest by the Russo-Asiatic Bank as well as by the French government. The result was an agree-

[56] This includes a deficit of rubles 4,513,000 which was met by the Russian government in 1914.

[57] Based upon the Military Agreement of September 6, 1918, between China and Japan. MacMurray, J. V. A., *Treaties and Agreements*, vol. II, p. 1413.

[58] A Subcommittee of the Committee of the Whole on Pacific and Far Eastern Questions stated concerning the ownership of the Chinese Eastern, "the railway is in effect the property of the Russian government." The statement concerning inter-allied control is not by Mr. Serebrennikov. (C. F. R.)

ment, on October 2, 1920, between the bank and the Chinese government.[59]

This agreement was superseded in the spring of 1924 when, on May 31, the Soviet government concluded a new agreement with the Peking government which dealt with outstanding questions and, among them, with the Chinese Eastern Railway.   Details were left for settlement at a conference to be called within a month and in the meantime "the rights of the two governments arising out of the contract of September 8, 1896, for the construction and operation of the Chinese Eastern Railway, which do not conflict with the present agreement and the agreement for the provisional management of the said railway and which do not prejudice China's rights of sovereignty, shall be maintained." [60]

A further agreement was concluded by the Soviet government with the Mukden authorities (that is, with the representatives of Marshal Chang Tso-lin) on September 20, 1924.   This agreement was necessary because of the refusal of the Mukden authorities to recognize the validity of the agreements of May.   An important new provision of the Mukden agreement was one which shortened the period, after which China was to recover the railway without payment, from eighty years to sixty years.   In other respects the Mukden agreement was similar to Peking agreements of May.[61]

[59] This agreement was made "pending an agreement which the Chinese government will come to with the Russian government recognized by China regarding the Chinese Eastern Railway." It contained a stipulation that the "rights and obligations of the company will henceforward and in every respect be of a commercial nature." The agreement is printed in the *China Year Book*, 1923, pp. 660–2.

[60] The "present agreement" is that "on general principles for the settlement of the questions between the Republic of China and the Union of Soviet Socialist Republics." *China Year Book*, 1924, pp. 1192–4. For the agreement concerning the provisional management of the railway, see pp. 1194–6. See also Young, C. W., *The International Relations of Manchuria*, App. G.

[61] The text of the Mukden agreement, and of the Peking agreements, is to be found in Young, C. W., *The International Relations of Manchuria*, App. G. It is difficult to find an accurate text of the Mukden agreement elsewhere. (C. F. R.)

The provisions of the 1924 agreements brought about joint Sino-Soviet control of the Chinese Eastern. An effort was made to guarantee equality to each side by equal representation on the board of directors and by other devices. The Soviet authorities insisted upon Soviet citizens for all places on the railway but did not insist upon dismissal of all Russian employees who were not Soviet citizens "for the sole purpose of enforcing this principle." [62] The agreements of 1924 provided, however, that the manager was to be a "national of the Union of Socialist Soviet Republics." [63]

The financial clauses of the agreements of 1924 are tentative, "pending a final settlement," and vague. Concerning the net profits the provisions were that they were to be held by the board of directors. Concerning the redemption of the railway, that is, its redemption by China before the expiration of sixty (or eighty) years, the provisions were that "the two contracting parties shall determine what the Chinese Eastern Railway had actually cost and it shall be redeemed by China with Chinese capital at a fair price." A conference to be held within one month was provided for in the Peking agreement and at this conference "the amount and conditions governing the redemption" were to be settled. So far as is known these questions and others concerning the railway were not settled during the following years. This made the situation worse and resulted finally in the conflict of 1929.[64]

[62] Declaration in connection with the agreement for the Provisional Management of the Chinese Eastern Railway, Peking, May 31, 1924. Young, C. W., *The International Relations of Manchuria*, p. 293.

[63] Article 3 of the Peking agreement and Article 1, Section 8, of the Mukden agreement. Boris G. Ostroumoff was removed from the general managership October 3, 1924, as a result of these agreements. He was placed under arrest and his case is briefly recounted in the *Report of the Commission on Extraterritoriality in China*, Washington, 1926, pp. 95–7. He was succeeded as manager by A. N. Ivanhoff. (C. F. R.)

[64] The conflict of 1929 brought about the so-called Habarovsk agreement of December 22, 1929 (Wheeler-Bennett, *Documents on International Affairs*, 1929, pp. 281–4). This agreement again was tentative and called for a conference "to regulate all outstanding questions" to be held in Moscow,

The sum to be set down to represent the investment in China of the Soviet government may be determined for 1930 as for the earlier dates. According to official information the entire cost of construction of the railway to the first of January, 1927, was rubles 391.6 million.[65] In a later publication the cost of construction is presented with somewhat less detail for January 1, 1930. The total is rubles 410.3 million. It is this sum which is accepted as the investment in China of the U. S. S. R. for the end of 1930.

The total obligations of the Chinese Eastern Railway to the Russian government reach a sum many times as great as the value which has been accepted, if other items are included. The first of these other items is the payment to cover deficits which amounted on January 1, 1930, to rubles 178.6 million. The second is an item which includes interest payments, refunds, and other charges. Some of the interest payments may have been made by the former government of Russia. In any case the total obligation of the Chinese Eastern Railway under this heading is said to have been rubles 1,221.6 million. If these items are added to the rubles 410 million reported above, a total of 1,810 million is reached. It is quite unreasonable to suppose that a debt of this amount is taken seriously either by the Russian or the Chinese government.[66]

In conclusion some information may be given concerning the net profits of the railway. It is believed that only one payment was made by the company to the Russian exchequer before the Russian revolution, amounting

1930. This conference was begun but no results had been arrived at by the end of the year. The Chinese Eastern Railway is, therefore, to be regarded as entirely the property of the Russian government, subject to conditions concerning control, profits, and redemption. In Harbin in June, 1931, the impression was general among Chinese and Russians that the effective control of the railway was in Soviet Russian hands. (C. F. R.)

[65] Economic Bureau, Chinese Eastern Railway, *Statistical Yearbook for 1928*.

[66] See footnote 66 on page 592.

to rubles 12,363,000. During the years 1916–1919 the railway was obliged to meet losses owing to the rapid fall of the Russian ruble and to the uncertain political situation. It is practically impossible to ascertain the operating revenue and expenses of the railway for these years. The net profits of the railway for the years 1920–1929 were reported to be as follows:

	Rubles
1920	2,827,000
1921	2,596,000
1922	1,275,000
1923	2,303,000
1924	7,162,000
1925	15,453,000
1926	16,119,000
1927	5,856,000
1928	
1929	5,672,000

After 1924 the profits of the railway were to be divided equally between the Chinese authorities and the U. S. S. R.

[66] THE VALUE OF THE CHINESE EASTERN RAILWAY ON JAN. 1, 1930

(The Economic Bureau of Chinese Eastern Railway, *Statistical Yearbook for 1930*.) In gold rubles

Construction expense incurred during the period from 1898 to 1905, both inclusive		365,649,451.17
Expenses for improvements and new construction work incurred from assignments according to appraisals during the period from 1906 to 1917	5,462,104.73	
Expenses for improvements, new construction work, etc., incurred during the period 1918 to 1929	39,188,617.84	
		44,650,722.57
Total		410,300,263.74

Note: (1) During the period of operation of the Chinese Eastern Railway there were received from the Russian government to cover deficits in the operation of the railway from 1903 to 1914   Rls.   178,579,617.95

(2) Unpaid interest and refunds on the capital of the railway, on loans obtained for equipping and improving the road and on surplus payments to cover deficits, amounted on January 1, 1930, approximately to:

Interest	1,203,213,536.14
Refunds	18,403,908.01
	Rls. 1,221,617,444.15

in accordance with the agreements of 1924.[67]   This division was made for the first time in 1928 when rubles 25,505,726 were so divided. The sum divided did not represent the net profit for the one year 1928. It would, therefore, be misleading to enter this amount as net profit in the table above.

It is to be noted, also, that the net operating revenue of the railway has had charged against it since 1924 (1) new construction, (2) losses from fixed exchange in connection with local traffic, (3) subsidies to Chinese government institutions. The sum expended for Chinese government institutions in 1929 was rubles 3.2 million and the total for the six years 1924–1929 was about rubles 21 million. The Chinese Eastern Railway has in the past supported a variety of institutions of an educational and philanthropic nature, some of which were more generally used by the Russian community than by the Chinese. Disagreements over the use of the net revenue from the railway have frequently turned upon the question of the use of funds in China; the question of the remittance of funds from China has not been involved.[68]

The government of the Union of Soviet Socialist Republics is the owner of railway property in China the construction of which cost about rubles 410 million. It is highly probable that competent engineers would put about this value upon the line. To bring this property into existence the Russian government of the past spent large sums in addition to construction costs, some of which are reported in deficits of rubles 178 million. Upon this investment the actual remittances out of China have been about rubles 25 million.[69] This railway, undertaken

[67] Mr. Serebrennikov's reference here is to the section which provides that the profits be held by the board of directors. I am informed that they are to be equally divided but the particulars of this agreement for equal division are not known to me. (C. F. R.)

[68] A large part of the funds turned over to the Soviet government in 1928 was actually remitted from China. The remittance was to England and other European countries rather than to Russia.

[69] Rubles 12,363,000 in 1916 and half of rubles 25.5 million in 1928.

before 1900 as a part of a venture in Russian expansion in the Far East, was, at the end of 1931, a foreign holding of the U. S. S. R. As a business investment it has not been a great success, and its status has been a matter of uncertainty since 1917 and was not finally determined by the summer of 1931.

Russian Business Investments

In China Proper: We must consider here the changes brought about by the European war and by other events since 1914 in the commerce between China and Russia. The first result was an increase in the Russian demand for manufactured goods from outside of Russia. Such goods were re-exported from China to Russia in considerable quantities.

This was followed, after the Russian revolution, by the cutting off of trade. The tea trade, for example, was greatly reduced. The following figures, showing the quantity of tea exported to Russia, make this clear.

	Piculs
1914	902,716
1915	1,162,842
1916	1,049,933
1917	733,653
1918	95,705
1919	165,334
1920	11,566
1921	21,154
1922	27,594
1923	12,064 [70]

The year 1915 was a record year in the Chinese tea trade with Russia. The rapid decrease in the export of tea to Russia after the Russian revolution resulted in the total suspension and stoppage of the trading activities of the Russian tea firms in Hankow, Foochow, and Kiukiang. It is impossible to suppose that new investments

[70] Torgashev, B. P., " China, a Supplier of Tea for Russia." *Manchuria Monitor*, 1925, no. 5–7, p. 164.

were made and the actual holdings of the Russian firms are difficult to estimate.[71]

There is to be recorded also a change in the position of the Russians in China. Previous to 1921 the consulates and consular officials of the former Russian government were active. After that year they were closed by the Chinese government and ceased to function. Russians in China were brought under the jurisdiction of the Chinese government and lost their extraterritorial rights.[72] In 1924 the Soviet Republic was recognized by China and Soviet diplomatic and consular officials appeared in China. At the same time Soviet trade representatives undertook to promote commercial relations between the two countries.

The position of the Russian emigrants [73] continued to be uncertain and difficult since they had lost their extraterritorial rights, privileges, and protection. This encouraged the Chinese to take advantage of their condition and caused them to act in a manner that violated former Sino-Russian treaties.[74] Russian emigration into China, in so far as it was due to the Russian revolution, began in 1918. It has grown rapidly, particularly since 1920. The emigrants brought to China some capital in the form of gold and jewelry and, sometimes, of other mov-

[71] The quickness of the change is shown in the following comments by the Customs authorities at Hankow. Of the tea season of 1915 we are told that it was "the most profitable in the history of the port," and of the season of 1918 that it was "the most calamitous on record." Remer, C. F., *The Foreign Trade of China*, p. 190.

[72] By a presidential mandate of September 23, 1920, in which the action of the Chinese government was based upon the fact that China no longer recognized the Russian minister and consuls. The formal surrender of extraterritoriality was made by Russia in the Peking agreement of 1924, Article 12. See Willoughby, *Foreign Rights and Interests in China*, vol. II, pp. 579–86. (C. F. R.)

[73] A name applied to Russians who are not Soviet citizens, whether they have come to China since the revolution or were in China before 1917. (C. F. R.)

[74] The position taken by the Russian minister no longer recognized by the Chinese government was that the safeguarding of Russian rights must continue to be in accordance with the existing treaties upon this whole question. *China Year Book*, 1921–1922, pp. 621–59. The treatment of the Russians is dealt with at some length.

able property. The total value of such property brought from Russia could hardly be ascertained if a special investigation were made. We think it would amount to many million gold rubles and there is no doubt that a part of the funds realized have been invested in China.

The chief center of the Russian emigrants was at first Harbin and the zone of the Chinese Eastern Railway. From this center the Russians gradually scattered over China. They are now to be found in considerable numbers in Shanghai, Tientsin, Mukden, Dairen, Tsingtao, Peking, and Hankow. Of the Russians in Tientsin and Peking some have come from Mongolia, Chinese Turkestan, and the adjacent areas of Siberia. A number of the Russian emigrants in China have come through Korea, having left Vladivostok when it was occupied by Soviet troops in 1922.

For a variety of reasons, but chiefly because of the growth of Soviet influence in Harbin, many of the older Russian residents and business men as well as a number of the newcomers have emigrated from this city to Mukden, Tientsin, and Shanghai.

The amount of capital invested by these Russians in China proper under the new conditions cannot be accurately estimated. It may be accepted as certain that it was not less than rubles 5 million.

Taking into account the whole of the available information concerning Russian property in the various open ports and cities of China, outside of Manchuria and Mongolia, we may put down the figure of their investments at rubles 15 million for the year 1930.[75]

[75] In November, 1930, the death occurred at Tientsin of a Russian woman reported to have been, with one exception, the wealthiest person in the Russian community. She was the owner of forty-three houses in the British Concession and had other interests. My informant, who was fairly familiar with the affairs of the family, put her holdings at Tientsin at a total which was certainly no less than a million dollars in Chinese currency. The wealthiest Russian in Tientsin is believed to be worth Chinese $20 million. His holdings are all in China but he has more in Harbin than elsewhere. Russian interests in Tientsin were estimated at certainly no less than Chinese $5 million. (C. F. R.)

In Mongolia: New political conditions in Outer Mongolia brought about the growth of Russian influence there both before and after the Russian revolution. In 1911 Outer Mongolia declared its independence of the new Chinese republic. A Russian protectorate, under Chinese suzerainty, was constituted by a tripartite Sino-Russian-Mongolian agreement concluded at Kiakhta on June 7, 1915. The Russian government, desiring to assist in the economic field, granted two loans in 1914 of rubles 2 and 3 million respectively. In 1915 a Mongolian National Bank was established at Urga, the capital. This bank was capitalized at rubles 1 million, of which rubles 800,000 were paid in by the Siberian bank.[76]

During the years 1917–1921 grave events took place in Mongolia. The country suffered from the consequences of the Russian revolution and of the activities of those opposed to the revolution.[77] In 1921 there was set up virtually under Soviet protection the so-called Mongolian Peoples Republic. During the following years Soviet influence was extended over Mongolia and the region may be held to be practically annexed to the U. S. S. R.[78] Mongolia was reorganized economically to bring the country into line with the neighboring Soviet republic. Private trade was suppressed and the result of this and other measures was to increase the trade between Mongolia and the U. S. S. R. and to decrease the trade between Mongolia and China.[79]

[76] Maisky, J., *Present Day Mongolia*, p. 210.
[77] The rule of Baron Ungern von Sternberg, February–June, 1921, was a fantastic and cruel climax. (C. F. R.)
[78] Outer Mongolia does not appear to have been represented at a Mongolian Affairs Conference held at Nanking in May, 1930. (C. F. R.)
[79] This is shown in the following figures presented by Mr. Serebrennikov in an article on Mongolia in *Foreign Affairs*, April, 1931, p. 514.

Year	Percentage of Trade with China	Percentage of Trade with Soviet Russia
1924	85.7	14.3
1925	78.3	21.7
1926	68.7	31.3
1927	63.6	36.4

In 1924 a Mongolian Trade Bank was established by the Mongolian Republic jointly with Soviet Russia. This bank was capitalized at rubles 500,000, divided equally between the two. During the years from 1921 to 1926 the institutions of the Soviet government operating in Mongolia invested not less than rubles 2 million in landed property and in the building of residences in the town of Urga.

It must be noted, also, that the Mongolor Gold Mining Company continued to operate during the years 1914–1919. During these years the total gold production in the gold fields of the company was 43,406 troy ounces with a value of rubles 1.6 million.[80]   In 1920 the Mongolor Company leased its concession to the newly formed Peking-Mongolor Mining Company, of which the shareholders were Chinese, British, and American.[81]   So far as is known the Peking-Mongolor Company had not undertaken operations at the end of 1930 on account of the difficult conditions set by the Mongolian government.

The estimates of Russian investments may be summarized.   The total investments of the Soviet government may be set down at rubles 2,250,000. It is difficult to assign them but they may be regarded as, in general, similar to business investments.   The new business investments of the period from 1914 to 1930 may be considered to have been rubles 2 million. When this sum is combined with the total of the earlier period we reach a total of rubles 10 million as the private business investments. The total business investments are then rubles 10 million if private holdings alone are considered, or rubles 12,250,000 if the holdings of the Soviet government are included.[82]

[80] The annual figures in troy ounces were given as follows in the Report on the Mongolor Gold Concessions, p. 7:

1914	11,027	1917	6,408
1915	9,879	1918	3,064
1916	9,957	1919	3,071

[81] *China Year Book*, 1921–1922, p. 586.

[82] Deductions from the private holdings are considered later when business investments are summarized.

In Manchuria: The Russian revolution weakened the economic ties between Russia and Manchuria. It was the main cause of the great changes that have come about in local trade and industry. It put an end to the free flow of Russian capital into Manchuria. This was partly compensated for by the influx of Russian emigrants and refugees with their capital. In 1918 the continued and extreme depreciation of the paper ruble ruined many Russian firms and for some time economic organization in Manchuria was on the verge of a complete breakdown. It was necessary to undertake reconstruction, to build up trade, and to seek for new markets. Business had to adapt itself to a new currency. The changes of this period in northern Manchuria offered a great opportunity to others and the Japanese, in particular, took advantage of it. The banks of other nations through their Manchurian branches helped to meet the dearth of capital. Import and export firms found new trade connections and the trade and industry of the region began to revive.

During the years which followed the Russian revolution some of the old and well-known Russian firms closed their doors and sold their stock in trade to Chinese or foreigners. In place of some of the old firms, new firms appeared, organized and operated by Russian emigrants. Because of the uncertain position of the Russians in Manchuria after they came under the jurisdiction of the Chinese authorities, a number of Russian firms transferred their business to foreign flags. This explains the appearance of many joint concerns such as Russo-Japanese, Russo-French, and in some cases Russo-Chinese firms.

In this connection it is to be noted that the economic influence of the Chinese in northern Manchuria increased during this period. In Harbin and in the railway zone there appeared a considerable number of large Chinese industrial concerns run on Western lines. Examples might be given in the manufacture of flour, bean oil, and bean cake.

The new Russian investment of the period has been estimated at rubles 50 million. No complete investigation can be made in the complicated and changing situation in which the Russians have found themselves. To support the estimate of rubles 50 million the following facts are offered for consideration.

1914–1916. In 1914 the Harbin firm of Chourin and Company established a tobacco factory. During the following year a new sugar refinery was installed at Ashiho on the eastern section of the Chinese Eastern Railway. In 1916 a large flour mill was built in Harbin by a Russo-Chinese firm. During these three years the Harbin merchants and war-supply contractors made large profits.

1917–1919. During this period the disturbances due to revolution and civil war were at their height in Siberia. A large number of Russian emigrants and refugees entered Manchuria. Many of the all-Siberian co-operatives transferred their activities to Manchuria. In 1920 the influx of emigrants was probably greatest. They brought with them what they could and undertook in many cases to set up commercial or industrial enterprises. In 1918 many Russian shipping companies transferred their steamers from the Amur region of Siberia to the Sungari in northern Manchuria in order to avoid confiscation. Many of these Russian steamers were sold to Chinese at a later time.[83] During the years 1918–1919 there was an intensive sale of land by the Chinese Eastern Railway in and around Harbin. New suburbs were formed around Harbin at this time.

1920–1921. There was much building activity in Harbin during these years. Some millions of rubles were invested by Russians for this purpose. This intensive house building was held to offer opportunities for profit because of the rapid increase in the Russian population. It is to be noted that during the single year 1921 the Harbin Mu-

[83] In 1922 there were eighty-three steamers on the Sungari of which thirty-three were Russian owned, twelve belonging to the Chinese Eastern Railway.

nicipal Council granted no less than four hundred building permits. The Siberian co-operative societies, having lost all connection with Siberia, were reorganized. Some of the co-operatives have gone under foreign flags and there are cases in which the co-operatives have gone in for the investment of their funds within China. During the years 1920–1921 new factories were established in Harbin and the railway zone in the following lines: the tanning of leather, the manufacture of sheepskin coats and felt boots, canning, the manufacture of butter and cheese, printing and publishing, and others. The Eastern Russo-Chinese Transport, Insurance and Commission Company, the Ural-Siberian Company, the Volga-Baikal Trading Company, and the Far Eastern Jewish Bank of Commerce were all established at about this time.

1922–1928. In 1922 Messrs. Borodin and Takata established a distillery with a capital of Yen 2 million (Russo-Japanese). In 1923 Chourin and Company enlarged and improved their tobacco factory. In 1924 an aërated water factory was built at one of the stations of the Chinese Eastern. During the same year the Dalbank (Far Eastern Bank), a Soviet credit institution, was opened in Harbin as well as the Interurban Telephone Company (Russo-French). In 1925 the Mulin Coal Mining Company, a Russo-Chinese enterprise, was undertaken with a capital of rubles 3 million. During the same year three new distilleries were established, all Russian owned, and a veneer factory.[84] There were additional flour mills established in 1927 and 1928. Motor bus routes in which Russians are interested increased in 1928 and in 1929 there was an extension of the Harbin street car lines. It is estimated that there were in 1925 minor Russian concerns with small workshops employing 530 workers. The number of such small concerns continued to increase until 1929.

[84] Sourin, V. I., *The Manufacturing Industry of Northern Manchuria and Harbin*, Harbin, 1928, pp. 109–10.

1929–1930. Open hostilities between the Chinese and
the Soviet representatives in northern Manchuria broke
out in July, 1929. When hostilities ended in December,
1929, recovery proved impossible because of the world
depression. It is estimated that about 15,000 Russians
were unemployed and seeking employment in Harbin
in the summer of 1931. Industrial development and commercial progress had not been renewed by the end of 1930.

The direct business investments of a private sort in
Manchuria in 1930 may be estimated at a total of rubles
125 million. This means an addition of rubles 50 million
during the period under consideration. The total of rubles
125 million will not be considered as too large by anyone
acquainted with the details of Russian business activity
in northern Manchuria.

The total investment in Harbin and the Chinese Eastern
Railway zone may be roughly divided into rubles 50
million in trade and industries and rubles 75 million in
land and buildings.[85]

Summary of Business Investments

The total business investments of a private sort in the
hands of Russians in China, according to the estimates
presented above, was as follows:

	Rubles
Business investments in China proper	15,000,000
Business investments in Mongolia	10,000,000
Business investments in Manchuria	125,000,000
	150,000,000

From this sum of rubles 150 million there must be deducted a sum which represents Russian enterprises which
have passed into the hands of Chinese or have been sold
to others. This sum is difficult to calculate since it is not
always possible to be certain as to the conditions of ownership which have accompanied changes in control and in

[85] The following estimate of Russian business investments in Harbin in
1926 is by Mr. N. M. Dobrohotov, Secretary of the Committee of the
Harbin Bourse and author of the *Commercial Companion* published in

legal status. The estimates of Mr. Dobrohotov presented above show sales to Chinese and Japanese to the amount of rubles 14,550,000. As the result of further investigation the total to be deducted has been estimated at rubles 30 million. This leaves the total private Russian business investments in China in 1930 at a sum which may be estimated at rubles 120 million.

Harbin in 1926. This estimate was prepared at the request of Mr. Serebrennikov.

PRINCIPAL INDUSTRIES IN HARBIN AND THE INVESTMENTS OF RUSSIAN
CAPITAL, 1926

(Figures are in thousands of gold rubles)

Denomination	Capital Invested	Sold To Chinese	Sold To Japanese
Flour mills	14,000	11,000	
Distilleries	5,000	1,250	
Breweries	1,200	200	
Vodka distilleries	1,300		
Bean oil mills	2,000	1,000	
Metal working factories	2,000		
Glass factories	100	100	
Tanneries	500		500
Electric plants	1,000		500
Sausage factories	1,000		
Bakeries	600		
Candle factories	250		
Drying oil factories	250		
Veneer factories	1,000		
Saw mills	500		
Timber concessions	6,000		
Mining concessions	3,000		
Sugar refineries	2,000		
Match factories	250		
Butter and cheese dairies	500		
Tobacco factories	1,000		
Sheepskin coat and felt boot factories	200		
Shoe factories	200		
Canneries	500		
Confectioneries	250		
Soap factories	150		
Others	500		
Total	45,250	13,550	1,000
Residential houses, storehouses, and other buildings, not including buildings of the Chinese Eastern Railway:			
in Harbin	50,000		
on line	2,000		
Land property (not built)	25,000		
	122,250		

Obligations of the Chinese Government, 1930

Under this heading we must draw attention to the final activities of the Russo-Asiatic Bank. In March, 1916, the bank signed an agreement with the Chinese government providing for the construction of a railway from Harbin to Aigun via Mergen with a branch line to Tsitsihar. The loan agreement was for £5 million and the loan was not to be floated until after the World War.[86] An advance of Shanghai taels 500,000 was made upon this loan. During the same year the bank advanced Kuping taels 300,000 to the Ministry of Education.

In 1918 the Russo-Asiatic Bank was nationalized by the Soviet government and all of its branches in Russia became the property of the state. The agencies abroad did not recognize the nationalization and the bank continued to exist with a head office in Paris. It has already been pointed out that from 1920 to 1924 the bank played an important rôle in the affairs of the Chinese Eastern Railway.

From 1918 to 1922 the bank made a series of loans to the Chinese government. Converting these and the loans of 1916 mentioned in the previous paragraph into rubles we find the total of these Russo-Asiatic Bank loans to have been rubles 4,054,000. On September 25, 1926 the Russo-Asiatic Bank was ordered to close its doors and its liquidation was undertaken by the Chinese government. The real property of the bank in Shanghai, Tientsin, Chefoo, and Hankow was sold and realized about rubles 3 million. Its total property in China may have come to rubles 5 million. The liquidation of this bank removes the obligations due to it from the list of obligations of the Chinese government.

If we could accept the place of issue as the basis for the assignment of the other known loans, the 4% Loan of 1895 and the Reorganization loan of 1913, we could

[86] MacMurray, J. V. A., *Treaties and Agreements*, vol. II, p. 1267.

show a total obligation to Russia of U. S. $13,878,811 as of December 31, 1930.[87] We find, however, that both the Russian and the Chinese governments regard these obligations as having been cancelled or in any case as non-existent. Taking into account the Mongolian loans mentioned above, the total of the obligations no longer recognized as outstanding reaches a total of about rubles 57 million.[88] At whatever amount we may put the outstanding amount on the basis of the place of issue it may be accepted as a fact that the Russian loan obligations of the Chinese government have been wiped out.

This is true also of the obligation under the Boxer indemnity agreement which came to an end with the Peking agreement of 1924.[89] Having disposed of the obligations of the Chinese government to the Russo-Asiatic Bank, the holders within Russia of Chinese loan bonds, and the Russian government under the Boxer agreement, there remain no other obligations of the Chinese government to be considered.

Summary of Russian Investments, 1930

Russian investments in China are summarized in the following table. It is to be borne in mind that the obliga-

[87] Russian share of the 4% Loan of 1895 U. S. $1,456,160 and of the Reorganization loan U. S. $12,422,651.

[88] Concerning the 4% Loan of 1895 it may well be that a large part of these bonds were in France and England at the end of 1930. Concerning the Reorganization loan bonds it may be remarked that their sale in London brought about an issue of "green" bonds to take their place. The "green" bonds were issued in Paris in exchange for bonds of the original Russian issue owned outside of Russia since 1917. The obligation which may exist as a result of the issue of the bonds of both loans is not an obligation to Russia. (C. F. R.)

[89] Article 12 of the Agreement on General Principles . . . Young, C. W., *The International Relations of Manchuria*, p. 286. A declaration of the same date contained provisions for the creation of a fund for the promotion of education in China administered by a commission of three, one member to be appointed by the Soviet government. This arrangement has not been made, so far as is known. As a matter of fact, the Chinese government suspended all payments to Russia on the Boxer indemnity from July 31, 1920. For a brief account see Bordelongue, J., *The Russian Portion of the Boxer Indemnity*, Bureau of Industrial and Commercial Information, Shanghai, 1929 or 1930.

tions of the Chinese government have been removed for reasons given above. This summary is, therefore, at the same time a total of Russian business investments in China and a total of all investments.[90]

TABLE 7

RUSSIAN INVESTMENTS IN CHINA, 1930

		Rubles	U. S. Dollars
In Manchuria			
Chinese Eastern Railway	410,300,000		
Private investments	100,000,000	510,300,000	261,783,900
In Mongolia			
Holdings of the Soviet government	2,250,000		
Private investments	8,000,000	10,250,000	5,258,250
In China proper			
Private investments		12,000,000	6,156,000
		532,550,000	273,198,150

The above table shows Russian business investments of rubles 532,550,000 or U. S. $273,198,150. The geographical distribution of these investments shows 95.8 per cent in Manchuria, 1.9 per cent in Mongolia, and 2.3 per cent in the rest of China. Other general statements concerning Russian investments are to be found in the concluding section below.

Remittances from and to China in Recent Years.[91]

The investments which have been called private Russian investments have been estimated at a total of rubles 120 million for 1930. These investments are entirely in the hands of Russians who have been in China since the

[90] The situation of the Russian Orthodox Mission and of other religious institutions is not entirely clear. The property involved may be considered to have had a value of rubles 2.5 million in 1930.

[91] Mr. Serebrennikov is not responsible for this section or for the sections which follow. (C. F. R.)

Russian revolution or who have fled from Russia as a result of the revolution. It has been estimated above that the property brought from Russia by Russian refugees chiefly in the form of gold and jewels was at least rubles 5 million during the years immediately following the Russian revolution. This property may be supposed to have come to China for permanent investment. There is some remote possibility that the Russian owners of business property in China may at some future time undertake to return to Russia or to go elsewhere. This is unlikely.

It may be pointed out, also, that this business property does not involve any remittance of profits or of dividends to Russia. The owners of the property are in China, that is in northern Manchuria, and they expect to continue to live there. They are a group of persons who are frequently said to be without a country. This may be true from the political point of view. From the economic point of view their country is China.

The holdings of the Russian government in China brought about a remittance from China of rubles 25 million, one-half of this sum having been remitted to the former Russian government in 1915 and the other half to the order of the Soviet government in 1928.

Remittances from Chinese in Siberia to their homes in China reach a considerable total. In a statement prepared by the Harbin office of the Bank of China these remittances are shown for the period from September, 1929, to the end of 1930. The remittances came through the Dalbank and through the Bank of China. During the last quarter of 1929 they amounted to Yen 56,709 and, in addition, Chinese $1,448. For the year 1930 the sums were Yen 215,568 and, in addition, Chinese $544,663. The total for the sixteen months was nearly a million Chinese dollars.

These sums are from Chinese laborers in Russia. In view of the strict control over foreign exchange exercised by the Soviet authorities, these payments are evidence of the power of Chinese family ties. It is probable that only contract laborers in Siberia are permitted to remit home to China. The local manager of the Bank of China in Harbin was of the opinion, however, that all Chinese in Siberia are granted this privilege.

Remittances from Russians in northern Manchuria to Russia were put at so small a figure by local bankers as to be negligible. Stories that turn upon the difficulty of making such remittances are heard daily in Harbin.

The outstanding facts are small inpayments into China and outpayments from China in connection with Russian investments when the value of the investments is considered. At the same time remittances from Chinese in Siberia to their homes are permitted by the Soviet government and are large enough to be significant.

Russian Population in China

It is impossible to arrive at figures of the Russian population of China which are entirely satisfactory. The reliance for such statistics for other nationals has usually been upon the annual reports of the Chinese Customs. A study of these reports raises doubts as to their usefulness in the Russian case.

Consider first the figures showing the number of Russian firms in China. Here we find changes which are difficult to explain. The number of such firms is reported as 964 for 1926, 595 for 1927, and 1,112 for 1928. Again the number of Russian firms is reported as 323 for 1912 and 1,229 for 1913. It is most unlikely that such changes actually took place. With this warning the figures may be given which show the number of Russian firms in China for each of the years selected for the estimates of Russian investments.

1903	24
1913	1,229
1930	1,073

The Customs figures showing the Russian population in China are probably somewhat more to be trusted than those showing the number of firms. In this case we find changes in the figures which can hardly be accepted as reflecting actual changes in the number of Russians but the changes in the figures are usually explainable. The Russian population in China, for example, is reported at 479 for 1907 and at 9,520 for 1908. It may be pointed out in explanation that the Customs show the foreign population of the treaty ports only and that Dairen and Manchouli were opened to trade during the year 1907. Again, the Russian population is reported as 9,952 for the year 1909 and as 49,395 for the year 1910. The explanation of the sudden change probably lies in the fact that Harbin became a treaty port in 1909 and was reported upon for the first time in 1910. There is no doubt that the total number of Russians in China in 1904 was nearer to 50,000, as reported for 1910, than to 308, the number found in the Customs report for 1904.

The Russian population, to take still another example, was reported as follows for the years immediately following the Russian revolution.

1918	59,719
1919	148,170
1920	144,413
1921	68,250

It is, of course, well known that Russian refugees came to China in great numbers during these years. It is true also that the disorganized state of northern Manchuria made it difficult to arrive at estimates of Russian population. Nevertheless the sharp fall in 1921 is to be questioned.

For 1930 the Customs figures showed a Russian population of 65,361. In this case an estimate prepared by Mr. Serebrennikov is available for comparison. This estimate is from various sources and has involved the securing of new estimates from Russian officials or from others who are well informed. The total of this estimate

for 1930 was about 140,000 and the details are shown in
the following table.

TABLE 8

RUSSIAN POPULATION IN CHINA IN 1930

Manchuria			
Harbin: Emigrants	30,044		
Soviet citizens	27,633		
Chinese citizens	6,793		
		64,470	
Chinese Eastern Railway zone		38,114	
Barga, outside the railway zone		7,000	
Elsewhere in Manchuria		2,000	
Total for Manchuria		111,584	78.9%
Mongolia			
Outer Mongolia		8,000	
Uriankha (Tannu Tuva)		7,000	
Chinese Turkestan (Sinkiang)		2,613	
Total for Mongolia		17,613	12.4%
China proper			
Shanghai: French Concession	3,879		
International Settlement	3,387	7,266	
Tientsin		3,000	
Elsewhere		2,000	
Total for China proper		12,266	8.7%
Grand Total		141,463	100.0%

The total of 140,000 for 1930 is certainly nearer to the
truth than is the Customs figure of 65,000. It is not to
be supposed that this implies that the Customs authorities
failed to take into account more than half the Russians
in China. The Customs figure, it may be repeated, covers
the treaty ports only and it could not be expected to
include the Russian population in the Barga region, in
Mongolia, and in Sinkiang. If 140,000 may be accepted
as the Russian population in China in 1930, is it possible
to arrive at a comparable figure for 1904 and for 1914?

The information is most inadequate, but some facts may be found.

The figures of the Shanghai Municipal Council show the Russian population of the International Settlement at Shanghai to have been as follows for the years nearest to those for which figures are desired:

1905	354
1915	361
1930	3,487 [92]

It is known also that the Russian population of Tientsin was 140 in 1915 and about 3,000 in 1930. We know, as has been pointed out above, that the Russian population of Harbin was about 30,000 in 1902. A report for 1903 put the Russian civilian population of Port Arthur at 4,024 for the year 1903.[93]

It may be regarded as reasonable, on the basis of the available information, to suppose that the Russians in China numbered about 40,000 in 1904, about 65,000 in 1914, and about 140,000 in 1930. It is undoubtedly true, also, that the greatest increase in numbers took place during the years immediately following the Russian revolution. The available figures from Tientsin and Shanghai make it fairly certain that the number of Russians in China, outside of Manchuria and Mongolia, has greatly increased since 1918. It may well be ten times as great. In other words the Russians who came to China after the revolution came first to Manchuria. They have spread to other ports of China in recent years.

In general, it may be said that the increase in the Russian population of China reflects the eastward spread of the Russian people, the policy of the former Russian government, and the consequences of the Russian revolution. No less than 91 per cent of the Russian population is in Manchuria and Mongolia, and almost 98 per cent of the Russian investment is in the same regions.

[92] *Feetham Report*, vol. 1, p. 51.
[93] Bank of Chosen, *Economic History of Manchuria*, p. 47. There were at the same time 13,583 Russian soldiers and sailors at Port Arthur.

Conclusion

The total Russian investment in China at the dates which have been selected is shown in the following table.

TABLE 9

Russian Investments in China, 1904–1930

(In millions of U. S. dollars with relatives)

1904	246.0	91.3
1914	269.3	100.0
1930	273.2	101.4

The outstanding fact is the slow growth of Russian investments. The rate of growth was more rapid before 1914 than since, but there has been no great increase in Russian investments in China since the building of the Chinese Eastern Railway. If it were possible to present figures showing Russian investments at the close of the Sino-Japanese War the total would be a negligible sum. The great increase in Russian investments was associated with the Chinese Eastern Railway and the Manchurian policy of the Russian government of which the railway was the evidence. Russian investments in China are in this respect similar to Japanese investments. In each case an interest in Manchuria brought a remarkable increase, which preceded the Russo-Japanese War in the Russian case and followed it in the Japanese.

Russian investments by chief divisions are shown in the table which follows. This table shows the complete

TABLE 10

Russian Investments, 1904–1930, by Main Divisions

(In millions of U. S. dollars with relatives)

	Business Investments		Government Obligations	
1904	220.1	93.1	26.0	79.3
1914	236.5	100.0	32.8	100.0
1930	273.2	115.5	—	—

elimination of the obligations of the Chinese government. Loans to the Chinese government had grown more rapidly than had business investments during the years from 1904 to 1914 but they were not great at any time. This fact is brought out by the percentage distribution of the investments by the main divisions.

TABLE 11

PERCENTAGE DISTRIBUTION OF RUSSIAN INVESTMENTS BY MAIN
DIVISIONS

	Business Investments	Government Obligations	Total
1904	89.4	10.6	100.0
1914	87.8	12.2	100.0
1930	100.0	—	100.0

The Russian population in China and the Russian investments in the country have been concentrated in Manchuria since the construction of the Chinese Eastern Railway. The percentage of Russian investments in Manchuria was 87.8 per cent in 1904, 84.6 per cent in 1914, and 95.8 per cent in 1930. These percentages do not reveal the significant change, however. This is shown by taking investments in Manchuria and Mongolia as a percentage of the total business investments of the Russians in China. The figures are as follows:

1904   98.8%
1914   98.0%
1930   97.7%

There has been a slight tendency toward a spread of Russian business into China proper.

The percentage of Russian investments which are at Shanghai is probably smaller than in the case of any other foreign group. The Russians have, in recent years, come to Shanghai in great numbers. There were about ten times as many in 1930 as in 1914. But they have come without capital and in most cases with little business experience. They have made a place for themselves in the business life of Shanghai under the greatest difficulties. The business holdings of the new arrivals together with the investments of those who were in Shanghai in 1918 probably do not come to more than U. S. $3 or 4 million. It is fairly certain that not more than 1.5 per cent of the total Russian investment in China is at Shanghai.

The distribution of Russian investments in China by the nature of the business is shown in the next table. It is obvious that none of the investments were for the general purposes of the Chinese government.

TABLE 12

RUSSIAN INVESTMENTS, 1930, DISTRIBUTED BY THE NATURE OF THE BUSINESS

	Millions of U. S. Dollars	Per Cent of Total
1. Transportation	210.5	77.0
2. Public utilities *	—	—
3. Mining	2.1	0.8
4. Manufacturing	12.8	4.7
5. Banking and finance *	—	—
6. Real estate and land	32.5	11.9
7. Import and export and general trading	12.2	4.5
8. Miscellaneous	3.1	1.1
	273.2	100.0

* Insufficient information to make an estimate possible.

The attitude of the Soviet government toward Chinese securities held within Russia has made direct business investments, important at all times, the only form of Russian investment in 1930. If at the same time the Soviet government had renounced its ownership of the Chinese Eastern, as it seems at one time to have intended,[94] the result would have been the wiping out of a

[94] This intention was expressed to the people of China by Ambassador L. M. Karakhan on July 25, 1919, "The Soviet government returns to the Chinese people without demanding any kind of compensation the Chinese

large part of Russian investments, of the whole of the investments which the Soviet government could control. Since this has not been done the Soviet government was in 1931 the largest Russian owner of business investments in China, holding 77.5 per cent of the total, with the rest in the hands of Russian business men in China.

The Soviet authorities who were consulted in Moscow in June, 1931, held it incorrect to set down anything as Russian investment in China.   The government loans were, they said, wiped out so far as Russia was concerned. The holdings of Russian business men in China were not to be counted as Russian investments since the holders were, in fact, the political enemies of the Soviet government.   The Chinese Eastern Railway, they said, was not to be regarded as a Russian investment in any sense in which that term is used in capitalistic countries. The railway, they maintained, is a *condominium* under the joint control of China and Russia.

The contention of the Soviet authorities has been accepted so far as concerns the obligations of the Chinese government. It cannot be accepted so far as concerns the Chinese Eastern Railway, for no document or other evidence is available to show that the ownership of the Chinese Eastern Railway has been given up in any part by the Soviet government, or had been given up at the end of 1931. The agreements of 1924 and the supplementary arrangements deal with management and with profits, they do not deal with ownership.

The contention that the investments of the Russians living in China are not Russian investments requires examination. Consider, for example, the property of a Russian business man who was in China when the Rus-

Eastern Railway, as well as all mining concessions, forestry, gold mines, and all other things which were seized from them by the government of the Tsars, Kerensky, and the brigands Horvath, etc." *China Year Book,* 1924, p. 869. However, the "rights and interests of the Soviet government in the Chinese Eastern Railway appeared in a somewhat altered light four or five years later." Young, C. W., *International Relations of Manchuria,* p. 222.

sian revolution began and has remained in China since, or the property of a Russian who came to China to escape from the revolution and its consequences. In the latter case he may have brought with him gold, furs, and jewels of sufficient value to enable him to set up in business or he may have come with nothing and have built up a small holding since his arrival. Is the property of such Russians to be regarded as a foreign investment in China?

The Soviet authorities take the point of view that it is not, basing their conclusion on political grounds. The Chinese point of view is that the property is a foreign investment and they take this position even when, as in some cases, the Russian owners have become Chinese citizens. It may be said of such Russians that they are without a country. It is probable that they would by this time have been accepted in their new home if it were not for the difference in race between themselves and the Chinese, but it is true also that they have brought their political differences with them and this helps to explain the Chinese attitude toward them.

The case of the "white" Russians is interesting because certain characteristics that mark most foreign groups in China are absent. One is frequently told in China that it is extraterritoriality which prevents the Chinese from accepting as desirable the economic development of their country by the foreigner or by foreign groups. The Russians, however, have been without extraterritorial rights since 1922. One is told, also, that it is the danger of political domination on the part of the home government of the foreign group. The Russians, however, have been at variance with their home government and are disowned by that government. I have no desire to minimize the dangers, from the Chinese point of view, that lie in extraterritoriality or the obvious fact that foreign economic development may lead to foreign political domination. It is important, however, to observe that the absence of extraterritoriality has not led to the acceptance of economic development by the "white" Russians as desirable. The conclusion seems unavoidable that legal and political arrangements are not the fundamental difficulty.

The property of the Russians who seem permanently domiciled in China has been included with Russian investments for a variety of reasons. In the first place it is practically impossible to distinguish between the property of, say, the Dalbank, a Soviet institution, and other Russian business property. A second reason lies in the fact that some part of the property of every foreign group in China is held by persons who are permanent residents of China. There was no good ground for making a distinction in the Russian case.

The total which is presented is the total of property which is normally expected to yield an income and which is in the legal possession of Russians. It is not to be supposed that the Russian ownership of this property necessarily involves annual payments of dividends or profits out of China. The question of the international payments involved is a different one. It has been shown that Russian investments in China have brought discoverable outpayments from China to the amount of no more than about U. S. $12.5 million since 1914. The estimating of foreign holdings is a first step toward discovering the annual international payments but it is no more than a first step. And there are additional reasons for estimating the total of foreign holdings. It is a significant fact that a very large part of the industrial development of northern Manchuria is in Russian hands.

The Chinese Eastern Railway, it may be repeated, has at all times since 1900 constituted the chief Russian investment in China. This railway is frequently referred to by Russian writers as a bridge connecting two parts of Siberia. The Soviet students of Chinese affairs, who were consulted in Moscow, used this metaphor and asserted

that Soviet Russia had no political ambitions in connection
with the railway.   The Soviet government, they said,
merely desired to keep the bridge open and usable.   The
statement was added that the Soviet government could
hardly fail to act if there were an effort on the part of any
other power to close the bridge to traffic or to destroy its
usefulness.   The conclusion seems unescapable that the
underlying economic and geographical conditions determine the objectives of Russian economic policy in China
whatever may be the form that Russian interest takes
or the manner in which it is expressed.

Under the Monarchy government borrowing in France
enabled the Russians to secure the capital required for
the forwarding of their economic policy in China.   In this
way Russia, a capital importing nation, was enabled to
play a rôle of importance in China from 1895 to 1914.
If we may take it for granted that foreign capital is still a
requirement, we may then ask concerning Soviet Russia
whether she will find the means of playing an important
rôle in the near future.

TABLE 13

THE POSITION OF RUSSIA IN CHINA'S INTERNATIONAL ECONOMIC RELATIONS

Customs Statistics Used for Trade Only

TRADE	Direct Trade Millions of Hk. Tls.	Relatives	Per Cent of China's Total Trade
1899	10.1	15.0	2.2
1903	15.1	22.5	2.8
1913	67.0	100.0	3.3
1930	74.4	111.0	3.4
POPULATION	Russian Population in China	Relatives	Per Cent of Total Foreign Population in China
1904	40,000	61.5	42.5
1914	65,000	100.0	37.8
1930	140,000	215.4	32.1
INVESTMENT	Russian Investment Millions of U. S. Dollars	Relatives	Per Cent of Total Foreign Investment
1904	246.0	91.3	31.3
1914	269.3	100.0	16.7
1930	273.2	101.4	8.4

CHAPTER XIX

FRENCH INVESTMENTS IN CHINA *

INVESTMENTS IN 1902

Information concerning French investments in China at the beginning of the century is difficult to find and is usually too general for our purposes. R. G. Levy, for example, estimated French interests at half a billion francs in 1897.[1] Detailed information is available only in the results of an inquiry instituted in 1902 by the French Minister of Foreign Affairs under the caption, French Wealth Abroad. By means of a questionnaire the Minister secured from the consular and diplomatic agents of the Republic around the world a considerable amount of economic data.[2] According to the French report a total of francs 650 million was invested in China in 1902. The total included the following items: "Commerce," francs 60 million; "Propriétés françaises," 47 million; "Mines," 5 million; "Emprunts," 539 million. The 60 million francs of "commercial" capital is divided among sixty firms in

---

* For the earlier years the preliminary work was done by Professor Howard S. Ellis of the Department of Economics of the University of Michigan, who wrote a report on *French and German Investments in China* (Honolulu, 1929) in connection with the general study of foreign investments in China.

[1] Levy, R. G., "Fortune Mobilière de la France à l'Etranger," *Revue des Deux Mondes*, March 15, 1897, p. 439.

[2] The Report was published in the *Journal Officiel de la République Française*, 34th year, no. 261, p. 6386, September, 1902. A summary was published in the *Journal of the Royal Statistical Society*, December, 1903, p. 730. The reliability of the report has been questioned. See Feis, H., *Europe: The World's Banker, 1870–1914*, New Haven, 1930, p. 50 footnote. It may be said, however, that the Chinese estimate is probably more to be trusted than the rest of the report, for under extraterritoriality French consular officials in China must have had fairly reliable information.

Shanghai, Tientsin, and Hankow.[3] Of the "Propriétés françaises," francs 37 million were reported as belonging to mission organizations, the remainder being partly accounted for by a single steamship company (francs 125,000) and by cotton and tobacco companies in Shanghai and Hankow (francs 500,000). If we wish to arrive at an estimate of direct investments from the French report, we must include not only the 60 million of "Commercial" capital and the 5 million in mines, but also 10 millions of other real property remaining after the deduction of 37 millions in missions, and, what is of greatest importance, the entire capital of the Yunnan Railway. The inclusion of this latter amount in the French report under "emprunts" is misleading as the company is both owned and operated by the French. With the 78 millions of Yunnan Railway capital added in, French business investments reached the sum of 153 million francs. By the same operation we reduce the figure for French loans to China from 539 million francs to 461, but this figure is too high. We may deduct a mysterious item of "Divers 50 million" which can be accounted for by none of the recorded French issues. In this way we arrive at a total of 153 million francs for business investments and 411 million francs for government obligations.

The figures at which I arrive by the method used for calculating the loans of other countries provides a total of U. S. $61,519,726 (about francs 318 million). In the second loan listed in the table there is uncertainty as to the percentage issued in France [4] and in neither case is the actual holding in France known. A total of 318 million francs is, I believe, much nearer to the truth than even the corrected estimate, 411, of the French report.

[3] The Chinese Maritime Customs reports put the number of French firms in China at seventy-one for 1902 and the number of French nationals at one thousand two hundred thirteen.

[4] Kent, P. H., *Railway Enterprise in China*, p. 102, states it to be 80 per cent. In an article by Emile Galland, an abstract of which was published in the *Board of Trade Journal* for December 19, 1901, vol. 35, pp. 545–6, it is stated to have been 60 per cent.

TABLE 1

FRENCH LOANS TO CHINA AS OF DECEMBER 31, 1901

	Total Outstanding U. S. Dollars	French Share	
		Per Cent	U. S. Dollars
4% Gold Loan of 1895	70,400,521	62.5	44,000,326
Peking-Hankow of 1898	21,899,250	80.0	17,519,400
			61,519,726

Accepting the total of the French report for business investments and the above total for loans, we arrive at a total of U. S. $91.1 million or francs 471 million. It is to be noted that the property of mission societies, all of them Roman Catholic societies, came to francs 37 million or about U. S. $5.4 million. It is fairly certain, if we may judge from our knowledge of the situation at the present time, that a considerable part of these mission holdings were for the purpose of securing an income and ought, therefore, to be included under direct investments, but in the absence of adequate information this has not been so included.

TABLE 2

FRENCH INVESTMENTS IN CHINA, 1902

	U. S. Dollars
Business investments	29,600,000
Government obligations	61,520,000
	91,120,000

INVESTMENTS IN 1914

French holdings of the obligations of the Chinese government reached a total of about U. S. $111 million by the end of the year 1913. This is to be compared with the total of somewhat more than 60 million dollars for 1902. If, however, the French share of the Boxer indemnity were added, the total would come to about U. S. $160 million.

Between 1902–1913 the French participated in but one

general loan to the Chinese government which was out-standing at the end of the period, that is the Reorganiza-tion loan of 1913.[5]

French participation in railway development was in co-operation with Russian and with Belgian interests.   In the case of the Chinese Eastern Railway funds were so provided as to give the French no actual holding in China and no legal claim against property in China.   The claim which the French had was against certain Russian cor-porations and the Russian government, but the invest-ments in China were entirely Russian.   The French par-ticipated on different terms, however, in the financing which followed the agreement for the Shansi Railway, a line connecting Taiyuanfu, the capital of Shansi province, with the Peking-Hankow Railway.[6]   The obligations in-volved in this contract were taken over by the French company concerned in it and the loan has always been regarded as entirely French.

French and Belgian interests co-operated in two loans for the construction of a railway which is now known as the Lunghai.   This name is given to the whole projected railway which is to run from Lanchow, the capital of Kansu province, to the sea at Haichow in the northern part of Kiangsu.   The first agreement covered a line from Kaifeng to Honanfu, which is known as the Pienlo, and was for 41 million francs.   The second was for the exten-sion of the Pienlo in both directions and involved the issue of bonds to the amount of £4 million.   Both con-tracts were with a Belgian company, one-half of whose shares were issued in France.   The loan bonds for the Pienlo were issued in France and Belgium, and those for the Lunghai were issued in Belgium alone, but the second loan is to be found in lists of French obligations drawn

[5] Certain smaller loans in which the French had participated were repaid from the proceeds of the Reorganization loan. These loans are listed in MacMurray, J. V. A., *Treaties and Agreements*, vol. II, pp. 1017–8.

[6] MacMurray, J. V. A., *Treaties and Agreements*, vol. I, p. 356, and Baylin, J. R., *Foreign Loan Obligations of China*, p. 31.

up by French officials and must be regarded as, in part, French. French and Belgian interests are so closely united in these loans that one can do no better than make an equal division between them. The same statement may be made concerning an obligation which appears in my list as an advance for the Tatung-Chengtu Railway, part of an ambitious plan to connect French Indo-China with Peking by rail.

The loans dealt with above are listed in the following table.

TABLE 3

FRENCH SHARE OF THE OBLIGATIONS OF THE CHINESE GOVERNMENT, 1914 *

	Outstanding Dec. 31, 1931 U. S. Dollars	French Share	
		Per Cent	U. S. Dollars
General purposes of the Chinese government			
1. 4% Gold Loan of 1895	51,527,728	62.5	32,204,830
2. 5% Reorganization Gold Loan of 1913	121,662,500	29.7	36,093,176
Subtotal			68,298,006
Railway obligations			
3. Imperial 5% Gold Loan of 1902 (Shansi Railway)	7,486,952	100	7,486,952
4. 5% Gold Loan of 1908 (Anglo-French)	24,332,500	50	12,166,250
5. 5% Hukuang Ry. Sinking Fund Gold Loan of 1911	29,199,000	25	7,299,750
6. Imperial 5% Gold Loan of 1903 and 1907 (Pienlo)	7,913,000	50	3,956,500
7. 5% Gold Loan of 1913 (Lung-hai)	19,466,000	50	9,733,000
8. Tatung-Chengtu Ry. advance of 1913	4,867,375	50	2,433,687
Subtotal			43,076,139
Grand Total			111,374,145

* The French share of the Boxer indemnity—U. S. $51,000,000.

French business investments in China in 1914 include in the first place the value of the Yunnan Railway. Fortunately we have available the results of an agreement of April 13, 1908 between the French and Chinese as to the cost of the line.[7] The total cost was put at francs 165,466,888 and the funds were reported to be from the following sources:

	Francs
Share capital	14,930,441
Debentures	86,494,962
Subventions of the colonial government	64,041,485

We may then consider French investment in the Yunnan Railway in 1914 to have been approximately U. S. $32 million.[8]

French business investments in addition to those in the railway can only be conjectured. Such investments were U. S. $15 million in 1902, a sum about equal to that which was then reported for the railway. If this proportion persisted, the business investments now being considered would come to about U. S. $30 million in 1914. We know that the number of French firms reported by the Chinese Maritime Customs increased from 71 in 1902 to 113 in 1914. If the size of these firms underwent no diminution, their business investment may be supposed to have increased from U. S. $15 million in 1902 to about U. S. $25 million in 1914. We may, then, estimate the total French business investment in 1914 to have been about U. S. $60 million; 32 million in the railway and 28 million in commercial and business undertakings.

Further support for a total of this size may be found if we assume, as we may from our knowledge of business investments, that the proportion between direct investments and government obligations did not greatly change between 1902–1914. Direct investments were about half

[7] Made in connection with the provisions of Article 34 of the railway loan contract.   MacMurray, J. V. A., *Treaties and Agreements*, vol. I, p. 461.

[8] The above sums are from a report drawn up at my request by an official of the railway.

the value of loans in 1902, and one-half of the figure for government loans in 1914 comes to U. S. $55 million.

It is impossible to say what sum ought to be added to cover income-yielding property in the hands of French mission societies. If this sum were known it would increase French holdings somewhat but, taking everything into account, they could hardly have been greater than U. S. $185 million.[9] A summary for 1914 is given in the following table.

TABLE 4

FRENCH INVESTMENTS IN CHINA, 1914

	U. S. Dollars
Business investments	60,000,000
Government obligations	111,374,000
Total	171,374,000

INVESTMENTS IN 1931

To estimate the obligations of the Chinese government to the French, as they were in 1930–1931, is to make one's way over a difficult bit of ground. The final figure involves more doubts and uncertainties than in the case of any other country. I shall proceed as in the other cases to consider, first, obligations for the general purposes of the Chinese government, secondly, railway obligations, and, finally, the French share of the "unsecured" loans. There are, however, two matters upon which general comments may be made.

The first of these is the whole set of obligations connected with the Banque Industrielle de Chine. If one turns to the figures of China's unsecured loans drawn up by the Financial Readjustment Commission for 1925, one finds that the Commission arrived at a total for France of Chinese $1,230,000. The French creditors' figure came

---

[9] Moulton and Lewis hazard the opinion that "the total French investment in China was probably more than one billion francs in 1914," *The French Debt Problem*, p. 339. My estimate comes to somewhat less than one billion francs.

to Chinese $73,549,000.[10] The difference is due to the inclusion by the creditors of obligations to the Banque Industrielle. The 1927 document of the Ministry of Finance lists no less than twenty items as "unsecured" obligations to the Banque Industrielle which totaled nearly francs 200 million. This sum does not appear in the final figures of this document. On the other hand an official report to the French Foreign Office in July, 1927, to which reference will be made again, listed, as valid, obligations of the Chinese government to the Banque Industrielle to the amount of gold francs 260 million. I have omitted entirely any obligations in connection with the Banque Industrielle, unless the obligation under the French Boxer settlement of 1925 may be so regarded. The elimination of the Banque Industrielle requires a word of explanation.

In 1913 this French bank began a career in Chinese finance which was active, colorful, and short. It closed its doors in June, 1921, after futile efforts had been made to prolong its life. The settlement of its affairs forms a long and complicated story which I will do my best to summarize. When the bank failed, its Far Eastern branches had numerous obligations, including, of course, many to Chinese. At the same time the bank was the creditor of the Chinese government on account of unpaid subscriptions to its shares and on account of numerous advances made from time to time. A plan was worked out by which the payments from China on the French share of the Boxer indemnity, when they were finally resumed after the gold-franc controversy,[11] became the basis for an issue of U. S. dollar bonds to the amount of

[10] Lieu, D. K., *Foreign Investments in China, 1929*, p. 37.

[11] The Chinese contention was that the Boxer indemnity payments were to be made in "paper" francs when payment was resumed in December, 1922, after the five-year postponement. The French contended that payment was to be made in "gold" francs, i.e. at the pre-war mint par. The French contention prevailed. There is reason to believe that the controversy would never have become acute but for the political connections and failure of the Banque Industrielle. The whole matter is fairly presented in Wright, S. F., *The Collection and Disposal of the . . . Customs Revenue*, pp. 118–24.

U. S. $43,893,900. These bonds were to be used to pay the Far Eastern creditors of the Banque Industrielle de Chine and the creditors were to turn over to the Chinese government the acknowledgment they held of the bank's obligation to them, the so-called *bons de repartition*. These *bons de repartition* were finally to be settled by funds realized from the assets of the Banque Industrielle and these funds were then to be turned over to a Sino-French commission for education and philanthropic purposes.

I am informed by the Banque Franco-Chinoise pour le Commerce et l'Industrie, successor to the Banque Industrielle, that the bonds (for U. S. $50 each) had been disposed of as follows at the end of March, 1931:

	Number of Bonds
To Far Eastern creditors of the Banque Industrielle	705,600
To the Sino-French Commission for Education and Philanthropic Purposes	63,250
In settlement of the Chinese government's obligation for shares in the Banque Industrielle	37,378
In settlement of other obligations of the Chinese government to the Banque Industrielle	71,563
In suspense	87
	877,878

There is no reason to doubt that these arrangements carry with them a settlement of all obligations connected with the Banque Industrielle. The French government provided for the ultimate remission of the Boxer indemnity. In the meantime the obligation of the Chinese government persists and takes the form of responsibility for the service of the loan bonds of this indemnity loan which is usually referred to as the 5% Gold Loan of 1925. I have included this loan in my list and have omitted the Chinese government's obligations to the Banque Industrielle. It may be added that many of the bonds of this loan are held within China.

The second matter for general comment concerns certain obligations in French francs. When this currency is specifically mentioned in loan agreements and bonds, I have taken it for granted that capital sums may be calculated in current francs. This was done by the Ministry of Railways of the Chinese government in drawing up the 1929 table on which my totals, in part, depend. Such obligations as those for the Shansi and Pienlo railways are thus reduced to about one-fifth of their former U. S. dollar values. In both the French and Belgian cases I am informed that payments in current francs have been accepted under protest. In view of all the facts I have accepted the Chinese figures.

Obligations of the Chinese Government

The first list of obligations is that for the general purposes of the Chinese government and is as follows:

	Amount Outstanding Dec. 31, 1930 (in U. S. Dollars)	French Share	
		Per Cent	U. S. Dollars
4% Gold Loan of 1895	3,883,092	62.5	2,426,932
5% Reorganization Gold Loan of 1913	111,915,776	29.7	33,238,985
5% Gold Loan of 1925 (Boxer indemnity)	40,602,450	100.0	40,602,450
			76,268,367

For the French share of China's railway obligations I turn to the table prepared by the Ministry of Railways of the Chinese government showing foreign obligations of government railways, as of December 31, 1929, classified according to nationalities. This table shows secured obligations in the French case of £2,652,660, francs 18,089,-930, and Chinese $174,987, and unsecured obligations of Chinese $440,795. These come to secured obligations of U. S. $13,688,574 and unsecured of U. S. $176,318, making total railway obligations of U. S. $13,864,892 at the beginning of 1930.[12]

[12] I have been obliged, in view of the difficulties in the way of securing complete information, to accept this. It is to be noted, however, that the

The French share of the "unsecured" loans of the Chinese government, omitting obligations to the Banque Industrielle, is shown in the 1927 document of the Ministry of Finance to be Chinese $848,880. Taking these at the rate of exchange at which they were calculated, namely Chinese $2=U. S. $1, the total is U. S. $424,440.

The obligations shown above are brought together in the following table.

TABLE 5

FRENCH HOLDINGS OF CHINESE GOVERNMENT OBLIGATIONS, 1931

	U. S. Dollars
General purposes of the Chinese government	76,268,367
Railway obligations	13,864,892
Unsecured loans	424,440
	90,557,699

The above total shows French holding of Chinese government obligations on the principle of the place of issue. Certain corrections may be made which bring us nearer to the correct total of actual holdings in France but it is to be borne in mind that the present distribution of issues in which the French and Belgians co-operated cannot be estimated by the bankers concerned. No correction is attempted in this case and the equal division is allowed to stand. The British bankers reported the ownership in England of bonds issued in France to the value of U. S. $19,952,650. This sum is to be deducted from the total shown above. There are on the contrary certain sums to be added.

French share of two loans in which the Belgians did not participate, the Anglo-French of 1908 and the Hukuang of 1911, comes to U. S. $13,468,965 on December 31, 1930. The sum outstanding on the advance for the Tatung-Chengtu Railway in which French and Belgian interests participated was on the same date U. S. $5,546,554. Half of this may be regarded as French. The total sum outstanding on the Pienlo and Lunghai Railways was reported to me by the Shanghai office of the Belgian company concerned as U. S. $52,819,040 on the same date. A part of this is certainly held in France. If a successful attempt could be made to calculate the total French interest in Chinese railways on the principle of actual holding, it would come to at least U. S. $10 million more than the U. S. $13.9 million shown by the Chinese Ministry of Railways.

In the first place there is the whole of the Russian share of the 4% Gold Loan of 1895. The history of this loan leads me to accept without question the statement made in Paris that the French hold the entire loan. This involves an addition of U. S. $1,456,160.

In the second place we have to consider the present location of the Russian issue of the Reorganization loan. The total Russian issue was U. S. $13,518,066. Of this the British report holdings of U. S. $3,163,225. It is well known that the Russian issue was, in part, sold in Paris and that the so-called "green" bonds issued in place of the original Russian issue are very largely held in Paris. It is reasonable to assign to France the whole of the Russian issue not held in England.[13] The Russian issue of the Reorganization loan involves an addition of U. S. $10,-354,841.

The present location of bonds originally issued in Germany is a matter upon which it is difficult to secure adequate information. French bankers have informed me that the French have made considerable purchases of these bonds. I estimate French holdings of bonds originally issued in Germany to be at most U. S. $15 million, which is also to be added. The result of these additions and subtractions comes to a net addition of U. S. $6,858,351. I therefore estimate the actual holdings by the French of the securities and obligations of the Chinese government to have been in 1931 U. S. $97,416,050.

Business Investments

Yunnan Railway: The first step in estimating French business investments at the end of 1930 is to accept the sum of U. S. $32 million as representing the investment in the Yunnan Railway. This is a direct business investment on the part of a French corporation with a sub-

---

[13] I disregard the bonds of the original Russian issue to the value of U. S. $2,500,000 reported to have been sold to Americans.

vention from the colonial government of Indo-China, and the property involved is the legal possession of the French corporation. Whatever may be the relation between the French corporation and its creditors as the result of the devaluation of the French franc, this devaluation cannot be held to have changed the value of property in China. I have, therefore, accepted the figure of francs 165 million, taking the franc at its pre-war value.[14]

Holdings in Shanghai: The value of French holdings in Shanghai has been carefully estimated by a well-informed French business man in that city. I have the assurance of two French officials in China that this business man's report is to be preferred to the official report contained in the French document of July, 1927, to which I have already referred. The estimate of this French business man enables me to arrive first at a total of French land holding in Shanghai. He found land owned by French business concerns and individuals in the whole of Shanghai to have a value of Sh. Tls. 42,865,000. French mortgages on non-French property he found to be Sh. Tls. 9 million, and French interest in non-French local companies, Sh. Tls. 6.5 million. This makes a total of Sh. Tls. 58,365,000. From this must be deducted Sh. Tls. 1 million, representing non-French interest in French concerns. This gives us a final total of French interests in land in Shanghai of Sh. Tls. 57,365,000.

In addition to land holdings French business interests at Shanghai were estimated at Sh. Tls. 40 million, which brings the Shanghai total for business investments to Sh. Tls. 97,365,000. This estimate was made early in 1931. At Sh. Tls. 2.5 to the U. S. dollar, the rate which I have accepted for the end of 1930, French business investments in Shanghai come to U. S. $38.9 million.

Holdings Outside Shanghai: Business investments are

[14] I disregard an increase in the capital of the Compagnie des Chemins de Fer de l'Indochine et du Yunnan of francs 1,750,000 on May 31, 1929, mentioned in the report sent to me by an official of the company.

estimated, on the basis of personal interviews and the French 1927 document, as follows:

	U. S. Dollars
Tientsin	1,200,000
Hankow	600,000
Other places	600,000
	2,400,000

This makes a total of French business investments for the whole of China, aside from the investment in the Yunnan Railway, of U. S. $41,300,000.

Mission Property: We have next to consider land held by French missions in China. This is reported by the French business man already quoted at Sh. Tls. 58 million for Shanghai alone. This sum is further divided into Sh. Tls. 8,532,000 directly used for mission purposes and Sh. Tls. 49,468,000 as land holdings, the income from which is used for the support of mission activities in China, including, of course, work of an educational and scientific character. The French Catholics maintain, for example, a university at Shanghai and a well-known observatory at Siccawei, just outside of Shanghai. The land held by mission societies for income presents difficulties of classification. I believe it best to regard such income-yielding property as direct business investments. This means the addition of the following sums to cover the holdings of French Catholic missions in China:

Shanghai	U. S. $19,787,200
Tientsin	1,200,000
Hankow	500,000
Canton	200,000
	U. S. $21,707,200

It may be added that one item of some importance has been omitted from this calculation. This is the French share of the holdings of an important Belgian firm, the Credit Foncier d'Extreme-Orient. Real estate owned by French missions was turned over to this Belgian company as the result of the fear on the part of certain religious orders that their property might be confiscated by the French government. The property has continued to be so held. No estimate of this property is available but it would probably add less than 20 per cent to the figure for French income-yielding mission property in Shanghai.

A summary of French business investments is shown in the following table:

TABLE 6

FRENCH BUSINESS INVESTMENTS IN CHINA, 1931

	U. S. Dollars
Yunnan Railway	32,000,000
Business investments, Shanghai	38,900,000
Business investments outside of Shanghai	2,400,000
Income-yielding mission property, Shanghai	19,787,200
Income-yielding mission property outside of Shanghai	1,920,000
Total	95,007,200

TABLE 7

FRENCH INVESTMENTS IN CHINA, 1931

	U. S. Dollars
Business investments	95,007,200
Government obligations	97,416,050
Total	192,423,250

CONCLUSION

This review of French investments in China, brief as it is, enables certain general statements to be made. French investments increased fairly rapidly during the years before 1914 and the two forms of investment grew together. After 1914 there was a marked difference, French holdings of Chinese government obligations fell off while business investments continued to grow. The French have long been known to prefer government obligations to investments in commercial and industrial undertakings and it is, therefore, significant that even in the French case business investments have increased more rapidly than loans since 1900.

TABLE 8

FRENCH INVESTMENTS IN CHINA, 1900–1931

By Chief Divisions with Relatives

(Values shown in millions of U. S. dollars)

	Business Investments	Rela- tives	Government Obligations	Rela- tives	Total	Rela- tives
1902	29.6	49.3	61.5	55.2	99.1	53.2
1914	60.0	100.0	111.4	100.0	171.4	100.0
1930	95.0	158.3	97.4	87.4	192.4	112.2

In spite of a relatively rapid increase business investments were, in 1930, no more than half of the French
total. In 1902 and 1914 they had been slightly under
and slightly over a third. The distribution between these
two divisions is shown in the following table. A study of
the two general tables shows the course of events.

TABLE 9

FRENCH INVESTMENTS IN CHINA, 1900–1931

Percentage Distribution by Chief Divisions

(Values shown in millions of U. S. dollars)

	Business Investments		Government Obligations		Total	
	Dollars	Per Cent	Dollars	Per Cent	Dollars	Per Cent
1902	29.6	32.5	61.5	67.5	91.1	100
1914	60.0	35.0	111.4	65.0	171.4	100
1930	95.0	49.4	97.4	50.6	192.4	100

There are other general statements which may be made.
French investment in China was in close co-operation
with Russia and Belgium in the days before the war and
reflected the political situation in Europe. Since the war
Chinese obligations to France have fallen off and this
may well reflect the declining importance of China in the
international economic situation as it has been viewed
from Europe in recent years.

A large fraction of the business investments of the French take the form of a single railway which is an extension into China of a railway across the French colony which forms China's southern boundary. This railway, while it is legally the property of a French corporation, has received subventions from the government of Indo-China and is, in some degree, under French governmental control. Its position may be compared to that of the South Manchuria or the Chinese Eastern.

An unusual feature, in the case of the French, is that a second large fraction of the business investments consists of the property held for income by the Roman Catholic missions under the protection of the French government. These investments are not to be considered as devoted to mission purposes, although it is clear that the income from them is so used. Total Catholic holdings are considerably larger than the sum of U. S. $20 million shown above and they play an important part in the financing of the missions of the Catholic orders. This is important in estimating remittances to China for missions in general.

It is highly probable that the considerable direct investments of the French in commercial and industrial undertakings has been increased in China by its proximity to French Indo-China where French undertakings have been encouraged. Finally, it may be said that the French, in common with other nationals, hold a considerable part of their investments in land at Shanghai. The rise in land values in that city, which was unusually rapid in 1929 and 1930, indicate that the remittances to China in connection with French business investments, which have been estimated at U. S. $95 million, have been relatively small.

To estimate remittances from China we must, of course, eliminate mission land holdings which involve no outpayment. The investment in the Yunnan Railway has brought outpayments which are difficult to calculate but

which must have been small.[15]   The remaining U. S.
$40 million brought its owners a larger return but this
income was, in part, retained within the French "colony"
in China or paid to Chinese.   Whatever may be the value
of these conjectures concerning remittances, the fact
remains that international political considerations and
French mission holdings have played an important part
in French economic relations with China.

TABLE 10

THE POSITION OF FRANCE IN CHINA'S INTERNATIONAL ECONOMIC
RELATIONS

Customs Statistics except for Investments

TRADE	Direct Trade Mills. Hk. Tls.	Relatives	Per Cent of China's Total Trade
1905	22.7	49.3	3.4
1913	46.0	100.0	4.7
1930	59.7	129.7	2.7
POPULA-TION	French Population in China	Relatives	Per Cent of Total Foreign Population in China
1899	1,183	51.6	6.8
1913	2,292	100.0	1.4
1930	8,575	374.1	2.4
FIRMS	French Firms	Relatives	Per Cent of Total Foreign Firms in China
1899	76	71.6	8.1
1913	106	100.0	2.7
1930	186	175.4	2.2
SHIPPING	French Tonnage in Millions	Relatives	Per Cent of Total Chinese and Foreign Shipping
1899	0.6	50.0	1.8
1913	1.2	100.0	1.3
1930	1.8	150.0	1.2
INVEST-MENTS	French Investment Millions U. S. Dollars	Relatives	Per Cent of Total Foreign Investment
1902	91.1	53.2	11.6
1914	171.4	100.0	10.7
1930	192.4	112.2	5.9

[15] They were little more than 3 or 4 per cent from 1924 to 1928. *Annuaire
Financier France Extreme Orient, 1928–1929*, Martin & Cie, Paris, pp. 143,
147.

CHAPTER XX

GERMAN INVESTMENTS IN CHINA

INVESTMENTS IN 1905

Our earliest official data on German investments in China come from a government survey in which the Germans followed the example set by the French Ministry of Foreign Affairs in 1902.[1] Prior to this report a certain amount of information is to be gleaned from the letters of two American consular agents.[2] Only scattered bits of intelligence are to be found in Hughes' report, but Harris, who apparently had access to some sort of official estimates, put the total German investment in China and Japan in 1900 at U. S. $90 million. He mentions German cotton and silk mills in Shanghai to the value of U. S. $1 million, warehouses in Hongkong, Swatow, Amoy, Foochow, Tientsin, and Shanghai worth U. S. $30 million, the Shantung Railway, and the Deutsch-Asiatische Bank with a capital of U. S. $3 million.

The survey of the German admiralty, which was made public in 1905, makes no mention of German loans to China, nor does it undertake to give a separate place to mission property. Direct business investments, however, are treated in some detail and the conclusion is reached that they amounted to some marks 350 million, outside of Kiaochow, the German leased area in Shantung province. The number of German firms is stated to be 150 and the capital of these firms is put at marks 125 million.[3]

[1] *Die Entwicklung der deutschen Seeinteressen im letzten Jahrzehnt*, Reichsmarineamt, Berlin, 1905. Portion on China, pp. 155–6.

[2] Oliver J. D. Hughes, Consul General at Coburg; cf. *Consular Reports*, vol. 72, p. 99 ff.; Ernest L. Harris, Consular Agent at Eibenstock, cf. *Consular Reports*, vol. 63, pp. 461–2.

[3] The Chinese Maritime Customs reports 197 German firms and 1,850 German residents in China for 1905.

We find the further statement that, at the end of 1900, twenty German wholesale houses and eight retail shops were doing business in Hongkong. German investments in industrial establishments at Shanghai were put at marks 20 million. The Shantung Railway Company accounted for marks 54 million and the Shantung Mining Company for 12 million. Other mining ventures were set down at marks 6 million.

The information by which to check this estimate of marks 350 million is not available. The sum of marks 20 million for industrial plants at Hongkong, for example, seems to me too large. The greatest difficulty, however, is the estimating of German business investments at Tsingtao and in the rest of the leased area of Kiaochow. The report of the German admiralty states that Kiaochow is omitted in arriving at the total of marks 350 million. At the same time the Shantung Railway Company and the Shantung Mining Company are included and these corporations held property of considerable value within Kiaochow. In addition, I am convinced that the sum given for land holdings, outside of Hongkong, in the 1905 report is reasonable if Kiaochow is included, and is unreasonably large if Kiaochow is not included. I am, therefore, driven to the conclusion that a large part of German property at Kiaochow is in the mark 350 million estimate.[4] I propose to accept marks 350 million, U. S. $83.3 million, as a total for German business investments, adding enough to make the sum U. S. $85 million to cover property in Kiaochow not otherwise reported. It is to be pointed out that this is presumed to include mission property as well.

For German holdings of the obligations of the Chinese government, I propose to go back to the end of the year 1901 in order to arrive at a figure which may be com-

[4] Consul General Hughes in his report, cited above, gives a figure of U. S. $14.9 million as the value of permanent improvements made by the German government. This has been omitted since government holdings of this sort are not regarded as investments.

pared with that for other countries. The German interest in the various loans, all for the general purposes of
the Chinese government, is shown below:

	Total Outstanding Dec. 31, 1901 (U. S. Dollars)	German Share	
		Per Cent	U. S. Dollars
5% Gold Loan of 1896	73,374,654	50	36,687,327
4½% Gold Loan of 1898	76,104,882	50	38,052,441
6% Gold Loan of 1895 (Arnhold Karberg)	4,542,070	100	4,542,070
			79,281,838

The totals for 1902 are shown in the following table:

TABLE 1

GERMAN INVESTMENT IN CHINA, 1902–1904

	U. S. Dollars
Business investments	85,000,000
Government obligations	79,282,000
	164,282,000

INVESTMENTS IN 1914

By 1914 German holdings of the obligations of the
Chinese government had reached a total of U. S. $127,-
596,000. The German share of the various loans is shown
in the table on page 640.

German loans to the Chinese government began early
and had reached a comparatively large total when the
war began in 1914. The early start is to be explained in
part by the fact that the Germans were of considerable
importance in the trade and shipping of China before the
end of the nineteenth century. The 6% Gold Loan of
1895, for example, was undertaken by one of the great
German firms of the China coast. Business investments
facilitated government financing. A factor of more importance was the political situation in Europe and the
Far East, by which it came about that the Germans were

TABLE 2

GERMAN SHARE OF THE OBLIGATIONS OF THE CHINESE GOVERNMENT, 1914 *

	Outstanding Dec. 31, 1913 in U. S. Dollars	German Share	
		Per Cent	U. S. Dollars
General purposes of the Chinese government:			
5% Gold Loan of 1896	56,869,554	50	28,434,777
6% Gold Loan of 1895 (Arnhold Karberg)	648,870	100	648,870
4½% Gold Loan of 1898	66,208,732	50	33,104,366
5% Reorganization Loan of 1913	121,662,500	24	29,199,000
Subtotal			91,387,013
Railway obligations:			
5% Hukuang Rys. Sinking Fund Gold Loan of 1911	29,199,000	25	7,299,750
5% Tientsin-Pukow Ry. Loan of 1908	24,332,500	63	15,329,475
5% Tientsin-Pukow Ry. Supplementary Loan of 1910	14,599,500	63	9,197,685
Tientsin-Pukow Advance, 1912	4,381,913	100	4,381,913
Subtotal			36,208,823
Total			127,595,836

* German share of the amount outstanding on the Boxer indemnity U. S. $64,859,000.

shouldered out of the Franco-Russian financial program in 1895 and, at about the same time, entered into closer relations with the British. The co-operation of the Deutsch-Asiatische Bank and the Hongkong and Shanghai Bank brought it about that half of two of the great Chinese loans to meet the Japanese war indemnity was issued in Germany.

A further factor enters into the explanation of the large total for 1914. The German acquisition of Kiaochow in 1898 carried with it an increasing German interest in the development of Shantung province. During the early discussion of plans for a line from the lower Yangtze to

Tientsin the Germans made it plain that they would insist upon the right to finance and build that part of the railway lying within the province of Shantung or to participate in the contract on the basis of such a right. In short, it was German policy in the international political field and within China more than the active participation of the Germans in Chinese trade and industry which explains her large holdings of government securities in 1914 and in 1902.

The business investments of the Germans in China in 1914 must remain unknown if we are to depend upon direct evidence. Neither the German writers on China nor those upon Germany's overseas holdings estimate German business investments. If we turn to the various indices of Germany's position in China which are to be found in the table at the end of this chapter there is evidence of vigorous growth. Figures for 1905 and 1913 are necessary for our present purpose. We find them to show an increase in German firms of 71 per cent and an increase in German population of 58 per cent. If business investments increased by 60 per cent the total for 1914 would be U. S. $136 million. We may approach the matter from another direction by supposing that German loans and business investments showed the same relation in 1913 as in 1905. The British figures tend to support such a generalization. Such calculations show German business investments to have been U. S. $144 million. It is an interesting fact that a German business man, a German banker, and a German government official, each one of whom had been in China before the war, undertook to estimate German property and business holdings in China as they were in 1914. The three guesses were between U. S. $130 million and U. S. $150 million. It seems to me reasonable to accept a total of U. S. $136 million, without attempting to make any adjustment or correction for mission property. Scattered information is available about certain aspects of German holdings in China but it does not help in judging the reasonableness of the estimated total.[5]

The following table shows the situation in 1914:

TABLE 3

GERMAN INVESTMENTS IN CHINA, 1914

	U. S. Dollars
Business investments	136,000,000
Government obligations	127,596,000
	263,596,000

INVESTMENTS IN 1931

Business Investments

It is convenient to divide the period from 1914 to 1931 and to consider first the decline in German business investments between the beginning of the war and the year 1921 when the Chinese government began to release sequestrated property to its German owners.

German property in the concessions and leased areas in China under the political control of the allied powers was taken over by those powers shortly after the war began in 1914. Much of this property was in British and French Concessions, the German holdings in the French Concession at Shanghai being particularly large. This property, or the proceeds from its sale, entered into the clearing house system established in the Treaty of Versailles [6] and was entirely lost to its former German owners.

German property in the Kiaochow area, that is at Tsingtao and in the immediate neighborhood, was taken over by the Japanese authorities after Japanese military

[5] Sartorius von Waltershausen instances the memorial of the German Colonial Secretary Dernberg giving the total investment in German colonies outside Kiaochow as marks 370 million in 1908, whereas in 1914 it had risen to 500 million. If German investment in China increased at the same rate over the period 1905–1914, we would arrive at a figure of U. S. $125 million. A. Sartorius von Waltershausen, *Deutsche Wirthschaftsgeschichte, 1815–1914*, Jena, 2nd ed., 1923.

[6] Temperley, H. W. V., *A History of the Peace Conference of Paris*, London, 1920, vol. III, pp. 254 ff.

occupation became effective and the British troops who had participated in the capture of the territory had been withdrawn.[7] The German-owned railway and mines, though outside the leased area, were occupied as well. The disposition of the public property and the German interest in the railway and mines was determined by Articles 156–8 of the Treaty of Versailles. This property was turned over to Japan [8] without any provision for the interest in the railway and mines which German corporations or individuals may have had. German private property within the Kiaochow area was taken over by the Japanese authorities. The real property of German individuals was sold and the sums realized turned over to the owners.[9] On the average the sums received seem to have been about 40 per cent of the value at which the property was held in 1914. A small number of Germans repurchased their own property, but German holdings in Tsingtao were small in 1931.

China declared a state of war with Germany and Austria to be in existence on August 14, 1917. As a result of this the German concessions in Tientsin and Hankow were taken over by the Chinese government and German property in China, outside of the concessions of the allied powers, was made subject to seizure. Some of this property was sold and the proceeds held.[10] The state of war with Germany was ended by presidential mandate dated September 15, 1919.[11] A preliminary

[7] Regulations governing the Japanese military administration were issued on November 19, 1914. MacMurray, J. V. A., *Treaties and Agreements*, vol. II, p. 1159.

[8] The railway and public property was turned over to China under arrangements dealt with in the discussion of Japanese investments.

[9] The owners received the whole sum up to Yen 10,000 and 70 per cent of any additional sum. My information comes from a German lawyer in Shanghai who referred to a German-Japanese liquidation agreement of 1924 which I have been unable to find.

[10] Regulations issued by the Chinese government concerning enemy property are reprinted in MacMurray, *Treaties and Agreements*, vol. II, pp. 1378–9.

[11] China did not sign the Versailles Treaty chiefly on account of the Shantung settlement contained in it.

agreement between China and Germany was reached on May 20, 1921, in which the German government accepted the fact that extraterritoriality no longer existed for German citizens. In an explanatory letter from W. W. Yen, the Chinese Minister of Foreign Affairs, we are told: "as to the indemnity for war losses Germany undertakes to pay in advance a portion thereof in a lump sum, which represents the equivalent of one-half of the proceeds from the liquidated German property and one-half of the values of the sequestrated but not yet liquidated German property, which amount will eventually be agreed upon and will consist of Chinese $4 million in cash and the balance in Tsin-Pu (that is, Tientsin-Pukow) and Hukuang railway bonds." The Chinese agreed to cease all liquidation of German property and to return to the German owners all proceeds and property still held. The affairs of the Deutsch-Asiatische Bank were to be settled by a separate agreement.[12] In June, 1924, correspondence was published concerning final settlement. From this correspondence we discover that the value of the property released to Germans from 1921 to 1924 and to be released under the new agreement was between Chinese $69 and 70 million.[13]

The sum stated above, say U. S. $35 million, ought, it seems, to represent the low point of German holdings in 1921. I am informed, however, that some of the proceeds from the sale of German property were entirely withdrawn from China.   The Shantung Mining Corporation, for example, is said to have invested in South America whatever small sums it received. The German interest in the Chinhsing (Kinsing) coal mine in Chihli (Hopei) province was reduced from one-half to one-third.[14] The Deutsch-Asiatische Bank, on the other hand, received back its land and buildings in Peking and Hankow and a sum of

[12] *Chinese Social and Political Science Review*, October, 1924, vol. 8, no. 4, pp. 183–9.
[13] *Ibid.*, pp. 190–4.
[14] Lieu, D. K., *Foreign Investments in China, 1929*, p. 65.

U. S. $975,000 in Tientsin-Pukow and Hukuang Railway bonds.

Since 1922 German trade has grown and the number of German firms in China in 1930 was almost exactly the same as in 1913. Of these firms, fifty-three were in Shanghai and ten were found to be the actual owners of industrial plants or landed property. The sale of commercial fertilizers has increased greatly in recent years and the chief corporations in this and in the dye business hold immense stocks of goods. German interests in Tientsin are small, but there has been some recovery in recent years. Estimates of total German business investments made in China in 1931 justify a total of about U. S. $75 million.

It may be added here that I was unable to secure an estimate of German mission holdings. They are said by officials to be extremely small. "The remittances from Germany,"—I quote a German official,—"for mission purposes do not amount to more than a few tens of thousands of dollars."

Obligations of the Chinese Government

The problem is to determine for the year 1931 the actual holding, by Germans or within Germany, of the securities and obligations of the Chinese government. I propose to attempt a solution of this problem by presenting, first, the German total on the principle of the place of issue and, secondly, the probable total on the principle of the place of actual holding, together with the available information as to where the bonds now are.

Consider, first, the total sums outstanding on the German issues of Chinese government securities. Taking the loans for the general purposes of the Chinese government, that is, the older secured loans, we find the situation to be this:

	Total Outstanding Dec. 31, 1930 in U. S. Dollars	German Share	
		Per Cent	U. S. Dollars
5% Gold Loan of 1896	8,749,724	50	4,374,862
4½% Gold Loan of 1898	39,304,885	50	19,652,442
5% Reorganization Loan of 1913	111,915,776	24	26,859,786
			50,887,090

The railway obligations are taken from the table for December 31, 1929, prepared by the Ministry of Railways of the Chinese government. This table was drawn up on the principle of the place of issue and its use for our present purpose is, therefore, appropriate. The table of the Ministry of Railways shows the following obligations as German:

Secured obligations	U. S. $31,021,670
Unsecured obligations	63,336
	U. S. $31,085,006

No "unsecured" German loans were listed by the Financial Readjustment Commission in 1925. None are shown in the 1927 document of the Ministry of Finance. This is consistent with the statement that all outstanding claims on both sides were settled by the agreement of 1924.[15] I am informed that German claims will appear in the new estimate which is being brought together by the recently appointed Commission for the Consolidation of Foreign and Domestic Obligations.

The German share of the Boxer indemnity was canceled by the agreement of May 20, 1921, which carried with it the acceptance on both sides of Article 128 of the Treaty of Versailles.[16] It need not be considered in any total for 1931.

[15] In so far as they originated before July 1, 1921. *Chinese Social and Political Science Review*, October, 1924, vol. 8, no. 4. p. 194.
[16] *Chinese Social and Political Science Review*, October, 1924, vol. 8, no. 4, p. 185.

From the sums shown in the preceding paragraphs we arrive at a total of U. S. $81,972,096, or roughly U. S. $82 million. This sum represents the normal value of the securities of the Chinese government which would have been in Germany on January 1, 1931, if all the securities issued in Germany had stayed within the country.

It is well known, however, that these securities did not stay in Germany. Every German banker to whom I talked in China and Germany during the year 1930–1931 was quite certain of this. Mr. Franz Urbig, for example, who is Chairman of the board of the Deutsch-Asiatische Bank, pointed out that the efforts of the German government in 1919 and 1920 to acquire foreign securities brought about the surrender of a considerable number of Chinese holdings which are not now in Germany. He took the trouble to estimate the total holdings of the Deutsch-Asiatische Bank and the Deutsche Bank-Disconto Gesellschaft in connection with all of their operations, and found the amount to be insignificant. There are no quotations on the Berlin Stock Exchange of Chinese government securities, which would hardly be the case if there were any considerable amount of such securities in Germany. He was willing to consider a sum of U. S. $10 million as the possible German holding, but this sum he was inclined to regard as too large. A German banker in Shanghai and a German broker undertook to make estimates for me and they arrived independently at guesses of U. S. $12 million and U. S. $10 million. I am entirely convinced that some figure of this sort is as near to the true figure as we can come and I, therefore, accept U. S. $12 million as the probable German holding of the obligations of the Chinese government in 1931.

The export of Chinese securities from Germany is supported by additional information. It is known that figures of German issues validated as having been in the possession of citizens of allied or neutral countries before China declared war on Germany came to a total of about

£10 million in 1923 or 1924.[17] The bonds held "invalid" came to about the same total, but these bonds were not necessarily in Germany.

The distribution of the bonds to the value of about U. S. $70 million, which were issued in Germany and are now held elsewhere, may be estimated. We know that British bankers report that U. S. $7,908,062 in bonds of German issues were in England in 1930. This is probably no more than half of the bonds actually in the possession of British citizens. The British probably held at least U. S. $16 million. French bankers reported considerable holdings which I estimate at U. S. $15 million.

The settlement of affairs between China and Germany in 1914 involved the surrender to China of certain sums in Tientsin-Pukow, and Hukuang railway bonds. The face value of the bonds so surrendered has been calculated and found to be £2,731,000.[18] In addition certain bonds were turned over to the Deutsch-Asiatische Bank. These I calculate to have had a nominal value of £340,000. Other evidences of indebtedness turned over were drawn bonds and unpaid coupons which may be disregarded here. The settlement of 1924 involved the turning over to China of bonds issued in Germany to the value of £3,071,000 or U. S. $14,945,022.[19]

Holdings within China of the bonds of the Chinese government issued elsewhere were estimated in China at about U. S. $40 million. If we suppose U. S. $15 million of the net movement to China to be accounted for by the

[17] A table is printed in the *China Year Book*, 1924, p. 817 and it is supported by comments in the *London Times*, February 18, 1924, p. 19b.

[18] Tientsin-Pukow 1908 £1,400,000; Tientsin-Pukow 1910 £950,000; Hukuang £381,000. See *Chinese Social and Political Science Review*, October, 1920, vol. 8, no. 4, p. 192. The reported sum of £400,000 for the first item is evidently a typographical error and should be £1.4 million. See pp. 190–1 for the settlement with the Deutsch-Asiatische Bank.

[19] There is good reason to believe that many of these bonds were disposed of outside of China by the Chinese government at the time. I am convinced, however, that purchases abroad by bankers in China between 1924 and 1930 brought a net increase of U. S. $40 million. It is the net movement out of Germany and into China with which I am now concerned.

1924 settlement, we find U. S. $25 million still to be accounted for. If we suppose the total holdings within China to have been U. S. $39 million in 1931, our estimates show the total disposition of the bonds issued in Germany to be as follows:

Great Britain	U. S. $16 million
France	15 "
China, 1924 settlement	15 "
China, bankers' purchases	24 "
	U. S. $70 "

The estimates above represent conclusions as to the net movements of Chinese bonds. It is not to be supposed, for example, that Chinese purchases have been of German bonds only, though, as a matter of fact, many of the bonds imported into China have been those of German issues. It is to be borne in mind, also, that bonds of French issues have moved to Great Britain while bonds issued in Germany have moved to France. The situation as it existed in 1931 is as if the German bonds had moved as I have indicated.

If we may trust the estimates of Germans who know most about the financial relations of their country with China, we may accept as reasonable the conclusion that German holdings of Chinese government obligations came to about U. S. $12 million in 1931. We may summarize the estimated German investments:

TABLE 4

GERMAN INVESTMENTS IN CHINA, 1931

	U. S. Dollars
Business investments	75,000,000
Government obligations	12,000,000
	87,000,000

CONCLUSION

The outstanding fact revealed in the general tables of German investments in China since 1900 is the effect of the World War on the position of Germany. German investments showed what may be called a normal increase between 1904–1914. In 1931 German investments were about a third of their value in 1914 and this situation reflects a recovery from a low point in 1921, when German holdings of all sorts were probably less than U. S. $40 million. In other words, the post-war development in the case of Germany began with holdings which were less than a sixth of the 1914 total.

TABLE 5

GERMAN INVESTMENTS IN CHINA, 1900–1931

By Chief Divisions with Relatives

(Values shown in millions of U. S. dollars)

	Business Investments		Government Obligations		Total	
	U. S. Dollars	Rela- tives	U. S. Dollars	Rela- tives	U. S. Dollars	Rela- tives
1902–1904	85.0	62.5	79.3	62.1	164.3	62.3
1914	136.0	100.0	127.6	100.0	263.6	100.0
1931	75.0	55.2	12.0	9.4	87.0	33.0

It is to be noted that German loans to China were relatively large in 1902 and that they increased as rapidly as did business investments to 1914. This, it has been pointed out, was due to the political situation in Europe and to German ambitions in Shantung province. The decline in security holdings after the war reflects the general German decline in the holdings of foreign securities. In the Chinese case there was the added fact that direct payments to the Chinese government were made in bonds of the German issues of certain Chinese obligations.

The relatively high percentage of the total German investments formed by government obligations in 1904 and in 1914 is shown in the second general table. The situation since 1914 reflects an increase in trade at a time when China was not borrowing abroad and when Germany had no money to lend. Stocks of goods play a large part in German holdings at the present time and the few contracts which involve advances, such as that in connection with aërial transportation between China and Europe, are closely associated with trade.[20]

TABLE 6

GERMAN INVESTMENTS IN CHINA, 1900–1931

Percentage Distribution by Chief Divisions

(Values shown in millions of U. S. dollars)

	Business Investments		Government Obligations		Total	
	U. S. Dollars	Per Cent	U. S. Dollars	Per Cent	U. S. Dollars	Per Cent
1902–1904	85.0	51.7	79.3	48.3	164.3	100
1914	136.0	51.6	127.6	48.4	263.6	100
1931	75.0	86.2	12.0	13.8	87.0	100

German trade and German business investments in China have grown rapidly since 1921. In discussions of this, such as one hears in China, it is frequently forgotten that German investments are much smaller than they were before the war. Attention is directed to the recent situation and the opinion is often expressed with some confidence that the rapid growth of trade bears a close relation to the absence of extraterritoriality. The German merchants and officials are less dogmatic than many others but they believe, rather generally, that their altered position does bring them a certain good-will, the importance of which cannot be measured.

The position of Germany is shown in the following table. Data for 1921 are included except in the case of shipping. German shipping was negligible until 1923 and the German share in the coast trade was insignificant in 1930.

[20] A summary of this contract was published by the Kuo Min News Agency on August 20, 1930, and appeared in various newspapers. It is reprinted in the *China Year Book*, 1931, p. 253.

The data for 1921 are given because the position of Germany today is to be judged by comparison with these figures as well as those for 1914.

TABLE 7

THE POSITION OF GERMANY IN CHINA'S INTERNATIONAL ECONOMIC RELATIONS

Customs Statistics except for Investments

TRADE	Direct Trade Mills. Hk. Tls.	Relatives	Per Cent of China's Total Trade
1905	20.2	44.6	3.0
1913	45.3	100.0	4.7
1921	20.1	44.4	1.3
1930	92.5	204.1	4.2
POPULA- TION	German Population in China	Relatives	Per Cent of Total Foreign Population in China
1899	1,134	38.4	6.6
1913	2,949	100.0	1.8
1921	1,255	42.6	0.5
1930	3,006	101.9	0.8
FIRMS	German Firms	Relatives	Per Cent of Total Foreign Firms in China
1899	115	38.8	12.3
1913	296	100.0	7.7
1921	92	31.1	0.9
1930	297	100.3	3.6
SHIPPING	German Tonnage in Millions	Relatives	Per Cent of Total Chinese and Foreign Shipping
1899	1.8	28.5	4.6
1913	6.3	100.0	6.3
1930	4.2	66.6	2.7
INVEST- MENT	German Investment Millions U. S. Dollars	Relatives	Per Cent of Total Foreign Investment
1902–1904	124.3	62.3	20.9
1914	263.6	100.0	16.4
1931	87.0	33.0	2.7

CHAPTER XXI

BELGIAN, DUTCH, ITALIAN, AND SCANDINAVIAN INVESTMENTS IN CHINA

It is possible to estimate fairly closely the investments of certain European countries for the year 1930 or 1931, but no estimate can be offered for the earlier years, 1900 and 1914. These countries are: Belgium, the Netherlands, Italy, and the three Scandinavian countries, Denmark, Norway, and Sweden.

BELGIAN INVESTMENTS, 1931

Belgian interests in China have been of considerable importance since the negotiations for the original contract for the Peking-Hankow Railway carried on during the years 1895–1898. An effort was, therefore, made to arrive at estimates of Belgian investments for 1902 and 1914, but it was abandoned after it became clear that no such estimate was possible.[1]

The obligations of the Chinese government to the Belgians at the end of 1930 is to be arrived at by estimating the totals under the headings which have been used in other cases.

The well-known secured loans for the general purposes of the Chinese government in which the Belgians have played a part include, first, an issue of bonds of the 5% Reorganization loan of 1913 to the amount of £1,338,880. Belgium was not represented in the five-power group that made the loan, but a certain part, equal to a large fraction

---

[1] It may be worth while to record the fact that our estimates for Belgian holdings of the obligations of the Chinese government were: for 1902 U. S. $4,379,400 and for 1914 U. S. $22,882,172. This is based on the allocation of the loans set forth in the discussion of French investments.

of the Russian share issued outside of Russia, was assigned to Belgian banks. The amount outstanding on these bonds on December 31, 1930, was U. S. $6,155,369.

The second item is a sum of U. S. $4,248,400 which is the amount outstanding on the Belgian indemnity loan of 1928. This loan is based upon an obligation of the Chinese government to make the payments called for by the Boxer indemnity agreements of September 5, 1925, and December 8, 1927.[2] The Belgian position at the termination of the "gold" franc controversy was that Belgium, having won its point in the controversy, decided not to take advantage of it. The government accepted payment in full in "paper" francs from the Banque Belge pour l'Etranger and the Chinese government undertook to pay the bank in "gold" francs. After the bank had received the amount of its advance to the Belgian government a loan for U. S. $5 million was issued on the basis of the annual sums due from China and, in the agreement of December 8, 1927, it was determined that 75 per cent of the sum realized was to be spent in Belgium for railway material and 25 per cent to be placed at the disposal of a committee charged with the supervision of educational and philanthropic activities. It seems to me best to regard the Boxer indemnity obligation as no longer in existence and to set down the outstanding amount of this new loan in its place.

Railway obligations to Belgium, as reported by the Ministry of Railways of the Chinese government for the end of 1929, were U. S. $37,353,982. This sum is accepted as the best available. Figures from the creditors are in substantial agreement with this total. For the Pienlo and Lunghai Railway the sums due have been reported to me by the Belgian company which has made practically all of the advances. No payments of any sort, I am told, have been made on these loans since 1927. On January 1,

[2] Wright, S. F., *The Collection and Disposal of the . . . Customs Revenue,* pp. 114, 124–5.

1931, the amount outstanding, covering principal and interest due but unpaid, was as follows:

			U. S. Dollars
Pienlo, 1903–1907	French Frs.	28,200,000	1,105,440
Lunghai, 1913	£	5,100,000	24,819,150
Lunghai, 1920	Belgian Frs.	198,449,920	5,516,900
Lunghai, 1920	Guilders	44,280,000	17,800,560
Lunghai, 1924	Chinese $	1,112,000	317,700
Lunghai, 1925	French Frs.	30,600,000	1,199,520
Advances:	Belgian Frs.	57,685,000	1,603,640
	£	11,122	54,1°0
	Guilders	1,000,000	402,000
Total			52,819,040

Deducting the sums due to the Netherlands, shown in guilders, we have a total obligation of U. S. $34,616,480 on the Pienlo and Lunghai. The Belgian share of the advance for the Tatung-Chengtu Railway (U. S. $2,773,-280) brings the total to U. S. $37,389,760. There may be sums outstanding for materials and supplies but, allowing for such sums, it is still true that the figures of the Ministry and of the Belgian creditors are, as has been said, in close agreement.

The Belgian total of about U. S. $37 million is based upon the principle of the place of issue. If the whole of the facts were known and we were able to estimate the actual holding of these bonds in Belgium and in France, it would then appear that the Belgian investor holds less than U. S. $37 million in Chinese railway obligations. In discussing French investments it was estimated that at least U. S. $10 million reported as Belgian is actually held in France. In the absence of detailed information, the Belgian total has been allowed to stand at U. S. $37 million.

There were no obligations to Belgians for communications other than railways and I turn to the 1927 document of the Ministry of Finance for the amount of the "unsecured" loans. This comes to U. S. $285,655.

The totals are shown in the following table:

TABLE 1
BELGIAN HOLDING OF THE OBLIGATIONS OF THE CHINESE GOVERNMENT, 1931

	U. S. Dollars
Loans for the general purpose of the government	10,403,769
Railway obligations	37,353,982
"Unsecured" obligations	285,655
	48,043,406

The business investments of the Belgians have recently been carefully estimated by a well-informed Belgian business man in Shanghai. The estimate was made for a conference in Brussels on the general subject of Belgian interests in the Far East. The total, for the beginning of 1931, came to somewhat less than Belgian francs 1,500 million, that is, to U. S. $41 million. This sum, together with the government obligations, brings the Belgian total to nearly U. S. $90 million.

TABLE 2
BELGIAN INVESTMENTS IN CHINA, 1931

	U. S. Dollars	Per Cent
Business investments	41,000,000	46.0
Government obligations	48,043,000	54.0
	89,043,000	100.0

DUTCH INVESTMENTS, 1931

The Dutch holdings of the obligations of the Chinese government consist of two items: a loan for the Lunghai Railway and a share of the "unsecured" loans of the Chinese government.

The share of the Boxer indemnity due to Holland need no longer be considered. As Wright points out, the Netherlands government has declared its intention to follow the example of others and has made arrangements to devote the balance of the indemnity payments to a scientific study of the Yellow River and to the drawing up of a plan for its permanent improvement.[3] Proposals for the creation of a Sino-Dutch Commission to administer the funds have been accepted by the Chinese government.[4] The funds have been accumulating in China since the beginning of 1926. Political disturbance has prevented the work from actually being undertaken but it is certain that no funds are being remitted from China to the Netherlands on account of the Boxer indemnity and that none will be remitted in the future.

The Dutch loan for the Lunghai Railway took the form of an issue at Amsterdam of certain 8 per cent treasury notes of the Chinese government. Guilders 16,-667,000 were issued in 1920 and Guilders 14,083,000 in 1923, making a total issue of Guilders 30,750,000. In addition a later advance of Guilders 1 million is reported without date by the Belgian company, and the Belgian report states the interest in arrears on January 1, 1931, to be Guilders 13,530,000. The total obligation reported by the creditors is, then, Guilders 45,280,000, or U. S. $18,202,560. The Chinese Ministry of Railways reports the obligation to the Netherlands at Guilders 31,752,025 or U. S. $12,764,314. My information agrees with the statement of Kann and Baylin that interest has been in arrears since July 1, 1925.[5] The Dutch case, involving as it does but one obligation, is so clear that I propose to accept the larger amount and put down the sum due to the Netherlands at U. S. $18,202,560.

Dutch obligations were reported by the Financial Readjustment Commission of 1925. The sum reported as among the "unsecured" loans in the 1927 document of the Ministry of Finance comes to U. S. $503,928. This

[3] Wright, S. F., *The Collection and Disposal of the . . . Maritime Customs Revenue*, p. 126.
[4] *China Year Book*, 1929–1930, p. 669.
[5] *China Year Book*, 1931, p. 359.

obligation, together with that reported above, brings the total for the Netherlands to U. S. $18,706,488.

The business investments of the Dutch in China have been estimated after consultation with Dutch bankers and with the Secretary of the Netherlands Chamber of Commerce at Shanghai. There are two Dutch banks of some importance in China, the Nederlandsche Handel Maatschappij and the Nederlandsch Indische Handelsbank.[6] A Dutch firm holds the contract for the improvement of the harbor at Hulutao and has engaged in similar work at other places. It owns considerable equipment in China. The estimate that which I have arrived is U. S. $10 million for business investments. This does not take into account the problem of the relation between China and Java. Here no more can be done than to estimate remittances from Chinese in the Netherlands Indies to China, though it is well known that there are Chinese, who are Dutch nationals, living in China who own property in the Dutch Colonies, and Chinese living in the Netherlands Indies who own property in China.

TABLE 3

DUTCH INVESTMENTS IN CHINA, 1931

	U. S. Dollars	Per Cent
Business investments	10,000,000	34.8
Obligations of the Chinese government	18,706,000	65.2
	28,706,000	100.0

ITALIAN INVESTMENTS, 1931

In the case of Italy the obligations of the Chinese government form a single item among the "unsecured" loans, which was reported at £8,648,633, or roughly U. S. $42 million in the 1927 document of the Chinese Ministry of Finance, the usual source of information for the accepted estimates in this field. This obligation be-

[6] Usually referred to, in English, as the Netherlands Trade Bank and the Netherlands India Bank.

gan as a series of loans, usually called the "Austrian," in 1912, 1913, and 1914, which involved contracts for munitions, torpedo boats, and destroyers. The contracts were interrupted by the war. An attempt was made in 1922 by an Italian bank, acting for the bond-holders of these Austrian loans, to bring all the obligations into a single agreement whose nominal amount was £5,777,190. Provision for payment of British income tax in this 1922 agreement gives some color to the conclusion that some of these bonds are held in England.[7] I was informed in Paris that French money was involved. The 1927 document of the Ministry of Finance cites an agreement of September 30, 1925, as its authority for the sum of £6,866,-046, which it gives as the amount of the original loan. The obligation is a tangled international transaction, the complete history of which will probably never be known. I have accepted the total shown in the 1927 document.

Italian business investments in Shanghai were carefully calculated for the end of 1927 by the Italian Chamber of Commerce at Shanghai. Returns were received from thirty-one firms. Six of these firms reported investments of Sh. Tls. 100,000 or more. Chinese capital was excluded in every case. The Sino-Italian Bank, which participated in the agreement of 1922 mentioned above, came to an end in 1925. Its place has been taken by the Italian Bank for China which had, at the end of 1930, a paid-up capital of U. S. $1 million and reserves of U. S. $171,212. There was no industrial plant owned by Italians anywhere in China in 1931 except, perhaps, that of a firm in Tientsin dealing in marble. The total business investment at Shanghai was, according to the returns of the Chamber of Commerce, U. S. $2,611,-200. Upon the basis of changes since the end of 1927,

[7] For some of the original contracts see MacMurray, J. V. A., *Loans and Agreements*, vol. II, pp. 1004–7. For information concerning the 1922 agreement see Baylin, J. R., *Foreign Loan Obligations of China*, p. 22.

the Secretary of the Chamber was of the opinion that U. S. $500,000 ought to be added to this, making the total for Shanghai U. S. $3,111,200. His studies had led him to the conclusion that the investment at Shanghai formed 70 per cent of the total Italian investment in China and, on this basis, an estimate of U. S. $4,445,000 was arrived at for the whole of China at the end of 1930.

The Chinese import of artificial silk, which has increased rapidly since the World War, is very largely from Italy and through Italian firms in China. Of a total import of Hk. Tls. 16 million in 1929, Italy supplied Hk. Tls. 11 million, and she supplied about 60 per cent of an import of Hk. Tls. 15 million in 1930. For each of these years the import of artificial silk was nearly three-fifths of the total imports from Italy.

The Italian share of the Boxer indemnity has been dealt with in much the same way as for France and Belgium. After the five-year deferment, the Chinese government in December, 1922, offered payment in "paper." This was refused. At the end of the "gold" franc controversy a settlement was reached.[8] The payments to December 31, 1925, were turned over to the Chinese government. From January 1, 1926, they were made to the Italian Bank for China in U. S. dollars. The Italian government accepted payment of the whole outstanding amount in "paper" from the Italian Bank and by the end of 1931 the whole sum due the Italian government had been paid. Payments in U. S. dollars are still being made to the Italian Bank by the Chinese government. It was expected at the end of 1931 that the annuities still to be paid would become the basis of a loan. The proceeds are to be devoted to education, philanthropic and public works, the materials for the public works to be purchased in Italy. Payments to Italy had come to an end by 1932 and the loan had not yet been floated. These facts seem to justify the omission of the

[8] On October 1, 1925. Printed in the *China Year Book*, 1927, pp. 125–6.

Boxer indemnity from the government obligations shown in the table below.

TABLE 4

ITALIAN INVESTMENTS IN CHINA, 1931

	U. S. Dollars	Per Cent
Business investments	4,445,000	9.6
Government obligations	42,000,000	90.4
	46,445,000	100.0

THE INVESTMENTS OF THE SCANDINAVIAN COUNTRIES, 1931

The obligations of the Chinese government to Denmark are of some importance. They include the Danish share (50 per cent) of three loans reported in the British case as for communications other than railways. The items are:

	U. S. Dollars
Shanghai-Taku cable	302,139
Taku-Chefoo cable	70,087
Telegraph charges advance	250,043
	622,269

In addition to this sum the 1927 document of the Ministry of Finance shows "unsecured" obligations to the amount of U. S. $205,557. This makes a total for Denmark of U. S. $827,826.

Norway has had no share in loans to the Chinese government for general purposes or for communications. No sum appears in the 1927 document of the Ministry of Finance. It is to be noted, however, that Mr. Johan Michelet, who represented Norway at the Tariff Conference of 1925–1926, called specific attention to an item of Hk. Tls. 50 million which had been sold in special bonds to one of his compatriots.[9] My efforts to trace an item as large as this led to a correction which brought it down to Tls. 50,000. This I propose to add, at U. S. $25,000,

[9] *The Special Conference on the Chinese Customs Tariff*, Peking, 1928, p. 300.

to the "unsecured" loans. The claim is not found in the Chinese lists of "unsecured" obligations which means, in this case, not, I believe, that it was rejected by the Financial Readjustment Commission but merely that it was not presented.

The obligations of the Chinese government to Sweden comprise the single item of U. S. $3,924 listed in the 1927 document of the Ministry of Finance as "unsecured."

I turn now to the business investments of the Scandinavian countries. Denmark is represented in China by no less than forty firms, nineteen of which have offices in Shanghai. A reasonable estimate of Danish business investments is U. S. $1 million. Norway is represented by business investments that were about U. S. $500,000 at the end of 1930.[10] The business investments of Sweden are at least U. S. $500,000. This amount is somewhat uncertain since it was found impossible to secure accurate information as to Swedish investment in match manufacturing in Manchuria.

The Boxer indemnity settlement of 1901 included a sum of Tls. 62,820 due to Sweden and Norway.[11] This obligation was unaffected by the changes of the war period and forms, with the Portuguese and Spanish share, the outstanding portion of the indemnity. The annuities still due justify the inclusion of a capital sum of about U. S. $30,000 as an obligation of the Chinese government to Sweden and Norway at the end of 1930.

Reports from the mission societies and from the officials in China of the various countries enable me to estimate the total holdings of property for mission purposes at U. S. $925,000 and the remittances to China by these societies for the year 1929 at U. S. $710,000. In the case of Norway, for a recent year,[12] no less than half of the total of 3,140,000 crowns remitted from the country for

[10] The transfer of the Union Brewery to a corporation under the laws of Hongkong in 1931 made this total considerably smaller.

[11] At a fixed rate of U. S. $.742 to the tael.

[12] *Norwegian Year Book*, Oslo, 1931, p. 115.

mission purposes went to China. The Danish Mission Society reported no less than sixty-nine missionaries in China in 1929 and a net remittance to China of about 350,000 crowns.

A table showing the investments of the Scandinavian countries follows:

TABLE 5

INVESTMENTS IN CHINA OF DENMARK, NORWAY, AND SWEDEN, 1931*

	U. S. Dollars		
Business investments			
Denmark	1,000,000		
Norway	500,000		
Sweden	500,000		
			2,000,000
Government obligations			
Communications other than railways			
Denmark	622,269		
		622,269	
"Unsecured" obligations			
Denmark	205,557		
Norway	25,000		
Sweden	3,924		
		234,481	
Boxer indemnity			
Norway and Sweden	30,000		
		30,000	
			886,750
Total			2,886,750

* Of the total investments, business investments formed 69.3 per cent and government obligations, 30.7 per cent.

APPENDIX

CAPITAL IN THE CHINESE ECONOMY*

The term "capital" is less fundamental in the analysis of the economists than is "land" or "labor." I believe that this is reflected in the emphasis upon land utilization and upon population in the studies of China that have been carried on in the United States and in other western countries. Studies of Chinese population have been pursued with considerable zeal and with results which would be more significant if the basic information were more plentiful. Capital formation within China and the flow of capital into and out of the country have seldom been the subjects of examination and study.

Now it may be quite correct to view the Chinese economy in terms of population and of the relation between population and land. To do this is probably to direct attention to the matters of ultimate importance. It may be remarked, however, that the subordination of all other problems to that of population has often had unfortunate consequences. It seems to limit the view so that one would suppose that the study of Chinese economic problems is, and can be, nothing more than a melancholy exercise in Malthusianism.

Even if one believes that the ultimate economic problem for China is one of population, it is still true that there are more immediate questions which demand attention. Japan offers an example of an immediate question which is obviously important; in the Japanese case, it is in the field of international trade. Whether one takes the position that foreign trade has prevented a disastrous pressure of population upon limited

---

* This is the edited text, in English, of an article which originally appeared in the Weltwirtschaftliches *Archiv* for July, 1936.

resources or that it has provided the opportunity for the rapid growth of population since the opening of the country, the outstanding importance of foreign trade in Japan must be recognized.

For the Chinese economy it is less easy to select an immediate problem of similar importance. There is no doubt that foreign trade is significant to China as well as to Japan, but it seems to be relatively less so. Much has been written about the necessity of finding a solution for the difficult problems of political organization in China. Such comment is not very illuminating if it does no more than point out that China could solve her economic problems more effectively if she had a strong and highly organized central government. But capable students have gone beyond this; they have reflected upon the disintegration of the old political system in China and upon the questions of political economy, in the true sense of that term, which are involved in the building up of a political organization for the future.

For China there seems to be an immediate problem of outstanding importance in the provision of capital. I believe that the importation of capital into China, and its effective application, has an importance for the Chinese economy similar to that which, for Japan, lies in the expansion of foreign trade.

How, one may ask, did it happen that traditional China entered upon modern economic relations with the West so poorly provided with capital equipment? Why did China have so little surplus, or potential surplus, with which to provide herself with the necessary equipment? Why did China have such relatively ineffective methods and devices for collecting and applying whatever surplus funds were available or might be made available? What changes in these respects have come about since contact with the West was initiated? What are the chief channels by which foreign capital has reached China in the past, and by what channels may one look to see it do so in the future? It is such questions as these that I propose to discuss, and the discussion is undertaken with a full realization that information is inadequate and that accepted conclusions in the field of Chinese economic history are lacking.

CAPITAL IN TRADITIONAL CHINA

My first question concerns "traditional" China and I mean by traditional China the economic, social, and political organization of the country as it was before the influence of the modern West began to be felt. When it is borne in mind that the modern foreign trade of China did not really begin before the opening of the five ports by the Treaty of Nanking in 1840 and did not really begin to count in the economic life of the country before about 1870, it is clear that the word "traditional" may be used of recent times. The truth is that in many respects traditional China is still in existence. To get the full picture of traditional China one may think of the China of Ch'ien Lung or of K'ang-hsi. The term "traditional" fixes attention upon a powerful element in the social organization of China as it has come down from the past and it seems to me preferable to the term "Asiatic" which Wittfogel employs in his work.[1]

How did it happen, I ask in my first question, that traditional China brought to modern China so little in the way of capital equipment? There are two aspects to this question. In the first place, traditional China had a relatively meagre industrial outfit and in the second place, the capital equipment which traditional China did have was of relatively little assistance in the developments of the last half century.

Traditional China was by no means without capital equipment. The oldest and most important forms had to do with the control and use of water. In the Loess region of the north, and throughout the rice-growing regions of the central and southern parts of the country, irrigation was necessary. The control of water on the Chengtu plain in the province of Szechuan is carried out by means of ancient and effective

[1] Wittfogel, K. A., *Wirtschaft und Gesellschaft Chinas*, Leipzig, 1931, p. viii.

devices which are in use at the present day. The Grand Canal brought water under control for purposes of navigation and it was at an earlier time one of the greatest and most useful of the public works of China. The lower valley of the Yangtze River is provided with what is probably the most extensive network of canals in the world. In addition, there were, according to usual estimates, about two thousand miles of imperial roads in China before the beginning of the nineteenth century. These facts are well known but it is useful to review them for the purpose of making the picture as complete as it can be made. Much of this equipment is, of course, useful at the present time, and it constitutes modern China's most valuable heritage from the past. But even this equipment is by no means all of use under the new conditions. Modern transportation facilities have rendered obsolete much that has come down from earlier times. Steam has made the Grand Canal less important. The motor car requires roads of a new sort. The railway has played its part in the creation of a new situation.

The Chinese handicraftsman of the past had tools of an effective sort for the work he had to do. The household looms of China represent a very considerable investment. But modern industry requires power-driven machinery rather than hand-driven tools. In general the technology which China slowly began to learn from the West required so different a supply of capital goods from those required by the traditional economy of the country that it is no matter for surprise to find that China had relatively little equipment of immediate usefulness under the new conditions. In this China did not differ greatly from Japan, from the other nations of the East, or, for that matter, from the nations of the West.

The second question brings us nearer to the heart of our problem. Why did China reach modern economic relations with so little in the way of reserve, with so little surplus? The same question applies, of course, to present-day China. Why, it may be asked, is there so little surplus available for the purchase or creation of the capital equipment required for modern industrial development? Here we face first the problem of the facts. Is it true that the surplus available in China is small? Some maintain that under favorable conditions the Chinese economy could provide funds on a considerable scale.

Those who take this position usually point first to the stock of silver in China which is hoarded or held in such forms as to constitute a reserve quickly available. A period of peaceful development, we are told, would bring large amounts of silver out of hiding in China and so into use in the country or into the world's markets. There is, of course, no reliable statistical information on this matter. Mr. Eduard Kann has given it some attention. Mr. Kann's estimates and those of Mr. J. A. Yavdynsky have been reviewed by Mr. Dickson Leavens, who accepted an estimate of 1,700 million fine ounces as the monetary stock of silver in China and 800 million ounces as the non-monetary stock. This estimate of non-monetary stock is little more than a guess, but it is an informed guess and is by no means to be disregarded.[2] It is significant that the estimate of 800 million ounces puts the figure for China at less than a quarter of the non-monetary stock of silver in India. This difference between China and India is made the more reasonable when one considers that the statistics of the Chinese Maritime Customs show that silver moved from China to India during the period of high silver prices at the end of the World War. China, it may be concluded, holds less silver than does India and holds it less tenaciously.

The smallness of the non-monetary stock of silver in China makes it reasonable to hold that silver stocks will play no great part in equipping China with the capital goods required for modern industry. The currency situation created by the proposed abandonment of the silver standard in November, 1935

[2] *The Review of Economic Statistics*, Cambridge, Mass., Nov. 1935, p. 6. Kann's estimate appeared in the *Chinese Economic Journal*, April, 1931, pp. 410-20, and that of Yavdynsky in *Finance and Commerce* (Shanghai), October 9, 1935.

may enable China to dispose of some part of her monetary stock of silver.[3] It is most unlikely, however, that China will be able to sell more than the amount of silver required to set up funds for the control of exchange. It is not unreasonable, even under the present changed circumstances, to disregard for our purposes the monetary stock of silver.

It may, however, be maintained that the Chinese economy, whether or not it has a reserve in the form of hoarded silver, does nevertheless show a potential surplus. This potential surplus, it may be claimed, is either prevented from coming into existence by forces which may be overcome or unproductively consumed in ways which may be altered. If every act of consumption to which the name unproductive may be applied were prevented throughout the whole of China, a surplus might be brought into existence. Whether a potential surplus in this sense is a possibility in China will be dealt with below. It is sufficient to observe here that it would require changes in long-established habits and in customs which are firmly rooted in the emotions of the mass of the people. The Chinese peasant, to give but a single example, feels that a wedding or a funeral must be properly celebrated whatever the cost. But the immediate problem concerns the possibility of checking military expenditure, banditry, and communist uprisings, which, it is frequently said, waste the substance of the people and prevent China from finding within her borders the means of economic development.

There is no doubt that the expense of civil war in China has been great during the period since 1911, and that the real cost has been borne by the Chinese people in some form. The significant question is whether these forms are such that under different circumstances the "surplus" so consumed might have been made available for capital equipment. As a matter of fact, much of this cost has been taken out of the Chinese

[3] Looking back in 1968 it may be said that the monetary stock of silver at the disposal of the Chinese government as the result of the abandonment of the silver standard in 1935 was used in large measure for defense expenditures after the outbreak of war with Japan in 1937.

people in ways which offer no possibility of use for the provision of funds for economic development. Illegal exactions levied upon merchants and farmers, forced labor by coolies and carters, the destruction of railway rolling stock, the deterioration of railway roadbeds and equipment; these are costs of civil war which do not demonstrate the existence of a surplus in any sense in which we are interested. Such costs as these were more common during the years before the establishment in 1928 of the nationalist government. After 1928 expenditures were more usually of such sorts as would, if they had not been made, have offered an opportunity to secure funds for economic development.

The most obvious of these is the item of military expenditure in the budget of the national government of China. In recent years this item has come to a total of about Chinese $300 million. How far a complete picture of the public finances of China would increase this by the addition of expenditures on the part of provincial and local governments is not known. It is not unlikely that the actual payment of funds on the part of governmental units of all sorts comes to a total of Chinese $500 million for the whole country. This represents a potential source of funds for economic development which is of first importance.

In view, however, of the problems which China faces at the present time, and must continue to face in the near future, it seems quite certain that a military establishment of considerable size will be maintained. There is little doubt that a thoroughly effective army and air force, to say nothing of other forms of defense, would require more than is now being expended, and that no important reduction in this expenditure may be expected. It is possible, of course, that a better army might be maintained at a smaller expense than is now being incurred, but the possible saving cannot, in any case, be great. It is more likely that an effective central government will continue to spend at least as much for military purposes as is now being expended.

With peace and order in China, and with such a solution of

Japanese relations as to make continued peace and order possible, there would be some return of hoarded silver to investment and there might be some reduction in military expenditures. Little more than this may be said. It is, of course, highly important in a country as poor as China to avoid every waste and to make use of every dollar; but our problem lies in the poverty of the Chinese people, rather than in the unconvincing evidence that they are not as poor as they seem. This leads us back to further comment upon traditional China.

Observation in a variety of fields leads to the conclusion that the Chinese economy presents very little potential surplus which might, under any circumstances, be used for the provision of capital equipment. The evidence for this lies in many studies of economic conditions in China. It will probably be sufficient to point to the relevant conclusions which have been reached in a few of these studies. Before doing so I wish to emphasize certain well-known facts about China. China is a country of agricultural villages. There is little doubt that three-fourths of the Chinese people live in such villages. Their chief dependence is upon farming. If it can be shown that Chinese agriculture brings little or nothing in the way of reserve, this demonstration will go far toward establishing the generalization that traditional China in general had little surplus.

It is the opinion of Professor Sarvis, an economist who has spent many years in China, that the majority of the population of China is below the poverty line, that four-fifths of those above the poverty line consume each year all that they produce, and that no saving for investment can be expected from 90 per cent of the population.[4] This is supported by the results of seven studies of family expenditures brought together by Professor L. K. Tao.[5] These studies show that the expenditures for food on the part of the laborers and poorer

---

[4] Sarvis, G. W., "The Standard of Living in China and Its Meaning," *Journal of Applied Sociology*, vol. 1X (1924-25), pp. 187-95.

[5] Tao, L. K., "Livelihood in Peking," China Foundation for the Promotion of Education and Culture, Peking, 1928.

classes come to an average of 70 per cent of the total expenditure.

The most complete and the most reliable study of the economics of Chinese agriculture has been made by Professor J. Lossing Buck of the University of Nanking.[6] The results of his studies were made public in 1930. Professor Buck studied nearly 3,000 farms in seventeen localities in China over the years 1921 to 1925. He found that the value of the buildings on these farms per hectare was Chinese $250, less than one-tenth of the corresponding figure for the United States; that the value of the equipment was about Chinese $50, one-sixteenth of the figure for the United States; and that the value of the livestock on the Chinese farms was about $70 per hectare, one-twentieth of the American figure. Professor Buck's studies show also that the application of labor in the United States, over a larger area and with much greater capital equipment, bring it about that "production per unit of labor is apparently at least twenty-five fold greater than in China."[7]

When one turns to the examination of these facts in terms of income, expenditure, and standard of living, it is no matter for surprise to find Professor Buck saying that "in general there is dearth of capital," that the absence of credit has been one of the chief factors impeding the progress of Chinese agriculture, and that an adequate and dependable transportation system is highly important. Professor Buck found the average payment per year to farm laborers to be Chinese $58, which includes the value of board; he found the average value of all goods consumed by the farm families to be Chinese $38.44 per capita, "a startlingly low figure upon which to maintain existence," and he found such illuminating facts as these: that many farmers are so poor that they retire early to save the expense of oil, and that in only one region studied was window glass used. When it does happen that an unusually large income is available as the result of a sudden rise

[6] Buck, J. Lossing, "Chinese Farm Economy," China Council of the Institute of Pacific Relations, Shanghai, 1930.

[7] Buck, op. cit., p. 23.

in prices, the farmers spend their extra funds in gambling, excessive drinking, and gorging themselves with food. Such a picture of life in the agricultural villages of China is a fairly effective answer to those who maintain that there is any considerable potential reserve for the provision of capital equipment.

More recent studies confirm the conclusions of Professor Buck in a striking manner. Certain investigations have been carried on under the National Economic Council of China in cooperation with the technical delegates of the League of Nations. Chekiang province, which is popularly held to be one of the richest in China, was given special attention.[8] The picture of Chekiang is that of a province given over almost entirely to the production of food for local consumption. "Five-sixths of the total human effort," says Sir Arthur Salter in his introductory comment, "is devoted to producing food consumed by the resident population." In addition there is some importation of food, and there is practically no surplus. Industrialization is upon the smallest scale. "Excluding public utilities, the total capitalization of all modern and semi-modern industries (the latter including even factories with very primitive equipment) is estimated at well below 10 million dollars." This is, it is to be borne in mind, for a province with a population of about 20 million people, and with an area of about 40,000 square miles, a province which has the reputation for being progressive. The whole picture presented in the detailed studies of such capable men as Professors Ho and Feng may be regarded as a demonstration that there is practically no surplus in Chekiang province in an ordinary year.

We may conclude then from the discussion up to this point that traditional China had relatively little capital equipment which was usable in the technology introduced from the West.

[8] The reports on Chekiang are to be found in *Annexes to the Report to the Council of the League of Nations of the Technical Delegate on his Mission in China from Date of Appointment until April 1, 1934*, Nanking, 1934, pp. 71, 166.

We may conclude also that there was in the Chinese economy
an absence of surplus or reserve by means of which to bring
such capital equipment into existence at home or to buy it
abroad. In short the Chinese economy was but poorly adapted
to modern methods of production and had little adaptability.

The explanation of this state of affairs may not be attempted
without careful study, and no one may say in advance of such
study where the explanation lies; but, if it were known, it
would probably prove to be fundamental to the explanation of
the disintegration of traditional China and thus of the course
of events in the Far East during the past forty years. It may
lie in the history of the growth of China's population. This is
a subject which remains obscure in many of its important
aspects, as competent students of China's population will
admit. If we can trust the information which is available to
us, we are forced to the conclusion that the population of
China increased rapidly between the years from about 1700
to about 1850. The evidence seems to show that the increase
in population was at a less rapid rate before 1700 and that the
growth has been at a much more moderate rate since 1850.
If this is true it may prove to be equally true that the growth
of the population of China reached such a point by 1850 as
to remove from the Chinese economy the resilience and adaptability which it needed when it met the new technology from
the West. It is an interesting fact that it was during the same
century and a half (1700-1850) that the population of Japan
is known to have remained stationary. We may have here a
population problem, but in the sense that it is one for the
economic historian of the Far East. What were the reasons
for so striking a difference between China and Japan during
the critical period before the beginnings of the industrial
revolution in the two countries? How did it happen that the
increase in the population of Japan has accompanied the
recent industrial changes while in China it preceded such
changes? There is no answer. It may be, however, that a
century and a half of peace and relatively effective govern-

ment brought about an increase in numbers and reduction in reserves in China which was to prove of critical importance at a later time.

THE AGENCIES OF CAPITAL FORMATION

Traditional China did bring together capital, and apply it, and my next question concerns the means or agencies by which this was done. This, in turn, leads to a related question as to how far the agencies which provided capital in traditional China have been effective in securing capital abroad for modern China. Here again we enter upon matters which must be dealt with rather tentatively for the study of the formation of capital in traditional China has hardly been touched.

Certain capital equipment was provided by the government of traditional China. Public works on a considerable scale, such as dikes, canals, and roads have been mentioned above. My immediate interest is in the methods by which the cost of such public works was met. In part such works were carried out by forced labor; in part they were paid for out of the revenues of the court raised by taxation. Forced labor seems to have been more common as we go back to earlier times. During the dynasty which came to an end in 1911, forced labor was seldom resorted to except for local purposes, at the command of local officials and to meet an emergency obvious to all, such as the repair of dikes to avert a threatened flood. The public revenue was more generally used for the construction of public works, especially in more recent periods. The public revenue was regarded as the income of the Emperor or the imperial court rather than as funds provided for public purposes. The application of such funds to the repair of dikes and the building of canals was looked upon by both the imperial court and the people as evidence of the gracious kindness of the Son of Heaven. The creation of capital equipment by the government in such ways as have been indicated played no great part in the economic life of traditional China.

In fact, the imperial government did not look upon it as its function to participate directly in the economic and industrial life of the people.

Below the imperial government was the actual day-by-day government by the officials. The point of view of the officials and of the people was to make official participation in economic matters unusual. From the point of view of the merchant, the handicraftsman, and the farmer, official participation of any sort was undesirable. A group of merchants contemplating some important venture were usually anxious to keep their plans from the knowledge of the officials. It has been pointed out by Morse and Burgess that a general reason for the creation and maintenance of guilds in China lies in the desire to present a united resistance to the demands of officials.[9] Forced labor at a time of emergency might be undertaken under their direction, but beyond this they had little to do with the provision of capital.

It may be pointed out also that the political organization of China did not promote the formation of capital by public borrowing. The public debt did not play the part in China that it did in the West. This seems difficult to explain when it is recalled that the issue of paper money was undertaken on more than one occasion. The transition from government paper money to government securities seems not to have been made. It is an interesting fact that Chinese merchants and bankers could not be persuaded to interest themselves in the bonds of the Chinese government when an effort was made to get them to do so by a British bank on the occasion of a loan by the bank to the Chinese government in 1875 or 1876. I mention this early case instead of later ones because there does not seem to have been at this time any prejudice against the loan for nationalistic reasons. We must conclude that the officials and the imperial court, that is, the government of traditional China, played no part in the formation of capital

[9] Morse, H. B., *The Gilds of China*, New York, 1909; Burgess, John Stewart, *The Gilds of Peking*, New York, 1928.

beyond the provision of certain public works.

When we turn to the private economy of traditional China, it is necessary to make distinctions. We must deal separately with agriculture, with handicraft industry, and with commerce. This is, of course, too neat a division. Domestic industry may be said to lie between agriculture and handicraft industry, and commercialized industry, the putting-out system, between handicraft industry and commerce. If we regard industrial organization in traditional China as reaching from agriculture at one extreme through domestic industry, handicraft industry, and commercialized industry to commerce at the other extreme, we may state it as generally true that capital was less available as we move from commerce toward agriculture.

Funds for the purchase of agricultural equipment and advances required for the carrying on of agriculture were secured by the Chinese farmer with difficulty and at rates of interest that seem shockingly high. It was usual to find rates of from 3 to 6 per cent a month and one does not dare to guess at the upper limit. The attempt was made to secure advances within the family or through friends of the family. If funds could not be secured in this way it was usual to apply to the pawnshop or to a merchant or large landowner in the neighborhood. There were also mutual aid societies of a variety of sorts, but they amounted to little as a source of capital since their membership was entirely local, and they did not have access to sources of funds outside the neighboring villages. Practices varied in different parts of China, and there have been such recent changes as the introduction of cooperative credit societies into parts of the country. In general it may be said that the Chinese farmer paid a high price for whatever advances he could secure. He had little equipment which he did not make for himself, he acquired this equipment with difficulty, and paid for it as he could. The capital available in traditional China was meagre and agriculture had but narrow access to it.

The tools and materials of the handicraft worker required

a greater outlay in money on the average than was necessary in the field of agriculture. The handicraftsman like the farmer found it difficult to secure the funds he required. He was accustomed to go first to members of his family and then to local merchants or moneylenders. He, also, paid a high price for funds. He was a member of a guild, but it was most unusual for the guild to concern itself with advances to its members. In the cases of both the handicraftsman and the farmer there seems to have been no access to or relation with the banking institutions of traditional China except as the banks advanced money to the pawnshops.

It is only when we turn to such operations as come under the control of merchants that we find a difference. Some industrial activities were under their control in ways which involved ownership by the merchant of equipment or raw material, or both, the turning over of such raw material and equipment to the worker for production within the household, the immediate payment at piece rates by the merchant for the finished product. This may be called the merchant-manufacturer system, or the putting-out system. Theatrical costumes, for example, were made at Soochow (Kiangsu province) under this plan. One element in the persistence and the spread of this system in China has undoubtedly been the fact that capital was more easily secured by the merchant than by the craftsman. The capital for the merchant-manufacturer system came in ways which were worked out for commerce rather than industrial operations, and we may turn to the provision of capital for commerce for further light upon this matter.

The merchant, of course, found it quite necessary to have funds for the carrying on of his business. The fact that the operations of the merchant were spread over a period of time seems to have been a less important factor in the development of commercial banking in China than the fact that these were spread over a fairly large territorial area. Exchange banking, that is, the transfer of funds between cities within China, was an early and a relatively well-developed form of banking in traditional China. It is probable that commercial banking in the usual sense of that term developed from exchange banking. The Shansi bankers were the best known in the country during the nineteenth century and exchange banking formed an important part of their business. But bankers and merchants provided funds for the financing of commerce on a scale which is surprising when one considers the poverty of the country. It was in this field that traditional China came nearest to bringing together adequate capital. Traditional China seems to have been better organized, in this as well as in other respects, for trade than for industry.

In the brief references above to the economic organization of traditional China, we have a part of the answer to my next question, which may be put thus: Why were the means which traditional China worked out for the provision of capital funds and capital equipment not applied to the development of modern industry when modern methods became available to the Chinese? The general answer lies in the poverty of the Chinese economy. What has been frequently referred to as the conservatism of the Chinese is in part the result of poverty. Those who are without any surplus or reserve do not readily undertake things that are new or experimental. This was, I may repeat, particularly true of agriculture and handicraft industry. In these fields the provision of capital was so inadequate that the question need hardly be considered. Even the growth in the early export industries, such as tea and silk, brought no notable changes in these industries so far as the Chinese farmer was concerned. There was, it is true, a fairly early introduction of silk filatures, but this change was introduced by the merchants, both Chinese and foreign, rather than by the farmers who produced the silk. It is not easy to see why the Chinese merchants and bankers did not introduce modern equipment into other fields. Among the reasons one may mention the power of custom, the attitude of the officials and the government, and the whole economic condition of the country dominated by poverty and the absence of a surplus.

THE IMPORTATION OF CAPITAL

If the capital at home was inadequate, why did not those

who were most effective in bringing together such capital as was available within China turn to foreign sources and import capital? We may eliminate the farmer and the craftsman once more and direct the question to the merchant and banker. Why did not the Chinese merchants import capital from abroad and in this way provide the Chinese economy with modern capital equipment? The merchants and bankers were the most effective means of bringing together capital in the domestic field; why did they not enter the foreign field? As a matter of fact they have played a very modest role in Chinese industry and economic development based upon foreign capital, and agencies less effective within the country have played a role of greater importance in the importation of capital. This situation requires some examination.

In the first place it is to be observed that the Chinese business man has brought some capital into the country from abroad in his own way. The Chinese merchant has gone into every country on the shores of the Pacific Ocean. The Chinese laborer has gone to these countries also and he has in many cases become a merchant, a landowner, or business man. Chinese are engaged in the greatest variety of enterprises. They run rice mills in Siam, tin mines in Malaya, sugar estates in the Netherlands Indies, wholesale and retail establishments in the Philippines. In short, the Chinese has made money and he has brought funds back with him to China or he has sent them back to the family in China. Insofar as these funds have gone to meet the ordinary expenses of the family, they have not been available for investment in industry. But funds have been remitted to China for investment on a fairly large scale. In the past such funds have gone very largely into the purchase of land. There has been relatively little modern industrial development in the parts of China, the southeastern coast especially, to which Chinese abroad have sent large sums. And there is no doubt that funds on a much larger scale have at all times been at the disposal of the Chinese business man overseas. In the holdings of Chinese abroad we have the greatest reserve available to the Chinese economy. That it has not been more effectively used in the development of China is a constant source of wonder to the student of China's economic problems.

It is true that Chinese have gone overseas and have made money which has been remitted to China, but the question still remains as to why the Chinese merchants at home have not imported funds to be invested within the country. That they have not done so finds confirmation in the following facts. In the study of foreign investments in China[10] I gave particular attention to investments by foreigners in Chinese corporations. Such investments were found to be extremely small and to be confined to the Japanese only. What is more, the Japanese business men and bankers who had made such investments were inclined to the opinion that their efforts had been a failure. There were perhaps U. S. $39 million in such investments in 1931, but even this small sum includes Japanese loans to Chinese corporations which had special relations with the Chinese government. If we look beyond Japanese investments and undertake to make an estimate for 1935, the total sum would be somewhat larger, but it would certainly be less than 2 per cent of the total foreign investment in China. It must be repeated that the Chinese merchant and banker, relatively effective in securing capital within the Chinese economy, have not been successful in bringing capital into China from outside.

This generalization may be illustrated by the facts from another related field. Foreign investment in China is, and has been, very largely direct investment. Direct investment takes the concrete form of business property in China owned by the foreigner or by the foreign corporation and under foreign control and management. It is such investment as that of the Standard Oil Company or the British-American Tobacco Company. It is foreign investment in China which leaves the business risk with the foreigner. Direct investment is the result of the fact that the foreign business man has come to China, which means that the Chinese business man has not gone abroad for funds.

[10] See pp. 82, 104-6, 412-14, 507-13.

My estimate of the total foreign investment in China in 1931 was U. S. $3,300 million. Of this total I found no less than 78 per cent to consist of direct investments, and the remainder, 22 per cent, to be investment in the obligations of the Chinese government. China is, I maintained, probably the world's outstanding example of the preponderance of direct investments. When it is added that I was able to disregard in reaching my totals the foreign borrowings of Chinese corporations, merchants, and bankers, the evidence is quite conclusive. China's most effective means in the domestic field of bringing together capital funds was ineffective in the foreign field. The Chinese economy was not adaptable to modern industry and modern economic relations.

The Chinese government, as has been pointed out above, was not, in traditional China, an important factor in the formation and application of capital. Nevertheless, the Chinese government has been the chief agency, on the Chinese side and under Chinese control, of bringing capital into the country. The new place of the Chinese government in this field has been one of a whole set of adjustments and changes which indicate to the student the nature of the new political institutions which were, it seemed, being built up in China in the 1930's. In other words, Chinese political organization of an enduring sort must be founded upon economic realities, among them the need of the Chinese economy for capital from abroad.

When China became acquainted with the technology of the West, the weight of tradition was against the introduction of this technology under the leadership of the government. An observer of Chinese economic conditions in 1835 or 1845 would probably have looked for the introduction of modern industry by the business men of China. Early efforts were, indeed, made by business men. The first important Chinese corporation in the field of steam shipping was the China Merchants' Steam Navigation Company. This Company was not, in spite of its name, entirely free of participation by government officials. Moreover, it was granted special privileges by the Chinese government. But it was not a government-owned and government-controlled corporation.[11] Fears and hopes were freely expressed during the early years of the China Merchants' Steam Navigation Company that foreign shipping would shortly be driven from the river and coastwise trade, when once the Chinese business man seriously entered the field. In 1935, however, steam shipping on the rivers and along the coast of China continued to be under the control of foreign corporations. Foreign flags covered fully half of such shipping, and, what is more significant from our point of view, the Company was now entirely in the hands of the Chinese government. The railways of China in 1935 were owned and operated either by foreign corporations or by the Chinese government. Failure had marked the efforts of the Chinese business man to enter this field. Air transportation was in the hands of government-owned corporations with participation by American and German capital. In general modern transportation was introduced into China by the government or by the foreigner; the Chinese business man has been of little importance.

There were, of course, fields in which private business played a larger part than in modern transportation. The cotton textile industry was developed in China by the Chinese business man and by the foreign corporation. This industry and flour milling were the chief examples of the activity of the Chinese business men in the introduction of modern equipment and in securing the assistance of foreign capital. In these industries, and in a number of others of minor importance, some investment of foreign capital was brought in by the purchase of machinery and equipment under long-term credits. The terms under which such equipment was purchased make it difficult in particular cases to determine whether we have to do with an importation of capital by the Chinese business man or a direct investment by the foreigner.

[11] The Company was formed in 1872, and information concerning it is to be found in the annual reports of the Chinese Maritime Customs of about this period, as for instance in the *Reports on Trade*, 1876, p. 99, where an account is to be found of the purchase during that year of the river fleet of a well-known American corporation.

Conclusion

The Chinese economy had been in touch with the West for about a century. If the technology revealed to China by these contacts was to be brought into the country, it was necessary to secure capital from abroad. The traditional economic organization of China was such as to make her merchants and bankers the only effective means of securing and applying funds. Agriculture and handicraft industry had no effective means at their disposal. The imperial government was remote and looked from a lofty height upon business and economic life. The officials were not without willingness to give attention to business, but this attention was something that the merchants and bankers desired to avoid. Government and officials took little part in the formation of capital or in economic leadership. But after a century of modern international economic relations and of possible access to foreign capital, the chief Chinese agency for importing capital has been the agency least effective in capital formation at home, that is, the government. Chinese business men have gone abroad and have been successful throughout the Pacific area. They have brought funds into China, but such funds have played only a small part in the development of modern industry. Modern technology has come to China through the direct investment of foreigners or through the borrowings of the Chinese government.

The explanation of this situation lies in a whole set of related facts. The merchants and bankers of China have been dominated by custom and tradition to so great an extent as to take the flexibility and adaptability from their business organization. They have not succeeded in making effective use of the corporation, or in working out another form of business organization which would give them access to foreign funds. They have been fearful of the officials of their government, and have hesitated to embark upon enterprises involving borrowing abroad. Both business men and officials have had brought home to them the political dangers involved in foreign borrowing under the conditions which have prevailed in the Far East during the past century.

From the point of view of the Chinese government, the explanation lies in part in the fact that it had foreign borrowing forced upon it. The government was obliged to borrow in order to meet the indemnity payments which it agreed to make in the Treaty of Shimonoseki, at the end of the Chinese-Japanese War in 1895. The government found itself a debtor on a large scale as a result of the Boxer settlement. Boxer indemnity payments brought a close contact with foreign financial institutions, and this facilitated borrowing. The Chinese government had, in fact, paid out over the fifty years before 1935 more in the way of indemnities and upon indemnity loans than it received for economic development through its borrowings from abroad.

But the Chinese government has imported capital. This has been pointed out above. The government has come to understand something of the part which modern Western governments and the Japanese government play in the economic life of their respective countries. In addition, modern foreign relations and modern economic development within the country have been accompanied by a rise of nationalism which had by 1935 forced upon the Chinese government a stronger and more immediate interest in agriculture and industry. The spread of socialism and the rise of Soviet Russia have produced their effect, for the Chinese government, although it stood aloof from economic activities in the past, has behind it a tradition of competence in all fields which is quite consistent with modern socialism. The Chinese government is adapting itself to the modern world in ways which have included the importation of foreign capital.

Chinese business organization is adapting itself to the modern world in its way, but this adaptation has not, so far, included the development of effective means for importing capital. In considering future possibilities, the Chinese overseas are not to be forgotten. China may well enter upon a new period when the Chinese abroad begin to invest in China on a large scale. If the Chinese overseas are able to develop access to capital funds in the countries to which they have gone, they may come to play a major role in the economic reorganization of the country.

Throughout the preceding pages it has been maintained that capital for China is of fundamental importance, and that capital must come in large part from outside the country. By "capital" I mean either capital equipment or funds destined to bring capital equipment into existence. A student of China's history during the past hundred years might assert that foreign capital for China in the 1930's has not consisted of capital equipment or funds destined for its creation, but has consisted rather of funds destined for the creation of political ascendancy or for the establishment of special political position in China.

The difference here is, in part, one of exposition or of emphasis in exposition. It is not possible to proceed as if international economic and political problems could be entirely separated. It is a question of which to put first. But the difference is, in part, deeper than this. It rests upon one's judgment as to whether, at the present stage of China's history, the solution of the economic or the political problem is the more fundamental, granted, again, that they cannot be entirely separated. My own estimate of the situation is that the poverty of the mass of the Chinese people presents the problem which is, after all, fundamental.

BIBLIOGRAPHY

This book list is not exhaustive. The preceding study has, however, involved a search for information over a fairly wide field and those who have occasion to deal with China's economic relations may find the list convenient. It includes few publications which have not been found directly useful. Titles are brought together under general headings with an indication of the chapters which fall under each heading. Works containing general or commercial statistics published by the League of Nations or by national governments have not been listed.

PART I

General

Chapters I, II, III, IV, XIII, XIV

Adams, Henry C. "International Supervision over Foreign Investments," *American Economic Review*, Vol. X, March, 1920

Arnold, Julean. *China—A Commercial and Industrial Handbook*, Trade Promotion Series No. 28, Dept. of Commerce, Washington, 1926

Arnold, Julean. "The Commercial Problems of China," *The Annals of the American Academy of Political and Social Science*, Vol. 152, Philadelphia, November, 1930

Bain, H. Foster. *Ores and Industry in the Far East*, Council on Foreign Relations, New York, 1927

Baker, John Earl. *Explaining China*, London, 1927

Baker, O. E. "Land Utilization in China," *Problems of the Pacific, 1927* (edited by J. B. Condliffe), Chicago, 1928

Beaulieu, Pierre Leroy. *The Awakening of the Far East*, translated by Richard Davey, London, 1900

Becqué, Emile. *L'Internationalisation des Capitaux*, Imprimière Général du Midi, Montpellier, 1912

Beresford, Lord Charles. *The Break-up of China*, New York, 1899

Bishop, Carl Whiting. "The Geographical Factor in the Development of Chinese Civilization," *The Geographical Review*, Vol. XII, No. 1, New York, January, 1922

Blakeslee, George H. *The Pacific Area*, World Peace Foundation Pamphlets, Vol. XII, No. 3, Boston, 1929

Brown, H. D. "A Survey of Fifty Farms on the Chengin Plain, Szechwan," *Chinese Economic Journal*, Vol. II, Peking, January–June, 1928

Buck, John Lossing. "Agriculture and the Future of China," *The Annals of the American Academy of Political and Social Science*, Vol. 152, Philadelphia, November, 1930

Buck, John Lossing. *Chinese Farm Economy*, China Council of the Institute of Pacific Relations, Shanghai, 1930

Buck, John Lossing. *An Economic and Social Survey of 150 Farms, Yenshan County, Chihli Province, China*, Nanking, June, 1926

Burgess, John Stewart. *The Guilds of Peking*, New York, 1928

Buxton, L. H. Dudley. *China: The Land and the People*, Oxford, 1929

Chen, Chang-heng. *China's Population Problem* (XIX° Session de l'Institut International de Statistique, Tokyo, 1930), Shanghai, 1930

Chen, Huang-chang. *The Economic Principles of Confucius and His School*, Columbia Studies, New York, 1911

Chen, Ping Tsang. "Nationalist Policies of Financial and Economic Reconstruction," *St. John's Echo*, Vol. XL, No. 1, Shanghai, January, 1929

Chen, Warren H. *An Estimate of the Population of China in 1929* (XIX° Session de l'Institut International de Statistique, Tokyo, 1930), Shanghai, 1930

China and the Far East, Clark University Lectures (edited by George H. Blakeslee), New York, 1910

Christian Occupation of China, The, China Continuation Committee, Shanghai, 1922

Clyde, Paul Hibbert. *International Rivalries in Manchuria, 1869–1922*, Contributions in History and Political Science, Columbus, 1926

Conant, Charles A. *The United States in the Orient*, Cambridge, 1900

Condliffe, J. B. *China Today: Economic*, Boston, 1932

Condliffe, J. B. "Industrial Development in the Far East," *The Chinese Social and Political Science Review*, Vol. XII, No. 3, Peking, 1928

Couling, Samuel. *The Encyclopaedia Sinica*, London, 1917
Cressey, George B. "The Geographic Regions of China," *The Annals of the American Academy of Political and Social Science*, Vol. 152, Philadelphia, November, 1930

Daszyńska-Golińska, Sophie. *La Chine et le système physiocratique en France*, Varsaviae, 1922
D'Elia, The Rev. Pascal M. "The Life of Dr. Sun Yat Sen," *North China Daily News*, Shanghai, October 25, 26, 27, 28, 29, 1930
Dittmer, C. G. "An Estimate of the Standard of Living in China," *Quarterly Journal of Economics*, Vol. 33, No. 1, Boston, November, 1918
Dolsen, James H. *The Awakening of China*, Chicago, 1926

Elliston, Herbert B. "China in the World Family," *Foreign Affairs*, New York, July, 1929
Erkes, Eduard. *China*, Gotha, 1919

Feis, Herbert. *Europe: The World's Banker, 1870–1914*, Council on Foreign Relations, New Haven, 1930
Feng, Chaoi. *Der Aussenhandel Chinas von 1913–1923*, Leipzig, 1926
Foreign Policy Association. "The Rise of the Kuomingtang," *Information Service*, Vol. IV, No. 8, New York, June 22, 1928

Gamble, Sidney D. (assisted by John Stewart Burgess). *Peking: A Social Survey*, New York, 1921.
Giles, Herbert A. *The Civilization of China*, New York, 1911
Granet, Marcel. *Chinese Civilization*, New York, 1930
Great Britain, Dept. of Overseas Trade:
The Commercial, Industrial, and Economic Situation of China to September 1, 1928, report by H. H. Fox. Together with a *Report on the Trade of South Manchuria*, by E. M. Dening, London, 1928
Economic Conditions in China to September 1, 1929, report by H. H. Fox. Together with *An Annex on the Trade of South Manchuria*, by W. B. Cunningham, London, 1930
Economic Conditions in China to August 30, 1930, report by E. G. Jamieson. Together with *An Annex on the Trade of South Manchuria*, by W. B. Cunningham, London, 1930

Harris, Norman D. *Europe and the East*, Boston, 1926

Hobson, C. K. *The Export of Capital*, New York, 1914

Holcombe, Arthur N. *The Chinese Revolution*, Cambridge, 1930

Hornbeck, Stanley K. *China Today: Political*, World Peace Foundation Pamphlets, Vol. X, No. 5, Boston, 1927

Hornbeck, Stanley K. *Contemporary Politics in the Far East*, New York, 1916

Hovde, Brynjolf J. "Socialistic Theories of Imperialism," *Journal of Political Economy*, Chicago, October, 1928

Hsia, Ching-lin. *The Status of Shanghai*, China Council of the Institute of Pacific Relations, Shanghai, 1929

Hsieh, Pao Chao. *The Government of China (1644–1911)*, Baltimore, 1925

Hsu, Leonard S. "The Population Problem in China," *Sociology and Social Research*, Vol. XIII, No. 5, Los Angeles, May–June, 1929

Hu, Shih. *The Development of Logical Method in Ancient China*, Shanghai, 1922

Hu, Shih. "The Civilizations of the East and the West," in Charles A. Beard's *Whither Mankind*, New York, 1928

Inouye, Junnosuke. *The Economic and Industrial Development of Modern Japan*, Japanese Council of the Institute of Pacific Relations, Tokyo, 1929

King, F. H. *Farmers of Forty Centuries*, Madison, Wisconsin, 1911

Kries, Wilhelm von. "Entwicklungstendenzen in der Chinesischen Volkswirtschaft," *Weltwirtschaftliches Archiv*, Jena, 1914

Kulp, Daniel Harrison. *Country Life in South China: The Sociology of Familism*, New York, 1925

La Fleur, Albert, and Foscue, Edwin J. "Agricultural Production in China," *Economic Geography*, Vol. III, No. 3, 1927

Latourette, Kenneth Scott. *The Development of China*, Boston, 1929

Laufer, Berthold. "Some Fundamental Ideas of Chinese Culture," *Journal of Race Development*, Vol. V, Worcester, 1914–1915

Lee, Mabel Ping-hua. *The Economic History of China*, Columbia Studies, New York, 1921

Lefort, J. "Les Physiocrates et la Chine," *Journal des Economistes*, 6ᵉ serie—Tome LXXX, Paris, January, 1925

Li, Chi. *The Formation of the Chinese People*, Cambridge, 1928

Liang, Chi-chao. *History of Chinese Political Thought During the Early Tsin Period*, London, 1930

Lieu, D. K. *China's Industries and Finance*, Chinese Bureau of Economic Information, Peking, 1927

Lieu, D. K. *Statistical Work in China* (XIXe Session de l'Institut International de Statistique, Tokyo, 1930), Shanghai, 1930

Lin, D. Y. *Some Economic Features of Chinese Agriculture*, Shanghai, February, 1922

MacMurray, John V. A. *Treaties and Agreements With or Concerning China, 1894–1919* (Vol. I, Manchu Period, 1894–1911) (Vol. II, Republican Period, 1912–1919), Carnegie Endowment for International Peace, Washington, 1921

MacNair, H. F. *China in Revolution*, Chicago, 1931

MacNair, H. F. *Modern Chinese History: Selected Readings*, Shanghai, 1927

MacNair, H. F. "The Political History of China Under the Republic," *The Annals of the American Academy of Political and Social Science*, Vol. 152, Philadelphia, November, 1930

Mallory, Walter H. *China: Land of Famine*, American Geographical Society, New York, 1926

Marakueff, A. V. *Foreign Trade of China and Its Place in World Trade* (Manchuria Research Society, Ser. D., No. 10), Harbin, 1927

McCordock, R. Stanley. *British Far Eastern Policy, 1894–1900*, Columbia Studies, New York, 1931

Meadows, T. T. *The Chinese and Their Rebellions*, London, 1856

Moon, Parker Thomas. *Imperialism and World Politics*, New York, 1926

Morse, Hosea Ballou. *The International Relations of the Chinese Empire*, Shanghai, 1918

Morse, Hosea Ballou, and MacNair, Harley Farnsworth. *Far Eastern International Relations*, Boston, 1931

"Nationalist Government of the Republic of China," *European Economic and Political Survey*, Vol. IV, Nos. 11–12, Paris, February 15, 1928–1929

Nearing, Scott. *Whither China*, New York, 1927

Nelson, John H. *Changing Factors in the Economic Life of China*, U. S. Dept. of Commerce: Trade Information Bulletin No. 312, Washington, 1925

Norton, Henry Kittredge. *The Far Eastern Republic of Siberia*, London, 1923

Otte, Friedrich. *China: Wirtschaftspolitische Landeskunde*, Gotha, 1927

Peffer, Nathaniel. *The White Man's Dilemma*, New York, 1927
Pott, F. L. Hawks. *A Sketch of Chinese History*, Shanghai, 1923
Pott, William S. A. *Chinese Political Philosophy*, New York, 1925
Problems of the Pacific, 1927 (edited by J. B. Condliffe), Chicago, 1928
Problems of the Pacific, 1929 (edited by J. B. Condliffe), Chicago, 1930
Problems of the Pacific, 1931 (edited by Bruno Lasker), Chicago, 1932

Quigley, Harold S. *Chinese Politics and the Foreign Powers*, International Conciliation, February, 1927

Remer, C. F. *The Foreign Trade of China*, Shanghai, 1926
Remer, C. F. *Readings in Economics for China*, Shanghai, 1922
Rockhill, William Woodhill. *An Inquiry into the Population of China*, Annual Report of the Board of Regents of the Smithsonian Institution for the year ending June 30, 1904, Washington, 1905
Roxby, Percy M. "The Distribution of Population in China," *The Geographical Review*, Vol. XV, No. 1, New York, January, 1925

Sakuda, S. "Some Characteristics of the Chinese National Economy," *Kyoto University Economic Review*, Vol. I, No. 2, Kyoto, December, 1926
Sargent, A. J. *Anglo-Chinese Commerce and Diplomacy (Mainly in the Nineteenth Century)*, Oxford, 1907
Sarvis, Guy W. "The Standard of Living in China and Its Meaning," *Journal of Applied Sociology*, Vol. IX, Los Angeles, 1924–1925
Scholz, Oskar. *China*, Berlin, 1928
Schrieke, B. *The Effect of Western Influence on Native Civilizations in the Malay Archipelago*, Batavia, Java, 1929
See, Chong Su. *The Foreign Trade of China*, Columbia Studies, New York, 1919
Shing, T., and Wong, W. H. *An Outline of the Power Resources of China*, Transactions of the First World Power Conference, London, 1925
Simon, G. Eug. *La Cité Chinoise*, 6me edition, Paris, 1890

Smith, Wilfred. *Coal and Iron in China*, Liverpool, 1926

Soong, T. V. "The Taxation Policy of the Nationalist Government," *St. John's Echo*, Vol. XL, No. 1, Shanghai, January, 1929

Spykman, Nicholas J. "The Social Background of Asiatic Nationalism," *American Journal of Sociology*, Vol. XXXII, No. 3, Chicago, November, 1926

Stamp, L. Dudley. *Asia: An Economic and Regional Geography*, New York, 1929

Steiger, George Nye. *China and the Occident: The Origin and Development of the Boxer Movement*, New Haven, 1927

Su, Sing Ging. *The Chinese Family System*, New York, 1922

Sun, Yat-sen. *The International Development of China*, Shanghai, 1920

Sun, Yat-sen. *San Min Chu I*, translated into English by Frank W. Price (edited by L. T. Chen), China Committee of the Institute of Pacific Relations, Shanghai, 1927

Suranyi-Unger, Theo. "Der Wirtschaftskampf um dem Stillen Ozean," *Weltwirtschaftliches Archiv*, Jena, January, 1930

T'ang Leang-li. *The Foundations of Modern China*, London, 1928

T'ao, L. K. "Handicraft Workers of Peking," *Chinese Social and Political Science Review*, Vol. XIII, No. 1, Peking, 1929

T'ao, L. K. *Livelihood in Peking*, China Foundation for the Promotion of Education and Culture, Peking, 1928

Taylor, J. B. *Farm and Factory in China*, London, 1928

Tegengren, F. R. *The Iron Ores and Iron Industry of China*, Peking, 1924

Théry, François. *Les Sociétés de Commerce en Chine*, Tientsin, 1929

Ting, V. K., and Wong, W. H. *General Statement on the Mining Industry*, Special Report of Geological Survey of China, No. 1, Peking, 1921

Torgasheff, Boris P. *Coal, Iron, and Oil in the Far East* (a digest prepared by the Institute of Pacific Relations), Honolulu, 1929

Treaties and Agreements With and Concerning China, 1919–1929, Carnegie Endowment for International Peace, Division of International Law, Pamphlet No. 50, Washington, 1929

U. S. Dept. of Commerce. *Changes in the Economic Life of the Chinese People*, Trade Information Bulletin No. 5, Washington, 1922

Viallate, Achille. *Economic Imperialism and International Relations During the Last Fifty Years*, New York, 1923

Vinacke, Harold M. *A History of the Far East in Modern Times*, New York, 1928

Vinacke, Harold M. *Problems of the Industrial Development of China*, Princeton, 1926

Viner, Jacob. "International Free Trade in Capital," *Scientia*, Vol. XXXIX, Bologna, January, 1926

Voskuil, Walter. "The Iron and Steel Industry of China," *The Annals of the American Academy of Political and Social Science*, Vol. 152, Philadelphia, November, 1930

Ware, Edith E. *Business and Politics in the Far East*, New Haven, 1932

Weber, Max. *General Economic History* (translated by F. H. Knight), New York, 1927

Whyte, Sir Frederick. *China and the Foreign Powers*, London, 1928

Wilhelm, Richard. *A Short History of Chinese Civilization* (translated by Joan Joshua), New York, 1929

Wilkinson, H. P. *The Family in Classical China*, Shanghai, 1926

Willcox, Walter F. "The Population of China in 1910," *Journal of the American Statistical Association*, Vol. XXIII, New Series No. 161, New York, 1928

Willcox, Walter F. "A Westerner's Effort to Estimate the Population of China and Its Increase Since 1650," *Bulletin de l'Institut International de Statistique*, Tome XXV, 3eme livraison, La Haye, 1931

Williams, E. T. *China Yesterday and Today*, New York, 1929

Willoughby, W. W. *China at the Conference*, Baltimore, 1922

Wittfogel, K. A. *Wirtschaft und Gesellschaft Chinas*, Leipzig, 1931

Wong, Ching-wai. *China and the Nations*, London, 1927

Wong, William. *Mineral Wealth of China*, Shanghai, 1927

Woolf, Leonard. *Economic Imperialism*, London, 1920

Wu, Kuo-cheng. *Ancient Chinese Political Theories*, Shanghai, 1928

Yashnov, E. E. *Chinese Farming in Northern Manchuria* (digest and translation by Lewis L. Lorwin of a volume published in Russian by the Economic Bureau of the Chinese Eastern Railway, Harbin, 1926), prepared for the Institute of Pacific Relations, Honolulu, 1929

Foreign Investments

Chapters V, VI, VII, VIII

American Chamber of Commerce, *Memorandum Relative to Extraterritoriality in China*, Tientsin, 1925

Baker, John Earl. "Transportation in China," *The Annals of the American Academy of Political and Social Science*, Vol. 152, Philadelphia, November, 1930

Bank of China, *Chinese Government Loan Issues and Obligations*, Shanghai, 1930

Barry, Arthur John. "Railway Development in China," *Journal of the Royal Society of Arts*, Vol. LVII, London, 1909

Baylin, J. R. *Foreign Loan Obligations of China*, Tientsin, 1925

Bratter, Herbert M. *Public Finances of Far Eastern Countries, Fourth (1929) Survey*, Dept. of Commerce, Washington, 1929

Chai, Hay Tsau. *La Situation Economique et Politique de la Chine et ses Perspectives d'avenir*, Louvain, 1921

Chamberlain, J. P. *Foreign Flags in China's Internal Navigation*, American Council of the Institute of Pacific Relations, New York, 1931

Chang, Ying-hua. *The Financial Reconstruction of China*, Peking, 1923

China, Republic of, Government Bureau of Economic Information:
Statement of Short Term Internal Loans of China as of January, 1920, supplement No. 4
Statement of Foreign Debts of Chinese Government Railways as of January, 1922, supplement No. 5
Foreign Loans of China Secured on the Customs and Salt Revenues as of October 1, 1922, supplement No. 10, January 20, 1923
Foreign Loans of China Which Are Not Definitely Secured, as of October 1, 1922, supplement No. 14
Comparative Statement of Salt Revenue Deposited in and Withdrawn from the Group Banks During the Two Years, 1920 and 1921, supplement No. 6
Comparative Statement of Receipts and Disbursements of Salt Revenue for the Years 1919 and 1920, supplement No. 16

China, Republic of, Financial Readjustment Commission:
Outstanding Debts of the Ministry of Communications, October, 1925

Tables of Inadequately Secured Domestic Loans of the Ministry of Finance, October, 1925

Tables of Inadequately Secured Foreign Loans of the Ministry of Finance, October, 1925

China, Republic of, Ministry of Finance:
Annual Report for the Fiscal Year, July, 1928 to June, 1929, Nanking, 1930

Annual Report for the Fiscal Year, July, 1929, to June, 1930, Nanking, 1931

Coons, Arthur G. *The Foreign Public Debt of China*, Philadelphia, 1930

"Foreign Investments in China," *The China Critic*, Vol. 1, No. 19, Shanghai, October 4, 1928

Foreign Policy Association, "Foreign Interests in China," *Information Service*, Vol. II, No. 25, New York, February 16, 1927

Funatsu, Tatsuichiro. *Nationalist Attitude Towards Foreign Industrial Establishments in China*, Japanese Council of the Institute of Pacific Relations, Tokyo, 1929

Great Britain, Foreign Office, "Correspondence Respecting Chinese Loan Negotiations," *China*, No. 2, 1912 (Cd. 6446), London, 1912

Grünfeld, Ernst. *Hafenkolonien und Kolonieähnlich Verhaltnisse in China, Japan, und Korea*, Jena, 1913

Harvey, T. Edmund. "International Extortion in China," *Contemporary Review*, Vol. 105, London, March, 1914

Ho, Franklin L., and Fong, Hsien Ding. *Extent and Effects of Industrialization in China* (a data paper submitted to the Biennial Conference of the Institute of Pacific Relations, October, 1929), Tientsin, 1929

Hodges, Charles. "China's 'Credit Power' and the Consortium," reprint from the *China Review*, January and February, 1922

Hornbeck, Stanley K. "Trade, Concessions, Investments: Conflict and Policy," *Academy of Political Science Proceedings*, Vol. VII, New York, July, 1917

Hsu, Mongton Chih. *Railway Problems in China*, Columbia Studies, New York, 1915

Huang, Feng-hua. *Public Debts in China*, Columbia Studies, New York, 1919

Joseph, Philip. *Foreign Diplomacy in China, 1894–1900*, London, 1928

Kann, Eduard. *Chinese Government Secured Foreign Loans Outstanding on January 1, 1929* (compiled by E. Kann, Shanghai, with the co-operation of Mons. J. Baylin, Peiping), *China Year Book, 1929–1930*, p. 658a
Kann, Eduard. "The Foreign Loans of China," *Finance and Commerce*, Vol. 19, Nos. 84, 85, 86, 87, Shanghai, January 7, 14, 21, 28, 1931
Kann, Eduard. "Chinese Internal Loan Issues Outstanding on January 1, 1931," *Finance and Commerce*, Vol. 19, Shanghai, December 31, 1930
Keeton, G. W. *The Development of Extraterritoriality in China*, New York, 1928
Kent, Percy H. *Railway Enterprise in China*, London, 1907
King, Miss S. T., and Lieu, D. K. *China's Cotton Industry* (a paper presented at the Conference of the Institute of Pacific Relations, 1929), Shanghai, 1929
Koch, Waldemar. *Die Industrialisierung Chinas*, Berlin, 1910

Laboulaye, Edouard de. *Les Chemins de Fer de Chine*, Paris, 1911
Li, Chuan Shih. *Central and Local Finance in China*, New York, 1922
Lieu, D. K. *Foreign Investments in China* (a paper prepared for the Kyoto Conference of the Institute of Pacific Relations), Shanghai, 1929
Lieu, D. K. *Foreign Investments in China, 1931*, China Council of the Institute of Pacific Relations, Shanghai, 1931
Lieu, D. K. "Problems of Economic Reconstruction," *The China Critic*, Vol. I, No. 2, pp. 35–6, Shanghai, June 2, 1928
Liu, S. Y. "China's Debts and Their Readjustment," *Chinese Economic Journal*, Vol. V, No. 3, Peking, September, 1929
Lobengier, Charles S. "Extraterritoriality," *Corpus Juris*, Vol. XXV, New York, 1921

MacMurray, J. V. A. "Problems of Foreign Capital in China," *Foreign Affairs* (New York), Vol. III, No. 3. Reprinted in Arnold, Julean, *China, A Commercial and Industrial Handbook*, Washington, 1926
Maguire, C. R. (compiler). *The China Stock and Share Handbook, 1929, 1930*, Shanghai, 1929, 1930

The Nanking Government's Laws and Regulations Affecting Trade, Commerce, Finance, etc. Issued annually by British Chamber of Commerce, Shanghai.

Padoux, G. *The Financial Reconstruction of China and the Consolidation of China's Present Indebtedness*, Peking, 1924

Quigley, Harold S. "Foreign Concessions in Chinese Hands," *Foreign Affairs*, Vol. VII, pp. 150–5, New York, 1928–1929

Railways of China, The, The National Review (China), Shanghai, 1913

Shanghai Municipal Council, *Report of the Hon. Mr. Justice Feetham, C. M. G.* (three volumes), Shanghai, 1931
Shaw, Kinn Wei. *Democracy and Finance in China*, New York, 1926
Shotwell, James T. *Extraterritoriality in China*, American Council of the Institute of Pacific Relations, New York, 1929
Special Conference on the Chinese Customs Tariff, The, Peking, 1928
Stringer, H. *The Chinese Railway System*, Tientsin, 1925

Tcheou, Jeungens. *Des Dettes Publiques Chinoises*, Paris, 1927
Thomas, E. P. "Investment and Trade in China," *Academy of Political Science Proceedings*, Vol. VI, pp. 154–62, New York, October, 1915
Tribolet, Leslie Bennett. *The International Aspects of Electrical Communications in the Pacific Area*, Baltimore, 1929

U. S. Dept. of Commerce:
    Far Eastern Markets for Railway Materials, Equipment, and Supplies, Frank Rhea, Trade Commissioner, Washington, 1919
    Public Finances of Far Eastern Countries, Washington, 1929
    Financial Developments in the Far East During 1929, Washington, 1930
    Chinese Currency and Finance, Ferrin, A. W., Special Agents Series, No. 186, Washington, 1919
U. S. Dept. of State:
    Report of the Commission on Extraterritoriality in China, Washington, 1926

Vinacke, Harold M. "Obstacles to Industrial Development in China," *The Annals of the American Academy of Political and Social Science*, Vol. 152, Philadelphia, November, 1930

Willoughby, Westel W. *Foreign Rights and Interests in China*, Baltimore, 1927

Winston, A. P. "China's Finances under the Republic," *Quarterly Journal of Economics*, Vol. XXX, No. 4, Boston, August, 1916

Woodhead, H. G. W. "Extraterritoriality in China," reprinted from the *Peking and Tientsin Times*, September and October, 1929

Wright, Stanley F. *The Collection and Disposal of the Maritime and Native Customs Revenue Since the Revolution of 1911*, Statistical Department of the Inspectorate General of Customs, Shanghai, 1927

Young, C. Walter. "Economic Factors in Manchurian Diplomacy," *The Annals of the American Academy of Political and Social Science*, Vol. 152, Philadelphia, November, 1930

China's Balance of International Payments
Chapters IX, X, XI, XII

Chinese Government, Commission of Financial Experts, *Project of a Law for the Gradual Introduction of a Gold-Standard Currency System in China Together with a Report in Support Thereof*, submitted to the Minister of Finance, November 11, 1929

Chinese Government, Tariff Board of Enquiry and Appeal, *Import Tariff Provisional Rules*, Ministry of Finance, Shanghai, 1929

Foreign Policy Association, "Foreign Troops and Warships in China," *Editorial Information Series*, 1925–1926, No. 7, January 9, 1926

Hinton, W. J. "A Hint on Some Anomalies in the Currency of Hongkong," *Indian Journal of Economics*, Vol. II, London, December, 1918

Ho, Franklin L. *An Index of the Physical Volume of Foreign Trade in China, 1868–1927* (a paper prepared for the Kyoto Conference of the Institute of Pacific Relations), Tientsin, 1929

702   BIBLIOGRAPHY

Hsieh, T'ing-yu. "The Chinese in Hawaii," *The Chinese Social and Political Science Review*, Vol. XIV, No. 1, pp. 17–40, Peking, January, 1930

Huebner, S. S. "Insurance in China," *The Annals of the American Academy of Political and Social Science*, Vol. 152, Philadelphia, November, 1930

Kann, Eduard. *The Mystery of the Hongkong Dollar* (Booklet Series No. 12), Bureau of Industrial and Commercial Information, Shanghai

Kann, Eduard. *The Currencies of China*, Shanghai, 1927

Lewis, Cleona. *The International Accounts*, New York, 1927

Matsukata, M. *Report on Adoption of the Gold Standard*, Tokyo, 1899

Mears, Eliot G. *Resident Orientals on the Pacific Coast*, The Institute of Pacific Relations, New York, 1927

Miller, Hugo H. *Economic Conditions in the Philippines*, Boston, 1920

Morse, H. B. *An Inquiry into the Commercial Liabilities and Assets of China in International Trade*, Chinese Maritime Customs, Shanghai, 1904

O'Toole, G. B. "Work of Catholic Christianity in China," *China Christian Year Book*, Christian Literature Society, Shanghai, 1928

Otte, Friedrich. "Commercial Statistics in China," *Chinese Economic Monthly*, Vol. III, No. 9, Peking, September, 1926

Pinnick, A. W. *Silver and China*, Shanghai, 1930

Remer, C. F. "International Trade between Gold and Silver Countries, China, 1885–1913," *Quarterly Journal of Economics*, Vol. XL, Boston, August, 1926

Renner, George T. "Chinese Influence in the Development of Western United States," *The Annals of the American Academy of Political and Social Science*, Vol. 152, Philadelphia, November, 1930

Spalding, William F. *Eastern Exchange Currency and Finance*, London, 1918

U. S. Dept. of Labor, Bureau of Labor Statistics Bulletin No. 340, *Chinese Migrations with Special Reference to Labor Conditions* by Chen, Ta, Washington, 1923

Wagel, Srinivas R. *Finance in China*, Shanghai, 1914
Wu, Ching-ch'ao. "Chinese Immigration in the Pacific Area," *Chinese Social and Political Science Review*, Vol. XII, No. 4 and Vol. XIII, Nos. 1, 2, Peking, 1928–1929

PART II

American Investments

Beach, Harlan P. "China as a Mission Field," *Missionary Review of the World*, Vol. XII, pp. 87–98, February, 1899
Bennett, C. R. "American Banks Taking Their Place in China," *Millard's* (now *China Weekly Review*), Vol. XIII, No. 3, Shanghai, June 19, 1920

Chronicle and Directory for China, Japan, Straits Settlements, Indo-China, Philippines, etc., for the Year 1899, Hongkong, 1899
Consortium, The, Carnegie Endowment for International Peace, Washington, 1921

Dennett, Tyler. *Americans in Eastern Asia: A Critical Study of the Policy of the United States with reference to China, Japan and Korea in the Nineteenth Century*, New York, 1922
Dunn, Robert W. *American Foreign Investments*, New York, 1926

Feis, Herbert. "The Export of American Capital," *Foreign Affairs*, Vol. III, No. 4, pp. 668–86, New York, July, 1925
Field, Frederick V. *American Participation in the China Consortiums* (a preliminary paper prepared for the fourth general session of the Institute of Pacific Relations held at Hangchow, China, October 21 to November 4, 1931), New York, 1931
Foster, John W. *American Diplomacy in the Orient*, Boston, 1903

Goodrich, L. Carrington. "American Catholic Missions in China," *Chinese Social and Political Science Review*, Vol. XI, Nos. 3, 4, Vol. XII, No. 1, 1927–1928
Great Britain: *Reports from the Foreign Commissioners at the Various Ports in China for the Year 1865*, London, 1867

Hitchcock, Frank H. *Our Trade with Japan, China, and Hong-kong, 1889–1899*, Washington, 1900

Hughes, Sarah Forbes. *Letters and Recollections of John Murray Forbes*, Cambridge, 1899

Latourette, Kenneth Scott. *A History of Christian Missions in China*, New York, 1929

Lee, Frederic E. *Currency, Banking, and Finance in China*, Washington, 1926

Long, Breckinridge. "Limitations upon the Adoption of Any Foreign Investment Policy by the United States," *Annals of the American Academy of Political and Social Science*, Vol. 126, pp. 92–4, Philadelphia, July, 1926

Pan, Shü-lun. *The Trade of the United States with China*, China Trade Bureau, Inc., New York, 1924

Patton, Cornelius H. *The Business of Missions*, New York, 1924

Pott, F. L. Hawks. *A Short History of Shanghai*, Shanghai, 1928

Remer, C. F. *American Investments in China*, The Institute of Pacific Relations, Honolulu, 1929

Rockhill, W. W. *Treaties and Conventions, with or concerning China and Korea, 1894–1904*, Washington, 1904

"Shanghai Electricity Department, The," *Chinese Economic Journal*, Vol. IV, No. 3, pp. 223–31, Shanghai, March, 1929

Straight, Willard. *The Politics of Chinese Finance*, Address at the dinner of the East Asiatic Society of Boston, Boston, May 2, 1913

Tan, Shao Hwa. *The Diplomacy of American Investments in China*, Chicago, 1927. An unpublished dissertation in the University of Chicago Library

U. S. Dept. of Commerce:
  A New Estimate of American Investments Abroad, Trade Information Bulletin, No. 767, by Paul D. Dickens, Washington, 1931
  American Direct Investment in Foreign Countries, by Paul D. Dickens, Washington, 1930

U. S. Dept. of State:
  List of Contracts of American Nationals with the Chinese Government, etc., with fourteen annexes. Submitted in pursuance of Article II of the Resolution No. XI, adopted

by the Conference on Limitation of Armament, February 1, 1922, Washington, 1925

Report upon the Commercial Relations of the United States with Foreign Countries, Washington, 1875, 1878

Report on the Commercial Relations of the United States with all Foreign Nations, 34th Cong., 1st Sess., Ex. Doc. No. 47, Washington, 1856

Warnshuis, A. L. "Christian Missions and the Situation in China," *Annals of the American Academy of Political and Social Science*, Vol. 132, Philadelphia, July, 1927

Winkler, Max. "The Dollar Abroad," *Information Service*, Foreign Policy Association, Vol. V, supplement No. 1, March, 1929

Wright, P. G. *The American Tariff and Oriental Trade*, Chicago, 1931

Young, A. N. "Department of State and American Enterprise Abroad," *Commercial and Financial Chronicle*, September 5, 1925

Young, C. Walter. *The International Relations of Manchuria*, American Council of the Institute of Pacific Relations, Chicago, 1929

Japanese Investments

C. C. S. and H. K. L. (Former Justices of the Supreme Court). *Notes on the Inadequately Secured Loans of China*, Peking, 1926

Chinese Government, Ministry of Foreign Affairs, *Agreement Concluded between the Republic of China and the Empire of Japan*, Nanking, May 14, 1930

Economic History of Manchuria, Bank of Chosen, Seoul, 1920

Foreign Policy Association, "Recent Japanese Policy in China," *Information Service*, Vol. III, No. 16, New York, October 12, 1927

Go, Toshi, *A Brief History of Japanese Investments in China* (an address given at the Council on Foreign Relations, January 6, 1931), New York, 1931

Ho, Franklin. "Population Movement to the Northeastern Frontier," *Chinese Social and Political Science Review*, Vol. XV, No. 3, Peking, October, 1931

Hsiao, Chu. *Manchuria* (a preliminary paper prepared for the Conference of the Institute of Pacific Relations, 1929), Tientsin, 1929

Itani, Zenichi. *The Export of Japanese Capital to China*, Tokyo, 1931

Japanese Investments and Expenditures in Manchuria (from the year 1907 to 1926), New York Office of the South Manchuria Railway, February, 1929

Kinney, Henry W. *Manchuria Today*, Dairen, December, 1930

Lin, T. C. "Political Aspects of Japanese Railway Enterprises in Manchuria," *Chinese Social and Political Science Review*, Vol. XIV, No. 2, Peking, 1930

Manchuria Year Book, 1931. East Asiatic Economic Investigation Bureau, Tokyo, 1931

Moulton, Harold G. *Japan—An Economic and Financial Appraisal*, Brookings Institution, Washington, 1931

Myers, Denys P. *The Sino-Japanese Conflict*, World Peace Foundation, Boston, 1931–1932

Nagano, Akira. *The Capital War of the Powers with China as the Stage*, Society for the Study of Chinese Problems, Tokyo, 1928 (in Japanese)

Nasu, S. *Land Utilization in Japan*, Japanese Council of the Institute of Pacific Relations, Tokyo, 1929

Odagiri, Masnoske. *Japanese Investments in China* (a paper prepared for the Kyoto Conference of the Institute of Pacific Relations, 1929)

Ogawa, G. *Conscription System in Japan*, New York, 1921

Ogawa, G. *Expenditures of the Russo-Japanese War*, New York, 1923

Ono, G. *War and Disarmament Expenditures of Japan*, New York, 1922

Orchard, John E. *Japan's Economic Position*, New York, 1931

Royama, Masamichi. *Japan's Position in Manchuria* (a paper prepared for the Third Biennial Conference of the Institute of Pacific Relations by the Japanese Council), Tokyo, 1929

South Manchuria Railway, *Report on Progress in Manchuria, 1907–28,* Dairen, 1929. *Second Report on Progress in Manchuria to 1930,* Dairen, 1931

U. S. Tariff Commission, *Foreign Trade of Japan,* Washington, 1922

Young, C. W. "Economic Bases for New Railways in Manchuria," *Chinese Economic Journal,* Peking, April, 1927

Young, C. W. *Japan's Special Position in Manchuria,* Baltimore, 1931

Young, C. W. *Chinese Colonization and the Development of Manchuria,* Institute of Pacific Relations, Honolulu, 1929

Russian Investments

Apostol, Paul N. *Russian Public Finance During the War,* New Haven, 1928

Bordelongue, J. *The Russian Portion of the Boxer Indemnity* (Booklet Series No. 9), Bureau of Industrial and Commercial Information, Shanghai, 1929

Chinese Eastern Railway, *North Manchuria and the Chinese Eastern Railway,* Harbin, 1924

Foreign Policy Association. "The Chinese Eastern Railway," *Information Service,* Vol. II, No. 1, February 27, 1926

Karamisheff, W. *Mongolia and Western China,* Tientsin, 1925

Lattimore, Owen. "Political Conditions in Mongolia and Chinese Turkestan," *The Annals of the American Academy of Political and Social Science,* Vol. 152, Philadelphia, November, 1930

Romanov, B. A. *Russia in Manchuria, 1892–1906* (in Russian), Leningrad, 1928

Serebrennikov, J. J. "Soviet Satellite: Outer Mongolia Today," *Foreign Affairs,* Vol. IX, No. 3, New York, April, 1931

Sokolsky, George E. *The Story of the Chinese Eastern Railway,* North China Daily News and Herald, Shanghai, 1929

Tong, Hollington K. *Facts About the Chinese Eastern Railway Situation, with Documents*, Committee for Public Enlightenment of the North-Eastern Provinces, Harbin, 1929

British Investments

British Chamber of Commerce Journal, British Chamber of Commerce, Shanghai

British Documents on the Origins of the War, 1898–1914 (Vol. I, The End of British Isolation; Vol. II, The Japanese Alliance and the French Entente), London, 1927

"British Investments Abroad," *Quarterly Review*, Vol. 207, No. 412, pp. 245–72, July, 1907

Cotton Industry Since the War, The, issued for private circulation by the Cotton Trade Statistical Bureau, Manchester, 1931

Great Britain, Department of Overseas Trade. *Report of the British Economic Mission to the Far East, 1930–31*, London, 1931

Hinton, Wilfred J. "Present Economic and Political Position of Great Britain in China," *The Annals of the American Academy of Political and Social Science*, Vol. 152, Philadelphia, November, 1930

Kindersley, Sir Robert. "A New Study of British Foreign Investments," *Economic Journal*, Vol. XXXIX, No. 153, March, 1929

List of the Principal Foreign and Chinese Industrial Enterprises in China and Hongkong, Shanghai, 1918

Willert, Sir Arthur. *Aspects of British Foreign Policy*, New Haven, 1928

French Investments

Annuaire Financier France Extrême-Orient, 1928–29, Ernest Martin & Cie, Banquiers, Paris

Bray, Ferdinand Joseph. *La Chine et ses Besoins au point de vue de l'Utilization des Belges, de leurs Capitaux et de leur Industrie*, Louvain, 1898

Ellis, Howard S. *French and German Investments in China*, Institute of Pacific Relations, Honolulu, 1929

French Ministry of Finance. "La Fortune Française à l'Etranger," *Bulletin de Statistique et de Legislation Comparée*, twenty-sixth year, October, 1902. Imprimière Nationale, Paris

"Indo-China," Special number of *La Vie Technique et Industrielle*, Paris, 1922

Levy, R. G. "Fortune Mobilière de la France à l'Etranger," *Revue des Deux Mondes*, March, 1897

Mackenzie, John A. P. "Investments of French Capital Abroad," *Journal of the Royal Statistical Society*, Vol. LXVI, Part IV, December, 1903

Moulton, Harold G., and Lewis, Cleona. *The French Debt Problem*, New York, 1925

Neymark, Alfred. "Les Valeurs Mobilières en France," *Journal de la Société de Statistique de Paris*, Vol. XLV, No. 1, January, 1904

German Investments

Baker, Dwight Condo. *Germany and the Far East* (an unpublished dissertation in the Library of the University of California, 1927)

Bericht der China-Studienkommission des Reichsverbandes der deutschen Industrie, Berlin, 1930

Die Entwicklung der deutschen Seeinteressen im letzten Jahrzehnt, Reichsmarineamt, Berlin, 1905

Steinmann-Bücher, Arnold. *Deutschlands Volksvermögen im Kriege*, Stuttgart, 1916

Waltershausen, A. Sartorius von. *Deutsche Wirtschaftsgeschichte, 1815–1914*, Jena, 1923

Works in the Chinese Language

Chi, Shu-feng. *China under Economic Exploitation*, Shanghai, 1925

Chia, Shih-yi. *Financial History of the Republic*, Shanghai, 1916

Confidential Papers of the Parliament, Peking, June, 1923

Liu, Yo-yun. *Kwang Hsu Accounts*, Peking, 1901

Ministry of Communications, Department of Railways, *Railway Loan Agreements of China* (edited by C. C. Wang), Peking, December, 1923

Tseng, Kun-hwa. *History of Chinese Railways*, Peking, 1924

Wu, Yu Kan. *The Trade Between China and Foreign States*, National Central University Series, Shanghai, 1930

Yen, Tsai-chi. *China's Public Debt*, Peking, 1921

INDEX

Agreement of 1924, between Soviet Russia and China, 589, 605; between Germany and China, 646

Agriculture in China, traditional, 34; Japanese families in, 503

Aigun, project for railway to, 266–67; Russian interests in railway to, 604

Alaskan Code, the, 319–20

Altai region, 567

American and Foreign Power Company, 287

American business investments, early, 66, 67, 243–45; in shipping, 67, 242, 246–47, 249, 251, 262, 285; in motor cars and accessories, 69–70, 88, 285, 289–90; share of total, 84, 85, 86, 98–99, 100; in public utilities, 96, 285, 286–88; geographically distributed, 97; in import and export, 243, 245, 246, 251–52, 284 86; in the 'seventies, 245–48; in real estate, 247–48, 254–55, 263, 278, 285, 312–13; in 1875, 249; in 1900, 249–59; in 1914, 260–74; in banking and finance, 264, 265, 285, 288–89; total 1930, 275; according to size of firm, 281; according to geographical distribution, 282; according to age of firm, 283–84; in transportation, 285, 286; in aviation, 285; in railway equipment, etc., 285; total, 285; in mining, 285; in manufacturing, 285, 289–90; textiles, 285, 289; others, 285; totals, 285; in miscellaneous, 285; according to nature of business, 285; remittances on, 290–95; their overwhelming importance, 333; Shanghai as center of, 335

American China Development Company, and the Canton-Hankow railway loan, 258, 272

American Cigarette Company, 252

American Express Company, 289

American firms in China, early, 242–44; in the 'seventies, 246; in 1900, 250–52; in 1914, 262; age of, 264, 283–84; investments of, 264, 280, 281; in 1930, 280; size of, 281; nature of, 281, 285; locality of, 282, 283, 284, 286

American holdings of the Chinese Government Debt, 1931 share of total obligations, 135–38; share of all railway obligations, 143, 256–59, 268–72, 295–96, 298–99; in 1875, 248; in 1900, 256–59; in 1914, 265–72; in 1930, 295–301; European issues, 300–01; 135, 136, 138, 143 (*See also* Boxer Indemnity)

American International Corporation, 299

American investments in China, *Chapter on, 239–338;* early, 66–67, 249; compared with other countries, 74–76; totals, 239, 241, 332, 338; American attitude toward early investments, 252, 253; in 1900, 260; in 1914, 274; Chinese participation in, 289, 291; in 1930, 308; estimate of 1924, 312; estimate of 1928, 314; recent estimates of, 316; in general table, 338 (*See also* American · business investments and American holdings of Chinese Government Debt)

American missionaries and mission holdings in China, rapid increase in, 251; in 1900 compared with 1875, 259; in 1900, 259–60; in 1914, 272–74; in 1930, 302–04; values, 302–05; geographical distribution of, 305; distribution according to nature of work, 306; other estimates, 314, 315

American Oriental Banking Corporation, 289

American population in China, in Canton a hundred years ago,

711

of total obligations, 135–38; in
1904, 570–71; in 1914, 581–84,
587 (*See also* Boxer Indemnity)
Russian investments in China,
Chapter on, 554–618; in 1904,
572–73; in 1914, 585–87; in
1930, 605–06; in general table,
618 (*See also* Russian business
investments and Russian holdings of Chinese Government
Debt)
Russian Ministry, of Communications, 560*n;* of Finance, 562,
563; of War, 563, 565
Russian Orthodox Mission, 571,
585, 606*n*
Russian population in China, 567,
568, 576, 579, 608–11
Russian Revolution, the, 587–88,
595, 599
Russian Timber Company, 569
Russian Turkestan, 578
Russo-Asiatic Bank (Banque Russo-
Asiatique), 581, 583, 588, 604–05
Russo-Chinese Bank, 556–59, 569,
571, 581
Russo-Japanese secret treaty, of
1907, 526; of 1910, 526; of 1912,
526
Russo-Japanese War, cost of, 579,
580*n;* 443–44, 564, 571, 574

St. Petersburg, 557, 559, 560
St. Petersburg Discount Bank, 556
Salt Revenue Administration, 130,
162, 175, 516
Santai Oil Company, the, 499
Sargent, A. J., 67*n*
Sarvis, G. W., 25
Sawmills, 350, 568, 603
Scandinavian business investments,
85
Scandinavian investments in China,
share in total government ob-
ligations, 135, 136; summary, 663
(*See also* Danish, Swedish and
Norwegian business investments)
Schantung Bergbau Gesellschaft,
494*n*
Schantung Eisenbahn Gesellschaft,
494*n*
"Secured Loans" of the Chinese
Government, American share,
295–96; British share, 376–77;
Japanese share, 515–16; German

share, 645–46; Belgian share,
653–55, 656
Serebrennikov, J. J., 554, 609
Seward, William H., 9*n*
Shanghai, compared with New Orleans and New York, 12; foreign
settlement, 45; telegraphic communication established, 48; labor
problems in, 64; foreign investments in, 71–74, 79; importance
of, 101, 111–12, 335, 354, 552;
municipal obligations, 133, 378;
real estate holdings, 163; and
the Yangtze Valley, 227; American interests in, 247–48, 254–55,
282, 290; American firms in, 283;
American public utility holdings
at, 286–88; American mission
holdings at, 305; British population at, 340, 353, 364; British
interests in, 348–49, 360, 390,
392–95, 399–401; as a coasting
trade center, 349; Japanese interests in, 415, 471, 473–74, 495–
99, 504, 506; Japanese population at, 418, 422, 456, 473; Russian interests in, 558, 571; Russian population at, 596, 611;
French interests in, 631–33; German interests in, 637, 638, 645;
Italian interests in, 659–60; Scandinavian interests in, 662
Shanghai Conference, Institute of
Pacific Relations, 447
Shanghai Electric Construction
Company, 359, 399
Shanghai-Fenching Railway, 175
Shanghai Gas Company, 258, 399
Shanghai-Hongkong Wharf Com-
pany, 350
Shanghai International (Foreign)
Settlement, 45, 112, 248, 286–88,
350, 378–79, 391–92, 394, 455
Shanghai Land Investment Com-
pany, 401
Shanghai Mint, loan for, 298
Shanghai Mutual Telephone Com-
pany, 349, 350, 359
Shanghai-Nanking Railway, 141,
173, 175
Shanghai Power Company, 286–88,
378
Shanghai Pulp & Paper Company,
252
Shanghai Rice Mill Company, 252